AMERICAN GOVERNMENT TODAY

AMERICAN GOVERNMENT TODAY REVISED EDITION

Gaylon L. Caldwell
UNITED STATES INFORMATION AGENCY

AND

Robert M. Lawrence
UNIVERSITY OF ARIZONA

W · W · NORTON & COMPANY · INC · NEW YORK

Printed in the United States of America

2 3 4 5 6 7 8 9 0

Contents

Preface

The title *American Government Today* suggests timeliness. The reputation of the first edition was built upon usability and readability. To enhance these qualities in this revised edition the authors have taken into account the dramatic changes in the American political scene and important new findings in American political science, while preserving the spirit, and much of the content, of the first edition.

Recent problems which have arisen to tax the implementation of the "Principles of the American Democracy" and the operation of "The National Power in the Federal System" were added to the analyses contained in the first two chapters. The chapter on "The American Citizen" has been revised to include the most recent changes in immigration and naturalization laws. The "American Politics" chapter was substantially expanded to bring in new research concerning parties, voting behavior, and pressure groups as well as a discussion of the politics of protest, perhaps the most dramatic new element in the American political scene. To the chapters on "The Congress," "The Presidency," and "The Judicial System" was added recent material regarding the functioning of and behavior within the three branches, and new emphasis on the patterns of cooperation and conflict between them. The chapter on "Civil Rights" was revised to incorporate the great outpouring of legislation and judicial decisions in response to the urgent strains on the fabric of the American society. An examination of the flood of legislation bearing the LBJ brand, of the support for and opposition to Great Society programs, was added to the chapter on "The Business of Government." A new chapter on "National Security" was written and linked to the largely revised one on "U.S. Foreign Policy" to provide perspective and background for the national debate on the nation's role in world affairs.

The authors agree that students must know how government functions, and yet ought to know why discrepancies exist between what the men of the Constitution thought they had created and what their successors are doing within the framework of constitutional government. From the attempt to develop an understanding of both the "must" and the "ought" this book was born, and now revised: the intention remains to provide a functional account of American government, while stressing the interplay between *The Federalist Papers* and the *Supreme Court Reports.*

The revised edition was developed from materials the two authors have given students over a period of fifteen years—materials which were intended to provide the student with essential information, so that the teacher could be free to discuss the actualities of the American political system instead of merely describing its formal structure. The authors believe their classroom presentations, now combined, contributed to the waxing of student interest, the waning of complaints about "excessive" textbook reading, improved questions, and more vigorous discussion.

Finally, *American Government Today* has been redesigned to meet the students' request for an approach to American government that is relevant to current issues. The book affords many points of departure for the lecturer. Whenever the instructor wants to concentrate on a particular policy question or a specific aspect of the governmental process, he can do so with the assurance that the text has provided his students with the necessary background.

The compactness of the book provides justification for the assignment of outside reading. Accordingly, the revised bibliographies concentrate on classic sources to be found in any library and on easily obtainable paperbacks that the teacher might want to use as supplements to the text. Newly added to facilitate study and review are marginal side headings and summary statements at the end of each chapter.

Many thoughtful people contributed to the first edition. Professor Richard E. Neustadt of Columbia University, Professor R. Kent Fielding of Wesleyan University, Professor Gordon Cleveland of the University of North Carolina, and Samuel Monson, formerly of Brigham Young University, read the first few chapters and encouraged the writing of more. Comprehensive readings were undertaken by Professor William M. Beaney of Princeton University, Professor William Irwin of Western Reserve University, and Professor Charles Anderson of the University of Wisconsin. Detailed help was provided by Professor Alan Rosenthal of Hunter College in the final stages of writing.

In addition, thanks should be given to Currin Shields, Chairman of the Department of Government, University of Arizona, and Roy Amara, Executive Director of the Systems Sciences

Division, Stanford Research Institute, for the encouragement they gave to the writing of the revised edition. And, for adjusting their daily activities to our work, a word of gratitude is due to our wives, Vickie and Elaine, and to the children, Tom, Camden, Melissa, and Kimberly Caldwell, and Karen, Kay, Nancy, and Linda Lawrence.

G.L.C.
R.M.L.

January 1969

AMERICAN
GOVERNMENT
TODAY

1

Principles of the American Democracy

Powers and responsibilities in a government are distributed by a "constitution": the arrangements provided by the constitution are its body, but the principles are its spirit. The principles of American government are the ideals and attitudes which helped to mold the existing structure of the Constitution and which will continue to shape it in the years ahead. In addition to the influence which they have on the distribution of power and the procedures of government, ideals inform the practitioners of government what is expected of them.

The principles of American government which we know today were not originated by the framers of the Constitution. The idea that government belongs to the citizens, for example, is as old as the Greeks; one might trace the history of the conception of "the equality of every man before the law" to the ancient Hebrews; the Romans knew the advantages of dividing political power, and Lord Chief Justice Edward Coke attempted to use the courts to defend people from governmental power in the three-way struggle for governmental supremacy among the common-law courts, the Parliament, and the monarchy of seventeenth-century England. But even if the ideals expressed by the Constitution are not uniquely American, it is the combination of them within the American experience that largely accounts for the uniqueness of the theory and practice of American government. The structure of government can easily be learned; the constitutional phrases which allocate power might even be memorized; and certainly the hypotheses and supporting data of the social scientists who inquire into the behavioral aspects of the political process enlighten and enliven

Ancient heritage

3

our study; but without an appreciation of principles, the dynamics of government can never quite be grouped properly nor understood fully. In a constitutional system, it is certain, "the spirit giveth life." It must be emphasized that principles are *ideals*, not *facts*. Because they are ideals, they are incapable of ever being fully realized and completely expressed in writing or in practice. Ideals can, however, serve as goals for each generation which accepts them, and they can be interpreted anew by each age that seeks to "form a more perfect union, establish justice . . . and secure the blessings of liberty."

It really is not surprising that disputes over the interpretation and application of the various principles are readily observable in the contemporary American political scene. It has always been so. While almost all Americans normally support the broadly stated principles of government, there is substantial disagreement as to precisely how the principles are to be implemented and for whose benefit they should be used. Therefore the principles, each in its own fashion, continue to be the subject of controversy as various groups seek to interpret them to advance their own interests, or those of a wider constituency such as the nation, or on occasion, mankind.

Interpretation of principles

In the discussion which follows, nine principles are isolated from their context of Constitution and functioning government. It is essential that these basic principles be understood beforehand, since reference will often be made to them when the structure of the national government is considered in detail. Besides, anyone who teaches so exciting a subject as American government merely as a series of facts is guilty of mayhem.

Popular Sovereignty

Popular sovereignty is absolutely required of any governmental system that is "democratic," since it indicates that the people have both the right and the ways of controlling those who govern them. This means nothing less than that institutions and techniques must exist to enable the popular will to influence the conduct of government continuously and effectively. The mere acknowledgment by the governors that their power stems from the people is not enough—the Roman emperors made this concession. Lincoln expressed the principle clearly, if simply, by his words "government *by* the people."

That popular sovereignty may be found as the first principle written into the Constitution should not be surprising. The conception of government prevailing in the generation which subscribed to the Declaration of Independence and ratified the

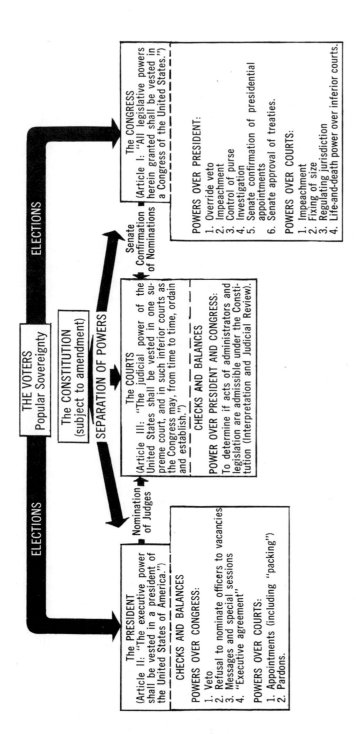

The VOTERS
Popular Sovereignty

The CONSTITUTION
(subject to amendment)

SEPARATION OF POWERS

ELECTIONS

ELECTIONS

Nomination of Judges

Senate Confirmation of Nominations

The CONGRESS
(Article I: "All legislative powers herein granted shall be vested in a Congress of the United States.")

POWERS OVER PRESIDENT:
1. Override veto
2. Impeachment
3. Control of purse
4. Investigation
5. Senate confirmation of presidential appointments
6. Senate approval of treaties.

POWERS OVER COURTS:
1. Impeachment
2. Fixing of size
3. Regulating jurisdiction
4. Life-and-death power over inferior courts.

The COURTS
(Article III: "The judicial power of the United States shall be vested in one supreme court, and in such inferior courts as the Congress may, from time to time, ordain and establish.")

CHECKS AND BALANCES

POWER OVER PRESIDENT AND CONGRESS:
To determine if acts of administrators and legislation are admissible under the Constitution (Interpretation and Judicial Review).

The PRESIDENT
(Article II: "The executive power shall be vested in a president of the United States of America.")

CHECKS AND BALANCES

POWERS OVER CONGRESS:
1. Veto
2. Refusal to nominate officers to vacancies
3. Messages and special sessions
4. "Executive agreement"

POWERS OVER COURTS:
1. Appointments (including "packing")
2. Pardons.

Constitution was the social contract theory as popularized by the English philosopher, John Locke. Locke's explanation of the origin and legitimacy of government included the ideas that men created government in order to make their "natural rights" secure, and that if government became destructive of life, liberty, and property, it could be overthrown and replaced by another one which would respect them. In America in 1789 few disputed that the people could create a national government, and the opening line of the Preamble recites:

The social contract theory

> We the People of the United States . . . do ordain and establish this Constitution for the United States of America.

There were heated disputes, however, as to whether this governmental compact had been made by the people of *independent* States or by the people of the *United* States. The argument was settled legally in favor of the champions of the latter position by a series of important decisions favoring the national government which were handed down by Chief Justice John Marshall's court (1801–35) in the formative years of the republic. The argument was settled for practical purposes in the staggering blow delivered to "states' rights" by the outcome of the Civil War.

Some of the Founding Fathers had read Locke carefully and had been enormously influenced by him, but they were also familiar with history. Many of them believed that history merely documented what their Christian theology had insisted—that human sinfulness was very real and ought not to be overlooked in the creation of social institutions. Others were not at all impressed with the sin argument but distrusted popular rule for other reasons (for example, that the multitudinous poor would engulf and exploit "the few, the rich, the well-born"). In any case, although the framers fairly unanimously agreed on the principle of popular sovereignty, most of them refused to define this principle as synonymous with unchecked majority rule. The anatomy of the Constitution discloses the deliberate attempts of the framers to restrain the power of the popular will of the sovereign people.[1]

Restraints on popular will

Today vocal, and sometimes violent, groups seek to bring about changes in public policy by means of demonstrations and

1. According to Richard Hofstadter, the men who drew up the Constitution combined a Calvinistic sense of human evil and a Hobbesian belief that men are selfish and contentious with practical knowledge of man's frailty. "They did not believe in man," writes Hofstadter, "but they did believe in the power of a good political constitution to control him." See the first chapter, "The Founding Fathers: An Age of Realism," in *The American Political Tradition* (New York: Vintage Books, 1954).

Drawing by Donald Reilly; ©1968 The New Yorker Magazine, Inc.

"While I disapprove of your bumper sticker, sir, I'll defend to the death your right to stick it on."

mass protests.[2] The chant, "We are the people," uttered as they clash with local police or Federal authorities, does not dampen the alarm felt by those who contend that popular feelings so expressed easily merge into anarchy when the more restrained avenues of public expression, such as balloting, are bypassed. On the other hand, those who participate in public demonstrations, and on occasion practice civil disobedience, assert that their methods of attracting and directing public pressure upon government officials are justified because of the magnitude of the wrongs they seek to right.[3]

The popular will today

2. The Winter, 1968, issue of *Daedalus*, Vol. 97, contains articles about the behavior of students who often constitute a majority of those found in protesting and demonstrating groups.

3. It should be recalled that acts of civil disobedience performed as a means of focusing attention upon government policy are not new in this country. More than 100 years ago the philosopher Henry David Thoreau went to jail rather than pay a poll tax to the state of Massachusetts, which at that time was tolerant of slavery, an institution which Thoreau opposed. Two views of Thoreau's act of protest, and of civil disobedience in general, are suggested by the conversation which traditionally is credited to having occurred between Thoreau and his friend and fellow philosopher, Ralph Waldo Emerson, who came to visit him in jail. Asked Emerson, "Why are you here?" Replied Thoreau, "Why are you not here?" Walter Harding, *A Thoreau Handbook* (New York: New York University Press, 1959), p. 8. See also Thoreau's *Walden and Civil Disobedience*, Owen Thomas, ed. (New York: W. W. Norton, 1967).

7

Limited Government

In America there are certain restrictions on the power of government. These limitations are to be found in the compact to which we adhere and in the procedures our governmental officials are obliged to observe. The written covenant is called our Constitution; but the practice of requiring governing authorities to follow regularized rules and procedures is known as constitutional government.

Constitutional government v. arbitrary rule

To be "constitutional," a government needs only to be regularized. This regularizing need not be done in writing, since time-honored practice has proved to be as powerful in regulating human actions as a written contract. The alternative to regularized government is arbitrary power—a system in which the officials are free to make the rules as they go and free to change the rules as frequently as they please.[4] Edmund Cahn suggested a fine analogy to distinguish between constitutional government and arbitrary rule: suppose that on a day in 1944, Adolf Hitler, strolling through his garden with a bodyguard, pointed to a gardener and said, "That man is a traitor, shoot him!" The soldiers, pledged to obey their Fuehrer, likely would have shot the unfortunate wretch without delay. If, on the same day and under similar circumstances, King George VI had said the same thing, his bodyguard would have assumed that His Highness had been overworking and would have called the royal physicians. The government of Nazi Germany permitted a great deal of arbitrariness; England's government is constitutional.

Limitations

A constitutional government is not necessarily a limited government. The power of the British Parliament is not subject to legal limitations: by a simple majority vote it could repeal the Magna Charta. In fact, it has also been said that Parliament can do anything except change a man into a woman. Not so in America, however, for there are certain things that Congress and state legislatures, the President and state governors may not legally do. These limitations are found throughout the Constitution, but especially in the first ten amendments to it which are called the Bill of Rights. Because our government deals with human beings in fluid situations, and because words

4. Of utmost importance to the modern citizen is the distinction between totalitarian dictatorship, where governmental power is unlimited and unrestrained, and democracy, where political power is limited by a constitutional framework providing that governmental authority be exercised in accordance with known procedures. For a brief but illuminating comparison of modern democracy and totalitarian dictatorship, see Gwendolen M. Carter and John H. Herz, *Government and Politics in the Twentieth Century* (New York: Praeger, 1961).

are capable of being interpreted in various ways, it is impossible to say precisely what limitations will always apply. Therefore, while the degree to which governments will be absolutely limited will vary from time to time, there is no doubt that an umpire exists who can blow the whistle. An excellent instance which illustrates how interpretation of the words of the Constitution can tip the scales in the constant struggle between ideal principles and practical government is the series of "Flag-Salute Cases."

LIMITATIONS ON NATIONAL GOVERNMENT: THE CONCERN FOR INDIVIDUAL RIGHTS

During the 1930's some states required each student in the public schools to begin the day by participating in a salute to the flag. The refusal to conform was to be regarded as insubordination, and insubordination meant expulsion. Members of the religious sect known as Jehovah's Witnesses considered the flag to be an "image" and held that to salute it would be to violate the second commandment of the Mosaic Law. The options open to the Witnesses appeared to be: (*a*) to violate their religious commitment and salute the flag; (*b*) to refuse to salute the flag and be expelled from school; or (*c*) to enroll in a private school which did not require a flag salute. The religious group insisted that option *a* was unthinkable; *b* was unsatisfactory; and *c* was incommodious. They appealed to the Federal courts to vindicate their "freedom of religion." *Conflict with religion*

In the first four cases to come before it, the Supreme Court unanimously found that the requirement of saluting the flag was within the constitutional power of the states. "Indeed," wrote Justice Frankfurter, "in the first three cases . . . the constitutional claim . . . was deemed so clearly unmeritorious that this Court dismissed the appeals . . ."[5] In the fifth case, a crack appeared in the solid front the judges had presented. Justice Frankfurter, speaking for an 8-1 majority, began: "A grave responsibility confronts this Court whenever in course of litiga- *Court tests*

5. Dissenting, West Virginia State Board of Education v. Barnette, 319 U.S. 624, 664 (1943). [Citations to the Supreme Court are given by volume number (*e.g.*, 319), the reporter (U.S.), and page where the case begins (624). If other pages are referred to, they are given after the first page of the report (*e.g.*, 664 in this footnote). The date is given at the end in parentheses (1943). In the first 90 volumes, however, the volume number varies with the name of the recognized reporter. These early reporters were Dallas (4 vols., to 1800); Cranch (9 vols., 1801-15); Wheaton (12 vols., 1816–27); Peters (16 vols., 1828–43); Howard (24 vols., 1844–60); Black (2 vols., 1861–62); and Wallace (23 vols., 1863-74). The citation of other Federal courts is discussed in the text of Chap. 7. State and foreign forms vary widely and are not explained in this book.]

tion it must reconcile the conflicting claims of liberty and authority." After a careful consideration of all the factors, the Court decided that in this instance authority must be given the nod, on the ground that "the mere possession of religious convictions which contradict the relevant concerns of a political society does not relieve the citizen from the discharge of political responsibilities."[6]

The Witnesses were not convinced, and brought up a sixth case. In West Virginia State Board of Education v. Barnette, the majority of the Court, evidently convinced by the argument of the previous dissent by Justice Stone, reversed the other five decisions, in ringing prose that captures the ideal of limited government so well that it deserves to be read. Speaking for the Court, the late Justice Jackson said:[7]

The ideal of limited government

> The very purpose of a Bill of Rights was to withdraw certain subjects from the vicissitudes of political controversy, to place them beyond the reach of majorities and officials and to establish them as legal principles to be applied by the courts. One's right to life, liberty, and property, to free speech, a free press, freedom of worship and assembly, and other fundamental rights may not be submitted to vote; they depend on the outcome of no elections.

Again:

> The case is made difficult not because the principles of its decision are obscure but because the flag involved is our own. Nevertheless we apply the limitations of the Constitution with no fear that freedom to be intellectually and spiritually diverse or even contrary will disintegrate the social organization . . . Freedom to differ is not limited to things that do not matter much. That would be a mere shadow of freedom. The test of its substance is the right to differ as to things that touch the heart of the existing order.

In a concurring opinion, Justice Black and Justice Douglas felt obliged to temper the liberality of the Court's language. Their words are quoted below, to indicate the practical problem of setting limits to government when the possibility always exists that constitutional limitations may be used as a blanket claim to cover disobedience. These judges found:

6. Minersville School District v. Gobitis, 310 U.S. 586, 591, 594–95 (1940).

7. The three quotations that follow are from West Virginia State Board of Education v. Barnette, 319 U.S. 624, 638 (1943). The full opinions in this case, as well as opinions in other First Amendment religious cases, are presented in Joseph Tussman, *The Supreme Court on Church and State* (New York: Oxford University Press, 1962).

No well-ordered society can leave to the individuals an absolute right to make final decisions, unassailable by the State, as to everything they will or will not do. The First Amendment does not go so far. Religious faiths, honestly held, do not free individuals from responsibility to conduct themselves obediently to laws which are either imperatively necessary to protect society as a whole from grave and pressingly imminent dangers or which, without any general prohibition, merely regulate time, place or manner of religious activity. Decisions as to the constitutionality of particular laws which strike at the substance of religious tenets and practices must be made by this Court.

A recent need to strike a reasonable balance between the requirements of individual conscience and the demands of duly

"Privately, I agree with you. Publicly, I've got to jail you."

**Objections to
Selective Service**

constituted authority has arisen as a result of the Vietnamese war. The problem involves the conflict between the moral and religious objections held by some Americans to the war and the Federal Government's requirements to draft men into the armed forces for duty in Vietnam. The confrontation between conscience and authority often has taken the form of draft-card burnings and other acts to thwart the operation of the Selective Service System. Congress in 1965 amended the Selective Service Act to outlaw the burning of draft cards. In 1968 the Supreme Court sustained the amendment and in so doing reversed the ruling of a lower Federal court.[8] Shortly thereafter a Federal court jury in Boston found the famous pediatrician, Dr. Benjamin Spock, and three others who had been prominent critics of the Vietnamese war guilty of conspiring against the Selective Service Act by aiding and abetting men to avoid the draft. The decisions in the two cases do not mean Americans are barred from voicing protests to the Vietnamese war or any other government policy. They do seem to mean that activity which is illegal remains illegal even if those participating in it claim to be exercising "symbolic" free speech by their action.

**The Lincoln
dilemma**

The memorable dilemma posed by Lincoln—"Must a government of necessity be too *strong* for the liberties of its people, or too *weak* to maintain its own existence?"—remains after the Civil War, the Flag-Salute Cases, and the Vietnamese war protest cases. The limits placed upon Federal power in regard to the preserve of individual conscience, as well as to other areas of activity, must be determined anew in each generation.

LIMITATIONS ON STATE GOVERNMENT

The "fundamental rights which may not be submitted to vote" are based on clauses in the Constitution. Probably the best-known limitation on the power of the national government is the Bill of Rights, which was designed to check the power of Congress. More and more frequently the Fourteenth Amendment has been interpreted to apply many of these limitations to the *states*. In the original Constitution, Article I, Section 9, limited the powers of the states. These guarantees will be considered in detail in Chapter 8; it is enough to recognize now that they are substantial contributions to the principle of limited government.

8. O'Brien v. U.S., 391 U.S. 367 (1968). In rejecting the lower court's contention that draft-card burning constituted "symbolic" free speech, Chief Justice Warren stated, "We cannot accept the view that an apparently limitless variety of conduct can be labeled 'speech' whenever the person engaging in the conduct intends thereby to express an idea."

Although the Constitution circumscribes the national government, state governments are limited by their own constitutions as well as the fundamental document. If states infringe the guarantees of the Constitution, the political and judicial branches of the central government will come to the aid of any person who is victimized. An example of this might be as follows: suppose a prisoner is serving a maximum sentence of 10 years in a state penitentiary for having written checks without funds. Now, assume that there has been such a rash of rubber checks that the legislature has amended the criminal code to increase the maximum prison sentence for such crimes to 15 years and that the prisoner's sentence has been increased by five years. His remedy would be to obtain a writ of habeas corpus (*i.e.,* protection against illegal imprisonment) from a state judge so that the courts could hold that the new law did not apply to convicted check artists like himself, since it clearly was a law passed after sentencing which was disadvantageous to the accused (*i.e.,* an ex post facto law). If the state courts refused to make the correction, he could appeal to the United States Supreme Court for help, since the national constitution (in Article I, Section 10) denies any state the power to apply ex post facto laws. Notice, however, that if the limitations set upon a state only by its *own* constitution are violated, the state itself must remedy the wrong. The national government may interfere in such cases only if it should be determined that the state has strayed so far from the accepted path that it has ceased to be a "republican form of government."[9] Suppose, for example, that a state constitution stipulated that juries in criminal trials must consist of 12 persons and the legislature has passed a law providing for a jury of 10 in criminal cases. If the signer of checks had been convicted by the smaller jury, he could appeal to his state's courts on the grounds that the jury law was in conflict with the state constitution. He could not go to the Federal Courts. While the Constitution has been interpreted by the Supreme Court as requiring a defendant in state criminal cases to be afforded a jury trial if the offense is "serious," there is no requirement that juries must be composed of 12 persons.[10]

9. The Supreme Court has consistently maintained that "political questions" such as this are to be determined by the "political branches" of government, *i.e.,* the Congress or the Executive. Presumably, if the Congress permits the delegation from a state to take their seats, the state they represent is "republican" in form. Luther v. Borden, 7 Howard 1 (1849); Pacific States Tel. & Tel. Co. v. Oregon, 223 U.S. 118 (1911); Coleman v. Miller, 307 U.S. 433 (1939).

10. Duncan v. Louisiana, 391 U.S. 145 (1968).

State and local law enforcement

Today much of the controversy over limitations placed upon state and local government activity is connected with the problem of law enforcement. Concurrent with the rapid increase in the crime rates of many areas the nation's judiciary, most notably the Supreme Court, has limited through court decisions the procedures which may be followed by state and local police and prosecutors in the apprehension, interrogation, and trial of suspected criminals.[11] These decisions have provoked outcries from police and other local authorities that the courts are significantly impairing law enforcement, and demands from politicians and citizen groups that more, not less, authority and flexibility be placed in the hands of the police and prosecutors.[12]

GOVERNMENT CONTROL OF PRIVATE ENTERPRISE

Growth in regulatory practices

Does a government that is "limited" mean a government that is powerless to intervene in the way legitimate businesses are conducted? There was a time when neither the states nor the central government could interfere with such matters as conditions of work. This was accomplished by the Supreme Court's insistence that the Fourteenth Amendment prohibited states from meddling with the "liberty of contract" between employer and employees—which liberty included determining hours of work and rates of pay. Without qualm, courts struck down regulatory statutes such as the New York law which imposed on bakers a 60-hour week. Next, Congress came to the aid of the states by refusing to allow articles produced under substandard working conditions from moving in interstate commerce, but the Court found interstate movement to be only incidental to the "local act" of production. When Congress attempted to fix minimum wages for women and children employed in the District of Columbia (over which it has jurisdiction), the Supreme Court voided the regulatory law over Justice Holmes's quotable protest: "It will need more than the Nineteenth Amendment to convince me that there are no

11. See, for example, Mapp v. Ohio, 367 U.S. 634 (1961); Gideon v. Wainwright, 372 U.S. 335 (1963); Escobedo v. Illinois, 378 U.S. 478 (1964); Miranda v. Arizona, 384 U.S. 436 (1966); Witherspoon v. Illinois, 391 U.S. 1770 (1968). These and other cases, some of which relate more directly to Federal law enforcement, will be examined in greater detail in Chapter 8.

12. During the 1968 Democratic National Convention in Chicago the nation watched on television the ugly scenes of violent confrontation between demonstrators of various persuasions and the police and National Guard. To some the Chicago violence seemed to offer additional proof that stricter law enforcement is needed. Others contended the events in Chicago should be interpreted as meaning more restraints ought to be placed upon the use of force by police.

differences between men and women ..." But Holmes's oft-repeated insistence that "a constitution is not intended to embody a particular economic theory" emerged triumphant as Franklin D. Roosevelt's "New Deal" steadily nudged twentieth-century American government into the public welfare business. The great depression of the 1930's, the "court fight" of 1937, and World War II effectively laid to rest any notions that government may not interfere with private enterprise. The tradition-shattering spectacle of a President pressuring a big business like steel not to increase prices did not disturb most of the people when Kennedy did it in 1962, and this suggests the tolerance and confidence with which the citizenry has come to view government interference with business. The limits on government regulation have shrunk, too, as the "police powers" of the states and the "general welfare" and "interstate commerce" powers of the Congress have been exercised more widely by legislative bodies and viewed more tolerantly by the courts.

There seems to be no return to the period when government refrained from the regulation of private enterprise. However, various groups continue to advance differing views regarding precisely how much, and what kind of, governmental regulation of private enterprise there should be. Current trends suggest that cooperation between government and the private sector of the economy will increase in importance during the 1970's. This development will involve the cooperation of big business, big labor, and the various levels of government in a concerted attack upon the human and material deterioration found in most large urban areas. Cooperative efforts involving business, labor, and government are not new. Certainly much such activity occurred during the two world wars. The impetus for cooperative ventures now stems from the mass violence which has exploded in the city ghettos, and the difficulty of making huge urban areas safe, clean, and enjoyable places in which to live.

How much regulation?

Representative Government

Except for the occasional "town meeting" (where all the residents meet together to discuss and determine community policy), local, state, and Federal government in America is carried on by representatives chosen by the people—not by the people themselves. Representative government means "government by a few people *for the many*." This way of arriving at decisions to bind the whole group is so common that even small student groups elect "senates" or "councils" to determine activities and allocate funds. Representatives decide policy for almost every type of organization—labor unions, business associations, and even churches, as well as political systems. We no longer seriously consider an alternative. Very few among us have ever even heard of Jean Jacques Rousseau's criticism of government by representatives. That eighteenth-century writer insisted that individuals under a representative system are free only during the split-second they vote—at which point they lose their freedom until the next election.

Madison states the case

The Constitutional framers weighed alternatives, however, and James Madison states the case for representative government in the brilliant Number 10 of *The Federalist Papers*.[13] The argument of Madison's essay was that groups of people who are united by common interests become factions which attempt to seek their own political advantage without regard for the interests of other groups or for the general welfare. Factions, Madison thought, always destroy the governments which permit them to exist. He saw only two methods of removing the causes of faction: by destroying liberty, or by giving every citizen the same opinions and interests. Clearly, the first remedy would be worse than the disease. He believed the second remedy would be impossible to achieve, since it was the amount and kind of property owned that accounted for the differences in human opinions and interest, and the first object of government was to protect the "different and unequal faculties of acquiring property."

Pure democracy

According to Madison, a pure democracy ("by which I mean a society consisting of a small number of citizens who assemble and administer the government in person") could not cure the mischiefs of these factional interest groups, but a republic ("by which I mean a government in which the scheme of representation takes place") could, because (he wrote) representatives

13. *Cf.* Alfred De Grazia, *Public and Republic: Political Representation in America* (New York: Knopf, 1951).

The Federalist consists of 85 essays explaining and urging adoption of the proposed national Constitution. The papers were published in New York State within the eight months preceding May, 1788, but attracted attention throughout all of the states. It was later revealed that the authors, who had originally signed the essays as "Publius," were Alexander Hamilton (who initiated the series and wrote about 50 essays), James Madison (who wrote about 30 of them), and John Jay (who wrote five). The articles were intended to ensure ratification of the Constitution by New York, but it was the practical political ability of Hamilton on the floor of the state convention (and the fact that 10 states had already ratified) which carried the state for the Constitution by the close vote of 30–27. *The Federalist* is widely read today not so much for its historical interest as for its superb analysis of the intent and interpretation of the basic document of American government. It is probably the best contribution Americans have made to political philosophy.

refine and enlarge the public views. That is, representatives must reflect the opinion of many different sorts of people as well as their own views, so their decisions will tend to be moderate. Madison believed that representative government might "be more consonant to the public good than if pronounced by the people themselves, convened for the purpose." Another advantage he saw was that the size of the representative body can easily be regulated. It can be made large enough to guard against "the cabals of the few" and yet kept small enough to prevent "the confusion of a multitude." The ability of a representative form of government to serve a large geographical area also increases its utility.

To the agrarian world of Madison's day it seemed only natural to choose representatives from territorial areas in the country. Territorial or geographic representation in the United States has meant that each electoral constituency or district returns one representative to the House of Representatives. Whatever the number of candidates in a district, the one who wins the highest number or "plurality" of the votes is elected. In the latter part of the nineteenth century, the single-member constituency system came under attack by those who advocated proportional representation or a multiple-member constituency system. The case for "PR" was based on the argument that the single-member district denied the smallest groups of voters any seats in the national assembly and reduced the minority's representation to a fraction of its actual strength throughout the country. Thus not every vote in the nation-at-large commanded an equal share of representation in the House.[14]

Territorial representation

As the nation became industrialized, there was increasing criticism of both territorial and proportional systems of representation. Critics challenged territorial representation—the dominant system in America—as being undesirable, and urged representation by economic interest. That is, they believed that people are more intimately concerned with their vocations than with the political subdivision in which they happen to live. Proponents of "corporate" (or "functional") representation think that teachers should elect their own representatives to the national legislature, auto workers should elect persons to represent their interests, and so on. These advocates of change assert that it is impossible for a single person to represent adequately such diverse groups as farmers, factory workers, engineers, and

Functional representation

14. Austin Ranney and Willmoore Kendall, *Democracy and the American Party System* (New York: Harcourt, Brace, 1956), pp. 65–71. Every student of American government should be familiar with John Stuart Mill's *Considerations on Representative Government* (New York: Liberal Arts, 1958), including his argument favoring proportional representation.

others, who live near each other but who have entirely different concerns to be presented and worked for in Congress.[15] It may be that the existence of bipartisan groups (such as the farm and textile blocs) in Congress constitutes an inevitable compromise between corporate representation and the single-member constituency.

Population shifts and the complexities of American life have recently produced two distinct challenges to the principle of representative government. One difficulty arose because Americans have increasingly migrated from rural areas to metropolitan centers. Such movement often resulted in urban congressional and state legislative districts containing far more inhabitants than corresponding rural districts. Thus a situation developed in which city voters were underrepresented in the United States House of Representatives and both houses of bicameral state legislatures while the less numerous rural inhabitants elected more representatives to those governing bodies than their numbers justified. During the 1960's the Supreme Court delivered a series of rulings, generally referred to as the "one-man, one-vote" decisions, which served to re-establish representative government on the basis of general equality in the numbers of persons contained within the congressional and state legislative districts of each state, and within certain types of local voting districts.[16] The Court held that when substantial inequities in population occur within a state's congressional or state legislative districts, the responsible state legislature must reapportion the state's inhabitants so that they are in voting districts roughly of equal population.[17] The Court's rulings on reapportionment have been criticized, particularly the finding in *Reynolds* v. *Sims* that both houses of a bicameral state legislature must be apportioned on the basis of population. To date the effort of Senator Everett Dirksen (R., Illinois) to obtain Congressional approval of a Constitutional Amendment permitting the states to apportion one house of a two-house state legislature on a non-population basis has failed.

In 1968 the "one-man, one-vote" principle was extended to

Equality of representation

"One man, one vote"

15. *Cf.* De Grazia, *Public and Republic,* pp. 214–34.

16. Baker v. Carr, 369 U.S. 186 (1962); Wesberry v. Sanders, 376 U.S. 1 (1964); Reynolds v. Simms, 377 U.S. 533 (1964); and Avery v. Midland County, 338 U.S. 905 (1968).

17. In the case of congressional districts the Court interpreted the Constitution's phrasing in Article I, Section 2, that representatives be selected "by the People of the several states," to mean also that the people must be roughly divided into equally populated districts. In regard to the malapportionment of state legislative districts, the Court chose to rule that the equal-protection clause of the Fourteenth Amendment was being violated.

apply to many types of local voting districts in towns, cities, and counties. Voicing the opinion of the Court's majority, Justice Byron White stated, "If voters residing in oversize districts are denied their constitutional right to participate in the election of state legislators, precisely the same kind of deprivation occurs when the members of a city council, school board, or county governing board are elected from districts of substantially unequal population."[18] The Court pointed out, however, that not all local voting units need be apportioned along roughly equal population lines. Some special-purpose units, for example a voting district concerned only with rural road construction, might under the Court's ruling be permitted to be apportioned so as to give greater voice to persons most concerned with county roads. The various decisions concerning reapportionment by the Court have already caused extensive redistricting of both state legislative and congressional districts, and no doubt will also lead to considerable reapportionment of certain local voting districts. The "reapportionment revolution" has generated substantial, but often ineffectual, opposition from those groups standing to lose political influence from such action.

The effectiveness of representative government is also put to a severe test by the increasing number and complexity of problems with which elected representatives, particularly at the national level, must contend. For example, during a recent session, Congressmen were expected to exercise judgment on such diverse matters as: the relationship between a tax rebate and industry's willingness to invest in plant modernization; the desirability of using Federal funds to assist in the faculty-improvement programs of local school districts; the repressive conditions which produce young people alienated from the general society; how to prevent criminals from obtaining guns while permitting sportsmen to buy them; the amount of emphasis which should be given research in theoretical physics vis-à-vis efforts to explore the solar system; and the motivations which guide the Communist Chinese rulers!

Demands upon the representatives

All of these matters, as well as much other business brought before the Congress, seems sufficiently complex to test the wisdom of the wisest, best-educated, and most experienced of men. If this is true, then one might ask whether elected representatives ought not be replaced by, or at least joined with, groups of experts and batteries of computers. Individual members of Congress, and congressional committees, do hire a range of experts as staff assistants and consultants, and do use

18. Avery v. Midland County, 388 U.S. 905 (1968).

machine-data-processing techniques and retrieval procedures. Still, it may be argued that the Executive Branch, with its proliferation of departments, commissions, and agencies, each with an army of specialists supplied with immense data bases and sophisticated electronic computation devices, is better equipped to cope with current problems of government than the 535 elected representatives on Capitol Hill.

Congress and public opinion

Both the pressures of tradition and the successful experience of American political institutions have dampened arguments for change. Although the Congress, including the popular-based House of Representatives, may not always mirror public opinion with full faith, Americans are little prone to tampering with constitutionally prescribed machinery. Despite difficulties which from time to time must be resolved, the American system of representation has over the long haul worked rather well. Strong sectional opinions have been moderated in the national legislature. The people's representatives, by and large, have demonstrated a willingness and an ability to harmonize strong pressure from their constituents with their own conceptions of the public good. It ought not be forgotten that during the crisis of the separation of the states more than 100 years ago, Congress was still functioning and its members still working for unity after churches and their ministers had abandoned hope and split into North and South.

Separation of Powers

Three branches

"The accumulation of all powers, legislative, executive, and judiciary, in the same hands," Madison's Number 47 of *The Federalist* asserts, "may justly be pronounced the very definition of tyranny." The logical reasoning of the French political thinker Charles de Montesquieu had convinced the Founders that governmental tyranny could be prevented by dividing political power. In order to prevent government from being concentrated, the framers separated its authority into three branches. The consequences of such division of power have been a mixed blessing, but one thing is certain: American government and politics have been profoundly influenced by it.[19]

19. Several efforts have been made recently to both study and redress the power distribution between the Congress, particularly the Senate, and the President. In 1967 Senator J. William Fulbright (D., Arkansas), chairman of the Senate Foreign Relations Committee, introduced a resolution calling for a return of the constitutional power of the Congress regarding the commitment of the nation to foreign ventures. In the same year the Senate created the Subcommittee on Separation of Powers to study the contemporary role of the separation of powers upon the three branches of the Federal Government.

Article I of the Constitution begins with the words: "*All leg-islative power herein granted shall be vested in a Congress of the United States . . .*" Likewise, Article II commences: "*The executive power shall be vested in a President of the United States of America.*" Similarly, Article III recites: "*The judicial power of the United States shall be vested in one supreme Court, and in such inferior Courts as the Congress may, from time to time, ordain and establish.*" The result of such frag-mentation of governmental power has been to require the coop-eration of all three branches to permit government to operate at all.

The requirement that cooperation among the three branches must be bought at the price of compromise seems implicit in the determination of the founders to separate power not only by function, but also by personnel. Officials do not serve in more than one branch of the national government simulta-neously. The Constitution requires a member of Congress to vacate his seat whenever he accepts a judgeship or an adminis-trative job in the executive branch. In 1916 Supreme Court Jus-tice Charles Evans Hughes resigned his position on the bench before engaging in an unsuccessful campaign for the Presi-dency. In addition, there is a different method for staffing each organ of government: members of the legislative branch are directly elected by the people for terms of either two or six years (although until the adoption of the Seventeenth Amend-ment senators were named by state legislatures); the President is chosen for a four-year term by an electoral college which is elected by the voters for that single purpose,[20] finally, Federal judges are nominated by the President, and when confirmed by the Senate, serve until retirement[21] at a salary which cannot be reduced but may be increased. "He who pays the piper calls the tune" is an adage which also has significance in politics, and officials of the national government play their tunes for differ-ent callers: members of the House of Representatives, in other words, are responsible primarily to the voters of their districts; senators must satisfy the people of an entire state; the President is accountable to the nation; Federal judges—at least according

Cooperation among the three branches

20. It should be noted that the Twenty-second Amendment states, "No person shall be elected to the office of the President more than twice, and no person who has held the office of President, or acted as President, for more than two years of a term to which some other person was elected President shall be elected to the office of the President more than once."

21. Article III uses the words "good behavior" for judicial tenure, but because few judges (and no Supreme Court justices) have been removed, a Federal judgeship, for practical purposes, is terminated by resignation or death.

to *The Federalist* Number 78—are responsible only to the Constitution.

Does the principle of separation of powers require that the legislative, executive, and judicial departments be wholly independent of each other? Madison concluded that it did not. Rather, "unless these departments be so far connected and blended as to give to each a constitutional control over the other," he wrote, "the degree of separation which the maxim requires, as essential to a free government, can never in practice be duly maintained." Number 48 of *The Federalist* explains how the three branches are to be "connected and blended"—and this explanation brings us to the next principle of American government.

Checks and Balances

Eight basic checks

This principle permits all group participants to frustrate the activities of other groups in government. It ensures that widespread agreement generally precedes action. Those who brandish the slogan "the government which governs least, governs best" view checks and balances with particular affection. Groups which cannot command the support necessary to achieve adoption of their philosophy view this principle as a means to thwart the majority which opposes them. It is a negative principle of government which was developed to a fine point by early American conservatives and which has endured to contribute to the impatience of latter-day liberals.

As originally conceived, the Constitution contained eight basic types of checks. These, with some examples, are as follows:

States vs. *Federal Government*. States may check the national government by refusing to concur in amendments endorsed by the Congress. On the other hand, Congress influences many important activities of the states by the offer of money known as "grants-in-aid." In order to receive the money, states must adhere to standards set by Congress. These grants are made for a wide variety of purposes—from highway construction to maternity benefits.

One House of Congress vs. *the Other House*. Since all bills must pass the two chambers of Congress in identical form, either house may defeat the legislation of the other. An interesting example occurred when the Senate refused to concur on a bill that would have increased the size of the House of Representatives beyond 435 members.

Executive vs. *Legislative.* The President may refuse to nominate officers to fill vacancies; he may veto bills that have passed Congress. Whether he is obliged to fight a war Congress has declared, or to enforce all laws vigorously, are interesting questions which probably could be settled only by an impeachment proceeding. On the other hand, presidential vetoes may be overridden by a two-thirds majority of each house. Congressional control of the purse strings, its powers of investigation and impeachment, and its authority to legislate are all effective checks on the executive branch.

Eight basic checks (cont.)

Senate vs. *Executive.* The Senate may refuse to confirm presidential appointments and decline to consent to treaties. The President, however, has ways to circumvent a recalcitrant Senate: he has power to make recess appointments (valid until the expiration of the "next session of the Senate"), so that positions need not remain vacant until the Senate will accept a nominee; and the use of the "executive agreement" often permits arrangements to be made with foreign powers without the consent of the Senate.

Courts vs. *President, Congress, and States.* Very early in constitutional history the Federal courts successfully asserted their power to determine whether or not the acts of administrators and the legislation of both national and state governments were permissible under the Constitution. However, by concerted action, the President and Congress may "pack" the courts by increasing their size and appointing sympathetic judges to fill the new vacancies. Also, under the Constitution, Congress may keep the Supreme Court from hearing many kinds of cases, and it has life-and-death power over the other Federal courts.[22]

Electoral College vs. *Popular Will.* The purpose of the Electoral College was to check the popular vote in the determination of who should be President. The theory was that the people would elect eminent persons who would, in turn, survey the field and select the Chief Executive. Today the system of political parties has pretty well obliged the electors to vote for the candidate of their party, but the right of an elector to vote

22. The balance of power between Congress and the Supreme Court is treated in fascinating detail by Walter F. Murphy, *Congress and the Court* (Chicago: University of Chicago Press, 1962).

for a candidate other than the one he was pledged to support still exists in some states and was exercised in 1968 by a Republican elector from North Carolina who chose to cast his vote for George Wallace rather than for the acknowledged national leader of his party. In 1960 a slate of "unpledged" electors from Mississippi (along with six electors from Alabama) accounted for Senator Byrd's 15 electoral votes, although Kennedy had carried their states.

Voters vs. *Congress.* The short term specified for the members of the House of Representatives was deliberately planned to provide the people with an effective check on their legislators in the lower house. This check by the voters has since been extended to the election of senators, although the six-year senatorial term remains.

States vs. *Senate (obsolete)*. Before the adoption of the Seventeenth Amendment in 1913, Senators were elected by state legislatures. At the present time legislatures have authority under the Constitution to permit a governor to make temporary appointments to the Senate in the event of a vacancy during an elected term.

Compromise It was through checks and balances that the framers sought to realize their conviction that "ambition must be made to counteract ambition." It is doubtful that they intended to institute a system where each branch checking the other would result in perpetual deadlock; instead, they intended to guarantee that all governmental actions would be moderated by compromise. The rise of political parties (viewed with alarm by the founders) has supplied the "axle grease" that has made the three branches work together as smoothly as they do. Whenever a President appeals to the voters for a "Republican" or "Democratic" Congress, he is attempting to weaken this principle of government. Yet checks and balances operate even in spite of a majority of Congress "friendly" to the President, and detractors of this principle point to the wreckage of many policies that never could be consistently maintained because of its operation, and even to situations when checks and balances prevented policy from being made at all. Without reaching a final judgment as to whether the times have brought forth strong Presidents, or whether certain Presidents have found the times conducive to the exercise of strong leadership, it is generally agreed that much of the twentieth century has been a period in which the power and checks of the Congress ebbed, and the power of the President increased. This situation, perhaps most noticeable regarding the use of presidential power in the Cold War context, and more particularly in regard to the American entry into—and prosecution of—the Vietnamese war, is of concern to laymen, scholars, and professional politicians. How power will be shared between the Congress and the Chief Executive, and what role the Supreme Court will play, as America moves through the 1970's remains to be worked out. Past experience suggests that all three branches will have their champions and critics, and that the balance of power established by the Constitution will be partially modified in practice by the flow of events and the appearance of new political personalities.

Future balance of power

Judicial Review

These two words refer to the power of the courts, in a case properly before them, to examine legislation and administrative actions and to determine whether or not such acts are, in Alexander Hamilton's words, "contrary to the manifest tenor of the Constitution." If found to be so, the courts declare such acts to be without force.

COURTS AND CONSTITUTIONALITY

There are observers of American history who insist that the power of the judges to pose as the official interpreters of the Constitution was "usurped," and they trace the usurpation to the federalistic fourth Chief Justice, John Marshall. Since the Constitution nowhere expressly states that the courts may nullify congressional legislation, laws of the states, or actions of the Federal administrators, what claim do the judges have to such enormous power? Thomas Jefferson considered that each branch of government should determine for itself the constitutionality of its acts. John C. Calhoun argued persuasively for the right of each state to review the acts of the national government and veto those found unconstitutional. Yet the only theory of review for constitutionality that has survived is judicial review.

Early theories

To other observers of the American scene, it seems apparent that from the very beginning, Federal courts were expected to determine constitutionality. In the celebrated Number 78 of *The Federalist*, Hamilton, while explaining the necessity for a completely independent judiciary in a limited government, argued: "Limitations of this kind can be preserved in practice

25

no other way than through the medium of the courts of justice, whose duty it must be to declare all acts contrary to the manifest tenor of the Constitution void." Two paragraphs after this he wrote: "No legislative act, therefore, contrary to the Constitution, can be valid." He refused to admit the familiar charge that authority to censor and kill laws made the judicial power superior to the legislative power, but held that "it only supposes that the power of the people is superior to both . . ."

A British precedent The effort of Sir Edward Coke, the English Lord Chief Justice in 1610, to hold a law of Parliament invalid was part of the history some Americans had learned. John Marshall was familiar with the case of Dr. Bonham: Parliament had given the London College of Physicians authority to grant licenses to practice medicine in the city and provided further that this licensing board would enforce its own decisions. Half of all the fines the board assessed were given to its members for their own use. The College of Physicians refused to give Dr. Bonham a license, and when he engaged in his profession without it, he was fined and imprisoned. Lord Chief Justice Coke decided that a law which permitted interested persons to refuse licenses to potential competitors was "against common right and reason." In such instances, he reasoned, "the common law will controul [sic] it and adjudge such act to be void."[23] Parliament simply reenacted the statute, thus refusing to permit censorship of its legislation by the courts. Dr. Bonham, presumably, moved to a more congenial city.

THE SHAPING OF JUDICIAL REVIEW

Marbury v. Madison Although individual Supreme Court justices were haltingly challenging the constitutionality of congressional statutes as early as 1792, it remained for the great Chief Justice Marshall to shape a petty affair into one of the most important decisions in judicial history. Before leaving office after an unsuccessful attempt to gain a second term as President, John Adams had his party create new judicial positions which he proceeded to pack with loyal partisans. The appointments were confirmed by the Senate, but not all the certificates of office had been delivered to the new judges when President Jefferson assumed office. The new President permitted some commissions to be delivered, but directed his Secretary of State, James Madison, not to distribute 17 of them. One of the disappointed office-seekers was William Marbury, who was to have been a justice of the peace in the District of Columbia. Relying on the provisions of the Judiciary Act of 1789, Marbury went before the Supreme

26

23. Dr. Bonham's Case, 8 Co. CCP 181a (1610).

Court to ask that a writ of mandamus (a court order directing an officer to perform a required duty) be served on James Madison to compel the delivery of the commission. Marbury's object apparently was to embarrass the Jeffersonian party rather than to secure such a paltry position for himself. Chief Justice Marshall (who, as the recent Secretary of State for President Adams, should have delivered the commissions before leaving office!) appeared to be in a tough spot. If he granted the writ of mandamus and Madison refused to obey, the Court would be powerless; if he did not grant Marbury the writ, Jefferson would have been triumphant. Marshall's cagey response was to find Section 13 of the Judiciary Act to be unconstitutional.[24]

The reason why Section 13 could be held unconstitutional was that it authorized the Supreme Court to issue writs of mandamus to "persons holding office, under the authority of the United States." The Constitution (Article III, Section 2) said that the only cases which could come to the Supreme Court for a first hearing were those "affecting ambassadors, other public ministers and consuls, and those to which a state is a party." Since William Marbury was not a foreign ambassador, a minister, a consul, nor a state, he was before the wrong court. The Supreme Court could not give him the help he sought. The mistake Congress had made, according to Marshall, was to add to the original jurisdiction of the Supreme Court. This aspect of the Court's power was set by the Constitution and so could be changed only by amendment, not by a mere law.

Justice Marshall's decision

The Chief Justice did not even discuss the constitutional problem, however, until after he had cloaked his political views in judicial robes and lectured his arch-enemy (and second cousin) Thomas Jefferson on the lack of morality displayed in the shameless denial of Marbury's "right." When he did get around to the constitutional issue, he relied heavily on Number 78 of *The Federalist*. Marbury, of course, could have gone to a lower Federal court for his writ of mandamus, but he evidently did not even bother to do so. And so an insignificant case, loaded with party politics, became the precedent for the principle of the power of the courts to kill laws of Congress.

24. Marbury v. Madison, 1 Cranch 137 (1803). The doctrine of judicial review expounded by Marshall in *Marbury* v. *Madison* has been seriously challenged several times. The basic opposition argument has been most clearly presented by Justice Gibson of the Pennsylvania Supreme Court in 1825. Eakin v. Raub, 12 Sergeant and Rawle 330 (Supreme Court of Pennsylvania, 1825). One of the most interesting discussions of judicial review as a political weapon is provided by Robert K. Carr, *The Supreme Court and Judicial Review* (New York: Holt, Rinehart, and Winston, 1942).

The monumental case of *Martin* v. *Hunter's Lessee*[25] allowed the Supreme Court to deny once and for all the position taken by a state court that "the Court is unanimously of opinion that the appellate power of the Supreme Court of the United States does not extend to this court under a sound construction of the Constitution of the United States..." Chief Justice Marshall disqualified himself in this instance because he had been involved in the litigation that had given rise to the challenge by the Virginia court. His cohort, Joseph Story, however, read a powerful argument for the necessity of a single final tribunal to ensure uniformity of decisions throughout the whole United States.

ULTRA VIRES

Under the common law, courts of justice had set aside official actions as *ultra vires* when an administrator had acted "beyond his powers." Under the principle of judicial review, there is no reason why the courts cannot declare *ultra vires* actions to be illegal. Although not the first of such decisions, the famous steel seizure case furnishes an excellent example of judicial review of the executive branch.

In April, 1952, President Harry S. Truman, by executive order, directed Secretary of Commerce Sawyer to take possession of, prescribe the terms of employment in, and operate some of the principal steel plants in the nation. At the same time, the President notified the company presidents of his action and invited them to serve as operating managers for the government. The President defended the drastic step of governmental seizure of private property as necessary, to halt the paralyzing strike in the steel industry at a time of national emergency, when American troops were locked in "deadly combat" with forces of aggression in Korea. The companies obeyed the order but went into a Federal district court to procure an injunction (a court order directing that a threatened wrong not be done) to prevent the Secretary of Commerce from continuing the possession of the plants. The district court granted the injunction; the government went to the court of appeals, which reversed the lower court; the companies then appealed to the Supreme Court, which denied that the President had authority to seize the mills.[26] In reviewing Truman's action the majority

25. 1 Wheaton 304 (1816).

26. Youngstown Sheet and Tube Co. v. Sawyer, 343 U.S. 579 (1952). A documentary portrait of the steel seizure decision is found in Alan F. Westin, *The Anatomy of a Constitutional Law Case* (New York: Macmillan, 1958).

opinion held: "The President's power, if any, to issue the order must stem either from an act of Congress or from the Constitution itself." It found no act of Congress granting the Chief Executive authority to seize the property; "indeed," Justice Hugo Black wrote, "we do not understand the Government to rely on statutory authorization for this seizure . . ." Neither could the order be sustained as an exercise of the President's position as Commander-in-Chief, nor from his constitutional charge to see that the laws are faithfully executed. President Truman promptly complied with the Court's decision. He was not the first President to be called to account by the courts,[27] and likely will not be the last.

RESTRICTIONS

Judicial review is a vital concept in American government and one so often in the headlines that it is familiar to most readers. However, two features about it need to be repeated: (a) all courts have the power of judicial review—not just the Supreme Court, although the highest court does have final determination; (b) a court may question the constitutionality of legislation or administrative actions only when cases raising the issues are properly before it. Congress may prevent the hearing of some cases simply by changing the power of the courts to handle appeals. This was done after the Civil War for the express purpose of preventing judicial review of questionable "reconstruction" laws. The Court meekly accepted the change in its appellate power in the McCardle case.[28]

The power of judicial review

It should be noted that some restrictions on the power of judicial review come from the judges themselves.[29] For example, courts are reluctant to decide an issue of constitutionality unless it is absolutely necessary to do so. Even when obliged to rule on invalidity, the judges attempt to confine their attack on a statute to as small a part as possible. In addition, courts in the past have flatly refused to determine "political questions"

27. For example, the Court repudiated Lincoln's suspension of the writ of habeas corpus. Ex parte Milligan, 4 Wallace 2 (1866). Franklin D. Roosevelt was not permitted to remove a Federal commissioner. Rathbun v. United States, 295 U.S. 602 (1935). However, each of these cases should be compared with instances when the Court subscribed to wide presidential powers. The Prize Cases, 2 Black 635 (1863); Myers v. United States, 272 U.S. 52 (1926).

28. Ex parte McCardle, 7 Wallace 506 (1868).

29. See Justice Brandeis' concurring opinion, Ashwander v. T.V.A., 297 U.S. 288 (1936). Also the brilliant essay by former Associate Justice Robert H. Jackson, "The Supreme Court as a Political Institution," in Alan F. Westin, ed., The Supreme Court: Views from Inside (New York: W. W. Norton, 1961).

such as whether or not a state has a "republican form of government," or if a proposed constitutional amendment may be reconsidered by a state legislature after it has once been rejected by that body. Judges have preferred to leave such determinations to the political branches of the national government.

Since the late 1930's the Supreme Court, and lesser courts, have shown a marked tendency to support social experimentation by the other two branches of government, to correct voting inequities caused by population shifts, and to protect the rights of various minority members of society, not only racial and religious groups but also accused and convicted criminals. For such action the courts, particularly the Supreme Court, have been applauded by some and castigated by others. Chief Justice Earl Warren, who has presided over one of the Court's most active periods (1953–1969), has drawn an unusual amount of praise and criticism during his tenure. Hailed by some as a truly great jurist deserving a place beside John Marshall,[30] he was condemned by others as a betrayer of the Constitution who should have been impeached. Attacks upon the courts and the justices may be expected to continue as judicial decisions are rendered that affect the ways in which Americans use government under the Constitution to solve the problems of living in an increasingly complex and crowded society.

Attacks upon the courts

Equality Before the Law

One of the most pervasive ideals of the American heritage is found in the ringing phrase of the Declaration of Independence: "We hold these truths to be self-evident, that all men are created equal..." It is an affirmation of the dignity of man that has roots in the genesis of history, and yet one would be unable to specify an historical time and a geographical place where the ideal was completely realized. We know that men are not equal in bodily strength, in intellectual prowess, in manual dexterity, nor in a hundred other ways of comparison; yet we believe that government and law should play no favorites.

Consider this hypothetical case:[31] Three men meet to dine together. They arrive simultaneously and leave their cars in the same block—where parking is prohibited. Two hours later they

30. John Marshall, Chief Justice in the first third of the 1800's, built the Supreme Court into a powerful third branch of government and did much to establish the strength of the Federal Government.

31. This case was suggested by Edmond Cahn, in his fascinating study *The Sense of Injustice* (1949).

return, and each finds a parking ticket. Appearing in traffic court together, each pleads guilty: one is dismissed with a warning; the second is fined $10; the third is fined $30 and given 30 days in jail. This would seem to most Americans to be incredibly unjust unless it were determined that the fines were scaled on the basis of prior convictions or some such reasonable classification. If, instead, the sentences were determined by status (the first man was identified as a university president; the second, a professor; and the third, an undergraduate student), a first impulse would be to quote the maxim, "let the punishment fit the crime." One who knew more history might flavor the complaint by reciting the protest from old England: "The poorest he that is in England has a life to live as well as the richest he." The symbol of justice is the blindfolded goddess.

Hypothetical case

If it were learned that, in the hypothetical instance of the three parking tickets, the distinguishing factor was race, religion, or color, today's citizen would very likely be much more disturbed than if the distinction had been based on educational or social status. If this assumption is correct, the fact provides an interesting comment on how the ideal of equality has changed in the century since the age of Jackson. Once the democratizing tide set in motion during Jackson's presidency had swept away social barriers to equality in public life, color was bound to become the next target of those who treasured the ideal of equality.

The attempt to apply the Declaration of Independence to the Negro has been underway for over 100 years. The Thirteenth, Fourteenth, and Fifteenth Amendments were advances to a new position as have been a number of court decisions which supported the ideal of equality before the law, and the series of Civil-Rights Acts which began with the 1957 statute. If they have not achieved the ideal of equality, they have established precedents in the struggle for equal treatment. The provision that "No state shall . . . deny to any persons within its jurisdiction the equal protection of the laws," was written into the fundamental document of American government after the Civil War. Despite enormous problems, history is vindicating the pithy statement Justice John M. Harlan made in 1896: "The Constitution is color-blind."[32] Yet, although it is everywhere recognized that even though legal equality is much more easily obtained than social—or even political—equality, it must be admitted that for two thirds of the twentieth century "equality before the law" remains, for many, more of an ideal

Racial equality

32. Justice Harlan, dissenting, Plessy v. Ferguson, 163 U.S. 537, 559 (1896).

than a fact. Whether the issue is presented in the form of non-violent protest by those associated with the name of the late Dr. Martin Luther King, by Black Power activists, or by white homeowners opposed to the open-housing legislation and judicial ruling of 1968—members of both races will continue to struggle with the problems inherent in the questions regarding equality: what kind? when? and at what cost? Examination of these and related problems occupy an entire chapter in this book because the resolution of racial and other minority-group problems constitutes a very major item on the American agenda for the 1970's.[33]

Civilian Control of the Military

Frozen into the Constitution, but rapidly melting from some citizens' conceptions of sound governmental principles, is the belief that, as Georges Clemenceau, France's World War I leader, is said to have put it: "War is too serious a business to leave to the generals."

Certainly, the Founding Fathers were convinced adherents to the "Cincinnatus theory" of military leadership. They knew the legend about the solid Roman citizen, Cincinnatus, who at the request of the senate forsook his plow to become dictator during a grave emergency, only to relinquish this power and return to his plowing when the danger to the state had passed. They also knew that a different sort of person, Julius Caesar, had crossed the river Rubicon with his victorious armies in violation of the law of Rome, and by leading his troops to the capital, sounded the death knell of the Roman Republic.

Roman precedent

The founders hoped to prevent the rise of Caesars by encouraging the Cincinnatus type. The Commander-in-Chief of the nation's armed forces was to be the President, and the President was to be a civilian. Checks and balances were invoked to prevent military control from resting with any branch of government, but its efficient exercise required the cooperation of Congress and President as suggested in the alleged relationship of the Roman Senate and Cincinnatus. The President, presumably, could command troops in the field, but the Congress alone could appropriate money to support the troops. In addition, no army appropriation might exceed a two-year period without congressional renewal. The President appointed all military officers, but only the Senate could confirm their commis-

---

33. *Cf.* Chapter 8. While the nation's attention may be attracted to the struggle for equality by black Americans, one should remember there are other minority groups with similar hopes and frustrations.

sions. Congress alone had the power to declare war, but the President's actions could make war inevitable. To the world of 1789 the provisions for civilian control of the military must have appeared to be as foolproof as could be devised.

But these are vastly different times. During the last few decades, when war or the threat of it have played an unusually large role in the conduct of American foreign policy, the civilian-control concept has both grown in importance and become more difficult to achieve. Contributing to the difficulty of precisely defining the proper relationship between the military establishment and civilian leadership is the immense size of the former. The military forces, combined into the Department of Defense by the Defense Reorganization Act of 1947, dramatically dwarf the rest of the Federal Government in regard to persons (civilians and military) employed and money spent.

A changing concept

Recent Presidents have sought by different means to implement the concept of civilian control of the military. During the Korean war President Harry S. Truman dismissed General Douglas MacArthur from command of the American forces on the charge of insubordination. The matter arose from a clash of views concerning the objectives to be secured in the Korean struggle. The President's policy was to limit the conflict in geographical scope and intensity to those levels necessary to restore the non-Communist status of South Korea. General MacArthur disagreed, and publicly expressed the opinion that the objectives should be expanded beyond the protection of South Korea to include a more forceful confrontation with Asian Communism. Writing of General MacArthur's dismissal in his memoirs, Truman stated:

Recent presidents and the military

Truman

> If there is one basic element in our Constitution, it is civilian control of the military. Politics are to be made by the elected political officials, not by generals or admirals. Yet time and again General MacArthur had shown that he was unwilling to accept the policies of the Administration. By his repeated public statements he was not only confusing our allies as to the true course of our policies but, in fact, was also setting his policy against the President's.[34]

Taking leave of the Presidency, Dwight D. Eisenhower, a five-star general in World War II, spoke to his countrymen of the unwarranted influence of the military and of the industrial suppliers of military equipment:

Eisenhower

> This conjunction of an immense military establishment and a large arms industry is new in American experience. The

34. Harry S. Truman, *Memoirs by Harry S. Truman*, Vol. II, *Years of Trial And Hope* (Garden City: Doubleday, 1956), p. 444.

total influence—economic, political, even spiritual—is felt in every city, every state house, every office of the Federal Government. We recognize the imperative need for this development. Yet we must not fail to comprehend its grave implications. Our toil, resources, and livelihood are all involved; so is the very structure of our society.

Then in an oft-quoted passage, the President issued this warning:

In the councils of government we must guard against the acquisition of unwarranted influence, whether sought or unsought, by the military-industrial complex. The potential for the disastrous rise of misplaced power exists and will persist.

We must never let the weight of this combination endanger our liberties or democratic processes. We should take nothing for granted. Only an alert and knowledgeable citizenry can compel the proper meshing of the huge industrial and military machinery of defense with our peaceful methods and goals, so that security and liberty may prosper together.[35]

Recent examples For his part, President John F. Kennedy held a tight rein over the military and on several occasions had shifted to lesser posts high-ranking officers he deemed were exceeding their authority or were failing to carry out his policies. Unhappiness on the part of some over the President's actions in controlling what the military officers said led to charges that Kennedy was "muzzling" the military. Kennedy also appointed as his Secretary of Defense a strong-willed businessman named Robert S. McNamara. The former Ford executive soon became the center of a number of controversies, many of which involved disagreements with the nation's highest-ranking military men. Amid rumors of differences over the Vietnamese war and other defense policies between the Secretary of Defense and other officials, McNamara left the Pentagon early in 1968 to become president of the World Bank. Upon his departure both critics and supporters generally agreed on one point: McNamara, for better or worse, was the Defense Secretary who had exercised the strongest civilian control over the military.[36]

35. Office of the Federal Register, *Public Papers of the Presidents, Dwight D. Eisenhower, 1960–61* (Washington: Government Printing Office, 1961), p. 1038.

36. Jack Raymond, *Power at the Pentagon* (New York: Harper and Row, 1964), Chapter XVI, pp. 277–293; and C. W. Borklund, *Men of the Pentagon* (New York: Praeger, 1966), Chapter XI, pp. 206–236, offer views of Secretary McNamara, and other Defense Secretaries, by two men with long experience in Washington.

Presidential interpretations of the civilian control concept have not always been shared by the defense establishment. The basic case against too much civilian control is that career military officers, experts in their profession, are better qualified to make policy decisions relating to national defense activity than are civilians whose competence has been largely acquired in other walks of life.[37]

Some scholars have suggested that the division of political power in the American system of government has contributed to frustrating the ideal of civilian control. A mid-1950 study of civilian control, applicable today, found the principle of separation of powers to be "a perpetual invitation, if not an irresistible force, drawing military leaders into political conflicts." It contended the provision of checks and balances to be "a standing invitation to military leaders to make an end run around the President to the Congress."[38] The major controversies often taken by the military to the Congress, or to various groups in the civilian society, arise over budget requests for procurement of major weapons systems (such as the Anti-Ballistic Missile system and new nuclear submarines), the degree to which executive-branch civilian judgment and analytical processes should override military experience in the conduct of military matters, and the relative worth of the views held by the military about the international situation and the menace of Communism vis-à-vis the views of those subjects expressed by the nation's executive leadership.[39]

Civilian control today

The questions of "how much is enough" in regard to missiles, nuclear bombs and warheads, aircraft, ships, and infantry divisions; and how the American military should be used to safeguard and advance national interests abroad, will no doubt continue to provide disagreement between the civil and military leadership in Washington.

37. A number of books have expressed the view that the military ought to be accorded an increased role in determining the national defense policies of the nation. See Barry M. Goldwater, *Why Not Victory?* (New York: MacFadden, 1963), Chap. 12, pp. 122–128; Major General Dale O. Smith (Ret.), *The Eagle's Talons* (Washington: Spartan Books, 1966); General Nathan F. Twining, (Ret.), *Neither Liberty Nor Safety* (New York: Holt, Rinehart and Winston, 1966), and General Curtis E. LeMay (Ret.), *America Is in Danger* (New York: Funk and Wagnalls, 1968).

38. Samuel P. Huntington, "Civilian Control and the Constitution," *American Political Science Review*, L (September, 1956), pp. 676–699.

39. A recent study of how one branch of the military service went about seeking its objectives in the Washington arena is Vincent Davis, *The Admirals' Lobby* (Chapel Hill: University of North Carolina Press, 1967).

35

Federalism

This word is derived from the Latin stem meaning "covenant." As a principle of the American variety of democracy, it describes an arrangement in which political power is divided between a central government and the local governments. According to the definition, this division of power is made by an authority superior to both (the "covenant," *i.e.*, the Constitution) and is made in such a way that the allocation may not be changed by either the central or local units acting independently (the amending process supposes cooperation of the two).

Origins To one who is familiar with the historical reasons why the early immigrants to America settled into separate colonies, the construction of a "more perfect union" on the base of self-governing states appears entirely sensible. The reader who lacks a background in American history might profitably make the simple subtraction of 1607 (the settlement of Jamestown) from 1788 (the year when 11 states had adopted the Constitution) and compare it with the difference in time from the inauguration of Washington on the last day of April, 1789 to the present date. Then he will see how a long history of local control contributed to geographical reality to make a federal form of government logical for the United States.

Even if federalism were logical—indeed almost inevitable—still it was a breathtaking experiment. The Founders aimed at

A cartoon by Benjamin Franklin calling for a union of the colonies in 1754.

nothing less than to apply their ideal of popular sovereignty to an area so vast that, considering the means of transportation and communication then available, only the most optimistic among them must have dared to hope for resounding success. It was generally known in 1787 that the history of the world afforded no instance of a large nation retaining self-government for a long period of time. The republican principles of ancient Rome, for example, stopped at the city walls.

If the principle of federalism was a successful experiment in sound government for America, it is one that has not uniformly yielded satisfaction for other countries which have attempted a dual government. Alexis de Tocqueville, an early and acute observer of American institutions, may have reported accurately when he wrote: "This Constitution, which may at first sight be confused with the federal constitutions that have preceded it, rests in truth upon a wholly novel theory, which may be considered as a great discovery in modern political science," but he was unquestionably correct when he continued that the Constitution "resembles those fine creations of human industry which ensure wealth and renown to their inventors, but which are profitless in other hands." He cited, for example, how in 1824 the Mexicans, neighbors to the South, "took the Federal Constitution . . . as their model and copied it almost entirely." "But," he continued, "although they had borrowed the letter of the law, they could not carry over the spirit that gives it life. They were involved in ceaseless embarrassments . . . and to the present day [he wrote in 1848] Mexico is alternately the victim of anarchy and the slave of military despotism."[40] In 1867 Canada, the neighbor to the North, profiting by the example of the American Civil War, adopted a form of federalism that reversed the division of power between central and local governments by giving the "enumerated powers" to the provinces. One is sure that Tocqueville would insist that the Canadian experiment has been successful because "the confederate states had been long accustomed to form a portion of one empire before they had won their independence," and not because Canadian federalism was based on cunning alterations of the American plan.

If federalism has been successful as a principle of government in the United States, it nevertheless must be recognized as a source of many problems. The important crises of American government and politics have a habit of turning on the question of "states' rights." The disputes between proponents of

The U.S. pattern

Problems of federalism

40. *Democracy in America* (New York: Vintage Books, 1955), Vol. I, Chap. VIII.

"The Present State of Our Country" as seen by an early nineteenth-century cartoonist (the pillars are labeled "Federalism," "Republicanism," and "Democracy").

state and national powers have been the most significant theme of American history since 1789. The dispute figures prominently in the build-up to the Civil War, and in 1948 the issue split the Democratic Party and led to the secession of "Dixiecrats" who nominated their own candidate for the Presidency. The unsuccessful Republican presidential candidate in 1964, Barry M. Goldwater, built his campaign to a large extent upon the contention that the Federal Government had by various means taken powers from the states and that these ought to be returned. The mammoth proportions of the loss Goldwater suffered to President Johnson did not signal the demise of states' rights as an issue in American politics. Former Alabama Governor George Wallace offered himself and his American Independent Party in 1968 to those voters who wished to reaffirm their belief in the strengthening of state powers, particularly in regard to racial matters, at the expense of the Federal Government. Within the Republican and Democratic parties discussion continues regarding ways to strengthen the abilities of the states to handle the many problems which beset them.

States' rights

Although they exercise authority over the same people and the same territory, state governments and their local subdivisions and the Federal Government tend to view mutual problems from somewhat different perspectives. It is then natural, when the two levels of jurisdiction attempt to cope with problems of concern to both, that states' rights will be an issue for continued assessment and redefinition.

Frequently it requires foreign eyes to see what the native readily assents to as being "natural." Tocqueville is only one who has been "struck by the good sense and the practical judgment of the Americans" in their ability to "elude the numberless difficulties resulting from their Federal Constitution." Someone has said that the American is a born constitutional lawyer. He has had to be. Tocqueville informed the Americans of today of something significant when he wrote: "In examining the Constitution of the United States, which is the most perfect federal constitution that ever existed, one is startled at the variety of information and the amount of discernment that it presupposes in the people whom it is meant to govern."[41] In the next chapter we will proceed to examine the facts about federalism that Americans are presupposed to know.

41. *Ibid.*

SUMMARY

• The operation of American government today, at local, state, and national levels, owes much to the form given it by the Constitution and later statutory enactments. However, there is more to the substance of government in the United States than constitutional phrases and laws. Principles of government, embodying both ideals and attitudes, have shaped, and will shape in the future, the kind of government Americans have. Many of these principles are being seriously questioned today, as indeed are many of the most basic strands of American life, to determine if they are sufficient to guide political life in the times ahead.

• Nine broad principles of American government may be identified:

Popular Sovereignty. An ancient requirement for a free people, popular sovereignty means that the people have both the right and methods to require those who serve in positions of authority to be responsive to the popular will.

Limited Government. The idea that government may not intrude in all areas of human endeavor far antedates the Constitution. All levels of government in the United States are enjoined from undertaking certain actions; for example, restricting an individual's right to observe the dictates of his conscience or religion.

Representative Government. The size of the nation makes pure democracy—that is, where everyone participates in governmental decision-making—an impossibility; the people therefore select a few individuals to represent their interests and enact their will.

Separation of Powers. Designed to prevent the accumulation of power in the hands of one person, or one group, this principle requires that power be shared among the executive, legislative, and judicial branches—meaning that no branch receives exactly what it wants.

Checks and Balances. Related to the separation-of-powers principle is the theory that each branch of government is empowered to block or modify the action of the others. During much of the twentieth century strong Presidents acting in crisis times have seized the initiative and operated in a fashion to lessen the influence of both the separation of powers and the checks and balances principles.

Judicial Review. The merit of the courts having the power to review actions by the legislative and executive branches, and subsequently to declare such actions null and void, has been debated by Americans as it was by Englishmen before them. While courts in general have the power of judicial review, the Supreme Court is the final authority.

Equality Before the Law. Despite the promise found in the Declaration of Independence regarding the equal creation of all men, "equality before the law" remains for millions of Americans more an ideal than a reality.

Civilian Control of the Military. America's almost constant involvement in serious military affairs since World War II has led some to suggest that the military be given increased control of military matters. Others contend that the "industrial-military complex" is so large and powerful that it threatens the most basic values in American life.

Federalism. This principle provides for the division of political power between the central government and the states and their subdivisions. Certain powers are delegated to the national government under the operation of this principle, and other powers not prohibited to the states or delegated to the national government are "reserved" for the states, by the Constitution.

SUGGESTED READING

* (*Books so designated are available in paperback editions.*)

* Almond, Gabriel A., and Verba, Sidney, *The Civic Culture* (Boston: Little, Brown, 1965).

* Beard, Charles A., *An Economic Interpretation of the Constitution of the United States* (New York: Macmillan, 1961).

* Becker, Carl L., *The Declaration of Independence* (New York: Vintage Books, 1968).

* Boorstin, Daniel J., *The Genius of American Politics* (Chicago: Phoenix, 1960).

* Lerner, Max, *America as a Civilization* (New York: Simon and Schuster, 1957).

* Lindsay, A. D., *The Modern Democratic State* (New York: Oxford University Press, 1962).

* McGiffert, Michael, ed., *The Character of Americans* (Homewood, Ill.: Dorsey Press, 1964).

2

The
Nature of
American
Federalism

**Federal and unitary
systems**

It is oftentimes explained that what is distinctive about a federal government is that it permits matters of state or local concern to be determined and managed by a state or local government while reserving items of nationwide concern for the central government. But this administrative convenience is no monopoly of federalism—any government might make a similar arrangement. The crucial point of difference between a federal government and others is that, under federalism, neither the central government nor the states may determine which areas they will control—the division of power has been made by a covenant. For example, in the United States (which has a *federal* form of government) Congress may not require the state of Louisiana to abandon the parts of her legal system which were inspired by the European civil law in order to be in step with her sister states which use the English common law. Neither may the Washington lawmakers require the Atlanta legislators to repeal the Georgia provision allowing persons to vote at the age of eighteen. On the other hand, the lawmakers for the state of California (which, like other states, has a *unitary* form of government) may require every city within her jurisdiction which has a population of more than 50,000 to have ten judges, even if the cities concerned have no need for more than one judge. Likewise, the state of North Carolina may in fact grant a great deal of local government to her counties—but she may take it back.[1] The difference is that since the governments of the states are unitary, not federal, the counties and cities within the states do not have the same relationship to their state governments as do the several states to the national government.

Powers Allocated to the National Government

One of the primary purposes of the Constitution was to allocate power between the national and state governments. According to the distribution, the national government may exercise the powers which are delegated to it by the Constitution. The most important enumeration is made by Article I, Section 8. Although not all of these grants have been (or are) equally important, they are discussed in order to indicate the kinds of power a central government requires if it is to be effective.

TAXATION, EXPENDITURE, AND THE GENERAL WELFARE

The sad experience of the penniless central government under the Articles of Confederation was not to be repeated after the adoption of the "more perfect union." Instead, Congress was given the power of the purse:

The power of the purse

> *The Congress shall have power to lay and collect taxes, duties, imposts and excises, to pay the debts and provide for the common defence and general welfare of the United States; but all duties, imposts and excises shall be uniform throughout the United States . . .*

The meaning of the phrase, "general welfare," for which the national government may tax and spend, has been, quite naturally, a fertile source for sharp debate. Even before the docu-

1. In granting varying amounts of authority to, and setting rules for, counties, metropolitan centers, and smaller communities within their jurisdiction, states may follow one plan or a combination of several plans. In wide use is the classification system under which the state classifies areas on the basis of population and then establishes rules and prerogatives for the different kinds of communities. Another method is for the state to grant substantial authority to an area in the form of a home-rule charter. This procedure is generally reserved for the larger cities whose governing problems set them apart from the other communities in a state. A third arrangement is to permit communities to select from several alternative forms of local-government structure that type which is thought best suited to local conditions.

THE CONSTITUTION

THE NATIONAL GOVERNMENT

Delegated Powers:

Taxation, expenditure, and the general welfare
Borrowing
Regulation of commerce
Naturalization
Bankruptcies
Coinage of money and the postal service
Patents and Copyrights
Establishment of lower courts
Upholding international law
Declaration of war
The military establishment
The national capital
etc.

Prohibited Powers:

To abridge the freedoms and rights set forth in the Bill of Rights
To pass bills of attainder or ex post facto laws
To grant titles of nobility
To levy export taxes
etc.

IMPLIED POWERS

(Article I, Section 8: Congress may "make all laws which shall be necessary into execution the foregoing powers and all other powers vested by this Constitution in the government of the United States...")

NATIONAL SUPREMACY

(Article VI, Section 2: "This Constitution and the laws of the United States ...and all treaties...shall be the supreme law of the land...")

CONCURRENT POWERS:

Taxation
Law enforcement
Social welfare
Interstate commerce
Implied powers, etc.

STATE GOVERNMENTS

Reserved Powers:

(Tenth Amendment: "The powers not delegated to the United States by the Constitution, nor prohibited by it to the states, are reserved to the states respectively, or to the people.")

Prohibited Powers:

To deprive persons of life, liberty, or property without due process of law
To deny persons equal protection of the laws
To abridge the privileges and immunities of U.S. citizens
To make treaties or alliances, coin money, emit bills of credit
To pass bills of attainder of ex post facto laws
To grant titles of nobility
To levy export taxes.
etc.

ment was finally drafted, disputes arose about it.[2] Alexander Hamilton and Thomas Jefferson, strong members of President Washington's first cabinet, differed profoundly on the subject. Hamilton maintained that the phrase conferred a power separate and distinct from those which follow it in Article I, Section 8. Jefferson, however, insisted that if such a broad interpretation were given the clause, the framers might as well have put a period after it and omitted the remainder of the Constitution. In view of the importance of the "general welfare" clause and the long history of debates concerning it, it seems incredible that the Court did not attempt to expound its meaning until 1936. On that occasion, after a survey of constitutional history, the judges concluded that the Hamiltonian position was the correct one. "While, therefore, the power to tax is not unlimited," Mr. Justice Roberts wrote in *United States* v. *Butler*, "its confines are set in the clause which confers it, and not in those of Section 8 which bestow and define the legislative powers of Congress." The opinion continues: "It results that the power of Congress to authorize expenditure of public moneys for public purposes is not limited by the direct grants of legislative power found in the Constitution."[3]

Hamilton vs. Jefferson

The words of Justice Roberts make it clear that the powers to tax and spend are not limited to the specific purposes set forth in the remaining clauses of this article, but the permissible areas have still not been clearly defined. When Congress attempted to bring child labor to an abrupt halt by levying a 10 percent tax on the net income of firms which failed to follow the provisions of the child labor statute, the Supreme Court found the law to be unconstitutional. Child labor was a state affair, the Court ruled, and taxation by the national government which had the effect of regulating a state concern was therefore out of order. The opinion was based, however, on a case which has since been explicitly reversed.[4] In other cases

Tests of the taxation powers

2. Max Farrand reports that the committee on style separated the general welfare clause from the preceding and following clauses by semicolons, making it an independent power of Congress. "The change may or may not have been intentional," he wrote, "but Albert Gallatin a few years later stated openly in Congress that 'he was well informed' that this modification was a 'trick' devised by 'one of the members who represented the State of Pennsylvania.' In the Constitution as it was finally engrossed the clause was changed back to its original form, and the credit for this Gallatin gave Sherman." Farrand, *The Framing of the Constitution of the United States* (1926), pp. 182–83.

3. United States v. Butler, 297 U.S. 1, 66 1936).

4. Bailey v. Drexel Furniture Co., 259 U.S. 20 (1922), disallowed the Child Labor statute. It was based upon Hammer v. Dagenhart, 247 U.S. 251 (1918), which was reversed in United States v. Darby Lumber Co., 312 U.S. 100 (1941).

the Court has found the "general welfare" broad enough to legitimatize a heavy tax on the transfer of sawed-off shotguns which effectively discourages their manufacture and sale; the tax due on narcotics provides the excuse for strict supervision by Department of Treasury officers. In the past, state bank notes were driven out of circulation by an uncommonly high federal tax. Because of the "uniformity clause," the federal tax on any item must not be higher in one state than in another.

Even if one concludes that Congress may tax to provide for defense and the "general welfare"—or even tax to regulate certain activities in the interest of the "general welfare"—many pressing problems have not been resolved. In a case testing the constitutionality of the Social Security Act the Court declined to draw a line between "particular" and "general" welfare, but held that this task was one for the Congress, not the courts.[5] Since neither a state nor a taxpayer apparently may challenge the federal spending power,[6] it would appear that the lawmakers in Washington are the sole authorities to decide how public money shall be spent. However, the Court has not closed the door completely to judicial review of public spending. A significant sentence from an opinion which dismissed another attempt by a taxpayer to bring the courts into his quarrel with congressional taxing is in the books: "It will require a very plain case to warrant the courts setting aside the conclusion of Congress in that regard."[7] Such a "plain case" would presumably involve a situation of taxing or spending so extreme as to threaten the destruction of individual liberties or the existence of the states.

BORROWING

Article I, Section 8 also grants Congress power

To borrow money on the credit of the United States ...

Interest and credit

"In the modern system of war," Hamilton wrote in Number 30 of *The Federalist*, "nations the most wealthy are obliged to have recourse to large loans." He argued that giving Congress the power to collect taxes in order to pay the debts of the government would have the effect of permitting government to borrow at low rates of interest. It is generally known today that government securities, the sale of which bring borrowed money into the treasury, attract buyers because of the confidence the lender has that the debt will be paid. Among such buyers are

5. Helvering v. Davis, 301 U.S. 619 (1937).

6. Massachusetts (Frothingham) v. Mellon, 262 U.S. 447 (1923).

7. Cincinnati Soap Co. v. United States, 301 U.S. 308 (1937).

both individual citizens and giant financial institutions. The interest rate paid by the Federal Government does not fluctuate as often as that paid by commercial banks and other lending institutions. However, it was raised in 1968 in recognition of the increased costs of borrowing money. The rate of interest paid by the government, although high, is not as high as that paid by private and commercial borrowers because the credit rating of the United States is good—and borrow it does.

REGULATION OF COMMERCE

One of the most important lines in the entire Constitution is deceptively simple. Congress may

> *regulate commerce with foreign nations, and among the several states, and within the Indian tribes . . .*

The meaning of regulation

When this clause was first interpreted by the Supreme Court, the strongly federalistic Chief Justice Marshall painted congressional powers over commerce with the widest brush he could find. "Regulate" was read to mean "prescribe the rule by which commerce is to be governed." Marshall found the prescription to admit of "no limitations."[8] Today the national government may regulate labor relations because interstate commerce is interrupted by strikes; it may determine maximum hours of work for persons employed by firms whose products are intended for sale across a state line.

NATURALIZATION

Since the central government must deal with national problems by uniform laws, Congress was delegated exclusive authority

> *To establish an uniform rule of naturalization . . .*

Congress may determine which foreigners may set foot inside the United States or its possessions and, from among these, which may become citizens. It may change the rules for persons specially favored. Congress may cause some aliens to be removed from the country. Obviously it would not make sense for such powers to be shared among the states.

BANKRUPTCIES

Congress was further delegated exclusive authority to establish

> *uniform laws on the subject of bankruptcies throughout the United States. . . .*

8. Gibbons v. Ogden, 9 Wheaton 1 (1824).

47

Since bankruptcies permit debtors to clean the slate of their debts by giving up all but exempted property (such as the homestead and occupational tools) to creditors, the terms governing this legal act must be uniform throughout all states if business by credit is to thrive. The provision had a practical political purpose, too: it brought many affluent persons who feared easy repudiation of debts to the support of the Constitution in the struggle for ratification.

COINAGE OF MONEY AND THE POSTAL SERVICE

Only the national legislature was to have the right

> To coin money, regulate the value thereof, and of foreign coin, and fix the standard of weights and measures;
> To provide for the punishment of counterfeiting the securities and current coin of the United States;
> To establish post-offices and post-roads . . .

Coinage by states

Under the first national government the states coined their own money—on a lavish scale. Financial chaos resulted when they insisted that such near-worthless money had real value. "All that need be remarked on the power to coin money, regulate the value thereof, and of foreign coin," wrote Madison, "is that by providing for this last case, the Constitution has supplied a material omission in the articles of Confederation." He concluded Number 42 of *The Federalist* with this comment: "The power of establishing post-roads must, in every view, be a harmless power and may, perhaps, by judicious management, become productive of great public conveniency. Nothing which tends to facilitate the intercourse between the States can be deemed unworthy of the public care."[9] Madison's words seem prophetic when one considers the 41,000 miles of Interstate and Defense highways built with 90 percent Federal funding, which are projected for completion in 1975.

PATENTS AND COPYRIGHTS

Congress was granted the power, under the Constitution,

> To promote the progress of science and useful arts, by securing for limited times to authors and inventors the exclusive right to their respective writings and discoveries . . .

Authors, composers, and artists, by federal law, may obtain an exclusive right to their work for 28 years for the payment of

9. By the late 1960's the Post Office Department had become so swamped with mail that some services had to be reduced, and serious consideration was given to various reforms. One proposal was to reorganize the Post Office into a public corporation directly responsible to Congress, which would have the power to set the postal rates.

a very small fee submitted with an application for copyright and several copies of their work. This copyright is renewable for another 28 years. Patents are given on new and useful discoveries for the same purpose but for the shorter term of 17 years.

ESTABLISHMENT OF LOWER COURTS
Article I, Section 8 also permits Congress

> To constitute tribunals inferior to the Supreme Court . . .

This clause gives the national lawmakers complete power over the birth and death of any Federal court except the Supreme Court. The life of the high court is insured by Article III of the Constitution. ·

UPHOLDING INTERNATIONAL LAW
Congress also may

> define and punish piracies and felonies committed on the high seas, and offences against the law of nations . . .

Piracy was a real problem in the era when the Constitution was adopted. By including the provisions of this clause in the fundamental document, the framers reduced the danger of foreign wars being provoked by capricious state action, but it did not end the danger entirely. Under our federal system the states have sufficient authority in local matters to precipitate war, or at least to jeopardize Washington's relations with foreign powers.[10]

Reducing danger of war

DECLARATION OF WAR
Another significant power granted Congress is

> To declare war, grant letters of marque and reprisal, and make rules concerning captures on land and water . . .

This line of the Constitution was intended to strengthen the principles of civilian control and of checks and balances by giving a power ordinarily associated with the executive to the

10. In the 1830's New York nearly provoked war with England when the state authorities arrested, imprisoned, and tried a Canadian citizen for arson and murder. Fortunately (for the British Foreign Secretary threatened war if the man were not released) the defendant was acquitted. In this century states, because of their actions, have made the Federal Government's dealings with other nations difficult at times. A Japanese war scare developed in 1906 when San Francisco authorities decided to segregate Oriental children in public schools. In 1961 the Federal Government was embarrassed when Alaska interned Japanese who were fishing in "her" waters. The situation was the more touchy because it followed the resumption of atmospheric nuclear testing by the United States—an event of understandable concern to the Japanese, who had suffered devastating effects from the atomic bombs that brought World War II to an end.

legislative branch. Letters of marque and reprisal were licenses whereby private individuals could legally attack the shipping of the enemy without becoming pirates. None have been granted in this century, and today the military forces, including the Coast Guard, effectively defend our sea lanes. But the power to declare war remains a live issue. Today, only Congress may declare war—although, if hostilities erupt, the Prize Cases (involving ships seized while attempting to run the Union blockade of Confederate ports) resulted in the declaration of the Supreme Court, a century ago, that "the President is not only authorized but bound to resist force, by force." He does not need to wait "for Congress to baptize it with a name."[11] The advent of intercontinental ballistic missiles, which carry thermonuclear warheads and can traverse the distance between the Soviet Union, China, and the United States in 30 minutes, has added techonological substance to the reasoning of the preatomic-age Court. In the event of certain types of nuclear attacks, or even perhaps of likely attacks,[12] the national existence could be imperiled should military action await the sanction of a Congress.

In the strange world of the Cold War, Congress has not declared war even in the face of actions that some of its members considered belligerent enough to warrant a declaration of war.[13] The cautious view of war declaration was clearly manifested in 1968 when the American intelligence-gathering ship *Pueblo* was seized by ships of the North Korean Navy (the crew, but not the ship, were released late in 1968). There have been times in American history when such an affront to the United States could well have resulted in a declaration of war by a Congress seething with indignation and wounded pride. But the prevailing philosophy in Washington, although certainly not the unanimous one, was that the *Pueblo* incident would best be settled by negotiation. The same congressional restraint has been shown on occasions when U.S. planes have been shot down by Soviet and Chinese interceptors, or when

Cold War

Pueblo incident

11. The Prize Cases, 2 Black 635, 668, 669 (1863).

12. Those who assume the United States would never, and should never, "strike first," *i.e.*, launch an attack before it had sustained an attack, should read Herman Kahn, *On Thermonuclear War* (Princeton: Princeton University Press, 1960), pp. 27–39, for some provocative ideas on the subject.

13. An American President has not asked for a declaration of war from the Congress since December 8, 1941. However, on several occasions since then a President has requested and received a joint resolution supporting the Commander-in-Chief's stated intent to use force in certain foreign-policy situations. The resolutions dealing with the Taiwan Straits, Middle East, and Tonkin Gulf are discussed in Chapter 6.

American embassy personnel have been killed or injured and embassy property destroyed during anti-American activity in foreign lands. The rationale for this restraint is drawn from several considerations.

In the thermonuclear era, when all-out war could destroy entire continents, nations have followed a pattern of gradually escalating the violence they employ toward each other in conflict situations. Thus they consciously move slowly up the "escalation ladder" whose top rung is tantamount to national suicide, pausing to allow themselves and their adversaries a chance to step down should it appear that the conflict is likely to expand toward the level of thermonuclear destruction.[14] A declaration of war might have the effect of "locking" a nation into an upward climb from which escape would be difficult if not impossible. Furthermore, a declaration of war, carrying with it the impression of greater commitment in terms of taxes, military mobilization, and participation, might cause the other side to overrespond and contribute to thermonuclear exchanges. Waging a conflict without a declaration of war provides more room for maneuver. Of course, the opponents of congressional restraint stubbornly contend that a declaration of war in regard to the Korean or Vietnamese struggles, or in response to the Soviet invasion of Czechoslovakia in 1968, would have been the kind of dramatic move which could have led to "victory" in terms of American interests.

Escalation

THE MILITARY ESTABLISHMENT

Further, Congress may

raise and support armies, but no appropriation of money to that use shall be for a longer term than two years . . .

The amount of attention accorded discussions about a standing army and the ingenious attempts to keep it strictly accountable to civilian control convincingly documents the founders' apprehension over a military dictatorship. In his splendid treatment of the subject in Number 41 of *The Federalist*, James Madison assumed that "security against foreign danger is one of the primitive objects of civil society," and then recognized that "if one nation maintains constantly a disciplined army . . . it obliges the most pacific nations who may be within the reach of its enterprises to take corresponding precautions." Although Madison observed that "the veteran legions of

A standing army: dangerous necessity

14. Herman Kahn's "escalation ladder" is reproduced in Chapter 11. For a full explanation of the theory of escalation one should read his book, *On Escalation: Metaphors and Scenarios* (New York: Praeger, 1965).

Rome were an overmatch for the undisciplined valor of all other nations, and rendered her the mistress of the world," he also was aware that "the liberties of Rome proved the final victim to her military triumphs." Reviewing all the data, he concluded: "A standing army, therefore, is dangerous, at the same time that it may be a necessary, provision. On the smallest scale it has its inconveniences. On an extensive scale its consequences may be fatal." Checks and balances were relied upon to preserve the delicate balance between an army which protects liberty and one which destroys it. The two-year limitation on appropriations was defended from critics as not being excessively long since it matched the term of the members of the House of Representatives—the ones who originate money bills.

Power to raise armies

Although Congress was given power to raise armies, no one knew exactly how this was to be done. Before the adoption of the Constitution, General Washington had asked for drafts of men by the states to fill their quotas. In the War of 1812 compulsory drafting was proposed, but the war ended before a draft bill was enacted. The Mexican War presented no problem because volunteers and the militiamen were available in sufficient numbers. The Civil War began with volunteers and the militia, but finally the military draft raised a quarter of a million troops. Only one challenge to the draft came before the Northern courts, but a series of state cases in the Confederacy upheld compulsory service.[15] The most important challenge to the power of the national government to raise armies by the draft was not to arise until World War I. At that time the Court found that since an army without men is inconceivable, a constitutionally based objection to a draft to provide for such men appeared to be "too frivolous for further notice." Incidentally, the Court also disposed of the assertion that drafted military service amounted to "involuntary servitude."[16]

"Status of forces" agreements

An unusual situation, fraught with implications for the government's draft policy, developed after World War II, while thousands of American servicemen were stationed in foreign countries. The general problem was that the United States had entered into "status-of-forces" agreements with a number of countries. These arrangements provided for the stationing of American troops within sovereign nations, but generally gave the host nation legal jurisdiction over an American serviceman alleged to have committed a crime while off duty. The United

15. The history of the draft is sketched by Chief Justice White in Arver v. United States, 245 U.S. 366 (1917).

16. *Ibid.*

States retained jurisdiction where the crime was committed while the serviceman was on duty. Either government a party to a status-of-forces agreement was given the right to waive its jurisdiction for political or other reasons.

In 1957 a soldier stationed in Japan, William S. Girard, killed a Japanese woman while standing guard duty. After considerable disagreement whether the soldier had acted in the performance of his duty, the United States agreed to turn the prisoner over to the Japanese for trial. This event provoked a heated attack upon the Eisenhower Administration. Many agreed with Senator William Knowland (R., Cal.), who stated:

> Any young man drafted in peacetime, sent overseas against his will and assigned to duty, should not be turned over to any other government for trial; he's wearing the uniform of the United States.[17]

The Supreme Court unanimously upheld the government's right to surrender the soldier to the Japanese for trial and in so doing supported the government's power to draft men in peacetime for duty overseas where they might be tried in a court without the familiar guarantees of the American Constitution.[18]

The unpopularity of the Vietnamese conflict among groups which have little in common with the isolationist and conservative forces that supported Senator Knowland's view has given rise to considerable opposition to the draft of men for duty in Southeast Asia. Much of this opposition is based more upon objection to the war in Vietnam than to the general principle of the draft. But it also reflects widespread doubt concerning a draft policy which selects some for military service and exempts others, because their services are highly prized by society. Responding to increased manpower needs, and to the criticism that the draft favored college students over those (such as ghetto dwellers) who found it difficult to enter college, Congress eliminated draft deferments for many graduate students except those entering medicine, dentistry, related fields, and the ministry. While undoubtedly more democratic than the system it replaced, the move brought down upon the legislators' heads heavy criticism from many of the nation's educational leaders. Should America's foreign commitments continue to require

Draft policies

17. Quoted in Dwight D. Eisenhower, *The White House Years 1956–1961, Waging Peace* (Garden City: Doubleday, 1965), p. 143.

18. Girard was tried in a Japanese court and received a three-year suspended sentence. Details about the case may be read in Luther A. Huston, "High Court Rules U.S. Can Release Girard to Japan," p. 1, *New York Times*, July 12, 1957, and "Texts of Supreme Court Opinion and U.S. Affidavit on Girard Case," p. 6 of the same issue.

large-scale drafting of men for military service, the nation's draft policy may be expected regularly to flare into public debate.[19]

Since Congress could raise armies, it was not unreasonable that it might

provide and maintain a navy . . .

"If we mean to be a commercial people, or even to be secure on our Atlantic side," Number 24 of *The Federalist* insists, "we must endeavor, as soon as possible, to have a navy." The navy was not believed to be a threat to personal liberty as was an army, and so no two-year limitation was set for appropriating funds to keep it operational.

With the provisions for creating the military services, Congress needed the right

To make rules for the government and regulation of the land and naval forces . . .

It was inevitable that the power to raise and support such forces would entail their governance. But it is not always apparent to the newly inducted serviceman why the form of military justice by which the armed forces are governed varies in so many important respects from the law with which he is familiar in civilian life. The answer, of course, is that the exigencies of the military situation do not countenance the legal delays which may safely be made available to civilians.

Military justice

In 1950 the Congress, aware of public concern regarding military justice, endeavored to revise, consolidate, and codify the rules and regulations governing military personnel. The result was Public Law 506 which contains the Uniform Code of Military Justice that is applicable to all the military services. Shortly thereafter, and in extension thereof, President Truman issued an executive order which promulgated the *Manual for Courts-Martial United States* (1951) which serves as the guide for dispensing military justice. An examination of the manual discloses the effort which was made to harmonize the most basic rights possessed by American citizens with the unusual degree of discipline and obedience required in the military service. For example, the Constitution specifically denies to servicemen the time-consuming right of grand-jury indictment, which is guaranteed to civilians. However, Congress created a three-man court, the United States Court of Military Appeals, consisting

19. A collection of differing viewpoints and proposals regarding draft policy for the future is contained in Sol Tax, ed., *The Draft, A Handbook of Facts and Alternatives* (Chicago: University of Chicago Press, 1967).

of civilians appointed by the President and confirmed by the Senate, to review the most serious decisions handed down by military tribunals. Furthermore, the Fifth Amendment guarantee against self-incrimination is reflected in Article 31 of the Uniform Code of Military Justice.[20] What was once generally considered an advanced concept of military justice is now thought by some to have become outmoded. The complaint is that the 1951 code does not reflect recent Supreme Court rulings regarding the rights of the accused in civil society, nor does it make allowance for the deep moral convictions some servicemen feel in opposition to the Vietnam struggle.

The Constitution permits the national government

> To provide for calling forth the militia to execute the laws of the Union, suppress insurrections and repel invasions . . .

The militia

Congress has made certain that sufficient statutes are on the books to permit the President to call out the state militia (now called the National Guard) and also the armed forces of the United States if necessary to enforce the laws, suppress rebellions, or repel invasions. A President is the sole judge as to whether or not the emergency requires the use of such forces.[21]

Although many did not like it, nobody could legally quarrel with President Eisenhower's use of power in 1957 when he dispatched troops to Little Rock, Arkansas, to enforce the integration of Central High School according to a Federal Court order. In a similar situation President Kennedy acted legally when he ordered Army and federalized Mississippi National Guard troops to the campus of the University of Mississippi in 1962. They were used to help United States marshals stop a riot caused by the presence of a black student, James Meredith, on the campus for the purpose of enrolling in the university. With troops patroling the campus and the town of Oxford, Meredith did enroll as sanctioned by a Federal Court order. More recently Federal troops and National Guard units have been used to restore order in riot-torn cities across the land. In 1968 both the Federal Government and various state govern-

Domestic use of troops

20. It is interesting to note that Article 88 of the Uniform Code of Military Justice makes it an offense to use "contemptuous words against the President, Vice President, Congress, Secretary of Defense," etc. However, true to the freedom-of-speech principle enunciated in the First Amendment, the U.C.M.J. discussion of what comprises an offense under Article 88 states: "Adverse criticism of one of the officials or groups named in the article, in the course of a political discussion, even though emphatically expressed, if not personally contemptuous, may not be charged as a violation of the article." See p. 318, *Manual for Courts-Martial United States* (1951).

21. Martin v. Mott, 12 Wheaton 19 (1837).

ments took measures to prepare their forces for more effective responses to civil disorders. Nearly one-half million National Guard troops were given special training in riot-suppression tactics; the Federal Government created a new civilian disturbance training and operations center in the Pentagon under an Army lieutenant general, and broadened riot-control duty to include units from the Marines, Navy, and Air Force.

Since state militias may be ordered into the service of the national government, Congress may

> provide for organizing, arming, and disciplining the militia, and for governing such part of them as may be employed in the service of the United States, reserving to the states respectively, the appointment of the officers, and the authority of training the militia according to the discipline prescribed by Congress . . .

The National Guard

Congress cooperates with each state to maintain and train the National Guard. The national government furnishes financial and other types of help while the states provide officers and policy. Such concurrent power has led to serious difficulties because dual control of the militia was never logical, although politically popular. Referring to an occasion when militiamen refused to cross the international border to support a Federal army fighting in Canada during the War of 1812, a scholar has commented, "Objective civilian control of the militia, which in the nineteenth century was difficult in war, became in the twentieth century virtually impossible in time of peace."[22] He found that the "citizen-soldier," the symbol of the National Guard, has been unusually successful in influencing Congress to be liberal with financial help, while the claims of "states' rights" have prevented congressional control in peacetime and guaranteed the Guard a prominent role in wartime.[23] The Cincinnatus ideal, intended to apply to the President, has been captured by the National Guard and converted into a symbol of the part-time "citizen-soldier."

The control of the militia is not only divided between two governments, but is further encumbered by the checks and balances of the American system. The Guard comes under Federal control only when called by the President, and he may act only after authority has been granted by Congress.

As in the past the National Guard and Reserve units today possess strong political powers since they comprise a large

22. Samuel P. Huntington, "Civilian Control and the Constitution," *American Political Science Review*, L (1956), 676.

23. See on the role of the National Guard, Martha Derthick, *The National Guard in Politics* (Cambridge: Harvard University Press, 1965).

number of voters and since many members of Congress hold Guard and Reserve commissions. This influence was demonstrated when a five-star general, President Eisenhower, was rebuffed by Congress in his efforts to reduce the size of the National Guard and Army Reserve to conform with strategic views on the changed nature of modern war. President Kennedy encountered stiff opposition to his efforts to streamline the National Guard and intensify its training and that of Reserve forces. Kennedy believed both steps were necessary to meet the demands imposed by a policy of rapid and flexible reaction to Cold War emergencies about the world.[24] Defense Secretary Robert McNamara finally succeeded during his service in the Johnson Administration in using the legal authority of his office to make some organizational and training changes regarding the National Guard and Reserve forces.

Guard and Reserve: political power

THE NATIONAL CAPITAL

As a gesture toward the Southern states, which wanted the capital city near them, rather than in the North, Congress was authorized:

> To exercise exclusive legislation in all cases whatsoever, over such District (not exceeding ten miles square) as may, by cession of particular states, and the acceptance of Congress, become the seat of government of the United States, and to exercise like authority over all places purchased by the consent of the legislature of the state in which the same shall be for the erection of forts, magazines, arsenals, dock-yards, and other needful buildings . . .

The building of an entirely new city to serve as the national capital makes sense in countries with a federal type of government.[25] It is generally known that the selection of the tract on the banks of the Potomac, which was chosen to be the nation's capital, resulted from a compromise between Jefferson and Hamilton. The faith, expressed by Madison in the eventful year of 1787-88 that "a municipal legislature for local purposes, derived from their own suffrages, will of course be allowed" to the residents of the District of Columbia, has not yet been vindicated.[26] Today the President and Congress still exercise

24. On several occasions during the Kennedy and Johnson administrations National Guard and Reserve units were called to active duty as part of American reaction to situations such as the Berlin crisis of 1961 and the capture of the intelligence ship *Pueblo* in 1968.

25. Canberra, the compromise capital of Australia, is situated between the rival cities of Sydney and Melbourne. The dramatically new city of Brasilia has been constructed far inland to serve as the capital of Brazil.

26. *The Federalist*, Number 43.

considerable control over the local government in "D.C." However, in 1967 Congress approved a mayor-council form of government for Washington to replace the three-man Board of Commissioners previously in existence. The new officials are appointed by the President with approval of the Senate. They have the power to reorganize the local government, but in fiscal matters their actions are subject to review by congressional subcommittees created for that purpose. The citizen who maintains his residence only in the District of Columbia has no vote for representatives or senators, but may now help elect the President.[27]

D.C. government

THE "NECESSARY AND PROPER" CLAUSE

Finally, Article I, Section 8 stipulates that Congress may

make all laws which shall be necessary and proper for carrying into execution the foregoing powers, and all other powers vested by this Constitution in the government of the United States, or in any department or officer thereof.

There frequently is need to emphasize that Congress is not given a blanket power to make any law which it considers to be "necessary and proper," but to make laws which are *"necessary and proper for carrying into execution"* the powers delegated to the national government. Under the principle of judicial review, the courts determine whether or not the officials representing the national government act within the powers enumerated.

The Growth of National Power

After considering the constitutional authority of Congress, even the most casual observer of American government cannot escape the conclusion that the powers wielded by the national government are far greater today than when the covenant was established. For example, it is difficult to find, in Article I, Section 8, that congressional power extends to setting a minimum wage for an elevator operator whose regular passengers work for firms which produce goods that are intended to cross the state line.[28] When many people learn that this is permissible under

27. According to the Twenty-third Amendment, ratified in 1961 by the required three-quarters (38) of the states, the District acquired three votes in the Electoral College, the minimum awarded to the least populous states. Another amendment must be adopted if the District is to be represented in Congress.

28. The Tennessee Valley Authority was passed under the navigability clause. The Supreme Court recently called this "the power over interstate commerce." United States v. Grand River Dam Authority, 363 U.S. 229 (1960).

the "commerce clause," they conclude that the powers of the national government are interpreted very broadly—and they are, by Presidents, Congresses, and Courts.

THE NATIONAL BANK

The Constitution had not been in effect a year before issues began to arise with regard to the correct interpretation of the document. In 1790 Alexander Hamilton, first Secretary of the Treasury, urged the Congress to establish a national bank. His opponents, principally Thomas Jefferson, insisted that they could read the Constitution forward, backward, and in translation, and could not find authority to do what the Secretary of the Treasury had requested. Hamilton's political opponents believed in a *strict interpretation* of the document—that the national government had only those powers specifically enumerated. Hamilton argued that the national government was not restricted to such an extent—that there were certain powers *implied* in the document. He insisted that since Congress could "coin money and regulate the value thereof," it was "necessary and proper" for it to establish a national bank. President Washington and Congress accepted the Hamiltonian position: the bank was chartered the following year.

The institution chartered as the Bank of the United States was in reality predominantly under private ownership and control. Its wealth and character led to the spread of branches over the country, but it was extremely unpopular in the South and West. In order to drive the Baltimore branch out of business, the state of Maryland taxed the bank $15,000 a year, since it was not chartered by state law. McCulloch, a bank official, refused to remit and was held liable for nonpayment of the tax. In the litigation, he was represented by Daniel Webster, who, oddly enough, was also the champion of the bank in the Senate.

Bank of the U.S.

The crucial question apparently was whether or not Maryland could tax the bank, but the constitutional question was more important: Did Congress even have power to charter a bank? The judgment, handed down by Chief Justice Marshall, is one of the epoch-making decisions in constitutional history.[29] By finding the power of the Congress to charter a bank implied in the Constitution, the Court affected federalism in America for all time. In the decision of the case of

29. A detailed analysis of *McCulloch* v. *Maryland*, which demonstrates a most effective method of constitutional-law case study, is found in Appendix C, "How to Read a Constitutional Law Case," Robert S. Hirschfield, *The Constitution and the Court* (New York: Random House, 1962).

McCulloch v. Maryland

McCulloch v. Maryland, the Chief Justice held: "This government is acknowledged by all to be one of enumerated powers. That principle is now universally admitted. But the question respecting the extent of the powers actually granted is perpetually arising, and will probably continue to arise, so long as our system shall exist." John Marshall admitted that among the enumerated powers one cannot find that of establishing a bank, but, "we must never forget that it is a *constitution* we are expounding"—a constitution "intended to endure for ages to come, and, consequently, to be adapted to the various *crises* of human affairs." The great Chief Justice established the implied-powers position firmly when he concluded: "Let the end be legitimate, let it be within the scope of the constitution, and all means which are appropriate, which are plainly adapted to that end, which are not prohibited, but consist with the letter and spirit of the constitution, are constitutional . . ."[30]

The Jeffersonian alternative to such broad construction of the written word was to have each generation call a constitutional convention to rewrite the fundamental law in order to keep it up to date. But Jefferson had cause to appreciate the elasticity discovered in the document by his rivals when he became President: It was necessary to stretch the Constitution in order to purchase Louisiana from France. He stretched it—to a chorus of constitutional objections from the Hamiltonians!

Chief Justice Marshall's decision

In his answer to the question of the right of Maryland to tax the bank, Chief Justice Marshall stirred up some federalistic dust that has taken a long time to settle. This was accomplished by his catch-phrase, "the power to tax involves the power to destroy." When he wrote this, John Marshall looked to what might happen, not what was likely to occur, and saw the claim of a state to tax an institution incorporated by Federal law as a noxious theory to be rooted out once and for all:

> If we apply the principle for which the State of Maryland contends, to the constitution generally, we shall find it capable of changing totally the character of that instrument. We shall find it capable of arresting all the measures of the government, and of prostrating it at the foot of the States. The American people have declared their constitution, and the laws made in pursuance thereof, to be supreme; but this principle would transfer the supremacy, in fact, to the States. . . . This was not intended by the American people. They did not design to make their government dependent on the States.

30. 4 Wheaton 316 (1819).

INTERGOVERNMENTAL TAXATION

Since both central and state governments are provided for by the Constitution, and taxing can "prostrate" them, did this mean that the two governments might never tax instrumentalities of the other? Could a state levy a property tax on a United States Post Office, and could the national government corporate income tax reach into the profits of a state liquor store?[31] These were the questions that the Supreme Court had to hammer out over the years. Marshall's dictum muddied the tax waters for a century. Down to 1939 the Court steadfastly refused to permit one government to collect a nondiscriminatory tax from the employees of the other. These were golden years for government workers: state employees paid no Federal income tax; Federal employees paid no state income tax. Then, in a message to the Congress in 1938 Franklin D. Roosevelt requested legislation permitting state taxation of Federal employees and future issues of Federal bonds; with the provision, also, that Federal income tax apply to state employees and future issues of Federal, state, and municipal bonds. The Public Salary Tax Act of 1939 emerged from the Congress the same year as the Supreme Court, upon reconsideration, found that it was permissible for a state to tax the income of an employee of a national government corporation. Actually the specter of one government destroying the other by taxation might have been laid to rest at least eleven years before, when Mr. Justice Holmes had enunciated a phrase as quotable as Marshall's and even more accurate: "The power to tax is not the power to destroy while this Court sits."

THE ADMISSION OF STATES

In Number 43 of *The Federalist*, it is observed that one of the signal defects of the Articles of Confederation was the failure to provide for admission of new states to the Union. Madison charged that "the eventual establishment of new States seems to have been overlooked by the compilers of that instrument." If the compilers of the first constitution overlooked the possibility of extending statehood to new members, the Con-

From territory to statehood

31. The Post Office is required for the exercise of a "usual, traditional and essential governmental function" and so may not be taxed without express congressional consent. However, the national government gives local governments payments of money "in lieu of taxes" on Federal installations which impose burdens on local facilities. Federal taxes do apply to the proceeds of state liquor stores. When New York sought to avoid the collection of excise taxes on mineral water bottled and sold by the state, Justice Frankfurter found: "We certainly see no reason for putting soft drinks in a different constitutional category from hard drinks." State of New York v. United States, 326 U.S. 572, 575 (1946).

The Northwest Ordinance of 1787

gress under the Confederation did not. The Northwest Ordinance of 1787 provided for the organization of the area north of the Ohio River into territorial status with a coherent plan for eventual statehood. This ordinance was extended by the First Congress under the Constitution. If it is claimed that the Constitution remedied the deficiency of which Madison complained, in fairness it must be admitted that the remedy was so vague that some states were admitted almost haphazardly while others were obliged to submit to a series of highly formal acts. Ordinarily Congress, upon petition by a territory, passes a resolution, or "enabling act," which authorizes the residents of the area to elect a convention empowered to draft a constitution. When the proposed document is approved by a majority of both houses of Congress and signed by the President, the territory has crossed the threshold, and the national flag is redesigned. In the case of Alaska, President Eisenhower proclaimed the admission of the 49th state only after Alaskans had formally voted specifically to accept statehood and had elected state officials. Once an applicant has been permitted to join the "indestructible Union, composed of indestructible States" there is "no place for reconsideration, or revocation, except through revolution, or through consent of the States."[32]

ACQUISITION AND REGULATION OF TERRITORIES

Article IV, Section 3 of the Constitution, after conferring power upon the Congress to admit new states into the union and allaying the fears of the original members that a new state might be carved out of them without their consent,[33] continues:

> The Congress shall have power to dispose of and make all needful rules and regulations respecting the territories or other property belonging to the United States . . .

The absoluteness of the authority given Congress in this grant is difficult to grasp at first glance. However, an American "national" in a territory knows well the immense power conveyed by the clause. For example, a person in American Samoa is not a citizen even though born in this possession; he is not even permitted to come to the mainland without explicit per-

32. Texas v. White, 7 Wallace 700, 725, 726 (1869).

33. After Virginia had seceded from the Union, some of her western counties "seceded" from the state, and, without consent of the Old Dominion, entered the Union as the State of West Virginia. The Court's policy of broad construction enabled it to see the separation as an "agreement" between the two states consented to by Congress. Virginia v. West Virginia, 11 Wallace 39 (1870).

mission; he has no right to vote for the taxing authority; and he is not extended all the guarantees of the Bill of Rights. In short, a national (or even a citizen) in an unincorporated territory knows that the Constitution does not necessarily follow the flag, even though many stateside citizens do not realize this. How did this come about? What makes it constitutional?

Territories existed before the adoption of the Constitution. The very favorable terms of the Treaty of Paris ending the Revolutionary War deeded to the successful rebel colonies the land west to the Mississippi River. In fact, the excellent handling of the touchy situation of the rival state claims to western lands probably made the Northwest Ordinance the most brilliant accomplishment of the national government under the Articles of Confederation. The ordinance provided a three-step evolution from wilderness to "an equal footing with the original states in all respects whatsoever." The appointed territorial governor, secretary, and a trio of judges were to be supplemented by a representative body when the free population of an area reached 5,000. At this time, the territory also was granted a delegate in Congress who could speak and introduce legislation but could not vote. The appointed governor retained his veto over the territorial legislature, and Congress retained a final veto. The third step came when 60,000 free inhabitants enabled the territory to assume statehood.

Northwest Ordinance

The first great addition of territory after ratification of the Constitution was the purchase of Louisiana. By treaty, this territory was "incorporated" into the United States, and its residents were given citizenship. It was expected that the vast area would be subdivided into states in the future, and that the Constitution would safeguard its inhabitants. The same expectation applied to each new increment as the nation pushed westward. Alaska, purchased in 1867, was the first noncontiguous territory, but few were concerned whether it was "incorporated" or "unincorporated," since its population was so scanty. The acquisition of Puerto Rico, the Philippines, and Hawaii, however, raised grave constitutional issues. These were well-populated noncontiguous territories with long histories of their own and little in common with the Anglo-Saxon culture of the mainland. Problems arose immediately because these new territories were not assumed to be potential states—they were "unincorporated."

Louisiana Purchase and other acquisitions

For example, could tariff duties be imposed on goods coming from Puerto Rico? The Court recognized that the island was not an integral part of the United States and yet was not a foreign country. De Lima v. Bidwell decided that import duties

63

Territories and the Constitution

would need clear congressional action.[34] Congress then passed a statute stipulating tariff duties on certain items. The next case tested whether Puerto Rico was part of the United States for the purpose of the clause which requires "all duties, imposts, and excises shall be uniform throughout the United States." The majority of justices could not agree why, but Justice Brown wrote for the Court in *Downes v. Bidwell*: "The Constitution is applicable to territories acquired by purchase or conquest only when and so far as Congress shall direct."[35]

Must Mr. Mankichi, a Hawaiian, be granted the Bill of Rights guarantees of indictment by a grand jury and trial by jury in a criminal prosecution? The Supreme Court, in a 5-4 split, said not. Why? Because Hawaiian laws had not stipulated these protections in criminal cases.[36] Such procedural processes, peculiar to the Anglo-American system of jurisprudence, are not "natural rights" and so are not guaranteed. On the other hand, such rights as free speech, free press, and protection from ex post facto laws are "natural rights" and will be furnished inhabitants in all American possessions even when they are not incorporated as a part of the United States.[37]

Incorporation of territories

The next logical question is to inquire how an unincorporated territory becomes incorporated. The official answer must be, "By treaty or by act of Congress." An unofficial answer would include "by judicial interpretation." Louisiana provided an example of incorporation by treaty; Hawaii was incorporated by act of Congress in 1900 (but too late to help Mr. Mankichi, since he had already been indicted). In addition, when Congress is "silent," the Supreme Court will read its mind. It performed this feat in 1904 to find that Congress intended the Philippines to be unincorporated, and in the next year the Court found that Congress intended Alaska to be incorporated.[38] Why are some territories incorporated while others are not? It may be supposed that the former are considered to be on their way to statehood while the latter are not.

Approximately a decade after the situation in Hawaii was settled, Congress again presented the inhabitants of the territories with some interesting constitutional issues when it passed a bill still known on the books as the "Organic Act of Porto Rico."

34. 182 U.S. 1 (1901).

35. 182 U.S. 244, 279 (1901).

36. Hawaii v. Mankichi, 190 U.S. 197 (1903).

37. Downes v. Bidwell, 182 U.S. 244, 282 (1901).

38. The case concerning the Philippines was Dorr. v. United States, 195 U.S. 138 (1904); Alaska's status was determined in Rasmussen v. United States, 197 U.S. 516 (1905).

This statute gave Puerto Ricans citizenship, established territorial courts, extended some of the laws of the United States to them and much of the Bill of Rights, but withheld trial by jury. Mr. Balzac, convicted of criminal libel by a territorial court sitting without a jury, furnished the Supreme Court an opportunity to suggest ways in which the Organic Act had changed things for him. He was told that the crucial difference the act made between a Puerto Rican and a Filipino was this: "A citizen of the Philippines must be naturalized before he can settle and vote in this country. . . . Not so the Porto Rican. . . ." Señor Balzac, however, did not get a jury trial, because "Congress has thought that a people like the Filipinos or the Porto Ricans, trained to a complete judicial system which knows no juries, living in compact and ancient communities, with definitely formed customs and political conceptions, should be permitted themselves to determine how far they wish to adopt this institution of Anglo-Saxon origin, and when. . . ."[39]

Today Alaska and Hawaii are states, having been admitted to the union in 1959; the Philippine Islands are independent, having gained that rank in 1946; and Puerto Rico has assumed the title of "commonwealth," dating from 1952.[40] At the present time, Puerto Rico elects her own governor and resident commissioner (who is her delegate to Congress); remains subject to some Federal legislation (but not to its tax laws); and is within the national tariff walls. Puerto Ricans retain American citizenship and have free access to the United States, and their commonwealth constitution recognizes "our union with the United States of America." The evolution of an "associated autonomous commonwealth" status in a federal system can be expected to pose many delicate political, legal, and logical difficulties.

The Puerto Rican experiment

The other territories are watching the Puerto Rican experiment with great interest because their relationship to the mainland is analogous. The Virgin Islands, which were transferred from the Navy to the Department of the Interior in 1931 (four years after the inhabitants were granted citizenship), have an organic act similar to the traditional pattern but lack a delegate in Congress. Inhabitants of Guam received an organic act and citizenship in 1950, but the island was formally declared to be unincorporated. Other American islands in the Pacific have yet

39. Balzac v. Porto Rico, 258 U.S. 298, 310 (1922).

40. For a discussion of the various options open to Puerto Rico in regard to political development see, *Status of Puerto Rico*, a report by the United States-Puerto Rico Commission on the Status of Puerto Rico (Washington: Office of the Commonwealth of Puerto Rico, 1967).

to be accorded the dignity of an organic act, and their inhabitants remain nationals.[41]

Powers Reserved to States

STATES' RIGHTS

Although the Constitution may be viewed as a covenant dividing power between a central government and the local governments, one looks in vain for a section enumerating the powers of the states. This is because the states were considered to have reserved all the powers not specifically granted to the general government. The author of Number 32 of *The Federalist* certainly had this opinion. He wrote: "The State governments would clearly retain all the rights of sovereignty which they had before, and which were not, by that act, *exclusively* delegated to the United States." Those powers which are not entirely national in scope (*e.g.*, postal system, foreign affairs, coining money) are shared *concurrently* with the states (*e.g.*, taxation, law enforcement, social welfare). Even sectors of interstate commerce have been held to be areas of legitimate concern for states, and some regulation of persons and objects involved in interstate commerce has been permitted. In an additional guarantee of states' rights, the Tenth Amendment was adopted as part of the Bill of Rights. Its words underscore the residual powers of the states:

> The powers not delegated to the United States by the Constitution, nor prohibited by it to the States, are reserved to the States respectively, or to the people.

State control

Many people frequently assert that the states have been robbed of their "rights." Others insist that state powers have atrophied. Both groups might become better informed.[42] It is true that industrialization brought the national government into regulatory activities that once were the sporadic concern of states, that America's new role in international affairs has brought new powers into use, and that the national government has been increasing its intervention in behalf of individual

41. As a result of World War II the United States administers certain Pacific islands formerly under Japanese authority. In 1967 the Bonin Islands were returned to Japan. However, the United States has not acceded to the Japanese request for the return of the strategically placed island of Okinawa, upon which large American military forces are based.

42. An informative discussion of the nature of American federalism is Arthur W. MacMahon, ed., *Federalism: Mature and Emergent* (New York: Doubleday, 1955). See also Edward McWhinney, *Comparative Federalism* (Toronto: University of Toronto Press, 1962).

rights secured by the Fourteenth Amendment; but states retain prodigious powers. In fact, Federal control exercised over the states and their subdivisions is not as extensive as state control is of counties, cities, and other local-government units.[43] A glance at the comparative statistics on the amounts of revenue collected and expended by state governments over the past 30 years is instructive, for the growth is startling. People who profess to believe that states have lost their powers might profitably jot down items which are the exclusive concern of state governments—but they should be warned that it is a project which takes time. The list will be huge, and it must include such interesting items as the decision whether or not to have capital punishment; to punish murder;[44] to monopolize the sale of liquor or outlaw its sale entirely; to permit divorce for a fancied frown or forbid it for mayhem; and to spell out how delegates to the national party conventions are to be selected or leave this to the political parties concerned. A complainer about dwindling state powers who has a more active imagination might list what states *could* claim to do if they wished: adopting the Mosaic Law as the official legal system; insisting that automobiles be driven on the left side of the street; refusing to let persons vote until they reach the age of 80; or selecting their legislators by flipping coins. Of course, nobody can deny that the Fourteenth Amendment[45] robbed states of the power they once had of establishing a religion as official and prohibiting other churches from public worship, taking a person's property without due process of law, or denying equal protection of the laws to people within their borders.

Ordinarily, the champions of states' rights have something quite different in mind when they speak of a loss of state power. They sometimes lament that a sovereign state may not protect its citizens from the national government. This is true. Early in the nineteenth century John C. Calhoun had elaborated the argument that states could "interpose" themselves between their residents and the national government, but in 1923, the decision in *Massachusetts v. Mellon*[46] denied it. In that case, a state (Massachusetts) sued the Secretary of the

State power

43. Herbert Kaufman, *Politics and Policies in State and Local Government* (Englewood Cliffs: Prentice-Hall, 1963), p. 104.

44. Following the recommendation of the Warren Commission, which investigated the assassination of President Kennedy, Congress in 1965 made it a Federal crime to attack, kidnap, or kill a President, Vice President, President-elect, or anyone acting as President.

45. See Chapter 8 for a discussion of this amendment.

46. 262 U.S. 447 (1923).

Treasury (Mellon) on behalf of one of its citizens (Miss Frothingham) who objected to the spending of her tax money to provide states with money for parental care under the Maternity Act of 1921. The Supreme Court pointed out that citizens of Massachusetts were also citizens of the United States and failed to see what the state had complained about since the money had not come from its treasury. Miss Frothingham was assured that the few mills which conceivably could have been from taxes paid by her were trivial compared to the "general welfare."

GRANTS-IN-AID

Actually, "grants-in-aid" such as made by the Maternity Act have historically had opponents, and still do. As early as 1802 the national government made land grants to states in order to help them accomplish certain defined objectives over the objections of some citizens. The opposition grew more vocal, however, during the decades following 1932 when gifts to states of dollars collected "to pay the debts and provide for the common defense and general welfare of the United States" increased tenfold. By 1952 grants from the national government had become the largest single source of revenue for state and local governments.[47] By 1968 Federal grants to state and local governments and individuals were approximately $22.3 billion a year.

Eligibility for a donation hinges on the acceptance, by the states, of certain conditions. The conditions vary from grant to
Conditions grant, but they include that the money be spent only for the purpose stipulated, that the state contribute to the appropriation, that the state create an agency with which the national government can deal, that no person whose principal employment is financed by such a grant may take an active part in a political campaign, and that the national government may set the standards and inspect the results of the project. For example, a highway grant-in-aid might specify that roads built with the money have an even number of lanes (e.g., two, four, six). If a state stands on its right to build three-lane highways, it may do so—but not with Federal funds. Since passage of the 1964 Civil Rights Act, state agencies and other organizations must comply with the stipulation that programs receiving Federal funds be made available regardless of race, color, or national origin. Violation of the provision, as when a school dis-

47. U.S. Bureau of Census, *Historical Statistics of the United States: Colonial Times to 1957* (Washington: Government Printing Office, 1960), p. 727.

TABLE 2.1 Recent Trends in Federal Aid
(in millions of dollars; by fiscal years)

	1961	1962	1963	1964	1965*	1966*	1967*
Total Grants	$ 9,826	$10,386	$ 10,976	$ 12,854	$ 15,340	$ 17,820	$ 21,864
To state, local govts.	7,102	7,895	8,597	10,061	10,904	12,833	15,193
To individuals	2,724	2,491	2,380	2,793	4,436	4,987	6,671
Increase or Decrease Since Preceding Year							
Total Grants	+ 7%	+ 6%	+ 6%	+ 17%	+ 19%	+ 16%	+ 23%
To state, local govts.	+ 1%	+11%	+ 9%	+ 17%	+ 8%	+ 18%	+ 18%
To individuals	+26%	− 9%	− 4%	+ 17%	+ 58%	+ 12%	+ 34%
Increase or Decrease From 1958							
Total Grants	+32%	+40%	+48%	+73%	+107%	+140%	+195%
To state, local govts.	+44%	+60%	+74%	+103%	+121%	+160%	+208%
To individuals	+ 9%	0%	− 4%	+ 12%	+ 78%	+100%	+168%
Federal Tax Collections	$94,401	$94,329	$104,495	$106,317	$114,400	$134,480	$149,591
Portion of federal taxes returned to states as grants	10%	11%	11%	12%	13%	13%	15%

The figures for these years include certain farm program payments which, although in existence for several years, were not previously part of the grant-in-aid statistics.

Source: Congressional Quarterly Inc.

trict refuses to integrate its students, results in the withholding of Federal grants until compliance is obtained. Needless to say, this situation has produced considerable opposition which decries what is charged as being Federal intervention in matters of purely local concern.

Sometimes state officials, while accepting grants with both hands, complain that the money actually was taken away from their citizens. To say this is to demonstrate a failure to comprehend a crucial fact about federalism, namely, that "their citizens" are also citizens (and taxpayers) of the national government. Ordinarily state authorities are delighted to accept the grants, but they sometimes grumble about the invasion of their sovereignty, forgetting that they were free to refuse the money and the accompanying limitations it imposed. On one such occasion, in 1947, the Supreme Court answered this charge in these words:

> So even though the action taken by Congress does have effect upon certain activities within the state, it has never been thought that such effect made the federal act invalid. . . . We do not see any violation of the state's sovereignty. . . . The offer of benefits to a state by the United States dependent upon cooperation by the state with federal plans, assumedly for the general welfare, is not unusual.[48]

Ten years earlier, when a challenge came that the financing aspects of the Social Security Act coerced a state to cooperate with the congressional plan, the Court asked:

> Who then is coerced through the operation of this statute? Not the taxpayer. He pays in fulfillment of the mandate of the local legislature. Not the state. Even now she does not offer a suggestion that in passing the unemployment law she was affected by duress.[49]

It can be argued that one important objection to the grants-in-aid system is that the taxpayers of wealthy states are made to

Wealthy states vs. others

subsidize activities of the other states. Why should the residents of Connecticut help pay for Nevada highways? Ideally, the Connecticut citizen recognizes that good roads in an immense, sparsely populated state contribute to the welfare of the whole nation. Practically, the answer could be that he might be glad for those highways some day when he is in haste to reach Reno in order to be separated from what he has—or in

48. Oklahoma v. United States Civil Service Commission, 330 U.S. 127, 143, 144 (1947).

70

49. Steward Machine Co. v. Davis, 301 U.S. 548, 589 (1937).

TABLE 2.2   State Allocations of Federal Aid

States	1967 Total Grants	1967 Est. Population	1967 Per Capita Grants
Alabama	$ 448,017,000	3,540,000	$127
Alaska	115,412,000	273,000	423
Arizona	250,210,000	1,635,000	153
Arkansas	330,352,000	1,969,000	168
California	2,129,274,000	19,163,000	111
Colorado	286,125,000	1,975,000	145
Connecticut	228,576,000	2,925,000	78
Delaware	47,872,000	523,000	92
D. of C.	209,219,000	809,000	259
Florida	460,870,000	5,996,000	77
Georgia	523,310,000	4,511,000	116
Hawaii	113,141,000	741,000	153
Idaho	110,241,000	699,000	158
Illinois	847,209,000	10,894,000	78
Indiana	378,815,000	4,999,000	76
Iowa	428,941,000	2,753,000	156
Kansas	406,951,000	2,275,000	179
Kentucky	420,487,000	3,191,000	132
Louisiana	471,450,000	3,660,000	129
Maine	86,626,000	973,000	89
Maryland	262,210,000	3,685,000	71
Massachusetts	551,010,000	5,421,000	102
Michigan	654,813,000	8,584,000	76
Minnesota	495,273,000	3,582,000	138
Mississippi	421,733,000	2,348,000	180
Missouri	539,012,000	4,605,000	117
Montana	170,686,000	701,000	243
Nebraska	317,236,000	1,435,000	221
Nevada	75,773,000	444,000	171
New Hampshire	52,396,000	685,000	76
New Jersey	417,158,000	7,004,000	60
New Mexico	211,780,000	1,003,000	211
New York	1,507,505,000	18,335,000	82
North Carolina	457,584,000	5,027,000	91
North Dakota	214,396,000	639,000	336
Ohio	753,038,000	10,462,000	72
Oklahoma	444,575,000	2,496,000	178
Oregon	249,906,000	1,999,000	125
Pennsylvania	891,764,000	11,626,000	77
Rhode Island	96,534,000	901,000	107
South Carolina	248,037,000	2,603,000	95
South Dakota	165,337,000	674,000	245
Tennessee	437,030,000	3,888,000	112
Texas	1,301,121,000	10,873,000	120
Utah	147,155,000	1,022,000	144
Vermont	65,937,000	416,000	159
Virginia	350,512,000	4,533,000	77
Washington	364,911,000	3,089,000	118
West Virginia	215,039,000	1,798,000	120
Wisconsin	332,322,000	4,188,000	79
Wyoming	87,994,000	315,000	279
Territories	345,037,000		
Undistributed	726,563,000		
Total	$21,864,478,000	197,884,000	$110

Source: Congressional Quarterly Inc.

71

a rush to get away from Las Vegas with what he has left! Similar questions about Federal aid for education, Social Security, maternity benefits, and other causes can be raised and answered—although, perhaps, not quite so flippantly.

Although opponents of grants-in-aid programs show greatest reverence for the ideas of Thomas Jefferson and repeatedly announce their conviction that local governmental agencies are inherently wiser than the Congress, often these sentiments serve as smokescreens. The crux of the dispute is that Federal aid redistributes the nation's wealth downward while state responsibility for services and taxation redistributes the wealth upward. If we ask who pays for services rendered, we see practical reasons for opposition to Federal-aid programs. When the state or locality provides public services, the lower- and middle-income groups bear the brunt of taxation, for local property taxes and state sales and excise taxes fall proportionately heavier on the poor man or middle-class citizen than on the wealthier individual or large corporation.

The Federal tax system, on the other hand, places a far heavier burden on the more well-to-do. Progressive individual **Transfer of wealth** income taxes as well as Federal corporate taxes, upon which grants-in-aid programs depend, take the most money from those with the greatest ability to pay.[50] Consider the case of the relatively wealthy state of Wisconsin, for example. It has been estimated that Wisconsin taxpayers contribute $1.46 to the cost of Federal grants-in-aid programs for every grants-in-aid dollar they receive back from Washington.[51] The 46-cents difference goes to poorer states, through an equalization formula, and to pay for administrative costs. Hence Wisconsin residents pay more—to subsidize programs in less wealthy states—than they would if Wisconsin only supported programs within its boundaries. But different people pay: The lower-income families pay less when the grants-in-aid are financed by the Federal Government, and the higher-income families pay more than if Wisconsin taxpayers contributed only to their state's programs.

REVENUE SHARING

Other objections to, or suggested modifications for, the grants-in-aid approach to assisting the states and metropolitan areas solve their fiscal problems can be examined under another

50. *Cf.* Roy Blough, "Fiscal Aspects of Federalism," in MacMahon, *op. cit.*

51. See the address of former Congressman Melvin R. Laird (R., Wis.), "Strengthening the Federal System—The Case for Revenue Sharing," *The Congressional Record*, 113 (February 15, 1967), pp. H 1330–H 1349. Laird was appointed Secretary of Defense by President Nixon.

heading—revenue sharing. Within recent years considerable interest has been evoked by various plans calling for the Federal Government to share its immense tax revenue, particularly that derived from the income tax, with the state governments.

One general view is that tax sharing by the national government should constitute a supplement to the existing grants-in-aid programs.[52] Another widespread opinion is that revenue sharing should be considered more as a replacement for grants-in-aid than as a supplement thereto.[53] Those advocating that the Federal Government engage in some variant of revenue sharing draw support from one or several complaints charged against the current grants-in-aid arrangement.[54] For example, it is claimed by some that there has been a proliferation of Federal grants-in-aid programs among too many projects, with the resultant tendency to dilute the available funds. Another complaint is that by making money available for particular projects the national government in effect entices the states to invest their severely limited funds in programs which may not in fact represent the highest priority for the particular state. Related to both points is the argument that the states, being closer to the scene, are better able to understand and tackle their problems than are Washington-based Federal officials. Some opponents insist that the administrative costs required to operate the grants-in-aid programs constitute a waste which can be ill afforded. Another point often raised by revenue-sharing proponents is that the Federal Government, by heavily taxing personal and corporate income, has pre-empted a tax source of vital importance to the states, and consequently the national government should share the revenue derived from income taxes with the states.

Several objections to the revenue-sharing proposals should also be noted. One is that revenue sharing "with no strings attached" might result in some states' using their Federal reve-

Proposals

52. This view is discussed by Walter W. Heller, one-time chairman of the President's Council of Economic Advisers under Presidents Kennedy and Johnson, in *New Dimensions of Political Economy* (New York: Norton, 1967), pp. 117–172.

53. For more than a decade Secretary Laird has led an effort to reduce Federal grants-in-aid and to replace them with a revenue-sharing program.

54. Other proposals representing something of a compromise between revenue sharing and grants-in-aid have been made. An example of one is the suggestion for block grants. This proposal calls for Federal funds to be transferred to the states for general purposes such as education or crime prevention, and permits the states to be flexible within broad guidelines to use the moneys as they think best. Of course, the danger exists that some states will not use such funds as the national thinking, reflected by Congress, desires, as for example in regard to integration of various activities.

73

Objections

nue income in ways which would run counter to national policies on matters such as integration of various activities or facilities. Another stated fear is that the states cannot be counted upon to pass down a portion of the revenue to metropolitan centers where the need for funded programs is greatest within many states.[55] An additional objection to revenue sharing is that some of the poorer states would be less well off than under the current grants-in-aid approach. Also some objectors point out that the states may show a tendency, should they become recipients of Federal revenue-sharing funds, to slacken their own taxation programs and thus offset the assistance from Washington.

Equalization

In fairness to those arguing for revenue-sharing proposals it should be noted that they are cognizant of the general objections made against the principle they espouse, and they have devised what are to them satisfactory means for meeting the objections. For example, Professor Heller suggests the shared revenue received by a state be reduced if the state relaxes its own taxation program. Heller has also suggested the Civil Rights Act requirements to make federally funded projects open to all regardless of race, religion, or national origin be made applicable to any revenue-shared funds. Secretary Laird has noted that some form of equalization formula should be used in regard to shared-revenue funds to provide more moneys to the poorer states than they otherwise would be entitled to receive.

The Responsibilities and Benefits of Statehood

The grants-in-aid principle, and the revenue-sharing proposals, recognize the simple truth that all states are not equal in economic advantages. Both are designed to provide a minimum economic level below which no state would be allowed to sink. In theory, however, the states are equal. The language of Article IV of the Constitution, discussed briefly now, is interesting not only for its provisions but for the way in which the principle of equality is assumed in the delineation of the responsibilities and privileges of the several states.

"FULL FAITH AND CREDIT" CLAUSE

Article IV, Section 1 states:

Full faith and credit shall be given in each state to the public acts, records and judicial proceedings of every other

55. This possibility has been made less likely by Supreme Court rulings which require state legislatures to reapportion themselves in a fashion to give greater representation to urban residents than has previously been the case when rural districts were overrepresented. See for example Reynolds v. Sims 377 U.S. 533 (1964).

state. And the Congress may by general laws prescribe the manner in which such acts, records and proceedings shall be proved, and the effect thereof.

The courts have read this clause as applying, in the main, to proceedings under civil law. That is, a judgment from a state court cannot be evaded by moving into a different state. For example, if Y receives a $2,000 judgment from Z for a damaged automobile and Z moves into another state, the courts in the new domicile will give "full faith and credit" to the judgment and dispatch a sheriff to enforce it.

This simple system breaks down when a divorce decree is disputed. Since each state determines her own laws, some grant divorce only for proved adultery, while others award decrees more liberally. In 1945 the Supreme Court ruled that if one party goes to Nevada and lives at a dude ranch for six weeks (the requirement for becoming a Nevada resident), receives the divorce, and then returns to the old homestead with an intent to remain indefinitely, such a person did not really become a resident of Nevada. Naturally, Nevada courts can grant divorces only to persons within their legal jurisdiction (*i.e.*, bona fide Nevadans), so when the six-weeks residency law was questioned, the divorce decrees based upon it became suspect. The seriousness of the Supreme Court's decision is immediately apparent: does a person with a Reno divorce who remarries commit bigamy? If such a person has children by the second marriage, are these children to be considered illegitimate? This question becomes enormously important if the Nevada decree is challenged, or if the parent dies without a will, for bigamy is a criminal offense, and illegitimate children do not enjoy the same status in a property settlement as do legitimate offspring. After several cases had been decided, this much appeared certain: if both parties to a divorce appear before the court in a liberal divorce state and the issue of domicile is raised and decided, neither they nor any of their heirs may attack the validity of the decree on the ground of lack of jurisdiction.[56]

State laws in conflict

"PRIVILEGES AND IMMUNITIES"

Section 2 of Article IV provides:

The citizens of each state shall be entitled to all privileges and immunities of citizens in the several states.

This clause has been interpreted to mean that one state must permit nonresidents access to its courts for actions at law, allow them to own property, and the like. On the other hand, it may

56. Williams v. North Carolina, 325 U.S. 226 (1945); but see Sherrer v. Sherrer, 334 U.S. 343 (1948).

75

levy an out-of-state fee for attending public schools, for fishing and hunting, and similar advantages. Notice the word "citizens"—this means a state within constitutional bounds may impose restrictions on "nationals," aliens, and corporations.

Varying welfare benefits

The increasing longevity and mobility of the American population have produced a particular problem in regard to "privileges" enjoyed by all citizens. The more wealthy states are able to provide more welfare benefits of various kinds than the poorer ones. In California, for example, wealth is found together with a balmy climate. This combination may lure residents of colder and poorer states to retire or to seek work in the "Golden State," a situation not always greeted cheerfully by the gainfully employed residents who must foot the tax burden should new arrivals find themselves on the unemployed rolls.[57] The form the problem takes today is that many states require applicants for welfare who are new to the state to wait varying periods of time before being able to claim welfare payments. A number of cases have resulted from charges by potential recipients that such rules are not constitutional. In time the matter may be expected to reach the Supreme Court for a final decision.

INTERSTATE RENDITION

A second clause of Section 2 of Article IV promises the impracticable:

> A *person charged in any state with treason, felony, or other crime, who shall flee from justice, and be found in another state, shall on demand of the executive authority of the state from which he fled, be delivered up, and be removed to the state having jurisdiction of the crime.*

This clause is perfectly logical and the language is entirely clear, and yet there is in fact no simple method by which state

57. In 1941 the Supreme Court ruled that California's so-called "anti-Okie" law, a reference to the fact many persons of little means had migrated from Oklahoma and other midwest areas during the depression of the 1930's, was unconstitutional. In Edwards v. California, 314 U.S. 160 (1941) Justice Robert Jackson wrote, "It is a privilege of citizenship of the United States, protected from state abridgment, to enter any state of the Union, either for temporary sojourn or for the establishment of permanent residence therein and for gaining resultant citizenship thereof." He also stated, "Any measure which would divide our citizenry on the basis of poverty into one class free to move from state to state and another class that is poverty-bound to the place where it has suffered misfortune is not only at war with the habit and custom by which our country has expanded, but is also a short-sighted blow at the security of property itself. Property can have no more dangerous, even if unwitting, enemy than one who would make its possession a pretext for unequal or exclusive civil rights."

officials can be compelled to render a fugitive from justice to the state from which he has fled. Certainly the requesting state may not dispatch the militia to enforce its demands, and as early as 1860 the Supreme Court had said, "We think it clear that the federal government, under the Constitution, has no power to impose on a state officer, as such, any duty whatever, and compel him to perform it."[58] Although the overwhelming majority of requests for interstate rendition are honored, a few are denied. An example of one denial that became the talk of the nation concerned Robert Elliott Burns.

Mr. Burns, a veteran of World War I who was hungry and penniless in Atlanta in 1922, participated with two other men in a robbery which netted $5.80. They were apprehended, brought to trial, and although this was Burns's first crime he was sentenced to six to ten years. After serving approximately six months on a chain gang he escaped to Chicago and succeeded in publishing a business magazine which brought him an enormous salary for those times. In 1929, the woman he had recently divorced informed the Georgia authorities of his whereabouts, and state officials appeared in Chicago to return him to their jurisdiction. The officers allegedly promised him a pardon provided he would return voluntarily and pay the expenses of the rendition. He accepted the offer (which the particular Georgia officials had no power to extend), served for a year as a model prisoner, and then, despairing of release, escaped a second time. He made his way to New York where he wrote an account of life in a chain gang that promptly became a best-selling book. The movie industry brought him to Hollywood to serve as technical adviser to the film version, *I Am a Fugitive from a Chain Gang*. The Georgia authorities located him in New Jersey through his activities with the film and requested the governor to return him to their custody. Governor Moore held a public hearing on the request a few days before Christmas, 1932, and, to the cheers of the spectators, announced that he would not return the fugitive. Of course, Mr. Burns lived in fear that his protector might have a change of mind or be replaced by a governor who refused to violate the letter and spirit of the Constitution. Requests for the rendition of the escapee continued until 1941, and three different New Jersey governors refused to honor them.

Then, in 1942, Georgia elected Ellis Arnall to the governorship, and during his administration the chain gang system was abolished. In 1943 Governor Arnall asked the Georgia Board of Pardons to extend a full pardon to Burns. The Board refused

The chain gang fugitive

58. Kentucky v. Dennison, 24 Howard 66 (1860).

77

on the ground that the fugitive was not within its jurisdiction. Burns, a successful Newark businessman, refused to return to Georgia. Two years later Mr. Burns returned to Atlanta. Governor Arnall accompanied him to the Board of Pardons and again requested full pardon. The Board ruled that it was unable to do this since the escapee had admitted guilt, but it was able, and willing, to commute his sentence. On November 2, 1945, approximately 23 years after his first brush with the law, Mr. Burns could leave the safety of New Jersey without fear.[59]

"A REPUBLICAN FORM OF GOVERNMENT" AND "PROTECTION AGAINST DOMESTIC VIOLENCE"

The fourth section of Article IV states:

> *The United States shall guarantee to every state in this Union, a republican form of government, and shall protect each of them against invasion; and on application of the legislature, or of the executive (when the legislature cannot be convened), against domestic violence.*

A political question

The Constitution does not explain what a "republican form of government" is, and the courts have consistently refused to interpret the phrase. In cases brought before it, the Supreme Court has consistently held that the "political" (*i.e.*, executive and legislative) branches, not the judiciary, are the proper ones to determine what is required for a "republican form of government." If the President, House of Representatives, or Senate accords recognition to a state, the courts assume it has passed the test. Presumably, if both chambers of Congress refused to seat elected representatives from a state, the President would be obliged to "reconstruct" it along republican lines.

Protection against invasion

Protection from attack was likely a comforting guarantee in 1787, but today invasion of a state by a hostile force would be an attack on the United States without the article. When an attack came in December, 1941, Americans did not make a sharp differentiation between states and territories—even unincorporated territories. Enemy bombs on Pearl Harbor and Davao led President Roosevelt to declare in a message to the Congress, "Yesterday, December 7, 1941—a date which will live in infamy—the United States of America was suddenly and deliberately attacked by naval and air forces of the Empire of Japan."

States have been understandably slow to ask for Federal help to protect them from domestic violence. In 1842 when faced by

59. For a complete account of this case see Gaylon L. Caldwell, "The Legacy of a Fugitive," *Western Humanities Review*, XV (Winter, 1961), 59–72.

an insurgent "constitution" and an unofficial list of state officers, the governor of Rhode Island appealed to President Tyler for aid. When Tyler indicated he would support the established state government, "Dorr's Rebellion" ceased. Had the President declined to act, the state officials could have done nothing to force him to honor this clause, since separation of powers precludes the courts from compelling such action by writ of mandamus. Conversely, a half-century after the Rhode Island rebellion, President Cleveland sent troops into Illinois over the vehement protests of the governor of that state. The occasion was the "Pullman Strike"; because there was considerable violence, the President ostensibly acted to protect the United States mail, although the effect of his act was to turn soldiers into strikebreakers. Once the Federal troops appeared, Governor Altgeld preferred to oppose the uninvited guests with words, rather than to have his militiamen oppose the soldiers with force. Later, President Cleveland's action was sustained by the court.[60] As previously mentioned, Federal troops and/or National Guard units acting under Federal jurisdiction have been used during the Administrations of Presidents Eisenhower, Kennedy, and Johnson to enforce court orders and to restore order to areas of severe civil disturbance.[61]

Uses of Federal troops

Restrictions on State Powers

Finally, the Constitution specifies restrictions on the powers of the states, not so much to limit their activities vis-à-vis their own citizens as against the national government. These limitations help make federalism work. One of the most important is the "supremacy article"—Article VI, Section 2, which states:

> This Constitution and the laws of the United States which shall be made in pursuance thereof; and all treaties made, or which shall be made, under the authority of the United States, shall be the supreme law of the land; and the judges in every state shall be bound thereby, any thing in the constitution or laws of any state to the contrary notwithstanding.

This means that when the national government acts within the powers granted it by the Constitution, its actions are

60. *In re* Debs, 158 U.S. 564 (1895).

61. A case study of the Little Rock controversy, during which President Eisenhower used both Federal troops and the National Guard to enforce a court order to open a high school to black students, and which dramatically illustrates many problems of federalism, is provided by Corinne Silverman, *The Little Rock Story*, Inter-University Case Program #41 (University, Ala.: University of Alabama Press, 1959).

supreme over those of any state. In the Little Rock case, mentioned above, evasive action by legislators and executive officials

Federal power supreme

of the state of Arkansas was overruled by the Supreme Court, which reiterated the supremacy of the Federal judiciary in expounding the law of the Constitution.[62] "It follows," wrote Chief Justice Warren for a unanimous Court, "that the interpretation of the Fourteenth Amendment enunciated by this Court in the Brown case is the supreme law of the land. . . ." Thus a governor or state legislature could not nullify a Federal court order without violating his oath to support the Constitution. Although the Court admitted that the responsibility for public education was primarily the concern of the states, it noted that "it is equally true that such responsibilities, like all other state activity, must be exercised consistently with federal constitutional requirements as they apply to state action. . . ." Should any state law or constitution conflict with the national Constitution or with a law or treaty made by the United States, the state must give way. Since the treaty power of the central government will be discussed in some detail in Chapter 6, it need only be noted here that treaties must be constitutional in order to bind the states.

In addition to the explicit provision of the supremacy of the national government, the states are limited expressly by the

Prohibitions on treaties, etc.

three paragraphs of Article I, Section 10. Except for phrases in the first of these, the three clauses are concerned with the delimitation of the areas of Federal primacy. Only a minimum consideration need be given them:

> No state shall enter into any treaty, alliance, or confederation; grant letters of marque and reprisal; coin money; emit bills of credit; make any thing but gold and silver coin a tender in payment of debts; pass any bill of attainder, ex post facto law, or law impairing the obligation of contracts, or grant any title of nobility.

The civil liberties are reminiscent of the guarantees against the national government in Section 9 of Article I, and will be considered with civil liberties in Chapter 8. The powers denied the states are granted to the central government in Article I, Section 8. One new provision will be recognized as preventing states from allowing paper money to be used for paying debts—a practice which had alarmed many a man of substance when worthless paper money circulated freely under the Articles of Confederation.

The prohibition of laws impairing the obligation of contracts has been extremely important and frequently has been invoked

62. Cooper v. Aaron, 358 U.S. 1 (1958).

before state and Federal courts. The high-water mark of rigid interpretation was reached early in the history of the country in the famous Dartmouth College case. In this instance, the State of New Hampshire sought to convert a private college, chartered by George III in 1769, into a state university, but the trustees refused to recognize the amended charter and engaged Daniel Webster, an alumnus, as counsel. After days of florid oratory (in English and Latin) Chief Justice John Marshall found the charter to be a "contract" and the legislation to be an impairment of the contract. Few were distressed because Dartmouth remained a private school, but the construction of the clause by the Court suggested that private property might never have to give way to the general welfare. Later, Roger B. Taney, President Jackson's appointee to the chair vacated by John Marshall, unhooked some snaps in the legal strait-jacket imposed by the Dartmouth decision. Chief Justice Taney was unconvinced by Webster's argument that to permit the construction of a free bridge across the Charles River (when a previously built toll bridge had secured a seventy-year monopoly) would be "a revolution against the foundations on which property rests." Instead, Taney ruled that the new bridge could be built because ambiguities in the language of franchises must be construed to operate to the advantage of the public. The community also has rights.[63] The decision in the "battle of the bridges" checked an extravagant definition of "contract," but the protection of contracts by the Constitution still remains today.

Contracts

The final constitutional provisions (in Article I, Section 10) for establishing and maintaining federalism with which we need be concerned are these:

> No state shall, without the consent of the Congress, lay any imposts or duties on imports or exports, except what may be absolutely necessary for executing its inspection laws; and the net produce of all duties and imposts, laid by any state on imports or exports, shall be for the use of the treasury of the United States; and all such laws shall be subject to the revision and control of the Congress.

Other prohibitions

> No state shall, without the consent of Congress, lay any duty of tonnage, keep troops, or ships of war in time of peace, enter into any agreement or compact with another state, or with a foreign power, or engage in war, unless actually invaded, or in such imminent danger as will not admit of delay.

63. Charles River Bridge Co. v. Warren Bridge Co., 11 Peters 420 (1827). *Cf.* Dartmouth College v. Woodward, 4 Wheaton 518 (1819).

It is difficult for the citizen of today to recognize the need for such provisions, until, perhaps, he is stopped at a state line and watches agricultural inspectors examine the contents of his automobile for insects. The courts have held such routine inspections to be within the prerogatives of the states, but one trembles to imagine the chaos which might well exist in a cross-country trip without the restraints on state officials imposed by Article I, Section 10.

The prohibition of interstate compacts without prior consent suggests the fear of the framers that a league of strong states might destroy the "more perfect union" they hoped to erect, or place a sister state at a disadvantage.

It is impossible to overestimate the influence that the principle of federalism has had in every aspect of American life. In the pressures of the present age the complexities of a national government and fifty state governments serving, taxing, and regulating the same people demand a degree of political sophistication superior to that required in the past. An understanding and valid appraisal of the powers and limitations of both national and state governments would seem to be a condition of good citizenship and intelligent participation in government today.

The Future of Federalism

According to both scholars of and participants in the system, the nearly 200-year-old American arrangement of shared political powers called federalism is in serious need of overhauling. A simplified statement of the problem is that the money and power are in Washington, but the situations which might be cured by the application of the money and power are in the states, or more specifically in the metropolitan areas. A recent report to the President stated, "The major crisis threatening the political system and, indeed, the whole fabric of American society," is in the nation's cities.[64] It is often charged that the local and state governments nearest the troubled situations are neither well organized nor have the legal powers necessary to cope with the growing problems. Further complicating the difficulties of state and local governments is frequently a shortage of adequate funds.[65] For these reasons many would agree

Urban crisis

64. *Ninth Annual Report,* by the Advisory Commission on Intergovernmental Relations (Washington: January 31, 1968), p. 1.

65. See James N. Miller, "Dead Hand of the Past," *National Civic Review,* LVII (April, 1968), pp. 183–188, for a discussion of how many state constitutions established in the 1800's are not adequate to meet today's requirements. It was generally considered a hopeful sign that by the beginning of 1968 twenty-two states were engaged in some form of state constitutional activity.

that when the states fail to adopt modern constitutions geared to facilitate action at the state and municipal level,

> The nationwide result, of course, is that the Federal Government, whose broad and flexible constitution enables it constantly to adapt to change, is being pulled into the government-service vacuum created by the states.[66]

Despite the growth of such new efforts at governmental cooperation below the state level as the Councils of Government in metropolitan areas, there remains the problem of many "special districts" which exist to exercise governmental authority on the local level in regard to some matter such as sewers, mosquito control, fire-fighting, etc., and which, on occasion, impede the coordination of imaginative and cooperative governmental responses to problems on a larger scale.

The entire matter of whether federalism as it has been known in America can endure was put in stark perspective in 1968 by the Advisory Commission on Intergovernmental Relations. Commenting upon the number and seriousness of problems with which the Federal system must deal, the commission stated:

Cooperation

> The manner of meeting these challenges will largely determine the fate of the American political system; it will determine if we can maintain a form of government marked by partnership and wholesome competition among National, State and local levels, or if instead—in the face of threatened anarchy—we must sacrifice political diversity as the price of the authoritative action required for the Nation's survival.[67]

Obviously there are immediate and practical problems—none greater than the crisis in American cities—that put the Federal system to the test. In addition, however, there are abstract and moral reasons for questioning the worth of the Federal system. For example, a strong moral case can be made that federalism has permitted local majorities of white segregationists to keep black citizens, first, in slavery, and then in a condition of political and economic inferiority in many portions of the land.[68] It can also be argued that federalism, with decentralized centers of power located in state capitols and city halls, has often

Doubts about federalism

66. *Ibid.*, pp. 187–188.

67. *Ninth Annual Report, op. cit.*, p. 14

68. It has been suggested a new form of federalism should permit the operation of black communities and institutions by blacks, rather than the increased administration of blacks by whites—even if the whites mean well. Support for the idea comes from the belief that black pride in black accomplishments requires some autonomous black activity. For a discussion of the matter see W. H. Ferry, "The Case for a New Federalism," *Saturday Review*, LI (June 15, 1968), pp. 14–17.

enabled a dedicated minority to frustrate the will of larger groups. Examples might be business and agricultural interests which have availed themselves of the Federal system as they opposed consumer and laboring groups consisting of larger numbers of people.[69]

Toward a reevaluation of federalism

If in fact the nation wishes to achieve the goals about which so much has been written and spoken—such as the political and economic equality of opportunity for all—then a major item of domestic business of the 1970's must be the reevaluation and possible modification of the Federal system. One method by which such an assessment may begin is for individual citizens to reach conclusions as to which of the following situations are most likely to produce undesirable results, and how these might be ameliorated by changes in the structure and operation of federalism:

a) Tyranny by national majorities over various minorities.
b) Tyranny by local majorities over local minorities.
c) Frustration of majority desires by national or local minorities.

SUMMARY

• A conspicuous feature of the American system of government is the constitutional division of political power between the national government and the states called federalism. The national government created in Philadelphia was intentionally provided with strong powers to tax, borrow, spend, regulate, and protect in a reaction to the dissatisfaction over the weak and short-lived government under the Articles of Confederation. Since 1789 the Federal Government has grown in power, and has expanded its sphere of activity to the point where some decry its size as a danger to individual freedom.

69. A trenchant critique of federalism in twentieth-century America, in which an examination is made of the moral implications of the system, is William H. Riker, *Federalism: Origin, Operation, Significance* (Boston: Little, Brown, 1964). Professor Riker concludes his study in this fashion: "If one approves of the goals and values of the privileged minority, one should approve of federalism. Thus, if in the United States one approves of Southern white racists, then one should approve of American federalism. If, on the other hand, one disapproves of the values of the privileged minority, one should disapprove of federalism. Thus, if in the United States one disapproves of racism, one should disapprove of federalism." p. 155.

For other studies and commentaries upon the subject of federalism see Nelson A. Rockefeller, *The Future of Federalism* (New York: Atheneum, 1963); Alpheus T. Mason, *The States Rights Debate, Antifederalism and the Constitution* (Englewood Cliffs: Prentice-Hall, 1964); and Daniel J. Elazar, *American Federalism: A View from the States* (New York: Thomas Y. Crowell, 1966).

• Those powers not delegated to the Federal Government by the Constitution, nor denied to the states, are "reserved to the states respectively, or to the people." Although the actions of the Federal Government draw the largest headlines, the states and lesser governmental units carry on an immense amount of necessary activity. This includes operation of educational systems running from kindergartens to universities, provision of police protection, zoning, street and highway construction and maintenance, and many other aspects of civilized life too often taken for granted.

• Interaction between the national government and the state and lesser governments have proved throughout American history to be a fertile area for dispute and bitterness, the worst of which was evidenced during the Civil War. States' rights disputes figure prominently in American politics today. Those who make the states' rights case argue that the Federal Government is unconstitutionally infringing upon state and local prerogatives in matters regarding integration, education, welfare, etc. Critics hold that the term "states' rights" is often a screen to hide what is essentially a bigoted and reactionary political philosophy.

• In some areas—taxation, for example—the Federal and state and local governments share concurrent powers. Besides "reserved powers," the states under the Constitution are assigned certain responsibilities and they receive stated benefits.

• The disparity in power and money between the Federal Government and the state and metropolitan governments has led to various attempts to utilize the assets of the former to assist in solving the problems of the latter. Much used today is the grants-in-aid approach. Under this plan grants of money from the Federal Government are made to state and local governments and other organizations to be used for a variety of specified purposes.

• Proponents of the grants-in-aid approach claim that in this fashion policies accepted by the Federal Government, presumably reflecting the national will, can be effectively transmitted to all portions of the nation. Opponents argue that grants-in-aid utilize the financial power of the Federal Government to coerce or bribe state and local governments into doing things which the local residents frequently do not favor. Something of a compromise is the block-grant plan, whereby grants of money are made by the Federal Government for broad categories of activity with the recipients having more flexibility concerning how the money is to be used than is the case with grants-in-aid. A more recently suggested approach is called revenue sharing, whereby the Federal Government would return some of the funds it collects in taxes to the states.

• More and more Americans are looking to Washington for money and knowledge with which to cope with the problems facing both rural and metropolitan areas. This situation has led to concern that the Federal system is eroding as the national government increasingly expands into the vacuum created by state and city inactivity. A few observers feel the demise of federalism in favor of a stronger central government is needed.

SUGGESTED READING

* (Books so designated are available in paperbound editions.)

Anderson, William, The Nation and the States: Rivals or Partners (Minneapolis: University of Minnesota Press, 1955).

Commission on Intergovernmental Relations. Report to the President (Washington: United States Government Printing Office, 1955).

* Elazar, Daniel J., American Federalism: A View from the States (New York: Crowell, 1966).

Holcombe, Arthur, Our More Perfect Union (Cambridge: Harvard University Press, 1950).

Maass, Arthur, ed., Area and Power (Glencoe, Ill.: Free Press, 1959).

MacMahon, Arthur W., ed., Federalism: Mature and Emergent (New York: Doubleday, 1955).

* Mason, Alpheus T., The States Rights Debate, Antifederalism and the Constitution (Englewood Cliffs: Prentice-Hall, 1964).

* Riker, William H., Federalism, Origin, Operation, Significance (Boston: Little, Brown, 1964).

* Rockefeller, Nelson A., The Future of Federalism (New York: Atheneum, 1963).

Wheare, Sir Kenneth, Federal Government, 3rd edn. (London: Oxford University Press, 1953).

3

The American Citizen

The Greeks of the classical period furnished much more to American government than the architectural style that characterizes our public buildings: they bequeathed concepts of government, together with a vocabulary which makes it possible for us to talk about the concepts. For example, the crucial word "politics" and all of its derivations come from the Greek term for "city-state." When Aristotle wrote his famous passage, "Man is by nature a political animal," he was merely stating what most of his fellows considered axiomatic—that a person who lacks a desire for human companionship and an interest in participating in civic affairs must be either a "beast or a god." The Greeks assumed that institutions civilized men and that the chief institution, the state, existed not merely to give its people protection, but to bring them the good life. Although we use a descendant of the Middle English word *citizein* (which traces through the Old French back to Latin) rather than the Greek *politēs*, the status of the person called a "citizen" was also a Greek invention. The proud participant in the concerns of government was a new actor on the ancient political stage. Before his time government consisted only in rulers and subjects; since his time the western world has never been permitted to forget the ideal that government should be a public affair—a concern of the people involved. As Aristotle put it, "The salvation of the community is the common business of them all."

Interestingly enough, Aristotle was not a citizen of Athens. Since his adopted city required a blood-tie for full-scale participation in civic affairs, he could not qualify. In modern America, however, the blood-tie is only one of the ways by which a person may obtain citizenship. In addition to being born of

American parents, one may become a citizen merely by being born in the United States, or through a legal process known as naturalization. The framers had several options in determining citizenship. They might have limited it to the descendants of the free inhabitants as of the time the Constitution was adopted. This would have imposed an hereditary civic aristocracy on the country. They might have stipulated the terms and procedures for naturalization, thereby effectively removing the subject from politics. Instead, the Founding Fathers granted Congress power "to establish an uniform rule of naturalization." The ideal of making government a public affair was furthered by the early congressional policies which encouraged immigration and then readily made citizenship available to those who wished it, and by the willingness of states, until recently, to permit resident aliens to vote.

The Constitutional ideal

America's Immigration Policies

The United States is a country of immigrants and descendants of immigrants. Except for those who are descended from slaves and from inmates of English jails, or the aboriginal American Indians, all of the present inhabitants either voluntarily left their homelands to take a chance in this country or trace their ancestry back to someone who did. In general, the people known as "Americans" have been transplanted a very short time, as the western world records history.

The salty ocean air did not purge the immigrants of their patterns of thought and behavior: these legacies have persisted and are reflected in the politics of the present day. For example, when one recalls that the dread of being conscripted for military duty led many people to leave their homes and come to America, the persistent disinclination of the American people to institute compulsory military training becomes understandable. Almost everyone knows that many settlers came to these shores to avoid religious persecution at the hands of their governments. Religious bigotry abroad led to religious diversity in the New World, and the result was the pioneer attempt to separate church from state. The immigrant nature of our population has always created difficulties in the formulation and maintenance of a consistent foreign policy. The fact that Americans vary more than people of any other nationality with the exception of the Soviet Union helps explain why the tasks of American politicians are very different from those of their coun-

Immigrant nature of U.S. population

terparts in countries where the population is relatively homogeneous and stable—countries like England, for example.

THE EARLY ATTITUDES

During the first century of its history under the Constitution, the United States consistently encouraged immigration. There was room for all, and many early Americans had a sentimental **Changing patterns** desire to provide a new kind of life to those across the Atlantic who sought relief from onerous political, religious, and economic constraints often found in Europe. Despite such sentimentality, however, there was a sordid side to immigration: immigrants frequently were exploited, for both national and state governments failed to safeguard their interests, and neither was seriously concerned in helping them adjust to their new homeland.[1] Then, because immigrants furnished a large supply of cheap labor, organized labor pressured for the restriction of immigration. Under the first immigration law (1882) paupers and feeble-minded and diseased persons were double-checked—and sent back. Other factors pressed for a revision of the traditional immigration policy. Public fear of anarchism accounted for a law in 1903 which excluded persons believing

Immigrants Made Welcome   (Puck, 1880).

1. Probably the best account of the immigrants' struggles in America is Oscar Handlin, *The Uprooted* (New York: Universal Library, 1957).

in assassination or overthrowing the government by force, those who belonged to organizations which taught such doctrines, and anarchists. The Chinese Exclusion Act had become law in 1882 upon the demand of citizens of the West Coast. Chinese, brought across the Pacific by labor contractors to work on railroad construction and in the mines, became so numerous as to make Westerners apprehensive. As Japanese immigration figures moved upward, President Theodore Roosevelt arranged a "gentleman's agreement" with the Japanese government in 1907 whereby the latter would not issue passports to prospective immigrants to America without the specific approval of the United States. In this way the President salved the pride of the Japanese by sparing them the insult of an exclusion act and satisfied the pressures at home for a curtailment of Japanese immigration.

By the 1880s' the "old immigration" from northern and western Europe began to be displaced by a "new immigration" from eastern and southern Europe. The Nordic majority watched with dismay as Italians, Poles, Croatians, Slovenes, and others disembarked and began to compete for work. Political societies to curb the immigration mushroomed, and pressure on Congress mounted.

The Era of the National Origins Quota System

In 1921 Congress passed the first of several laws which limited the immigration of Caucasians on the basis of national origin as well as personal fitness. After some modification in 1924 the principle was firmly imbedded into law in 1929. Although no quotas were imposed upon persons seeking to immigrate from the Western Hemisphere, which meant in practice primarily Mexico and Canada, restrictions were placed upon immigration from the rest of the world. The quota system thus established heavily favored immigrants from northern Europe, particularly individuals from England, Scotland, Wales, Ireland, and Germany.[2] Immigration from southern and eastern Europe was severely limited by the quota formulation, and that from the nonwhite areas of Africa and Asia was nearly nonexistent. The national origins quota legislation embodied into law the feeling that persons from northern Europe, who were most like the majority of Americans, were best qualified to become future citizens.

Favored ethnic groups

2. The formula for determining the quota for each country was to take one-sixth of one percent of the number of inhabitants of that nationality who lived within the United States in 1920, except that no quota was smaller than 100.

Pacific Chivalry: Encouragement to Chinese Immigration (Thomas Nast, 1869).

The Immigration and Naturalization Act of 1952 retained the national origins features of the previous legislation but added several changes.[3] Among these were more stringent rules **Exclusion of** designed to prevent subversives from entering the nation, the **subversives** elimination of race as a barrier to immigration and naturalization of Asiatics, and the introduction of a system to provide preference in the awarding of immigration slots to persons having close relatives as citizens of the United States, or to those with unusually desirable personal qualifications. The concern with subversives in the 1952 Act reflects the national interest at the time in such matters which was associated with the activity of the late Senator Joseph McCarthy (R., Wisconsin), whose crusade to ferret out Communists and "fellow-travelers" was briefly popular with many Americans.

In the early 1920's various minority ethnic groups sought to change the national origins quota policy. Later they were joined **Opposition to the** by others who were concerned with the racial and religious bias **quota system** evidenced in America's immigration laws.[4] Opponents of the national origins quota policy also noted that quotas for nations such as England went unfilled while many more southern and eastern Europeans were eager to immigrate than there were quota spaces assigned to their nations. The unfilled quotas of one nation were not transferable to another. In 1952 President Truman vetoed the McCarran-Walter Act only to see Congress override his action. President Eisenhower charged in 1953 that the McCarran-Walter Act was discriminatory. In a posthumously published book, President Kennedy argued for a new immigration policy, and President Johnson, in his first State of the Union address, asked Congress to remove the discriminatory bars from the nation's immigration legislation.[5]

The Current Policy

On October 3, 1965, while standing by the Statue of Liberty in New York Harbor, President Johnson signed an immigration bill into law which eliminated the national origins provisions of

3. The 1952 Act is more commonly known as the McCarran-Walter Act after the names of its authors in the Senate and House of Representatives.

4. The more than 40 years of political maneuvering which preceded adoption of the current policy offer an example of how a minority point of view has, over time, the opportunity of becoming the majority opinion in a pluralistic society.

5. John F. Kennedy, *A Nation of Immigrants* (New York: Harper and Row, 1964).

the McCarran-Walter Act. As the President said at the time, the new policy will not affect the lives of millions, nor reshape the structure of American society. In fact, it does not greatly increase the numbers of immigrants allowed each year to enter the United States.[6] The 1965 provisions do not abolish the quota procedure—a quota was established ·for immigration from the Western Hemisphere where before there had been none. What has been changed is that the United States no longer sets immigration quotas on the basis of a person's place of birth, which in practice had meant quotas established along racial and religious lines. Thus the concern about the removal of racial and religious bias in American national life, which has come to occupy a central place in contemporary politics, changed one of the nation's long-standing discriminatory practices.

McCarran-Walter Act

The Immigration and Nationality Act of 1965, which became fully operative July 1, 1968, after a three-year transition period, assigns a quota of 120,000 immigrants a year to the Western Hemisphere and 170,000 a year to the rest of the world. In addition the immediate relatives, persons defined as being minor unmarried children, spouses, and parents of United States citizens, and certain small categories of individuals such as ministers, may enter quota-free.[7] It is anticipated that such persons will annually number approximately 30,000.

Western Hemisphere and non-Western Hemisphere quota

In place of the national origins criteria and derivative quotas for each nation previously applied to immigrants from beyond the Western Hemisphere, the 1965 Act prescribes new criteria for determining the preference given to a person seeking a quota space, and assigns a percentage of the 170,000 spaces to each preference category. Unlike that portion of the McCarran-Walter Act which it replaces, the 1965 statute permits unused quota spaces in one preference category to be

Quota transfers

6. The number of individuals admitted in 1967 was 361,972. In 1965 the number was 296,697.

7. Each year a number of persons come to the United States who are not expected to remain permanently. These non-immigrants include foreign officials and their families, students, vacationing visitors, foreign correspondents, and others. The reasons for limiting the number of visas (an endorsement by the proper authority on a passport denoting that it has been examined and that permission is given to enter) for this group is to prevent undesirable persons from entering the country.

A particular group of persons, migrant workers from Mexico called braceros, who once were welcomed into the United States, are now legally restricted from entering. The move was made to protect American labor from cheap competition. "Wetbacks," individuals who swim or wade the Rio Grande or otherwise illegally enter the United States from Mexico to work, continue to be a problem. Some Mexican nationals who commute at border crossings are still permitted to work in the United States.

93

TABLE 3.1 Quota and Nonquota Immigration to the U.S., 1967

Country or Region of Birth	Number Admitted	Quota Immigrants	Total Nonquota Immigrants	Selected Nonquota Categories		
				Spouses, Children of U.S. Citizens	Natives of W. Hemis. and Families	Admitted Under Special Acts*
Britain	23,778	19,676	4,102	2,627	855	5
Czechoslovakia	297	191	106	61	1	7
Germany	16,595	7,075	9,520	8,759	199	104
Greece	14,194	11,361	2,833	2,483	9	76
Hungary	582	262	320	185	1	11
Ireland	1,991	1,743	248	131	10	0
Italy	28,487	20,585	7,902	3,600	113	1,926
Poland	4,356	3,574	782	551	4	6
Portugal	13,400	11,802	1,598	872	116	31
Other	25,586	16,729	8,857	3,978	2,849	836
EUROPE	129,266	92,998	36,268	22,305	4,157	3,002
China†	7,118	5,302	1,816	672	9	4
Hong Kong	15,737	12,988	2,749	1,496	12	3
India	4,129	3,793	336	267	6	3
Philippines	10,336	6,729	3,607	2,957	8	17
Other	19,763	10,888	8,875	7,231	109	551
ASIA and MIDDLE EAST	57,083	39,700	17,383	12,623	144	578
Africa, Oceania and Other Countries	5,388	3,905	1,483	967	169	80
SUBTOTAL	191,737	136,603	55,134	35,895	4,470	3,660
Canada	34,768	8,941	25,827	1,012	23,811	10
Mexico	43,034	185	42,849	56	40,562	1
Cuba	30,869	856	30,013	16	4,497	0
Other	43,002	4,259	38,743	869	36,245	24
NORTH & CENTRAL AMERICA	151,673	14,241	137,432	1,953	105,115	35
Argentina	3,013	517	2,496	48	2,343	1
Colombia	4,679	89	4,590	22	4,513	0
Other	10,870	1,629	9,241	186	8,841	1
SOUTH AMERICA	18,562	2,235	16,327	256	15,697	2
SUBTOTAL	170,235	16,476	153,759	2,209	120,812	37
ALL COUNTRIES	361,972	153,079	208,893	38,104	125,282	3,697

*Admitted under Acts of July 14, 1960, Sept. 26, 1961, or Oct. 24, 1962.
†Includes Taiwan.

Source: Annual Report of the Immigration and Naturalization Service, Department of Justice, 1967.

transferred to other categories, or to be made available to other qualified immigrants on a "first come, first served" basis.

The preference categories for non-Western Hemisphere immigration, and the percentage annually assigned to each, is as follows: (1) 20 percent of the over-all quota (170,000) for unmarried adult sons and daughters of American citizens; (2) 20 percent for spouses and unmarried sons and daughters of aliens permanently residing in the United States; (3) 10 percent for members of the professions or those possessing special training or talents; (4) 10 percent for married sons and daughters of American citizens; (5) 24 percent for brothers and sisters of American citizens; (6) 10 percent for skilled and unskilled laborers required to meet labor shortages; (7) 6 percent for refugees from political and religious persecution, or persons made homeless by a natural disaster. The last provision was made to replace the former practice whereby the Congress would pass special legislation from time to time to permit entry of a particular group of refugees.[8] No more than 20,000 individuals a year, excluding immediate relatives, may enter the United States from any one non-Western Hemisphere nation.[9]

Preference categories

Prospective immigrants from Western Hemisphere nations are selected for spaces in the annual 120,000 quota for that region on a "first come, first served" basis provided certain standards applied to all immigrants are met. These standards include provisions prohibiting the entry of the mentally retarded, sexual deviates, criminals, members of a Communist Party, and persons afflicted with certain diseases. The Immigration and Naturalization Service, in the Department of Justice, administers the immigration laws with the assistance of the Department of State and the Department of Labor.

"First come, first served" basis

In a world faced with a "population explosion" it is not likely that the United States, troubled by its own urban crowding, will significantly or soon increase the number of immi-

---

8. Examples of special immigration legislation for groups of individuals are the Displaced Persons Act of 1948, under which refugees from World War II were admitted, and special legislation enacted to admit Hungarians who fled their land after the Soviet Union crushed the 1956 uprising. Congress has also passed legislation to admit "war brides" outside the quotas. In 1965 the United States arranged with Cuba to fly persons wishing to leave the Castro regime to America.

9. Persons entering the United States under the employment preferences [(1) and (3) above] must be certified by the Department of Labor that their entry will not adversely affect the American labor market, and that the job sought cannot be filled by American working people. Concern has been voiced that this provision will encourage the so-called "brain drain"—exodus of highly skilled people from nations desperately needing them.

Fitzpatrick in The St. Louis Post-Dispatch
"The not so very free world."

grants permitted entry under the 1965 law.[10] The nation which once was new and empty and in need of immigrants is full, or at **Future policy** least generally thought by its inhabitants to be so, and Emma Lazarus' famous lines at the Statue of Liberty,

> Give me your tired, your poor,
> Your huddled masses, yearning to breathe free . . .
> I lift my lamp beside the golden door,

are more a relic of America's past than an accurate description of the present.

CONGRESSIONAL EXCEPTIONS AND THE IMMIGRATION AND NATURALIZATION SERVICE

Since Congress is vested with the authority to admit into the United States whom it pleases, it can and does make individual exceptions to the immigration laws. Exceptions are defended on the grounds that laws are impersonal and apply to general problems, whereas individuals are persons with particular problems. Thus exceptions humanize government, and many an

10. Some Irish members of Congress have complained that Irish immigrants have a difficult time meeting the new immigration requirements and hence the law should be changed to permit larger numbers from the Emerald Isle to enter the United States.

immigrant favored by an exception to the rules has good reason to thank Congress. Exceptions are made by what are known as private laws whereby Congress waives certain requirements so that a designated individual may enter the country, or, having entered, remain.

By private law, Congress quite frequently waives requirements in order to permit the entry of an individual who otherwise would be ineligible. Consider, for example, the case of **Special cases** Mrs. H—— P——: After having survived a Communist concentration camp and escaped from hard labor on a road gang in Yugoslavia, she came to Italy, where she met and married a naturalized American citizen. Mrs. P—— wished to immigrate to the United States, but at her physical examination an X-ray disclosed spots on her lungs indicative of tuberculosis. Because she was physically unfit, Mrs. P—— was denied a visa, but by passing a private law, Congress authorized her entry.[11]

Ought an exception be made for Mr. Y——? One day the people in a small Southern town must have been astonished to learn that their Chinese grocer was in serious trouble with the national government. They had known him for nearly 20 years as a model resident who had nothing to mar his record except a 30 day suspension of his beverage permit (he had sold beer on a Sunday). Now they learned that he had entered the country illegally in 1934—a stowaway on an unnamed oil tanker. Mr. Y—— was given the opportunity to depart voluntarily, with the unlikely prospect that he would become eligible during his lifetime for one of the 100 quota numbers annually allotted to China. The Congressman for his district introduced a private bill, which would give him permanent residence upon payment of the visa fee and would deduct one number from the first available Chinese quota. The Congress passed the bill in 1955.[12]

Congress has admitted, by public law, entire groups of people (such as "war brides") outside of quotas. Displaced persons (those uprooted because of political upheavals) included per- **Exhausting the** sons dislocated as a result of World War II, those fleeing the **quotas** Soviet suppression of the 1956 Hungarian revolt, and refugees from Castro's Cuba. But since Congress has too many concerns to be occupied with the determination and adjustment of quotas to meet the needs of international politics, it has delegated much authority in this area to the Executive Branch.

The Immigration and Naturalization Service has broad

11. *Priv. L. No. 378, 69 Stat.* A130 (1955). See *S. Rep. No. 772*, 84th Cong., 1st Sess. (1955).

12. *Priv. L. No. 53, 69 Stat.* A19 (1955). See *H.R. Rep. No. 280*, 84th Cong., 1st Sess. (1955).

powers of applying the rules. An interesting instance of the authority of the Service was its interpretation of a divorce law.

Marriage, divorce, and citizenship

A female resident of California obtained a divorce in Mexico from her husband, who was not a California resident. The husband was not present at the divorce proceeding but was represented by an attorney. The divorcée then married an alien. The acceptability of the Mexican divorce became of crucial importance to the second husband and the immigration authorities because if the Immigration and Naturalization Service recognized the divorce, the alien received all the advantages of an immigrant who is married to a citizen; if the divorce were not recognized, the new husband could not remain in the United States as a nonquota immigrant. The district commissioner in San Francisco found the foreign divorce had not legally terminated the domestic marriage, and the subsequent remarriage, therefore, was illegal. The Board of Immigration Appeals, however, interpreted the California law concerning foreign divorces differently and reversed the commissioner's decision.[13]

ALIEN CONTROL AND DEPORTATION

An alien living within the United States is required to register with the Immigration and Naturalization Service and to keep the government informed as to his address. Failure to abide by the regulations may lead to deportation.

Reasons for deportation

The power to admit and exclude aliens includes the power to deport those who have been admitted. Several thousand aliens are made to leave each year for such reasons as illegal entry, fraudulent statements, membership in a subversive group, or conviction of various crimes. If deported, an alien may not return. Since aliens are "persons," they receive the safeguards of the Constitution—even if they should be in the country illegally.

Naturalization Procedures

Most aliens admitted for permanent residence expect to become citizens of the United States. The process whereby one changes his nationality is known as naturalization. In America, naturalization can be effected in either of two ways: collectively or individually.

Collective naturalization is the blanket bestowal of citizen-

13. In the matter of B——, 5 I. & N. Dec. 659 (1954).

ship. There are three ways citizenship might be given to large groups of people: by treaty (as was accorded the residents of the Louisiana territory in the purchase agreement); by act of Congress (which transformed the "nationals" of Guam into citizens in 1950); or by joint resolution of the Congress (such as that which admitted the independent republic of Texas into the Union and converted Texans into American citizens). In such instances, all the alien need do is be included in the category affected.

Collective naturalization

Individual naturalization is by law a lengthy and involved process.[14] The immigrant must be 18 years of age and must have resided in the United States continuously for five years prior to filing application for naturalization. The applicant must be able to read and communicate in English in most instances, and is required to demonstrate a knowledge of American history, political institutions, and government principles.[15] Additionally an applicant for citizenship must be, in the words of the law, "a person of good moral character, attached to the principles of the Constitution of the United States, and well disposed to the good order and happiness of the United States."[16]

Individual naturalization

The Immigration and Naturalization Service administers the preliminary examination for citizenship applicants, with the final examination being held in open court with a judge presiding. It is at this stage of the process that one comes to understand the enormous power of the judge: one judge might find a person who has been issued a traffic ticket to lack the qualities of "good moral character," while another might find no fault in one who had once been convicted of rape. The petitioner must formally renounce any former national allegiance. In this respect he must satisfy the judge of his unequivocal loyalty to America, and in assuring himself of this a judge may convert a simple ceremony into a public ritual reminiscent of the test of

Examination

14. For the details of the naturalization process see the pamphlet, "Naturalization Requirements and General Information" (Washington: Immigration and Naturalization Service, May 1, 1967); and Louise Boggess, *Journey to Citizenship* (New York: Funk and Wagnalls, 1967).

15. There are special cases to which the naturalization procedures do not apply in their entirety. For example, although Uncle Sam does not give the spouse of a citizen the gift of citizenship as a wedding present, the residence requirement is reduced. Special provisions are made for alien children, persons who have served honorably in the United States armed forces, individuals who lost their citizenship through serving in the military service of nations allied with the United States in World War II, and women who lost their citizenship in the early part of the century when they married an alien. Women no longer lose their citizenship by marrying an alien.

16. 8 United States Code 1427.

99

conversion in a seventeenth-century New England church. If the petitioner passes all the tests, he takes the oath of allegiance, and the judge congratulates him as a new citizen.

Easing the process

The naturalization process has become less difficult as ideas concerning equality and an individual's rights have expanded at home, and international friendships have broadened overseas. In 1946 the Court ruled that one no longer need swear to "bear arms on behalf of the United States," and Congress has removed the racial bars to the naturalization of Orientals.[17] Today aliens not eligible to apply for naturalization include: habitual drunkards; adulterers; polygamists; persons illegally connected with prostitution or narcotics traffic; criminals; anarchists, Communists, and others who advocate the violent overthrow of the Government of the United States; individuals convicted of desertion from the armed forces of the United States or avoiding the draft; and those who have applied for and received a discharge from the military service of the United States because of their alien status.

Revocation of citizenship

A certificate of naturalization once granted may be revoked by a proceeding in a Federal court if it is proved that citizenship was obtained by fraud. Congress has also classified certain activities as "presumptive fraud," which, when committed, should be judged by courts as sufficient reason for loss of citizenship gained through naturalization. Examples are: when a naturalized citizen takes up continuous residence in the nation of which he was formerly a citizen, joins a subversive organization within five years of naturalization, or refuses to testify before a congressional committee regarding subversive activities within 10 years of his citizenship award. Within recent years, however, the will of Congress has clashed with the rulings of the Supreme Court concerning discrimination between native-born and naturalized citizens. In 1964 the Court held a naturalized citizen could not have his citizenship revoked because he had resided more than three years in the nation where he was born. In the Court's words, "This statute proceeds on the impermissible assumption that naturalized citizens as a class are less reliable and bear less allegiance to this country than the native-born."[18] This direction taken by the Court reflects an earlier injunction that denaturalization should only be imposed after "clear, unequivocal and convincing" evidence, because "while it is our high duty to carry out the will of Con-

17. Girouard v. United States, 328 U.S. 61 (1946).

18. Schneider v. Rusk, 377 U.S. 163 (1964).

gress in the performance of this duty, we should have a jealous regard for the rights of the petitioner."[19]

Citizenship on the Basis of Jus Soli and Jus Sanguinis

The first section of the Fourteenth Amendment, written to erase the ruling in the celebrated Dred Scott case that Negroes were not citizens, provides:

All persons born . . . in the United States, and subject to the jurisdiction thereof, are citizens of the United States and of the state wherein they reside.

One may be "born . . . in the United States" both in terms of the *place* wherein the birth occurs and through *parentage.* The phrase "subject to the jurisdiction thereof" excludes from automatic citizenship the children born to foreign diplomats and others not subject to the laws of the United States. Children born to anyone else may claim citizenship—even if born on a beach to a mother who jumped ship and swam to shore without checking through customs.

A person born in any of the 50 states, or in a commonwealth or territory where the inhabitants have citizenship, may claim citizenship under the *jus soli* ("right of the soil"), provided of course, that he is subject to the jurisdiction of the United States. Children born to American citizens in a foreign country have the opportunity to gain citizenship derived from parentage under the *jus sanguinis* ("right of the blood"), provided the parents file an application for naturalization in behalf of their children before the latter reach the age of 18.

Jus soli and jus sanguinis

Individuals who owe their citizenship to either *jus sanguinis* or *jus soli* have in the past, like naturalized citizens, involuntarily lost their citizenship, but of course not for reasons of fraudulent naturalization. The cause of involuntary expatriation has been the action of Congress in declaring that certain acts committed by a citizen must lead to loss of citizenship. Among the acts Congress designated as causes for loss of citizenship were voting in a foreign election, conviction of desertion from the armed forces during wartime, leaving the country during a period of national emergency to evade military service, treason, and serving in the armed forces of another nation without government permission to do so. Within recent years, however, the Supreme Court has looked with an increasingly critical eye upon such congressional activity. In several cases the Court held that Congress does not have the authority to deprive one

Loss of citizenship

19. Schneiderman v. United States, 320 U.S. 118, 120 (1943).

101

of citizenship because a specific act had been committed.[20]
Then in 1967 the Court issued an extremely broad ruling which
indicates that in the future a citizen, native-born or not, may
only lose his citizenship by voluntary renunciation. In a 5-4
decision, based upon the citizenship guarantees of the Fourteenth Amendment, Justice Hugo Black spoke for the majority:
"Congress lacks the constitutional authority to pass laws that
strip American citizens of their nationality without their
consent".[21]

Travel Abroad by Aliens and Citizens

Passports

While it is clearly within the power of the Federal Government to regulate the entry and departure of aliens into and out
of the nation, efforts by the Congress and the Executive
Branch to establish the conditions under which citizens may
travel abroad, and where they may go, have been a matter of
considerable controversy. For a number of years it has been the
practice of the government to require that a passport be
obtained before citizens may legally travel to most foreign
nations—Mexico and Canada being notable exceptions.

Power to deny passports

Because of the dangers of the Cold War, Secretaries of State
began denying passports to citizens believed traveling abroad to
advance the interests of Communism. This practice came
under the scrutiny of the Supreme Court in 1958 when the
judges decided that while the Secretary of State possessed the
power delegated by Congress to issue or deny passports, such
power is limited. Specifically the Court ruled that the Secretary
of State did not have authority to deny a citizen's request for a
passport because of the individual's political beliefs or
associations.[22] In 1964 the Court ruled that a statutory provi-

20. Trop v. Dulles, 356 U.S. 86 (1958). In this case the Court ruled
Congress does not have authority to deprive one of citizenship for conviction or desertion from the armed forces of the United States during wartime. The Court held in Kennedy v. Mendoza-Martinez, 372 U.S. 144
(1963) that leaving the country during wartime or a period of national
emergency in order to evade military service was not a valid reason for
depriving one of citizenship. See also John P. Roche, "The Expatriation
Decisions: A Study in Constitutional Improvision and the Uses of History," *American Political Science Review*, LVIII (March, 1964), pp.
72–80.

21. Afroyim v. Rusk 387 U.S. 253 (1967). The immediate matter at
issue in this case was whether Mr. Afroyim should be deprived of citizenship, as stipulated by Congress, because he had voted in a foreign election.
Under the broadly worded decision in the case, the Court held Congress
had no authority to act in the matter.

22. Kent v. Dulles 357 U.S. 116 (1958).

sion declaring it a criminal offense for a registered Communist to make application for a passport was unconstitutional. It was also the Court's view that to deny traveling abroad on the grounds that a person belonged to a Communist organization constituted a restriction on freedom far too broad to be permitted.[23]

The "right to travel"

However, in the following year the Court apparently reconsidered and backed away from its liberalizing attitude when it declared that the Department of State did have authority to restrict where Americans can travel when, in the opinion of the Secretary of State, such travel is not in the interest of the United States.[24] In practice this meant the Department of State could and did deny passports for travel to certain Communist nations. Then, several years later, the Court again moved forward on the "right to travel" road when it stated that area restrictions—for example, in regard to China, Cuba, North Korea, and North Vietnam—upon the use of a valid passport could not be enforced by imposition of criminal sanctions.[25] The case arose out of a trip by a woman possessing a valid passport to a proscribed area, Cuba. Following the lead suggested by the Court, the Department of State in 1968 announced that it would no longer attempt to punish persons who travel to "off limit" countries.[26]

SUMMARY

- With few exceptions the United States is a nation of immigrants and the descendants of immigrants. The important responsibility for establishing immigration policy was vested by the Constitution in Congress. For a century immigration was generally thought to be a good thing because people were needed to develop the new nation.
- Pressures began building in the late 1800's to restrict and control immigration. Today the United States employs strict limitations upon how many may enter the United States to live, and imposes complex standards regarding who can qualify for immigration.

23. Aptheker v. Secretary of State, 378 U.S. 500 (1964).

24. Zemel v. Rusk, 381 U.S. 1 (1965).

25. Travis v. United States, 385 U.S. 491 (1967).

26. See "Passport Revocation," *Congressional Quarterly Weekly Report,* XXVI (April 12, 1968), Part II of two parts, p. 821.

• For most of this century immigration policy was based upon the national origins quota concept and the personal fitness of individuals wishing to immigrate to the United States. The former operated to favor heavily immigration from countries which had contributed the largest number of immigrants in the past, such as the British Isles and northern Europe. Immigration during the national origins era was difficult, and in some instances practically impossible, for those from southern Europe, the Middle East, Africa, and Asia. Immigration from the Western Hemisphere was not numerically limited. In 1965 a numerical quota was imposed for the first time upon immigration from the Western Hemisphere (120,000 each year), and the quota for the remainder of the world was set at 170,000 each year (with some provision for non-quota immigration). The national origins basis for allocating spaces in the quota for each year was abolished.

• Today an individual seeking to immigrate to the United States is accorded a quota space on the basis of relationship with individuals already in America, possession of certain occupational skills, and personal fitness. In addition to controlling who may enter the nation, Congress establishes by law who may become a naturalized citizen.

• Within recent years the Supreme Court has clashed with Congress over the latter's efforts to deprive native-born and naturalized citizens of their citizenship following participation in proscribed behavior. The Court has held that neither kind of citizen can lose citizenship unless it is voluntarily relinquished by the individual, or in the case where fraud was used to gain naturalized citizenship. In addition the Supreme Court on one side, and Congress and the Administration on the other have disagreed over the government's powers to regulate travel abroad by citizens. The trend of the high court's recent decisions has been to support the right of citizens to journey beyond the borders of the United States.

SUGGESTED READING

* (*Books so designated are available in paperbound editions.*)

Auerbach, Frank L., *Immigration Laws of the United States*, 2nd rev. edn. (Indianapolis: Bobbs-Merrill, 1961).

* Handlin, Oscar, *The Newcomers* (Garden City: Anchor Books, 1961).

* ———, *Race and Nationality in American Life* (Garden City: Anchor Books, 1962).

* ———, *The Uprooted* (New York: Universal Library, 1957).
* Kennedy, John F., A *Nation of Immigrants* (New York: Harper & Row, 1964).
  Stephenson, George M., *History of American Immigration, 1820-1924* (New York: Russell & Russell, 1964).

4

American Politics

People are involved in politics if only because they are concerned about their own problems. One does not frequently encounter a human being who is so detached that decisions touching his liberty or property mean nothing to him. "To say that private men have nothing to do with government is to say that private men have nothing to do with their own happiness or misery," an ancient Roman senator insisted. Cato did not mean that one achieves joy in performing civic duties—rather, that men are obliged to be interested in government because government determines "whether they be naked or clothed, fed or starved, deceived or instructed, protected or destroyed."

Most people care about being clothed, fed, instructed, and protected. Naked human beings generally are not at all averse to having government clothe them; if hungry, to having government feed them. Others, conversely, who are well-fed and fully clad may be understandably unenthusiastic about having government use tax money for such purposes—particularly since they contribute most of it. It should surprise no one that the naked and the fed will try to influence government social welfare policies.[1] Governmental decisions touch many more aspects of life than the primitive economic needs of food, clothing, and shelter, of course, and so individuals are affected to a varying degree by all decisions made—to build a new sewer line, to extend military service, to grant the telephone company permission to increase rates, or to change the national anthem.

"Politics" has been defined as "the art of the possible"—that

1. For example, the 1968 Poor People's March to the nation's capital, and their subsequent habitation called "Resurrection City," was a highly visible effort directed at obtaining government action which would be favorable to millions of persons scattered across the land. Before it was closed down, the encampment had attracted considerable news coverage and its presence had afforded the Poor People's leader, the Rev. Ralph D. Abernathy, numerous occasions to speak out in behalf of the nation's needy.

is, the talent for getting done as completely as practicable that which one wants done.[2] Politics is a method by which decisions are influenced. It is not limited to international, national, state, local, or even campus governments: to speak of "office politics" or "church politics" is to speak of something very real. Even within a family one may observe the operation of politics. In fact, any time decisions are being made which affect the "outputs" of government to their citizens and others, or which affect the "outputs" of groups to their members and others, politics is in season.[3] In democratic societies the individual not only is encouraged to concern himself with the politics of his group, but has the means whereby he can effectively influence the decision-makers—or even supplant them. In the United States, the procedure for replacing government officials is through elections held at regular intervals; and the means of influencing them by personal contact is protected by the Constitution. In authoritarian societies, even if the leaders never

Dictators and democracies

Drawing by D. Fradon; © 1968 The New Yorker Magazine, Inc.
"That's the trouble with a *truly* enlightened electorate."

2. During the spring of 1968 Governor Nelson Rockefeller (R., New York) disclosed in an unusually candid discussion how he got the things done which really mattered. What needed doing, in the governor's judgment, was passage of a six-billion-dollar slum rebuilding program. His method of convincing reluctant members of the New York Assembly to vote for his measure was to threaten to stop doing "personal favors" for the legislators, such as signing pet bills and appointing friends of the legislators to jobs. Rockefeller said of his arm-twisting tactics, "Now I don't like to take this position, but I think that one has to use whatever authority one has when something of major importance to the people comes before you." Quoted in Sidney H. Schanberg, "How to Twist Arms: The Rockefeller Way," *New York Times*, April 11, 1968.

3. See for a discussion of an "input-output" analysis of political activity David Easton, "An Approach to the Analysis of Political Systems," *World Politics*, IX (April, 1957), pp. 383–400.

have to face the hazards of really free elections, they cannot immunize themselves from politics, for dictators, too, depend on influential elites and the mass public for support or at least acquiescence.[4] Dictators may exercise powers of coercion, since they control the army and policy, or of indoctrination, through their control over education and the media of communication. A citizen of a totalitarian regime generally has little chance to influence policy, but if his personal security or ideals are seriously enough affected by deprivations imposed by the regime, he will probably attempt to exert influence through whatever means are possible, including violence. All he needs is sufficient impetus and a reasonable prospect that his form of politics can be applied successfully. If any ruling clique has ever been so monolithic, or any individual official has ever been so impervious, that some form of politicking has not been effective, history does not preserve the memory.

The policy-makers

Policy-makers may attain their positions by any of various ways. The assumption of office on the strength of bayonets is not at all uncommon in history and is almost the norm in some countries. Less often now, heredity is important: few persons assume power because of their birth. Sometimes rule is by a self-perpetuating elite, where the "in-group" chooses its colleagues or retiring officials name their successors. In a few instances, people have been accorded leadership because they are accepted as enjoying the special favor of the local deity. In democratic societies the most usual methods are by *election* and *appointment*. For example, in the national government members of Congress and the Chief Executive are elected, whereas judges and the remainder of the top-level policy-makers of the executive branch are appointed. American congressmen, senators, and the President are chosen by different groups of people, and, generally speaking, the bulk of the adult population is permitted to participate on the basis of "one man, one vote."[5] However, the right to elect has frequently been limited to a few in other systems, and it has not been long since Great Britain permitted some of her citizens to have two votes in the selection of members of Parliament.

4. Carl J. Friedrich and Zbigniew K. Brzezinski, *Totalitarian Dictatorship and Autocracy* (New York: Praeger, 1961). In the fall of 1964 the premier of the Soviet Union, Nikita Khrushchev, was summarily removed from all power. Presumably he had lost the political support of those groups in the Soviet Union which are necessary even for the leader of a totalitarian society.

5. This principle and the cases decided by the Supreme Court which are relevant to it are discussed in Chapter 5.

The concern of this chapter is the politics of the national government. Since the policies of this leviathan are designed and implemented by those who occupy key positions, emphasis will be on *political parties* (which seek to control policy by furnishing the officials who make and execute government decisions) and *pressure groups* (which are primarily concerned with influencing the officials who fill government offices). Since the officials must reflect the wishes of the people or be eventually returned to private life, consideration will be given *public opinion* and *voting behavior*.

Parties, pressure groups, and public opinion

In the United States, political parties are relied upon to nominate, campaign for, and be responsible for policy-makers who range in dignity from the local dog-catcher to the President. When political parties are mentioned, Americans are so familiar with the two-party system that they think of Republicans and Democrats, even though as shall be seen later in this chapter, American political history has often been spiced with the activities of third parties. Once officials are selected, favorable decisions from them can be procured by a variety of techniques extending from outright bribery to cogent argument. In America, although there are many talented amateurs engaged in influencing decision-makers, pressure groups have mastered the art. When pressure groups are mentioned, one thinks of "lobbies" maintained by labor unions, professional societies, veterans' organizations, business interests, and less self-oriented organizations working for the "public interest." Public opinion is much more elusive, but in the American democracy it is certainly reflected in governmental policies and activities and at the same time persuaded by governmental and pressure-group arguments and propaganda.

The American Party System

The two large political parties in the United States are loosely knit, extra-constitutional organizations which make the election process meaningful and exciting. The Constitution is hopelessly silent as to how competing issues are to be presented, candidates selected, or campaigns financed. The drafters of the fundamental document apparently had no expectation of the rise of nationwide parties, since they provided for the states to manage elections. Although the Founding Fathers were veterans when it came to politicking, they disapproved political

The silent Constitution

competition between large organized groups.[6] Washington cautioned against political parties in his memorable "Farewell Address" for essentially the same reasons Madison had advanced a decade earlier in Number 10 of *The Federalist*. As Madison put it, "the public good is disregarded in the conflicts of rival parties, and . . . measures are too often decided, not according to the rules of justice and the rights of the minor party, but by the superior force of an interested and overbearing majority."

Madison's view

Yet if Madison was right when he charged that the "latent causes of faction" (which he found to be "sown in the nature of man") account for the existence of political parties, the Constitution he had so carefully helped to write required nation-wide political organizations if it were to operate smoothly. The principles of separation of powers, checks and balances, and federalism were certain to cause the national engine of government to grind to a halt unless some form of lubrication were provided. Today it is the political parties—their leaders, rank-and-file members, and the sharing of attitudes and obligations—which provide the needed axle grease.

The foreign view

Foreigners, familiar with political parties based on single issues such as agrarianism, monarchism, religion, socialism, and nationalism, profess to find the organization of the mass, classless American parties as practically unintelligible; the wide measure of agreement between the two parties, almost indecent; and American political behavior as approaching naïveté. Lord Bryce, in a famous statement, compared America's great parties to two bottles of the same size and shape, with different labels—and both empty.[7] Half a century before this Englishman's judgment, Tocqueville had found the political scene in the United States lacking in disputes about substantial issues.

The campaigns

He saw political campaigns chiefly as a way of determining who would gain office rather than a clash between opposing views as to which policy should be pursued. The shrewd visitor suspected, however, that ambitious men would somehow manage to invent artificial "principles" around which they could create issues—since it was awkward for one group of politicians to try

6. The framers of the Constitution were not alone in their distrust of political parties. Although few 18th- and 19th-century political participants or observers even commented on parties, the majority of those who did viewed parties either as destructive of good government or unavoidable evils in a free society. See Austin Ranney and Willmoore Kendall, *Democracy and the American Party System* (New York: Harcourt, Brace, 1956), Chap. 6.

7. See Bryce's description, *The American Commonwealth* (New York: Capricorn Books, 1959), I, 134–279.

to push another group out of office merely on the ground that they wanted the positions too.[8]

On the other hand, those who have witnessed the exciting, rowdy, slam-bang campaigns which keep American political life vital are disinclined to agree that the speeches, handshaking, and (in the earlier days) mass picnics with free food and drink are "full of sound and fury, signifying nothing." Sometimes campaigns are not concerned with political issues common in other nations because the American people *are* in basic agreement on such essentials as popular control of government, encouragement of religion without special cooperation with any church, and a regulated capitalistic economy. The issues which divide parties and candidates are often about how the widely supported generalities should be applied in specific instances.[9]

THE EFFECT OF PARTIES ON CONSTITUTIONAL DEVELOPMENT

The Federalists, the first political group in control under the new Constitution, encountered substantial opposition to their plan for implementing the basic document with a powerful central government. Because they were successful, the structure and functions of American government were profoundly affected. Without the broad construction of the Constitution which Alexander Hamilton proposed and Chief Justice Marshall disposed, central power likely would have been considerably weaker than it is now. The Jacksonian Democrats destroyed religious and property voting qualifications in the states and irrevocably placed political control in the hands of the ordinary citizens—over the anguished cries of the "gentlemen" that government should be the prerogative of "the few, the rich, the well-born."[10] Many Americans today are not even aware that the franchise was ever restricted by qualifications of religion or wealth. Or, consider the penchant of the Republican Party in the late nineteenth century of favoring a government which governed but little. Since during the period from 1888 to 1932 they were chiefly interested in a protective tariff and "sound"

Federalists, Democrats, and Republicans

8. Alexis de Tocqueville, *Democracy in America* (New York: Vintage Books, 1955), I, 181–87

9. For a modern study suggesting the presence of a basic consensus among Americans which permits them to argue heatedly over policy alternatives yet still support the framework in which the arguments take place, see Robert A. Dahl, *A Preface to Democratic Theory* (Chicago: University of Chicago Press, 1956), pp. 132–133.

10. For historical background on how Americans won the franchise, see Robert E. Lane, *Political Life* (Glencoe, Ill.: Free Press, 1959), pp. 8–26, and Alfred de Grazia, *Public and Republic: Political Representation in America* (New York: Knopf, 1951), *passim*.

money, there was little need for governmental involvement in other areas of economic and social life. This policy of passive **Passive vs. active** government received its challenge from William Jennings **government** Bryan, who stumped the country as the defender of the poor, urging Federal legislation to assist those who he suggested were about to be "crucified on a cross of gold." The campaign of 1896 charted the course for the future progressivism which was to have momentous significance. And, despite the vague party platform and the enigmatic speeches of the Republican nominee in 1920, what reasonably interested citizen did not know that a vote for Warren G. Harding was a vote against Wilsonian liberalism in domestic affairs and the League of Nations in foreign policy? Certainly the "New Deal" of Franklin D. Roosevelt had at least one unequivocal and hard-fought test at the polls. If today the voters are in general agreement as to the propriety of having the national government vigorously and actively attack problems at home and abroad, then another area of disagreement has been largely removed. Much contemporary political argument is not about whether the Federal Government should be active, but rather where and how it should act. Members of both great parties insist that there is a difference in emphasis between them due to their views of the roles of Congress and the President and the degree to which the national government should be involved in the affairs of its citizens. These differences might be questioned, but it is certain that the charge that American political parties have never had substantial disagreements is not entirely accurate.[11]

It should be noted that a minority of Americans are displeased with the similarities they detect between the Republi- **Party similarities** cans and Democrats on a number of issues. For example, in the 1964 presidential campaign, supporters of Senator Goldwater believed their man offered something distinctly different from the "standard" nominees so often put forward by both major political parties.[12] In 1968 former Alabama Governor George Wallace, running for President as a third-party candidate, told his audiences, "We intend to give the people a choice."[13] Wal-

11. A concise and lucid analysis of the differences between the Democratic and Republican parties is Clinton Rossiter, *Parties and Politics in America* (Ithaca: Cornell University Press, 1960), Chap. IV. See also Wilfred E. Binkley, *American Political Parties: Their Natural History* (New York: Knopf, 3rd edition, 1958).

12. The feeling that the Republican candidates in the past had too often merely been reflections of the Democratic candidates was set forth in strongly partisan terms in Phyllis Schlafly, *A Choice, not an Echo*, (Alton, Ill.: Pere Marquette Press, 1964).

13. Quoted in Ray Jenkins, "George Wallace Figures to Win Even If He Loses," *New York Times Magazine*, April 7, 1968, p. 27.

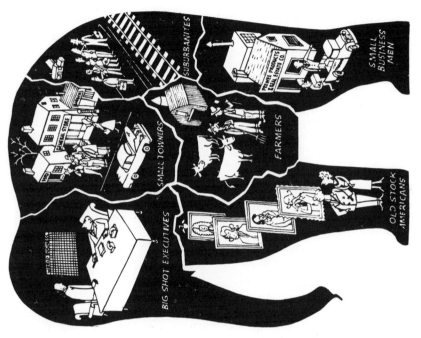

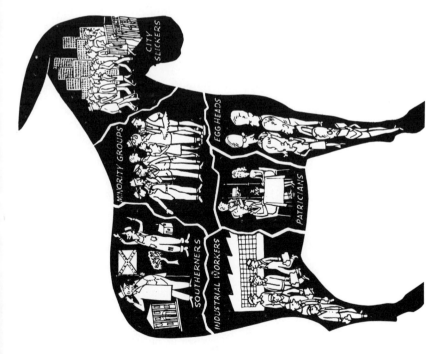

Political X-Ray

lace hammered on the theme that "The two national parties are just tweedledee and tweedledum. There's not a dime's worth of difference between them."

THE EFFECT OF CONSTITUTIONAL DEVELOPMENT ON PARTIES

Weak party organization

Parties, no doubt, have provided meaningful alternatives and a measure of coherence necessary for the continuous and successful functioning of a Constitution drafted in the eighteenth century. The beneficial influence of political parties on constitutional principles is only one side of the coin. As E. E. Schattschneider puts it in a wonderful metaphor: "If the parties are the river of American politics, the stream of the living impulse to govern, the Constitution is the river bed, the firm land whose contour shapes the stream. In the long run the river can transform the landscape, but it is also the prisoner of the land."[14] The tradition of the two-party system was inherited from Great Britain, and the theory and utility of having two powerful and disagreeing groups compete for power is frequently praised as indicating the "Anglo-American genius for government." Yet the two-party system and the weak party organization in the United States clearly reflect the principles of the American democracy: the prescription of separation of powers discourages effective presidential leadership over the Congress, while the principle of checks and balances prevents a single congressional leader from cracking a political whip effectively enough to keep his party members in line. The principle of federalism compounds the weakness of our national parties by emphasizing local issues and loyalties (which result in a lack of coherence in matters of major policy) and by allowing each state to legislate regarding political organizations and practices (which tends to decentralize power).[15] It is possible to have 50 different definitions of "a political party" in the United States, and a definition has practical consequences since, if a political group is not defined as a "party," it faces serious obstacles in getting its candidates on the ballot. If the names of candidates are not printed on the ballot, it is almost

14. *Party Government* (New York: Holt, Rinehart, and Winston, 1960), p. 124.

15. *Cf.* David B. Truman, "Federalism and the Party System," in Arthur W. MacMahon, ed., *Federalism: Mature and Emergent* (Garden City, N.Y.: Doubleday, 1955). A contrasting argument is that because the party is decentralized and interested primarily in relatively trivial local affairs, the President has unusual freedom of action to formulate national policies. See James Q. Wilson, "Politics and Reform in American Cities," in Ivan Hinderaker, ed., *American Government Annual: 1962–1963* (New York: Holt, Rinehart and Winston, 1962).

impossible to get them elected, since "write-in" campaigns are notoriously difficult to win. Federalism also enhances localism by reserving many governmental matters to regional determination. For example, it is possible for voters to become so belligerent about such a local matter as the location of a new junior college that an unpopular stand on the issue by a candidate for the United States House of Representatives could cost him election, even though Congress is not even remotely concerned with the location of state schools.

Organization of a Major Party

It is in the fantastically incoherent organization of the two great parties that the influence of federalism is most easily discernible. In popular conversation one speaks of "the Democratic Party" and "the Republican Party," but in theory each has 51 independent organizations. The picture is even more confusing when one examines those 50 states and the District of Columbia, and finds that they are based upon more than 200,000 governmental units at county, municipality, town, and election district levels. In addition, there are special organizations for different candidates—groups such as "United Citizens for Nixon-Agnew" and "United Democrats for Humphrey-Muskie" were found throughout the land in 1968. All of the different groups active in campaigns are more or less united at the top, in the national committee.

The many organizations below the national committee level deserve brief explanation.[16] The reader must remember that local organizations vary widely as a result of state laws, party **Precinct to nation** practices, and the degree of organization of the parties in different areas, but a strong, well-organized party might follow this pattern:

The Precinct. This is the smallest unit, varying from a neighborhood to a section of town or city. If the organization is so efficient that it functions like a "machine," this acreage will be carefully nursed by a "boss" who pays frequent visits to his partisans. Where a political machine exists, the local contact man performs favors for his flock ranging from getting the electric-

16. For detailed description and analysis see Ranney and Kendall, op. cit., pp. 213–64. For an examination of changes in community political activity see Samuel P. Hays, "Political Parties and the Community-Society Continuum," in William N. Chambers and Walter D. Burnham, eds., The American Party Systems: Stages of Political Development (New York: Oxford University Press, 1967), pp. 152–181.

Political machines

ity turned on promptly to getting Junior out of the clutches of the police. In return, the people of the area support at the polls the man to whom they are indebted—a simple *quid pro quo.* The holder of local political power represents his precinct at the ward (in urban areas), city, or county level. But since political machines are breaking down in America today, party representatives are more often chosen at caucuses held biennially or in the spring preceding a presidential campaign. Although party members of the precinct are invited, caucuses are generally poorly attended if popular interest has not been aroused. If the party has no neighborhood headquarters, the meetings are held in private homes. "Eisenhower Republicans" in 1952 charged that the "Taft Republicans" held party caucuses in some Texas precincts in moving automobiles (to prevent "grass-roots" party members from attending and making their preferences known to the precinct leaders).

The Ward. This is an urban unit, not found in rural areas. It is typically a group of precincts which are linked together under a leader. The dubious title "ward heeler" refers to a person who tags along at the heels of a ward leader with the hope of obtaining petty favors.

The City. If political organization exists at this stratum as separate from the precinct or county, it will have a recognized leader who directs the smaller subdivisions within its geographical limits.[17] Most of the famous (and infamous) "bosses" in American political history have operated at this tier, although many of them have controlled counties (especially in New York), and a few have dominated an entire state. The difference between a "boss" and a "leader" is not, as some cynics suggest, whether or not he belongs to the opposition party! The term "boss" suggests political power based upon illegal or extra-legal favors, force, or tricks.

The County. This unit has a definable leader (the county chairman) and organization. It is generally at this level that precinct and city leaders meet in convention. The most important function of the convention is to nominate candidates for county offices, but it also serves to create enthusiasm for the forthcoming campaign and to select representatives to the state convention.

The State. The 50 state parties are the constituent members of the federations known as "national parties." The organization

17. The political process in one American city, New Haven, Connecticut, is examined in detail by Robert A. Dahl in *Who Governs?* (New Haven: Yale University Press, 1961).

of state parties depends either upon law or, in the absence of legislation, on party practice. The state party officials trace their normal source of power to the state convention which elected (or at least ratified) them. The state convention is a meeting of partisans who are either elected as representatives by party members, or are appointed as delegates by local party organizations.

The Nation. The national party is an alliance of 50 state parties and that in the District of Columbia. Its supreme governing body is the national convention, but since this huge and unwieldy body sits only a few days every four years, it is not suitable for managing party affairs beyond selecting candidates and framing a party platform.

The national committee is supposedly the executive of the national convention, and its members are cursorily approved by the latter. In practice, members are chosen by the states in any of four ways: (1) by convention, (2) by caucus, (3) by state delegations at the national convention, or (4) in state primaries. The Democratic National Committee numbers over 100 members, since each state is accorded one committeeman and one committeewoman, with the District of Columbia and the territories also given representation. The Republican counterpart is even larger, since the state chairman is included for each state which voted Republican for the President at the previous election, which has a Republican governor, or which has a majority of its congressional delegation of that party. The national committee meets perfunctorily during three years of its four-year term, and its most important function during this time apparently is to choose the site for the national convention.[18] Directly following the convention its powers increase. Should the candidates for President and Vice President be found ineligible, resign, or die, the committee may make replacements; it will participate actively in the campaign, administer much of the party finances, and may contribute to the candidate's strategy.

The national chairman is charged with the task of liaison and organization for the party. This officer allegedly is elected by

The National Committees

18. For an examination of the National Committees see, Cornelius P. Cotter and Bernard C. Hennessy, *Politics Without Power: The National Party Committees* (New York: Atherton Press, 1964). During the time which intervened between the Republican disaster of 1964 and the effort to recoup by 1968, the Republican National Committee made a considerable effort to replace the ideological splits within the party with unity and to revamp the party organization. See Robert B. Semple, Jr., "Skill Replaces Ideology at G.O.P. Headquarters Under Bliss," *New York Times*, February 1, 1968.

The national chairman

the national committee but actually is tapped by the presidential candidate. If his candidate is successful, the chairman may be rewarded with a cabinet position (the Postmaster-Generalship has been a favorite assignment). If the candidate is unsuccessful, the chairman will be confronted with demands for his resignation by those who hope to carry the party banner in the next election. If the defeated candidate is strong in the party, or the opposition is divided, the unhappy chairman may continue in his party office for years.

Campaign committees: senatorial and congressional

Two additional kinds of national party organizations exist because of the principles of separation of powers and checks and balances. These are the Senatorial Campaign Committee and the Congressional Campaign Committee of each party. The primary concern of each is to aid colleagues who are seeking re-election and, to a lesser extent, help party candidates in the states who are seeking election to their houses of Congress. These two completely separate entities sometimes cooperate fully neither with each other nor with their party's national committee.[19]

Party deadlock

While it is customary to speak of the "two party" system in American politics, some scholars have voiced concern about a "four party" system.[20] The contention is that there are Republican and Democratic "Presidential Parties" both of which are positively oriented toward social legislation and racial equality, and both of which derive support from the metropolitan areas so important in terms of the electoral vote needed to win the White House. Opposed to the "Presidential Parties" are the two "Congressional Parties." It is held that these are likely to reflect the interests of rural and small-town America, which are not always in sympathy with the needs and philosophy of the big urban centers. At times the "Congressional Parties" operate in cooperation to block legislation supported by the "Presidential Parties"; at other times the latter can muster the power to push through Congress wide-ranging social and racial legislation as was especially the case during portions of Franklin D. Roosevelt's Presidency and that of Lyndon Johnson.[21]

19. For an analysis of what Americans term their "two party" system see Frank J. Sorauf, *Party Politics in America* (Boston: Little, Brown, 1968), pp. 26–53.

20. James MacGregor Burns, *The Deadlock of Democracy* (Englewood Cliffs: Prentice-Hall, 1963).

21. Burns describes the operation and composition of the Republican and Democratic "Congressional Parties" on pp. 295–300, and 311–316 respectively in *op. cit.* It should be noted that the redistricting of congressional districts which followed population movement to the cities and their suburbs may have an effect upon both presidential and congressional constituencies.

From *The Herblock Book* (Beacon Press, 1952).
"I have the same trouble."

"Third Parties" in the United States

"Third parties" are a consistent phenomenon in American history and have enriched the field by their crusading spirit; under such picturesque names as "Locofoco," "Barnburner," "Know-Nothing," "Bull Moose," "Dixiecrat" and, in 1968, "American Independent" and "Peace and Freedom." They have been important in influencing policies, but they rarely control offices. They have never elected a President,[22] and it is

The Electoral College factor

22. It is sometimes said that the Republican Party which elected Lincoln in 1860 was a "third party," but this is not accurate. In the campaign of 1852 General Winfield Scott, the Whig candidate, was buried under an electoral avalanche by Pierce (Democrat) of 254–42. The Whigs then ceased to be a factor. In the following campaign, Buchanan, the Democratic candidate, defeated General Fremont, the first Republican candidate, by an electoral count of 174–114. Millard Fillmore, the Whig Vice President who succeeded to the Presidency on the death of Zachary Taylor in 1850, ran in the 1856 campaign as a "Know-Nothing" and won 8 electoral votes. Thus the Republicans had assumed major party status by 1856.

a crucial point of American politics that a national political party cannot long exist without the hope of capturing the Presidency. Although a President needs a majority of the electoral votes, he can be elected by a mere *plurality* of popular votes, since when a candidate carries a state by any margin, he receives all of its electoral votes. This is why third parties have not managed to throw a presidential election into the House of Representatives.[23] If a majority of the popular votes were required to elect, or electoral votes were apportioned to the popular vote, third parties might have real bargaining power, since America has had many Chief Executives who were elected by a minority of the voters.[24]

The 1968 election In 1968 George Wallace, running for President on the American Independent Party ticket, was unable to capitalize on the provisions of the Electoral College as he had apparently hoped to do. Before the presidential election he had mentioned his candidacy might serve to withhold a majority (270) of electoral votes from the major-party candidates. Had this happened, Wallace's plan was to strike a bargain with one of the major-party candidates—trading his support for some kind of agreement by the recipient that he would implement Wallace's policies regarding states' rights, school segregation, and anti-Communism.[25] As it turned out the former Alabama governor's campaign mixture of advocacy for "law and order," states' rights—most notably in regard to decisions concerning desegregation of public schools—and a "hardline" on Vietnam carried five southern states (Arkansas, Louisiana, Mississippi, Alabama, and Georgia) with a total electoral vote of 46. In addition he

23. The House of Representatives chose between Jefferson and Burr (nominees for President and Vice President by the same party) in 1800 because of a tie. The Twelfth Amendment was adopted to prevent a recurrence of this kind of situation. In 1824, four strong candidates, each claiming to be a "Jeffersonian," precluded an electoral majority for any of them, and the House selected John Quincy Adams to be President rather than Andrew Jackson, who had received more popular votes and more electoral votes than had Adams.

24. On two occasions the Democratic Party polled more popular votes than its rival and yet won fewer electoral votes. These were in 1876 (Hayes) and 1888 (Harrison). Ten presidents have received a majority of the electoral college votes but only a plurality· of the popular votes: Polk (1844), Taylor (1848), Buchanan (1856), Lincoln (1860), Garfield (1880), Cleveland (1884, 1892), Wilson (1912, 1916), Truman (1948), Kennedy (1960), and Nixon (1968). See also the preceding footnote for the unique cases of Jefferson (1800) and John Quincy Adams (1824).

25. Jenkins, *op cit.*, pp. 76, 79, 82. Fear that Wallace might throw the election into the House of Representatives prompted both Democrats and Republicans to propose a pledge that members would vote for the presidential candidate with the greatest number of popular votes, thus undercutting the former governor's bargaining power.

received 15 per cent or more of the three way vote in nine other southern or border states (Florida, Kentucky, Maryland, North Carolina, South Carolina, Oklahoma, Tennessee, Texas, and Virginia). Wallace's popular vote was nearly 10 million, which amounted to 13.5 per cent of the votes cast for President. Despite the failure of Wallace's plan to use the Electoral College for his own purposes the closeness of the 1968 election caused many more persons to wonder about the utility of that venerable institution of American politics. Had Hubert Humphrey received a few more per cent of the vote in California (40 electoral votes) and Illinois (26 electoral votes) Richard Nixon would not have gotten the 270 electoral votes necessary to win and there would have been no President-elect the day after the election. As it was, Nixon received 301 electoral votes, and Humphrey 191.

Voters are reluctant to support a candidate who has no chance to win, which handicaps a nominee for national office today who is neither a Democrat nor a Republican. Third parties sometimes have elected members of Congress, since they may be chosen by a plurality in a much smaller district. The organization of Congress is, however, geared to a two-party system, and so senators and congressmen who represent minor parties are at a disadvantage in the national legislature, primarily because the organization of Congress and assignments to standing committees is the responsibility of the two major parties.

Third-party candidates

Third parties have tended to be based either on a dynamic personality or the appeal of a single idea.[26] An example of a great personality was the insurgent progressive Theodore Roosevelt who, in the three-way presidential race of 1912, pushed the regular Republican nominee, William Howard Taft, into third place. But his party had no candidate in the succeeding presidential race, and it died. In 1948 Henry Wallace, a dissident Democrat, appropriated the time-honored name of "Progressive Party," garnered over a million votes, but failed to carry a single state. His party also bloomed for but one season.[27] The strength of a personality party is its greatest weakness.

"Great Idea" parties

"Great Idea" parties vary from those which oppose generally accepted notions about food (Vegetarian Party) and drink

26. An excellent analysis of the place of minor parties in the American political system is V. O. Key, Jr., *Politics, Parties, and Pressure Groups*, 5th edition (New York: Thomas Y. Crowell, 1964), pp. 280–309.

27. In the following campaign (1952) Vincent W. Hallinan ran as a Progressive but received only 132,000 popular votes.

(Prohibition Party) to antislavery groups (Free Soil, Liberty), agrarian crusaders (Populists), and proponents of economic change (Socialist Party). Historically such parties either disappear completely or wither away to mere shadows of their former selves. Some, with ideas attractive to the public, survive in the sense that their policies are incorporated into the programs of one or both of the major parties. For example, the Free-Soilers died with the Lincoln Republicans; the Populists lost force when Bryan captured the Democratic nomination in 1896; and after Roosevelt's New Deal got under way, Norman Thomas, perennial candidate of the Socialists, decided to stop running for the Presidency. The strength of the idea party is its greatest weakness.[28]

Major parties as coalitions

The fact that the major parties can embrace ideas which have been popularized by others and which they had previously attacked or ignored indicates something important about them. The Democratic and Republican parties are coalitions of dissimilar smaller groups which, at times, seem only to share a common name. Not so the minors, composed primarily of people who are devoted to a common cause, who formally join the organization, who pay dues and contribute time. (Perhaps this is why they are small!) The majors, on the contrary, are apparently more concerned with political success than with political philosophy and will even refuse to nominate the obvious party leader if they believe he "can't win" (*e.g..*, Bryan in 1904, Robert A. Taft in 1952). Although they actively solicit and gratefully accept donations of money and time from Americans, the two parties do not count on such a high level of mass participation. Consequently, they usually are satisfied with the contribution of an "X" for their candidates on election day. (This popular apathy toward partisan activity accounts for the fact that an energetic newcomer can ordinarily find an important place for himself in the party of his choice.)

Parties and Individual Political Behavior

"REGULARS," "LOYALS," AND "NOMINALS"

The two large parties have a core of *regulars*—those members who are as much dedicated to the cause as are the stalwarts of

"Regulars"

the minor parties.[29] This hard core is made up of different types of people who are active in politics for different kinds of

28. *Cf.* Rossiter, *Parties and Politics*, pp. 4–6.

29. See Robert E. Lane, *op. cit.*, Chapter 4 and *passim* for an account of the levels of partisan involvement and their causes. For a comparative analysis of party membership and the degrees and nature of participation see Maurice Duverger, *Political Parties* (New York: Wiley, 1954), pp. 61–132.

reasons. For example, some citizens become regulars because they are sincerely convinced that the goals of their party are more in the public interest than those of its rival. Many are dyed-in-the-wool partisans because of remembered past, experienced present, or anticipated future favors. A number of them are highly motivated by the excitement and prestige which are by-products of active political participation. A few men and women are dedicated to their party strictly because being on the inside affords opportunities for "honest graft"—and there are those who have no scruples about making an easy dollar through dishonest graft. The regulars carry the brunt of party activity: organizing, financing, and campaigning. They always vote and, since their idea of party loyalty includes voting a straight party ticket, rarely vote for candidates from other parties, i.e., "split their ticket." Experts in the field of politics estimate that on the crucial Election Day the regulars of the two parties often come close to canceling each other in national elections.

Each party also has identified with it a group much larger than the regulars who are known as *loyal* party members. These are less actively involved. They generally have inherited their allegiance from strong partisans or undergone a political conversion. Loyal members can be identified by their campaign buttons and conversation. They can be counted on to help in a particularly difficult campaign and generally do not need much prodding to get them to vote. They may cross party lines for local offices, but support party candidates for major offices. **"Loyals"**

An enormous pool of *nominal* supporters exist for each party. Their allegiance, in most cases, reflects that of family or friends who are politically lukewarm. Nominal sympathizers rarely are sympathetic enough to donate either time or money although they may contribute arguments on behalf of a candidate—or, more likely, arguments *against* the opposition candidate. Many of them will fail to vote if the weather is unpleasant or if going to the polls involves personal inconvenience. Others among this group are convinced that voting is the hallmark of a good citizen and that voting a straight ticket is the earmark of a bad one. Therefore, they split their ballots with abandon, proudly wear an Election Day tag which proclaims "I've voted, have you?"—and feel genuine satisfaction for their contribution to good government. **"Nominals"**

THE "INDEPENDENT" VOTER

The "independent" voter is a question mark: how many are there? do they exist? The status of being independent is claimed by some people who believe it increases their prestige.

The label also affords a refuge for those who are uncomfortable about making their views known, and serves as an excuse for nominal supporters who haven't really been interested enough to have a point of view. If the "independent" analyzes his past voting record, he very likely will see a definite pattern of support for one of the parties. However, he will often claim that he puts the nation's interest above consideration of party label, and therefore votes solely on the basis of the qualifications shown by the competing candidates. Of course it is always possible that there *are* interested citizens who actually do study the campaigns of all parties, appraise the candidates, and then vote without any traditional bias. There might also exist true "floating" voters who fluctuate from one big party to the other on the theory that such behavior preserves the two-party system—but these appear to be a minute portion of the electorate.

THE NONVOTER

The most shocking aspect of the American political scene is that the kinds of voters described above represent only about 50 to 60 percent of the electorate. The other 50 to 40 percent are nonvoters. After the 1960 presidential race it was abundantly apparent that every single vote counted, for Kennedy moved into the White House on the strength of a well-distributed plurality of 113,057 votes out of a record-shattering 68,832,818 votes cast. Among the approximately 40,000,000 eligible voters who failed to vote, Richard Nixon needed only 4,500 to carry Illinois which, with another 28,000 Republican votes in Texas, would have given him the Presidency. On the other hand, those in this enormous reservoir who favored Mr. Kennedy could have strengthened his position in the country and abroad by increasing the margin by which he won.

Every vote counts

It may be argued that disenchantment with both major party candidates led to considerable voter apathy in the 1968 election. Compared to the voting statistics in European countries, the American turnout in 1968 was miserable. The 60 percent of Americans voting in 1968 may be contrasted to the 75 to 85 percent regularly voting in Italy, Great Britain, France, and West Germany. In nonpresidential elections, when voter enthusiasm traditionally falls off in the United States, none of the States can compare at all favorably with democratic participation in Western Europe. If it is true that the good citizen is a voter, the sad conclusion must be that Americans are poor citizens. What can be said in defense of the American "nonpolitical animal?"

Sometimes it is argued that, instead of marking X's for candidates, better tests of citizenship are low levels in the rates of crime and tax-dodging and high degrees of willingness to accept community responsibilities and to risk life in the service of the country. In spite of the obvious validity of such arguments, however, most of us have an uneasy feeling that the poor voting statistics in the United States *do* reflect unfavorably on the American government. We hope, with Clinton Rossiter,[30] that the mass nonparticipation is really an evidence of strength, since it indicates that the citizens trust both parties and have no doubt that "the next election will take place on schedule." Yet we fear, with E. E. Schattschneider,[31] that even if a voter's silence is interpreted to give consent, consent is not participation. Viewed in this way, the appallingly low participation figures do indicate the "soft underbelly" of American democracy.

What is good citizenship?

Every political analysis indicates that the nonvoters comprise the most poorly educated and the lowest income segments of American society. For example, one study found that 52 percent of the college-educated become politically active; most of them vote regularly. Only 26 percent of the high-school graduates and 16 percent of those who fail to go beyond grade school are politically active, and the voting percentages fall proportionately. In the "A" (highest) economic category, 69 percent participate actively; on the "B" level, 50 percent; of the "C's" only 30 percent; and in the lowest, or "D" economic group, about 12 percent care enough about politics to try to do something about it. Or, consider that 63 percent of executive and professional people are actively engaged in politics, while farmers plod along with 25 percent and laborers and housewives trail behind with 20 percent each.[32] Some observers conclude that it is just as well that these people do not participate, since they do not have the stake in society that the better-educated and more affluent do: the nonvoters, if brought into active participation, would likely support radical programs financed by unsound economic policies. It has also been pointed out that it is politically and morally doubtful if, as a result of a friendly rivalry between neighboring governors to produce higher voting percentages, an intense campaign succeeds only in prodding droves of eligible but uninformed citizens to beef up the statistics, thereby canceling out the ballots cast by voters who are interested and well-informed. A public-minded citizen, before devoting his life

The nonvoters

30. In his *Parties and Politics in America.*

31. *The Semisovereign People* (1960).

32. *Ibid.*

to getting out the vote, might well ponder the disturbing comment of Rossiter that "if America ever 'goes to hell' in a national election, it will be one, I suspect, in which a very high turnout is marked up."[33]

The student of politics cannot, however, afford to ignore the psychological and mechanical factors which might account for the large number of nonvoters. If it is true, as Schattschneider suspects, that the citizens in lower social and economic strata do not participate because they have abandoned hope in the present two-party system, then the situation is extremely serious. If *this* attitude explains why almost 40 million eligible Americans fail to vote in presidential elections and upwards of 60 million stay away from other elections, it means that about half of the electorate do not have faith in the system of government existing in the United States. They may be psychologically ready for a less constitutional way of obtaining political changes. Without doubt, many of the nonvoters are dissuaded by inconvenient registration laws in some states and by long residence requirements which grow more onerous as the population becomes more mobile. The existence of many effective one-party areas surely discourages voting: a vote for the dominant party doesn't help it much; a vote against doesn't hurt it much.

It is devoutly to be wished that the tens of millions of nonvoters will become more politically active as they come to real-

Intelligent voting ize that their opinions do matter and can be determinative. However, Americans should not be permitted to lose the Jeffersonian idea that *intelligent* voting is of greater value than mere *voting* to the democratic form of government. Certainly, in a country where schools, libraries, the free press, radio and television facilities are more widespread than in any nation in the world, failure to be informed as a citizen can only be a confession of blame. The possibilities for Americans to nourish the rationality which, Aristotle held, distinguishes the "political animal" from other animals is almost unlimited.

A Structural-Functional View of Political Parties

Another way to view a political party is to think of a tripartite structure consisting of the organizational component; the party members holding public office, either elective or appoin-

33. Rossiter, *op. cit.*, p. 185.

tive; and "the party-in-the-electorate."[34] The party organization contains the "regulars" mentioned previously, and it is much like other organizations which must handle administrative matters and in so doing assumes some bureaucratic aspects. Like other organizations, parties undertake recruitment to and promotion within their hierarchy, the objectives being in their case the winning of elections, and after that the implementation of policy through the machinery of government controlled by the second component—the party members holding public office. Frank Sorauf notes that party members in office develop their own system of norms, rewards, and punishments which differs from that of the party organization.[35] This observation would appear valid whether one is discussing the Democrats or Republicans in office. As can be seen from the Washington news accounts, the party members holding office do not always agree with members of the other two party components and sometimes they do not agree among themselves. On Election Day the party independents may number into the tens of millions. On less politically stimulating days such membership may be hardly visible, although individuals in the electorate may use party identification and affiliation to provide benchmarks with which to arrange their political thinking.[36]

Party purpose

VOTING BEHAVIOR

Even though the ordinary citizens tend to be lethargic about their politics, those engaged professionally and academically are not. As the study of politics has sought to become more "scientific" and less "philosophical," there has been among some a decreasing emphasis on *what ought to be done and why*, and a surge of interest in *what is done and why*. Although Aristotle's dictum that "politics is a contingent science" has rarely been directly challenged, modern political behaviorists believe that voting patterns, among other things, can be both predicted and understood with an acceptable degree of accuracy and that the variables are not such a formidable obstacle to the scientific method when applied to human beings as was once supposed. From rudimentary beginnings voting prediction has reached a

Predicting the vote

34. This type of analysis is made by Frank J. Sorauf, "Political Parties and Political Analysis," in Chambers and Burnham, *op. cit.*, pp. 37–39. Sorauf attributes the quotation to V. O. Key, Jr., who in turn attributed it to Ralph Goldman.

35. Chambers and Burnham, *op. cit.*, p. 37.

36. *Ibid.*, p. 38.

From *The Herblock Book* (Beacon Press, 1952).

"Well, let's see what's in the crystal ball today."

high stage of sophistication.[37] It is based upon scientific sampling of voter preference among small but representative fractions of the general population. Using historical data regarding

37. Polling, and the resulting prediction of election outcomes and voters' views, has become so widespread that fears have been voiced that the practice may affect actual voting rather than measure and predict it. For example, some wonder if the announcement that candidate X is the front-runner in the week's poll will pull additional votes to him in a "bandwagon" effect, or cause voters to rush to back the other candidate who is the "underdog." One may also speculate that in some cases a false sense of security is associated with the front-runner to the extent that some supporting him do not bother to vote, for they believe his lead is so great he no longer needs them. Questions have been raised as to whether candidates are tempted to say only those things the polls indicate are popular, regardless of the national interest.

previous patterns, "bellwether" districts are identified as are "swing" areas, and these receive particular attention. Using the past voting data and interviews with selected potential voters, the researchers are able to predict with considerable accuracy what the percentage of the vote will be in a particular election for various candidates.[38] The standing of such investigations is so high that the major political candidates employ their own voting prediction and behavior experts, in addition to studying the findings of others.[39]

A more difficult aspect of voting behavior analysis goes beyond how people will vote to the question of why they vote as they do. Considerable research has been done in this area. For example, on the basis of available evidence, it is apparent that an individual's orientation toward political affairs in general, and often a party in particular, typically begins before the individual attains voting age and reflects, at least initially, the disposition of the parents.[40] Of course, any member of the "younger generation" may come to reject the political philosophy and party identification of his parents. It was not uncommon in 1968 to find young people from conservative Republican homes working for Democrats such as Eugene McCarthy and Robert Kennedy, and to a lesser extent Hubert Humphrey. On the other hand, some persons born in working-class families, which had supported the Democrats from the New Deal to the Great Society, backed Nixon or Wallace because they no longer identified with the welfare and employment security image which had attracted their parents to the Democrats. In 1968 such individuals worried more about "law and order" and what they viewed as encroachments by blacks than about the economic fears which had clouded their parents' lives. In some

Why people vote as they do

38. If large numbers of voters do not make up their minds until just before Election Day, or if significant switches of opinion occur late in the campaign, the task of the voting prediction specialists is made difficult. This was the case in the close presidential race of 1968 where Hubert Humphrey came up sharply in the final polls after trailing Richard Nixon by a wide margin earlier in the campaign.

39. One estimate of the cost of such polling by presidential, gubernatorial, and senatorial candidates runs between $4 and $6 million. Homer Bigart, "Pollsters Find Credibility Imperiled," *New York Times*, July 15, 1968.

40. A number of studies have been made of children and their formulation of political beliefs. See Herbert Hyman, *Political Socialization* (Glencoe, Ill.: Free Press, 1959), Chapter IV. More recent studies include David Easton and Robert D. Hess, "The Child's Political World," *Midwest Journal of Political Science*, VI (August, 1962), pp. 229–246; Fred Greenstein, *Children and Politics* (New Haven: Yale University Press, 1965); and David Easton and Jack Dennis, "The Child's Acquisition of Regime Norms: Political Efficacy," *American Political Science Review*, LXI (March, 1967), pp. 25–38.

instances young people argued with their parents and switched parties because of their feelings concerning the Vietnamese war.[41]

Categories of voters From the increasing amount of information available one may draw certain conclusions regarding voting behavior. For example, the findings of one prominent group of researchers suggests that voters may be generally categorized into four groupings on the basis of the motivation underlying their voting behavior.[42] The study found one group composed of those who vote on the basis of an ideological position which they hold relative to the parties and issues. This group represents only a small percentage of the voting population, and overlaps the next category—persons who vote on the basis of group interest. Such persons view the party of their choice as one which will further the interests of the particular groups with which they identify. For example a labor union member "voting the dictates of his pocketbook" would likely believe the Democratic

Party images Party most solicitous of the workingman's interests. There is of course some basis in fact for such a view, since recent Democratic Administrators have tended to support legislation favorable to labor. Another individual motivated by considerations of a different group interest—for instance, a businessman concerned over high taxes, high spending by the government, and plagued with labor problems, might logically support the Republican Party. Again, given the group identification of the individual, the choice is reasonable, for the Republicans have shown considerable interest in the welfare of the business community.[43] It has been observed that in areas where the two major parties are competitive both tend to seek out various

41. In 1968 some parents switched their long-standing political allegiance for the same reasons as their children.

42. Angus Campbell, Philip E. Converse, Warren E. Miller, and Donald E. Stokes, *The American Voter*, An Abridgement (New York: John Wiley & Sons, 1964), pp. 124–144. Another major study by the same individuals is *Elections and the Political Order* (New York: John Wiley & Sons, 1966).

43. Any single individual may belong to or identify with a number of groups having differing interests (a person having only one all-consuming passion is ordinarily considered to be a fanatic). Some of these interests are perceived with varying intensity, some reinforce each other, and some conflict and so modify or cancel each other. There are laboring men who vote Republican because the total calculus of their interest motivation produces an interest orientation different from that of many of their peers, or because other considerations are more important than group interest. The same is true of those found in other interest group classifications.

identifiable groups in order to solicit their support by indicating concern for what concerns the groups.[44]

A third category of voters consists of persons less group-interest oriented except in a very narrow and personal fashion, who tend to make their political choices on the basis of whether the times are "good" or "bad." The barometer used by such individuals to indicate the "goodness" or "badness" is the economic condition in which they find themselves. When prosperous, they tend to support the party in power; when under economic strain, they turn to the party out of power.

Group-interest voters

The fourth and last category in which voters were classified is less clear-cut. Persons in this category frequently support a particular party without being able to distinguish how "their" party differs from the competing one. Some persons in the fourth category also identify with a particular political candidate because of the appeal of his personality.

Since the majority of voters whose motivational behavior was studied in *The American Voter* were in the second and third listings—group interest and condition of the times—one understands why politicians give attention to various identifiable segments of the population. When it is further learned that the knowledge of the issues and other relevant political information declined from the small numbers of voters in the first category (ideological motivation), where it was high, to the other categories, where it was lower, one understands more fully the worry expressed by the Founding Fathers over the dangers of "mass democracy." Today politicians seeking to gain the White House make use of computer technology to project past voting patterns and to determine which groups may be won by particular arguments and promises. In campaign years one frequently hears the charge that some candidate is catering to the selfish interests of the various publics.[45] Such a charge is often coupled with another: that the candidate is seeking to win votes by

"Mass democracy"

44. Duane Lockard, *New England State Politics* (Princeton, N.J.: Princeton University Press, 1959), pp. 326–327. More recently it has been noted that Southern blacks who have settled in Northern cities, where two-party competition is often substantial, are sought out for their votes and so brought into the political process as another group for which the parties must indicate solicitude. This process is discussed by Richard E. Dawson, "Social Development, Party Competition, and Policy," in Chambers and Burnham, *op. cit.*, p. 209.

45. This view was well portrayed by Senator Barry Goldwater (R., Arizona). Goldwater has warned of demagogues who ". . . might persuade a majority of the people to confer on government vast powers in return for deceptive promises of economic gain." *The Conscience of a Conservative* (New York: Hillman Books, 1960), pp. 18–19.

projecting an image that will appeal to the voters who base their decision mainly on personality.

The preceding analysis suggests that, to be successful, political parties in the United States must compete with each other in making promises that will match group interests. Critics will undoubtedly cite the disadvantages of such a system as being the pressure for parties to oversell candidates who are only human, and to promise more than they can possibly deliver should they win control of the government. Furthermore, it will be pointed out that the consequences of responding to such pressures could be the overstimulation of the electorate, followed by political disappointment and disenchantment with democratic processes. Up against these liabilities of political party activity in America one may list advantages. In a large and diverse nation like the United States the major parties may differ somewhat in emphasis and composition, but essentially they must be broadly based in their appeals and not situated too far away from the "middle-of-the-road" if they are to win a majority of the electorate. In other words, a presidential candidate has considerable incentive to offer a program of reasonable compromise taken from many competing interests instead of meeting the desires of only one segment of the population. The requirement of a broadly based appeal when seeking national office means that the major parties and their candidates must listen to, evaluate, and modify different points of view.[46]

Overselling the candidate

This process in theory, and to a large extent in practice, constitutes a sound method of resolving conflicting demands made of government by citizens with varying backgrounds, interests, capabilities, and characters.[47] Whether pluralistic democracy, consisting of political parties seeking to amass majorities from diverse groups of citizens, works well or badly at a given moment probably depends upon more than its potential for conflict resolution. A system that seems to work when individuals and groups display patience, reason, and understanding, could fail utterly when a nation's mood is irrational and dogmatic.

46. In some subdivisions of the nation the majority of the population is so similarly inclined on certain very major questions as to be conducive to the tyranny of only one point of view. Black citizens would certainly argue that this is the condition under which they must often live.

47. Robert Dahl has observed what he described as an "inescapable fact" of American politics. "In the United States, any group of people who have virtually the same views on political questions, the same political loyalties and identifications is certain to be a minority." *Pluralist Democracy in the United States: Conflict and Consent* (Chicago: Rand McNally, 1967), p. 455.

The Importance of Political Success: Party Self-Control and Compromise

It has been suggested that political parties must include within their component parts a number of differing elements if they are to be successful. The empirically observable fact has its reflection in the old saying, "Politics makes strange bedfellows." This situation may lead to political victory; it may also prove to be an Achilles heel in the event of intraparty argument about policy and intraparty struggles for nomination to high public office. At times discord results when one faction seeks to impose its particular view upon another, as happened when the Democrats split over the civil-rights plank of the party platform in 1948, leading to the secession of a "Dixiecrat" wing of the party that year. In 1968 the Democrats were badly sundered at their convention and during much of the campaign when the "peace" faction failed in its efforts to modify the pro-Johnson Vietnam plank in the platform. Often division comes from a plot of challengers to seize control of the party from the old guard, or if a dominant group refuses to give adequate representation to other factions within the party: at the Republican convention of 1948 the liberals refused to nominate a conservative for the Vice Presidency to balance Governor Thomas E. Dewey; the disgruntled regulars did not bolt the party, but their lack of fervor was reflected in the failure to "get out the vote." In 1968 some Democrats vented their displeasure over rejection of their bid to change party leadership by refusing early in the campaign to support Hubert Humphrey. When squabbles occur, the success of the leaders in patching up quarrels determines, to a very large extent, the success the party will have at the polls. In 1952, for instance, General Eisenhower, after having defeated Taft for the Republican nomination, met with his rival in order to unite the party. Eight years later Senator Kennedy, having beaten Senator Lyndon Johnson for the Democratic presidential nomination, immediately chose the Texan as a running mate, primarily to placate the southern wing of the party and keep the South as solid as possible in the coming campaign.

The fatal potential of deep party splits, whether over personalities, issues, or ideology was demonstrated in both the 1964 and 1968 elections. In 1964 the Republicans suffered from the defection, or lack of support, of "Eastern Wing" liberals unhappy over the nomination of Barry Goldwater and the elevation of conservative elements in the party to positions of

"Strange bedfellows"

Deep party splits

133

dominance.[48] In 1968 dissident groups within the Democratic Party were so alienated by their convention's rejection of their views on the Vietnam war and racial matters they did little or nothing to support Hubert Humphrey.[49] Disaffection among some was so high that talk was heard about tearing down the Democratic Party so that it could be rebuilt along new lines. The increasing polarization of extreme conservative and liberal groups little inclined to accept compromise within the Republican and Democratic party frameworks could severely sap the vitality of the two-party system.[50]

Political compromise

Since success in national elections turns on the ability of the parties to motivate their own nominal supporters while capturing the nominal supporters of the opposition, theory holds American parties today can be neither radical in their present doctrines nor necessarily consistent with their past ideas. Each party tries to guess what the same blocs of voters want to hear and then tries to say it first and most frequently. This factor accounts for the similarity between the platforms of the major parties and why, in a close election, the speeches delivered by the same candidate in different parts of the country often disclose flat contradictions which even the most adroit apologists cannot reconcile. But propagandistic language helps to obscure the similarities in programs and the contradiction of promises. On the local level, Republicans from Maine and Republicans from Hawaii face different problems, and even if they adopt different views on similar state issues, the chances are excellent that they will not be aware of the other's position. When they meet in a Washington caucus room or at an annual governors' conference, the common name and tradition make common cause possible. If the party leadership is astute, the possibility becomes a powerful reality. Although the framers of the Constitution were right when they accused political factions of being a potential source of conflict, they failed to see that nationwide parties could also serve to effect compromises among factions and so increase national unity and decrease radical movements. Compromise is necessary because every one of the larger groups

48. For a discussion of this matter see Theodore H. White, *The Making of the President: 1964* (New York: New American Library), pp. 242–243, 261.

49. Unsuccessful presidential candidate Eugene McCarthy waited until a week before the election before announcing a qualified endorsement of Hubert Humphrey. Some thought the endorsement came too late for maximum effect.

50. See Dahl's *Pluralist Democracy in the United States: Conflict and Consent*, Chapters 10–14, for an examination of varying levels of political conflict and polarization.

within each political party (farmers, trade unions, business interests, religious and racial groups, "senior citizens") has the threat of a veto to protect its interests.[51] Compromise makes sense because each of these groups is reluctant to use its veto for fear of being isolated. Political isolation means political ineffectiveness in a country as large and diverse as the United States. Radicalism might thrive locally, but it is kept in check on the national level by the very nature of the two mass parties.

Political parties serve more purposes than to compromise the diverse views of individuals, groups, and sections, and to harmonize government personnel and policies adversely affected by the principles of American democracy already considered. Although times are changing, politicians still intercede for people or organizations with government administrators. In varying ways, however, the traditional stereotype of party organization, the big city "machine," which could "deliver" the vote for both local and national elections in exchange for little favors to voters, is dying. A number of factors account for the decline of "machines." One is the increased use of merit, indicated by performance in competitive examinations, as the criterion for government employment, instead of the applicant's party affiliation. Another factor is the relationship between the local party organization and the voter as it now exists. Some years ago local politicians frequently delivered food and fuel to destitute families—and never forgot the turkey on Thanksgiving Day and basket on Christmas. Now the growth of the welfare state and the enlargement of activities by private organizations on behalf of the disadvantaged have undercut the requirement for "machine" assistance.[52]

Decline of the "machine"

Another service of political parties which is frequently overlooked is their role as bonding agents for the persons they nominate and elect. Many candidates have been dropped by their parties because of past or threatened scandals, undesirable per-

Other party services

51. David Riesman explores the psychological and characterological bases of political compromise and the power of veto groups in his study, *The Lonely Crowd* (New Haven: Yale University Press, 1961), especially Chap. X.

52. For examples of the new and the old in American political party organization see William L. Riordan, ed., *Plunkitt of Tammany Hall* (New York: Knopf, 1948) and Frank J. Sorauf, *Political Parties in the American System* (Boston: Little, Brown, 1964). Edwin O'Connor's novel, *The Last Hurrah* (Boston: Little, Brown, 1956), explains the fall of the fictional boss of Boston (who bears a marked resemblance to the late James M. Curley) in terms of the altered political/welfare climate. Despite the trends, some strong big-city politicians remain in control of their organizations. Mayor Richard Daley of Chicago, although unpopular with many Democrats inside and outside of the Windy City, probably is the strongest such figure.

135

sonal habits, or questionable friends. Parties serve as public informants, too. Their arguments are slanted, but so are those which opposing attorneys give in court.[53] During the campaign they formulate and discuss issues, listen to suggestions, and crystallize opinions. When in power they attempt to "educate" the electorate by explaining the problems they see facing the nation and defending their proposed solutions to these problems. When out of power they expose the mistakes of the party in power and by this negative function help prevent ill-conceived actions, corruption, and injustice. The task of being "the Opposition" is not one coveted by political parties, but it does provide a vital service to the nation. The political organizations are best known, of course, for their part in determining candidates for public office, in attempting to get them elected, and in financing the campaign. These functions require discussion in some detail.

The Party Selects a Candidate

Basic nominating procedures

Because of the dynamics of federalism in America, it appears inevitable that the selection of candidates for national office be done on the local level. This is why state legislation and/or state party practices account for most of the regulations governing nominations to national positions. State statutes outline requirements for getting the name of a candidate on the ballot and specify the officials with whom the name must be filed, the fee, and the number of bona fide voters whose signatures must be on the petition—if a petition is required. Either the state law or party rules will then determine the method of making the final choice of party candidates. Three basic nominating procedures are used.

THE CAUCUS

The oldest method

This American Indian word is one of the New World's contributions to the vocabulary of politics. It signifies a meeting restricted to a few leaders whose purpose is to reach agreement on a position before submitting alternatives to a larger group. In a caucus the party chieftains "draw up the slate"—that is, determine which candidates will be supported by the party as its nominees for office. Naturally, the strategy of a hopeful candidate is to cultivate members of the caucus. On occasion, the

53. Cf. Stanley Kelley, Jr., *Political Campaigning: Problems in Creating an Informed Electorate* (Washington, D.C.: The Brookings Institute, 1960).

caucus will co-opt a person who has not indicated an interest—that is, attempt to persuade him to accept the position offered.

The caucus is the oldest method of nominating candidates, the most simple, and the least expensive. It has an additional advantage in that it strengthens party control, since each nominee knows precisely to whom he owes his candidacy. The method has disadvantages, too. Chief among these are that it is considered to be undemocratic and that it invites questionable arrangements between the nominee and the slatemakers.

THE CONVENTION

This is an assembly of delegates and/or representatives from the district or state the nominee seeks to represent. The convention usually chooses among avowed candidates (one becomes an "avowed candidate" by "tossing his hat into the ring"). Candidates also must have met the legal requirements set by the state. Conventions have been known to draft persons who have not been active candidates.

An assembly of delegates

In theory, since it is "straight from the people," the convention is believed to cure the disadvantages of the caucus method of nomination. In practice, a convention also can be manipulated by professional politicians or dominated by a political machine. If it has power to select one nominee for each office to the exclusion of other hopefuls, the convention method definitely links the candidate to the party in an effective way. However, party discipline may be weakened by a public display of disagreement.

THE DIRECT PRIMARY

This method permits interested party members to select the individual who will enter the final election race as the candidate of the party. It is widely used by states. In a primary election the voter chooses among two or more fellow partisans who are seeking nomination, but it is possible in some states to select a person who has not declared his candidacy by the "write-in" device. The write-in is accomplished by having a majority of the voters properly enter the name of an unavowed candidate in the space provided on the ballot. It is the direct primary equivalent of co-option by a caucus and the convention draft.

Vote of party members

The direct primary is undoubtedly the most democratic system yet devised for nominating; it also has been an effective tool by which dedicated reformers could unseat a political machine. These advantages, however, are priced high:[54] an immense amount of money is required to administer the primary elections and to finance the expensive pre-primary campaigns the potential party nominees undertake. A heated primary may have a costly divisive effect on party harmony, since differences are brought into full public view. Party discipline is further weakened if one who has contributed nothing to the party in the past becomes its official candidate—particularly if he insists that his nomination is owed to "the people" rather than the party. Still another problem arises if a majority vote is required for nomination and if the number of candidates is large, since a primary frequently cannot produce a single candidate with a clear majority of all the votes cast. When this occurs, a "run-off" (second primary) is held between the two (or sometimes three) office-seekers who have received the largest pluralities in the first primary election. The run-off primary is used in about ten Southern or border states and is extremely important in preserving a meaningful choice for voters, since the Democratic nomination in these states is usually tantamount to election. However, the development of party competition in the South should reduce the importance of the run-off primary. In order to retain the advantages of the direct primary and still preserve a modicum of party control, some states have provided for a "pre-primary endorsement" of candidates—indicating on the ballot the ones the leaders of the party prefer.[55] A few states have required the state convention to narrow the field of hopefuls for each office to two, thus permitting party voters to choose between them at the primary election.

The form the direct primary may take, as well as the determination of participants, depends upon state legislation or party practice. Since the type of primary promises special advantages to individual candidates and parties, direct primary lawmaking has been a fertile field for political activity, and the imagination reels before the variety which have been, or may be, conceived by nimble minds. In general, there are four distinct types which are easily recognized.

The Open Primary. When a primary is "open," the voter is not obliged to reveal his affiliation when he votes nor to ask for the

54. Probably the best analysis of the drawbacks of the direct primary for healthy political parties is V. O. Key, Jr., *American State Politics* (New York: Knopf, 1956), *passim.*

55. In the 1962 primary struggle for the Massachusetts Democratic senatorial nomination, President Kennedy's brother, "Ted" Kennedy, received his party's convention endorsement. Nevertheless, his opponent (and nephew of the Speaker of the House of Representatives), "Ed" McCormack, contested the convention decision in the primary election.

Margin notes:
Advantages and disadvantages

The run-off primary

ballot of a particular party at the primary election. Instead, he selects the party ballot in the privacy of the voting booth. The chief complaint about the open primary is that it encourages raiding—that is, members of one party may conspire to help nominate the weakest candidate of their rival so that he may be more easily defeated in the final election. The chief argument in favor of the open primary is that it permits a voter to keep his political preference a personal matter. Those who consider the primary to be a party affair are distressed that members of rival parties may participate in what is essentially none of their business.

The Closed Primary. This arrangement permits a voter to receive only the ballot of the party of which he is a registered member or which he has publicly declared his intention to support. Although the closed primary discourages raiding, it also discourages voting, since some people are unwilling to state their political affiliations. One who "declines to state" is limited, in primary elections, to voting for candidates who are nonpartisan by law. He has no voice in the selection of candidates for any federal office or most state offices.

The Mixed Primary. This is the "open primary gone mad." Under this system the voter may range, pencil in hand, over a comprehensive list of names, voting for a Democratic aspirant for one office and a Republican hopeful for another—the voter has the best of all possible worlds. The person from each party who receives the most votes for the particular office he seeks is declared to be the nominee of his party and faces the nominee of the rival party in November.

The Nonpartisan Primary. Due to a persistent idea in American politics that party membership is inappropriate for some offices (judgeships, school board members, etc.) and unnecessary for others (local positions, where it is assumed that the townspeople know personally the individuals seeking office), some ballots list the names of candidates without an indication of their political affiliation. The two persons with the highest primary vote then face each other in the final election—again without disclosure of party membership.

The Presidential Nominating Primary

Of the many offices across the land for which primary elections are held the presidential primaries naturally evoke the

(margin note: Types of primaries)

greatest general interest.[56] Such primaries may be conducted for several purposes: (1) They may indicate which candidate the party voters wish their delegates to the national convention to support, although the expressed wish of the voters in the primary may or may not be binding upon the delegates. (2) They may be used to select the actual delegates who will represent the state party at the national convention. Delegates selected for this purpose may be "pledged" to a certain candidate or they may go to the convention "unpledged." The number of roll-call votes at the convention for which a "pledged" delegation is required to support a particular candidate varies among the states. At times a state delegation will support a "favorite son" candidate from the particular state on the first roll call, as a compliment to the individual, then will cast its votes in earnest for a bona-fide candidate. At the present time the majority of states do not have presidential primaries.

The Party Wages a Campaign

When a candidate has been selected, the objective of the political party shifts to getting him elected. People who actively engage in politics find the problems and pleasures of the campaign even more intense than those of the nominating process. This is the stage where, it appears to the uninitiated, the parties take off the gloves and begin hitting their rivals hard, often—and, sometimes, low. To the seasoned politicians, however, the campaign appears to be something quite different: it is the time to convince loyal members that the party will lose without their help; to rally nominal supporters to the party flag by adroitly fanning the embers of traditional loyalty; and to seize the opportunity to persuade the independents and those with weak leanings toward the rival party that the American Way of Life (at least, and, more likely, that Western Civilization itself) is at stake and that they must cross the faint line between parties to preserve it.[57]

56. In 1968 the Senate Majority Leader, Mike Mansfield (D., Montana) suggested that the national nominating conventions be replaced by a nationwide primary as the means for selecting presidential nominees. He noted the likely difficulty of getting his suggestion adopted. See also the discussion of presidential primaries and nominating conventions in Chapter 6.

57. An amusing example of the flight campaign oratory can take is this passage taken from a sermon delivered during the generally apathetic presidential campaign of 1920: "There are only three great documents in the world today and they are the decalogue, the Constitution of the United States, and the platform of the Republican Party. Wilson, if allowed to have his way, would have linked this glorious God's country up with the territory of the devil, Europe. Thank God he did not succeed." *Chicago Tribune* (July 15, 1920), p. 15.

To undertake the tasks of activation, reinforcement, and conversion, prodigious quantities of money must be raised and spent; the candidate must appear under the most advantageous circumstances; and the campaign should ideally improve every week, reaching a climax just before the Tuesday following the first Monday in November. An effective campaign requires sound organization and expert timing: these are the responsibility of the political organizations.[58]

The party does a great many other things for its candidates: it gives them the aura of a tradition which traces back through many illustrious statesmen to Jefferson or Lincoln; it affords **Aura of tradition** them a ready-made core of solid support; it brings nationally known personalities into their districts to add interest and prestige to the campaigns. In short, it helps get the candidate before the people. The party also furnishes headquarters staffed with such necessities as secretarial help, registration and election-day workers. Special *ad hoc* committees must be formed to arrange and pay for radio and television time and to finance speech-writers and research and publicity experts. All of these activities cost a great deal of money, for even though some of the work is volunteered and unpaid, much of it is not. Full-time employees generally draw salaries; rent, utilities, and travel must be paid; and the use of mass media must be bought.

CAMPAIGN FINANCES: RAISING MONEY

In America today the means of financing political parties is almost universally condemned as unsatisfactory. The unfortunate situation is primarily due to the loose organization of the parties, compounded by legislation which is not only unrealistic but sometimes downright harmful. A brief survey of the traditional sources of political funds and pertinent legislation will indicate the problem of money in politics and the costs of democracy.

For a number of years the spending to elect candidates to public office has been of such a magnitude as to justify its cate-

58. Accounts and analyses of political campaigning are numerous. A good summary of campaign techniques is provided by V. O. Key, *Politics, Parties, and Pressure Groups*, pp. 501–30. A participant's view is well stated by Stimson Bullitt, *To Be a Politician* (Garden City, N.Y.: Anchor, 1961), Chaps. 5, 6, and 7. Stanley Kelley, Jr., examines political campaigning with particular emphasis on the role of public relations men and techniques, *Professional Public Relations and Political Power* (Baltimore: Johns Hopkins University Press, 1956), Chaps. IV, V, and VI. Recent campaigns are the subject of fascinating books by Theodore H. White, *The Making of the President: 1960* (New York: Pocket Books, 1962) and *The Making of the President: 1964* (New York: New American Library, 1966).

Election costs

gorization as "big business."[59] An exact accounting of how much is actually spent in campaign years by the contesting parties is difficult to obtain. There is considerable difference between the figures reported by the parties and candidates and the actual expense figures, due to the laxity in accounting and reporting procedures. For example, the reported total spending in the presidential election year of 1960 was $28,326,322, but the estimated figure given by political experts was $175,000,000.[60] In 1964 it was estimated by the *Congressional Quarterly* staff that a total of nearly $200,000,000 was spent in political campaigning.[61] The expenditure of such an amount could, under certain conditions, threaten the continued operation of democracy.[62]

Office-Holders and Candidates. The Civil Service Act (1883) prohibited kickbacks of money to be used for political purposes by classified employees of the national government. Since this law was rigorously enforced, a steady source of party revenue quickly dried up. However, many appointed officials are exempt from the law and are said to be lavish donors. Parties expect, and receive, contributions from candidates. Sometimes parties actually seek out wealthy individuals (affectionately known as "fat cats") for nomination, with the expectation that they will more than pay their own freight. This hope would be realized if the Federal Corrupt Practices Act of 1925 were observed in spirit, since it attempted to limit the maximum expenditure for a candidate for the House of Representatives to $5,000 and a senator to $25,000. Unfortunately, campaigns cost much more

59. In the California Republican senatorial primary in 1968 the losing candidate reported spending $822,355, or about 80 cents for each vote received. For the winning candidate, expenditures were reported of $1,075,984, or slightly less than a dollar a vote. "Max Spent $1 Million To Beat Kuchel," *San Jose Mercury*, July 10, 1968. After the primary it was reported that Texas oil millionaire H. L. Hunt had contributed to the victory of conservative challenger Max Rafferty over liberal Senator Thomas Kuchel. "Hunt Aided Kuchel Loss," *San Jose News*, July 27, 1968. The money spent in behalf of both Kuchel and Rafferty was spent in a sense in vain, for Democrat Alan Cranston won the senatorial election in November.

60. These figures are found in "Political Contributions and Campaign Spending," *Politics in America 1945–1966*, 2nd ed. (Washington: Congressional Quarterly Service, 1967), pp. 86–91.

61. *Ibid.*, p. 89.

62. A study of this subject is by Alexander Heard, chairman of President Kennedy's Commission on Campaign Costs, *The Costs of Democracy* (Chapel Hill: University of North Carolina Press, 1960; also available in abridged, paperback edition published by Anchor Books).

than these amounts, and few candidates contribute enough to meet even the expenses of their own campaigns.[63]

Party Projects. Lincoln and Jefferson-Jackson Day dinners which feature $100-a-plate specials are a time-honored source of raising funds, and various testimonial affairs add extra money to the party coffers.[64] The sale of party neckties, magazines, and books perform a useful ritual function, but they probably drain money from the party accounts. Champion fund raisers have been Presidents Eisenhower and Kennedy. One of the most lucrative of the testimonial affairs was one entitled 'Salute to Eisenhower' in January, 1956. The appearance of the President via closed-circuit television before 53 banquets in 37 states is reported to have brought in between four and five million dollars. Between the evening of his inauguration and a dinner tribute in Houston, Texas, the night before he was assassinated, President Kennedy raised over $10 million for the Democrats.[65] Donated performances by Hollywood and Broadway stars mean that most of the money from ticket sales (prices run up to $1,000) to such events can go directly to the party treasuries.

Champion fund raisers

Special Interests. Contributions by business and labor unions are an important source of party revenue, despite legislative attempts to outlaw such donations. Federal legislation enacted in 1907 prohibited contributions by corporations "in connection with any election to any political office." The Taft-Hartley Act (1947) extended this prohibition to primaries and placed labor unions and corporations in similar positions—neither could contribute to the campaigns of national officers in a caucus, convention, primary, or final election. Loopholes exist, however, through which both corporations and unions may contribute to "independent" organizations (which somehow appear to be extremely active in partisan politics), and unions canvass their members for voluntary contributions. Critics of the unions point out that the contributions exacted are hardly "voluntary," and critics of corporations charge that business executives are sometimes given "bonuses" to reimburse private

63. The late Robert A. Taft, running for the Senate in 1950, reported spending $1,553 for his campaign. However, 45 "citizens' committees" spent $400,000 on his behalf, and the Ohio State Republican committees spent an additional $1,600,000. Jean Begeman, "Million Dollar Senators," *New Republic*, CXXIV (April 9, 1951), p. 15.

64. Senator Thomas Dodd's (D., Connecticut) difficulties with testimonial appearances and the Senate and House efforts to establish codes of ethics in regard to financial matters are discussed in Chapter 5.

65. "Political Contributions and Campaign Spending," *op. cit.*, p. 87.

political donations. For a number of years business firms which wished to support either or both of the major parties were given the opportunity to purchase advertising space in publications put out by the party organizations. The cost for the ads, sometimes running as high as $15,000 for one page, were deductible for tax purposes.[66]

Wealthy Donors. Contributions which run into tens of thousands of dollars are given by wealthy individuals and families. Such large-scale donations supply a chief source of party funds. The Hatch Acts (1939, 1940) stipulate that no individual, committee, or association may donate more than $5,000 to a campaign committee for a candidate for national office in any calendar year; so the donors give the maximum amount to many committees and arrange for other members of the family to do the same.

Interested Citizens. Small individual contributions are increasing in number as Americans have come to recognize the enormous cost of political campaigns and to acknowledge that good citizenship requires more from them than voting on Election Day. Private foundations, aided by free newspaper space and radio-television pleas, have begun a concerted drive to encourage small donations. Voters are urged to support with money the "party-of-your-choice" as an indication of good citizenship and fair play, probably with the hope that the voters will become aware of the danger when sky-rocketing campaign costs are paid for by a relatively few organizations and private individuals.

During the 1960's momentum built to have the Federal Government act to relieve the dependence of the political parties upon large contributors. In 1966 the Presidential Election Fund Act was passed and signed by the President. Its major provision was for a voluntary taxpayer checkoff whereby those paying Federal taxes could contribute one dollar to the Presidential Election Campaign Fund and have that amount deducted from their taxes. The money was then to have been divided between the two major parties, with a dollar a vote going to minor parties if they attained a minimum of two million votes. Later, in 1967, the Senate Majority Leader Mike Mansfield successfully led a fight to make the 1966 law inoperative until additional guidelines can be worked out regarding the allocation and control of funds generated by the taxpayers' checkoff plan. Mans-

Taxpayer checkoff

66. *Ibid.*, p. 91. In 1966, at the urging of Senator John J. Williams (R., Delaware) Congress approved and the President signed a provision prohibiting tax deductions for such advertisements.

field was quoted as saying his action did not discard the principle of public financing of presidential election campaign costs, but merely required more precise guidelines before the principle was implemented.[67]

CAMPAIGN FINANCES: ACCOUNTING

Another significant problem, and a twin to that of raising money, is accounting for money spent for political purposes. In America today states have enacted corrupt practices laws which vary widely both in coverage and effectiveness. National legislation, beginning in 1883, has sporadically attempted to control money spent in national political campaigns—an attempt generally considered to be futile because it is unrealistic. Reports have been required which include the name and address of each person who contributes a hundred dollars or more and information furnished as to whom payments of ten dollars or more have been made. The Hatch Acts limitations on donations and the ceiling of $3,000,000 imposed on spending by each committee have resulted in the proliferation of committees, each spending and reporting (if they *do* report) separately. The officials who are supposed to receive the reports have no power to force committees to submit them; they may not audit reports if and when received; nor may they prosecute for violations of the laws. It requires no clairvoyance to predict that some campaign funds are ineffectively spent—if not actually embezzled. To remedy these problems, the Heard Commission and President Kennedy recommended repealing the $3,000,000 limit and also the $5,000 ceiling on annual individual contributions to the political committees, and tightening up reporting requirements through the creation of a Registry of Election Finance in the General Accounting Office.

The primary obstacle to efficiency in controlling and publicizing campaign funds traces again to the principle of federalism, this time augmented by the natural inertia of successful politicians to change a system which has served them well. The principle of federalism provides for the election of the President, representatives, and senators from *states*; many people insist, therefore, that the purity of elections should be the responsibility of the state rather than of the national government. Regarding the reluctance of the elected representatives of the people to improve the system, two contradictory arguments are advanced as to why it is not done: in order not to let constituents know the large expenditures made to win election, and to

Reporting donations

Reluctance to change

67. "Final Action on Campaign Fund Issue," *Congressional Quarterly Weekly Report* (May 12, 1967), p. 777.

keep alive the idea of the high cost of campaigning in order to discourage challengers. A third reason might be that since many different committees support his candidacy, a national office-holder is less liable to be subject to control by the national party organization. Any realistic proposal for reform will have to take such factors into account.

ELECTION DAY COSTS

On Election Day the parties pay a substantial amount of money to "get out the vote." Calls are made by telephone and personal visit to assure that qualified voters get to the polls. Transportation is sometimes hired, and babysitters are furnished. The campaign costs for political parties end with the election-eve parties which are held at headquarters for workers, candidates, and well-wishers.

The expenses of holding the elections are borne by the states. These costs include renting polling places, paying election officials (party faithful rewarded with a small check), and the costs of ballots or voting machines.

Equal Time on Radio and Television

Over the years the increased use of radio and, later, television, plus the fact that there are often more than candidates from just the two major parties in contention for public office, created what is known as the "equal time" problem. The legislative history of the matter began in 1934 when the Communications Act of that year became law.[68] The act contained a provision (in Section 315) that whenever a radio broadcasting station permits a "legally qualified" candidate for public office to use its facilities it must "afford equal opportunities" to the other candidates running for the same office. Section 315 became the subject of considerable practical controversy in the late 1950's. A write-in candidate complained that he was not being given "equal time" in comparison with news broadcasts showing his major-party opponent engaging in various activities. The Federal Communications Commission agreed with him in a close vote. It therefore appeared that the 1934 law would be interpreted to give "equal time" not only to paid political broadcasts but to newscasts featuring candidates as well. Congress and the President reacted to the FCC ruling in 1959 by

The 1934 law

68. For an account of efforts to deal with the "equal time" problem see "'Equal Time' Problems Part of TV Impact," in *Politics in America 1945–1966, op. cit.*, pp. 92–94.

amending the law to make it read that news broadcasts and news documentaries would not require "equal time" treatment.

Legislation was adopted in 1960 which suspended the "equal time" provisions of Section 315 as they applied to presidential and vice presidential candidates. This cleared the way for the series of televised debates between Vice President Richard Nixon and Senator John F. Kennedy, which were estimated to have been viewed by more than 115 million persons.[69] In 1964 Congress did not again suspend the "equal time" provisions, and Senator Goldwater did not debate President Johnson on television although he challenged the President. A bill to suspend the "equal time" requirements died in the Senate in 1964 because Democrats did not support it, presumably according to the wishes of President Johnson.[70] In 1968 the tables were turned. Vice President Humphrey, trailing Richard Nixon in the polls, tried vainly to debate the Republican candidate. A Democratic effort to suspend the "equal time" requirements failed in the Senate because of Republican opposition.

The Nixon-Kennedy debates

Future attempts to square the theories of pluralistic democracy with television costs and the practical political power to be found in mass television utilization may be difficult. The crux of the problem was suggested several years ago by a spokesman for the American Civil Liberties Union who testified against permanent suspension of the "equal time" provisions. His argument ran that such suspension would guarantee to the Republican and Democratic parties what would amount to permanent monopolistic control of the most widely used means of communication employed in American politics.[71] A complicating factor emerged regarding the "equal time" matter in 1968. Because of the rash of political assassinations in the 1960's, and widespread heckling at campaign speeches, the suggestion was often heard that even greater use of television ought to be made.

"Equal-time" problem remains

Ballots and Local Elections

The ballots currently in use in the 50 states are adaptations of a type first used in Australia. They are uniform, with no distinguishing marks, issued only at the polling place and furnished by the states. Voting is done secretly in private booths. State law determines whether the names of the nominees are

69. *Ibid.*, p. 93.

70. *Ibid.*, p. 94.

71. Lawrence Speiser, as quoted in *Ibid.*, p. 93.

arranged in a single column under the party emblem or classified according to the office sought. The "party-column" ballot
permits voting a straight ticket and is preferred by well-
established political organizations, whereas the "office-group"
ballots are preferred by strong candidates and most reformers.
In highly urbanized areas voting machines are used. Machines
are extremely convenient, since a voter merely steps into a
booth, closes the curtain, and pulls down a lever over the name
of each candidate he wishes to support (or closes a master lever
which will record a vote for every candidate of one party, if
straight-ticket voting is permitted). When the voter opens the
curtain to step out of the booth, the vote is recorded, and the
machine is cleared. Voting machines are secret and accurate,
and they save time-consuming ballot counts, but their large initial cost and the problem of storage have restricted their use.

In most elections the ballot consolidates the names of candidates for national, state, county, and city offices, as well as pro-

The long ballot posed state constitutional amendments, referenda, and even
bonding issues. Since one of the legacies of "Jacksonian Democracy" is the idea that all public officials should face the voters,
ballots tend to be very long—it is said that one used in Omaha
in 1946 measured 13 feet! There is general agreement among
political scientists that the "long ballot" is a reason for the generally poor turnout of American voters; that it causes many of
the ballots which are cast to be disqualified; and that it encourages voters to follow the path of least resistance and vote a
straight ticket. Hilarious stories are told about long ballots, but
most voters fail to see the humor. Instead, the conscientious citizen is frustrated by the implication that he should know the
qualifications of candidates seeking election as Public Weigher
or Hide-and-Animal Inspector. If he refuses to cast a straight
ticket, the voter chafes at the time required to fill out a ballot.

States could ease the situation by scheduling local elections
in odd-numbered years, when national officers were not being

Shortening the ballot elected, but this practice would surely reduce sharply the
number of votes for local offices and would make local govern-
ment less democratic. A more promising solution would be for
states to follow the logic of the national government and elect
only policy-makers (governors, legislators, county commissioners, mayors, and city councilmen), leaving judgeships and administrative positions for appointment. Actually, there is no
more need to elect a county assessor or a state treasurer than
to have a nation-wide campaign for the Director of the Bureau
of the Budget. Democratic participation is not measured so

much by how many officials are elected by the voters, but by the availability of the right to vote, the presentation of meaningful choices to the voters, and the provisions for keeping policy-makers responsible to the people.

Pressure Group Activities and Targets

The successful candidate, despite his debt to the political party which nominated, financed, and elected him, is not permitted to forget that he represents all the people in his constituency—including those who did not vote for him. The official knows that free men will not tolerate entrusting their liberty and property to one who presumes that the mere fact of election places a stamp of approval on all decisions he will make during his term of office. If he is a national official (elected or appointed), he should know that the First Amendment guarantees to the American people their right of access to him, because he will soon find out that the people will register their requests and complaints vehemently and frequently—through personal calls and visits, letters, telegrams, editorials, and by representatives of their organized interest groups.

Public officials and pressure groups

How should a public official respond to pressures from his friends and foes? Representative Emanuel Celler (D., New York), a veteran congressman, answered the question: "The 'good' representative . . . is he who effectively accommodates conflicting interests within his constituency; who successfully relates the needs of his constituents to those of the people as a whole; and who, at the same time, harmonizes his responses to the demands made upon him with the dictates of his conscience."[72] He suggested that the alternative to being a sympathetic "message center" was to assume that a person was elected so that he might "function exclusively by Divine guidance or personal intuition." Far from being annoyed or alarmed at countless "pressures" applied to himself by hundreds of "interests," Congressman Celler insisted, "After thirty-six years as a target for such messages, I still regard them as the bloodstream of the democratic process and the *sine qua non* of effective legislation."

72. Emanuel Celler, "Pressure Groups in Congress," *The Annals* of the American Academy of Political and Social Science, CCCXIX (September, 1958), 1–9. The quotations are found on pages 2 and 3. The entire issue is concerned with pressure groups and lobbies.

PRESSURE ON ELECTED OFFICIALS

This is not to say that the congressman approved of every aspect of pressure groups.[73] He was ashamed of the overt and covert bribery of a century ago (such as the Crédit Mobilier scandal which disclosed that a member of Congress who was employed by a railroad had distributed, among his colleagues, free gifts of stock in the construction company in return for give-away legislation) but found such practices not typical of American government today. Instead, "public relations men" (the new, polite name for "lobbyists") have adopted the more subtle technique of distributing a variety of gifts to policy-makers without even hinting for a *quid pro quo*, or giving campaign contributions at crucial times (such as in 1956 when an oil lobbyist wanted to donate $2,500 to the campaign of a senator who was undecided on a vote to withdraw national control from natural gas which moved in interstate commerce). Such refined lobbying practices not only avoid the criminal penalties meted out to those who try to influence votes by buying them, but also are more effective than bribery would be today.

On the other hand, Congressman Celler found that many groups employ contact men of the highest caliber, who are able to present busy lawmakers with succinct and helpful arguments on pending legislation.[74] Some policy-makers even schedule their own meetings with representatives of various interest groups in order to hear their views on important issues. Of course, most pressure groups will have their advocates present at congressional hearings, fully equipped with statistics and charts in an attempt to nail down the points they wish to make. Frequently, hearings are accompanied by the flutter of telegrams and letters drummed up from all over the country by the interested parties, but veterans soon come to distinguish the standard form letters from those written by persons who are sufficiently interested in pending legislation to register their

Subtle techniques (margin note)

High – caliber contact men (margin note)

73. An introduction to the literature of "interest-group theory" is contained in Chapter I of Harmon Zeigler, *Interest Groups in American Society* (Englewood Cliffs: Prentice-Hall, 1964). See also the "Introduction" by Phillip R. Monypenny, in H. R. Mahood, ed., *Pressure Groups in American Politics* (New York: Charles Scribner's Sons, 1967), and the contributions by Earl Latham and Robert Golembiewski. Those interested in the work which triggered much subsequent study of groups in the political process should read Arthur Bentley, *The Process of Government* (Bloomington, Ind.: Principia Press, 1949). The book was first published in 1908.

74. *Cf.* Donald R. Matthews, *U.S. Senators and Their World* (Chapel Hill: University of North Carolina Press, 1960), Chap. VIII; also David B. Truman, *The Governmental Process* (New York: Knopf, 1958), Chaps. XI and XII.

private opinions.[75] On occasion, the pressure groups resort to planted witnesses, such as purported "spokesmen for labor" who have been brought to the Washington committee room at the expense of the management. Like the evidence of lawyers in the courts and the pleas of political parties during campaigns, the presentations of special interest groups are not the whole truth, but if the opposing forces are ably staffed and well prepared, the resulting choice is believed to be better informed and more in accordance with the public good than if the legislator relied merely upon his own convictions buttressed by whatever private study he could give the problem.

PRESSURE ON APPOINTED AND JUDICIARY OFFICIALS

Activities of pressure groups are not limited to the legislative branch of government. The increasingly wide regulatory powers of the executive agencies have naturally led interest groups to concern themselves with the nonelected adminstrators who both make and administer public policy.[76] Ideally, the interest groups would like to name the appointees, but will be satisfied to have a veto over appointments. To this end they apply pressure to the elected officials who do have appointive power. After an administrator has been selected, the techniques for applying pressure directly to him are practically the same as with elected officials—from providing information to the deluge of letters and the provision of relatively minor favors, adroitly given.

Since judges have the power to affect adversely the liberty and property of citizens and corporations, they are involved in politics and cannot escape unscathed the activities of special interest groups. The deep-rooted concept of the "independent judiciary" in America has, however, removed judges from being subjected to the same types of pressure to which legislators and administrators are heir. Pressure groups do attempt to control the selection of judges (appointed in the Federal system and some states), since it is reasonable to suspect that the political and economic philosophy of a judge will influence his interpretation of the law. On the other hand, the history of the Federal courts, beginning at least with Jefferson, has consistently indicated that once a judge has assumed the bench, he feels no particular obligation to the person or groups which elevated him and strongly resents any suggestion that he should. Therefore,

Independent judiciary

75. See Estes Kefauver and Jack Levin, *A Twentieth-Century Congress* (New York: Duell, Sloan and Pearce, 1947), pp. 170–84.

76. On the role of pressure groups in influencing executive branch policies see Truman, *The Governmental Process*, Chaps. XIII and XIV.

although the use of personal and social contacts for grinding political axes does not cease, it becomes more discreet. Most interest groups ignore the courts entirely; but some (such as the American Civil Liberties Union and the American Legion) seek to appear before the judges as *amici curiae*—"friends of the court"—in order to get their views, in writing and orally, before the bench and bar; and a few (*e.g.*, the National Association for the Advancement of Colored People) have been extremely active in initiating litigation with the hope of realizing their aims by way of judicial decisions. Interest groups before the courts, like those before the other branches, have a spotty record of useful and useless presentations.[77]

PRESSURE ON THE PEOPLE

Pressure groups in a democracy cannot limit their activities to the three branches of government which make and administer public policy. When government is by the people, the people themselves must be influenced. Actually, the attitudes favored by pressure groups are more widely disseminated than more tangible products like motion picture personalities and soap. In their long-range campaigns to influence public opinion the pressure groups flood schools and libraries with books, pamphlets, and films, and treat teachers to well-endowed workshops, seminars, and conferences where the views of the sponsor are inculcated. Sometimes even comic strips are subsidized. Effective public speakers and well-known writers are constantly being sought to peddle the attitudes of the group. Despite frequent assertions that the American public has developed an immunity to propaganda after having been incessantly bombarded with it, many serious scholars have expressed grave fears about the influence "Madison Avenue" is having on "Main Street."

The maintenance of Washington (and frequently, state capital) offices staffed with qualified personnel to accomplish the research and contact work necessary to influence legislators, administrators, and judges alone involves an outlay of over a

A billion dollars a year

77. For studies of interaction between pressure groups and the courts see Chapter XI, Zeigler, *op. cit.*; Clement E. Vose, "Interest Groups, Judicial Review, and Local Government," in Mahood, *op. cit.*; Chapter XV in Truman, *The Governmental Process*; Glendon A. Schubert, *Constitutional Politics* (New York: Holt, Rinehart and Winston, 1960), Chapter 3; and Clement E. Vose, "Litigation as a Form of Pressure Group Activity," *The Annals* of the American Academy of Political and Social Science, CCCXIX (September, 1958) pp. 20–31. For a study demonstrating the role of pressure groups in a particular legal battle, the case of *Burstyn* v. *Wilson* (1952), see Alan F. Westin, *The Miracle Case: The Supreme Court and the Movies*, Inter-University Case Program (University, Ala.: University of Alabama Press, 1961).

billion dollars a year.[78] The cost of hiring big New York and San Francisco public relations firms and supplying them with the expensive media they need to propagandize the public reaches staggering sums.[79] Even if one ignores the attempt to "educate" the general public, the prospect of presenting "competent, well-matched advocates on the opposite sides of a legislative issue," which Congressman Celler appreciated, is a difficult assignment for groups which do not have the wealthy donors of the American Liberty League, a general levy of the membership as is possible for the American Medical Association, or a share of the monthly dues of a giant like the American Federation of Labor-Congress of Industrial Organizations. Although it might be discouraging for groups of modest means to realize that they must make up in resolution what they lack in riches, some encouragement might come from the fact that there are few areas in politics where dedication without dollars has a better chance of success.

Examples of Pressure Group Activity

While some pressure groups "win," they rarely obtain all they set out to accomplish. When pressure groups "lose," however, they do not lose the right to try again so long as their methods are in accord with the Constitution. In between the more clearly defined winners and losers are found numerous groups whose yearly activities must be described by the terms "draw," "stalemate," or "no decision." Of these groups many return to legislative, executive, and judicial halls or public platforms each year with renewed vigor and funding.

"Winners and losers"

The importance of pressure group activity within the greater framework of a pluralistic democracy may be gauged by recalling some of the prominent national arguments in which pressure groups were conspicuous participants during the 1960's.[80]

78. For a humorous account of lobbyists in Washington see Larry L. King, "Washington's Money Birds," *Harper's Magazine,* 231 (August 1965), pp. 43–54.

79. The cost of the American Medical Association campaign against President Truman's national health insurance plan was reported at $4,678,000. Stanley Kelley, *Professional Public Relations and Political Power* (Baltimore: Johns Hopkins University Press, 1956), p. 106.

80. One should not fall into the trap of easily explaining all governmental activity as merely resulting from some form of pressure group activity or interaction. The words of a student of pressure groups should be remembered: "In the process whereby rewards are distributed, organized groups may, under certain conditions, be major actors; but in other situations they may be no more than peripheral and ineffective participants." Zeigler, *op. cit.*, p. iv.

153

The labor unions

Among the most powerful such groups in the nation are the labor unions which have organized American workers along industry and craft lines since the last century. Although the unions have won many victories as they sought to improve the environment for laboring men and women, they have not been able to date to repeal Section 14(b) of the Taft-Hartley Act.[81] After years of argument "Medicare" was passed by Congress and signed into law by President Johnson in 1965. Greatly broadening the role of the Federal Government in providing health care to specified age groups, the passage of the bill was applauded by such organizations which had worked for it as the AFL-CIO and the National Council of Senior Citizens. A different reaction to what the government had done came from the American Medical Association, which had actively opposed the measure for years.

Veterans and real-estate groups

A powerful group which both "won" and "lost" in the 1960's was the American Legion. The group was pleased with the passage of Public Law 89-358, the "Cold War GI Bill," which it supported; and unhappy over failure of a proposed constitutional amendment to permit voluntary prayers in public schools to pass the Senate. In the contest between various civil-rights groups and the National Association of Real Estate Boards, the latter was unable to prevent inclusion of an "open housing" provision in the 1968 Civil Rights Act.

The gun lobby

In 1968 one of the nation's most powerful lobbies, the National Rifle Association, lost some ground in its fight against increased Federal regulation of guns. Partial winners in regard to gun regulation were groups which had become particularly active after the political assassinations which marred the 1960's. Despite the 1968 gun-control legislation many, including President Johnson, considered the regulations too mild and narrow in scope—and the battle lines for additional legislative skirmishing were plainly evident. Another battle in which the outcome was not a clear-cut victory was the confrontation of lumbering interests and the Sierra Club and other conservation groups. The latter secured passage of a bill creating a Redwoods National Park in Northern California, but some were disappointed that more land could not be secured than was.

Conservationists vs. lumber interests

Lobbying activity is not confined only to groups from the private sector: citizens also seek to advance their own special interests, trade associations seek to obtain advantages for the industries they represent, and so forth. An increasingly familiar

81. This section deals with the right of states to permit a condition known as the "open shop," wherein association with a union is not necessary as a condition of employment.

sight in Washington are groups representing in various ways the interests of some governmental entity or its employees. Thus one finds representatives from the larger states, such as California, New York, and Illinois. Among the cities maintaining offices in Washington to keep themselves abreast of Federal activities are New York and Los Angeles. In view of the complexity of city-Federal and state-Federal relationships, and the amount of funds available from the central government, the establishment of offices to assist in maintaining contact with the Federal Government is understandable.

State and city groups

Even segments of the Federal Government have lobbying powers which are exercised by various organizations composed of government employees or others with some particular interest in the fortunes of a specific governmental agency. For instance, the United Federation of Postal Clerks actively lobbies for better wages and fringe benefits for themselves. The Air Force Association, through its magazine *Air Force & Space Digest,* and by other means, brings considerable pressure to bear on both Congress and the executive branch to provide the weapons systems and adopt the defense policies which it advocates. Membership in the organization is open to past and current United States Air Force personnel and other interested persons.[82]

Government-employee lobbies

Controlling Pressure Groups

Although activities of pressure groups among the American people are fraught with significance, attempts by government to control or limit such activities would be bound to founder on the rock of the Constitution. Publicity appears to be the most effective way of ensuring that the conduct of the interest groups does not become outrageous, and the many articles and books on the subject attest to the determination of scholars to make their contribution to the national welfare in this area. Congress, however, has not taken all the steps available under the Constitution either to control or to publicize the activities of pressure groups operating in Washington. The Federal Regulation of Lobbying Act (1946) was the first general law on the subject and remains the basic one.[83] Its language is vague, and the most important point appears to be that "any person who

82. The Association of the United States Army and the Navy League perform similar functions for those branches of the military establishment.

83. *Cf.* Belle Zeller, "The Regulation of Pressure Groups and Lobbyists," *Annals,* CCCXIX (September, 1958), 94–103.

shall engage himself for pay or for any consideration for the purpose of attempting to influence the passage or defeat of any legislation by the Congress . . ." must register with the Clerk of the House of Representatives and the Secretary of the Senate, listing his employer and salary. The act created no special enforcement agency to investigate compliance nor to punish fraudulent statements. The searchlight of publicity was given a feeble bulb by providing that quarterly reports, limited to money spent for the purpose of directly communicating with members of Congress, be published in the *Congressional Record*. Lobbying of executive agencies was completely ignored, activities before the courts were overlooked, and the practice of propagandizing the people was not considered.

Perhaps the regulation of lobbying is not considered to be crucially important because the Congress recognizes that the

Checks and balances principle of checks and balances operates among special interests as well as within government and party politics. Everyone who reads the newspapers knows that the aims of the large occupational groups such as farmers, businessmen, and labor often conflict with each other. Closer observation discloses that even within their own societies the various groups are far from unified. For example, spokesmen for the many different labor organizations which maintain Washington offices frequently disagree heatedly on specific legislation. It is evident that the two large farmers' groups (the American Farm Bureau Federation and the National Farmers' Union) are poles apart on agricultural policy. Lawyers from the American Bar Association have seldom agreed with their counterparts in the National Lawyers' Guild. "Big business" has interests and goals quite different from small business. Even big business, which apparently enjoys much more internal harmony than other groups, has squabbles over important items such as tariff policy.

It is apparent that the conflict between interest groups does not narrow down to "business *vs.* labor," but to "big *vs.* small"

"Big" and "small" (in business, labor, and agriculture), and even to "big *vs.* big" and "small *vs.* small." Pressure groups in America today might be described as a kaleidoscope of hundreds of organizations which actually and potentially fall into innumerable patterns of cooperation or opposition. Whether or not groups will cooperate, conflict, or remain neutral depends upon the specific issue at the time, the personalities of leaders, and strategy.

Pressure Groups and Public Opinion:
Diversity vs. The Band Wagon

Pressure groups are most effective when they can convince policy makers that public opinion supports their cause. To demonstrate that it does, they hire public relations experts first to sample the public mood and then to spend millions in order to win friends and influence people in those segments of the population which are not favorably disposed toward them or their aims. Although the meteoric rise of professional public relations is a phenomenon of our times, throughout history leaders of political, economic, and religious groups have sought to convince both their own members and people on the outside that their particular organizations basked in the favor of the gods and men. In "closed" societies the controlling few inevitably have sought a preferred position for communicating ideas and have originated many ingenious techniques for accomplishing it. They have traditionally insisted upon the exclusive right for determining standards by which "deviationists" can be judged and accorded appropriate punishment or curses. In "open" societies, where ideas must compete for favor, more expensive and time-consuming methods have been necessary. The prospects for success are less likely since opposing ideas are protected and the use of physical force against recalcitrants is not permitted.

The task of welding public opinion into a unity is especially difficult in the United States where the rich diversity of the people, encouraged by history and institutions, has prevented **No single "public"** easy formation of a single "public." Instead, there are thousands of little "publics" with strong opinions on matters which touch them directly and with weak (or no) opinions on matters which do not. Since government does not permeate every aspect of their lives, Americans belong to several unrelated publics at once. One might think of himself as a "Southerner," "Caucasian," "Presbyterian," "Small Businessman," "Rotarian," "Democrat," "Mason," "Member of the Country Club," "Supporter of the Fine Arts," and "Veteran of Foreign Wars" all at the same time.

Most people want to be accepted in the small societies to which they belong and find that acceptance is most easily achieved by conforming to group values. Membership in more groups than one often requires one kind of behavior and opinion on Saturday and another on Sunday, but if the inconsistencies are not too great, they can be accommodated. Membership in different groups also permits a check and balance system to operate.[84] For example, one might test an idea gained during a Sunday sermon on his colleagues at a club meeting and find, after the encounter, that the concept needed modification, that it should be abandoned, or that it appeared even more valid than he had thought at first. In the area of opinion (as in government and politics) the principle of checks and balances weeds out radical ideas and encourages moderation. If, however, the dominant values and ideas of some of the little publics appear unalterably opposed to those of others and the individual cannot reconcile them, he tends to drift out of the groups least important to him. If a person effectively detaches himself from all groups but one, he is on the road to becoming a "fanatic." This is a principle well understood in dictatorships, where groups are either converted into "fronts" for the government or abolished. On the other hand, if the positions of all groups with which an individual is identified tend to coincide on an issue, he is fortified in his opinion. There is comfort in being "on the band wagon," for as the author of Number 49 of *The Federalist* put it, "The reason of man, like man himself, is timid and cautious when left alone, but acquires firmness and confidence in proportion to the number with which it is associated."

Conformity of opinion

Long before *The Federalist* was written or psychologists talked about the "herd instinct" and sociologists worried about the "organization man," canny leaders knew the enormous appeal of the band wagon. If their techniques for creating the illusion that "everybody thinks so" were not as polished as those of modern tacticians, still they were employed just as seriously and for the same reason: to capitalize on the awesome power public opinion has over most people. Public opinion, and the social pressure it generates, probably is more effective in producing conventional behavior than is overt force.[85] Follow-

84. A logical analysis of the relationship of American pluralism to the American political system is Robert A. Dahl, *A Preface to Democratic Theory* (Chicago: University of Chicago Press, 1956).

85. Tocqueville, writing of the United States in the 1830's, perceived majority opinion as tending toward the most coercive form of tyranny, *Democracy in America*, Vol. I, Chap. XV. Recent observers have stressed—perhaps overstressed—the dangers of conformity in American society: Riesman, *op. cit.*, and William H. Whyte, Jr., *The Organization Man* (Garden City, N.Y.: Anchor, 1957). For an excellent analytical survey of the scholarly literature on American values, including "conformity," see Clyde Kluckhohn, "Have There Been Discernible Shifts in American Values During the Past Generation?" in Elting E. Morison, ed., *The American Style* (New York: Harper, 1958).

ing the logic of *The Federalist*, perhaps the unconventional person could acquire firmness and confidence from frequent rereading of John Stuart Mill's remarkable essay, "On Liberty," an eloquent attack on the tendency of public opinion to rob society of new ideas and spontaneity by crushing eccentricity.

In addition to launching band wagons for everything from breakfast cereals to religious revivals, public relations experts are employed for political purposes: they "sell" attitudes for pressure groups with amazing efficiency and even invent "personalities" and market profiles for political candidates.[86] Experts inform government officials as to the state of the public mind so that announcements, proposals, and disclosures can be timed most effectively. Despite the insistence of some commentators that public opinion polls before elections are "immoral if not unconstitutional," candidates follow the results feverishly—fearing that a band wagon psychology will develop (if they are behind) or that an "underdog" appeal will be created (if they are ahead). Some agencies of the national government are said to make analyses of public opinion regularly for use by their planning staffs.

Molding public opinion

The discussion of the role professional public relations is playing in America today should not obscure the fact that opinion is much too dynamic to be entirely created and manipulated—even by the experts.[87] Whenever vocal segments of the population become interested in a "cause," public policy and actions can be influenced. In the case of the "fugitive from a chain gang," for example, enough little publics mobilized on behalf of the escapee to flood the governor of New Jersey with letters and telegrams for a week. The "more than a thousand" messages received at the governor's office from dissimilar groups and individuals might not seem an impressive number in the cold light shed after 30 years, but it appeared to be an almost irresistible tide at the time. Incidents like this illustrate the crucial point about public opinion: it is a phenomenon which defies full quantitative analysis because it is a state of mind.

When the people speak

This conclusion brings us back to the beginning of the discussion of applying politics. Officials of all organizations are more or less responsive to the wishes of their constituents, but in America the combination of governmental principles, tra-

86. When cries of anguish were heard after the first televised debates between the presidential candidates in 1960 that improper television make-up had severely hurt Mr. Nixon's "image," one wondered if any make-up artist could have hidden the scars, pockmarks, and moles on Washington's face and if not, whether his distinguished record would have been forgotten by critical viewers.

87. For the contrary argument, however, see Vance Packard, *The Hidden Persuaders* (New York: Pocket Books, 1961).

159

dition, and diversity has made public officials especially alert to the voices of the people. Channels for effective politicking have been kept open by the Constitution, the nature of the party system, and the agreeable environment which permits interested little publics to flourish. But, government officials, party leaders, and group managers only hear the opinions of their articulate members.[88] Today, as always, if one wants to influence efficiently the decisions which have a bearing on his own happiness or misery, he must work at it. Politics implies activity.

The Politics of Protest, Disruption, and Violence

Violence re slavery

The United States has always had practitioners of protest against the *status quo*. Often such persons have resorted to disruptive and violent means to call the public's attention to their beliefs and to try to force changes in society. Every American schoolchild is taught that his nation was born in revolution, at a time when the political and economic system imposed by England apparently could be changed only by resort to violence. Later, violence settled questions concerning the extension of slavery to new states entering the Union, whether or not human beings could be sold like cattle, and, ultimately, the question of whether the Union itself would endure was determined by a particularly bitter civil war. The powerful and almost sedate labor unions of today trace their origins to bloody labor conflicts of the last century, and some in this century.[89]

Assassination

For a number of years people were killed illegally in America as mobs took the law into their own hands. Negroes were lynched by racists who were resolved to "keep the Nigger in his place".[90] Neither draft riots nor marches on Washington are new. Similarly, violence reflected in successful and unsuccessful assassination attempts on the lives of political leaders is not

88. *Cf.* V. O. Key, *Public Opinion and American Democracy* (New York: Knopf, 1961), especially Chap. 21.

89. For example, the Haymarket Riot of 1886 in Chicago took the lives of seven and injured 66. It followed efforts by labor to obtain an eight-hour working day. Four were hanged for their part in the strife. Labor violence in 1892 at the Carnegie steel works, Homestead, Pennsylvania, resulted in the death of seven guards and 11 strikers and spectators. James Q. Wilson notes that as late as 1934 nearly 30 persons were killed in labor disputes. "Why We Are Having a Wave of Violence," *New York Times Magazine*, May 19, 1968, p. 23.

90. Today, when the slogan "law and order" is heard so frequently about the land, black citizens must ruefully remember the times when few cared about legal protection and processes for members of their race.

unknown in the United States. Presidents Lincoln, Garfield, McKinley, and Kennedy were victims of assailants. Attempts were made on the lives of Presidents Theodore Roosevelt, Franklin D. Roosevelt, and Harry Truman.[91] Senator Huey P. Long of Louisiana was shot to death in the Louisiana State Capitol in 1935.

In spite of the thread of violence which can be discerned in American history, the use of civil disorder as a political instrument reached bewildering and unprecedented heights in the 1960's. There was a spectacular increase in the number of public demonstrations of a political character. Many of these demonstrations took the form of peaceful protests; some spawned outrageous behavior including, in too many cases, rioting, arson, beatings, and looting. The demonstrations were mounted primarily by groups associated with civil-rights movements, racial minorities, students, those concerned with pover-

Violence in the 1960's

"Well, it wasn't very pretty before, either."

91. After he left the White House, Theodore Roosevelt was wounded by an assailant but recovered; President Franklin D. Roosevelt escaped injury in an attack in which Mayor Cermak of Chicago was killed; and President Truman was not hurt in an attack on his residence by two gunmen identified as members of a Puerto Rican nationalist movement.

161

ty in America, and ending the Vietnamese war. They often faced, and sometimes clashed with, counterdemonstrations by groups opposed to them. Most of the protesters had limited aims, but some among the rioters and demonstrators wished, for varying reasons, to destroy American society in order to make way for other political structures.[92]

The murder of persons participating in different ways in the political process increased to an alarming degree in the 1960's. Among those shot and killed were President John F. Kennedy; his brother, Senator Robert F. Kennedy (D., New York), who at the time of his death was celebrating his presidential primary victory in California; the leader of a major segment of the civil-rights movement, the Rev. Dr. Martin Luther King, Jr.; Medgar Evers, National Association for the Advancement of Colored People leader in Mississippi; an active figure in a Black Nationalist group, Malcolm X; and the head of the American Nazi Party, George Lincoln Rockwell.[93]

Americans in increasing numbers became concerned over the size and demeanor of the protesting groups. They wondered **Civil disobedience** how the excesses associated with some of the demonstrations could be curbed without destroying freedom, and they were aware of the world which was watching to see whether the vaunted American way of life would be able to meet the challenges facing it.

As citizens pondered the basic causes of the political unrest which engulfed much of their land, a number of theories were advanced to explain the sudden use of violence and the departure from "normal" political processes.[94] Some argued that

92. An important aspect of much of the demonstrations and protests against the Federal Government which serves well to distinguish American pluralistic democracy from other forms of political organization was amply observable in the 1960's: the frequent practice of government officials to provide the protestors with an opportunity to present their views. For example, Robert McNamara, when he was Secretary of Defense, invited Vietnamese war protesters who had been picketing the Pentagon to discuss their views in the quiet of his office. Even more impressive (those who do not understand democratic principles found it "incredible") was the granting by the government of permission to the Poor Peoples' Marchers to camp upon 15 acres of public land. From this plot near the Lincoln Memorial in the center of the nation's governing complex, groups of poor people sallied forth each day to demonstrate against policies of the very Administration that extended their camping permit. "Resurrection City," as the camp was called, cost the local and Federal governments involved nearly $500,000 in public services and cleanup work.

93. In addition a number of civil-rights workers • (or agitators, if one strongly disapproved of their efforts in attempting to educate and organize blacks for political activity) were slain.

94. Many books written by civil-rights leaders are available to those seek-

Americans still thought they were living in a frontier environment where the settling of arguments by the six-shooter was not unusual; others attributed the excesses to conspiracies in which the Communists (or extreme Rightists) figured prominently. There were those who traced the flow of violence to a decay in the moral fiber of the "affluent" or "permissive" society—particularly in regard to the "coddling of criminals." Others attributed it to the violence freely depicted in television programs, novels, movies, magazines, and the daily press. Of course there were those who did not find the recourse to violence excessive in view of the complex problems which faced an expanding and highly mobile population living in uncertain times.

Explanations of violence

The Task Ahead

While bits and pieces of the problem of political protest, disruption, and violence have been analyzed, no clear answers supported unambiguously by scientific research have yet emerged.[95] Criminologists, psychiatrists, sociologists, psychologists, anthropologists, and others are seeking to learn more about the aspects of human behavior which contribute to violence.[96] Political scientists also are concerned with the problem—particularly as it relates to the political process.

ing to understand the goals and means for achieving them, sought and used, by the major strands of the civil-rights movement. Two particularly significant ones are Stokely Carmichael and Charles V. Hamilton, *Black Power the Politics of Liberation in America* (New York: Vintage, 1967); and the last book written by the late Rev. Martin Luther King, Jr., *Where Do We Go From Here: Chaos or Community?* (New York: Bantam Books, 1968). A collection of articles by persons protesting the Vietnamese war in particular, and concerned with the conditions of race relations and poverty in general, is James Finn, ed., *Protest: Pacifism & Politics* (New York: Vintage, 1968).

95. Some of the bits and pieces may be found in works such as the following: Richard Hofstadter, *The Paranoid Style in American Politics and Other Essays* (New York: Vintage, 1967); Eric Hoffer, *The True Believer* (New York: Perennial Library, 1966); Arnold Forester, "Violence on the Fanatical Left and Right," *The Annals* of the American Academy of Political and Social Science, CCCLXIV (March, 1966); and James Q. Wilson, *op. cit.* Centers such as the Lemberg Center for the Study of Violence at Brandeis University exist where studies of violence are made. In the wake of Senator Robert F. Kennedy's assassination President Johnson appointed a National Commission, headed by Dr. Milton Eisenhower, to study violence in America.

96. It has been suggested that the death penalty should be abolished so that convicted individuals may be subjected to prolonged and intensive psychiatric examination to determine the causes of criminal behavior. In practice it may be set aside for other reasons discussed in Chapter 8. Some scientists have noted that a genetic abnormality may in some cases account for the excessively violent behavior of individuals who have committed ser-

What basic questions ought to be asked regarding the ability of American governmental institutions and theories to meet the problems of today? Several come to mind, and the reader will have others. For example, has the government itself contributed to political unrest, the disruption of public life, and the increase in violence? Can the political system as it is presently constituted materially assist in the peaceful resolution of conflicts which arise from competing philosophies in a nation with finite resources but a continually increasing population with a seemingly limitless appetite for material goods? Is the democratic framework adequate for selecting national policies from among competing alternatives, some of which are presented with the touch of the political demagogue and huckster?

Those who are sufficiently interested to ask these questions must sooner or later come to grips with some fundamental facts of American political life. They will need to examine, for example, how "values are authoritatively allocated" within the political system.[97] Such an exercise involves an appraisal of the values, their distribution, and the way they are distributed. That is to say, an honest examination of the political system requires the setting aside of myths and determining "who gets what, when, how?"[98]

Role of political and social scientists

Professor David Easton has noted that although political scientists are understandably interested in assisting democratic governments to survive and prosper, they must learn much more about the basic motivational forces of government in general before they attempt to apply themselves to solving specific problems. In his words, social scientists "also serve who only

ious crimes. Out of such research has come the suggestion that society may wish to test persons to determine who is most likely to be violence prone. Obviously much clinical and judicial study will be required before any such activity can be set forth into law. See Richard D. Lyons, "Ultimate Speck Appeal May Cite a Genetic Defect," *New York Times*, April 22, 1968; and "Chromosome Test for Flaws Costly," *New York Times*, April 23, 1968.

97. The quotation is from David Easton, *The Political System* (New York: A. A. Knopf, 1953), p. 135. This and other works by Easton offer a frame of reference for the study of the political process which features the examination of the demands made upon political entities by those dependent upon them, the demands made by one political entity upon another one, and of the outputs of the political entities in both cases. See also *A Systems Analysis of Political Life* (New York: Wiley, 1965).

98. This quotation is from the title of a book written by one of the senior scholars in the contemporary study of politics, Harold D. Lasswell, *Politics: Who Gets What, When, How* (New York: Meridian Books, 1958).

stand and think".[99] It is certain that more heat than light will be generated by those who brandish slogans and neglect facts. For example, in the days following the assassination of Robert F. Kennedy it was said that the United States was "composed of 205 million sick people." It would be more accurate to state that the country is inhabited by 205 million individuals, each of whom bears responsibility for the current condition of American society whether it is judged to be good, bad, or somewhere in between.

There are those who choose to ignore social ills which pockmark the nation. Others wish to perpetuate society as it is currently constituted for various reasons. Some want to effect social changes as quickly as possible and believe that "quick" must equate with "violent." There are those who work earnestly for social adaptation to today's problems but insist that change must occur nonviolently if it is to last. There are a few who encourage resort to violence with absolutely no program in mind. Interspersed among the millions are leaders, situated along various points on the political spectrum, who knowingly or unconsciously heighten fears and/or expectations in their drive for power.

Social scientists can be relied upon to furnish a statistical count and an analysis of the strengths and weaknesses of each competing group. Behavioral scientists will seek to explain why the various groups and individuals act the way they do. Experts can devise ways to assure order at the price of individual freedom, or they can help form a harmonious expansion of personal freedom and creativity extending across the national population within a framework of law. But one thing is certain: the decisions as to what kind of future it will be, and the techniques used to achieve it, will be heavily "political" in character.

SUMMARY

• Politics has been defined as activity designed to influence decisions by which a group exercises its authority over members or in regard to other groups. Such activity is found most extensively in democratic societies. But even in totalitarian nations leaders are subject to some pressures designed to influence state action.

99. *A Systems Analysis of Political Life*, p. 482. Today's college activists who are understandably impatient and unhappy with many things as they now are might do well to ponder Easton's advice.

- The Founding Fathers were skeptical of the competition between large political groups. They feared that the selfish and divisive characteristics of partisanship would ill serve the nation as a whole. Nevertheless, national political parties quickly assumed an important place.

- Unlike some ideologically oriented European parties, the major American parties exhibit considerable agreement on basic principles, but they disagree on the implementation of those principles and about specific solutions to immediate problems. The parties have served to give life to the Constitution regarding such major matters as strengthening the Federal system, extending democracy, and involving government with the health, education, and welfare of the people. A minority of Americans feel the two major parties are too similar regarding fundamentals, and that parties based upon marked ideological differences would be preferable.

- The presence of the constitutional imperatives such as federalism and the checks and balances arrangement have significantly influenced the development and operation of the parties. Thus major American parties are organized along geographical and functional lines.

- A characteristic of the American party system is the "third party." Traditionally these organizations criticize the philosophies of the two major parties and offer alternative proposals to theirs. Such political movements have never elected a President, but they have served to proclaim graphically dissatisfaction with the *status quo* on the part of some, and on occasions their proposals have been adopted by one or both of the major parties and thus translated into law.

- The individual unit of the political process, the citizen voter, may be classified according to the amount of support given a party and the party role performed. Predictions by "pollsters" of how persons will vote are an important and sometimes controversial aspect of the political scene.

- The necessity for major American parties to attract a vast array of persons having different desires and fears forces the Democrats and Republicans, particularly at the national level, to accommodate rather diverse groups and to promise compromise proposals. Their success in doing so has important implications upon their success at election time. Badly split parties unable to compromise and offer broadly appealing programs are severely handicapped.

- Because of the operation of federalism local, state, and national candidates for political office are selected by persons representing in different ways the local and state party organization. The caucus, convention, and primary, or combinations of them, are the means whereby a party's candidate is selected to run in the general election.

• After a candidate has been selected by the party he must spend more time and money in campaigning against the opposition party nominee except in one-party areas where nomination is tantamount to victory in the general election. In such efforts money has assumed an increasing importance, arousing concern that democratic government may be subverted to financial power.

• Once elected, the officeholder will be under pressure from many elements to perform in ways which they desire. In particular the American system of democracy and diversity has bred the political creature known as the pressure group. Representing too small a constituency to operate as a political party, the pressure group seeks its political goals through attempts to influence politicians, bureaucrats, and legislation. The two broad categories of pressure groups, those operating to achieve goals particularly advantageous to themselves, and those contending their objectives are beneficial to all, also operate to influence the population in general. Because of the power wielded by well-organized and well-financed pressure groups, attempts have been made to regulate their activities and to preserve the national interest as factions battle for their particular ones.

• American politics has always included a certain amount of protest. In the 1960's this aspect of politics expanded into numerous and often violent demonstrations and even riots. Assassinations claimed the lives of an unusually high number of political figures. The increase in political violence seemed to serve notice that the American political system may need modification if conflicting political demands amid rapidly changing times are to be successfully met.

SUGGESTED READING

* (*Books so designated are available in paperbound editions.*)

Binkley, Wilfred E., *American Political Parties: Their Natural History* (New York: Knopf, 1958).

* Bryce, James, *The American Commonwealth*, 2 vols. (New York: Capricorn Books, 1959).

* Campbell, Angus, Philip E. Converse, Warren E. Miller, and Donald E. Stokes, *The American Voter*, an abridgement (New York: Wiley, 1964).

* Carmichael, Stokely, and Charles V. Hamilton, *Black Power: the Politics of Liberation in America* (New York: Vintage, 1967).

* Chambers, William N. and Walter D. Burnham, eds., *The American Party Systems: Stages of Political Development* (New York: Oxford University Press, 1967).

Dahl, Robert A., *A Preface to Democratic Theory* (Chicago: University of Chicago Press, 1956).

———, *Pluralist Democracy in the United States: Conflict and Consent* (Chicago: Rand McNally, 1967).

* De Tocqueville, Alexis, *Democracy in America*, 2 vols. (New York: Vintage, 1955).

Duverger, Maurice, *Political Parties*. Barbara and Robert North, tr. (New York: Wiley, 1954).

Easton, David, *The Political System* (New York: Knopf, 1963).

———, *A Systems Analysis of Political Life* (New York: Wiley, 1965).

* Finn, James, ed., *Protest: Pacificism & Politics* (New York: Vintage, 1968).

* Heard, Alexander, *The Costs of Democracy* (Garden City: Anchor Books, 1961).

* Herring, Pendleton, *The Politics of Democracy* (New York, Norton Library, 1966).

* Hoffer, Eric, *The True Believer* (New York: Perennial Library, 1966).

* Hofstadter, Richard, *The Paranoid Style in American Politics and Other Essays* (New York: Vintage, 1967).

Key, V. O., Jr., *Politics, Parties, and Pressure Groups*, 5th ed. (New York: Crowell, 1964).

———, *Public Opinion and American Democracy* (New York: Knopf, 1961).

* King, Martin Luther, Jr., *Where Do We Go From Here: Chaos or Community?* (New York: Bantam Books, 1968).

Lane, Robert E., *Political Life* (Glencoe, Ill.: Free Press, 1959).

* Lasswell, Harold, *Politics: Who Gets What, When, How* (New York: Meridian Books, 1958).

Leiserson, Avery, *Parties and Politics* (New York: Knopf, 1958).

* Lubell, Samuel, *The Future of American Politics* (Garden City: Anchor Books, 1956).

Mahood, H. R., ed., *Pressure Groups in American Society* (New York: Charles Scribner's Sons, 1967).

* Packard, Vance, *The Hidden Persuaders* (New York: Pocket Books, 1961).

Ranney, Austin, and Willmoore Kendall, *Democracy and the American Party System* (New York: Harcourt, Brace, 1956).

* Riesman, David, *The Lonely Crowd* (New Haven: Yale University Press, 1961).

* Rossiter, Clinton, *Parties and Politics in America* (Ithaca: Cornell University Press, 1960).

* Schattschneider, E. E., *Party Government* (New York: Holt, Rinehart and Winston, 1960).

————, *The Semi-Sovereign People* (New York: Holt, Rinehart and Winston, 1960).

Sorauf, Frank, *Party Politics in America* (Boston: Little, Brown, 1968).

Truman, David B., *The Governmental Process* (New York: Knopf, 1958).

* White, Theodore H., *The Making of the President: 1960* (New York: Pocket Books, 1962).

————, *The Making of the President: 1964* (New York: New American Library, 1965).

Zeigler, Harmon, *Interest Groups in American Society* (Englewood Cliffs: Prentice-Hall, 1964).

5

The Congress

A Washingtonian on his way home late at night looks up, sees the light in the Capitol dome (the signal that Congress is at work), and mutters, "Who wants to be a congressman?" A factory worker leafs through the comics after dinner and sees the familiar characterization of a United States senator as fat, big-mouthed, and stupid, and chuckles, "Who wants to be a congressman?" A student of American government, realizing the perilous political and economic obstacle course a person must successfully complete before taking the oath and reflecting on the harassment that is in store for him, wonders, "Who wants to be a congressman?" And a businessman, reading a political biography, learns that one member of Congress spent 20 percent of his annual salary for Christmas cards, and asks the same question.[1]

RESPONSIBILITIES

Even overlooking the representative's occupational hazard— elections every two years—it is certainly true that the congress- man's lot is not an easy one. Congress has been the object of more jokes than the other two branches combined.[2] The aver- age citizen stands in awe of the President, has enormous respect for the Federal judges, rages or trembles before bureaucrats, but Congress is his favorite whipping-boy. Visitors to Washington have little hesitation in stopping at the offices of their congres-

1. As a freshman senator, Richard M. Nixon spent $4,237.54 for his Christmas cards in 1951 (Earl Mazo, *Richard Nixon*, Avon Books, 1960, p. 94).

2. Bertram M. Gross, in *The Legislative Struggle* (New York: McGraw-Hill, 1953, p. 364), tells the story of the little boy, who after watching the chaplain open the floor session of Congress with a prayer, asked his father, "Why does the minister come in every day and pray for Congress?" His father replied, "You've got it all wrong, son. The minister comes in every day, looks over Congress, and then prays for the country."

sional delegation for a visit; they expect a ride on the private subway train to the Capitol and are sometimes annoyed if they are not invited to lunch. Constituents bombard their delegations with letters and telegrams asking for every kind of information and favor, or offering unsolicited advice—and expect a personal letter in return. Usually, the congressman is politely responsive to an inquiry or demand from a constituent. But many a member must have the urge to follow the example of a California congressman, who in 1934 wrote a constituent:

> One of the countless drawbacks of being in Congress is that I am compelled to receive impertinent letters from a jackass like you in which you say I promised to have the Sierra Madre mountains reforested and I have been in Congress two months and haven't done it. Will you please take two running jumps and go to hell.[3]

The workload The pay is not princely, but the recipient is expected to contribute handsomely to every worthy project in his district, state, and country. The work load is enormous, with between 15,000 and 20,000 bills and resolutions to peruse each two years, a budget of approximately $180 billion to raise, spend, and safeguard, committee meetings and hearings to attend, floor debate, frequent sallies home to deliver speeches and mend political fences, and a constant round of social functions.[4] One former congressman wrote that the basic difficulty facing a member of Congress is finding time for legislative study and innovation.[5]

Yet every two years several thousand of the nation's most capable and substantial citizens gird for the race to the white-domed building which sits on the eighty-foot elevation known as "The Hill." The losers are rarely sufficiently discouraged to abandon hope, and the winners almost always come back home insisting they have been impoverished, imposed upon, and insulted—but intending to run again for the national legislature. In Great Britain candidates "stand" for Parliament, but in

3. Quoted in John F. Kennedy, *Profiles in Courage* (New York: Pocket Books, 1957), p. 8.

4. The volume and complexity of legislation which is overwhelming has a disquieting effect on the congressman. For a brilliant analysis of the sources and types of strain on a legislator, see Edward A. Shils, "The Legislator and His Environment," *University of Chicago Law Review*, XVIII (1950–51), 571–84.

5. Charles L. Weltner, "Congress Needs Reform," *Saturday Evening Post*, 240 (October 7, 1967, pp. 12, 16.)

the United States they "run" for office, and no nominee runs harder than one who has contracted "Potomac Fever."[6]

REWARDS

The lures which attract the 535 senators and representatives to Capitol Hill are probably still "duty, gratitude, interest, ambition itself"—the cords which the writer of *Federalist* Number 57 predicted would bind the members of the House of Representatives to their constituents. It is *something* to have a seat in the policy-making body of the world's largest democracy. Congressional office provides a unique opportunity to serve fellow men both inside and outside the national borders. Article I, Section 8 of the Constitution indicates the power this legislative body has over the liberty and property of the American people, and almost every newscast suggests the influence Congress has on the lives and fortunes of people all over the world. A seat in Congress rewards its holder with the satisfaction of seeing his own ideas and ideals affecting the law of the land. The oath of office opens the door to the pleasant prospect of hobnobbing with the famous and powerful—if not becoming one of them. The excitement of playing the great game of politics in the center ring is another benefit of membership in Congress.

Realignment of seats

Members of Congress receive the same annual salary of $42,500, which is taxable. They are provided with office space; given an allowance for hiring aides and clerical staffs; and allotted money for telephone and telegraph expenses and trips back to their home districts. Offices are assigned on the basis of seniority, and senators from states with large populations are allowed larger staffs than those from less populous states. Although Congress controls the purse-strings of the nation, its own salaries have always been extremely difficult to increase. In 1815, when congressional salaries were raised to $1,500, only a few members of the whole Congress were re-elected. Even those who had voted against the bill were contaminated. As the work load of Congress increases, more and better trained staff members are necessary but, again, difficult to obtain. In 1959 a proposal that each member of the House of Representatives be provided a professional administrative assistant was linked with an "exposure" by a newspaper story that many wives and some relatives were among the 7,500 congressional employees; public

Salaries and staff

6. The powerful attraction of Washington is amusingly described by Donald R. Matthews in *U.S. Senators and Their World* (Chapel Hill: University of North Carolina Press, 1960), pp. 74–79.

opinion was believed to be so unsympathetic that the bill was hastily buried.

The Road to Congress

Qualifications
for office

While almost anybody can legally qualify for Congress, few have the financial assets needed to wage a successful campaign in the expensive age of air travel and television campaigning. The Constitution merely requires that members of the House of Representatives be at least 25 years of age (30, in the Senate); must have been citizens for seven years (nine in the case of senators); be inhabitants of the states they represent; and during their periods of service hold no other office under the United States. Today the claim made in 1788 by Number 52 of *The Federalist* that "the door of this part of the government is open to merit of every description, whether native or adoptive, whether young or old, and without regard to poverty or wealth, or to any particular profession of religious faith," does not fully square with the facts of actual political life. A recent study, suggesting it is becoming increasingly more difficult to become a member of the House of Representatives, documents the fact that the "turnover" in the House is steadily decreasing as the same members tend to be returned term after term.[7]

ELECTION

Getting elected is, of course, another matter. The most successful path to nomination lies through "party regularity." Occasionally a political parvenu with a good organization and sufficient economic backing can snatch the nomination in a direct-primary state, but the people who turn out to vote in primaries (party regulars and loyal party members) are generally disinclined to support the pretensions of one who has done nothing for the party in the past. More often, the success of a candidate who has not been known for party service can be traced to the fact that the party leaders, in searching for a suitable nominee, have approached him to urge that he run for the office on their ticket. Farsighted organizations "groom" likely political material for years, pushing them into the limelight through civic activities and then advancing them into elective office until the opportunity comes to make the congressional race. A campaign for Congress depends on the local situation

7. Nelson W. Polsby, "The Institutionalization of the U.S. House of Representatives," *American Political Science Review*, LXII (March, 1968), pp. 144–168.

to an astonishing degree. In many districts throughout the United States the voters are so overwhelmingly loyal to one party that its candidate needs merely to stay alive in order to win. In such a relaxed atmosphere, the veteran frequently abandons campaigning on the ground that he is so devoted to public business that he has little time for handshaking and speechmaking. The newcomer finds the time useful for getting more solidly entrenched with party leaders and community opinionmakers, but if he enjoys large groups he can make stirring speeches on issues no more controversial than being in favor of God, motherhood, and the locality. In a district which could go either way, the battle is hard, and strategy is important. If the campaign is fought in a presidential election year, the candidate must determine whether he would have a better chance of riding into the Capitol on the coattails of the party's presidential nominee or whether he should detach himself and "fight this local election on local issues." If the political struggle is against an incumbent who has been solicitous of his constituents, the challenger might see foreign policy as "*the* issue in this campaign"—or if the incumbent has been preoccupied with national and international concerns, he could be attacked as "having done nothing for this district."

"Stay alive— and win"

THE MAKING OF A CONGRESSMAN

Let us look at the process of election to Congress from the point of view of a single freshman representative.[8] In November, at the age of 36, John H. Legislator was swept into office with a national political tide. He put his personal affairs in order and, the day after Christmas, left for Washington, where he moved his family into a hotel. While his wife looks at suitable houses or apartments (including those of defeated incumbents who are going home to try again) and schools for the children, the new congressman waits for Congress to convene on January 3 (unless, by law, another day has been set). During these few days he has an opportunity to reflect upon the House of Representatives and how he had been brought to its threshold.

He has known from his school days that the United States has a bicameral legislature (*i.e.,* consisting of two chambers or legislative bodies) because of an expedient compromise reached at the Constitutional Convention between delegates from the

Two chambers

8. This is based in part on a true story. For a profile of the hypothetical congressman, see the introductory chapter, "The Congressman and His World," in James MacGregor Burns, *Congress on Trial* (New York: Harper, 1949).

175

large states (who wanted a single body based upon population) and those of the small states (who urged one chamber based upon equality of states). The House of Representatives was given *unequal* representation, reflecting states' populations, with the guarantee that every state would have at least one representative and the promise of a census every 10 years to assure equitable distribution. The size of the House was left to the determination of law. An "upper House," the Senate, had been designed for *equal* representation from states, to confirm their parity. Each state was allotted two senators, with the guarantee that this number would not be reduced without its consent. Having studied American history and government, John H. knows that the Yankee genius for compromise created the two-house Congress; that British parliamentary experience gave it historical precedent; and that the principle of federalism made it dynamic.

The new congressman can easily recall the steps by which he achieved official status in Washington. As an undergraduate he had been interested in national and international affairs, but the only politics he had participated in were on the campus—and with indifferent success. When he went to Washington to attend law school, he needed part-time work and so applied at the office of the Senate Sergeant-at-Arms; he was given a position as Capitol guard (which was charged to the patronage allowance of a senator from another section of the country). Some months later he applied for a clerkship in the office of a senator from his home state. John H. was given the position, even though he was a nominal member of the opposition party, but since he was loyal to his employer and not particularly committed politically, he drifted into identification with the senator's party. The senator indicated a genuine interest in John's progress at law school and frequently talked to him about his plans after graduation. John always said he intended to return and practice law in his home town. One day John H. was invited into the senator's private office, where he was introduced to other members of his state's congressional delegation who shared the common party tie: after a brief conversation about his family and background, he was informed that he had been marked as a "comer," and that they would be willing to help him prepare for a career in government if he were interested. He was very much interested.

After passing the state bar examination, John H. Legislator married, hung out his shingle, and began to participate actively in community affairs. He joined professional, social, and civic clubs, activated his church membership, and became a party

Introduction to politics

regular. He worked with Little League baseball, Boy Scouts, and other worth-while projects. Soon he was directing the Community Chest drive and chairing the Fourth of July committee. The governor named him, quite unexpectedly, to a "citizens' committee" to investigate a proposal to consolidate rural schools. A year later he was defeated for a position on the county school board, but on his next try for public office he was elected County Attorney. He earned the reputation as an interesting public speaker and frequently appeared at high school commencements and patriotic programs. His sincere interest in Latin America was converted into a series of talks that brought invitations to speak to a variety of groups in his section of the state.

First steps

Two years before he came to Washington as a member of Congress, John went to the state capitol as a freshman legislator. He had barely been sworn in when news arrived that the congressman from his district had died suddenly. That weekend he attended a caucus consisting of state party leaders and most of the party's delegation in Congress. He emerged some hours later knowing he would be supported for the vacancy. His district was not represented in the House for 18 months, since representatives (unlike senators) may not be appointed, and his state did not hold a special election to fill the vacancy. John H. used this time to campaign. He accepted every invitation to speak at schools and civic groups about the state legislature and his part in it. His wife's name moved from the society page to the news columns as she began to increase her activity in community affairs. When the time came to file for nomination as representative from the 4th District in his party's closed primary, his only opposition was a used-car dealer. John easily won the nomination.

Entering the race

The primary in the opposition party had been a stormy affair with three strong contenders. John had hoped that the rifts in the opposition would be slow to heal, but the party apparently rallied around the successful candidate, a respected state judge and an adept campaigner. John decided to identify himself as closely as he could with his party. In his public appearances during the months which followed, John H. Legislator always insisted that the important issue before the voters was the election of the President. The presidential nominee never got into his district, but willingly posed for pictures with him. When his party's popular nominee was elected by a landslide, John was carried to Washington with him.

Election to Congress

At noon on January 3, John H. and 434 other newly elected representatives assemble in the House for swearing in. This

177

Sworn in ritual is required for all members, because the House is not a continuing body as is the Senate: all members face the voters at once, instead of only a third every two years. The clerk of the previous House calls the roll of members-elect (alphabetically by states) from a list compiled from certificates of election forwarded by state officials. The "dean" of the Congress administers the oath to the Speaker (chosen beforehand in caucus by the majority party), who in turn administers it to the other members as a group, provided their elections have not been challenged.[9] The House then organizes (actually a formality, since the officers have been determined in advance during caucuses by the two major parties)—and John H. is ready to begin the first session of the two-year "Congress."

The Problem of Proper Representation

Too many representatives? Although merely reading the Constitution would lead one to infer that the apportionment of representatives among the states is a simple matter, actually it has not been. In the first Congress there were 65 representatives, one for each 30,000 "free persons" (excluding Indians not taxed and counting "other persons," i.e., Negro slaves, as three-fifths each of a "free" person). As the population grew, the size of the House was increased, but by 1910 it had reached what many people considered to be the unwieldy number of 435. Further increase seemed undesirable,[10] yet the 1920 census showed that California and Michigan were badly underrepresented in the House (and thus in the Electoral College). The alternatives seemed to be either to reapportion by decreasing the representation from states which had grown slowly, or to increase the member-

9. If an election is contested, the person involved stands aside until the others have received the oath of office. He may then be directed either to take the oath and serve while the Committee on Administration conducts an investigation or to wait until an investigation has been concluded. The former practice apparently is firmly entrenched. The Constitution gives each house the power to "judge the elections, returns, and qualifications of its own members," and in the past determinations seem frequently to have been made on partisanship. In Great Britain contested elections are for the courts to determine.

10. The aim of the Founding Fathers, according to the author of Number 55 of The Federalist, was to construct the House of a size small enough "to secure the benefits of free consultation and discussion" and yet large enough "to guard against too easy a combination for improper purposes." The implication is that it is better to err on the size of a small body, for "in all very numerous assemblies, of whatever character composed, passion never fails to wrest the sceptre from reason. Had every Athenian citizen been a Socrates, every Athenian assembly would still have been a mob."

ship of the chamber. In desperation, the House proposed that its number be set at 470. The Senate refused the bill, and the House refused to take the first alternative—so, for the first time, the Constitutional mandate was ignored. Congress solved the dilemma by giving it to the executive branch. The Legislative Reapportionment Act (1929), amended by an act of 1941, directed the Bureau of the Census, after each decennial census, to work out reapportionment by giving each state a representative and dividing the remaining seats on a method known as "equal proportions"—a difficult formula for laymen to understand but, fortunately, a simple task for statisticians. Thus the shifts in population are reflected in the number of seats each state has in the House of Representatives. For example, the realignment of seats in the House of Representatives following the 1960 census added eight seats to California and four to Florida, reflecting the fact those two states showed the greatest population growth. On the other hand, states with a population decline or a much lower population growth than other states lost seats, as did Pennsylvania, which lost three seats, and New York, Arkansas, and Massachusetts each of which lost two seats. The Bureau presents the plan to the President who, in turn, sends it on to Congress. If Congress does not adopt a different arrangement within 60 days of receipt, the reapportionment proposal automatically becomes law. The number of the House swelled temporarily to 437 with the admission of Alaska and Hawaii, and in 1961 there were various proposals to increase the permanent size of the House. The late Speaker, Sam Rayburn (D., Texas), however, opposed any increase, and the proposals died in the Judiciary Committee. In 1962, with John McCormack (D., Massachusetts) the successor to Rayburn as Speaker, a bill to add three seats—one each for Massachusetts, Pennsylvania, and Missouri—came to the floor for a vote but died after a confused fight over division of the spoils.[11] Although the size of the House now stands at 435, or approximately one representative for every 471,000 inhabitants, many members are convinced that it must be increased. They argue that since the populations they represent are increasing and the hours in a day remain constant, there is less time available for each constituent. These congressmen point out that as much as 50 percent of their working day is already devoted to

Realignment
of seats

11. See *New York Times*, March 9, 1962, p. 1, and Washington *Post and Times Herald*, March 9, 1962, p. 1. The politics of House enlargement can be seen clearly in hearings held before the House Judiciary Committee, "Increasing the Membership of the House of Representatives and Redistricting Congressional Districts" (Hearings before Subcommittee No. 3, 87th Cong., 1st Sess., August 24 and 30, 1961).

servicing requests for, and corresponding with, people from their districts.

REDISTRICTING, THE GERRYMANDER, AND "ONE-MAN, ONE-VOTE"

As a result of population shifts between states, after every decennial census some states gain congressional seats, others lose, and many see no change in their delegations. If a state gains a representative, it must redistrict; otherwise the new district borders are identical with state boundaries, and the congressman must run in an "at large" election. When a state loses representation and does not redistrict before the next congressional election, the entire delegation is obliged to campaign "at large."

Gerrymander The job of determining congressional district boundaries as well as the boundaries of districts sending state representatives and senators to the state capitol has provided state legislatures with an opportunity for political intrigue for a century and a half and has added another distinctively American word, "gerrymander," to the political lexicon. By 1812 a canny Massachusetts governor named Elbridge Gerry learned that by studying the voting patterns in his state, the political map could be drawn for congressional districts to favor the party which controlled the state legislature. The first celebrated design looked

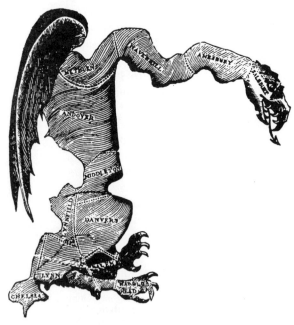

The Original Gerrymander (drawn by Elkanah Tisdale, 1812).

like a salamander (hence the term, "gerrymander"), and others bear marked resemblances to streaks of jagged lightning, dumbbells, and shoestrings. Congress has, from time to time, sought to assure "compact and contiguous" districts with "as nearly as practicable an equal number of inhabitants," but the phrases were omitted in the Reapportionment Act of 1929, and the Supreme Court ruled that Congress had not intended the injunctions to apply after that date.[12] The failure of a state to redistrict after important shifts in population is known as the "silent gerrymander." An outraged citizen in one such state sued his governor on the ground that he had been denied equality, since his vote was only one ninth as important as a vote in another congressional district, but the Supreme Court declined to interfere with the powers of the state legislature: this was a "political," not a "legal," question.[13] It is doubtful if the plaintiff was surprised at the decision, since he was a professor of constitutional law, but the publicity of his case had the desired effect—the state was redistricted.

In 1962 the Supreme Court, in a rather dramatic 6-to-2 vote reversal of its past reluctance to involve itself in apportionment questions, either of congressional districts or state legislative districts, issued a landmark ruling in *Baker v. Carr.* It was the Court's view that the equal protection clause of the Fourteenth Amendment provided Tennessee citizens with the right to challenge their legislature's failure to reapportion state legislative districts since the first years of this century.[14] The Court's decision that the alleged malapportionment of a state's legislative district was justiciable (*i.e.*, the matter could be argued out and decided before a court of law) obviously hinted that malapportionment among congressional districts within a state might also be justiciable. So it was in 1964 that the Supreme Court ruled in *Wesberry v. Sanders* that, "as nearly as is practicable one man's vote in a congressional election must

One man, one vote

12. Wood v. Broom 287 U.S. 1 (1932). In 1964 a case reached the Supreme Court which raised the question of racial makeup in congressional districting. The facts were that the Republican-dominated New York Legislature had drawn the 17th Congressional District in New York City to conform to the upper-income area of the East Side. The action produced a "silk stocking" district which was wealthy, 90 percent white, and Republican. In contrast, nearby areas were poor, Negro and Puerto Rican, and overwhelmingly Democratic. The Court could find no motive for racial discrimination in the drawing of the district's boundaries and therefore declined to take any action. See Wright v. Rockefeller 376 U.S. 52 (1964).

13. Colegrove v. Green, 328 U.S. 549 (1946).

14. Baker v. Carr 369 U.S. 186 (1962). Much of the history of apportionment in the United States is found in Gordon E. Baker, *The Reapportionment Revolution* (New York: Random House, 1966).

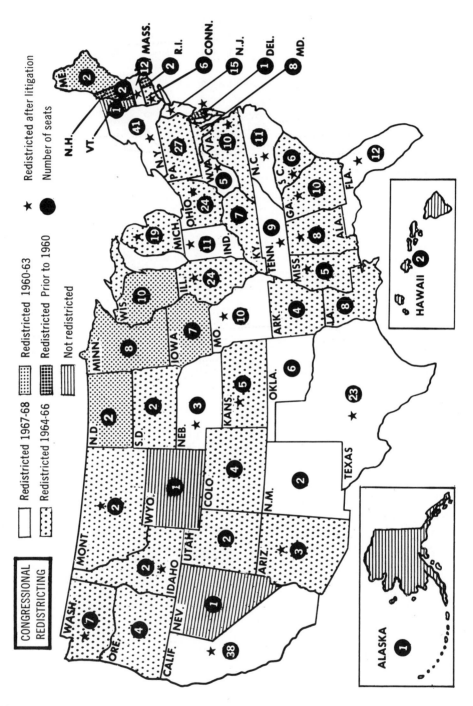

CONGRESSIONAL
REDISTRICTING

Redistricted 1967-68
Redistricted 1960-63
Redistricted 1964-66
Redistricted Prior to 1960
Not redistricted

★ Redistricted after litigation
● Number of seats

be worth as much as another's."[15] The facts were that the 5th Congressional District of Georgia (the area around Atlanta) had a population of 823,680. However, the average population of all 10 Georgia Congressional Districts was 394,312, or less than half that of the 5th District. One district held only 272,154 persons. Residents of the 5th District complained of being grossly discriminated against because their congressman had to represent two to three times as many people as those from Georgia's other congressional districts. In accepting the complaint as a valid one requiring correction the Court held that Article I, Section 2 of the Constitution, which states that representatives be chosen "by the People of the several States," requires state legislatures to ensure their congressional districts are essentially equal regarding numbers of inhabitants.[16] In a strongly worded dissent, Justice John Marshall Harlan contended that the historical background to, and the wording of, Article I, Section 2, meant that the authors of the Constitution were concerned with apportionment among the states, not within them. Furthermore, Harlan felt, "what is done today saps the political process. The promise of judicial intervention in matters of this sort cannot but encourage popular inertia in efforts for political reform through the political process. . . ."[17]

The impact of the Wesberry decision, and subsequent Court orders, has been national in scope as legislatures in state after state have redrawn the boundaries of their congressional districts to confer fairer representation upon urban and suburban voters. What the resulting reapportionment will mean in political terms for the 1970's is not clear. However, one may be sure that Congress, particularly the House of Representatives, will increasingly turn its attention to the problems and promise of the metropolitan areas where more than 70 percent of Americans live.[18]

Fairer representation

The Constitution requires that a congressman live in the state from which he is elected, but political reality has reinforced the tradition that he also live in his district. Occasionally a candidate only maintains a legal or mailing address there, but

15. Wesberry v. Sanders 376 U.S. 1 (1964). By late 1968 37 states with 395 congressional seats, out of a total of 435, had been redistricted.

16. In the various apportionment decisions the Supreme Court has not stated precisely how equally populated voting districts must be.

17. Wesberry v. Sanders 376 U.S. 1 (1964).

18. The Bureau of the Census lists 29 Standard Metropolitan Statistical Areas with populations above one million. The largest such SMSA is New York City and several nearby New York counties, with slightly over 11 million. The smallest is composed of San Bernardino-Riverside-Ontario, California, with just above one million.

usually he has grown up in the district in which he runs for election. This is unlike the situation in Great Britain, where the famous politician, Edmund Burke, was elected to Parliament from a district in which he had never been until he went there to thank the voters for electing him!

IN THE SENATE

From time to time one hears complaints about the "undemocratic" nature of the Senate, since populous states like New York and California are on a par with such sparsely settled states as Alaska and Nevada; sometimes elaborate schemes are publicized which would give "bonuses" of senatorial seats to heavily populated states. If one remains convinced that a change should be made—even after reading the logic of Number 62 of *The Federalist* that "in a compound republic, partaking both of the national and federal character, the government ought to be founded on a mixture of the principles of proportional and equal representation"—the words of the Constitution guaranteeing equality, together with state pride, suggest that an attempt to change would be futile. One who has observed the Senate over a period of time would be reluctant to see it much enlarged because its small size is one of its great assets. The membership of 100 is much like that of a fraternity, and the six-year term permits senators to come to know each other.

Advantages of small size

The Road to the Senate

Under the original Constitution, senators were to be elected by state legislatures. The Founding Fathers believed that this arrangement would enhance federalism by linking states with the national government and provide an effective check to prevent absorption of the states by the central government. In practice, several flaws developed. Oftentimes, when legislatures could not agree on a choice, the state lacked full representation in the upper house: Louisiana had only one senator from November, 1872, to January, 1876. It was frequently charged that powerful economic interests controlled some state legislatures and, in fact, named their favorites to office. Some members were called, not "United States Senator," but "Railroad Senator" or "Senator for Standard Oil." Critics charged that Senate seats were bought, and they referred to the chamber as the "Millionaire's Club." Amendment XVII, proclaimed in 1913, provided for the direct election of senators at large.

Election to the Senate involves processes quite different from those leading to election for the House of Representatives. In the first place, there are fewer "one-party" seats. Secondly, since their terms are staggered in order to keep the Senate a continuing body, only a third of the seats are available each two years, and so voters may elect but two senators (four or more candidates) every six years, increasing voter interest. Thirdly, since senators always run at large, they must stump the entire state rather than a district composed of a few counties (or sometimes, even only part of a city) and so are widely known. Fourthly, because of the larger constituency, candidates for the Senate must spend considerably more money in their campaigns than is generally the case with representatives from the same state. Finally, the office has more prestige, and hopefuls are almost always men and women with more experience and renown than their colleagues in the House.[19] A glance at the biographies of successful candidates for the Senate indicates that their political reputations have usually been established in the House of Representatives. The next most popular training ground is the governorship. It is not surprising that about one out of 10 men first went to the Senate as appointees to fill vacancies, for once seated, the senator may campaign as an incumbent and thus improve the odds of being elected in his own right. Frequently, when vacancies occur, a politically ambitious governor will resign his office with the understanding that he will be named to the Senate by his successor.

Election to the Senate

Restrictions, Immunities, and Ethics

Both houses are authorized to refuse to seat a person who has been duly elected if a majority of the members are persuaded that the member-elect would offend the dignity or moral atmosphere of their chamber. Members of the House have declined to sit with a polygamist (1900) and with one who was considered to have violated espionage laws during World War I. The Senate refused to seat a man who had become notorious for his excessive campaign spending. It is much easier to stop a member-elect at the door than to expel a member who has taken the oath (unless it is found that he was not qualified when he

Expulsion

19. The greater prestige of Senate office can readily be seen if one determines the number of representatives who run for Senate seats as opposed to the number of senators who run for House seats. The traffic flow is in one direction only. In the 91st Congress, for example, there were 39 former House members serving in the Senate, but no former senators serving in the House.

assumed office). Expulsion requires an extraordinary majority of two thirds, and this margin is extremely difficult to muster. The Constitution also provides that a member may be punished by his colleagues for improper behavior. Members are subject to prosecution in the regular courts for treason, felony, and breach of the peace. The Constitution is silent regarding impeachment of members of the Congress, and proceedings have been instituted against only one (a senator, 1788) in history; since he resigned before trial, there is no clear precedent, and the question is still debatable.

Recent cases

In the 1960's three notable cases, one involving the House of Representatives and the other two the Senate, focused attention upon the problem of congressional ethics.[20] The first case involved Bobby Baker, the Secretary to the Senate Democratic Majority who had worked under Senator Lyndon B. Johnson. Baker's business activities were investigated and reported on by the Senate Rules and Administration Committee in 1964 and 1965. A year later he was indicted by a grand jury and in 1967 was convicted in a Federal District Court on charges of income-tax evasion, theft, and conspiracy to defraud the government.[21] Baker's conviction raised the larger problem of future conflict-of-interests situations developing in regard to other congressional employees.

in the House

In 1967 House Democrat Adam Clayton Powell, who had represented Harlem's 18th Congressional District for 22 years, was excluded from his House seat by a 307 to 116 vote. The action taken by the House came as a result of an investigation by a select committee which proved, at least to the majority of the House, that Powell had misused funds allocated to his committee. The Powell case attracted special attention because of its racial overtones. Many in and out of the black community believed what United Nations Under Secretary Dr. Ralph Bunche was quoted as saying: "If Adam Powell had been white he would have his seat today."[22] Others agreed with Representative Morris K. Udall (D., Arizona) that Powell had consistently escaped punishment because he was black. "If he had

20. For a discussion of the ethics problem in Congress see "Ethics in Congress," *Congressional Quarterly Guide to Current American Government* (Washington: Congressional Quarterly, January 1968), pp. 80–84. For a former senator's views on congressional ethics see Paul H. Douglas, *Ethics in Government* (Cambridge: Harvard University Press, 1952).

21. In 1968 attorneys for Baker began arguments that his conviction was gained by means of illegal wiretapping activities by the Federal Government, and that Baker should receive a new trial.

22. David Holmstrom, "Powell Case Leaves 'Harlem Throne' Empty," *Christian Science Monitor*, November 27, 1967.

been a white man we'd have gotten him a long time ago," Udall was quoted as saying, "but this racism thing held a lot of people off."[23] The Harlem voters, in a futile rejection of the verdict by the House, gave Powell 75 percent of their votes in a special election in 1967 to fill the vacant seat. The next year a United States Court of Appeals refused to intervene in the case, stating that to do so would interfere with the legitimate sphere of congressional authority. Then, in the 1968 general election, the voters of Harlem again returned Powell to Washington. Early in 1969 the House voted 252 to 160 to seat Powell on the condition that he pay $25,000 as a fine and forfeit his seniority. Powell accepted the conditions and once more became a member of the House.

In the Senate Thomas J. Dodd (D., Connecticut) received the censure of his colleagues on charges of spending campaign and testimonial dinner funds for personal use.[24] During the Senate investigation of the charges, Dodd maintained he was innocent of wrongdoing. The Dodd investigation caused argument to swirl around the questions of how money given to a senator ought to be used, and to whom staff employees of senators owed their loyalty.[25] **in the Senate**

An outgrowth of the Baker, Dodd, and Powell disclosures was the adoption by both houses of Congress in 1968 of formal codes establishing behavior standards for senators, representatives, and certain employees of Congress in the conduct of their financial affairs. In regard to the Senate, the new rules permit senators to use contributions to defray various expenses associated with maintaining their offices. However, they and certain Senate employees must file a confidential financial statement which may be examined by the Senate Select Committee on Standards and Conduct when a majority of the committee **Formal codes adopted**

23. *Ibid.*

24. Only three other times in its history has the Senate considered a censure of one of its members. In 1955 the Senate voted censure for the first time in 26 years. The recipient was the controversial Joseph McCarthy (whose name had given birth to a new word, "McCarthyism," which describes the practice of making unsubstantiated charges of political disloyalty). The effect of the vote of censure was to isolate Senator McCarthy politically and socially, thus making him ineffective in the Senate. The attitude of the institution toward McCarthy is detailed by William S. White in *Citadel: The Story of the U.S. Senate* (New York: Harper, 1956), pp. 126–33.

25. The investigation of Dodd followed the taking of documents from Dodd's files by an administrative assistant, with a resultant exposé by Drew Pearson and Jack Anderson. James P. Boyd, the assistant who helped launch the investigation of the senator, has written a book on his experiences and senate ethics entitled, *Above the Law* (New York: New American Library, 1968).

votes to do so. Other provisions prohibit most Senate employees from handling campaign contributions and from engaging in outside financial activities which would not be consistent with their official duties.

The problem of contributions

Some dissenting voices were raised against the ethics code. Senator Clifford Case (R., New Jersey) branded the measure a fraud. He criticized his colleagues for causing the voters to believe the Senate had purified itself, "when actually we are making it worse."[26] Case was objecting to that portion of the code which permits contributions to be used for office expenses. During the ethics debate one of the self-appointed holders of the Senate's conscience, Senator Joseph S. Clark (D., Pennsylvania) suggested that permitting senators to accept contributions to pay their expenses was a corrupting practice. His point was that it might be less expensive in the long run for senators to vote themselves the salaries necessary to maintain their offices and families in a dignified style so that contributions could be more stringently controlled. For its part, the House

Herblock from *The Herblock Gallery* (Simon and Schuster, 1968).

"We are met to honor a fine, upstanding statesman—that is, if he actually uses this money for his campaign."

26. Quoted in the *New York Times* (March 23, 1968).

established a Committee on Standards of Official Conduct as a permanent standing committee of 12 members divided equally between the two major parties, and added a Code of Official Conduct to the Rules of the House. The code prohibits members or employees to accept gifts of "substantial value" from persons or groups with a direct interest in legislation being considered by Congress, and prohibits honorariums of more than "the usual and customary value" for articles and speeches. Specified employees are required to do the work for which they are hired, not other activities. Representatives are required to keep campaign and personal funds separate. They and their principal assistants are required to file for the public record a list of sources whence they derive income, and to file the amounts of income from the sources which may be examined by the Committee on Standards of Official Conduct. Although the House overwhelmingly adopted the ethics code, a voice of dissent was heard again from New Jersey. Republican Representative Peter H. B. Frelinghuysen stated his belief the new rules were too unclear to be meaningful.[27]

Members of Congress are accorded certain "immunities" (borrowed from ancient British practices), which are of varying importance today. The "privilege from arrest during attendance at a session of their respective houses and in going to and returning from the same" originated in medieval Britain to prevent the harassment of Parliament by unsympathetic elements. In modern America "treason, felony, and breach of the peace" are excepted; however, a congressman may not be subpoenaed to defend a civil action in court. "For any speech or debate in either house they shall not be questioned in any other place"—an extremely important immunity. It gives a member speaking from the floor freedom to say what he thinks and to criticize the activities of anyone without being liable for slander or defamation. The fact that the privilege has been abused on occasion (such as to heap vilification on personal enemies or make reckless charges that cannot be proved)[28] has not led many to wish to abandon such a firm bulwark of a free and independent legislature. Rules permit calling a member to

Congressional privilege

27. "House Adopts Code of Conduct by 406–1 Vote," *Congressional Quarterly Weekly Report*, XXVI (April 5, 1968), pp. 692–693 summarizes the debate.

28. An example of one such charge is Mississippi Senator James O. Eastland's attack on the Supreme Court, particularly Chief Justice Warren. In debate on civil-rights legislation in 1962, Eastland alleged that the Chief Justice "decides for the Communists" whenever there is a choice between them and the security of the United States. *New York Times*, May 3, 1962, p. 1; also *Congressional Record* (daily edition), May 2, 1962, pp. 7026–7034.

order if remarks become too scurrilous, or if he criticizes the actions or members of the sister chamber. In practice public opinion often swings to the side of a private individual who is victimized if his attacker will not repeat his remarks off the safety of the floor.

A Bicameral Legislature:
Differences Between House and Senate

In an attempt to provide equality for the two houses of Congress and yet permit them to check and balance each other, the Founders wrote certain prerogatives for each into the Constitution. Following British practice, bills for raising revenue must originate in the House of Representatives (but once originated, the Senate may amend them to the extent that they become practically new measures). The House has the sole power of impeachment against officers of the executive and judicial branches of the national government. The Senate alone, however, has the sole authority to try impeachment charges. The Senate also must "advise and consent" before treaties and certain appointments of the Chief Executive become binding on the United States.

SIZE AND ORGANIZATION

Centers of power

One of the most important differences between the two houses of Congress is their different sizes. An old political observation, discernible long before *The Federalist* was written but well stated in Number 58, is that "in all legislative assemblies the greater the number composing them may be, the fewer will be the men who will in fact direct their proceedings." The 435 members require that the House of Representatives be tightly organized, and the prodigious powers of the Speaker, the Rules Committee, and committee chairmen appear to be the alternatives to chaos. Parliamentary devices to limit debate and speed up procedure are mandatory with so many participants.[29] The "Big Six"—the Speaker, Majority

29. Parliamentary rules and procedures are explained by George B. Galloway, *History of the United States House of Representatives* (New York: Thomas Y. Crowell, 1962), especially Chapter V. For discussion of the operation of the House see Charles Clapp, *The Congressman: His Work as He Sees It* (Washington: The Brookings Institution, 1963); Neil MacNeil, *Forge of Democracy: The House of Representatives* (New York: McKay, 1963); Clem Miller, *Member of the House* (New York: Charles Scribner's Sons, 1962); and Robert L. Peabody and Nelson W. Polsby (eds.), *New Perspectives on the House of Representatives* (Chicago: Rand-McNally, 1963).

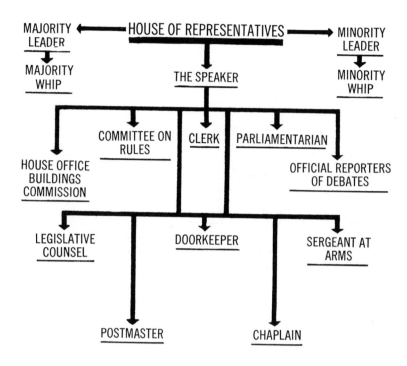

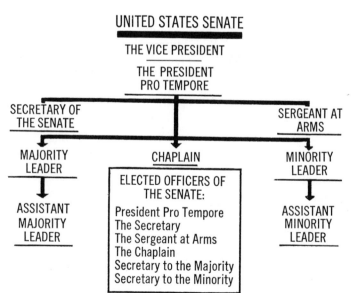

Herblock from *The Herblock Gallery*
(Simon and Schuster, 1968)

Moment of truth.

Leader, Minority Leader, and the chairmen of the Rules, Appropriations, and Ways and Means Committees—dominate the
House. In the Senate power is more dispersed, although the
Majority and Minority Leaders as well as the chairmen of
standing committees are clearly figures of considerable authority. The membership of 100 in the Senate has maintained its
president merely as a presiding officer; there is no Rules Committee; and although committee chairmen have great power,
they do not equal their counterparts in the House of Representatives.[30]

Because the small membership makes it practicable, individual senators may employ the useful, if sometimes frustrating,
Filibuster weapon of the "filibuster." In the House a member's remarks
are limited to one hour unless he has the unanimous consent of
his colleagues to continue, but all debate halts when "the previous question" is moved and passed by a majority. In the
Senate, however, unless agreed to by unanimous consent, rules

30. For views of the methods by which the Senate operates see Joseph
S. Clark, *The Senate Establishment* (New York: Hill and Wang, 1963);
Ralph K. Huitt, "The Outsider in the Senate: An Alternative Role," *Amer-
ican Political Science Review*, LV (September, 1961), pp. 566–575; and
William White, *Citadel: The Story of the U.S. Senate* (New York: Harper,
1956).

for limitation require that a petition to end debate by imposing cloture be signed by 16 senators, voted on the second calendar day following, and passed by an extraordinary majority of two thirds of those senators present and voting. This deliberately cumbersome arrangement to prevent a majority steamroller on matters as controversial as civil rights has the practical effect of allowing endless talk if a third of the members favor it, and if such a minority is adamant, it can force either compromise or abandonment of a bill before the Senate. On occasion a "one-man filibuster" has been attempted, and although it is unlikely to be successful, the spectacle of one senator talking for upwards of 24 hours focuses nationwide attention on an issue and provides an opportunity for public opinion to mobilize. Unwritten rules, reinforced by political sense, preclude the use of the filibuster for frivolous causes.[31]

Act of Closure on a Filibuster

Since the 435 members of the House are divided among 21 standing, or permanent, committees, most of them may serve only on one committee. The 16 standing committees of the Senate permit the 100 senators to serve on at least two, and usually three or four. The smaller Senate affords each member an assigned desk (bearing an inkwell, penholder, and glass shaker filled with blotting sand), whereas the House provides only unassigned chairs for its occupants. In the House, stenographers have given way to mechanized operators, but the Senate still relies on shorthand reporters who range about the room, pencils in hand, ready to sit at an unoccupied desk near the person having the floor.

Committees

TERMS OF SERVICE AND RESPONSIBILITY TO THE ELECTORATE

The House of Representatives must completely reorganize each new Congress, after the entire membership has stood for election the previous November. This requirement has denied the House a tradition of continuity and stability available to the Senate. More important are the facts that a two-year term does not give a Congressman an adequate chance to learn his job and that the potentially short tenure makes it difficult for him to establish the contacts and build the reputation requisite for becoming a national figure. However, able members from

31. A brilliant description of how Senate procedures, including the threat of filibuster, affect the substance of policy is provided by Howard E. Shuman, administrative assistant to former Senator Paul Douglas of Illinois, in "Senate Rules and the Civil Rights Bill," *American Political Science Review*, LI (1957), 955–75. The 1961 attempt of a coalition of liberal Democrats and Republicans to change the present cloture requirement to cloture by a majority of three fifths of those senators present and voting is recounted in Alan Rosenthal, *Toward Majority Rule in the U.S. Senate* (New York: McGraw-Hill, 1962).

safe districts do become as influential as senators, particularly if they serve as the chairmen of powerful committees, and accrue so much power within their own bailiwicks that few of them are interested in exchanging a chair in the House for one of the private desks in the Senate.[32]

Short vs. long terms

The member who represents a genuinely two-party district is obliged to begin campaigning for re-election the day he takes the oath of office. Although it is often said that voters have short memories, the 435 representatives know that two years is a very short time. The result is that they are generally more tightly bound to their constituencies and important interest groups in their districts than are senators. The latter's six-year terms afford them greater independence, which enables them to be freer to follow the dictates of conscience, party, or President. In his 1966 State of the Union Address President Johnson suggested a constitutional amendment which would lengthen the terms of congressmen from two to four years. The suggestion was greeted with loud and prolonged applause, presumably from the House members in the audience.[33] Proponents of the measure claim that the greater time between elections would enable representatives to participate more fully in the business of the Congress before having to return home for campaigning. Some who oppose the proposal note that its passage would make it more difficult for popular political changes to be reflected in the lower house.

A former distinction between the Senate and House, the overrepresentation of rural interests in the latter due to the failure of state legislatures to reapportion congressional districts to reflect population shifts to the cities, is fading into history. As previously mentioned, most state congressional districts have been reapportioned since the *Wesberry* decision in 1964.

SENIORITY

Committee chairmen

If a representative successfully completes the hurdles of re-election every two years, he stockpiles the essential raw material for power in the House: seniority. The chairmanship of standing committees goes to the ranking (*i.e.*, senior) member

32. Representative Carl Vinson of Georgia, for example, began his service in the House in 1914 and was chairman of the Armed Services Committee for more than 10 years. His influence in the Pentagon was so immense that when someone suggested that he would be the logical choice for President Truman's Secretary of Defense, he replied: "Hell, I'd rather run the Pentagon from up here on the Hill" (James Reston, "Take to the Hills, Men—The Swamp Fox's Loose," *New York Times*, March 9, 1962).

33. For a study of the two-year term, its effects on the House of Representatives, and some alternatives, see Charles O. Jones, *Every Second Year* (Washington: The Brookings Institution, 1967).

of the majority party, and this is the plum all congressional politicians seek. Committee chairmen may resemble feudal lords, with life-and-death power over legislation that finds its way to their realms. Although a despotic chairman might be tamed by an aggressive majority of committee members, his control of the agenda and staff of the committee, and his prerogatives to accord recognition and assign chairmen and members to subcommittees, usually induce his colleagues to go along with his leadership. Seniority is important in the short run too, since assignment to a major committee like Appropriations, Rules, or Ways and Means generally goes to members who have already served their apprenticeship and have learned the arts of flexibility, compromise, and moderation, all of which are highly regarded by the House leadership.[34] As the tides of party fortune change and party representation on committees is reduced to reflect the change, the junior members are the first to lose their positions on desirable committees.

Because of the power associated with the seniority principle much controversy swirls about it, most particularly as it is applied in the selection of committee chairmen in the House of Representatives.[35] Seniority is criticized for giving power to legislators who come from stagnant, one-party areas of the nation, removed from the mainstream of political development. Other critical views are that seniority is often associated with age, which may mean it is associated with senility and a tendency to cling to outmoded ways. Furthermore, it is claimed that seniority undercuts party responsibility and presidential leadership.[36]

Seniority in the House

34. Assignments to standing committees are made by the two party "committees on committees." House Democrats use their Ways and Means committee members as a committee on committees. Republicans use a committee made up of members from each state with Republican representation, with votes weighted according to the number of Republicans in the House from their states. In assignments to the major committees, the party leaders also play an extremely influential role. An intensive analysis of the processes of committee assignments is Nicholas A. Masters, "Committee Assignments in the House of Representatives," *American Political Science Review*, LV (June, 1961), 345–57.

35. Those who make claims for, or charges against, the seniority system might do well to temper their thinking by reading the thoughts of Heinz Eulau concerning the human factor in matters of organization. "Whatever system of chairman selection be adopted by a legislative body, for instance, there will always be good and bad presiding officers, and many who are in between." See "The Committees in a Revitalized Congress," in Alfred de Grazia, ed., *Congress: The First Branch of Government* (Garden City: Doubleday, 1967), p. 206.

36. Arguments for and against the seniority principle can be found in: George Goodwin, Jr., "The Seniority System in Congress," *American Political Science Review*, LIII (June, 1959), pp. 412–436; and Emanuel Celler, "The Seniority Rule in Congress," *Western Political Quarterly*, 14 (March, 1961), pp. 160–167.

Among congressmen most sympathetic to such charges are new-comers and representatives from genuine two-party districts outside the "safe" areas of the Midwest (for Republicans) and South (for Democrats).[37] Among the chief arguments in support of the seniority system are that it eliminates intraparty feuds for committee positions, that it emphasizes experience and wisdom, and finally that there is no suitable alternative. To date the congressional critics have not been able to convince most of their colleagues that the seniority system ought to be changed.

Seniority is important in the Senate for the same reasons, but the longer term and the smaller membership make a senator **Seniority in the** less dependent upon seniority as a requisite for establishing a **Senate** reputation. Furthermore, with limited manpower, the chances for a senator to become a subcommittee chairman in his first term are extremely good. Seniority has several interesting by-products in the Senate which are not available in the House. The member of the state delegation who has longer service is known as the "senior senator" and, if he belongs to the President's political party, he receives little favors denied to the "junior senator." For example, in 1960 the senior senator from a western state was notified five minutes before his colleague that the government was granting a large contract to a defense plant in his state. This gave him an opportunity to make the announcement first, and thus get the credit. Had the senior senator not been of the same party as the President whereas the junior senator had been, harassed agency officials would have had to decide between the competing claims of seniority and party. If the news had been unfavorable to the "folks back home," either the state's entire congressional delegation would have made the sad announcement together or, more likely, would have left to the agency the task of breaking the bad news.

Another facet of the role of seniority is found in the custom of "senatorial courtesy." According to the "self-help" tradition **Senatorial courtesy** of the Senate, appointments to Federal offices entirely within one state must be cleared with the appropriate senators before

37. In the Second Session of the Democratically controlled 90th Congress Southerners held 20 of the 36 standing-committee chairmanships. Texas led with five chairmanships, followed by Louisiana and Arkansas with three apiece, Mississippi, Maryland, and South Carolina each held two, and North Carolina, Alabama, and Georgia had one each. Theories concerning Southern influence in Congress are examined by Raymond E. Wolfinger and Joan Heifetz in "Safe Seats, Seniority, and Power in Congress," *American Political Science Review*, LIX (June, 1965), pp. 337–349.

being submitted for confirmation. If this is not done, and either of the senators share the party tie with the President, the nomination can be defeated if the offended senator wishes to make an issue of it. If either senator objects to a nomination (and is of the same party as the President), the Senate will almost surely reject the appointee. If both senators are in the same party with the President and disagree on the nomination, the attitude of the senior senator will almost always be adopted by the Senate.

Congressional Organization

The 535 members of Congress who come to Washington from farms and metropolitan areas stretching from Alaska to Florida come there to represent and further the interests of their constituents and to promote the general welfare of the entire nation. This is their job, the accomplishment of which requires them to initiate legislation, modify or ratify bills initiated elsewhere, gather information, deliberate and talk, adjudicate disputes, perform favors and express grievances for folks back home, and oversee the burgeoning administrative bureaucracy. With so many members of Congress, representing different constituencies and performing dissimilar and often contradictory functions, it is obvious that some system of authority is needed to bring order where chaos might otherwise prevail. The Constitution is extremely sketchy on the topic of congressional organization and merely gives the Representatives authority to choose their Speaker "and other officers," while it stipulates that the Vice President of the United States shall be President of the Senate (but not a member, and with no vote except in case of tie) and that "the Senate shall choose their other officers, and also a President pro tempore . . ." How the two chambers decided to organize is now to be considered.

THE HOUSE: THE SPEAKER

The Speaker of the House, a person of enormous power and responsibility, is rewarded for his efforts by an annual salary of $43,000 with $10,000 for expenses, both of which are taxable. It is probably not an exaggeration to place him second only to the President in terms of formal political power. Unlike the Speaker in the House of Commons, who is traditionally impartial, the Speaker of the House of Representatives is the leader of the majority party in the House, and even when he wields

The Speaker's power

197

the gavel, he is not entirely impartial.[38] Theoretically elected by the chamber, he is in practice nominated by the majority party (having been selected in caucus) and elected by a strictly partisan vote in the House. (In 1962, for example, in voting for a successor to the late Speaker Sam Rayburn, every Democrat present supported John W. McCormack, while every Republican supported the G.O.P. Minority Leader, Charles A. Halleck.)

Among the responsibilities of the Speaker is that of maintaining order in the House of Representatives, a body never famous for its tranquility. He may censure a disturber from the chair, but ordinarily mentioning the name of the offender is enough to silence him. The Speaker has the power of recognizing members who wish to have the floor, but this power is now rather narrowly limited by House rules and conventions. When committee bills are debated, recognition resides theoretically in the Chair, but actually time and debate are controlled by the committee members in charge of the legislation being considered. The Speaker also must rule on points of order, and, although he has about a dozen volumes of Hind's and Cannon's *Precedents of the House of Representatives* to guide him, he can himself establish precedents on occasion (Speaker Reed in 1890 ruled that a quorum was present when members who were physically in the chamber did not answer to the roll call). The Speaker names members to select and conference committees. Before 1911 he could also choose the membership of standing committees, but today he can only influence the choices made by the committee on committees. He has the power to refer bills to committee, and his choice of committee can determine whether the bill will ever come out again. As presiding officer, he puts questions and announces the vote, and signs all bills and legal papers of the House. As a top congressional leader, he frequently confers with the President, and if he and the Chief

The Speaker's responsibilities

---

38. There was a time when the Speaker was even more powerful. This was before the domination of Speaker Joseph Cannon was challenged by a "revolt" of the House in 1910–1911. At that time the Speaker was removed from membership of the Rules Committee and lost the power to appoint standing committees. For a recounting of the clipping of "Uncle Joe's" wings see Kenneth Hechler, *Insurgency* (New York: Columbia University Press, 1941). The Speaker's power is still formidable as suggested by the following poem.

> "I love Speaker Rayburn, his heart is so warm,
> And if I love him he'll do me no harm,
> So I shan't sass the Speaker one least little bitty
> And then I'll wind up on a major committee."

New York Times, April 8, 1958, p. 28, as quoted in George Goodwin, Jr., *op. cit.*, pp. 412–415.

Executive belong to the same party, he serves as liaison agent between the White House and the House of Representatives. The successful Speaker of the House, who follows in the great tradition begun by Henry Clay, is generally a man of long service with a reputation for fairness, character, and sense of humor.

THE HOUSE: THE RULES COMMITTEE

Subject of much controversy—defended by traditionalists and attacked by reformers—the House Rules Committee still wields extraordinary influence over the many bills which fall **Practices** under its jurisdiction. Much of the Rules Committee's power stems from its practice of issuing special orders which authorize a bill to be moved from the committee considering it to the floor of the House for debate, and a resultant vote. The special order is considered by the entire House immediately after it is issued, and upon a majority vote it is put into effect. This type of control, which prevents the jamming of the legislative ma-

Alexander in The Philadelphia Bulletin.
"In charge of arrangements."

199

chinery, also permits the Rules Committee to keep some bills from ever receiving consideration. In addition to releasing a bill to the floor for debate, the Rules Committee confers informally with leaders from both parties and (when backed by a majority vote in the House) sets the "rules" (the time for debates and amendments). Time is always divided equally between the two parties. If debate is strictly curtailed and kept in the hands of a few speakers, with no amendments permitted from the floor, the procedure is known as a "gag rule."[39]

Recent changes During the 1960's several important changes were made in the Rules Committee and the manner in which it operates. After several years during which the "conservatively" dominated Rules Committee refused to report special orders for legislation favored by "liberals," the House voted, in 1961, to enlarge the committee's membership. By a close vote of 217 to 212, the number of members on the Rules Committee was increased from 12 to 15, and thus "liberal" individuals were added who were favorably disposed toward the legislative program of President Kennedy.[40] Another change came in 1965 when the House reduced the Rules Committee's influence still further by constraining its authority to issue special orders. The change authorized the Speaker to permit a committee chairman, or other proper person, to bring a bill approved by a committee onto the floor of the House, despite the fact the Rules Committee had ruled against such a move or had not issued a special order favoring the move, provided the bill had been before the Rules Committee for 21 days.

A rarely used device to force the Rules Committee, or any other committee, to move a bill to the floor is the Discharge Petition. This difficult procedure requires 218 members, a majority of the House, to sign a petition to release a bill after it has been before a committee for 30 days.

THE HOUSE: PARTY LEADERS

Although party chiefs rather than House officials, the Majority and Minority Floor Leaders rank in power directly below,

---

39. The immense power of the House Rules Committee can be seen in Hugh Douglas Price's study of the legislative history of the 1961 Federal aid-to-education bill, "Race, Religion and the Rules Committee: the Kennedy-Aid-to-Education Bill," in Alan F. Westin, ed., *The Uses of Power* (New York: Harcourt, Brace & World, 1962). For an over-all examination of the operations of the Rules Committee see James Robinson, *The House Rules Committee* (Indianapolis: Bobbs-Merrill, 1963).

40. The vote for enlargement of the committee included 195 Democrats and 22 Republicans, the vote against consisted of 64 Democrats and 148 Republicans. *New York Times* (February 5, 1961).

the Speaker and are constantly in contact with him.[41] The Minority Leader is assumed to be the leader of his party and heir presumptive to the Speaker's chair whenever his party obtains a majority. He confers with the President often and, if they belong to the same political party, serves a liaison capacity between the members of the House and the Chief Executive. His influence on the agenda of the chamber depends largely on his relationship with the Majority Leader, but without close cooperation between the two parties the work of the House of Representatives could not get done. The Majority Leader is generally regarded as the "number two" man of his party—next in line for the Speakership or slated to be reduced to the position of Chief Whip of his party should lose its majority in the House and the Speakership change hands. The Floor Leaders, tacticians for their parties, are largely responsible for incorporating partisan views into matters before the chamber. When important bills are set for discussion, the party leaders meet with the Speaker, chairman, and ranking members of the committee in charge to decide who will be permitted to speak on the measures, thus reinforcing the tie which binds individual members to their leaders. The Floor Leaders are aided in their functions by the party whips, who serve as liaison between the members and the leadership and whose job it is to know the whereabouts of every member of the party at all times so that party strength can be mustered whenever needed. The task, which requires much stamina and patience, is generally undertaken as a good-will project to be rewarded by favors from the party leaders. The position of Chief Whip is considered to be an advanced steppingstone to the floor leadership.[42]

Majority and Minority leaders

ORGANIZATION OF THE SENATE

The system of authority which operates in the House of Representatives is not quite as visible in the more individualistic Senate. Unlike the Speaker of the House, the President of the Senate is a very dispensable cog in the congressional machinery. In fact, he is frequently absent since his official role as Vice President of the United States is more rewarding than presiding

Presiding office

41. A useful bibliography and research guide concerning party activity in Congress is Charles O. Jones and Randall B. Ripley, *The Role of Political Parties in Congress* (Tucson: University of Arizona Press, 1966).

42. A hint of changing times occurred early in 1969 when 46-year-old Morris K. Udall (D., Arizona) made a bid to wrest the Speakership from 77-year-old John McCormack (D., Massachusetts). Even though he lost (the vote was 178 to 58) Udall's effort drew considerable comment from political observers, and the seniority principle seemed a little less secure than formerly.

over the deliberations of a body of which he is not a member. To fill the anticipated vacancy of the presiding officer, the majority party elects one of its members to be President pro tempore. Generally, the official is chosen more out of respect than for his leadership since, unlike the Speaker, he is expected to be nonpartisan. According to Senate custom, he is expected to recognize the Majority Leader first when the party chief wants the floor. Before referring disputed bills to a committee, he usually consults not only with the Senate Parliamentarian but also with the leaders of both political parties. In short, his powers are nominal; he is generally limited to putting the vote, signing papers and deciding points of order. The Vice President receives a salary of $43,000 and $10,000 for expenses, all taxable. If he is elevated to the Presidency, dies in office, or resigns, this salary is paid the President pro tempore.

Party leaders   Although the senators, in conference (a word they and House Republicans prefer to "caucus"), elect Majority and Minority Floor Leaders and Whips, their individual freedom has prevented the rise of party managers with the power of those in the House of Representatives. Occasionally a leader with a happy combination of personality, political savoir-faire, and integrity has been able to weld his colleagues into a partisan unity by persuasion and the deft management of political I.O.U.'s. Former President Lyndon B. Johnson, who served as the Democratic floor leader from 1953 until his election as Vice President, was a master legislative craftsman whose power of persuasion consistently molded Senate majorities for Administration bills. For Johnson, persuasion depended not only on his ability to grant favors to other senators or on his mastery of parliamentary technique, but also on his personal influence with his colleagues. Johnson always worked closely with the Republican leader, who sat directly across the aisle from him in the Senate chamber. The Majority and Minority Leaders—whether Johnson or Mike Mansfield, William Knowland or Everett McKinley Dirksen—maintain contact with one another and with their party's leaders in the House of Representatives and the Administration. Working with committee chairmen and individual senators, the floor leaders are in a strategic position to influence the outcome of the legislative struggle, although they can neither dictate nor completely dominate.[43]

43. Party leadership in the Senate is analyzed by David B. Truman in *The Congressional Party* (New York: Wiley, 1959), pp. 94–144. In 1969 Senator Edward M. Kennedy (D., Massachusetts) defeated Senator Russell B. Long (D., Louisiana) for the position of Assistant Majority Leader. Speculation immediately began concerning the political consequences of the elevation for the last of the Kennedy brothers, and what it would mean for the operation of the Senate.

CONGRESSIONAL PUBLICATIONS

The utterances of congressmen, which are seldom heard by the majority of their colleagues, are recorded and preserved for posterity in a daily publication (later rebound into a permanent record) known as the *Congressional Record*. This rather unattractive production (which is printed in small print on poor-grade paper, lacks the delightful humor of the British *Parliamentary Debates*, and costs the taxpayers $113 a page) apparently gives a verbatim account of what was said in each chamber. In practice, however, the privilege is accorded members to edit, revise, and extend their remarks. The constitutional requirement that "each house shall keep a journal of its proceedings, and from time to time publish the same, excepting such parts as may in their judgment require secrecy" is met by the publication of the *House Journal* and the *Senate Journal*. These volumes do not contain speeches, but they are convenient sources for ascertaining the actions of each house. The *Senate Journal* does not include proceedings while that body is in executive (secret) session; these are printed years later by special Senate order in volumes known as the *Senate Executive Journal*. Since the *Executive Journal* is primarily concerned with treaties and nominations, possible personal and national embarrassment is prevented by delayed publication.

The Congressional Record

Bills Into Laws

The primary concern of Congress is the thousands of bills (public and private) and resolutions (joint, concurrent, and simple) which are introduced every year.[44] All bills and resolutions must be introduced by a member of Congress and are considered to be "alive" until the two-year "Congress" ends. The odds are that over 90 percent of them will be either killed or permitted to die in committee.[45] The number of bills and

44. A "public bill" is of concern to the country at large (*e.g.*, to extend the draft); a "private bill" is for the benefit of individuals (*e.g.*, to permit the immigration of a person outside the regular quota). A "resolution" uses the word "resolve" instead of "enact" in the enacting clause. A "simple resolution" is passed only by one house, and a "concurrent resolution" is passed by both houses. These usually convey attitudes of Congress and do not go to the President. "Joint resolutions" require the action of the President in order to have the force of law, except for amendments proposed to the Constitution which do not need his approval.

45. As Woodrow Wilson wrote in 1884: "As a rule, a bill committed is a bill doomed. When it goes from the clerk's desk to a committee-room it crosses a parliamentary bridge of sighs to dim dungeons of silence whence it will never return." *Congressional Government* (New York: Meridian Books, 1956), p. 63.

203

resolutions introduced in one Congress has numbered more than 44,000, but between 15,000 and 20,000 is more usual. Granted congressmen's talents, it is still impossible for 535 people to think up so many potential laws within a period of two years. Where do they come from?

THE ORIGINS OF BILLS

"Administration measures"

Most of the important public bills come from the executive branch of government. These "Administration measures" are accorded preferred treatment before the Congress because they are introduced by acknowledged spokesmen for the President. This does not guarantee that they will be approved, but the members know that the party leaders have a special interest in them. If the President is willing to fight for their passage, he has a bag of political tricks to employ, beginning with the subtle pressure of personal contact with the legislators and ending with an attempt to "light a fire under Congress" by appealing to the people. About two thirds of the major laws of Roosevelt's first term of the "New Deal" were Administration measures. In his frequent "fireside chats" by radio, F.D.R. successfully persuaded the voters to urge the Congress to support his legislation. Lyndon Johnson used his powers of persuasion effectively with the Congress. Although his legislative accomplishments were partially overshadowed in the public's mind by the Vietnamese war, Johnson left office in early 1969 with a monumental record of legislative accomplishments. Among the most important laws passed with his backing are the Civil Rights Act of 1964, the Voting Rights Act, the Open Housing Act, Medicare, consumer protection acts, housing acts, some controls upon the sale of firearms, and a series of Conservation and National Park bills. Other Presidents have been less successful or have been disinclined to pressure Congress, probably from the conviction that to do so would violate the principle of separation of powers. Today, whatever the President's conception of his role as legislative leader, Congress has come to rely upon him for what it needs most—a legislative agenda, including some determination of priorities.[46]

Interest-group proposals

Interest groups as well participate in the formulation of legislative proposals. For example, veterans' organizations prepare many bills to help their members. The Guffey Coal Act, one of the important laws of the 1930's, was written by lawyers from the United Mine Workers. Local interests, and even private cit-

46. The historian Wilfred E. Binkley has surveyed the relationship of the Presidency and the Congress in *President and Congress* (New York: Vintage Books, 1962).

izens, also provide a multitude of proposals which are more or less ably drafted. A member of Congress ordinarily has no hesitancy about introducing such measures. If he agrees with the purpose, he may even campaign actively for its passage, but if not he has the bill marked "by request," which indicates that he is merely introducing it for someone else. Request bills have a very high mortality rate, but the congressman can always go home with clean hands, telling the interest groups that he introduced their pet schemes only to have them killed by the reactionaries (or radicals).

SPONSORSHIP AND "FIRST READING"

The origins of a legislative proposal are complex indeed. Usually the ideas incorporated in a bill introduced in Congress stem from a multiplicity of sources—officials of the executive branch, spokesmen for interest groups, and legislators themselves.[47] Once a bill is drafted, it must be introduced and sponsored by a member of Congress. In the House a bill may carry only the name of one member, but any number of senators may sponsor the same bill. Where several similar bills are introduced, the standing committees consider them together and may report on only one (which incorporates ideas of others) or may choose to redraft a new one (a "clean bill") which will take the name of a member of the committee. The famous Taft-Hartley Law took the names of the Senate and House committee chairmen.

Although any bill (except one to raise revenue) may begin its long struggle for enactment into law in either chamber, the House of Representatives provides a better opportunity for discussion of the process, since it is much more complex than the Senate. Bills are introduced in the House by the member simply dropping them into "the hopper"—a box on the Clerk's desk. In the Senate a member must be recognized and formally announce that he wishes to introduce a bill. The parliamentary tradition provides for three "readings." In Britain, reading a bill was mandatory since not all members were literate, and three readings were considered necessary because the unpaid members of the House of Commons who had outside employment were frequently not present. In America today the "first reading" is reduced to the publication of the title of the bill in the *Congressional Record*.

A bill is introduced

47. For fascinating accounts of the involved history behind one bill, see Stephen K. Bailey's case study of the Employment Act of 1946, *Congress Makes a Law* (New York: Vintage, 1964), and a recent case study of the Education Act of 1965: Eugene Eidenberg and Roy Morey, *An Act of Congress* (New York: Norton, 1969).

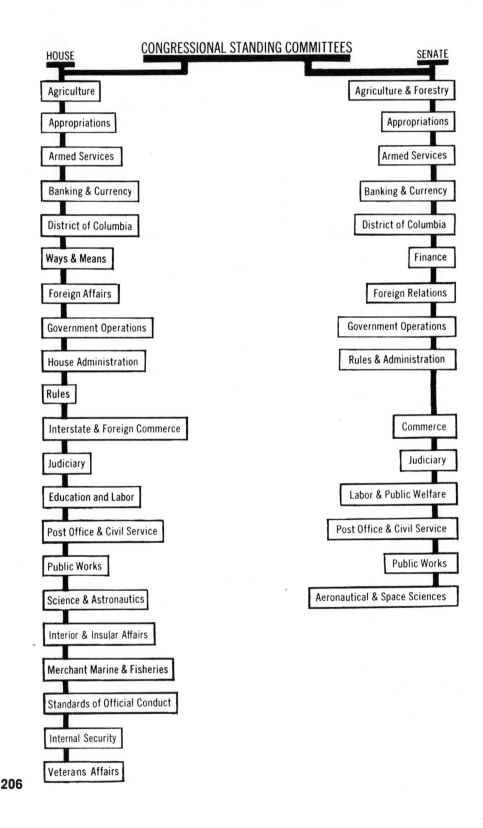

CONGRESSIONAL STANDING COMMITTEES

HOUSE

- Agriculture
- Appropriations
- Armed Services
- Banking & Currency
- District of Columbia
- Ways & Means
- Foreign Affairs
- Government Operations
- House Administration
- Rules
- Interstate & Foreign Commerce
- Judiciary
- Education and Labor
- Post Office & Civil Service
- Public Works
- Science & Astronautics
- Interior & Insular Affairs
- Merchant Marine & Fisheries
- Standards of Official Conduct
- Internal Security
- Veterans Affairs

SENATE

- Agriculture & Forestry
- Appropriations
- Armed Services
- Banking & Currency
- District of Columbia
- Finance
- Foreign Relations
- Government Operations
- Rules & Administration
- Commerce
- Judiciary
- Labor & Public Welfare
- Post Office & Civil Service
- Public Works
- Aeronautical & Space Sciences

THE BILL IN COMMITTEE

After the first reading a bill is sent to a standing committee for its action. Today, as in 1884 when Woodrow Wilson wrote his classic *Congressional Government*, the House of Representatives "virtually both deliberates and legislates in small sections." Because of the great pressure of a huge workload, the complexity of measures to be considered, and the inability of Congress as a whole to study and deliberate each bill introduced at a session, the division of congressional labor into the 21 permanent committees in the House and the 16 in the Senate is absolutely necessary.[48] But as a result, committees have come to exercise greater influence over affairs in their own bailiwicks than Congress as a whole. Power, as Wilson noted, is divided among subject-matter specialists, and today almost as much as in the past, committees rule "without let or hindrance." Since members spend approximately 30 percent of their time on committee work, they become experts over the years; their colleagues, therefore, who cannot be equally proficient on many subjects, generally defer to committee recommendations if committee members are in substantial agreement.

Recent research points out the special utility of the committee system. For example, one study noted that the opportunity for political bargaining is facilitated by the "intimacy of personal relations" found in the committee settings.[49] While efficiency may be reduced by the lengthy give-and-take of committee deliberations, there seems to be no other alternative than the undesirable one of Congress voting "blind" on bills insufficiently studied and debated.[50] According to this same study the evidence indicates that committee hearings reach their peak of utility when members participate as protagonist and antagonist.[51] Another student of politics contends that the rising complexity of the division of labor gives to House members the opportunity to specialize and so enhance their influence on particular policy matters within a large political system.[52] Of this situation he writes, "Considered separately,

Deliberation

Value of the committee system

48. The House and Senate each contribute members to joint committees, such as the Joint Committee on Atomic Energy, and conference committees established to resolve differences between Senate and House versions of the same bill. Each chamber establishes its own special or select committees. These are created for particular purposes, generally investigative in nature, and they serve for a limited time.

49. Eulau in de Grazia, *op. cit.*, p. 219.

50. *Loc. cit.*

51. *Ibid.*, p. 241.

52. Polsby, *op. cit.*, p. 166.

the phenomenon of specialization may strike the superficial observer as productive of narrow-minded drones. But the total impact of a cadre of specialists operating over the entire spectrum of public policies is a formidable asset for a political institution; and it has undoubtedly enabled the House to retain a measure of autonomy and influence that is quite exceptional for a twentieth-century legislature."[53]

Committee size and organization

Committees in the House vary in size from the large and powerful Appropriations Committee (50 members) to the nine members who comprise the Internal Security Committee. In the Senate the range is from 27 members (Appropriations) to seven (District of Columbia). Much of the spade-work in the committees is done by numerous subcommittees, some of which have become powerful in their own right. Congressional committees rely heavily upon various staff members to assist the representatives and senators in their legislative, investigative, and administrative functions. Hopefully these individuals are highly qualified specialists whose knowledge and abilities complement the skills and experience of committee members. Nagging questions concerning committee staffs continue over whether enough staff assistance is being provided to the committees and whether the salaries are sufficient to attract the most qualified individuals.[54] Committee members are also assisted by the Office of the Legislative Counsel, which is concerned with bill drafting, and the Legislative Reference Service of the Library of Congress, a research activity. The party membership on standing committees reflects the proportionate size of the two major parties in the chamber (with no quota assigned for minor parties). The influence of the members is largely determined by seniority. The chairman is traditionally the senior member of the majority party.

Doomed bills

The majority of bills which go to a committee never emerge. Their disappearance may be desirable in view of the many duplications and the large number of frivolous request measures, but many worthwhile bills are denied consideration simply because of the pressure of business and the lack of an ardent champion. A hostile chairman can virtually condemn a proposal to death in a "pigeonhole" of his desk. When a bill is improperly referred (by accident or design), the committee to which it goes has jurisdiction unless the House decides to

53. *Loc. cit.*

54. For a study of the staffing system used by Congress see Kenneth Kofmehl, *Professional Staffs of Congress* (Lafayette: Purdue Research Foundation, 1962).

re-refer it by a simple majority vote. Improperly referred bills, unless rescued, are practically doomed.

If committee members desire hearings on bills before them, and time permits, open hearings are held. Individuals and groups who are interested in the proposal, such as lobbyists, experts, and private citizens, are given an opportunity to read a statement to the committee and then answer questions raised by members. The transcript of the hearing is preserved and printed as a public document. After all the arguments have been heard, the committee members go into executive session in order to "mark up the bill"—that is, to decide how the language will be changed and what their decision will be. The public is denied entry to these closed meetings, or to hearings held in executive session where classified matters relating to national security are being discussed. Bills which survive the standing committee may emerge wholly intact, with amendments, or be revised entirely. The bill is reported out of committee by its chairman and is accompanied by a committee report explaining its provisions. If a minority of members disagree with the bill as reported, a minority report or separate minority views will generally accompany the committee or majority report. The attitudes toward a bill taken by members are not necessarily along partisan lines.

Committee hearings

THE BILL ON THE FLOOR

The reported bill is given a number (*e.g.*, H.R. 100) and assigned to one of the three calendars in the House: the "Union Calendar" is appropriate for public bills raising or appropriating revenue; the "House Calendar" receives other public bills; the "Private Calendar," as the name implies, is for private bills.[55] Theoretically, the bills are considered by the House in turn, according to the dates reported to the calendars, but in practice some bills, of vital importance to the nation, must be considered immediately; these are known as "privileged bills." With the exception of Appropriations Committee bills, which go directly to the floor, the crucial Rules Committee—as previously described—has the power to release bills from the calendars to the floor.

The "calendars"

55. There is also a special one known as the "Consent Calendar," to expedite passage of bills which have no opposition. Upon request by a member of the House, the Clerk will transfer a bill from the Union or House to the Consent Calendar. Then the bill will be taken in order and almost invariably passed. If, however, there is objection from one member, action will be postponed until the next call of the calendar. At that time, if three members object, the bill is removed from the Consent Calendar and may not appear there again.

The "second reading": Committee of the Whole

Tax, appropriation, and most public bills receive their "second reading" before the Committee of the Whole. This useful and interesting institution had its genesis in medieval England when, in order to rid itself of a Speaker who was believed to be a spy for an unsympathetic monarch, the House of Commons resolved itself into a committee ("The Committee of the Whole House") rather than a chamber of Parliament. Whenever this transformation occurred, the Speaker left his "throne," the mace (an emblematic war club symbolizing the government's power) was placed under the table, and the formalities of parliamentary behavior were relaxed. In America today some of these forms are preserved in the House of Representatives, although the aim is entirely different. The Speaker rises and is replaced by a chairman he has selected; the mace[56] is withdrawn; the quorum is reduced to 100 (instead of a majority of the qualified membership, which is more than twice that number); members are limited to five minutes of speaking at a time; roll call votes are not permitted; and motions for the previous question are out of order. In this streamlined atmosphere bills are given a full reading (unless the membership votes unanimously to waive it), and the give-and-take of debate is possible. It is here that the individual member may propose crippling or strengthening amendments and, if he has support, radically alter the bill. It is also during this stage that the House may waive its rules and permit the addition of amendments to appropriations bills which have nothing to do with

Riders

the proposal. Such amendments, called "riders," are resorted to when Congress believes the President would veto them if presented to him separately. By tacking them on bills appropriating money, it is hoped that the President will swallow the extraneous amendment in order to have the funds voted. This technique often works, for the President, unlike some governors, does not have the power of item veto.

When the Committee of the Whole has finished its considerations, it resolves itself back into the House of Representatives. The Speaker returns, the mace is exhibited, the formality revives, and the chairman informs the Speaker of the committee's action and moves passage of the bill as reported. Debate may be continued, but generally the previous question is ordered immediately and a vote is taken.

If a bill survives the "second reading," it is engrossed and given the "third reading." This reading is by title only unless a

56. The mace is the one physical symbol of government used in Congress; it consists of 13 ebony rods bound by silver strips; at one end is a silver eagle perched on a globe.

member requests that the bill be again read in full. The Speaker usually simply asks for a vote after the title is read, and the bill is either defeated or passed. Ordinarily, the "third reading" is merely a form, since the sentiments of the House have had opportunity for expression in the Committee of the Whole.

The "third reading"

THE BILL IN THE SENATE

A successful bill in the House of Representatives is sent with a message to the Senate. There it is obliged to submit to similar, although abbreviated, procedures including reference to a standing committee (usually with public hearings for a second time) and consideration on the floor. The Senate has only two calendars (one for general and one for executive business) and nothing comparable to the House Rules Committee. Instead, the bills that come before the Senate and the order in which they are taken from the calendar are determined by the Majority and Minority Leaders after informal negotiation. The different composition of the Senate, its freedom of debate, and its weaker leadership provide a very different environment for considering legislation than does the House of Representatives.

VOTING PROCEDURES

Since a bill en route through Congress is frequently subjected to the acid test of voting, some consideration of voting methods is required. One of the favorite forms is "viva-voce" (by voicing "aye" or "no"). This method saves a good deal of time and keeps the votes of the members fairly secret. Any member, however, may ask for a "division," which requires members to stand up and be counted. One fifth of a quorum in the House (but not in the Senate) may demand a vote by "tellers," which obliges the members to rise from their seats and file between two persons at the head of the center aisle. Those in favor of a proposal are counted first; those opposed are then counted. The final method is the "roll call," which must be insisted on by a fifth of those present. The Clerk calls the names of the entire membership, and the voter responds with a "yea" or a "nay"; the roll is read twice so that members not actually on the floor may be summoned by ringing bells and arrive in time to vote. The roll call method is required by the Constitution when voting to override a presidential veto. It is frequently employed by minorities as a tactic to delay action and is sometimes used by proponents of measures which are believed to be popular with the people on the expectation that many congressmen will change their minds when they know they are on record. Some

Roll call

state legislative assemblies use voting machines whereby the legislator merely presses a button for "aye," "no," or "not voting": the votes flash on a scoreboard over the name of the member; they are then photographed for permanent record. The Congress has not favored the adoption of this speedy electronic device for reasons of tradition and, one may suspect, politics.

Pairing

When a member of either chamber of the national legislative branch knows he will be absent, he may arrange to "pair" with a colleague of the opposition—a device which preserves his vote, since he will vote differently from his colleague on each measure. A "general pair" is a written agreement covering a stipulated period of time, while a "live pair" is used only for a particular question. The "paired" person who is present does not vote. Pairs are announced by the clerks and are printed in the *Congressional Record*.

Conference committees

Before a bill may go to the President for his consideration, it must have passed both houses of Congress in a form which is identical down to the last semicolon. Whenever a bill has passed the House and Senate in different form, the measure is referred to a Conference Committee, if one house does not immediately accept the bill as enacted by the other. These *ad hoc* committees, theoretically appointed by the Speaker of the House and the presiding officer of the Senate, are actually selected by the chairmen of the standing committees which had jurisdiction over the bill in dispute. Membership on Conference Committees ordinarily consists of five to seven members from each chamber and reflects both majority and minority views. Sometimes the "managers" (conferees) cannot reach agreement and have to step down, but they can usually iron out differences. The same report must be submitted to each house to be accepted or rejected as a package. If all the differences cannot be adjusted the bill dies.

Final passage

After a bill has been passed in identical form by both houses, it is "enrolled" (printed on parchment with so little space between lines and paragraphs that forgery is impossible), examined by committees for correctness, signed by the Speaker and his Senate equivalent, and forwarded to the President.

THE BILL GOES TO THE PRESIDENT

Upon receipt of a bill from Congress, the President has four options. (1) He may sign the bill, thus making it a law. After final passage, acts are generally published in a temporary form as "slip laws" before they find permanent publication in the official volumes known as *Statutes at Large* (often abbreviated to *Stat.*). Since laws appear in the *Statutes* chronologically, a topical index of all valid laws is needed. This need is met by the publication of the *United States Code* (*U.S.C.*). The *Code* is kept up to date by frequent additions of supplements and occasional reissues of the entire series of volumes. Private laws appear in a special section of the *Statutes at Large*, but are not found in the *U.S.C.* (2) The President may decide not to sign a bill sent him. After 10 days (Sundays excepted) such bills become law without his signature if Congress remains in session. (3) He may not sign a bill, and if Congress adjourns before the 10-day period has expired, the bill dies. This is known as the "pocket veto." Franklin D. Roosevelt initiated the practice of indicating on his pocket vetoes that he did not approve of a bill, thus informing interested persons that had the measure not come with the avalanche of bills which accompany the end of a congressional session, he would have returned it to the proper house with a veto message. (4) He may decline to sign—*i.e.*, he may veto—a bill, returning it to the house of origin with a message explaining his decision. If a two-thirds roll-call vote to pass the measure in spite of the President's attitude is successful, the bill is referred to the other chamber. The bill can be killed in the second house if the extraordinary majority cannot be obtained, but, if it is, the bill becomes the law of the land without the approval of the President.

Presidential options: signature or veto

Private Bills, Traditional "Pork," and Spending for National Security

Although the progress of important public bills through the labyrinth of Congress is followed attentively by many groups in the nation, the lawmakers themselves, and especially the members of the House of Representatives, know that they must not neglect private bills. The little favors they do for constituents and constituency are the best insurance they can buy when it comes to job security. Before the passage of the Legislative Reorganization Act (1946) much of the average congressman's time was devoted to cases such as that of W—— R——. This individual had been dishonorably discharged from the Army for sleeping while on sentry duty in December, 1917. He had been confined until February, 1918, when he was released because of poor physical condition. His congressman set about to change his service record and steered a private law into the statutes in 1946 which provided: "W—— R—— shall hereafter be held and considered to have been honorably discharged from the military service of the United States as a private . . . Provided,

Job-security insurance

213

that no bounty, back pay, pension, or allowance shall be held to have accrued prior to the passage of this Act."[57] Today, the "correction" of military records has been transferred to civilian boards in the Department of Defense—but still the contacts occupy congressional time. Another private law of 1946 compensated certain persons for the loss resulting from their failure to plant crops and save roughage crops in their silos in the early years of World War II (they had been notified by military authorities that their land would be taken to expand an Army post).[58] These days such claimants take their causes to the heads of the governmental departments concerned, or they sue for recovery in Federal courts. Congress no longer need give specific authorization for constructing bridges over navigable streams, having given blanket approval to other officials to exercise judgment in such cases. Even with these changes, the annual volume of private laws is thick, and each of the little acts represents time devoted by a member of Congress and, he hopes, gratitude from someone in his district.

"Pork barrel" legislation

However, the staff of life for the average congressman often has been "pork" ("pork barrel" legislation refers to appropriations of government money for local projects, where politics plays an extraordinary role, sometimes proving to be more important than the usefulness of the project). Some appropriation bills resemble a hodgepodge of private bills "logrolled" through Congress; a research contract here, a new post office there, a river dredged in one section, and a harbor enlarged in another. Many of these improvements are necessary, some are not, but all are accomplished with the cooperation of colleagues and the leadership. Members of Congress soon learn that by trading votes ("logrolling") with other members they can secure majorities for their projects. A congressman from Idaho votes for a new national park in California, a new custom house in Chicago, or deepening a stream in Texas—and goes home with a new dam in his own state. If he has gone along with his party leaders on an important public bill (such as supplying American dollars for use by the World Bank), he can expect their help on the little local projects which mean so much to him.[59]

57. Priv. L. 463, 60 *Stat.* 1144 (1946).

58. Priv. L. 517, 60 *Stat.* 1167 (1946).

59. There are many subjects of traditional pork-barrel legislation—veterans' hospitals, post offices, flood-control projects; etc.—but the most comprehensive vehicle is the annual or biennial rivers and harbors flood-control bill. A close-up of such a bill is given by Stephen K. Bailey and Howard D. Samuel, *Congress at Work* (New York: Holt, 1952), pp. 166–93.

While the long-standing "pork barrel" activities of Congress may be regrettable, rarely has it been charged that they endanger the fundamental character of the nation. Such is not the case with the more than one trillion dollars authorized for defense expenditures by the Congress since the onset of the Cold War.[60] Although it has a humorous side—to the suggestion that another military installation be placed in Georgia, a courageous general is said to have replied, "One more base will sink the state"—the impact and influence of spending for national defense has become a major concern for a number of Americans.[61] The subject of national defense spending is so important that it must be examined in more detail. This is done in Chapter 11.

Nonlegislative Functions of Congressmen

Dipping into the "pork barrel" requires a great deal of time and effort which might be spent on policy decisions of more importance to the nation, but it is, at least, legislating. Some members of Congress bewail the demands made on them which lack the remotest relationship to lawmaking. They complain that they are regarded by their constituents merely as "glorified errand boys" who are in Washington to arrange appointments with government officials for them, to keep in constant contact with Federal agencies in order to ascertain progress on their claims, and to find them jobs. Despite their private resentments, however, congressmen know that "case work" for constituents brings political rewards, especially at election time.

In addition to their tasks of looking out for the needs of their constituents, making laws for the country, and debating proposals inside the Capitol, members of the Congress have an additional function: discussing issues before the people of the nation on television and radio programs, by press interviews, and by numerous public speeches. The presence of so many prestigious and popular orators in Congress has made Washington a gold mine for organizations looking for speakers. Almost every weekend at the Washington airport one can see dozens of popular senators and congressmen coming from and going to all parts of the United States for such appointments. Indeed, a

Public speech-making

60. The reader will recall President Eisenhower's warning regarding the "military–industrial complex" mentioned in Chapter 1.

61. See "The 'Military Lobby'—Its Impact on Congress, Nation," *Congressional Quarterly Weekly Report*, XIX (March 24, 1961), p. 469.

good number of congressmen whose districts are relatively near Washington are referred to as the "Tuesday to Thursday Club," since they spend Mondays, Fridays, and the weekends back in their districts. Some of the absent members are away in order to keep in touch with their law firms or businesses at home, but most are out of town to speak or for reasons directly associated with their congressional functions. Committees often hold hearings in various parts of the United States in order to permit the attendance of people who would not or could not come to the Capitol.

"Junkets"

Very frequently members are off to various parts of the world for what they call "on the spot investigations" and what their critics dismiss as "junkets." On occasion these travelers pay their own expenses, but more often the bills are paid from funds voted to each house for such contingencies. Although the shortcomings of such trips have been pointed out, some of our domestic and many of our important foreign policies have been initiated or revised because of this sort of investigation. It is no doubt true that many a "junketeer" (who is unable to read or speak any language except English) is wined and dined like the V.I.P. that he is, and returns home having learned only what the local ambassadors or military commanders wanted him to learn. It is also true that a few of the visiting congressmen are extremely acute observers and effective agents of goodwill.[62]

CONGRESSMEN AS INVESTIGATORS

The type of investigation that Congress is popularly known for, however, is the probe into domestic matters: subversion, labor racketeering, civil rights, crime and domestic unrest, or questionable business practices.[63] At times an investigation captures the interest of the public to such an extent that the press, radio, and television afford it wide coverage. Hitherto obscure members of Congress gain national publicity, and people argue heatedly as to the methods and propriety of congressional investigations. Investigations do have the potential for being both enormously worth while and dangerous. Certainly, congressmen as legislators need the subpoena power

62. For some of the harmful effects resulting from visits by congressmen to Vietnam, see William R. Corson, *The Betrayal* (New York: Norton, 1968).

63. A notable exception to the normal pattern of investigation into domestic matters has been the activities during the late 1960's of the Senate Foreign Relations Committee. Under the chairmanship of J. William Fulbright (D., Arkansas) this committee repeatedly challenged the American participation in the Vietnamese struggle by "grilling" Administration spokesmen and offering a rostrum to nongovernmental critics of the war.

in order to bring otherwise recalcitrant witnesses and privately owned papers before them so that they may legislate more intelligently. Just as certainly, congressmen as politicians face the constant temptation of using investigations for purposes other than legislative.[64]

The eye-catching headlines usually tell us only about one type of investigaton—those by specially appointed ("select") committees. But actually every standing committee in Congress is charged by law to keep a watchful eye over the Federal agencies within its jurisdiction—a responsibility which requires constant unpublicized probing.[65] The Congress is assisted in its general watchdog responsibilities by the General Accounting Office. Created by statute in 1921, the GAO helps Congress check the operation of the many departments, bureaus, and agencies in the executive branch by auditing the receipts, disbursements, and uses of public moneys.

"Select" committees

All Senate committees, and the House committees on Appropriations, Un-American Activities, and Government Operations, are authorized to use subpoenas to compel people to appear before them and to produce records for examination. The Constitution is silent regarding the power to secure information by forcing private individuals to appear before Congress to testify, but the permissible limits have been, and are being, hammered out by interaction among the three branches of government.

In a leading case which emerged from the congressional investigation of the Teapot Dome Scandal, the Supreme Court pointed out that legislative investigation was an ancient practice in Britain and in the colonies and that Madison himself ("the architect of the Constitution") had voted for such a committee.[66] The Court has established that a house of Congress may punish for contempt since this power is implied in its ability to examine, but when there is no need or intent to legislate, a reluctant witness may not be punished for contempt.[67]

Historical precedents

64. See Douglass Cater's analysis of the publicity purposes of congressional investigations, *The Fourth Branch of Government* (Boston: Houghton Mifflin, 1959), pp. 56–74. A thorough history of congressional investigations is provided by Telford Taylor, *Grand Inquest* (New York: Ballantine Books, 1961).

65. For a study of the control Congress exercises over the "administrative state," and suggestions for more effective control, see Joseph P. Harris, *Congressional Control of Administration* (Washington: Brookings Institution, 1964).

66. McGrain v. Daugherty, 273 U.S. 135 (1927).

67. Anderson v. Dunn, 6 Wheaton 204 (1821). Kilbourn v. Thompson, 103 U.S. 168 (1880).

In the rash of cases which accompanied investigatons of subversion in the 1950's, the Court protected witnesses from being obliged to divulge their private affairs to prying congressmen unless such information was absolutely essential for a legitimate legislative function. In so doing, the Court applied judicial brakes to the speed with which committees, such as the House Un-American Activities Committee, sought public exposure of persons whose loyalty was doubted by its members, thus arousing public opinion against the alleged offenders.[68]

Protecting witnesses

The "due process of law" clause has been used to protect witnesses from committees with vaguely drafted powers, and from answering questions apparently designed to rummage through their personal lives with the hope that something would be turned up. In 1957 the Supreme Court defended a witness' right to refuse to answer questions put to him by the House Un-American Activities Committee which he claimed were improper on the grounds that violence was being done to the "due process" clause.[69] In explaining its decision the Court held that an investigating committee must make clear to its witnesses precisely what topic is under investigation and how the questions being asked are pertinent. In subsequent cases the Court attempted to define even more sharply the precise limits over which a congressional committee must not transgress in questioning a witness.[70] Public indignation arose as many witnesses refused to answer pertinent questions and sought refuge behind the Fifth Amendment, but the Court ruled that the self-incrimination clause was to be accorded a liberal construction in favor of the right it was intended to secure, and refused to allow the state of New York to discharge a college professor who had invoked the privilege.[71] In 1954 the Congress provided an "immunity path" whereby two thirds of a committee may vote to force a witness, in investigations concerning national security, to cooperate in spite of the alleged danger of self-incrimination. The person so obliged is protected from pro-

68. The "father" of the House Un-American Activities Committee, the late Martin Dies (D., Texas) stated during debate on the establishment of the committee, "I am not in a position to say whether we can legislate effectively in reference to this matter, but I do know that exposure in a democracy of subversive activities is the most effective weapon we have." Quoted in Robert E. Cushman, *Leading Constitutional Cases*, 12th Edition (New York: Appleton-Century-Crofts, 1963), p. 379. In February 1969 the Un-American Activities Committee was renamed the Internal Security Committee.

69. Watkins v. United States, 354 U.S. 178 (1957).

70. Barenblatt v. United States, 360 U.S. 109 (1959); Braden v. United States, 365 U.S. 431 (1961); Deutch v. United States, 367 U.S. 456 (1961); and Russell v. United States, 369 U.S. 749 (1962).

218

71. Quinn v. United States, 349 U.S. 155 (1955). Slochower v. Board of Higher Education, 350 U.S. 551 (1956).

secution by either Federal or state courts for any information divulged under this law.[72]

The principle of separation of powers has protected executive and judicial officials from punishment for refusing to appear or give testimony to Congress. In 1949 President Truman forbade any officer of the executive branch to give information concerning the loyalty of employees, and five years later President Eisenhower instructed the Department of the Army not to cooperate with investigations by congressional committees on certain questions. In late 1953, a Justice of the Supreme Court refused to answer a subpoena of the Un-American Activities Committee as did a private citizen, former President Truman. Neither was cited for contempt. More recently President Kennedy invoked the doctrine of executive privilege—the Chief Executive's right to withhold information from Congress. Acting on behalf of his Secretary of Defense, who refused to reveal the identification of a Pentagon censor before the Special Senate Preparedness Subcommittee of the Armed Services Committee, President Kennedy invoked the doctrine on the ground that "it would be contrary to the public interest" to make such information available. There was little Congress could do. Kennedy's position was quickly accepted by the subcommittee chairman, and no member appealed his ruling.[73]

It is very likely that the investigative function of Congress will become increasingly more important. If the demand continues for more direct action by the central government to meet problems at home and abroad, the President will assume more and more of the policy-making power the drafters of the Constitution expected to be exercised by Congress. The increased prominence of the Presidency will be reflected in the number and power of administrative agencies in the executive branch, making Congress more of a critic and less of an initiator of legislation. Critics are most useful when they are informed. Thus should Federal agencies proliferate and expand, they can best be kept responsible by constant scrutiny—a purpose which Congress can serve.[74] If the people continue to fear subversion,

A growing function

72. 68 *Stat.* 745, 18 *U.S.C.* Supp. II § 3486 (1954), sustained in Ullman v. United States, 350 U.S. 422 (1956). See, also, Adams v. Maryland, 347 U.S. 179 (1954).

73. *New York Times*, February 9, 1962, p. 1.

74. Professor Alfred de Grazia has suggested in testimony before Congress that what he terms "legislative postaction review" is developing as a means to enable Congress to supervise executive agencies. He further suggested that Congress must see to it that the agencies respect areas of freedom into which they should not intrude. See Subcommittee on Separation of Powers of the Committee on the Judiciary, United States Senate, 90th Congress, First Session, *Separation of Powers*, Part 1 (Washington: United States Government Printing Office, 1967), p. 166.

the alternative to having Congress make investigations is to leave the probing to executive agencies, which are not nearly so sensitive to the public mood as are elected representatives.

The Congressman and His Constituents

The trustee concept

Any student who has visited Washington or his state capital, and has had a brief meeting with his Federal or state representatives, knows the interest taken in constituents by elected members of any legislative body. However, the precise kind of relationship which does, or ought, to exist between a representative and those who selected him, and the reasons therefore, are still matters about which those who study politics speculate.[75] Perhaps the most quoted statement on the subject was made by Edmund Burke, a member of the British Parliament known for his conservative theory of government. In 1774 Burke told his constituents in Bristol:

> Parliament is not a *congress* of ambassadors from different and hostile interests, which interests each must maintain, as an agent and advocate, against other agents and advocates; but parliament is a *deliberative* assembly of *one* nation, with *one* interest, that of the whole—where, not local purposes, not local prejudices, ought to guide, but the general good, resulting from the general reason of the whole. You choose a member indeed; but when you have chosen him, he is not a member of Bristol, but he is a member of *Parliament*. If the local constituent should have an interest or should form a hasty opinion evidently opposite to the real good of the rest of the community, the member for that place ought to be as far as any other from any endeavour to give it effect.[76]

The delegate concept

Many after-dinner "bull sessions" about politics would reveal another theory of representation—the delegate concept. According to this view representatives are basically similar in interests to those electing them, and they are expected to vote as would their constituents were they sitting in the legislature. Suggestive of this philosophy is the statement by the late Senator Robert S. Kerr (D., Oklahoma) who frankly said this about his interests and those of his constituents:

> I represent the financial institutions of Oklahoma, I am interested in them, and that is the reason they elect me. They

75. See for example Lewis A. Dexter, "What Do Congressmen Hear: The Mail," *Public Opinion Quarterly*, 20 (Spring 1956), pp. 16–27; and Warren Miller and Donald Stokes, "Constituency Influence in Congress," *American Political Science Review*, LVIII (March, 1963), pp. 45–56.

76. Ross J. S. Hoffman and Paul Levack, eds., *Burke's Politics* (New York: Knopf, 1959).

wouldn't send a man here who has no community of interest with them, because he wouldn't be worth a nickel to them.[77]

Within recent years behaviorally trained political scientists have made the point that both the trustee concept described by Burke, and the delegate view expressed by Senator Kerr, are insufficient to explain the relationship between constituents and representative. It has been suggested that the representative-constituent relationship needs to be studied with the overt assumption that the representatives achieve a status different from that of their constituents by virtue of having been elevated by the latter.[78] More research needs to be done to understand and predict the tensions which may arise from the status differences between constituents and representatives, and the role expectations the constituents have for their representatives.

The need for further study

What Is the Matter With Congress?

In an age when the King and the King's justice were suspect, the Founding Fathers established Congress in Article I of the Constitution as the preferred branch of government. Their action contributed to an age characterized by the presence of powerful legislative assemblies. That was nearly 200 years ago. Today the lodgement of political power, particularly since the 1930's, is substantially different from the situation existing in the early days of the nation. For more than three decades the dramatic increase in the power of the executive branch has been noted, generally at the expense of Congress.[79] While all

Executive vs. legislative power

77. Quoted in "Ethics In Congress," *Congressional Quarterly Guide to Current American Government* (Washington: Congressional Quarterly, January, 1968), p. 81.

78. Heinz Eulau, "Changing Views of Representation," in Ithiel de Sola Pool, ed., *Contemporary Political Science: Toward Empirical Theory* (New York: McGraw-Hill, 1967, in cooperation with the American Political Science Association), pp. 53–85.

79. Pendleton Herring wrote in 1934 of President Franklin Roosevelt's power vis-à-vis the Congress in these terms: "Disagreement with his proposals was interpreted by the general public as obstructionism . . . His radio talks to the nation served the double purpose of reassuring the people and breaking down resistance in Congress. Legislators were made only too well aware of the temper of their constituents." "First Session of the Seventy-third Congress, March 9, 1933, to June 16, 1933," *American Political Science Review*, XXVIII (February, 1934), p. 67. In the late 1950's David Truman noted that the "cardinal fact of maturing American federalism in the twentieth century, a fact agreed to almost unanimously," is "the pivotal position achieved for the Presidency under a series of 'strong' Chief Executives dealing with an almost unbroken series of domestic and world crises." *The Congressional Party* (New York: John Wiley & Sons, 1959), p. 9. In the 1960's former Senator Joseph Clark (D., Pennsylvania) observed, "In times of peril the President can act because the Congress will recede. If he can cite statute, he will; if not, he will act anyway, as Lincoln and FDR did." *Congress—The Sapless Branch* (New York: Harper & Row, 1964), p. 105.

the evidence is not yet in, and the inquiry continues, one may state with confidence that a preeminent characteristic of American government in the mid-portion of the twentieth century has been the growth of executive power in the Federal Government at the expense of legislative power.[80]

Congress has officially taken cognizance of the decline in its power. In 1967 the Senate established a Subcommittee on separation of Powers to inquire into the current power relationship between Congress and the two other branches of government, and to ascertain means of reestablishing the authority of Congress. The comments of Senator Sam Ervin (D., North Carolina), the subcommittee chairman, are illustrative of widely held views as to why power has gravitated into the hands of the President and other officials in the executive branch:

> In short, all three of our basic concepts—constitutionalism, federalism, and separation of powers—are thought by many to be outmoded means of carrying on affairs in the 20th century when all governments are "crisis governments" and the great need is for strong central leadership able to make decisions and take action before the opportunity for constructive action is past. Instead of encouraging such leadership and facilitating the decision-making process, the critics say, our system of federalism and separation of powers invites delay, obstruction, obfuscation, and even deadlock.[81]

Separation of powers

Senator Ervin further noted that central authority can provide efficiency in times of crisis whereas the separation-of-powers arrangement can not so easily do so. He hastened to indicate his doubt whether efficient government, *i.e.*, a government which does things quickly, is necessarily a good government. Many would join the senator in contending that the "inefficiency" of the separation-of-powers system is a welcome price to pay for purchasing the ability to deliberate at length, and even

---

80. The centralization of political power in the hands of Chief Executives or ruling juntas abroad may be noted. See for example Arthur S. Banks and Robert B. Texter, *A Cross-Polity Survey* (Cambridge: MIT Press, 1963), pp. 98–101, 110–111. Elsewhere the thesis is advanced that in the developing nations the locus of power is generally in the hands of strong, if not dictatorial, executives. Furthermore, it has been noted that where the office of Chief Executive is unstable, with considerable turnover in occupants, the cause is generally not a powerful legislature. See Bruce M. Russett, Hayward R. Alker, Jr., Karl W. Deutsch, and Harold D. Lasswell, *World Handbook of Political and Social Indicators* (New Haven: Yale University Press, 1964), pp. 103–104.

81. Senator Sam Ervin (D., North Carolina) in Subcommittee on Separation of Powers of the Committee on the Judiciary, *op. cit.*, p. 2.

block on occasions, the use of government to effect rapid social change.[82]

THE DECLINE OF CONGRESSIONAL POWER

While there are those who question the validity of the "crisis government" theory as an explanation and justification for the decline in congressional power and the growth in executive power, it is clear that during the last four decades, the American people have tended to rely on the man in the White House and the burgeoning Federal bureaucracy rather than the Congress for help in times of national crisis. A brief look at recent American history may be instructive in documenting the influence of these crises upon the decline of congressional authority.[83]

Crisis government

Following the stock market crash of 1929 came nearly a decade of unemployment, economic frustration, and despair for millions of Americans. With enormous numbers of unemployed, with the alien and violent philosophies of Communism and Fascism gaining recruits, with confidence in the capitalistic economic system and the democratic political system shaken, the people—including the Congress—accepted strong leadership from a man who declared, "The only thing we have to fear is fear itself." In such circumstances it is scarcely astonishing that President Franklin D. Roosevelt's proposals for creating a vast bureaucracy of Federal agencies were speedily accepted as the surest way to help the nation out of its economic doldrums.[84]

The Depression

World War II loomed as a far-away crisis in the late 1930's

82. The 1964 Republican presidential candidate Barry Goldwater suggested the time will come when the American people would elect as their President a man who would proclaim, "I have little interest in streamlining government or in making it more efficient, for I mean to reduce its size. I do not undertake to promote welfare, for I propose to extend freedom. My aim is not to pass laws, but to repeal them. It is not to inaugurate new programs, but to cancel old ones that do violence to the Constitution, or that have failed in their purpose, or that impose on the people an unwarranted financial burden." *The Conscience of a Conservative* (New York: Hillman Books, 1960), p. 23.

83. The term "crisis management" is now in common use. Whole research staffs, such as those at the Hudson Institute in New York, devote much of their time to studying possible future crises and ways to manage such situations in order to maximize the outcomes for the United States.

84. Representative "alphabet soup" agencies were the CCC, Civilian Conservation Corps; WPA, Works Project Administration; and PWA, Public Works Administration. See Paul K. Conkin, *FDR and the Origins of the Welfare State* (New York: Thomas Y. Crowell, 1967), for a discussion of Roosevelt's impact on social and economic life.

Wartime powers

but became America's primary concern after the attack by the Japanese upon Pearl Harbor on December 7, 1941. Scarcely a voice was raised to protest the wartime aggregation of power which quickly developed in the executive branch, and its use in further enlarging the central bureaucracy. The power and effectiveness of the Federal Government were attested to by its achievements during the war.[85] In the great democracies assumption and use of "wartime powers" was well received by the public. Such centralization of power has been customary in wartime—both Lincoln and Wilson had acted in similar fashion during the Civil War and World War I—and it has always worked, which commended the arrangement to the American sense of pragmatism.[86]

Executive "alphabet" agencies

During World War II a new brew of "alphabet soup" agencies was created by the Congress, vested with extensive powers, and given to the executive to operate. The OPA (Office of Price Administration), the OEM (Office of Emergency Management), the ODT (Office of Defense Transportation), and others relied upon centralization to organize the nation for winning the war. The Manhattan Engineer District, as the nuclear-bomb project was called, secretly spent nearly two billion dollars to develop the first atomic bombs. This activity, which had the full blessing of President Roosevelt, was so highly classified that the Vice President, Harry Truman, first learned of it upon being sworn in after President Roosevelt's death.[87]

The Cold War

Before there was time to dismantle much of the wartime machinery with which Congress had equipped the executive branch, the nation moved from the brief respite following the end of World War II to the threatening confrontation with the Soviet Union which came to be called the Cold War. This extended critical situation, now in its third decade, has been

85. It should be noted that America's allies in World War II, England, the Soviet Union, and China were also led by powerful executives heading vast central-government bureaucracies. Of course, considerable difference could be observed between the wartime executive leadership in the two western democracies in contrast to the two totalitarian states.

86. Perhaps the most arbitrary use of power by the executive branch in World War II was the detention of approximately 100,000 Japanese, of whom about 70,000 were native-born citizens, in "War Relocation Centers." Although the Supreme Court regretted the difficulties encountered by American citizens in this forced evacuation of homes and businesses, it upheld the right of the government to the action because of the pressures of war. See Korematsu v. United States, 323 U.S. 214 (1944) and the discussion of this and related cases in Cushman, *op. cit.*, pp. 86–98.

87. Harry S. Truman, *Year of Decisions* (Garden City: Doubleday, 1955), pp. 10–11.

punctuated by numerous specific crises, of which the Korean conflict and the Vietnamese struggle were particularly dangerous and lengthy.

The onset of the Cold War was accompanied by the addition to the executive branch of still another generation of the "ABC" agencies.[88] Among the most notable were the AEC (Atomic Energy Commission), the NSC (National Security Council), and the CIA (Central Intelligence Agency). Created in 1958, NASA (National Aeronautics and Space Administration) was partially the child of the Cold War and partly of the government's growing involvement with science and technology. AID (Agency for International Development), dating from 1961, was created to coordinate various projects designed to oppose Communism with foreign aid, and to pursue humanitarian aims divorced from the Cold War. In 1961 President Kennedy asked for, and received from Congress, an agency designed in part to de-escalate the Cold War. ACDA (Arms Control and Disarmament Agency) seeks to implement presidential objectives regarding arms-control measures which might be a prelude to lessened tensions between the United States and Communist nations.

"Cold War" agencies

Finally, as America was organizing to oppose Communism abroad, the people through their Congress provided the Chief Executive with new powers for a new kind of "war." Whether called the "Fair Deal" by Harry Truman, the "New Frontier" by John Kennedy, or the "War on Poverty" by Lyndon Johnson, the basic concerns have generally been the same.[89] In domestic affairs Americans supported legislation by the Congress, often sought by the Chief Executive, to give the latter broad new powers to improve the quality of life in America. Concern with social values in the United States led to creation by Congress, for operation by the President, of three new Departments: the Department of Health, Education, and Welfare; the Department of Housing and Urban Development; and the Department of Transportation. The enactment of the Medicare program added bureaucrats to those already reporting at least nominally to the President.

The new welfare state

If by now the reader is still unconvinced about the immense

88. The agencies created because of the Depression and World War II emergencies had mostly disappeared, but some of their functions were found in other parts of the government.

89. President Eisenhower did not have a particular slogan or catch phrase for his participation in the attack upon domestic social problems, but participate he did. For example, Social Security benefits were extended during the Eisenhower years, and the Department of Health, Education, and Welfare was established.

size to which the executive branch of government has grown, and unsure of the reasons for it, a graphic form of evidence should be considered. *The United States Government Organization Manual,* issued periodically by the Government Printing Office, lists and describes all major functions within the three branches of the Federal Government. The 1967-1968 issue of this document required 26 pages for the legislative branch, nine for the judicial branch, and 533 pages for the executive branch. Of course it would be utterly erroneous to suggest that the legislative branch is only one-twentieth as powerful or important as the executive branch. Nevertheless the sheer size and diversity of the executive branch remains as mute testimony to the era of "executive dominance." Many of the departments, agencies, bureaus, and commissions over which the President exercises some manner of control suggest in their titles the kind of crises they were intended to help the President resolve. This is true of the largest function of the American government, the several-million-strong Department of Defense, to one of the smallest, the President's Council of Economic Advisers, with its chairman and two other members supported by a small staff of specialists.

"Executive dominance"

Efforts by Congress to Strengthen Itself

Congress, aware of and concerned about the change in power relationships between itself and the two other branches of government, particularly the executive branch, has launched a number of different efforts to investigate and realign the power balance. The Senate Subcommittee on the Separation of Powers has already been cited. Several other major activities also deserve discussion.

Senator Vance Hartke (D., Indiana) has proposed the creation of a Congressional Counsel General. This individual would serve as a congressional advocate, "an attorney of knowledge and prestige who would be of substantial help to the Congress in reaffirmation of the doctrine of separation of power."[90] The office of the Congressional Counsel General would be expected to check the administration of the laws by the executive branch to determine if the intent of Congress was being carried out. The Congressional Counsel General and his staff would also represent Congress in the courts when the question

Congressional advocate proposal

90. Subcommittee on the Separation of Powers, *op. cit.,* p. 8.

of constitutionality arose concerning the validity of congressional acts.[91]

Another senator, J. William Fulbright (D., Arkansas), chairman of the Senate Foreign Relations Committee, has been particularly active during the 1960's in seeking to reestablish the authority of Congress regarding the waging of war and the entering into of various international commitments.[92] To this end the Senate Foreign Relations Committee issued a report recommending that in the future the United States should, unless repelling an attack upon itself or protecting American citizens and property, enter into hostilities on foreign soil *only* with the "affirmative action by Congress specifically intended to give rise to such commitment."[93] By "affirmative action" the committee meant a declaration of war or the issuance of a joint resolution specifically authorizing the President to initiate some form of hostilities, in some definite place, for some stated purpose. The insistence on specifics by the committee resulted from concern over the practice of the past two decades whereby four Presidents have either (1) committed American military forces after only informing the congressional leadership of the action; or (2) obtained a joint resolution so broad that a wide spectrum of military activity could be claimed as being justified.[94] Furthermore, the committee suggested that in the future joint resolutions carry with them a time limit, the expiration of which would signal a congressional review of the military activity underway and a congressional decision to extend or terminate the commitment.

Authority to commit military forces

91. Senator Hartke has compiled a list of Court decisions particularly significant in regard to the powers of Congress, and wherein statutory interpretation by the courts was at odds with the intent of Congress. *Ibid.*, pp. 11–18.

92. Article I, Section 7 of the Constitution states, "The Congress shall have power to . . . declare war . . . raise and support armies . . . provide and maintain a navy."

93. Senate Foreign Relation Committee, *National Commitments*, Report No. 797, 90th Congress, 1st Session, November 20, 1967 (Washington: United States Government Printing Office), p. 1. For a study of Congress' influence upon foreign policy see James A. Robinson, *Congress and Foreign Policy-Making*, rev. ed. (Homewood, Ill.: 1967). Robinson suggests that increasingly the influence of Congress on foreign policy is to approve or amend positions taken by the Executive. A major explanation for this relationship, according to Robinson, is the changing nature of information and intelligence data collection and evaluation—an activity in which the Executive has outstripped Congress.

94. Examples of the former are the sending of troops by President Truman to Korea (1950), by President Eisenhower to Lebanon (1958), and by President Johnson to the Dominican Republic (1965). An example of the latter was the joint resolution broadly supporting the possible use of force in regard to the Tonkin Gulf crisis (Vietnam) in 1964.

To some observers, the constitutional arguments supporting the case for greater congressional participation in authorizing the use of force abroad run counter to the realities of the times. For instance, there is the belief that declarations of war are not always compatible with the ambiguities of waging limited conflicts in the nuclear age.[95] It may also be pointed out that the compression of political reaction time resulting from the advent of missiles and supersonic aircraft may mitigate the advantages, under certain circumstances, which are normally associated with the deliberative function of Congress. Finally, one may argue that the President, as Commander-in-Chief (Article II, Section 2, of the Constitution states, "The President shall be commander-in-chief of the army and navy . . ."), already possesses the necessary powers to utilize military force when in his judgment the national interest requires it. As is often the case when Congress examines the decrease in its power vis-à-vis the growth of power exercised by the executive branch, the Senate Foreign Relations Committee noted that Congress itself was partially to blame for the current situation. While decrying the inability of Congress to adapt its war powers to the nuclear age, the committee ended its somber report with this warning:

Executive power: a warning

> The concentration in the hands of the President of virtually unlimited authority over matters of war and peace has all but removed the limits to executive power in the most important single area of our national life. Until they are restored the American people will be threatened with tyranny or disaster.[96]

Beginning in 1965 the Congress began a specific effort to revitalize itself by appointing a bipartisan Joint Committee on Organization of the Congress. The committee's recommendations, known as the Legislative Reorganization Act of 1967, were largely left unacted upon by the 90th Congress, which concluded its life in 1968. Nevertheless, the committee's suggestions represent the first reorganizational attempt by Congress since 1946, and they may point to important changes in the future and therefore deserve a brief examination: The committee's report echoed the common theme—That, under the pressures generated by increasingly complex domestic and foreign problems, Congress "has tended to delegate authority to the executive branch of the Government. While it has not abdi-

Reorganization moves

95. See the views expressed by former Under Secretary of State Nicholas deB. Katzenbach before the Senate Foreign Relations Committee, *op. cit.*, p. 22.

96. *Ibid.*, p. 27.

cated its role, it has permitted its power to become diluted."[97]

The report contained the hope that through reorganization the Congress might regain and refocus its power upon national policy problems.

Major provisions of the Legislative Reorganization Act of 1967 outlined in the committee's report called for Congress to be supplied with greater fiscal and budgetary data by the Comptroller General, Budget Bureau, and Treasury Department, and for the President to report each June on budgetary changes regarding revenue and expenditures. The President was also required to present to the Congress each June an estimate of the budgets for the ensuing four years. Supporters of the proposed legislation hoped that in the hands of an energetic "cost-effectiveness"-minded Congress the increased fiscal data could materially increase Congress' traditional "power of the purse."[98] Additional provisions of the proposed reorganization legislation included more effective control of lobbying activity, appropriation of more funds for congressional staffs and research, a "bill of rights" regarding the increased democratization of congressional committees, and the establishment of the Committee on Congressional Operation as a continuing group.

To increase the "power of the purse"

Proposals for Strengthening Congress

The concern over the "sick man" among the trio of separated power centers has extended far beyond the Congress itself, and has generated a number of studies containing suggestions for reorganization and reinvigoration.[99] One of the most challeng-

A recent study

97. Special Committee on the Organization of the Congress, *Legislative Reorganization Act of 1967, Report No. 1*, 90th Congress, First Session, January 16, 1967 (Washington: United States Government Printing Office), p. 2.

98. In Washington the term "cost-effectiveness" is most often associated with the fiscal reforms introduced by Robert S. McNamara in the Department of Defense. In practice the term means that alternative programs may be judged on the basis of their comparative effectivenss for each dollar expended. A classic study of the use by Congress of its "power of the purse" is Elias Huzar, *The Purse and the Sword: Control of the Army by Congress Through Military Appropriations, 1933–1950* (Ithaca: Cornell University Press, 1950).

99. As long ago as 1950 the American Political Science Association issued a report which suggested, among other things, that the effectiveness of Congress could be enhanced by the development of greater party unity within a more democratic framework. See "Toward a More Responsible Two-Party System," *American Political Science Review*, XXXXIV (September, 1950), Supplement. An earlier effort at reform by the same group

(Continued on next page)

ing and provocative of recent studies appeared in 1967 as a collection of 12 essays, entitled *Congress: The First Branch of Government*. The prominent scholars who contributed to the study singled out three problems of contemporary American national government 'for which the strengthening of Congress would in part be an answer. The study's first chapter asserts:

> The first of these is the danger represented by an excessive reliance for the handling of all issues on an escalating bureaucracy, consisting of huge agencies of permanent civil servants who are not made effectively responsible to the larger society. The second is the danger of the kind of militarism that arises in the course of efforts to solve the issues of foreign affairs and their related domestic aspects. The third problem results from the increase of presidential personalism: the exaltation of an office above its stated powers and the capacities of the incumbent, which poses a veritable threat of dictatorship—or whatever one may wish to call the phenomenon of the people's overly great dependence upon the magical qualities of a person occupying an outstandingly prominent office.[100]

Revolutionary proposals

Among the more revolutionary proposals put forth in the study were the following: scrapping the traditional annual budget process in favor of "a continuous consideration of incremental changes to the existing base [budget]; granting Congress the power to reverse Supreme Court decisions declaring laws unconstitutional by reenactment of the offending statute by two-thirds vote in two consecutive sessions of Congress; and appointing outstanding individuals who are not members of Congress to serve on committees almost as if they were members.[101]

Perhaps the most provocative proposals of the study are to be found in the appendix.[102] These include suggestions for: A

100. Alfred de Grazia, "Toward A New Model of Congress" in de Grazia, *op. cit.*, p. 17.

101. Alfred de Grazia, *op cit.*, Aaron Wildavsky, "Toward a Radical Incrementalism," p. 141; Cornelius P. Cotter, "Legislative Oversight," p. 70; Lewis A. Dexter, " 'Check and Balance' Today": What Does It Mean for Congress and Congressmen?" p. 102.

102. *Ibid.*, Alfred de Grazia, "47 Propositions for the Strengthening and Stabilization of Congress," pp. 466–471.

had many of its recommendations adopted in the Legislative Reorganization Act of 1946. See *The Reorganization of Congress* (Washington: Public Affairs Press, 1945). Other sources may be consulted for the view that Congress is in a period of decline. For example see Sidney Hyman, "Inquiry Into the Decline of Congress," *New York Times Magazine*, January 31, 1960; and David Truman, "Introduction: The Problem and Its Setting," in Truman, ed., *The Congress and America's Future* (Englewood Cliffs: Prentice-Hall, 1965), pp. 1–4.

Social and Behavioral Sciences Institute, funded by Congress, to pioneer pure and applied social science not connected with the immediate needs of Congress; shortening the President's occupancy of the White House to a single six-year term; and establishing a Supreme Court of the Union, comprised of members from the United States Supreme Court and state supreme courts, to decide matters of constitutional law affecting federalism.

A remark here is in order to those who may fear that the various efforts meant to strengthen the Congress may in time be too successful—with the result that a tyrannical legislature will threaten the republic. In this respect it should be recalled that more than 100 years ago, when the Congress was on the verge of substantially reducing the power of the Presidency—the occasion was the impeachment trial of President Andrew Johnson—a lone senator from Kansas committed political suicide by voting "No" to conviction and thus helped preserve the independence of the Presidency.[103]

A tyrannical legislature?

SUMMARY

- United States representatives and senators lead busy and hectic lives. During the 1960's their workload increased, and both chambers had scandals which raised questions concerning ethics. As a result the House of Representatives and the Senate passed formal codes in 1968 to govern the behavior of members and certain staff employees in regard to financial affairs. The former had to adjust to the "one-man, one-vote" decision of the Supreme Court which requires that the 435 members be chosen by districts as nearly equal in population as it is practical to make them.

- Important differences exist between the two chambers. The much larger House of Representatives features relatively tighter control by the Speaker and committee chairmen. The two-year term of the House, in contrast to the six-year term of the Senate, has been criticized as being too short for effective work to be performed before preparations must be made for the next election.

- A controversial matter in the House of Representatives and the Senate, but of greater significance in the lower chamber, is seniority. According to this principle, chairmanships of

103. The story of Edmond G. Ross and his refusal to cast the guilt-producing vote in the Johnson trial is told in John F. Kennedy, *Profiles in Courage* (New York: Pocket Books, 1957), pp. 107–128.

committees go to the senior, in terms of years of service, member of the majority party on the committee.

- In the House of Representatives the Speaker, although not possessing the power of past times, still ranks as one of the most powerful men in Washington, perhaps second only to the President in formal authority. A unique feature of the House of Representatives is the Rules Committee. Like the Speakership it has been shorn of some powers, but it remains an important and controversial entity.

- The Senate operates with a committee system as in the House of Representatives, but there is no Rules Committee, and the President of the Senate, the Vice President, is not comparable in power to the Speaker. Depending upon the individual's personality and talents, the most influential member of the Senate is often the Majority Leader.

- The primary responsibility of Congress is to enact legislation. However, most of the important bills considered by the Congress originate in the executive branch. Some proposed legislation is generated by interest groups seeking laws to benefit their members or the nation at large.

- Much of the work of Congress is done in standing, joint, conference, and select committees. The committee system permits a division of labor and specialization of abilities which contribute order and expertise to the operation of the Congress. Considerable "spadework" for the committees is done by subcommittees and committee research staffs.

- Most bills never emerge from the committees to which they are assigned. The few which do, sometimes in modified or mutilated form, are sent to the entire body of the House of Representatives or Senate to be voted upon, and if passed to be sent to the other chamber, and then to the President.

- The President may sign a bill or veto it, in which case a two-thirds majority of both chambers is sufficient to override the veto. Should the President decide not to sign a bill, after 10 days (Sundays excepted) the bill becomes law without his signature if Congress remains in session. If Congress adjourns, the bill dies and the action is called a pocket veto. The President, unlike some governors, does not have the power of item veto, i.e., the ability to strike out portions of a bill while leaving the remainder intact.

- The Congress has other responsibilities besides legislating. A time-consuming aspect of congressional life results from the many requests made of congressmen and senators by their constituents. Pursuant to their legislative responsibilities members of Congress engage in various types of investigations. Considerable controversy has surrounded the power of Congress to subpoena a witness to appear before an investigating committee. The Supreme Court has attempted to clarify rules which protect the rights of such witnesses while enabling congressional investigators to pursue their proper purposes. From time to time it has appeared that individual members have used their investigatory power to enhance their own political fortunes rather than to contribute to legislation or to check upon the activity of the executive branch.

- Theories vary as to the relationship which does and ought to exist between the elected representatives and the constituents. Notions of representatives' voting for the general good above narrow local interests vie with the belief that representatives ought simply to represent the views of those who elect them.

- Although Congress was born in an age of great legislative activity, much has changed in the last 180 years. Today most observers agree that the branch of government first mentioned in the Constitution has been far surpassed in power by the executive branch. Much of this has happened since the early 1930's. A frequently advanced reason for the decline in the power and prestige of Congress vis-à-vis the Executive is the "crisis environment" which has characterized much history of the past few decades.

SUGGESTED READING

* (Books so designated are available in paperbound editions.)

* Bailey, Stephen K., Congress Makes a Law (New York: Vintage, 1964).

* Bolling, Richard, House Out of Order (New York: Dutton, 1965).

* Clapp, Charles, The Congressman: His Work as He Sees It (Washington: The Brookings Institution, 1963).

* Clark, Joseph, Congress—The Sapless Branch (New York: Harper & Row, 1964).

* de Grazia, Alfred, Congress: The First Branch of Government (Garden City: Doubleday, 1967).

* Eidenberg, Eugene and Roy Morey, An Act of Congress (New York: Norton, 1969).

Galloway, George B., History of the United States House of Representatives (New York: Thomas Y. Crowell, 1962).

———, The Legislative Process in Congress (New York: Thomas Y. Crowell, 1953).

* Griffith, Ernest S., *Congress: Its Contemporary Role*, 3rd edn. (New York: New York University Press, 1961).

Gross, Bertram M., *The Legislative Struggle* (New York: McGraw-Hill, 1953).

* Jones, Charles O., *Every Second Year* (Washington: The Brookings Institution, 1967).

* Kennedy, John F., *Profiles in Courage* (New York: Pocket Books, 1957).

* Lowi, Theodore J., *Legislative Politics U.S.A.* (Boston: Little, Brown, 1962).

Matthews, Donald R., *U.S. Senators and Their World* (Chapel Hill: University of North Carolina Press, 1960).

* Peabody, Robert L., and Nelson Polsby, eds., *New Perspectives on the House of Representatives* (Chicago: Rand-McNally, 1963).

* Robinson, James, *The House Rules Committee* (Indianapolis: Bobbs-Merrill, 1963).

* ———, *Congress and Foreign Policy-Making*, rev. ed. (Homewood, Ill.: Dorsey Press, 1967).

* Taylor, Telford., *Grand Inquest* (New York: Ballantine Books, 1961).

Truman, David B., *The Congressional Party* (New York: Wiley, 1959).

———, ed., *The Congress and America's Future* (Englewood Cliffs: Prentice-Hall, 1965).

Wahlke, John C., and Heinz Eulau, *Legislative Behavior* (Glencoe: Free Press, 1959).

White, William S., *Citadel: The Story of the U.S. Senate* (New York: Harper, 1956).

* Wilson, Woodrow, *Congressional Government* (New York: Meridian Books, 1956).

6

The
Presidency

When the members of the Constitutional Convention met in Philadelphia, they recognized that the creation of a Chief Executive was one of the most delicate problems they faced. Under the British monarchy the American people had chafed because the government had too much executive power; under the Articles of Confederation important segments of the population had become impatient because their central government had too little executive power. The framers had no clear precedent for the official they had in mind: a vigorous leader who would not destroy republican institutions, a chief officer who would ultimately be responsible to the people but not entirely dependent upon them. Although many of the plans and predictions sometimes went awry, the founders succeeded. In this chapter we will consider the office of the President of the United States which, through accident and design, has become one of the truly remarkable achievements in the political history of the world.

The creation of the office

The Highest Office in the Land

The formal qualifications for the nation's highest office, as Hamilton described them in *Federalist* 68, were the essence of republican simplicity. The individual needed only to be a natural-born citizen (or a citizen when the Constitution was adopted), at least 35 years of age, and a resident in the United States for 14 years. Mothers yet unborn should be able to visualize their infants in the presidential chair, but only persons "preëminent for ability and virtue" should be chosen; *i.e.*, the final selection should be entrusted to people "most capable of analyzing the qualities adapted to the station." The principle of popular sovereignty dictated that "the sense of the people

Qualifications for the office

235

should operate in the choice of the person to whom so important a trust was to be confided," although it was also important "to afford as little opportunity as possible to [the] tumult and disorder" which could be expected to result from popular election. "Nothing was more to be desired than that every practicable obstacle should be opposed to cabal, intrigue, and corruption," which was bound to come from more than one source, but "chiefly from the desire in foreign powers to gain an improper ascendant in our councils . . . by raising a creature of their own to the chief magistracy of the Union." Finally, the executive "should be independent for his continuance in the office on all but the people themselves."

THE ELECTORAL COLLEGE IN THEORY

Reasons for the electoral college
A hereditary monarch was out of the question after the successful propaganda generated in the heat of the Revolution against King George III. Popular election was unthinkable to the conservative men at the Constitutional Convention. Election by Congress appeared to be the only way, although the founders suspected (as has since become obvious in foreign governments which elect chiefs this way) that the President would become a mere figurehead if he owed his election to the legislature. In despair, the Convention voted several times to have the office filled by Congress and then produced the idea of the Electoral College which, although it bore marked similarities to the election system of the Holy Roman Empire, was probably the most original provision in the Constitution.

"The mode of appointment of the Chief Magistrate of the United States," wrote Alexander Hamilton in *The Federalist*, Number 68, "is almost the only part of the system, of any consequence, which has escaped without severe censure, or which has received the slightest mark of approbation from its opponents." He concluded that the election of the President by an electoral college (his own suggestion at the Constitutional Convention), "if . . . not perfect . . . is at least excellent. It unites to an eminent degree all of the advantages the union of which was to be wished for." The astonishing thing is that this applauded system worked only for the elections of Washington and has produced serious problems ever since.

The plan was that each state should choose as many electors as it had members in its congressional delegation. None of these could hold an office of trust or profit under the United States, thus excluding those who "might be suspected of too great devotion to the President in office" and making it more difficult for corrupting influences to reach electors scattered over all the states. The electors would meet at a place designated by the state legislature (usually the state capitol) and vote by ballot for two persons (at least one who was not of their own state), certify the result, and send it to the president of the Senate. The certificates were to be opened in a joint session of the Congress, and the person with a majority of the votes was to be declared elected. If no majority resulted, the House of Representatives would choose among the five most popular candidates; in this selection each state was to have a single vote. The scheme appeared promising because it provided for deliberation by distinguished persons removed from the hysteria of campaigns and elections, and prevented band wagon movements. "It will not be too strong to say," wrote the champion of the proposal, "that there will be a constant probability of seeing the station filled by characters preëminent for ability and virtue."

THE ELECTORAL COLLEGE IN PRACTICE

All went well for the first two presidential elections, in which Washington, a "character preëminent for ability and virtue," was elected unanimously. But the third time (in 1796), party politics reared its head in the savage contest between Adams and Jefferson. The former Vice President won by three electoral votes when a Virginian and North Carolinian, evidently disagreeing with the voters of their states on the ability and virtue of the two contestants, cast their votes for the Yankee Adams, and under the original provision of the Constitution (altered by Amendment XII), the runner-up took second place: Jefferson became Vice President. Four years later, the Jefferson party was so united and strong that Aaron Burr, its candidate for second place tied the party leader and so threw the election into the House of Representatives. Since the House had a liberal number of "lame duck"[1] Federalists who could not resist the temptation to deprive their hated enemy, Jefferson, of the Presidency, a week of voting resulted before Hamilton could persuade his Federalist cohorts to accept Jefferson as the lesser of two evils. (This interference increased Burr's enmity for his fellow New Yorker, which culminated in the duel in which Hamilton was killed.) The Twelfth Amendment was quickly adopted to require the electors to specify their choices for President and Vice President so that the fiasco

Electoral deadlock

---

1. A "lame duck" is an official who is still serving out his term but who was not re-elected to the office at the most recent election.

of 1800 would not be repeated. Lame ducks were not exterminated until the Twentieth Amendment was proclaimed, 133 years later.

The constitutional arrangement again came under fire 24 years after the Jefferson-Burr hassle: the Jeffersonians had become the only operational political party in America, and the entrance of four strong candidates into the presidential race precluded a majority in the Electoral College for any one of them. This time the House chose John Quincy Adams instead of Andrew Jackson, the better votegetter, and what, in other countries, would have been a pretext to seize control of the state by the popular general was dismissed as a "corrupt bargain." The tradition of swallowing the bitter pill created by the provision of an Electoral College instead of resorting to revolution was strengthened in 1876 when Tilden polled more popular votes than Hayes but lost the electoral vote to him. Again, in 1888, Cleveland accumulated 100,000 more popular votes than Harrison but trailed by 65 in the electoral count. The presidential race between John F. Kennedy and Richard M. Nixon in 1960 was so close in terms of the popular vote (49.7% to 49.5%) that some contend Nixon actually was the winner. The Electoral College vote, however, favored Kennedy heavily by 303 to 219.

It may seem strange that, despite the repeated anomalies, the Electoral College system has not been reformed by constitutional amendment—particularly in view of the eagerness of the people to write the "no third term" tradition into the Constitution after the death of the one President who had ignored it. The reason, of course, is the impact a change could be expected to make on the local political scene. At the present time the constitutional requirement that every state have a minimum of two senators and one representative gives states with small populations more representation in the electoral college than their populations entitle them to have, an advantage none is interested in losing. It is difficult to predict exactly the effects on the two-party system of a requirement for dividing the electoral vote of each state according to the percentage of party votes cast. The present arrangement of "winner take all" certainly has not encouraged the growth of a strong opposition in one-party states, and local politicians are not in favor of strengthening the opposition. Until the present time, there have been more than enough small states and one-party states to prevent the adoption of a constitutional amendment changing the Electoral College system. In addition, the present arrangement has increased the importance of the large urban

**'No third term"
tradition**

Copyright © 1968 Chicago-Sun Times; reproduced by courtesy of Wil-Jo Associates, Inc. and Bill Mauldin.

states and minority groups within these states, which must be wooed and won by presidential candidates who hope to capture big blocs of electoral votes. Nevertheless, pressures are building to change the Electoral College system, and an increasing number of plans are being introduced regarding alternative means to select the President.[2] These center about the proposi-

2. For a summary analysis of the operation of proposed changes in the Electoral College system see "Election Law," *Politics in America 1945–1966* (Washington: Congressional Quarterly Service, 1967), pp. 71–76. For a lengthy critique of the Electoral College system, and discussion of proposals for direct-vote selection of the President see Neal R. Peirce, *The People's President: The Electoral College in American History and the Direct-Vote Alternative* (New York: Simon & Schuster, 1968).

tion that the President ought to be selected on the basis of the popular vote.

Candidates and Conventions: How to Be Nominated

The search for a good candidate

The promise of Number 68 of *The Federalist* that the Presidency would "never fall to the lot of any man who is not in an eminent degree endowed with the requisite qualifications" has not always come true. To read Hamilton's prediction of 1788 in the light of subsequent American political history is to smile at the prophecy that "talents for low intrigue, and the little arts of popularity" would be insufficient to make a man a successful candidate for the distinguished office. Political parties cannot be entirely blamed for this development, for they had nominated excellent candidates from their caucuses; it is the national convention system which seems to be the culprit. Andrew Jackson's aim to democratize the process of selecting the party candidate has resulted in searches for *good candidates* rather than *good presidents*. The hope that "the office should seek the man, not the man the office," was undermined by the institution of presidential preferential primaries, which further democratized the procedure. As the Founding Fathers knew from their study of ancient history, talents for the art of popularity become increasingly important as selection machinery becomes increasingly democratic.[3]

There can be no doubt, however, that the increased popular participation in the election of the President has made the race to the White House the most spectacular sprint in politics anywhere. Foreigners watch the process with fascination, although few of them ever seem to understand the rules. This is not surprising, since many Americans do not appear to be very knowledgeable about it either. Actually, there are two races, the winner of the first (nomination) becoming qualified to enter the second (election).

PRE-CONVENTION STRATEGY AND THE PRIMARIES

The 50-state dash for the nomination is oftentimes referred to as a trial heat, but it has peculiar rules. Chief among them are that participants are not obliged to cover the same ground

3. H. L. Mencken, a caustic critic of American tastes, wrote: "As democracy is perfected the [presidential] office represents, more and more closely, the inner soul of the people. We move toward a lofty ideal. On some great and glorious day the plain folks of the land will reach their heart's desire at last, and the White House will be adorned by a downright moron." Malcolm Moos, ed., *H. L. Mencken on Politics* (New York: Vintage Books, 1960), p. 21.

and that it is possible to win without having entered the competition. The trial heat usually begins at least a year or two before the nomination prize is awarded, and hopefuls have a choice among several types of strategy. Some announce themselves and immediately begin their efforts to win commitments from state delegations before their rivals can begin. This was the strategy unsuccessfully selected by Robert A. Taft in 1952 and successfully used by Kennedy in the wide-open rush for the nomination in 1960; by Barry Goldwater in 1964, and by Richard Nixon in 1968.[4] If a candidate is not strong, he does better to wait, since it is easy to exhaust strength avoiding the obstacles in the broken field running toward the national convention. If the President is eligible for re-election, he is nearly always the front runner and can afford to wait in confidence, secure in the knowledge—to choose an example—that even the crisis of the Great Depression did not seriously threaten the renomination of Hoover by his party in 1932. This rule of thumb might not have held for 1968. That year, before President Johnson made the momentous announcement, "I shall not seek, and I will not accept, the nomination of my party for another term as your President," there were signs he might not be the choice of the Democratic convention.[5] The unfavorable signs included heated debate within the Democratic Party regarding the desirability of the President seeking re-election; the surprising strength shown by Minnesota Senator Eugene McCarthy in the nation's first primary (New Hampshire, March 12); and the sagging popularity of the President in the polls.

If, however, a potential nominee currently is the Vice President or was the defeated nominee in the previous election, or for some other reason is prominent in the party, he must plan his strategy in view of what his rivals are doing. Nixon in 1960 and 1968, Stevenson in 1956, and Goldwater in 1964 built up a following among rank-and-file partisans by frequent public

Getting an
early start

4. Kennedy's arduous road to victory at the Democratic convention in Los Angeles is the subject of the first part of Theodore H. White's *The Making of the President: 1960* (New York: Pocket Books, 1962). In his book on the presidential campaign of 1964 White noted that there was a "Goldwater movement," *i.e.*, people mobilized as receptive to Goldwater's philosophy, several years before the Arizona Senator officially declared his candidacy 10 months before the November, 1964, presidential election. See *The Making of the President: 1964* (New York: New American Library, 1965), pp. 111–112. The story of the Goldwater campaign is told by a key member of the Arizona senator's supporters in F. Clifton White and William J. Gill, *Suite 3505; The Story of the Draft Goldwater Movement* (New Rochelle: Arlington House, 1967).

5. President Johnson's remarks are contained in "A New Step Toward Peace," (Washington: United States Government Printing Office, April, 1968).

appearances and got such a head start that they coasted in to receive the prize. There is more dignity in being an unavowed, but willing, candidate, but if other strong contenders are **Late entries** actively pursuing support, the chance of a "draft" becomes remote. The aloof candidate is unlikely to be successful unless he gets into the thick of the fight in time, as General Eisenhower learned in 1952 and the supporters of Stevenson did not learn in 1960. The year 1968 was a curious one because three major candidates for their party's nomination, Senator Robert F. Kennedy (D., New York) and Vice President Hubert H. Humphrey for the Democrats, and the Republican governor of New York, Nelson A. Rockefeller, were late entrants in the primary races. President Johnson's unpopularity and his unexpected March 31, 1968, announcement he would not seek reelection may have encouraged the late-comers.

THE NATIONAL CONVENTIONS

The climax of the cross-country race comes at the national conventions. The huge, unwieldly meetings are generally held **Size of the** in late July or August preceding the election and are limited, in **convention** choosing a meeting place, to a half-dozen cities.[6] The official performers in these political circuses are the delegates and their alternates aided and abetted by the candidates and political leaders who come on their own and the representatives of the news media, some of whom are better known than those they interview before the television cameras.[7] In 1968, using different selection formulas to assign the number of delegates to various states, the District of Columbia, the Virgin Islands, and

6. Many cities do not have a large enough convention hall to hold a national convention nor enough suitable hotels to house delegates, alternates, visitors, and the representatives of the news media. Because of the strength of local political organizations some cities are particularly favored—for example, Chicago by the Democrats. The unfortunate incidents which occurred in Chicago during the 1968 Democratic Convention, as Democratic Mayor Richard Daley's police confronted demonstrators and some delegates, probably will preclude that city's being chosen again by the Democrats for some time. Cities may be selected for political strategy. When the Democrats intended to nominate a Roman Catholic in 1928, Governor Al Smith of New York, they chose Houston, likely with an eye to "hold the South." The Republican selection of Miami Beach for their 1968 convention site, the first time the party of Lincoln ever met in the South, may have been occasioned by the hopes of making further inroads into what was once the "solid South" for the Democrats. The large West Coast cities have great advantages of climate in July, but eastern delegates sometimes object to traveling so far and eastern television viewers object to the time differential.

7. The presidential nominating cycle is intensively explored by Paul T. David, Ralph M. Goldman, and Richard C. Bain, *The Politics of National Party Conventions* (Washington, D.C.: The Brookings Institution, 1960).

242

Puerto Rico, the Republicans called a national convention consisting of 1,333 delegates, each with one vote, while the Democrats had to make room for 3,099 delegates.[8] The latter cast 2,622 votes because some states gave each delegate only one-half vote, thus enabling more persons to attend. The 5,000-plus delegates and alternates formally called to the Democratic convention in August of 1968 is likely the largest convention assemblage in the history of either party.[9] The inability of such throngs as now gather to "deliberate" is rather obvious, and predictions that conventions will increasingly become "rubber stamps" may be well founded.[10]

In 1964 and again in 1968 the nominating conventions became focal points of national unrest. There was a massing of protesting groups, generally pro-civil rights, poor people, black, and anti-war demonstrators around and sometimes inside the convention halls and delegates' hotels. Such activities hit a peak at the 1968 Democratic convention in Chicago and resulted in the gloom of tear gas which was spread in the streets being mixed with forebodings concerning the political process in America. Some felt the nation had slipped a notch toward anarchy while others worried about the growth of police-state methods they feared would increase.

Conventions and protest movements

THE SELECTION OF DELEGATES

The delegates to the national conventions are chosen in any of three ways: by state and district party conventions, by state central committees, and by presidential preferential primaries. Since the first two methods are familiar from earlier discussion, only the preferential primary method needs amplification.

Like the direct primary, the presidential primary is designed to give the rank-and-file voter an opportunity to indicate his preference for the party standard-bearer. The states which use presidential primaries vary widely as to how they shall be conducted. Some require a formal petition in order to get a name on the ballot, and others permit the entrance of names of

The presidential primary

8. The practice of giving bonus delegates to states which cast a majority of their votes for the party's candidates for President, governor, or senator was originated by the Republicans to offset the otherwise disproportionate influence the Southern states had in their convention. Later, the Democrats gave a smaller bonus to states which had given their electoral votes to the party's nominee for President.

9. "The 1968 Conventions," *CQ Guide to Current American Government,* January 1968, p. 3.

10. For a discussion of the importance of the primaries in the selection of presidential nominees see James W. Davis, *Springboard to the White House: Presidential Primaries; How They Are Fought and Won* (New York: Thomas Y. Crowell, 1967).

potential candidates even without their approval. Candidates' names may be "written in" under the rules operating in some states. Primaries add much excitement to American political life, but they are extremely expensive and treacherous for the participants. If a hopeful nominee enters a primary, he must be prepared to spend a great deal of time and money to stump the state. If he loses, his chances may be ruined (Willkie in 1944); if he wins, he may have the vote of the state delegation at the convention for the first ballot only, and then stand helplessly by while he watches "his" delegates switch to a rival. State law stipulates how long the delegates must vote for the man to whom they are pledged, but political reality requires that delegates remain free to "get on the band wagon" of the candidate who is ultimately successful.[11] President Truman once called presidential primaries "eyewash," and he was partly right. Some hopefuls have stayed out of primaries altogether and still won the nomination (Willkie, 1940; Dewey, 1944; Humphrey, 1968). On the other hand, primaries can give a declared nominee necessary and valuable publicity. John F. Kennedy convinced many uncommitted politicians that the "Catholic issue" was dead when he won the primary in the overwhelmingly Protestant state of West Virginia in 1960, and thereby gained their support.[12] In 1968 Senator Eugene McCarthy's showing in Democratic primaries in New Hampshire and Oregon helped to make him a serious contender for the Democratic presidential nomination. Senator Robert F. Kennedy's victory over Senator McCarthy in the California primary seemed, until his fatal shooting a few hours after the polls closed, to presage a vigorous campaign which could have netted him the nomination.

Criticisms

The entire system of delegate selection to the national conventions of the two major parties received considerable criticism in 1968. Particularly critical were groups favoring Senator McCarthy and Governor Rockefeller and those who had followed Senator Kennedy. They charged that in some states delegates were picked by bosses or unrepresentative state conventions or committees without regard for voter preferences as

11. It is said that Democrats who came to Washington for political favors in 1933 were asked: "Were you for F.D.R. B.C. [before Chicago]?" Whether the story is true or false does not matter, since politicians know the rule of the *quid pro quo*.

12. That the "Catholic issue" was really very much alive through November, 1960, is evidenced by the election results. The narrow margin by which Kennedy won is attributable mainly to the adverse net effect of his religion on the American electorate. See Philip E. Converse *et al.*, "Stability and Change in 1960: A Reinstating Election," *American Political Science Review*, LV (June, 1961), 269–80.

"There's got to be a better way for us to travel."

reflected in the polls. The widespread discontent over the old
methods of nominee selection added support to suggestions
that the hodgepodge of primaries, state conventions, and state   **A uniform**
central committees which select the convention delegates, who   **national primary**
in turn pick the party nominees, be replaced by a uniform
national presidential primary.[13] Each party's winner in such a

13. A few weeks before the Republican convention in 1968 Governor
Rockefeller expressed his unhappiness with the delegate selection system by
suggesting a poll be used to indicate voter preference. His plan, which was
not adopted by the Republicans, was for a poll to be conducted in each
state to determine whether he or Richard Nixon would have the better
chance to beat selected Democrats. The winner of such trial runs would
then have been nominated as the Republican standard-bearer.

primary election would then be pitted against each other in the November general election. The major business of the national conventions would thus become the drafting of the party platform. Such an arrangement would probably feature some device—for example, the requirement for petitions with a significant number of signatures to be recorded before a candidate could have his name placed on a primary ballot, in order to separate serious contenders from unknown or eccentric ones. In this way it would be hoped to maintain the two-party system and prevent a disintegration into a multiparty system which could lead to an American variant of the weak and often indecisive coalition governments which have plagued some European nations. Adoption of a national presidential primary would also be likely to include some provision for the heavy costs of such an activity to be in some way borne by the Federal Government.

THE CONVENTION BEGINS

The opening gun of the convention is the keynote speech. This oration is a stylized political harangue in which the **The keynote speaker** speaker "points with pride" to his party's achievements, "views with alarm" the sinister plans of the rival party, and attempts to excite the delegates to a state of high emotion. The choice of the keynoter is frequently fraught with politics, since it is widely believed that he might influence the convention to favor a particular contender or even stampede the delegates into his own camp.

For the first day or two the convention is concerned primarily with the work of the Committee on Credentials and the **Committee on** Platform Committee. The former gets into the news only if it **credentials** must choose between rival groups from the same state who are fighting for the opportunity to represent the state, or when rival groups from the same state are pledged to different candidates.[14] This kind of intraparty fight has characterized recent Democratic conventions. The difficulty arises from struggles within some Southern states over the racial composition and philosophy of rival delegations, and reflects the changes which are taking place within the Democratic Party, particu-

14. In 1952 the Republican convention wrestled with the problem of rival delegations supporting different candidates from Louisiana, Texas, and Georgia. That same year the Democrats had their own controversy over the seating of several Southern delegations whose loyalty to the majority decision of the party was in doubt. This problem is explored by Allan P. Sindler in his case study, "The Unsolid South: A Challenge to the Democratic National Party," in Alan F. Westin, ed., *The Uses of Power* (New York: Harcourt, Brace & World, 1962).

larly its southern component. In 1964 the Democratic convention wrestled with the explosive problem of rival delegations from Mississippi. There was the Mississippi Freedom Party slate which had no legal right at the convention, for it had been chosen outside the legal party machinery of delegate selection. But the Mississippi Freedom Party delegates, composed primarily of black citizens, had in the words of Theodore White, chronicler of recent presidential campaigns, an "impeccable" moral case.[15] On the other hand there was the legally selected all-white regular delegation from Mississippi. It was, again using White's words, "morally absurd."[16] Thus the Democrats were faced again with the racial issue which looms behind the uneasy alliance of Southerners and Northerners in their party.[17] In 1968 the Democratic Committee on Credentials sought to avoid a floor fight over the seating of rival delegations from Georgia—the regular delegation composed of delegates selected by Governor Lester Maddox and the state party chairman faced an insurgent group headed by a young black politician, Julian Bond—by splitting the Georgia vote evenly between the competing factions. The closest vote of the convention ensued when the Bond delegation's motion to have all the Georgia votes given to it narrowly failed of adoption.[18]

The Platform Committee works hard to placate all the elements in the party by putting together a statement of policy which sounds wonderful but which few people believe and even fewer read. On occasion a minority group will be unable to force an acceptable compromise and will walk out of the con-

Platform committee

15. *The Making of the President: 1964*, p. 334.

16. *Ibid.*, p. 333.

17. Under the leadership of Hubert Humphrey, who was later selected as the vice-presidential candidate, a compromise was worked out. It provided for two delegates from the Mississippi Freedom Party to be seated as delegates representing their state, and it stipulated that in future conventions of the Democratic Party no delegations would be seated from states where the party election process denied citizens the right to vote because of race or color. *Ibid.*, pp. 334–335. The promise was kept in the 1968 convention as a delegation chosen by the regular (white) Democratic organization in Mississippi was replaced by a delegation representing the integrated interests in the state.

18. Another indication in 1968 of the changes within the Democratic Party in regard to racial matters was the placing into nomination for President the name of a black minister from Washington, D.C., Channing Phillips. He received nearly 70 votes. It should also be noted that the 1968 Democratic Convention scrapped for the 1972 convention the "unit rule"—the device which had required all of a state's delegate votes be cast the way the majority voted. Of course, this action will benefit other minorities besides racial ones.

vention, as the "Dixiecrats" did at the Democratic convention of 1948.

The work of the Platform Committee can be as productive as that of the Committee on Credentials when it comes to convention floor fights. In 1964 the Republicans participated in a party-splitting dispute which pitted the "liberal" Eastern wing of the G.O.P. against the "conservative" Southern and Western wings. The result was an uncompromising victory for the latter and their champion, Barry Goldwater, which helped to set the stage for the dismal showing made by the Republicans in the subsequent general elections. In 1968 it was the Democratic turn to publicly argue out serious differences. While the Republicans were healing the wounds of 1964, the Democrats vehemently argued over the Vietnam plank of their platform. The convention's adoption of a pro-Johnson Administration plank supporting the war effort, over the bitter opposition of the anti-war forces, badly split the party less than three months before the November election.

THE ANATOMY OF A CANDIDATE

The most important activity at national conventions is the selection of "the next President of the United States." If the party choice is obvious (Eisenhower in 1956, Nixon in 1960, and Johnson in 1964), the delegates merely go through the form of ratifying him; if there is a challenge (Harriman to Stevenson in 1956, Scranton to Goldwater in 1964, Rockefeller to Nixon in 1968, and McCarthy to Humphrey in 1968), a flurry of interest results; but if there are several strong contenders (Republican convention of 1952, Democratic convention of 1960), the excitement becomes electric. The politicians present are supposed to be looking for a winner, and the test is *availability*.

Looking for a winner

To be available, a candidate for the nomination is not merely willing and able to undertake the campaign; he meets in a satisfactory manner the political requirements which will win—or at least not lose—votes: one observer recognized nine rules of availability,[19] but, until the election of 1960, it was commonly agreed that the absolute minimum was that the candidate be a WASP.[20] It is likely that for years to come an acceptable nom-

19. The "Rules" of: Political Talent, Governors, Big Swing States, Northern Monopoly, Multiple Interests, Happy Family Life, Small Town, English Stock, Protestantism. Sidney Hyman, "Nine Tests for the Presidential Hopeful," *New York Times Magazine* (Jan. 4, 1959), p. 11.

20. White, Anglo-Saxon, Protestant. The term "Anglo-Saxon" applies especially to the name. This requirement may be fading, however, as the 1968 vice-presidential nominations of Spiro Agnew (Greek-American) by the Republicans and Edmund Muskie (Polish-American) by the Democrats suggest.

inee will have to be at least a W or, perhaps a WA, since the introduction of television has made *appearance* important. A candidate is extremely popular with the "plain folks" if he embodies the enduring American myths of having been born in the modern approximation of the log cabin and is happily married—preferably to a photogenic wife, the mother of attractive children. A personal fortune need not be a detriment unless the opposition candidate can make some invidious comparisons between himself and the more wealthy individual; in the cases of Franklin D. Roosevelt and John F. Kennedy, wealth appeared to be a positive asset. He is popular with practical politicians if he comes from a pivotal state with many electoral votes.

If a potential candidate can combine these traits of availability with experience in a high office which has not required him to speak out on controversial issues, he becomes formidable. A glance at the backgrounds of the 26 different candidates of the major parties who have participated in the 18 campaigns since the turn of the century is instructive as well as interesting:[21]

Backgrounds of candidates

Governor of a State	8
Private Life	4
Unelected Incumbent President	4
Senator	3
Cabinet Member	2
Federal Judge	2
Vice President	2
Military Service	1

Governors have been popular nominees in the past because their tasks look, to most voters, like those of the President, and because they have not been obliged to concern themselves with national or international issues and have made a minimum of enemies. Governors also come into the conventions with loyal delegations because they control state patronage, and if their

Governors

21. *Governors:* McKinley, Wilson, Cox, Smith, F. D. Roosevelt, Landon, Dewey, Stevenson. *Private life:* Bryan, Davis, Willkie, Nixon (1968). *Incumbent President not elected:* T. Roosevelt, Coolidge, Truman, Johnson. *Senators:* Harding, Kennedy, Goldwater. *Cabinet members:* Taft, Hoover. *Federal judges:* Hughes, Parker. *Vice President:* Nixon (1960), Humphrey. *Military service:* Eisenhower. Two of the four incumbent Presidents who had gained the office by the death of their predecessors had served as governor; the other two had been senators. All were elected in their own right. Three of the private citizens were defeated. Bryan (nominated twice this century) had served in Congress. Willkie, a lawyer, was "available" during the pre-war year of 1940 because he was a prominent internationalist in a political party whose leaders were identified with isolationism. No doubt helped by the "no third term" tradition, Willkie won more popular votes than any Republican until General Eisenhower. Davis, a lawyer nominated in 1924, won a smaller percentage of popular votes than any Democrat in history.

states are politically important, the kingmakers favor them on the supposition that local pride will carry their state for the party in the election. Prominent members of Congress, on the other hand, are widely believed to be too vulnerable to political attack because of their voting records and speeches. During the Cold War period to date, governors, who are primarily concerned with domestic problems, appeared to be less popular than candidates thought to have more international experience. The future seedbed for presidential timber may depend heavily upon the emphasis the United States gives to domestic policy vis-à-vis foreign affairs.

Since the Civil War, only the unelected incumbent President Lyndon B. Johnson of Texas, who succeeded to the Presidency upon the death of John F. Kennedy, has been nominated for President from a Southern state. Except for the unusual circumstances surrounding the nominations of Bryan (Nebraska, 1900, 1908), Landon (Kansas, 1936) and Humphrey (Minnesota, 1968), none has come from sparsely populated central states during this century—partially because such states do not have the crucial electoral votes of the large, two-party states such as New York, California, Illinois, Ohio, Michigan, Massachusetts, New Jersey and Pennsylvania.

THE CONVENTION'S CHOICE

Oratory and demonstrations

In an uncommitted convention, the nomination process is always a colorful, if sometimes a tiresome, affair. The name of each potential candidate is placed before the assembled delegates by a speaker (selected from another part of the country or faction of the party whenever possible) with a burst of oratory designed to convince the world that only his man can unite the party and win the election. Many "favorite sons" are offered; although taking the trouble of nominating local figures who have practically no chance to win seems futile to the uninitiated, it serves a useful political purpose, allowing state delegates time to maneuver and bargain with the real contenders. It is also considered an honor merely to have been placed in nomination, and each unknown governor or senator probably secretly cherishes the hope that the convention will deadlock the way the Republicans did in 1920 and turn to him as a "dark horse" who can gallop to the finish line first. It is no secret that public relations experts view with disfavor the parade of local personalities before the television cameras, which detracts from the show they are trying to produce. The entry of many hopeless hopefuls into nomination requires a good deal of time since the close of each nomination speech is the signal for a demonstration: while the chairman half-heartedly beats for order, hired bands play, and recruited marchers parade around the convention hall in an attempt to convince the delegates that their nominee has widespread support. If demonstrations are prepared carefully enough they look spontaneous.[22]

Traditional demonstrations

When all the names are before the convention, balloting begins. The roll of the states is called, and the world watches to see if a trend develops. Timing is all-important because states playing the favorite-son game must know when to switch, and delegates supporting a losing candidate must scramble to get on the bandwagon. If possible, practical politicians prefer to decide the contest on the first ballot, thereby minimizing the danger of party division and reducing the risk of the convention choosing a dark horse. If it is apparent to a candidate that he cannot get a clear majority on the first ballot, his managers attempt to farm out some of his votes so that he can appear reasonably strong on the first ballot and then begin increasing strength as the voting progresses. (The candidate who begins slipping is deserted like a sinking ship.) At a crucial time the switch in an important state can get the bandwagon in high gear. California is always an important state to watch since it combines the advantages of having many votes with being near the top of the alphabet. As soon as the nominee has received enough votes to win, it is customary for his rivals to move that his nomination be unanimous, and the main feature is over. Before 1932, it was considered proper for the successful candidate to be "notified" by his party and, after indicating great surprise, to make an acceptance speech. Franklin D. Roosevelt shattered the precedent by flying from Albany to Chicago (in a special plane, standing by) and accepting the nomination before the assembled candidates. Since then, candidates of both parties have stayed in nearby hotels and rushed over to make an appearance at the convention hall while the delegates were still in a frenzy.

Balloting

The nomination for the Vice Presidency is usually an anticlimax, since it is left for the determination of the party leaders. The considerations which go into the choice are the per-

22. It is possible for a sincere demonstration to overwhelm the delegates, as the galleries did for Wendell Willkie in 1940. But consider the observation of Theodore H. White after his description of the gigantic manifestation for Stevenson in the Democratic convention of 1960: "Yet if demonstration and noise alone can sway a national decision at a nerve center of national politics, then American politics would be reduced to that naked violence that has so frequently and tragically swayed the history of France and of Germany. To be effective, such a demonstration . . . must cap, not begin, a campaign that has long since previously established other bases of power." *The Making of the President: 1960*, p. 166.

Nomination of Vice President

sonal preferences of the presidential candidate, the extent of political I.O.U.'s resulting from the convention, and the observance of the political maxim of "balancing the ticket." It seems strange that although the Vice President may well assume the Presidency, the man chosen for second place on the ticket is ordinarily from a different faction of the party from that of the presidential nominee. The favorite types of balances are Easterner-Westerner, Northerner-Southerner, liberal-conservative, and Reformer-Party Machine Man.

The Election

The opening of the campaign

After the excitement of the nominating process, candidates are allowed about six weeks to develop a second wind before beginning the dash to the election finish line. This rest period is not due to the concern Americans have for the health of their presidential hopefuls, but because picnics, vacations, and baseball games tend to keep voters away from the hustings. In 1960, however, Nixon had campaigned in six states stretching from Rhode Island to Hawaii during the first 10 days following his nomination and had broken another precedent by attracting hordes of Atlantans to a rally held on a Friday afternoon in August—the precise time when city dwellers traditionally begin weekending out of town. In any event, by the last week of September the campaign has become serious, and the candidates have become used to 15 to 20 hours a day of speechmaking, handshaking, and examining livestock with great interest. The candidate has decided whether he wishes to be marketed as a scrappy fighter or an aloof Olympian, detached from politics; as witty or serious; as frank or evasive; and he knows that whichever role he assumes he is bound to lose some votes. Traditional campaign maxims have insisted that one should never provide his opponent with any publicity, that damaging remarks should be ignored, and that only the weakest and wildest charges should be answered. These maxims do not always hold true. In the campaign of 1960 Richard Nixon agreed to a series of televised debates with Senator John F. Kennedy, thus providing the latter with "exposure" beside the then Vice President. Some felt a new aspect had been added to presidential electioneering. However, the unhappy results of the debates for Nixon may be remembered in the future when prominent office holders are asked to debate and share the stage with those of less distinguished rank. President Johnson did not engage in televised debates with Senator Goldwater. In 1968 Senate Republi-

TABLE 6.1 Presidential Nominating Conventions

REPUBLICAN CONVENTIONS

Year	City	Presidential Nominee	No. of Ballots
1856	Philadelphia	John C. Fremont	2
1860	Chicago	Abraham Lincoln	3
1864	Baltimore	Abraham Lincoln	1
1868	Chicago	Ulysses S. Grant	1
1872	Philadelphia	Ulysses S. Grant	1
1876	Cincinnati	Rutherford B. Hayes	7
1880	Chicago	James A. Garfield	36
1884	Chicago	James G. Blaine	4
1888	Chicago	Benjamin Harrison	8
1892	Minneapolis	Benjamin Harrison	1
1896	St. Louis	William McKinley	1
1900	Philadelphia	William McKinley	1
1904	Chicago	Theodore Roosevelt	1
1908	Chicago	William H. Taft	1
1912	Chicago	William H. Taft	1
1916	Chicago	Charles E. Hughes	3
1920	Chicago	Warren G. Harding	10
1924	Cleveland	Calvin Coolidge	1
1928	Kansas City	Herbert Hoover	1
1932	Chicago	Herbert Hoover	1
1936	Cleveland	Alfred M. Landon	1
1940	Philadelphia	Wendell L. Willkie	6
1944	Chicago	Thomas E. Dewey	1
1948	Philadelphia	Thomas E. Dewey	3
1952	Chicago	Dwight D. Eisenhower	1
1956	San Francisco	Dwight D. Eisenhower	1
1960	Chicago	Richard M. Nixon	1
1964	San Francisco	Barry Goldwater	1
1968	Miami Beach	Richard M. Nixon	1

DEMOCRATIC CONVENTIONS

Year	City	Presidential Nominee	No. of Ballots
1832	Baltimore	Andrew Jackson	1
1835	Baltimore	Martin Van Buren	1
1840	Baltimore	Martin Van Buren	1
1844	Baltimore	James K. Polk	9
1848	Baltimore	Lewis Cass	4
1852	Baltimore	Franklin Pierce	49
1856	Cincinnati	James Buchanan	17
1860	Baltimore	Stephen A. Douglas	2
1864	Chicago	George B. McClellan	1
1868	New York	Horatio Seymour	22
1872	Baltimore	Horace Greeley	1
1876	St. Louis	Samuel J. Tilden	2
1880	Cincinnati	Winfield S. Hancock	2
1884	Chicago	Grover Cleveland	2
1888	St. Louis	Grover Cleveland	1
1892	Chicago	Grover Cleveland	1
1896	Chicago	William J. Bryan	5
1900	Kansas City	William J. Bryan	1
1904	St. Louis	Alton S. Parker	1
1908	Denver	William J. Bryan	1
1912	Baltimore	Woodrow Wilson	46
1916	St. Louis	Woodrow Wilson	1
1920	San Francisco	James M. Cox	43
1924	New York	John W. Davis	103
1928	Houston	Alfred E. Smith	1
1932	Chicago	Franklin D. Roosevelt	4
1936	Philadelphia	Franklin D. Roosevelt	Acclamation
1940	Chicago	Franklin D. Roosevelt	1
1944	Chicago	Franklin D. Roosevelt	1
1948	Philadelphia	Harry S. Truman	1
1952	Chicago	Adlai E. Stevenson	3
1956	Chicago	Adlai E. Stevenson	1
1960	Los Angeles	John F. Kennedy	1
1964	Atlantic City	Lyndon B. Johnson	Acclamation
1968	Chicago	Hubert H. Humphrey	1

cans successfully blocked a bill aimed at enabling the TV networks to provide time for debates between Humphrey, Nixon, and Wallace, without having to give "equal time" to minor candidates.

Campaign strategy

If the original intention of the founders were observed and 535 electors made the final decision, campaign strategy would be entirely different from what it is today; if the election were determined merely on the basis of popular votes, the candidates would concentrate on the North, South, East, and West— where the voters are. Instead, on Election Day, the voters *in the states* make the choice. Since 40 electoral votes of state A are won as securely by a plurality of 1,000 as the 40 electoral votes of state B are won by a majority of 1,000,000, the candidates dedicate their attention to the big states where they might win. They pay only courtesy calls to states where they expect to win, generally ignore states where they expect to lose, and stop off at the small "possible" states only between pivotal ones. This accounts for the fact that citizens of a metropolis in some states may never have the opportunity of seeing either candidate in person during a campaign. Instead, they read about shoppers in Long Island supermarkets shaking hands with one candidate while the other is campaigning in every farm town of central California. A candidate can reach the White House by winning the blue ribbon in a dozen states— provided they are the right ones. Dramatic proof of this hard fact about American presidential politics was reaffirmed in 1960 when Senator Kennedy, after his nomination, decided to concentrate on the nine most populous states. Vice President Nixon, on the other hand, told cheering Republican convention delegates that he would carry his campaign into every one of the 50 states. On the last weekend before the election Nixon, in order to redeem his pledge, was obliged to go to Alaska (which offered three electoral votes), while Mr. Kennedy was relaying among Illinois, New Jersey, New York, and New England. Candidate Kennedy won seven of the nine states singled out in his strategy—and became President. Candidate Nixon carried 26 of the 50 states he had reached for—and lost.

The prize

What is the prize for winning the greatest election of them all? Certainly not the money. It may seem incredible that most recent Chief Executives were unable to manage on the former annual salary of $100,000, but it was true. Just before the 1969 inauguration Congress raised the President's salary to $200,000. President Nixon may not find that income large enough. Even with his housing furnished and a general expense fund of $50,000 a year to maintain it, a variety of means of transportation (cars,

PRESIDENTIAL ELECTION RETURNS 1960, 1964, 1968

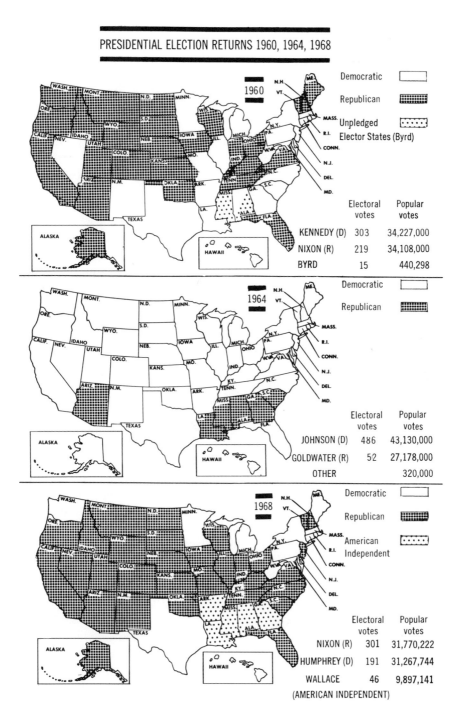

1960

Democratic

Republican

Unpledged
Elector States (Byrd)

	Electoral votes	Popular votes
KENNEDY (D)	303	34,227,000
NIXON (R)	219	34,108,000
BYRD	15	440,298

1964

Democratic

Republican

	Electoral votes	Popular votes
JOHNSON (D)	486	43,130,000
GOLDWATER (R)	52	27,178,000
OTHER		320,000

1968

Democratic

Republican

American
Independent

	Electoral votes	Popular votes
NIXON (R)	301	31,770,222
HUMPHREY (D)	191	31,267,744
WALLACE	46	9,897,141

(AMERICAN INDEPENDENT)

255

helicopters, airplane, and yacht) for his personal use, and $40,000 to spend while traveling, and for official entertainment, a President does well to leave the office with as much of this world's goods as he had when he entered. Taxes take some of the money, but the enormous costs incidental to living at 1600 Pennsylvania Avenue consume most of the rest. Former Presidents now receive lifetime pensions of $25,000 a year, free mailing privileges, free office space, and up to $65,000 a year for office help.

The Powers of the President

Precedents

The President of the United States not only is elected to office by a system almost completely different from that envisaged by the founders; he enters a position more powerful than they had intended. In fact, as the previous chapter indicated, a number of Americans fear that the President's power has grown beyond what is required, or even safe. According to Number 69 of *The Federalist* (written to assure the people that the President would not be another king), the office was simply that of chief magistrate, primarily concerned with administration and the occasional social chore of receiving ambassadors. The writer dismissed the other powers delineated in Article II as making the President less powerful than the governor of New York.

But over the years, as challenges and changes have confronted the American people, some Presidents have taken broad views of their constitutional powers and bequeathed precedents to those who followed them in office. Lincoln said that his role had been made possible by Jackson, who had ended one threat of secession by shouting, "Send for General Scott!" President Wilson was the first to go abroad while in office and the first to engage in international power politics on a "summit" level. The "strong" presidents always seem to have acted on the dictum Wilson later made explicit: "The President can be as big a man as he wants to be."

Whether or not a President will utilize the precedents and powers at his disposal depends on the conception he has of his position.[23] Jackson's memorable cry was certainly known to Buchanan, Lincoln's predecessor, but he was not a "strong" President, and he watched the crumbling of the United States into separate states without conceiving, apparently, that he was

23. Sidney Warren, ed., *The American President* (Englewood Cliffs: Prentice-Hall, 1967), contains essays by various authorities on the Presidency.

in a position to do anything about it. Wilson's predecessor, President Taft, had viewed his role as a balance wheel in the delicate mechanism of government, but *his* predecessor, the irrepressible Theodore Roosevelt, apparently regarded the President not only as the balance wheel but as the entire machine!

Since Franklin Roosevelt's election in 1932 American Presidents have exercised the power of office freely, with the partial exception of Dwight Eisenhower.[24] All have tended toward the view ascribed by Lyndon Johnson: "For Johnson, the Federal Government is the chief way of doing things—a vehicle of action."[25] FDR's unprecedented four terms, plus the increasing power of twentieth century presidents, largely accounted for the addition of the Twenty-second Amendment in 1951. Since then Presidents have been limited to two full terms in office, or two full terms plus two years of the previous President's term, should the Vice President succeed to the office upon the death of his predecessor.

The two-term limit

The enormous powers and discretion which a modern American President may employ have seldom been better illustrated than by two episodes in the short presidential career of John F. Kennedy. The first example occurred in the spring of 1962, when what could have been considered to be a routine newspaper announcement by a steel company was converted into a domestic "crisis" by President Kennedy.

THE STEEL CRISIS

The steel crisis was launched by a four-page mimeographed press release from the United States Steel Corporation stating that the company was increasing its prices by 3 ½ percent. During most of the 173 years under the Constitution such a decision would have elicited no response at all from a President of the United States. In the last three decades a President, however, might be expected to indicate his "disappointment" or even "dismay" about a policy of private enterprise which he felt was opposed to the national interest. President Kennedy's response was to provide one of the most dramatic displays of presidential power in American history. He may have created a precedent for the expansion of presidential authority as important as any bequeathed to him.

24. Emmet John Hughes, *The Ordeal of Power* (New York: Atheneum, 1963) examines the manner in which President Eisenhower handled presidential power. Former President Eisenhower tells his own story in two volumes entitled, *The White House Years—Mandate for Change*, and *Waging Peace* (Garden City: Doubleday, 1963 and 1965).

25. Theodore H. White, *The Making of the President: 1964*, p. 56.

Every Administration since the beginning of World War II had been concerned about the spiral of inflation in the country, but the Kennedy Administration proposed to do something about it through a policy of more active intervention by the executive branch without legislation. The logic of inflation, put simply, appeared to be this: workers demanded higher wages with each new contract because the prices of things they bought were continuously rising; producers raised prices because their labor costs increased with each new contract. This vicious cycle not only increased the cost of living for the consuming public, but higher prices meant that American businessmen were losing markets at home and abroad to foreign competitors. Yet if industry attempted to cut labor costs by laying off workers, crippling strikes could be expected as unemployment resulted. The government was deeply concerned both with unemployment and the flow of dollars out of the country, as Americans bought more and more foreign products, but to raise tariffs on imports would mean sure political repercussions and economic reprisals from abroad. The Kennedy plan was to persuade workers to ask only for wage increases which were "justified" by increased production per man-hour, and to convince businessmen that this kind of raise did not increase labor costs. The formula apparently had survived its acid test when the steel industry was dissuaded from hiking prices in the fall of 1961 and the unions moderated wage demands in bargaining for contracts early in 1962. Therefore, when the largest steel producer in the nation suddenly increased its prices, the President was forced either to intervene or to abandon his anti-inflation policy.

In the battle against "big steel," the President used practically every weapon in his arsenal. His enormous prestige as President carried his argument to the American people by press conference and television. By telephone, he probably persuaded at least one steel producer not to follow the leader of the industry. His relationship to Congress helped account for the threat of immediately forthcoming legislative investigations and restrictive legislation. The national committee of his political party contacted Democratic governors in strategic states to rally support behind the President and to solicit their public statements against price increases. His personal friends outside of government undertook negotiations with the chairman of the board of the steel company concerned. His subordinates in the executive branch took to their telephones to contact friends who were influential in the steel industry. The Chairman of the Federal Trade Commission talked publicly about investigating possible collusive price-fixing in steel; the Department of Justice dispatched FBI agents to verify statements which could be used against the offending corporations in the event that its announced investigations materialized; and the Department of Defense decided to shift steel contracts to producers which had not raised prices. Within 72 hours one of the most powerful corporations in the world capitulated to the irresistible pressure mustered by the President of the United States.[26]

THE CUBAN MISSILE CRISIS

Six months after the confrontation with Big Steel, President Kennedy took on a far more potent antagonist, the Soviet Union. On October 14, 1962, an American U-2 photo-reconnaissance plane flew over the island of Cuba. This was not the first, nor would it be the last such flight. However, it was during this flight that pictures were taken that might well have signaled the beginning of World War III.[27] By the following evening the photo interpreters had finished their analyses and were fairly certain they had discovered evidence not only of Soviet bombers but also of Soviet medium-range nuclear missiles being installed on the belligerent little country 90 miles off the American coast. A briefing of the President was scheduled for the following morning.

From October 16 until the President addressed the nation on October 22, preparations for peace and/or war were conducted by a small group in absolute secrecy. The President maintained his normal routine as much as possible. When he did return early from a speaking trip to attend to the deepening crisis, the

Secret preparations

26. A play-by-play account of the battle between the Kennedy Administration and the United States Steel Corporation may be found in the *New York Times*, April 23, p. 1, and in Grant McConnell, *Steel and the Presidency, 1962* (New York: Norton, 1963). In 1966 and 1968 steel companies were involved in less dramatic confrontations with President Johnson when they raised prices to levels thought by government to be dangerously inflationary. In both instances government pressure caused reductions in the price hikes.

27. Before this time the United States knew the Soviets had introduced SAM's—surface-to-air missiles—into Cuba. These, however, limited as they were to use against only aircraft flying close by, did not present the threat associated with medium-range missiles. The latter could obliterate cities within a rough arc drawn from Washington through St. Louis, to beyond Houston. Three accounts by men who participated in the American planning at the time are: Roger Hilsman (director of the State Department's Bureau of Intelligence and Research during the crisis period), *To Move a Nation* (Garden City: Doubleday, 1967); Theodore Sorensen (the President's Special Counsel), *Kennedy* (New York: Harper and Row, 1965); and the posthumously published book by the President's brother, Robert F. Kennedy (who at the time was Attorney General), *Thirteen Days* (New York: Norton, 1969).

cause given was "a cold." The group of men who were personally appointed to recommend a response to the Soviet move were principally from the executive branch and came to be known officially as the Ex-Com (the Executive Committee of the National Security Council).[28]

A number of alternative responses were considered and discarded as the Ex-Com focused more and more on two particular strategies. One was to initiate an air strike (with or without warning) designed to destroy the missiles and associated equipment. This plan, if implemented, would present the Soviets with a *fait accompli* which they could accept, or to which they could reply with war. The other plan, and the one finally recommended, was to impose a limited sea quarantine of Cuba to prevent additional Soviet missiles and bombers from being furnished the island. This action would be accompanied by a demand that the "offensive" weapons already in Cuba be dismantled and removed from the island.

Alternative strategies

At no time in this century was the power of the president more apparent than during the week when the United States, or, more accurately, a very few Americans, planned this nation's response to the threat of the Soviet Union in secret—in secret from the Soviets, in secret from the American people, and in secret from the Congress. Two hours before the President appeared on national television to confront the missile threat publicly, and one hour before Soviet Ambassador Dobrynin had been informed of American knowledge of the missiles and of the United States response, the President met with congressional leaders. Reports of that meeting record that both Senators Russell (D., Georgia), chairman of the Senate Armed Services Committee, and J. William Fulbright (D., Arkansas), chairman of the Foreign Relations Committee, spoke out in favor of invasion.[29] According to one report, "the President listened politely" to the objections to the quarantine idea. The same source relates that the President was "adamant" in rejecting suggestions from some of the congressional leaders that he order an invasion under the authority of the Joint Resolution concerning Cuba which Congress had passed several months earlier. According to Theodore Sorensen, the President "was

Unique crisis

28. Kennedy, *op. cit.*, pp. 30ff.

29. Sorensen, *op cit.*, p. 702; and Kennedy, *op cit.*, p. 53. Sorensen notes that senators and representatives were scattered about the nation the weekend before Kennedy's speech. Hale Boggs (D., Louisiana), the House Majority Whip, was found fishing in the Gulf of Mexico, where he was buzzed by an Air Force plane which dropped a note to him in a bottle. He was later picked up by a helicopter, deposited in New Orleans, and flew by jet to the President's briefing. Sorensen, *loc. cit.*

acting by Executive Order, presidential proclamation, and inherent powers, not under any resolution or act of the Congress."[30]

President Kennedy addressed the nation at 7 P.M. on October 22, 1962. He told of the discovery of the missiles and the grave threat which their presence constituted to the United States. He outlined the quarantine of "offensive" military equipment bound for Cuba and called upon Soviet Premier Khrushchev to halt future shipments of such equipment and to withdraw what was already on the island. The seriousness of the situation was captured in the President's words:

The President's warning

> It shall be the policy of this nation to regard any nuclear missile launched from Cuba against any nation in the Western Hemisphere as an attack by the Soviet Union on the United States, requiring a full retaliatory response upon the Soviet Union.[31]

A study of the speech reveals the fundamental concepts and psychological objectives of the President and his advisers:

Analysis of the U.S. position

1. The American plan rejected the immediate use of military force. An air strike likely would have entailed the loss of life by Soviet technicians at the sites and, therefore, might have triggered an unmanageable military confrontation.

2. The quarantine response left the door open for a gradual escalation of threat and violence. The American posture was calculated to reduce the chance of immediate hostilities to a minimum while maintaining the threat of a worsening situation to convince the Soviets that they should withdraw.

3. Since the quarantine actually went into effect against ships still on the high seas, the Soviets had time to think out their move.

4. A diplomatic escape route was left open through which the Soviet Government could retreat quietly while publicly trumpeting its "peace loving" aims.

5. The less-aggressive posture would at least postpone military invasion and, hopefully, avoid it completely. In either event the United States would be less liable to criticism from other nations.

6. This was the world's first serious nuclear confrontation. President Kennedy had no precedents to follow, but was instead setting precedents for those who would come later. If

30. Sorensen, *loc. cit.*

31. Kennedy reproduces the drama of the speech, *op. cit.*, p. 55, and the speech itself, *op. cit.*, p. 55.

firmness without bellicosity, an indication of some understanding of the other side's problems and, giving the other side time to weigh its acts without postponing American action, would meet the situation, useful guidelines for future encounters could be set.

Resolution of crisis

The Cuban missile crisis reached its apogee Saturday the 27th of October. After some preliminary signs that the missiles would be withdrawn, bad news arrived in quantity. Word was received that Khrushchev had changed his mind about removing the missiles and would not do it until American missiles had been removed from Turkey. Word was also received that a Soviet ship, which had previously turned about, was heading again for Cuba. Capping events, it was learned that an American U-2, piloted by Major Rudolf Anderson, Jr., the man who first took the pictures indicating the missile emplacement, had been shot down and the pilot killed. The Kennedy Administration rapidly communicated to the Soviet Union that the missiles must be removed and that time was quickly running out. In such a somber atmosphere the next day, Sunday October 28th, the world gratefully received Khrushchev's message that in order to reduce the chance of war the Soviets were removing the "offensive" weapons from Cuba. The crisis was over even though it took some time to work out the bomber removal.[32]

The missile crisis in retrospect

Two points of interest to students of the Presidency emerge from the Cuban missile crisis: First, the President, operating entirely within the executive branch, acted without the consent and, until the last two hours, the knowledge of Congress. Second, the President acted promptly, calmly, and effectively. Could 535 representatives and senators have done the same? Could they have done so well? Had the Congress been entrusted with the problem would secrecy have been forfeited? Would there have been an advantage to have had the American people know about and participate in the decision? These are all questions to ponder when the fear of increased presidential powers in the realms of war and peace are voiced in the nuclear age. The questions also raise some uncomfortable problems of democratic theory. While it is by no means certain that the pragmatic solution of the first nuclear confrontation will be

32. Actually, not all the points originally agreed to were implemented. Because Premier Castro objected to inspection on Cuban soil, no U.N. inspection was ever made to ascertain whether the weapons were in fact removed. This event, and the American pledge not to invade Cuba if the missiles were removed, caused some to doubt the worth of the settlement obtained by President Kennedy. Since 1962 it has been contended from time to time that the missiles are still in Cuba, stored in caves.

duplicated in succeeding ones, should they occur, the importance of elevating the right caliber of people to the highest level of decision-making is apparent.

The struggle with big steel, which began at 5:45 P.M. on Tuesday, April 10, 1962, and ended at 5:28 P.M. on Friday of the same week; and the confrontation with the Soviet Union, which required nearly two weeks to resolve, demonstrate the range of power possessed by an American President in both domestic and foreign affairs—if he chooses to use it. In addition it should be recalled that during the steel crisis the President carried out his normal duties (which included being host to a reception for members of Congress and their wives; working on tax legislation with the Secretary of the Treasury; meeting the Shah of Iran at the airport, giving a state dinner for him and his empress, and attending another at the Iranian embassy; and inspecting the fleet at Norfolk). During the Cuban missile crisis the President was similarly busy with a multitude of other activities.

Range of presidential power

No matter how the Founding Fathers may have envisaged the chief magistrate they created at the Constitutional Convention, the job today has become the most complex and difficult in the world. For purposes of exposition and analysis, the President's task can be divided into a half-dozen dissimilar but interrelated parts, of which administration is only one.[33]

Chief of State

The President is the symbol of America at home and abroad. His only rival is the Constitution, which he can constantly defer to, regard as an ally, or upstage—as he sees fit. In the role of Chief of State he has the power to pardon or reprieve all offenses against the United States except those punished by impeachment, and in his discretion he may withhold a pardon, give a qualified one or a complete one, lighten a sentence, or delay its execution. He may grant amnesties for entire groups of people.

Diversity of functions

Most people expect their Chief of State to be aloof from politics and to behave like someone more than mortal. He is expected to visit devastated areas, throw the first baseball of the

33. Clinton Rossiter's accounting of presidential functions differs somewhat: Chief of State, Chief Executive, Commander-in-Chief, Chief Diplomat, Chief Legislator, Chief of Party, Voice of the People, Protector of the Peace, Manager of Prosperity, and World Leader. See his excellent study, *The American Presidency*, rev. (New York: Harcourt, Brace & World, 1966).

season, congratulate the "Truck Driver of the Year," and award medals to the survivors of fallen servicemen—all with appropriate words and demeanor. He receives notable visitors and pays visits of state to foreign lands. Even the people who dislike him most would rise to avenge an insult to him.

In times of tranquility the people are willing to wait for hours just to see him; in times of trouble they turn instinctively to him. They read about him in the newspapers, hear about him on the radio, and see him on television, because they are interested in everything about him and his family: what he had for breakfast, how he relaxes from the cares of the world's biggest job, and his reactions to both trivial and earth-shaking events.

If a President has a flair for the dramatic, he can capture the attention of the world. When he speaks, his words are translated into dozens of languages and promptly distributed over the globe. He is frequently immortalized by having his name attached to everything from schools to subway stops, from Paraguay to Paris. While he is alive, he is showered with gifts and letters from humble citizens; if he dies in office, millions of people feel grief at what seems to be a private loss.

Chief of Party

The role of Chief of Party is one the President has been expected to play ever since the time of Jefferson. As partisan chief, he not only must lead but also must dispense political rewards to the party faithful. The two go hand in hand: the President was elected to office by an organized group of people who are willing to defer to his leadership as long as he fulfils their expectations. They want him to use the enormous prestige and power of his office to help them, and there are at least two ways he can do it.

PATRONAGE

Almost from the beginning a change of Presidents signaled a rush of jobseekers to the capital to take over government positions held by political appointees. Since the passage of the Civil Service Act, there have been fewer and fewer jobs for the administration to hand over to the "boys," but there are still thousands of positions on the higher levels at the disposal of the President: embassy posts, judgeships, and positions in Federal agencies. When such plums are wisely distributed, they gain influential friends for the Administration and strengthen the

Senate concurrence

party tie. Of course, the rule of "senatorial courtesy" applies to offices within the boundaries of single states and so effectively removes such assignments from the President's personal control.

Appointments to all "superior" offices require the confirming vote of two-thirds of the Senate, but most of them are agreed to automatically. In the few instances where the Senate indicates reluctance to approve a nominee, the President may decide to fight or to back down gracefully. Forcing individuals into positions against the wishes of party leaders is sometimes possible, but it is seldom an appropriate use of the power held by the Chief of Party. The Constitution provides that the President may fill vacancies "that may happen during the recess of the Senate" by granting commissions which expire at the end of the next session: a person may be given a "recess appointment" subject to Senate approval, but if confirmation fails to come, he may only serve until the expiration of the session. If a President is adamant, he can keep reappointing the same man to the same office, but such behavior would seem to breach the spirit of the Constitution however much it might delight the people. If a recess appointee is rejected by the Senate, it is customary for him to resign, but the President can remove him summarily at any time.

The power to appoint does not necessarily imply the power to remove all Federal employees. In 1926 the Supreme Court decided that postmasters could be removed without the approval of the Senate,[34] but a decade later the Court ruled that a member of the Federal Trade Commission could not be summarily dismissed by the President because of policy differences, since commissioners are appointed for fixed terms and the grounds for removal are explicitly set out in statutes.[35] Therefore, whether or not a President may remove an officer is determined by the character of the office. The Court has been especially solicitous of holders of "inferior offices" who have been forced from their positions because of alleged "security reasons."[36]

Removal of appointees

PRESTIGE

The office of the Presidency has more prestige than any other position in the United States. By channeling the glow to members of his party, the President can aid them enormously in the

34. Myers v. United States, 272 U.S. 52 (1926).

35. Rathbun v. United States, 292 U.S. (1935).

36. Cole v. Young, 351 U.S. 536 (1955).

eyes of their fellow citizens. He can virtually name his party's candidate for the office he is vacating. He can be of immeasurable help to a candidate who is having a hard fight for a seat in Congress through personal appeals on his behalf—or even by issuing the familiar statements and posing with candidates for the usual photographs. He can patch up quarrels between party leaders and unite party members into a fighting team by the judicious use of personal influence and invitations.

Limits
The prestige of a President has its limits. Franklin D. Roosevelt learned that his impressive victory in 1936 could not be translated into sufficient power to "purge" conservative Democrats when he decided to go into their districts in person to help defeat them in the primaries.[37] Eisenhower was obliged to abandon the plan to convert his party to his conception of "modern Republicanism" two decades later for the same reason. Although he is Chief of Party, the President cannot always dictate to it. His party is made up of autonomous local units which can preserve their independence because the tradition of local control in American politics reacts savagely against uninvited meddling by "foreigners" and because they are not dependent upon the President for their patronage. In short, as Chief of Party, the President must negotiate with local party leaders much as he, as Chief Diplomat, does with the leaders of foreign governments.

Commander-in-Chief

As supreme commander, the President, with the advice and consent of the Senate, recommends the commissioning of all military officers, advancements in rank, and appointments to special positions, an important responsibility because the safety of the nation depends upon his choices. Although Congress alone may declare war, Presidents have dispatched ships and men to fight undeclared wars since the time of Jefferson. Presidents may precipitate wars, too: Polk in 1846 ordered United States troops into disputed territory; when Mexico resisted, he interpreted her activities as an act of war. Had the Soviet Union responded to President Kennedy's demand for removal of the missiles from Cuba with war, the Congress would have had no part in the development.

When war comes, the President takes the final responsibility for crucial decisions, whether they be to raise and deploy troops

37. See William Riker, "The Purge of 1938," in Theodore J. Lowi, ed., *Legislative Politics U.S.A.* (Boston: Little, Brown, 1967).

without authorization by Congress, as Lincoln did; to concentrate on one of several enemies, as Franklin D. Roosevelt did; to approve the use of atomic weapons, as Truman did, or decide when and where North Vietnam would be bombed, as President Johnson did. The Commander-in-Chief may make secret agreements with foreign nations that are much more important than treaties which must have the consent of the Senate. He may authorize (at least he *has* authorized) the relocation of American citizens in other parts of the country under the pressure of military necessity, as was done in the early days of World War II.[38]

War requires unity, teamwork, and discipline, so the people turn instinctively to one man. The changed psychology is reflected by the wartime tendency to refer to the President principally as the "Commander-in-Chief." He becomes a kind of constitutional dictator, but emphasis must be on the word "constitutional." The Commander-in-Chief still must face the voters, and although Lincoln was not defeated in a wartime election, it appeared certain that the people were prepared to "trade horses in the middle of the stream" until several military victories rescued Lincoln's political fortunes. Checks and balances continue to operate. Lincoln, Wilson, and Roosevelt watched off-year congressional elections with apprehension. The courts have always sat, and although they generally have been generous in their interpretations of the Commander-in-Chief's power during wartime, judicial review and precedents built up in postwar periods seriously curtail activities of the Presidents.[39]

Chief Policy-Maker

Although the responsibility of Congress in determining national policy is vast, the lawmakers appear to have been

38. The relocation of American citizens descended from Japanese ancestors was accepted under the pressures of war by the Supreme Court. See Korematsu v. United States, 323 U.S. 214 (1944) and for a detailed account, Allen Bosworth, *America's Concentration Camps* (New York: Norton, 1967).

39. For example, *Ex parte* Milligan, 4 Wallace 2 (1866); Duncan v. Kahanamuku, 327 U.S. 304 (1946); and Youngstown Sheet & Tube v. Sawyer, 343 U.S. 579 (1952). In the latter case President Truman "seized" most of the nation's steel mills during the Korean conflict. The President gave as his reason for the seizure the fact that threatened work stoppage would jeopardize the Korean military effort and would constitute a national catastrophe. He justified his act as falling within the total constitutional powers he possessed as Chief Executive and Commander-in-Chief. The Court did not agree, and the seizure was speedily ended.

Basset in Scripps-Howard Newspapers

"Just remember . . . I'm an independent deliberative body!"

Working with Congress

maneuvered into the frustrating position where they must either cooperate with the Chief Executive on policy or be on the defensive. The position is not entirely a result of the refusal of strong presidents to treat the legislative branch as an equal (as is sometimes charged) but to the logic of the Constitution and to historical events. If the Founding Fathers thought that, by incorporating the principle of separation of powers into the Constitution, they had locked the door on the possibility of one person controlling the making of policy, they were right—but checks and balances prevented leadership coming from Congress. The provision that the President "shall from time to time give the Congress information of the state of the Union, and recommend to their consideration such measures as he shall judge necessary and expedient" has, over the years, come to mean that the legislators now wait to hear what he wants and then accept, reject, or modify his proposals. Although the first two presidents appeared personally before Congress to deliver their "State of the Union" addresses, the practice lay dormant for a century after Jefferson abandoned it (as violating separation of powers). Wilson revived the addresses, and Franklin D. Roosevelt seized the opportunity to draw the attention of the entire country to his legislative proposals. These speeches now receive a great deal of attention at home and abroad. On Capitol Hill they signal a flood of Administration bills—and, if the President is adamant about his program, a corps of White House aides to work for their passage.

From time to time the working of the election process results in the Congress being controlled by one party and the White House by the other. Such was the case after the election of 1968 when President Nixon had to work with a Democratically controlled 91st Congress—243 Democrats and 192 Republicans in the House and 58 Democrats and 42 Republicans in the Senate. To avoid deadlock under such conditions it is necessary for statesmanship to be exercised both on Capitol Hill and in the Executive Mansion.

THE ORDINANCE POWER

One of the greatest claims of the President to be the Chief Policy-Maker is the ordinance power. Ordinances are detailed rules and regulations prescribed by the executive branch. The President has inherent power to make ordinances for the administration of his branch of government, but this power has been enhanced by Congress when it passes many laws which are general in their nature and which contain the provision that the President may fill in the details. Congress is simply not suited to determine standard instrument approach procedures for the municipal airport in Centralia, Illinois, or to determine when and which public utilities companies may issue bonds for sinking funds. Such decisions are better made and revised by the experts who serve on the Federal Aviation Agency and the Securities and Exchange Commission. The Supreme Court has upheld the delegation of rule-making power from the Congress to the President, provided the statutes are carefully drafted to afford intelligible principles which guide the administrative officers.[40] If the transfer is made in vague language which

Detailed rules and regulations

40. J. W. Hampton Co. v. United States, 276 U.S. 394 (1928).

apparently sets no boundaries, the courts may disallow the authorization as unconstitutional.[41]

The ordinances, which have the effect of law, have appeared in the *Federal Register* since 1936 and take effect upon publication there. The arrangement follows the scheme of titles of the *United States Code* in order to facilitate the use of these volumes by lawyers, government administrators, and other interested persons. The *"Fed. Reg."* is printed several times a week and bears the same relationship to the executive branch as the *Statutes at Large* do to Congress. The constant flux of administrative rules appearing in the *Federal Register* makes codification mandatory, and the *Code of Federal Regulations (C.F.R.)* fills this need. It is kept fairly current by the use of supplements, cumulative supplements, "added pocket parts," and, on occasion, complete reissues.

THE VETO POWER

Although Alexander Hamilton feared that Presidents would use the veto power less frequently than they should, Andrew Jackson demonstrated its potency, and Presidents have employed it ever since as another bulwark to their position as Chief Policy-Maker. The veto is qualified by the checks and balances which allow extraordinary majorities in both houses of Congress to override a President, but the strength of the veto lies in the fact that such majorities are usually not obtainable. If two thirds of the members of Congress are unalterably arrayed against the President, the legislative branch can virtually assume control of the government.[42] This happened once in American history, and few would like to see the phenomenon repeated.

The strength of the veto

After the congressional elections of 1866, Andrew Johnson was faced with hostile odds of 3 to 1 in Congress. This handicap and some personal inadequacies put him into the helpless situation of vetoing bill after bill which he considered to be unconstitutional only to watch them pass; his work as Chief Administrator was hampered by the Tenure of Office Act (1867); his function of Commander-in-Chief was negated by the Command of the Army Act (1867); and finally, the pinnacle of the presidential office was attacked when the Chief of State was subjected to impeachment proceedings in 1868. The

41. Schechter Poultry Corp. v. United States, 295 U.S. 495 (1935).

42. By withdrawing appellate jurisdiction from the Supreme Court in habeas corpus matters and reducing the size of the Court, Congress brought the Supreme Court to heel before its showdown with President Andrew Johnson.

humiliated President was actually impeached but then was acquitted in the Senate trial by a single vote. In the long run, the dubious behavior of the 40th Congress no doubt did as much to weaken the legislative branch vis-à-vis the President as any historical "usurpation" by the Chief Policy-Maker.[43] Today, a national controversy is touched off whenever a rare bill is passed over a presidential veto, and usually the threat of using the negative power is sufficient to force compromise on legislation which has importance beyond political advantage.

CONTROL OF THE DEPARTMENT OF JUSTICE

It is curious that so few citizens are aware of the fact that the Department of Justice is a useful instrument in the President's medicine bag. When it is realized that this arm of the government is charged with the enforcement of Federal criminal statutes, the potential power of the person who decides which investigations will be made can be understood. The head of the department is the Attorney General—a presidential appointee and member of his Cabinet. It is desirable that political organizations, business corporations, labor unions, and private associations which have somewhere run afoul of Federal law need to be investigated and brought to justice. On the other hand, even groups which are as clean as a hound's tooth have no desire to have government agents checking them. Fortunately, the Department of Justice has an excellent record for fair play, but its potential danger for harassment should never be forgotten by the citizenry.[44]

Enforcement of statutes

Chief of Foreign Policy

In determining foreign policy the President's supremacy is firmly established, even though political and institutional checks and balances continue to operate. He is Chief of Foreign Policy, Chief Diplomat. "In this vast external realm, with its important, complicated, delicate and manifold problems, the President alone has the power to speak or listen as a repre-

43. In the campaign of 1948, while smarting under setbacks from the first Republican Congress in 16 years, President Truman toured the country denouncing the "no good, good-for-nothing Eightieth Congress" as "the worse since the Fortieth Congress." The voters responded by sweeping Truman back into office and returning the Congress to Democratic control.

44. This danger may be dramatically increased in the next decade by electronic devices available for wire-tapping, "bugging," and otherwise listening to the conversations of individuals.

sentative of the nation," a conservative Justice wrote for a conservative Supreme Court.[45] Six years later a liberal Justice for a liberalized Court said, "The powers of the President in the conduct of foreign relations include the power, without consent of the Senate, to determine the public policy of the United States."[46]

Dominant position

The very nature of international affairs requires such interpretations of the dominant position of the Chief of Foreign Policy. As Chief of State he alone represents the nation; as Commander-in-Chief he heads the military establishment; and he has access to diplomatic, military, and intelligence reports which even Congress may not force him to disclose. In addition, the Supreme Court has upheld his right to make "executive agreements" with the heads of foreign states.[47] These do not require the advice and consent of the Senate—even if they trade public property for island bases.[48] Although executive agreements bind only the *persons* who make them, the reluctance of the American people to break international commitments has obliged subsequent Presidents and Congresses to honor the agreements made.

Evidences of the pre-eminence of the President in making foreign commitments abound—in the popular names of specific policies, such as the "Monroe Doctrine," the "Truman Doctrine," and the "Eisenhower Doctrine," and in other well-known international positions intimately associated with Presidents: "Non-Entanglement" (Washington and Jefferson); "Open Door" (McKinley, T. Roosevelt); "Big Stick" (T. Roosevelt); "Good Neighbor" (F. D. Roosevelt); "Point Four" (Truman); "Alliance for Progress" (Kennedy), and "Containment" (Truman, Eisenhower, Kennedy, Johnson, Nixon). The recognition of some governments (*e.g.*, the Soviet Union by Roosevelt) and the refusal to recognize other governments (*e.g.*, Communist China on the part of Truman, Eisenhower, Kennedy, Johnson, and Nixon) have provoked a great deal of public discussion. Finally, every student of American history is aware

45. Mr. Justice Sutherland in United States v. Curtiss-Wright Export Corp., 299 U.S. 304 (1936).

46. Mr. Justice Douglas in United States v. Pink, 315 U.S. 204 (1942).

47. B. Altman & Co. v. United States, 224 U.S. 583 (1911).

48. President F. D. Roosevelt traded 50 "overage" destroyers to Prime Minister Churchill of Great Britain in return for long-term leases on Caribbean Sea islands. The President's Attorney General (later appointed to the Supreme Court) saw no constitutional problem created by the transfer. 39 *Ops. Att'y Gen.* 474 (1940).

of the attitudes and actions of Presidents which have encouraged, discouraged or settled wars.

The Supreme Court ruled the judicial branch out of inquiring into foreign relations on the ground that this area is the proper concern only of the political branches of the national government.[49] As previously mentioned, even Congress has had to be satisfied with a relatively passive role.[50] It may refuse to provide money required by the President's foreign policies and pass resolutions advising the Chief Policy-Maker of its attitudes. Its committees may investigate government agencies and installations at home and abroad, and the Senate may refuse to confirm ambassadors because it does not agree with their views or assignments. However, during the past decades, the Presidents have initiated and Congress has ratified nearly every major foreign policy undertaken by the United States. As one observer notes, "points of detail could be and often were compromised in the face of congressional objections. But the heart of what the President of the hour wanted, the Congress approved."[51] Everything considered, the complications in domestic affairs which result from policy differences between a nationally oriented President and a more parochial Congress are practically absent in the realm of foreign policy, except of course for serious disputes arising from the Vietnam war.

Other branches and foreign policy

Chief Administrator

The principle of separation of powers assigned the administration of government to the executive branch. The Constitution clearly conveys the responsibility to the President when it says that "he shall take care that the laws be faithfully executed." This requirement would have been a full-time job for the first Chief Administrators even when the laws were few and

49. United States v. Belmont, 301 U.S. 324 (1937).

50. In the early 1950's then-Senator Bricker (R., Ohio) sought a constitutional amendment which would have given Congress power to regulate "all executive and other agreements with a foreign power or international organization." The proposal was publicly disapproved by both Presidents Truman and Eisenhower and failed to muster the two-thirds vote required by the Constitution for submission to the states. Concern that the treaty power might be used for unconstitutional purposes probably was laid to rest by the decision of Reid v. Covert, 354 U.S. 1 (1957).

51. Sidney Hyman, "The Man on Top," *The New Republic*, CXLVI (June 11, 1962), p. 16. For analysis of the contrasting roles of the executive and Congress in foreign policy, see James A. Robinson, *Congress and Foreign Policy-Making* (Homewood, Ill.: The Dorsey Press, 1962), especially Chap. 2.

uncomplicated and the ordinance power so underdeveloped that neither special volumes nor a code was required to publicize and catalog them. Yet today's President has almost as many administrative subdivisions as the entire national government had employees in Jefferson's day, and the number of civil servants has increased more than 1,000 percent. How can a President possibly supervise over 3,000,000 Federal employees (scattered among all states and most foreign countries) when he can only allot part of his time to the task of administration?

The answer is that administrative control is one of the most difficult problems which the President faces. Too many Americans tend to think of the executive branch as an ordered hierarchy (just as it is portrayed graphically on government organization charts), with presidential commands flowing downward and immediate response flowing upward. As Richard Neustadt points out, however, the executive establishment, like the governmental structure as a whole, consists of separated institutions sharing power. Cabinet officers, agency administrators, and bureau chiefs all have many loyalties—not only to the President, but to Congress and its committees, to "clients" outside the government, and to their own staffs.[52] As a result, the President can seldom command even his own subordinates; instead, he must persuade them that what he wants them to do in the interests of his Administration is what they should do in their own interests as well.

The executive establishment

When a President assumes office, he inherits a Civil Service staffed with able and dedicated career personnel who have built up such a tradition for honest and efficient work that an occasional disclosure to the contrary surprises and angers the American people. Over the years the channels of communication up and down the hierarchy have been established so solidly that the bureaucracy could continue functioning for months even

Career personnel

52. *Presidential Power* (New York: New American Library, 1964), pp. 42–51. The difficulties encountered by the Chief Administrator are well illustrated by the remarks of one of America's most powerful Presidents, Franklin Roosevelt: "The Treasury is so large and far-flung and ingrained in its practices that I find it almost impossible to get action and results I want—even with Henry [Morgenthau] there. But the Treasury is not to be compared with the State Department. You should go through the experience of trying to get any changes in the thinking, policy, and action of the career diplomats and then you'd know what a real problem was. But the Treasury and the State Department put together are nothing compared with the Na-a-vy. The admirals are really something to cope with—and I should know. To change anything in the Na-a-vy is like punching a feather bed. You punch it with your right and you punch it with your left until you are finally exhausted, and then you find the damn bed just as it was before you started punching." Marriner S. Eccles, *Beckoning Frontiers*, quoted in Neustadt, p. 50.

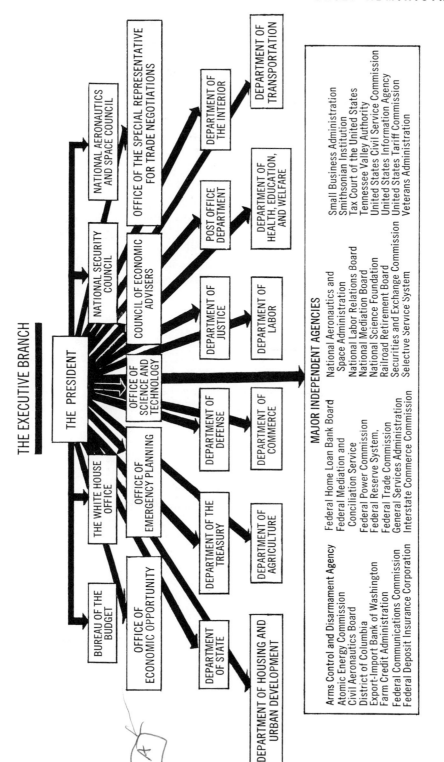

THE EXECUTIVE BRANCH

THE PRESIDENT

BUREAU OF THE BUDGET

OFFICE OF ECONOMIC OPPORTUNITY

THE WHITE HOUSE OFFICE

OFFICE OF EMERGENCY PLANNING

OFFICE OF SCIENCE AND TECHNOLOGY

NATIONAL SECURITY COUNCIL

COUNCIL OF ECONOMIC ADVISERS

NATIONAL AERONAUTICS AND SPACE COUNCIL

OFFICE OF THE SPECIAL REPRESENTATIVE FOR TRADE NEGOTIATIONS

DEPARTMENT OF STATE

DEPARTMENT OF THE TREASURY

DEPARTMENT OF DEFENSE

DEPARTMENT OF JUSTICE

POST OFFICE DEPARTMENT

DEPARTMENT OF THE INTERIOR

DEPARTMENT OF HOUSING AND URBAN DEVELOPMENT

DEPARTMENT OF AGRICULTURE

DEPARTMENT OF COMMERCE

DEPARTMENT OF LABOR

DEPARTMENT OF HEALTH, EDUCATION, AND WELFARE

DEPARTMENT OF TRANSPORTATION

MAJOR INDEPENDENT AGENCIES

Arms Control and Disarmament Agency
Atomic Energy Commission
Civil Aeronautics Board
District of Columbia
Export-Import Bank of Washington
Farm Credit Administration
Federal Communications Commission
Federal Deposit Insurance Corporation

Federal Home Loan Bank Board
Federal Mediation and Conciliation Service
Federal Power Commission
Federal Reserve System,
Federal Trade Commission
General Services Administration
Interstate Commerce Commission

National Aeronautics and Space Administration
National Labor Relations Board
National Mediation Board
National Science Foundation
Railroad Retirement Board
Securities and Exchange Commission
Selective Service System

Small Business Administration
Smithsonian Institution
Tax Court of the United States
Tennessee Valley Authority
United States Civil Service Commission
United States Information Agency
United States Tariff Commission
Veterans Administration

CIA

without direction from the Chief Administrator. Although there was a time in American history when a change of Presidents meant the wholesale replacement of personnel throughout the government service, today only the policy-makers change. These executives are appointed by the President and are responsible to him, while the career service personnel are expected to serve their new chiefs as faithfully as they did their former ones. The task of supervision is simplified, even though it is still difficult.

Ideally, an administrator should have fewer than a dozen people reporting directly to him, a principle of organization which should extend completely throughout the hierarchy. Unfortunately, the President is denied this luxury partly because of the gigantic size and widespread activities of the Federal bureaucracy, but more importantly because attempts to reorganize the executive branch scientifically have to be compromised for politics.

THE CABINET

There are 12 great departments in the executive branch: State (foreign affairs); Treasury; Defense (including Army, Navy, Air Force, and the Marine Corps); Justice; Post Office; Interior; Agriculture; Commerce; Labor; Health, Education, and Welfare; Housing and Urban Development; and Transportation. At first glance, the department heads or secretaries who make up the Cabinet would seem ideally suited to fill the President's needs for establishing uniform and coherent national policy—but they don't. The Cabinet has not been the lofty policy-making body most people mistakenly think it is, even though Presidents have met with it regularly since the time of Washington.[53] For some time, Presidents have preferred to rely on advisers outside the group—the "kitchen cabinet" (which dates from Andrew Jackson)—and disproportionately on some official advisers—the "inner cabinet." Wilson had his Colonel House, Franklin Roosevelt his Harry Hopkins, and Dwight Eisenhower his Sherman Adams. Coolidge leaned heavily on his Secretaries of State and Treasury (Charles Evans Hughes and Andrew Mellon) as did Eisenhower (John Foster Dulles and George Humphrey). Kennedy also made selective and differential use of his Cabinet and White House advisers. Although he delegated to each Cabinet member responsibility for the management of his department, he made little use of

Special advisers

53. The functions and relationships of the Cabinet are thoroughly investigated in Richard F. Fenno, Jr., *The President's Cabinet* (Cambridge: Harvard University Press, 1959).

the entire Cabinet as a group. Instead, as all-purpose advisers, he used his Vice President, Lyndon Johnson, and his brother, Attorney General Robert Kennedy. If the problem at hand concerned a domestic issue or the national economy, the appropriate Cabinet member as well as the Vice President, the Special Counsel to the President, the director of the Bureau of the Budget, the chairman of the Council of Economic Advisers, and perhaps the Secretary of the Treasury would work with the President on a solution. If the problem pertained to foreign policy, then the work group generally was composed of Secretary of State Dean Rusk, Secretary of Defense Robert S. McNamara, and the President's Special Assistant, McGeorge Bundy.[54]

President Johnson's use of the Cabinet was more akin to Eisenhower's than to Kennedy's, in that a regular agenda was followed. Those who attended Johnson Cabinet meetings reported them to be occasions when the President infused his high-level team with a sense of direction and solidarity.[55] Among the cabinet officers, Secretary of State Rusk, and, until his departure in early 1968, Secretary of Defense McNamara appeared to be the men upon whom the President relied most. As has been the case with other Presidents, Johnson sought advice from men not in the Cabinet, including individuals outside the government. Prominent among his Special Assistants were William Moyers, who also served as his press secretary for a time, and W. W. Rostow, who assumed the national security role played by Bundy under Kennedy. Abe Fortas, later appointed to the Supreme Court, and Clark Clifford, appointed to replace McNamara at the Pentagon, were advisers to the President before he brought them formally into government service.

There are good reasons today for the altered status of the President's Cabinet. First, political considerations, not personal

Johnson and the Cabinet

54. "I can't imagine," said one Cabinet member, "why the President would want to hear Bob McNamara talk about price supports on cotton or Orville Freeman [Secretary of Agriculture] talk about sending troops to Vietnam." Quoted in Richard F. Fenno, Jr., "The Cabinet: Index to the Kennedy Way," *New York Times Magazine*, April 22, 1962, p. 13. For a similar view of Kennedy's Cabinet by a leading Washington reporter, see Carroll Kilpatrick, "Is Kennedy Correct in Use of Cabinet?" *Washington Post and Times Herald*, March 25, 1962. p. E1. See also Robert F. Kennedy, *op. cit.*, for a discussion of what men President Kennedy relied upon during the Cuban missile crisis. President Nixon began his term by giving significant policy roles to his special advisers for national security affairs (Henry A. Kissinger) and urban problems (Daniel P. Moynihan).

55. "The President's Cabinet," *CQ Guide to Current American Government* (Washington: Congressional Quarterly Service, January 1968), p. 76.

affinity, are primary in the selection of Cabinet members. The group is expected to represent factions within the President's party and, recently, even members of the opposition party. Arguments are advanced for religious representation. Geographical sections insist on having a man on the Cabinet (*e.g.*, the Secretary of Interior is expected to come from the West). In addition, business, agricultural, and labor interests must be appeased in the selection of the Secretaries of Commerce, Agriculture, and Labor. Such representation is a fine way to cement unity, but it does not particularly encourage teamwork.

Secondly, since Franklin D. Roosevelt created the Executive Office of the President by executive order in 1939 to handle **The Executive Office** policy and administrative problems which were not amenable to Cabinet consideration, many of the Secretaries were pushed further into the periphery of influence. The free hand with which the President appoints his personal selections to key positions in the Executive Office and juggles their assignments to suit his immediate needs has brought them into more intimate contact with him than most of his other aides.[56] Indeed, even Cabinet members work closely with members of the White House staff, both before and after they take their problems to the Chief Administrator.

As the Executive Office of the President has grown in size so has it increased in importance. For example, the director of the Bureau of the Budget not only confers with the President and other executive branch officials on budgetary policy, but he and his staff also make suggestions on pending and passed legislation, as well as upon problems in improving governmental efficiency.[57] The three-man Council of Economic Advisers wields tremendous influence as it advises the President upon actions which the Federal Government should take, or refrain from taking, in regard to controlling the nation's economy. On occasions the National Security Council and the Central Intelligence Agency have dealt with the gravest threats found in the international arena. Although perhaps less spectacular in terms of the severity of the problems they handle, the other divisions of the Executive Office of the President direct their

56. The Executive Office of the President consists of 10 divisions: The White House Office, Bureau of the Budget, Council of Economic Advisers, National Security Council, Central Intelligence Agency, National Aeronautics and Space Council, Office of Economic Opportunity, Office of Emergency Planning, Office of Science and Technology, and Office of the Special Representative for Trade Negotiations.

57. The role of the Bureau of the Budget in reviewing and coordinating agency legislative requests—"legislative clearance"—is examined in Richard Neustadt, "Presidency and Legislation: The Growth of Central Clearance," *American Political Science Review*, LXVIII (September, 1954), 641–71.

efforts toward significant problems which the Founding Fathers never dreamed about.

INDEPENDENT OFFICES, ESTABLISHMENTS, AND REGULATORY COMMISSIONS

In addition to intimate contact with the members of his Executive Office and formal meetings with his Cabinet, the President as Chief Administrator generally supervises activities of a multitude of committees, commissions, and agencies outside the 10 divisions of his Executive Office and the 12 Departments of the Federal Government. The tasks of these independent entities range from managing the Arlington Memorial Amphitheater to atomic energy. As early as 1937, a committee on administrative management recommended that all independent agencies be incorporated within the departments in order to streamline administration. Congress implemented some of the suggestions along with those made later by the Hoover Commission Report on Organization of the Executive Branch (1949), but, for reasons of its own, has been reluctant to follow all the recommendations. It is doubtful if these reasons include concern about the logic of distributing subject matter. For example, a glance through the *United States Government Organization Manual* reveals that the Treasury manages the Coast Guard and the Bureau of Narcotics, whereas the enormous span of the Department of Health, Education, and Welfare does not include the Gorgas Memorial Institute of Tropical and Preventative Medicine. One can only imagine the political pressures generated by the independent agencies when faced with the threat of losing their status by being incorporated into the maze of bureaus, divisions, branches, and sections of one of the departments.

Attempts to consolidate

Congress has been adamant about retaining the independence of the great regulatory commissions.[58] These quasi-legislative, quasi-judicial administrative bodies were sporadically created by the demand of the citizenry for national regulation of private businesses concerned with banking, commerce, transportation, labor, and public utilities. Congress established fixed terms of five to fourteen years for the bipartisan members of the regulatory commissions; they are subject to removal only for cause (except for the FCC and SEC, where members may be removed for policy differences by a President). Recognizing the

Regulatory commissions

58. United States Atomic Energy Commission, Civil Aeronautics Board, Civil Service Commission, Federal Communications Commission, Federal Power Commission, Federal Trade Commission, Interstate Commerce Commission, National Labor Relations Board, Security and Exchange Commission.

279

facts of complicated modern life, Congress has outlined only vaguely the policies the commissions are to follow (such as requiring "fair and reasonable" rates, or granting licenses on the basis of "public convenience, interest, or necessity"). The commissions are staffed with experts who have adequate professional assistance allocated so that investigations may be made, regulations prescribed, and violations punished.

Cease and desist orders

"Trials" before the quasi-judicial agencies are informal, with flexible procedures not found in courts of law. The commissioners, experts in their field who are not necessarily trained in law, are aided by legal assistants and ordinarily settle disputes with dispatch and justice. They are authorized to issue "cease and desist" orders to enforce their regulations, and if violators do not comply, to implement the order with a decree from a Federal court. Similarly, a party before an administrative tribunal may petition an appropriate Federal court for judicial review of the commission's decision. The ever growing number of cases has led to the formation of a branch of legal science new in the United States but well-regarded in other countries—administrative law. Many traditional lawyers and judges view the rapid growth of administrative law with apprehension even though they recognize that ordinary courts of law have neither the time nor the talent to adjudicate the intricate disagreements which became inevitable when government began to regulate privately owned and operated business.[59]

THE OPERATION OF THE CIVIL SERVICE

In order to transform policy into programs, money and personnel are needed. Money for salaries and operating expenses are voted by Congress and approved by the President. Personnel are appointed on a basis of politics or merit. Appointments to the policy-making posts are made by the President with the advice and consent of the Senate, but over 90 percent of all Federal employees owe their positions to their own capabilities; they are assured of tenure until they resign, retire, or are removed for good cause. The Civil Service Commission, with regional offices in twelve cities, is responsible for recruiting, examining, training, and rating the classified employees and providing for their retirement. In addition to merit, the other chief criteria the Commission relies upon in making appointments are loyalty (to the government) and geography (to give each state an equitable representation).

The Civil Service Commission

Announcements for the competitive examinations, posted in Federal buildings, inform interested persons where application

59. See Peter Woll, *American Bureaucracy* (New York: Norton, 1963).

may be made and what qualifications (if any) are necessary in order to be considered for the examination. A number of types of examinations, both written and oral, practical and theoretical, are used to fill the spectrum of positions in the Federal Government. The majority of those seeking employment with the government in civilian status are required to take and pass the Federal Service Entrance Examination.[60] A score of 70 percent is necessary to pass. One who passes is ranked on a register according to his points. Veterans are given preference by the addition of 5 points to their earned scores, 10 if disabled in the service. The preference points are transferable to unmarried widows of veterans, and in some cases to the mothers of servicemen who were disabled or killed.

Competitive exams

When a vacancy occurs in a Civil Service position, the appointing officer is furnished a list of the three highest-ranking applicants, and if he decides not to choose one of them, he is obliged to explain in writing why he did not. The names of the applicants suggested but not hired are returned to the top of the register. After new examinations are held, the old register is discarded.

New civil servants under the merit system are employed on a probationary basis for six months. This permits easy weeding out of people who perform well in examinations but are unable to work with others. Once final appointment is given, it is extremely difficult to remove an employee without good cause. If dismissal were made easy, politics might reappear in the Civil Service under the cloak of "the good of the service." If dismissal is difficult, inept and lazy employees retain their jobs. Whenever a permanent employee is to be dismissed, he receives a copy of charges brought against him and has the right of appeal. The protection afforded by the system is illustrated in the famous case of an incompetent stenographer who clung to her job seventeen months before she had exhausted all her rights.

The merit system

The prestige of working for the government has never been as high in the United States as in Germany and Great Britain partly because of the odium cast on the Civil Service by decades of the "spoils system," when positions were handed out on the basis of political service rather than on ability. Other reasons probably include the traditional distrust Americans have had for government and the relatively low pay. Improvement began with the passage of the Pendleton Act (1883) which

Prestige

60. Special examinations and criteria are used to select individuals for the Department of State, for certain managerial positions, and for technical and specialized positions of various kinds.

established the merit system. Furthermore, a number of salary increase and benefit expansion laws have enhanced the appeal of working for the government, as has the general prestige of government service. Nevertheless, periodic efforts are made by the President to secure better pay for civil servants, and the problems of recruitment and retention of personnel remain.

Although political parties out of power frequently promise to "clean up the mess in Washington," the few instances of **Removal** proved misbehavior almost always trace to political appointees—frequently those subject to the rule of "senatorial courtesy." Among workers recruited through the merit system an extremely tiny minority were dismissed for cause during the security investigations of the early 1950's. Only a fraction of these were cited for "disloyalty," the remainder being "security risks" because they were potentially subject to blackmail for present or past activities, immoderate drinking, or questionable friends.

Responsibility of government employees to the Chief Administrator is implemented by the chain of command—everybody except the lowest on the totem pole reports to and takes orders from someone in the level above him and, in turn, directs those below him. Administrators are also responsible to Congress, although very few are impeached, and Congress may not remove a specific individual from his position. Congress can, however, abolish positions, and the powers it uses most effectively are its authority to investigate and its control of appropriations. Finally, Federal employees are responsible to the judiciary to an extent uncommon in most countries. Angry citizens, by challenging actions as *ultra vires*, may bring an administrator before the ordinary courts to determine whether or not he is acting within his powers. In a case properly before them, the judges can go even further and determine whether or not the statute under which a government employee operates is constitutional.

The Responsibility of Being a President

The President is hemmed in by checks and balances when he functions in his roles of Chief Administrator, Commander-in-Chief, and Chief Policy-Maker. However, when he ventures into foreign relations as Chief of Foreign Policy or Chief Diplomat, the President realizes that hundreds of millions of people at home and abroad depend almost entirely on his own character and wisdom. There may be no time, in a "worst possible case," to consult with allies, or even to allow a temperate discussion with his closest adviser. His is also the awesome responsibility for distinguishing sharply between his position as Chief of State and his tasks as Chief of Party, knowing that if he confuses the roles, he will bring the highest office in the nation into disrepute.

It is also apparent, even from this brief discussion of the different (and, sometimes, contradictory) roles he must perform in domestic life, that the requirements of the office of the President of the United States demand more skill and time than any one person can be reasonably expected to have. In addition to these worries, the primary place of the United States in world affairs has increased his responsibilities to a frightening degree: his attitudes can set off or prevent revolutions and invasions in other countries; a mistake in judgment or a loss of temper could plunge the entire world into war. The awful truth is that the President is officially alone, and the decisions, whether trivial or crucial, must be *his* decisions. Much as he might like to share his load, he cannot; much as others would like to assume part of it, they may not.

The Vice President

It has been a maxim from the first that the Vice Presidency is the least desirable position in the national government. The first person to hold the office suggested that a suitable title would be "Your Superfluous Excellency." In 1960 the newly nominated Democratic candidate John F. Kennedy offered the Vice Presidency to Senator Lyndon Johnson of Texas. Before Johnson accepted, he called John Nance Garner, a fellow Texan and former Vice President under Franklin Roosevelt, to inquire about the wisdom of accepting second place on the ticket. It is reported that Garner replied in colorful Texas style, "The Vice Presidency isn't worth a pitcher of warm spit."[61] Many outstanding men have refused the nomination, and one actually resigned from the office (John C. Calhoun in 1832). The Constitution relegates the Vice President to the fate of presiding over a body of which he is not a member, and thereby effectively reduces his influence for shaping policy. He cannot take a leading role in administration because the Constitution gives the charge directly to the President. He cannot take up the burden of Chief of Party because the policy (and, fre-

Views of the office

61. Theodore H. White, *The Making of the President: 1960*, p. 176.

quently, personality) differences—which made him suitable for "balancing the ticket" in the first place—rule him out. There can be only one Commander-in-Chief. In the past, Vice Presidents were virtually unknown to the people and so were not suitable for representing the nation at home or abroad.

However, Franklin D. Roosevelt's suggestion that his third-term Vice President pay a state visit to Latin America during the war years (aided by Mr. Wallace's efforts to learn Spanish before departing) resulted in an astonishingly successful debut of Vice Presidents into international relations; another minor revolution in American constitutional practice had evidently been introduced.

Changes in status

President Eisenhower included his Vice President, Richard Nixon, in high policy meetings, sent him abroad to Latin America and to the Soviet Union, and generally "used" him more than had been the custom of previous Presidents.[62] While Vice President, Lyndon Johnson chafed at the gap between his position and that of final authority. However, Theodore White notes that Johnson was a participant in every very high level council of state, such as meetings of the National Security Council, or the Cabinet, and conferences with the congressional leadership.[63] Furthermore, the Vice President under Kennedy was kept well briefed concerning major military and foreign affairs policies.[64] Under President Johnson the Vice Presidency continued to be a position about which more activity revolved than during most of American history. Hubert H. Humphrey actively participated in the councils of government, although perhaps not in all of the decisions regarding the increasing involvement of the United States in the Vietnamese war.[65]

62. The assumption of a major international role by the United States after World War II has required visits of state on a scale never imagined by the Americans of the past, and because the President is rarely free to travel abroad, the long-sought useful role for the Vice President apparently has been discovered. It seems appropriate that this officer, too, should fill a position never intended by the founders, just as the enormously increased importance of his position has given even greater force to the insistence of one founder that the Vice President be an "extraordinary person."

63. *The Making of the President: 1964*, p. 58.

64. White, *loc. cit.*

65. James Reston, "Vietnam Policy Root of Switch," *Arizona Daily Star*, September 27, 1968. Whatever the Vice-President's views of the war, Humphrey did defend his Commander-in-Chief's foreign policies in public. However, late in the 1968 presidential campaign Humphrey attempted to convince the voters he would be his own man regarding Vietnam, if elected.

Presidential Succession

One feature which has been consistent in the American system of government is that provisions made for the orderly transfer of power when a President dies have always been implemented. This has been true even under the traumatic conditions following the assassination of Abraham Lincoln, the sudden death of Franklin D. Roosevelt during World War II, and the assassination of John F. Kennedy.[66] The provisions for the transfer of power in case of the President's death flow from Article II, Section I of the Constitution, and the Presidential Succession Act of 1947.[67] Both constitutional and statutory requirements have been refined in practice through the years by a number of tragedies.

Constitutional provision

TABLE 6.2 Incompleted Terms of Presidents

President	Term	Succeeded by
William Henry Harrison	Mar. 4, 1841 - Apr. 4, 1841	John Tyler
Zachary Taylor	Mar. 5, 1849 - July 9, 1850	Millard Fillmore
Abraham Lincoln	Mar. 4, 1865 - Apr. 15, 1865 (second term)	Andrew Johnson
James A. Garfield	Mar. 4, 1881 - Sept. 19, 1881	Chester A. Arthur
William McKinley	Mar. 4, 1901 - Sept. 14, 1901 (second term)	Theodore Roosevelt
Warren G. Harding	Mar. 4, 1921 - Aug. 2, 1923	Calvin Coolidge
Franklin D. Roosevelt	Jan. 20, 1945- Apr. 12, 1945 (fourth term)	Harry S. Truman
John F. Kennedy	Jan. 20, 1961- Nov. 22, 1963	Lyndon B. Johnson

However, despite the Constitution's wording that the powers of the President "shall devolve on the Vice President" should the former suffer an "Inability to discharge the Powers and Duties" of the office, it is not clear what should legally occur should a President become seriously ill or succumb to mental incompetency. In a slower-paced age, when it took weeks to ship a cannon from Europe to America, the matter was less serious than in the second half of the twentieth century when the Soviet Union is only 30 minutes away by intercontinental mis-

Presidential incapacitation

66. Controversy surrounds most accounts of the transfer of presidential power which took place in Dallas, Texas, on November 22, 1963; in Air Force One as the President's jet flew back to Washington with the body of a slain President, the new President, and their advisers on board; and in Washington during the first few days of the Johnson Administration. A detailed account of those days is William Manchester, *The Death of a President* (New York: Harper and Row, 1967). The official investigation of the President's death, made by the President's Commission on the Assassination of President Kennedy (known as the Warren Commission), was published by the government in 1964.

67. The 1947 Act placed the Speaker of the House of Representatives next in line for presidential succession after the Vice President. Following the Speaker comes the President Pro Tempore of the Senate, and then the Cabinet officers in rank according to when their departments were created.

285

sile, and when a mistake, or failure to act, could cost the nation 120 million dead. The problem of what to do in case the President is seriously ill received considerable public attention in the 1950's when President Eisenhower suffered a heart attack while in Colorado.

The matter of mental competency is generally not considered a proper subject for public discussion; however, some popular novels were woven about the mental composure, or lack of it, a future President might display under stress.[68] Eisenhower and Nixon, Kennedy and Johnson, Johnson and House Speaker John McCormack (there was no Vice President when Johnson succeeded to the Presidency), and Johnson and Humphrey entered into agreements to permit the junior individual to serve as Acting President under certain contingencies. These informal arrangements did not satisfy those concerned about presidential disability, persons who contended that a "Constitutional gap" existed regarding the transfer of power in the event of presidential incapacitation.[69]

National concern over the problem led in 1967 to the ratification by the states of the Twenty-fifth Amendment. It pro-

The 25th Amendment

vides that when there is a vacancy in the office of Vice President the President shall nominate a Vice President. Confirmation is by majority vote of both Houses of Congress. The Vice President will serve as "Acting President" during periods when the President shall communicate to the Congress (specifically the Speaker of the House and President Pro Tempore of the Senate) that he is unable to perform his duties. The amendment also provides that when the Vice President and a majority of the Cabinet officers, or "such other body as Congress may by law provide," decide the President "Is unable to discharge the powers and duties of his office," the Vice President will become "Acting President." The President is authorized to resume his responsibilities when he states in writing to the Congress that he is able to do so. In case the President's decision is disputed by the Vice President and a majority of the Cabinet, or "other body as provided by Congress," the Congress is empowered to decide the issue by a two-thirds vote—"assembling within forty-eight hours for that purpose if not in session." The Twenty-fifth Amendment may provide imaginative writers and Hollywood producers with the material for

68. Fletcher Knebel, *Night of Camp David* (New York: Harper and Row, 1965).

69. The quotation is from Senator Birch Bayh (D., Ind.), who, with Representative Emanuel Celler (D., N.Y.), jointly worked to push the Twenty-fifth Amendment through Congress.

some exciting political scenarios. How it will operate in the real world can only be assessed with the passage of time.

SUMMARY

- The office of the Presidency is one of the distinctive features of the American political system. It was originally conceived to help correct the weaknesses of the government under the Articles of Confederation, while avoiding the excesses of central authority found objectionable under British monarchial rule. Modified over almost 200 years, the Presidency today is praised by some as being the innovative "spark plug" of the government, while others are concerned that too much power and initiative have accrued to the man in the White House at the expense of Congress.

- Fearing to entrust the election of the President solely to the common people, yet hesitant to permit Congress to handle the job lest the President would become the figurehead of the legislature, the framers of the Constitution devised the Electoral College system. In practice the arrangement has serious deficiencies. Within recent years dissatisfaction with the Electoral College has been mounting, and proposals to provide for the selection of President by a direct-vote method have increased in their support.

- Although no provisions were made for them in the Constitution, presidential nominating conventions have grown to become a spectacular feature of American politics. In the 1960's criticism of the convention system grew markedly; it is argued by some that delegates to the conventions do not reflect popular sentiment regarding the candidates. In addition to selecting the nominees, conventions must draft the party platforms and resolve disputes between rival delegations from the same states.

- The winner of the Presidency inherits an awesome array of powers and responsibilities. Since 1932 the trend has been toward strong Presidents, men who generally have believed that the apparatus of the Federal Government was meant to be used in a host of problem-solving activities.

- As Chief of State the President symbolizes American values to citizens as well as to foreigners. In his role as *Chief of Party* the President must lead those who selected him if he is to implement his political objectives for the nation. While he has the advantages of patronage and prestige, a President must confront the fact that his party is composed of autonomous local units often resentful of too much interference from Washing-

287

ton. As the *Commander-in-Chief* of the nation's armed forces the President is responsible not only for the security of the United States but also of that for the many nations allied with and dependent upon America.

• The actions of "strong" Presidents have resulted in the Presidency's acquiring the responsibility of *Chief Policy-Maker.* In addition to delivering executive recommendations for each year's legislative and budgetary programs to Congress, the President exercises significant authority in terms of the veto and ordinance powers. In his role as *Chief of Foreign Policy* the President's supremacy is firmly based upon the Constitution and Supreme Court decisions. Presidents have generally had their own way regarding foreign affairs rarely encountering serious dissent from the Congress.

• As *Chief Administrator* the President tops the apex of an immense Federal bureaucracy which includes the 12 Cabinet-level departments, the 10 divisions of the Executive Office of the President, and numerous agencies, boards, commissions, and other governmental entities. Much of the bureaucracy is staffed by the Civil Service, whose standards for selection and promotion have vastly improved from the days of the "spoils system" when individuals often obtained government positions more because of their party loyalty than their competence.

• During much of American history the office of Vice President has been notable for the paucity of responsibility given its occupant. However, since the 1950's, Vice Presidents have been pressed into greater service by their Presidents. In 1967 the addition of the Twenty-fifth Amendment established procedures whereby the Vice President could become "Acting President" during periods of presidential incapacitation.

SUGGESTED READING

° (*Books so designated are available in paperbound editions.*)

° Binkley, Wilfred E., *President and Congress,* 3rd rev. edn. (New York: Vintage Books, 1962).

° Corwin, Edward S., *The President: Office and Powers,* 4th rev. edn. (New York: New York University Press, 1957).

° Fenno, Richard F., Jr., *The President's Cabinet* (New York: Vintage Books, 1959).

Eisenhower, Dwight D., *The White House Years—Mandate for Change,* and *Waging Peace* (Garden City: Doubleday, 1963 and 1965).

Herring, Pendleton, *Presidential Leadership* (New York: Rinehart, 1940).

Kennedy, Robert F., *Thirteen Days* (New York: Norton, 1969).

* Laski, Harold J., *The American Presidency* (New York: Universal Library, 1940).

* Neustadt, Richard E., *Presidential Power* (New York: New American Library, 1964).

* Polsby, Nelson W., and Aaron B. Wildavsky, *Presidential Elections*, 2nd rev. edn. (New York: Charles Scribner's Sons, 1968).

* Pomper, Gerald, *Nominating the President* (New York: Norton Library, 1966).

* Rossiter, Clinton, *The American Presidency*, 3rd rev. edn. (New York: Harcourt, Brace, and World, 1966).

Schlesinger, Arthur M., Jr., *The Crisis of the Old Order* (Boston: Houghton Mifflin, 1957).

———, *The Coming of the New Deal* (Boston: Houghton Mifflin, 1959).

———, *The Politics of Upheaval* (Boston: Houghton Mifflin, 1960).

Sorenson, Theodore, *Decision-Making in the White House* (New York: Columbia University Press, 1963).

* ———, *Kennedy* (New York: Harper & Row, 1965).

Tourtellot, Arthur B., *The Presidents on the Presidency* (Garden City: Doubleday, 1964).

Truman, Harry S., *Year of Decisions* (Garden City: Doubleday, 1955).

———, *Years of Trial and Hope* (Garden City: Doubleday, 1956).

* White, Theodore H., *The Making of the President: 1960* (New York: Pocket Books, 1962).

———, *The Making of the President: 1964* (New York: New American Library, 1965).

White, William S., *The Professional: Lyndon B. Johnson* (Boston: Houghton Mifflin, 1964).

* Woll, Peter, *American Bureaucracy* (New York: Norton, 1963).

7

The
Judicial
System

When a visitor approaches the white-marble building (a replica of the Temple of Diana at Ephesus) at 1 First Street N.E., Washington, which houses the Supreme Court, he observes on the pediment four words: "Equal Justice Under Law." If he steps through the Corinthian columns into the building, he will encounter a small sign with *one* word: "Silence." In the quiet he has an opportunity to ponder the significance of the words on the building. If he asks himself "What is justice?", he is in the tradition of all the philosophers who ever lived—because that particular question is one of the few raised by every inquiring mind in every generation. Many of the attempted answers have been preserved in tradition and writing from the beginning of time, but no conclusion seems to have been completely satisfactory—especially to the thinker who arrived at it.

As the visitor sits in the ornate courtroom awaiting the entry of one of the most influential and powerful judicial tribunals in the history of the world, he cannot resist the desire to know more about the nation's court system, the distinguished judges who have served the bench, and the legal system they represent.

The Federal Judicial System:
Its Organization and Administration

Article III of the Constitution assigns the judicial power in America to "one Supreme Court, and in such inferior courts as the Congress may from time to time ordain and establish." The lack of a national court system had been, in truth, just what the writer of Number 22 of *The Federalist* alleged it to be—"a circumstance which crowns the defects of the Confederation."

Laws without courts

290

THE UNITED STATES COURT SYSTEM

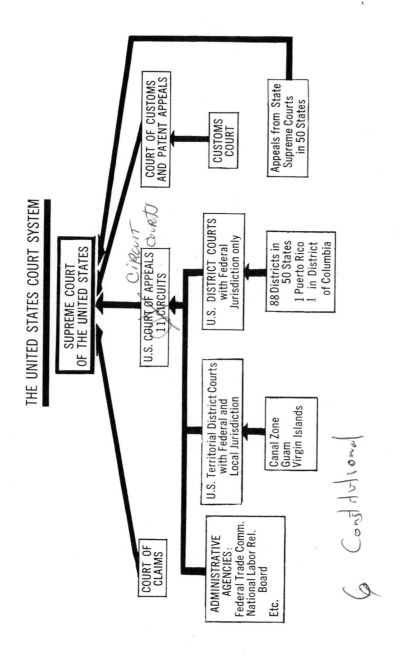

Then, as now, it was perfectly obvious to thoughtful citizens that "laws are a dead letter without courts to expound and define their true meaning and operation"; it was equally obvious that if the courts of each state were permitted to interpret Federal law, the result would be injustice as well as chaos. The institution of a Supreme Court was not difficult for the people to accept—although, interestingly enough, President Washington had a laborious time persuading prominent men to be appointed to it, and to remain on the Court after having accepted appointment. No one in the early days of the country suspected the prestige which the American people would come to accord their judges—especially those on the highest tribunal.

DISTRICT COURTS

Origins and current districts

There was, however, much debate in the first Congress regarding the necessity and propriety of establishing inferior Federal courts. The primary argument was that the state courts could easily adjudicate any cases involving Federal problems and that final appeal to one Supreme Court would assure uniformity. The "states' rights" champions lost the battle, but they won the concession that Federal judicial districts would be drawn within state boundaries. Since then, every state has been assured of having at least one Federal district court, but because of more litigation (and, one suspects, more effective politicians), many states have several districts. At the present time there are 88 of these courts of first instance in the 50 states. There is also one United States District Court in the District of Columbia, and in the Commonwealth of Puerto Rico. Each is presided over by a district judge, who is currently paid $40,000 annually. Again, for reasons of workload and politics, most districts have more than one judge.[1] Since ordinarily only one judge sits in a district court proceeding,[2] it is possible, where there are additional judges, for many cases to be heard simultaneously: the District Court for the District of Columbia can hear 15 cases at one time. Some districts are split up into "divisions," so that Federal court is held in several cities at least twice a year.[3] The United States (Prosecuting) Attorney and

1. In 1968 there were 316 permanent district judgeships in the 50 states, 15 in the District of Columbia, and two in Puerto Rico. The number may be increased at any time by legislation.

2. In specified instances, cases before district courts require three judges.

3. The immense area of Alaska is served by four divisions, with sessions held at Juneau, Nome, Anchorage, and Fairbanks. The court for the District of Connecticut, a small state in area, sits in Hartford, New Haven, Bridgeport, and Waterbury.

the United States Marshal are officers appointed for four-year terms to assist these courts. Other functionaries include baliffs, assignment commissioners, auditors, and clerks. District court decisions are published in volumes known as the *Federal Supplement* (cited: F. Supp.)

COURTS OF APPEAL

The first Congress arranged for the local district judge to sit with the two justices of the Supreme Court who were to travel a circuit in order to hear cases appealed from district courts. **Circuit judges** This arrangement was extremely unpopular not only with the justices who, in the days of poor transportation facilities, resented long arduous trips, but also with parties to litigation, since an appeal from a decision of the district court to the circuit court and on to the Supreme Court meant that in each instance one third of the judges had ruled on the case previously. Today there are 10 numbered circuits (which, of course, cross state lines) and a Court of Appeals for the District of Columbia. Since courts of appeal have three judges hearing each case, no circuit has fewer than that number, and the majority of them have between five and nine judges assigned. These judges may be temporarily assigned to other circuits by the Chief Justice in order to relieve crowded dockets, and the chief circuit judge may exercise the same power with respect to district court judges within his jurisdiction. Each circuit also has a Supreme Court justice assigned it (the Chief Justice and one Associate Justice each having two) who seldom sit, although they may. The individuals filling the 84 permanent judgeships on the Courts of Appeal each receive $42,500 as an annual salary. They travel a circuit, holding court at **Traveling** stated times in principal cities within their jurisdiction. Deci- **the circuit** sions of these courts are published in a series of volumes known as the *Federal Reporter* (cited: 100 Fed. 116, 100 F. 2d 116, etc.).

The Constitution gave Congress absolute power over these "inferior" Federal courts, specifying only that once a judge has been confirmed and sworn to one of them, he may serve during "good behavior" (*i.e.*, for life, unless he resigns or is impeached and convicted) and that his salary may not be reduced while he serves.

THE SUPREME COURT

Two guarantees are given the nation's highest tribunal: it may not be abolished, and its original jurisdiction (cases concerning "ambassadors, other public ministers and consuls, and in those in which a State shall be a party") cannot be interfered with by the Congress. Congress could, however, increase the size of the Supreme Court to a thousand judges or reduce it to one, and could change its appellate jurisdiction. As a matter of fact, the Court began with a Chief Justice and five associates, reached the high of ten, and then leveled off at nine members in 1869. Only one justice has been impeached (in 1804), but he was not convicted; none has been forced to retire, although a few have perhaps overstayed their usefulness. Today members of the Court receive an annual salary of $60,000 (with an additional $2,500 for the Chief Justice) and retire at full pay. Like other Federal judges, they are political appointees, but recent Presidents have not evidenced as much concern over their political party ties as over assuring regional and religious "representation." There have been unusual appointments, such as President U.S. Grant's nomination of Edwin M. Stanton (who had been a thorn in the flesh of Lincoln and sabotaged Johnson), but the Senate has usually given confirmation; indeed, only one nominee has been rejected during this century. This occurred in 1968 when President Johnson nominated Associate Justice Abe Fortas to replace Earl Warren as Chief Justice. The Senate did not have the opportunity to vote on the nomination. Following the failure of a motion to invoke cloture and so stop a filibuster against Fortas, the nominee withdrew his name from further consideration, and returned to his former position. In part, the opposition to Fortas reflected the hostility of many senators toward the Court, upon which Fortas had served since 1965, because of the high tribunal's decisions safeguarding the rights of criminal defendants, and its disinclination to censure movies and printed materials some senators thought were obscene. In addition, charges were made that Fortas lacked judgment and judicial propriety because he had, after his appointment as Associate Justice, accepted a $15,000 lecture fee and had continued to advise President Johnson. The latter charge gave rise to the contention the President's efforts to elevate Fortas were based upon "cronyism."

Appointees to the Supreme Court have not necessarily been notable for their judging experience. Of the nine members serving in 1968, three had been on the Federal bench before elevation to the high court, but none for more than four years, and one had served for 25 years as the chief counsel for the National Association for the Advancement of Colored People before sitting on a Federal court. Of the others, one had served briefly in the Attorney General's office, one had been an attorney general of a large state, one had been a government official,

Appointment of justices

The Fortas dispute

Previous experience

one had been a successful Washington lawyer, one had been a United States Senator, and one had served on a state supreme court.

It is impressive to observe the nine men who grace the highest bench in the nation arrive at the red-carpeted room in the Supreme Court building a few minutes before 10 on a weekday morning between the first Monday in October and June. One stands respectfully to hear the Court crier intone the chant which is a reminder of the Norman French days of old England: "Oyez, oyez, oyez! The Honorable, the Chief Justice, and the Associate Justices of the Supreme Court of the United States!" The heavy red draperies will part and the robed justices will enter, in order of seniority, and sit in their leather chairs. These are the persons who will apply the Constitution and the law to all kinds of situations involving every sort of person.

ADMINISTRATION OF THE FEDERAL JUDICIAL SYSTEM

The Judicial Conference of the United States serves as the governing body for the Federal Judiciary. It is chaired by the Chief Justice of the Supreme Court and has as members the Chief Judge of the Court of Claims, the Chief Judge of the Court of Customs and Patent Appeals, the Chief Judge from each judicial circuit and one district judge from each circuit. These individuals meet each year at the call of the Chief Justice to consider the nature, amount, and distribution of the work before the courts of the United States. The conference is empowered to make certain internal adjustments to fit judicial manpower to current workload, and its periodic reports to Congress may contain suggestions for legislation concerning judicial matters.

The Judicial Conference of the United States

In addition, the United States Courts of Appeal judges constitute the Judicial Council of each judicial circuit. They meet at least twice a year to "make all necessary orders for effective and expeditious administration . . ." of the Federal judicial business in the circuit.[4] The chief judge of each judicial circuit also holds annually a Judicial Conference of all circuit and district judges and sometimes members of the bar, to discuss the state of business before the circuit.

The Judicial Council

The Administrative Office of the United States Courts is charged with the responsibility of collecting various statistical data and preparing certain reports which indicate the nature and type of workload being carried by the various courts. Furthermore, this office supervises the administrative details of the

4. 28 U.S.C. 332.

The Administrative Office of the U.S. Courts

Federal judiciary, such as the purchase of law books, equipment, and supplies required by the courts, and it handles disbursement of moneys to operate the courts. The director prepares the budget for the Federal courts except the Supreme Court. Congress recently created a Federal Judicial Center within the Administrative Office of the United States Courts. The stated purpose of the center is to conduct research, training, and education leading toward more efficient judicial administration and a higher standard of justice.[5]

The Rise of English Law

COMMON AND CIVIL LAW

Common law

Every civilization has developed a legal system, but western civilization managed to produce two complete and influential ones. Although the Romans had created a magnificent legal system well over 1,000 years before the rudimentary beginnings of what became the Anglo-American law, it, like their cities and civilization, disappeared in Great Britain when Rome was obliged to contract her frontiers in the face of the barbarian onslaughts. Unlike the situation on the Continent, where the *civil law* systems of the various countries trace their concepts and practices directly to Roman origins, the complete withdrawal of Roman military power from England in A.D. 410 meant the disappearance of Roman culture, and so the invading Germanic tribes (who were on the cultural level of the Iroquois Indians of the seventeenth century) had to forge their own tools for the tortuous climb to civilization. The resulting lack of Roman influence in the formative stages explains why the *common law*, a unique legal system, was developed by the British.

After Rome recalled her legions from Britain in the fifth century, tides of invaders began to sweep from the Continent across the narrow English Channel to the islands in migrations which continued for the next 500 years. Each of the various

5. A problem facing the Federal courts, as well as the various state court systems, is that created by a backlog of cases which jam many courts throughout the land. In 1968 the Congress moved to reduce the load on Federal courts by abolishing the U.S. Commissioner system and replacing it with Federal salaried magistrates. The latter are authorized to try minor criminal offenses whereas the former were restricted to petty cases where the offense is committed on Federal reservations. It is hoped that the magistrates will relieve the regular courts of minor criminal cases so they may more speedily process felony and civil cases.

groups of arriving Angles, Saxons, Jutes, and Danes brought with them their own rules for regulating conduct and settling disputes. When these rude tribes were Christianized, some of their practices, written down as "dooms," approached the status of law. Over the centuries ambitious chieftains carved out petty kingdoms (*e.g.*, Essex, the land of the East Saxons) where tribal customs became so fixed that the hegemony of Wessex, under the grandfather of King Alfred the Great, did not disturb them. Even the final successful invasion of 1066, led by the Norman William the Conqueror, had a surprising lack of effect on the differing customary practices of the many little enclaves, although it revolutionized the political life of England.

It remained for Henry II (1154-89) to become the Father of the Common Law. Before his time, courtiers, who followed the king as he traveled about his domain, had served as representatives of the monarch in three important areas: land law (the basis of taxation and proprietary rights), breaches of the "King's Peace" (serious crime), and supervision of local officials. King Henry II regularized this practice by training his representatives (called "justices" from the title of "Justiciar," an official who presided in England during the king's absence on the Continent), giving them lists of instructions, and rotating their assignments frequently. In this way, judicial administration was made the same in all parts of the country, and differing customs were united into a law common to the entire kingdom.

When justices began keeping records of their decisions in disputes, a body of precedent was built up. They early developed a practice of following precedent called *stare decisis* (Latin for "let the decision stand"), which added the element of predictability to the growing legal system. Thus by referring to past situations they could make the same decisions in identical cases and, by logic, arrive at judgments in disputes which were similar, but not the same. For example, suppose it had become customary to fine a person a lamb if he enticed a servant away from another. Then, if a man came before the traveling justices to complain that someone had stolen his wife, the judges might decide that since the woman had cooked and kept house for her husband, the seducer should be required to pay one sheep as damages. The system of relying on precedent tended to make the law extremely conservative, but it fulfilled the minimum requirements of justice in that it was predictable, regular, and evenly applied. It also led to the rise of the first professional group of lawyers since Roman days.

Beginnings of precedent

297

EQUITY AND RELATED SYSTEMS

The origins of equity

Now suppose that an ancient Briton owned an oak tree into which Alfred the Great had carved his name and that a jealous neighbor threatened to cut it down. If the apprehensive owner sought the advice of a lawyer, he might be told that the common law would make sure he would be paid a pig if the property were destroyed. The owner, unsatisfied with this promised remedy, might have visited the Lord Chancellor—the "Keeper of the King's Conscience." This high official was always a clergyman (since it was necessary that he read and write) and, being a church official, had a knowledge of the *canon law* (developed by the Christian church from Roman law). Since the King was believed to be the fountain of justice, the keeper of his conscience was empowered to dispense super-legal justice, or "equity." If the Lord Chancellor believed it would be unjust to permit the destruction of such an antiquarian treasure as the tree on the pain of being fined a pig, he could issue a letter (a *writ*) called an *injunction,* which enjoined (*i.e.,* forbade) the jealous neighbor from destroying something irreplaceable. If, then, the wretch cut down the tree, he would not only forfeit a pig but would go to jail (perhaps permanently) for exhibiting "contempt" of the Lord Chancellor's command. Thus a second body of rules, *equity,* grew up to fill inadequacies of the common law and to afford higher principles of justice. Because of its Roman background, equity did not use a jury (an English invention);[6] its sophistication made it important for problems involving subtleties such as intent, mistake, and fraud, which the common law did not then recognize. Naturally, there were struggles between the judges of the two systems, but equity won out on questions of trusts, forfeiture, and redemption. It also provided a choice of remedies in cases involving breach of contract: where the common law provided damages, equity required specific per-

6. The Romans had used a form of inquest, by which persons were placed under oath and obliged to answer questions important to the government. The procedure passed to England with the Norman Conquest but was used only sporadically until Henry II recognized its potentialities. In one form it was used for criminal cases: 12 men from the local area and four from the town were sworn and then required to inform the justices of persons suspected of grave infractions against the King's Peace. The use of the jury in civil cases grew from Henry's idea of using a group of neighbors to determine ownership and possession of disputed land. The system was such a safeguard against rapacious manor lords that Henry provided that any freeman could claim the jury in cases concerning real estate. Once made available to the people, trial by jury established its superiority over trials by combat, ordeal, and swearing oaths which had been practiced in England for half a millennium.

formance, and the plaintiff (the one who went to court to complain of an alleged wrong) had his choice. The use of the injunction, which at first only could be invoked to protect "real property" (*i.e.*, land), was extended to other kinds of valuable property and has been used extensively in America to prevent crippling strikes and to protect civil rights.

The developing English law was filled out into a complete corpus by absorbing the independent systems of the law merchant (commercial law), admiralty (sea law), probate (wills), divorce, and others. Since these specialized legal rules had come to England from the Continent, they were heavily influenced by Roman principles and procedures and added immeasurably to the common-law system. Parliament began passing statutes, which not only took precedence over custom, but which pruned, shaped, and filled in the traditional law. In England, the legislative power became so strong that simply by passing a bill the lawmakers could nullify the decisions of the judges (*e.g.*, Dr. Bonham's Case). In the United States, curiously enough, the courts, which *Federalist* Number 78 insisted made up the weakest of the three branches of government, can be reversed only by subsequent court decisions or by constitutional amendment (*e.g.*, it took Amendment XIV to convert ex-slaves into "citizens" and "persons" after the Dred Scott decision had recognized them as property).

English law: consolidation

The Development of Law in America: Civil and Criminal Actions

After their successful rebellion, the new American states reacted against the common law as a legacy from Great Britain. Some of their legislatures passed laws making it a criminal offense to cite English cases, and judges turned hopefully to French law as a substitute. But the years of English predominance, the remarkable success in the American colonies of Blackstone's masterpiece, *Commentaries on the Laws of England* (1761), and the lack of a codified system (Napoleon's Code was still in the future) obliged the reluctant states to move back into the fold of the common-law system. Since that time the states have, by statute, decided what portions of the traditional law they would accept, and there are important differences among them. Idaho recognizes "common-law marriage" whereas, a few miles away, across the Utah border, a man and woman who publicly live together as man and wife, without having submitted to the prescribed ceremony, not only

Differences among the states

fail to create the legal rights and obligations of the marital status (of vital importance for inheritance), but may also be tried for crime. Today, Louisiana is the only one of the 50 states which does not have its legal system based on the common law—a holdover, of course, from its Spanish and French past. Louisiana has, however, chosen to follow common law on some important matters (such as criminal law and procedure, civil and criminal evidence, or torts), just as some common-law states have adopted sections of the civil law (such as community property). The national government has never had separate courts for law, equity, or admiralty, in contrast to England and some of the states. There is no national common law, of course, since acts of Congress are statutes. Whenever Federal courts apply state laws, they are bound by the common law of the state concerned, as interpreted by its highest court.[7] Federal judges and attorneys, however, bring the heritage of a thousand years of English legal development to the bench and bar with them.

When we consider that even games which are played for fun need rules, referees, and umpires to keep them orderly, it is obvious that struggles for the greater stakes of power and property require law and judges to keep them peaceful. If the players or referees made up the rules as the game progressed, chaos would result; if batters had the right to determine whether the pitcher was throwing balls or strikes, very few would ever strike out. Yet even if everyone concerned knows the rules and is willing to abide by them, there are always those doubtful instances where the best disposed men disagree. Experience has taught that since absolute certainty in human affairs is not possible, best results are achieved by setting rules to cover every possible contingency and choosing the most independent and impartial persons available to make the hard decisions and to apply the rules. It is true that sometimes umpires (and judges) have been successfully persuaded, by intimidation or greed, to favor one of the participants unfairly, but to dispense with courts and judges because of human weakness would result in justice becoming what one of Socrates' opponents said it was—merely "the interest of the stronger."

The cases which come before American courts can be divided neatly into two basic types: civil actions and criminal actions. **Civil and criminal actions** The former are disputes between two parties, usually over money or property. For example, Mr. White was offered a position with Mr. Black's company and, on the strength of the offer, resigned his former employment and reported for work, only to learn that Mr. Black had changed his mind; the Deep

7. Erie R.R. v. Tompkins, 304 U.S. 64 (1938).

Sea Delicacies Company contracted to provide pickled squids for the grand opening of a restaurant and delivered salted herring instead; an unsteady driver, disturbed by a bumblebee in the car, piloted her vehicle through the English rose garden and picture window belonging to one of the authors and brought it to a halt on the Persian rug in his living room; and a woman falsely named a prominent minister in a paternity suit. All of these were civil actions. Criminal actions are wrongs against the public, punished because they disrupt the peace of the community and endanger the people. For centuries in medieval Britain there were no public wrongs except those committed in the presence of the king or on the old Roman roads which were under the special protection of the monarch. Little by little, as the "King's Peace" was extended to towns for market days and eventually applied to the whole country, it became a crime to steal, assault, and murder. In America today these wrongs are still regarded as crimes, and statutes to which criminal penalties are attached have expanded greatly. One will be tried for crime if he prints his own supply of money, drives without a license, advertises chalked water as milk, or fails to tell the truth to a census taker. It is possible for a person to face both civil and criminal trials for the same act. For example, the lady who brought her car to rest in Professor Caldwell's living room had to pay damages for the destruction of his property (civil), and she was convicted for reckless driving (criminal).

The Scope of Federal Justice

Most civil and criminal actions in America are handled by state courts, since the jurisdiction of the Federal courts is restricted to the specific types of cases enumerated in the Constitution and determined by Congress. The extent of the power of the Federal courts to hear and try disputes is outlined succinctly in Article III, Section 2:

Jurisdiction

> The judicial power shall extend to all cases, in law and equity, arising under this Constitution, the laws of the United States, and treaties made, or which shall be made, under their authority; to all cases of admiralty and maritime jurisdiction; to controversies to which the United States shall be a party; to controversies between two or more States; between a State and citizens of another State,[8] between citizens of different

8. Amendment XI, proclaimed January 8, 1798, clarified the words "between a state and" as follows: "The judicial power of the United States shall not be construed to extend to any suit in law or equity, commenced or prosecuted against one of the United States by citizens of another State, or by citizens or subjects of any foreign State."

301

States; between citizens of the same State claiming lands under grants of different States, and between a State, or the citizens thereof, and foreign states, citizens, or subjects.

Two of the most important words in this grant of power are usually overlooked: *case* and *controversy*. Unlike some state and foreign courts, the Federal courts do not concern themselves with suits which appear to be collusive, or "friendly," and they do not give "advisory opinions." The adversary nature of the common law assumes that both sides to a dispute are trying equally hard to win and that in the clash of their best arguments an impartial judge can discern the "truth." If a president of a company sues his own firm merely to test the validity of a law, the courts will refuse to hear the case on the ground that it is collusive since the parties are not in actual conflict. Anglo-American judges do not enter into the argument of a case as frequently and actively as do their counterparts in civil-law countries, and so it is necessary that the opposing attorneys be really opposed. Similarly, the courts are not disposed to give advice to curious parties; they insist that their function is to exercise the judicial *power* and that, therefore, they can only hand down decisions which will be enforced.

Case and controversy

Consider the case of the Cherokee Indians of Oklahoma at the turn of the century. In 1901, Congress admitted them to citizenship and a year later provided for the distribution of tribal lands and other property to members of the tribe enrolled as of September 1 of that year. In 1906, at the request of the tribal council, Congress amended the law to include the papooses born before March 4, 1906, in the undistributed remainder. The congressional conscience was troubled; in an Indian Appropriation Act of the following year, Congress provided that Muskrat and other Cherokees could sue the United States in the Court of Claims "with the right of appeal, by either party, to the Supreme Court of the United States" to determine the validity of the 1906 legislation. When Muskrat sued the United States, the Supreme Court refused to rule on the constitutionality of the second law because the government and Muskrat were really not in a genuine dispute. The United States had nothing to gain or lose; Muskrat did. A justiciable case here could only arise between an old Indian and a papoose.[9]

The courts will, however, give "declaratory judgments." These differ from "advisory opinions" in that they arise out of *controversies*: the decision will be enforced in the future, when

9. Muskrat v. United States, 219 U.S. 346 (1911). The legislation was sustained the following year, when a real "case" was presented. Gritts v. Fisher, 224 U.S. 640 (1912).

a case is brought to court. Suppose a man has a life insurance policy with the provision that in the event he becomes permanently disabled it will be considered to be paid up. He stops paying premiums on the ground that he is permanently disabled. Justice is better served if the courts determine conclusively now whether or not he is in fact disabled, even though the payment of the policy will not be in dispute until his death. If the courts refused judgment, the alternative would be for the heirs to sue the company—an action which might take place many years later. By that time witnesses might have moved away or the policy holder would be unavailable for physical examination, and the opportunity to establish the true condition of the insured at the time he discontinued making payments would be lost. This situation is certainly "adversary."[10]

Declaratory judgments

Crimes against the United States (except when "ambassadors, other public ministers and consuls" are a party) are *always* heard first in one of the district courts. Similarly, these courts have exclusive jurisdiction on bankruptcy, admiralty, and a few other types of cases, and when the United States is plaintiff in a civil action unless, of course, the defendant is a foreign dignitary or a state. Otherwise, the Federal district courts share jurisdiction in civil suits with the 50 state courts (plaintiff's option) provided that: either the issue involves a substantial *Federal question* (*i.e.*, under the Constitution, laws, and treaties of the United States), *or* (1) there is a *diversity of citizenship* (*i.e.*, the suit is between people, including corporations,[11] from different states or persons of a state and a foreign government or its citizens), and (2) that the *amount in dispute exceeds $10,000* exclusive of interest and costs. If the driver of the automobile temporarily garaged in Professor Caldwell's living room had been from another state, he would have had the choice of suing her in a state court or in the Federal district court, provided the damage exceeded the minimum stipulated. If it had not, then his legal recourse was to a court within the state.

Crimes against the U.S.

Civil Actions in a Federal Court

The car caused damage conservatively estimated at $15,000. The first thing Professor Caldwell did was call the police, since it was up to them to decide whether or not to cite the lady for

10. Aetna Life Insurance Co. v. Haworth, 300 U.S. 227 (1937).

11. The Court held that corporations are "citizens" for rights under Article III and may not be obliged to resort only to state courts. Terral v. Burke Construction Co., 257 U.S. 529 (1922).

reckless driving or, if the buzzing was only in her head, for drunken driving. No one was available at the time, so Caldwell visited the police station (it could have been the office of the District Attorney) and signed a complaint. He was told that the alleged crime would be tried in a local (state) court at public expense; that he should expect to be served a subpoena to appear in court in order to testify; and that he might or might not have the satisfaction of seeing the home-wrecker fined or put in jail.

To recover damages to his property, however, the initiative was all with the homeowner. His second action, therefore, was to consult a lawyer who said that time and money could be saved by settling the case out of court, since costs are not paid by the government in civil actions, but if Caldwell wanted to sue, he would suggest whether or not to go to a state court or to the Federal district court. He said that if Caldwell delayed too long, the "statute of limitations" would prohibit the suit, since the defendant needed to be protected from living the rest of her life under the threat of being sued. It seemed best to begin suit in the Federal district court, hoping to settle out of court. Since the lady was from another state and owned property there, it would have been more convenient (had the case gone to trial) to have had a judgment from a Federal court nearby rather than have the trial take place in her state, miles away. Had the trial been held in a state court in Caldwell's state, the judgment would still have to be given effect by the courts of her state if she didn't pay on the spot.

A civil action begins with a complaint signed with a clerk of the court and the summons sent to the defendant. In a civil **Initiating a civil action** action, unlike a criminal proceeding, a summons does not have to be served to the defendant in person, and the trial can take place without his physical presence. Ordinarily, however, the defendant's attorney will file an answer to the complaint within the time prescribed in the summons (about 20 days), and the trial will be expected to settle the points in dispute. Before trial, most Federal and many state judges hold informal pre-trial conferences with the attorneys for both parties with the aim of reaching a satisfactory agreement without further resort to the courts. If it appears that a trial is necessary, the pre-trial conference aids in simplifying the issues.

If a case goes to trial before the Federal district court, either party may request a jury or, to save time and money, both may waive the right guaranteed them by the Seventh Amendment. The trial jury ("petit" or "petty") is selected in the presence of the judge, plaintiff, and defendant with their attorneys, court stenographer, and a few other court officers. Names of prospective jurors are taken from tax rolls; these persons are called in, put under oath, and asked questions designed to determine whether or not they are biased. If they indicate prejudice for either party they may be challenged "for cause" and dismissed. Each attorney is also allowed several "peremptory" challenges by which he can dismiss from duty prospective jurors who are otherwise qualified. In the trial, opposing arguments are presented to the jurors, who are instructed by the judge regarding the law applicable to the case just before they retire to determine a verdict. In civil actions, the jury decides for one of the two parties by "the preponderance of the evidence." The members return their verdict, and the judge renders his decision and assigns costs. The responsibility of the court officially ends with the judgment: the winner must take steps to secure satisfaction, an administrative process so automatic that it is frequently not recognized as such. If the loser does not pay the amount stipulated, his personal and real property may be seized and sold in order to give force to the judgment.

Jury trial in civil actions

Criminal Proceedings in a Federal Court

Suppose that, while examining the automobile in Professor Caldwell's living room, the police had found a cache of home-made postage stamps. Their duty would have been to notify the Federal prosecuting attorney. If investigation disclosed that there was probable cause to suspect the lady driver of complicity in the crime of forgery, she would have been arrested. Since she could not be given the death sentence if proved guilty, she could request release on _bail_—an amount of money set by the judge to be put up as security for her appearance at trial. If she should have failed to appear, the money would have been forfeited. Had the bail not been raised, or if the district judge had refused to accept it, the lady would have been obliged to remain in custody to await trial, unless released by the grand jury. These elaborate precautions are necessary since, in the United States, the accused must be physically present in criminal trials.

"No person shall be held to answer for a capital or otherwise infamous crime, unless on a presentment or indictment of a grand jury," the Fifth Amendment provides, "except in cases arising in the land or naval forces or in the militia when in

305

Le Pelley in The Christian Science Monitor © TCSPS
Outmoded Symbol

The grand jury *actual service in time of war or public danger.*"[12] The grand jury, which was invented in England and exported to America, has been abandoned in its native land and by many of the states, but it survives in the Federal system of criminal justice. The defenders of the system explain that it affords a person accused of serious crime the protection of having a large number (16 to 23) of independent, nonpolitical citizens summoned to hear the evidence, prepared by the prosecuting attorney, and to determine whether or not there is sufficient cause to bring the accused to public trial. The proceedings of the grand jury are

12. A "capital crime" is one where death may be the penalty; an "infamous crime" makes one liable to imprisonment in a federal penitentiary. If the accusation made by the grand jurors is from personal knowledge, it is known as a "presentment"; if from the basis of the evidence presented by the prosecuting attorney, it is called an "indictment."

kept secret so that, if the charges are dismissed, the fact that a person was suspected of crime will not be widely known. The defendant is never forced to appear; he may testify, however, provided he first signs a waiver of immunity, so that his testimony can be introduced against him should his case come to trial. If the grand jury had found the accusation of complicity in forging stamps to be a "true bill," the case would have come to trial; if not, the charges would have been dismissed.

The jury trial in criminal cases is essentially the same as in civil actions. The Sixth Amendment guarantees the accused a "speedy and public trial"—but not so "speedy" that the defense does not have time to prepare its case, nor so "public" that the courtroom may not be cleared if evidence of an especially embarrassing nature is to be presented, or if the courtroom becomes too boisterous. The jurors must come from the state and district in which the crime was committed. **Jury trial in criminal cases**

In the past, criticism was leveled at the jury selection system used by the Federal courts. It was contended that too often jurors were selected from lists of white, affluent persons with little representation from other economic groups or from the black community. While the system may have resulted in juries with a generally high level of education, it did not always produce juries of one's peers when the defendants happened to be from the less affluent strata of society, or when they were non-white. Congress acted to alter the situation by passing the Federal Jury Selection Act of 1968, which required the United States District Courts to change their means of jury selection. The courts complied, and now prospective jurors are selected at random from lists of registered voters. The jurors are chosen from counties in proportion to the population of the counties. In the South particularly, with more black voters being registered, the new system will produce more black jurors than previously was the case.[13] The accused has a right to know the charges brought against him, to confront the witnesses against him, and to obtain witnesses in his favor by the compulsory process of the *subpoena* (Latin for "under penalty"). The accused may not be denied the right to be represented by an attorney; he is generally provided free counsel if the crime is serious and he is unable to pay for legal assistance. Jurors must find the accused "guilty beyond reasonable doubt"—a degree of certainty not required in civil actions. Within recent years the **Rights of the accused**

13. Under the new procedures it is now more difficult to evade jury duty because the eligibility criteria have been broadened. The pay for jury duty has been increased, to reduce the complaint that jury duty constituted an economic burden.

Supreme Court has attempted to define further, and in so doing often increased, the procedures which must be observed in Federal Courts (also in state courts) to protect the rights of the accused.[14]

Appeals

TO COURTS OF APPEAL

Powers

A pervasive ideal of justice supports the claim of a litigant to have his case heard by two different courts. Except for a few instances, appeals from district courts go to one of the 11 courts of appeal.[15] Since Amendment VII forbids re-examination by another court of facts tried by a jury, the courts of appeal are rather effectively limited to cases tried without juries, alleged improper charges to the jury by the judge, and questions concerning evidence introduced in the trial. They have precedence in interpreting the law and have power to affirm, reverse, or remand a case before them. Finally, they hear appeals from cases that have been tried before the quasi-judicial regulatory agencies.

TO THE SUPREME COURT

Cases of national interest

Many cases from the district courts find their way to the courts of appeal, but few go beyond them. If the lady driver had threatened to "fight this case to the Supreme Court if it takes my last penny," she would have overestimated her chance of getting before the high tribunal, not to mention the cost of Federal justice. The fact is that the Supreme Court has almost reached the stage where it hears only the cases it wants to hear. It wants to hear, almost exclusively, cases concerning principles of broad national interest rather than disputes over amounts of money or prison sentences. The Court would be much less interested in hearing a case from a court of appeals in which $10,000,000 was disputed than it would be to hear a case where it was alleged that Orientals had been systematically excluded from grand juries in a Federal district. The cases which the Supreme Court *has* to hear (determined by law in appellate

14. The high court's rulings are examined in Chapter 8. The political controversy created over the court's actions is discussed later in this chapter.

15. If a district court rules that a Federal law or treaty, which has been invoked in a criminal case, is unconstitutional or enjoins a state statute, the appeal lies directly to the Supreme Court. Congress has also provided for appeals from antitrust laws and the Interstate Commerce Commission to go to the high court.

cases) are ambiguously called "appeals." In addition to appeals allowed directly from district courts, the Supreme Court is obliged to hear cases when a court of appeals has affirmed a decision that a state law is invalid under the Constitution.

Approximately five of every six cases heard in the Supreme Court building get there because petitions for writs of *certiorari* ("let it be certified") have been approved by at least four of the nine justices. Writs of certiorari occupy a disproportionate amount of the justices' time, since each member of the Supreme Court reads every request and well over 60 percent of the petitions are entirely without merit. The Court tends to grant certiorari to cases which involve issues important to the administration of justice; to those which require construing an important statute for the first time; to situations where two courts of appeal have given differing judgments on a similar issue; to cases when the Court believes a lower court has misconstrued one of its past opinions; and on the rare occasions when the Court changes its mind after having made a decision. It refuses to issue certiorari if fewer than four justices wish to hear a case; if review is sought too late; if the judgment of a lower court is not final; or if it appears desirable to have further illumination by state courts. Inferences as to why certiorari is denied are not trustworthy, since there is no implication that the Court has been concerned with the substantive merit of a case.[16] Sometimes the Supreme Court will dismiss a case summarily with a *per curiam* decision—a terse statement ("by the court") of its decision with one or two controlling precedents.

sur shio rari

Writs of certiorari

The Operation of the Supreme Court

A case which finally gets before the nine justices of the Supreme Court is assured only two hours for formal argument, the time being divided among the opposing parties. The attorneys dare not prepare even an hour's presentation since questions from the bench, humorous or serious interchanges among the judges, or even a justice's lecture consume much of the time. Three cases are heard each day the Court is in session: it sits at 10 A.M. and remains four hours before rising for a half-hour lunch; it then returns for another two hours. The judge's life is not an easy one, for the morning is taken up by reading and considering the flood of petitions for certiorari and by

16. "The Court has said this again and again; again and again the admonition has to be repeated," wrote Mr. Justice Frankfurter. Maryland v. Baltimore Radio Show, 338 U.S. 912 (1950).

briefings on the many cases on the docket. At the end of the week the Court meets in executive session to discuss the cases heard during the week and to arrive at decisions. After returning home from this conference the justices receive notes from the Chief Justice assigning them the cases they are to write for the Court. The actual writing is generally done during the two-week recess which follows each two-week session, and as drafts are completed, they are circulated among the eight colleagues for suggestions. Judges who cannot agree to the decision of the majority may team up to write a dissenting opinion. But group **Dissent** opinions and dissents may reflect compromises, and some judges prefer to write their own concurring or dissenting opinions in order to say exactly what they think. The positions of "great dissenters" such as Justices Harlan, Holmes, and Brandeis have been adopted by later courts: a dissent may serve an invaluable purpose.

Opinions are delivered by the justices who wrote them and are published in volumes known as *United States Reports* (U.S.). On days when opinions are handed down, the Supreme Court chamber is well attended, not only because the decisions made generally have repercussions over the entire naton, but also because it is almost impossible to obtain advance information on how the Court will decide any particular case. In fact, the secrecy which surrounds each decision is so carefully guarded to prevent "leaks" that the printing is not even entrusted to the regular Government Printing Office. Secrecy is necessary because, of course, knowledge of the decision prior to its general release could well be of enormous benefit to people on the inside.

The Supreme Court in Action: Judicial Interpretation, Judicial Decision-Making, and Judicial Review

The Supreme Court not only applies the law (a function any well-schooled lawyer could do); it also has the final power of *interpretation*. Words are not capable of being framed so precisely that differing interpretations are impossible, and the way the Court reads the words arranged by Congress, state legislators, or city fathers is final. For example, if, in an attempt to promote civic tranquility, a city ordinance prohibited "mechanical devices emitting loud and raucous noises" from its streets, the Supreme Court conceivably would be called upon to determine how loud is *loud* and how raspy is *raucous*. It might have to pronounce on whether or not a proscribed sound must be both loud *and* raucous or merely loud *or* raucous. The justices might have to decide if a city court interpreted the ordinance correctly when it permitted the beep of a small car but prohibited the honk of a truck horn. They, rather than the hometown court, will finally determine if music and the human voice are *noises* or if a megaphone is a *mechanical device*.

In ascertaining what the words mean the Court may choose among several techniques: it may study the "intent" of the law-makers from what was said in the general sessions, in commit-tees, at hearings, or from public utterances; it might engage in a semantic inquiry as to the real meaning of the words; it could conduct historical research into the problem which gave rise to the law in the first place. And, as has been observed, "the judges read the newspapers." Different judges may prefer differ-ent tests for the words, and, if their conclusions do not agree, who can say which is right?[17]

"Intent"

JUDICIAL DECISION-MAKING

One who examines cases decided by the Supreme Court will note that on a number of occasions the decision is by a 5-to-4 or 6-to-3 margin. If such close decisions involve the constitu-tionality of a law, it is possible for five justices voting against four to strike down a law passed by Congress, signed by the President, and presumably desired by the nation at large. This kind of situation, as well as others, cause one to wonder how judges decide cases.[18] A review of literature on the Supreme Court suggests that judges reach their decisions through a far more complicated means than that described by Mr. Justice Owen J. Roberts in 1936 when he said:

> When an act of Congress is appropriately challenged in the courts as not conforming to the constitutional mandate, the judicial branch has only one duty—to lay the article of the Constitution which is invoked beside the statute which is

17. How judges reach a decision is the subject of Benjamin N. Cardozo, *The Nature of the Judicial Process* (New Haven: Yale University Press, 1960). See also Felix Frankfurter, "The Process of Judging in the Supreme Court," in Alan F. Westin, ed., *The Supreme Court: Views from Inside* (New York: Norton, 1961).

18. Since there are fewer of them, and their decisions are therefore easier to study, the discussion of judicial decision-making is often confined to Federal judges. This does not mean that the variables examined do not also apply to state judges.

challenged and to decide whether the latter squares with the former.[19]

In studying judicial behavior one must take into account a number of variables that enter into judicial decision-making. For example, there is the law itself to be considered, and with it the precedent and judicial philosophy which extends back to the English Common Law, and in some instances beyond that to Roman times. Another variable is the political tide evident at a particular time in the nation. While the Supreme Court and lesser courts can deliver decisions running against the political currents for a time, they cannot do so indefinitely. The "switch-in-time-that-saved-nine," a reference to the change of mind evidenced by the Court after President Roosevelt's threat to enlarge the number of justices, underscores this point.[20] It must be generally assumed that judges are fully aware of political developments, if for no other reason than because of their background of extensive education and rearing in politically active families.[21]

Judicial behavior

Another variable is based upon the reasonable belief that judges, many of whom served in political posts before their appointment, have developed personal political philosophies regarding which kinds of legislation are beneficial to the nation and which are not. Despite the admonitions from former Justice Felix Frankfurter to the contrary, justices may permit their political views, perhaps unknowingly, to color their judgments.[22] Furthermore, justices are aware that the courts

Political views

19. U.S. v. Butler, 297 U.S. 1 (1936). Various theories regarding judicial decision-making are examined in Theodore L. Becker, *Political Behavioralism and Modern Jurisprudence: A Working Theory and Study in Judicial Decision-Making* (Chicago: Rand McNally, 1964). See also Glendon Schubert, "Academic Ideology and the Study of Adjudication," *American Political Science Review*, LXI (March, 1967), pp. 106–129. Schubert suggests that there are three schools of thought regarding the study of adjudication. These he terms "traditional," "conventional," and "behavorial." This article contains good bibliographic references to the works of all three groups which, incidentally, do not always agree with each other.

20. On this point, see below, p. 313, and H. J. Abraham, *The Judiciary* (Boston: Allyn and Bacon, 1965), p. 112. See in the same work on p. 116 the quotation from Wallace Mendelson, *Justices Black and Frankfurter: Conflict in the Court* (Chicago: University of Chicago Press, 1961) that if the Supreme Court is to prosper it must "respect the social forces that determine elections and other major political settlements. No Court can long withstand the morals of its era."

21. Abraham, *op. cit.*, p. 96, describes the typical justice of the Supreme Court. See also John R. Schmidhauser, *The Supreme Court: Its Politics, Personalities and Procedures* (New York: Holt, Rinehart and Winston, 1960).

22. See Justice Frankfurter's dissent, West Virginia State Board of Education v. Barnette, 319 U.S. 624 (1943).

play a political as well as a judicial role.[23] Some scholars, reflecting the impact of behavioral studies in political science, feel that eventually a better understanding of another variable—judges' personalities—will yield fruitful insights regarding judicial decision-making.[24]

JUDICIAL REVIEW

Closely allied to the problem of interpreting words in statutes is the awesome responsibility of judicial review. Any Federal court may declare a statute or government act to be "contrary to the manifest tenor of the Constitution" and, therefore, void; the Supreme Court, however, has the decisive last word. On questions of state law, Federal judges defer to the interpretations given by the state courts concerned, but since the Fourteenth Amendment prohibits any state from denying persons "equal protection of the laws" and "due process of law," local acts may be interpreted as unconstitutional invasions of individual rights. The delicate function of interpretation is complicated by the human tendency to allow personal bias to creep into decisions.

During the first years of Franklin Roosevelt's "New Deal," four of the justices considered the program to be foolish and dangerous; two of the members were lukewarm toward it; and three believed their personal opinions should not influence their decisions. The result is history: after a series of 5-4 and 6-3 decisions against the constitutionality of much important legislation (which had the approval of the President, the Congress, and, presumably, the people), Roosevelt proposed to increase the size of the Court. In a crucial decision, the Supreme Court

Roosevelt and the "Court-packing plan"

23. See Samuel Krislov, *The Supreme Court in the Political Process* (New York: Macmillan, 1965), for a discussion of the intertwining of political and judicial roles, particularly Chapter 3, pp. 55–78.

24. As one such political scientist has stated, "Judicial behavioralism is an attempt to construct a systematic theory about human behavior, analyzing data about judges and adjudicatory processes of decision-making by using theories and methods from all of the behavioral sciences, according to their relevance to the particular inquiry at hand." Glendon Schubert, "Ideologies and Attitudes, Academic and Judicial," *Journal of Politics*, 29 (February, 1967), p. 7. For a critical evaluation of the approach followed by Schubert, see Wallace Mendelson, "The Neo-Behavioral Approach to the Judicial Process: A Critique," *American Political Science Review*, LVII (September, 1963), pp. 593–603.

For earlier discussions of judges, their lives and personalities see the following: Max Lerner, *The Mind and Faith of Justice Holmes* (Boston: Little, Brown, 1943); Alpheus T. Mason, *Brandeis: A Free Man's Life* (New York: Viking Press, 1946) and *Harlan Fiske Stone: Pillar of the Law* (New York: Viking Press, 1956); and John P. Frank, *Mr. Justice Black: The Man and His Opinions* (New York: Knopf, 1949).

reversed its anti-New-Deal direction by a majority of 5-4;[25] the Congress killed the "Court-packing plan"; and the President is said to have remarked: "We have lost the battle, but we've won the war."

Many members have historically interpreted the role of the Supreme Court as striking a balance between the legitimate claims of local and national communities and thus being, in effect, the umpires of the Federal system.[26] Beginning with the critical decision in the Slaughterhouse Cases after the Civil War, when the Court refused to read the Fourteenth Amendment as virtually ending state legislative powers,[27] and extending down to the recent past, the judicial branch has undoubtedly had a more consistent "states' rights" position than either the executive or legislative branch of government. The Supreme Court has been able to accommodate state taxing powers and state regulation (even in areas of interstate commerce), and during much of the first half of the twentieth century it saw no problem in the segregation of the races. The results have not always been logical or popular, but the fact that the system of dual government has survived and remains potent is due, in large part, to the Federal courts.

Judicial vs. "political branches"

Is the Supreme Court Doing a Good Job?

Through the years the Supreme Court has been vigorously attacked by some as it was vigorously defended by others. The former contend the Court is usurping the legislative function of the Congress while the latter claim the Court serves the highest interests of justice. One can better understand the accumulation of criticism and praise heaped upon the Court when it is recalled that people tend to assess the Court in terms of their own political and economic views, or, as one observer has put it, in terms of "Whose ox is being gored."[28] For example, New Deal Democrats, much excited over the prospects for social reform they saw in Franklin D. Roosevelt's legislative program, were hostile to a Supreme Court which on numerous occasions handed down adverse rulings regarding "their" legislation

Champions and critics of the Court

25. National Labor Relations Board v. Jones Laughlin Steel Corp., 301 U.S. 1 (1937).

26. See Paul A. Freund, "Umpiring the Federal System," in Arthur W. MacMahon, ed., *Federalism, Mature and Emergent* (Garden City, N.Y.: Doubleday, 1955).

27. 16 Wallace 36 (1873).

28. Abraham, *op. cit.*, p. 106.

between 1934 and 1936. On the other hand, those opposed to Roosevelt's efforts to manipulate the economy viewed with favor the Court's actions, for they believed the high bench to be the last bastion holding back a dangerous flood of socialistic experimentation. When the Court began accepting New Deal legislation in 1937, the roles of Court critic and champion were reversed, and have remained largely so to the present. Those who today applaud the Court for protecting and extending the rights of black persons in the 1960's would have felt much differently about the Court which in 1896 handed down the "separate but equal" doctrine—that theory which served as an underpinning for segregation for nearly a half century.[29]

Any evaluation of the Supreme Court must also take into consideration contrasting attitudes toward judicial restraint and activism. Regardless of political and economic views, those favoring judicial restraint argue that the Court should leave the initiative in configuring American society to Congress. They assert that the legislature was given the responsibility for such matters, and that the Court should intervene only where very clear violence is being done the Constitution. Former Justice Felix Frankfurter is remembered for his ardent championing of judicial self-restraint:

Judicial restraint

> It can never be emphasized too much that one's own opinion about the wisdom or evil of a law should be excluded altogether when one is doing one's duty on the bench. The only opinion of our own even looking in that direction which is material is our opinion whether legislators could in reason have enacted such a law. . . .[30]

On the other hand, judicial activists believe that the Court should play a more prominent role in structuring American life. For example, Justice Hugo Black has spent considerable time on the bench working to ensure that society is organized so as to give full meaning to the Bill of Rights, most particularly the First Amendment.[31]

A related concern of some, although less so of judges and scholars, is that the Court engages in law-making, or politics, rather than limiting itself to law-applying, or strictly legal activity. Much has been written that in practice the two cannot be separated, and that it is only law-making (political activity)

Judicial activism

29. Plessy v. Ferguson, 163 U.S. 537 (1896).

30. Frankfurter, *op. cit.*

31. Justice Black stated his philosophy in his James Madison Lecture, "The Bill of Rights," New York University School of Law, February 17, 1960. It was reprinted in part in Alan F. Westin, ed., *The Supreme Court: Views from Inside* (New York: Norton, 1961).

315

which is not in accord with the Constitution, or which is not supported by current and dominant events, which constitutes inappropriate activity. For example, former Justice Robert H. Jackson wrote:

> The judicial power of the Supreme Court, however, does extend to all cases arising under the Constitution, to controversies to which the United States is a party, and to those between two or more states. Thus, the Court must face political questions in legal form, for surely a controversy between two separately organized political societies does present a political question, even if waged with the formalities of a lawsuit. And any decision which confirms, allocates, or shifts power as between it and a constituent state is equally political, no matter whether the decision be reached by a legislative or a judicial process. Our Constitution was the product and expression of a virile political philosophy held by those who wrote it. Controversies over its meaning often spring from political motives, for the object of politics always is to obtain power. Such controversies have to be solved either by consideration of the experiences and the statements of the framers which indicate the original will, or by reference to some relevant subsequent events and currents of opinion deemed controlling. And all constitutional interpretations have political consequences.[32]

THE "WARREN COURT"

Areas of activity The "Warren Court" (Earl Warren, former Republican attorney general and governor of California, was nominated for the Chief Justice position by President Eisenhower in 1953) was largely an "activist" body in the 1960's, as it had been in the 1950's.[33] Prominent among the areas in which the Court has been active are civil rights, particularly those of blacks and

32. Robert H. Jackson, *The Supreme Court in the American System of Government* (Cambridge: Harvard University Press, 1955), pp. 55–56.

33. In 1954 Chief Justice Warren indicated the kind of Court he would head when he delivered the opinion of an unanimous Court in the monumental case involving school desegregation, Brown v. Board of Education of Topeka, Kansas, 347 U.S. 497 (1954). C. Herman Pritchett, in his second edition of *The American Constitution* (New York: McGraw-Hill, 1968), wrote of the latter two thirds of the Warren Court: "The nine years that have elapsed since the first edition of this volume appeared have been years of unprecedented activity in constitutional interpretation. In no comparable period, even during what was then thought to be the 'constitutional revolution' which terminated the Supreme Court's battle with the New Deal in 1937, has the Court developed so much new constitutional doctrine in so many important fields or dealt simultaneously with so many controversial issues. Even more significant, never before has the Court so consistently taken an activist stance which so often challenges important conservative interests, institutions, and philosophies," p. vii.

other minority groups, and of persons accused of committing crimes; apportionment of state and congressional legislative districts; and the separation of church and state. As suggested previously, those who are favorably disposed toward the social and political trends supported by the Court's rulings tend to look with favor upon the high Court. On the other hand, someone concerned over the "coddling" of criminals attributed by some circles to the Supreme Court, or opposed to racial integration, might agree with former Governor George Wallace of Alabama, the unsuccessful presidential candidate of the American Independent Party, that Chief Justice Warren "doesn't have enough legal brains in his head to try a chicken thief in my home county."[34]

In addition to the attack by some senators upon the high tribunal during the filibuster against the nomination of Abe Fortas to the Chief Justiceship, the Congress specifically rebuffed the Court in 1968 and in so doing appeared to be casting a vote of no confidence regarding particular aspects of the Court's activities. The situation arose when the Court's decisions protecting the rights of those accused of crimes, and of convicted criminals, collided with the "law and order" issue which was prominent in the 1968 election campaign.[35] Widespread and severe criticism was directed at the limitations the Court placed upon the activities and methods of both Federal and state/local law-enforcement officials. This public outcry was responsible for provisions in the Omnibus Crime Control and Safe Streets Act of 1968 which negate some of the Court's rulings that the Congress thought had extended too great a measure of protection to those accused of breaking Federal law.[36]

"Law and order" issue

Legislative Courts

When one speaks of the "Federal courts," he ordinarily has in mind the hierarchy of district courts, courts of appeals, and the Supreme Court, which were established under Article III of

34. Quoted in "The Public Record of George C. Wallace," CQ *Guide to Current American Government*, p. 47. Of course many do not fit neatly into a pattern of complete approval or disapproval of the Court. For example, Samuel Krislov has noted that "Conservative, Southern, suburbanite Republicans, normally a major force in the anti-Court fight," must have mixed emotions about the Court, for they stand to gain much from its reapportionment decisions—judgments which serve to give areas where they live more representation.

35. The causes involved are discussed in Chapter 8.

36. The provisions of the law which struck at Supreme Court decisions are examined in Chapter 8.

Drawing by Lee Lorenz; © 1968 The New Yorker Magazine, Inc.

"Five years! I thought the courts were coddling punks like me!"

the Constitution. Under its grant of power in Article I, however, the Congress has established other courts to adjudicate
special kinds of questions. Judges of these "legislative courts"
do not automatically receive the guarantees regarding salaries
and tenure accorded their brethren on the Article III courts.
Congress is free, of course, to stipulate whatever arrangements
it wishes—even to converting them all into "constitutional
courts," as it did the Court of Claims in 1953 after that court
had existed for nearly a century under the Article I classification.

The ancient British legal maxim that "no writ runs against the king" has its counterpart in the American doctrine that the government may not be sued without its consent. Article I, Section 8, gave Congress the authority to "pay the debts ... of the United States," which meant that persons with claims against the Federal government were obliged for years to seek special appropriation legislation from Congress to reimburse them for breach of contract or tort damages (wrongs against persons) due to the Federal Government. In 1855 the Court of Claims was established, and since that time Congress has increased its jurisdiction, particularly in contract cases. The Federal Tort Claims Act (1946), which greatly expanded the permissible area of suits, provided some concurrent jurisdiction for the Court of Claims with the district courts. The Court of Claims consists of seven judges, appointed for "good behavior" at a salary of $33,000. It sits in Washington. The court publishes its decisions in a special volume (Ct. Cl.), and its position relative to the Courts of Appeal is observed by the fact that many of its decisions are also published in the *Federal Reporter* series. Litigants have no right of appeal from the Court of Claims, but may seek a writ of certiorari to the Supreme Court.

Claims against the government

The power given Congress to control "duties and imposts" led to the creation of courts concerned with imported products because of the subtle difficulties of classification, valuation, and the like. For example, the duties levied on chemicals are different from those on cosmetics, and it is possible that an important preparation could be typed as either one. The United States Customs Court, whose chief judge and eight judges sit in New York City (but hold sessions in other chief ports), determine such disputes. The members of this court are appointed for good behavior and receive $30,000 annually. Its opinions are printed in a special volume (Cust. Ct.) and frequently also are reported in the *Federal Supplement,* the official reporter for district court cases.

Customs Court

Appeals from the United States Customs Court may be carried to the United States Court of Customs and Patent Appeals, which received appellate jurisdiction in customs matters in 1909 and from the Patent Office 20 years later. This court sits in Washington and is composed of a chief judge and four associates. All are accorded tenure during good behavior at a salary of $33,000. Two books are printed for each volume of the court's reports (C.C.P.A.), one for customs and the other for patents; some cases are included in the *Federal Reporter* series. Dissatisfied litigants may petition for certiorari if they wish final review by the Supreme Court.

In addition to the special courts described briefly above are the Tax Court of the United States (formerly called the Board of Tax Appeals); the United States Court of Military Appeals (a tribunal established in 1951 to be administered by the Department of Defense while preserving its judicial independence); the territorial courts (with both local and Federal jurisdiction, but under the control of Congress); and inferior courts for the District of Columbia (Juvenile Court, Municipal Court of Appeals, and the Municipal Court). Although each may be accorded appeals as specified by Congress, certiorari is their only way of reaching the Supreme Court.

On a number of occasions bills have been introduced into the Congress for the purpose of creating another legislative court, an Administrative Court. To date all have failed of passage. Those pressing for such a court cite the fact there is considerable controversy between citizens and the Federal Government which ought to be—in their view—but is not in practice begun in a court. The controversies mentioned are those between government administrators and persons subject to the former's rules and regulations. In many instances the dispute is taken before whatever government commission is charged with regulatory responsibility in the subject matter, and the decision is rendered by that body. For example, the Federal Trade Commission may rule whether a tobacco company is deceiving the public when it makes certain claims for its product.[37] To some the practice of letting administrative bodies serve in judging their own cases is unfair. Argument to the contrary is that adverse decisions made by administrators can generally be carried from the administrative agency to a court, although at some extra cost. Those opposed to the creation of a special Administrative Court point out that the legislative courts previously described also serve in some instances as administrative courts.

State Courts and Federal Courts

The dual citizenship which Americans possess in the Federal system explains the existence of 51 distinct and separate judicial systems in the United States. Each of the 50 state systems is entirely independent of the others; each handles the bulk of the

---

37. Robert S. Lorch, "The Administrative Court Idea Before Congress," *Western Political Quarterly*, XX (March, 1967), pp. 65–81, discusses the reasons supporting creation of an Administrative Court and the efforts to create such a court by the Congress.

judicial business for its residents. The average American who goes to court for such matters as probate, divorce, and trusts, and even for civil and criminal causes, will go to a *state* court. The state systems are subject to review by only one court: the Supreme Court of the United States.

A litigant in a state court has the right of appeal out of his local system if he has invoked a national statute or treaty and the state court of last resort has held it to be invalid; if he challenged a state law as being incompatible with a law, treaty, or the Constitution of the United States, and the state court upheld it; or if a Federal right has been denied. In addition to these grounds for appeal to the Supreme Court, certiorari is available for state cases, but neither appeal nor certiorari will lie unless the litigant has "exhausted local remedies" (*i.e.*, been before the highest state court which has jurisdiction over the particular matter). Some cases must move up a hierarchy of a half-dozen courts before a controversy is ready to be considered in the replica of the Temple of Diana in Washington, but another case may go from the Justice of the Peace court to the nation's highest bench in one leap. This has happened—but it was a Civil Rights case, and the thorny question of civil liberties deserves a separate chapter.

SUMMARY

- The Federal judicial system is in the form of a pyramid. The base is composed of the 90 Federal District Courts which are courts of first instance, and which therefore handle most of the litigation brought before the Federal judiciary. Cases on appeal from the District Courts normally go to a Federal Circuit Court of Appeals, of which there are 11. Capping the Federal system is the Supreme Court of the United States, whose existence, unlike the other levels of Federal courts which were created by the Congress, is established in the Constitution.

- The Judicial Conference of the United States, comprised of representatives from the Federal bench, serves as the governing body of the Federal judiciary. There is also a Judicial Council for each judicial circuit. The Administrative Office of the United States Courts handles administrative matters, while the newly formed Federal Judicial Center conducts research and training directed toward more effective judicial administration and a higher standard of justice.

- The American legal system owes more to English common law than to the Roman legal system, whose influence is greater in Europe. In addition to the common law, American jurisprudence reflects the rules of equity developed in England to afford justice in cases not covered by the common law. After the Revolution both state and national governments commenced codifying their laws, and less reliance was placed upon the common law, although the influence of 1,000 years of English custom remains. Today the cases which come before the courts may be divided into civil actions, in which there is a dispute between two parties, and criminal actions, wherein a criminal statute has allegedly been broken. Rules of equity may be applied in particular circumstances.

• The states have their own trial, appeal, and supreme courts, and the bulk of American litigation is handled by the state judicial systems. The Federal courts handle only those cases enumerated in the Constitution or defined by Congress. In the Federal system the rights of litigants in criminal and civil cases are protected by constitutional safeguards, and in the states by state constitutional provisions. The efforts of the Supreme Court in particular to extend the Constitution's safeguards to state courts regarding persons accused of crimes, as well as to expand upon their application in Federal cases, has recently resulted in charges of "coddling the criminals."

• The right of a litigant to appeal his case in which the judgment went against him in the court of first instance is a fundamental aspect of the American judicial system. Many cases from the Federal District Courts are appealed up to the Circuit Courts of Appeal. A few, generally involving principles of broad national interest, reach the Supreme Court. By utilizing its power to approve writs of *certiorari*, the high bench may exercise considerable control over which cases it hears, although some types of cases it must hear as stipulated in the Constitution.

• Because it is the court of last resort, the Supreme Court is more involved in controversy and is more studied than lesser tribunals. Three aspects of its operations stand out as subjects for dispute and inquiry. The Court not only *applies* the law but it *interprets* it. This responsibility requires the Court to decide upon the meaning which shall be given words in a particular statute as it is applied in a specific case. *Judicial decision-making* has recently received considerable attention by scholars and some comment by critics of the Court, as efforts are made to understand the ways in which variables beyond the purely legal influence a justice as he renders a decision. The power of *judicial review*, by which the Court may overturn the declared will of the Congress and the President as embodied in a statute, has been a controversial matter since the doctrine was first practiced by John Marshall.

• The question of whether the Supreme Court is doing a good job is sharply debated today. Often it seems that one's views on the matter are related to whether the Court is furthering one's political and economic interests by its actions. Others make their judgments of the Court's behavior on the basis of whether they believe in judicial restraint or judicial activism. Some critics of the Court are upset because the Court engages in law-making instead of strictly confining itself to law-applying.

• The "Warren Court" handed down a number of landmark decisions—involving Civil Rights, apportionment of legislative and congressional districts, and separation of church and state—which attracted to the Court considerable praise and caustic criticism. In 1968 the Congress twice indicated its disapproval of the Court. By statute it negated some of the Court's rulings regarding safeguards to be extended to those accused of crimes in Federal cases. By refusing to invoke cloture on a filibuster designed to prevent a vote being taken on the nomination of Associate Justice Abe Fortas to become Chief Justice, Congress wrecked President Johnson's effort to make the Chief Justice appointment before leaving office, and in effect passed a kind of censure upon the liberal-voting Fortas.

• In addition to the regular Federal courts, the Congress from time to time has created what are known as legislative courts to handle particular kinds of cases. Examples are the United States Customs Court, the United States Court of Customs and Patent Appeals, the Tax Court of the United States, and the United States Court of Military Appeals. Efforts to obtain legislation for an Administrative Court to handle disputes between persons and Federal Government agencies which are heard by the involved agency have failed to date.

• The dual citizenship which Americans possess in their Federal system requires the presence of 51 distinct and separate judicial systems. Each state's court system is independent of the others; however, cases begun in any of them may move up into the Federal system if certain criteria are met.

SUGGESTED READING

* (Books so designated are available in paperbound editions.)

Abraham, Henry J., The Judiciary (Boston: Allyn and Bacon, 1965).

Becker, Theodore L., *Political Behavioralism and Modern Jurisprudence: A Working Theory and Study in Judicial Decision-Making* (Chicago: Rand McNally, 1964).

* Cardozo, Benjamin N., *The Nature of the Judicial Process* (New Haven: Yale University Press, 1960).

* Freund, Paul A., *The Supreme Court of the United States* (New York: Meridian Books, 1961).

Hyneman, Charles S., *The Supreme Court on Trial* (New York: Atherton Press, 1963).

* Jackson, Robert H., *The Supreme Court in the American System of Government* (Harper and Row, 1955).

* Krislov, Samuel, *The Supreme Court in the Political Process* (New York: Macmillan, 1965).

* Mason, Alpheus T. and William M. Beaney, *The Supreme Court in a Free Society* (New York: Norton, 1968).

* Peltason, Jack W., *Federal Courts in the Political Process* (New York: Random House, 1960).

Pritchett, C. Herman, *The American Constitution*, 2nd ed. (New York: McGraw-Hill, 1968).

* Rosenblum, Victor G., *Law as a Political Instrument* (New York: Random House, 1960).

* Schmidhauser, John R., *The Supreme Court* (New York: Holt, Rinehart, and Winston, 1960).

Schubert, Glendon, ed., *Judicial Behavior: A Reader in Theory and Research* (Chicago: Rand McNally, 1964).

* Westin, Alan F., ed., *The Supreme Court: Views From Inside* (New York: Norton, 1961)

8

Civil Rights

When the proposed Constitution of the United States was criticized for its lack of a Bill of Rights, Alexander Hamilton, like a true Englishman, argued that the principle of popular sovereignty "is a better recognition of popular rights than volumes of those aphorisms which make the principal figure in several of our State bills of rights, and which would sound much better in a treatise of ethics than in a constitution of government."[1] History, however, was on the side of the complainers, who, foreshadowing the American fascination for constitutional legalism, adopted a Bill of Rights and (wittingly or unwittingly) entrusted the protection of the "unalienable rights" for which they had fought to appointed judges rather than to elected representatives. The United States thus probably became the only country in the world where a fairly adequate description of civil liberties could be written with considerably less mention being made of the national executive and legislature than of the courts. However, during the 1960's particularly, both the executive and the Congress expressed an unusual interest in and solicitude for the civil rights of minority groups, in particular the black community. Late in the decade the Congress exerted its authority regarding the rights of those accused of crimes in a manner to cancel some of the liberal rulings made by the Supreme Court. In both instances the governmental activity reflected considerable interest on the part of the public, or at least articulate portions of it.

The Supreme Court and Civil Liberties

Despite the recent activity of elected officials the Supreme Court seems destined—subject to curbs enacted by the other

1. *The Federalist*, Number 84.

two branches—to continue in its customary role of being the agent for defining and protecting American liberties. The high bench early assumed the monopoly of interpreting the written Constitution, long ago aspired to the role of being the umpire of the Federal system, and probably is best qualified of all three branches of government to deal with problems as relative as civil rights. The rights of individuals cannot be absolute, because the community has rights, too. People can quote the principle found in the Declaration of Independence that "governments were instituted among men to secure their rights" and still agree that local, state, and national governments must make rules to govern the actions of each member of society. American society today is more permissive than formerly regarding such matters as: the frankness with which sex and all other types of human activity is treated in print, by the movies, and on the stage; the use of traditional drugs as well as the newer and more potent hallucinatory agents; appearance of "four-letter words"; and public nudity. The areas of proscribed behavior are in a state of flux and reexamination; nevertheless, the general principle remains that some behavior must be prohibited and the right to do absolutely as one pleases is not an absolute right.

Congress, state legislatures, and city councils can legislate many restrictions on freedom easily enough (e.g., that religious liberty does not include permission to indulge in human sacrifice), but it would be difficult and dangerous for them to attempt to draw the line where liberty turns into license in every case. One pales to imagine bills defining the nuances of the First Amendment freedoms or the meaning of a phrase such as "due process of law" finding their way through the labyrinth of readings, hearings, compromising, and voting which attend legislative assemblies. Independent judges appear better qualified by tenure and training to define the rights and obligations of people in the specific instances which inevitably arise.

The Bill of Rights and the States

The framers followed the affirmative grant of power to Congress (Article I, Section 8) with eight stipulated restrictions on the national legislature (Article I, Section 9) and a section of prohibitions on the states (Article I, Section 10) because they viewed all government with distrust. The fear that the national government would be the primary subverter of individual rights was still so strong in 1791 that the first 10 amendments to the

Constitution became a Bill of Rights guaranteeing protection against the national government.[2] It is significant that the First Amendment begins, "Congress shall make no law..." Even after state powers had been checked legally by new constitutional amendments (the Thirteenth, Fourteenth, and Fifteenth) and psychologically by the bloody Civil War, the Supreme Court rejected the argument of an ex-Confederate government official that the recently adopted Fourteenth Amendment meant that "privileges and immunities cannot be abridged by state authority; that state laws must be so framed as to secure life, liberty, property from arbitrary violation, and protection of law shall be secured to all."[3] Instead, Mr. Justice Miller, speaking for a 5-4 majority in the classic Slaughterhouse Cases,[4] read Amendments XIII, XIV, and XV, which had been invoked to protect a private business, *only* as ending slavery and assuring civil rights to emancipated Negroes—not as placing the United States in the role of protector of the people from their own state governments. The result of this decision was to leave to the states the responsibility of ensuring the "privileges and immunities" of their citizens and to delay for decades the active part the Federal courts could play in defending and expanding American freedom.

Civil War amendments

The direct use of the power of the national government to extend the prohibitions of the Bill of Rights to states was made possible by the decision of a 1925 New York criminal anarchy case when the Court publicly announced that feeedom of speech and the press are "fundamental" and are guaranteed by the Fourteenth Amendment.[5] No subsequent Court majority has accepted the logic that all the freedoms mentioned in the first eight amendments are equally "fundamental" and therefore are guaranteed against abuse by state, as well as national, government. But liberally allowing certiorari to an increasing

"Fundamental" rights

2. Barron v. Baltimore, 7 Peters 243 (1833). John P. Roche points out that the desire for a Bill of Rights reflected a concern for the Federal principle, under which the regulation of the individual was to be left to the discretion of his neighbors and the state government, rather than an abstract dedication to the freedoms detailed in the amendments to the Constitution (*Courts and Rights*, New York: Random House, 1961, pp. 58–59).

3. Campbell's argument in the Slaughterhouse Cases, when he urged that the Court strike down as unconstitutional a long-term monopoly given to a New Orleans slaughterhouse by the State of Louisiana. 21 L.Ed. 394, 398 (1873).

4. 16 Wallace 36 (1873).

5. Gitlow v. New York, 268 U.S. 652. Actually, this pronouncement did not seem necessary to the decision of the case since the Court found the defendant guilty over the protests of Justices Holmes and Brandeis.

number of cases from state courts, the Supreme Court has moved beyond the obvious requirements of the Fourteenth Amendment for "due process of law" and "equal protection of the laws" (such as ascertaining the fairness of trials and the existence of discriminatory state laws) to explore a wider range of civil rights. The reader may note in following sections of this chapter the great extent to which the provisions of the Bill of Rights have been extended to limit state governments. Recently, intricate problems involving speech in public parks and streets, "sit-ins" at lunch counters, various types of demonstrations in public places, admission of blacks to state schools, censorship, demagogy and group libel, loyalty investigations, searches and seizures, and a variety of claims to religious freedom have come up from lower courts to occupy the time and attention of the judges. In their exploration of the domain of freedom, the justices of the Supreme Court have generally been cautious, recognizing that the tensions which exist between government and individuals, and among national and state governments, are explosive. In the 1960's the Supreme Court moved too far and too fast for many. Displeasure over the Court's actions could be seen in the 1968 election (the polls showed "anti-Court" votes going to Wallace and Nixon) and in the critical view Congress took of the high bench.

Basic rights Although specific interpretations of civil rights may differ from one opinion to another, the liberties of the American people can be explained fairly simply. At the outset, however, it is necessary to recognize that the most important guarantees of the Constitution apply to "the people," "the accused," and "persons." The rights of "citizens" are limited to the two "privileges and immunities" clauses (Article IV, Section 2; Amendment XIV) which have never been especially important.[6] Any animal which can qualify as a "person" is thus afforded basic

---

6. In a confusing opinion in the case of *Corfield* v. *Coryell*, handed down in 1828, Mr. Justice Washington had "no hesitation" in confining "privileges and immunities" to "rights which are fundamental," and which he decided would be "more tedious than difficult" to enumerate. He did rule that the clause did not give non-residents of Maryland the right to fish for Maryland oysters (4 Wash. C.C. 380, Fed. Cas. No. 3, 230). Forty years later the Court struck down a state law which required every person to pay a dollar when leaving its jurisdiction as violating the guarantees of "privileges and immunities." Crandall v. Nevada, 6 Wallace 35 (1868). In the famous Slaughterhouse Cases, Mr. Justice Miller relegated the "privileges and immunities" clause of the Fourteenth Amendment to the mercy of the states, thus making it an ineffective guarantee. In 1935, for the first time, the Court held a state law invalid as abridging the guarantees of this clause (Colegate v. Harvey, 296 U.S. 404) but overruled its decision five years later (Madden v. Kentucky, 309 U.S. 83).

rights—even aliens who are illegally within the country.[7] "Enemy aliens" (*i.e.*, nationals of a country with which the United States is at war) are, of course, in a different category: they may have their liberty sharply curtailed (for their own protection as well as that of the United States) and may have their property confiscated. The Courts will only inquire as to the fact of their status.[8] In addition, there are many *state* laws which discriminate against "friendly aliens" with regard to voting, holding public office, receiving government pensions, and engaging in a variety of occupations from architect to osteopath. In the spirit of the decision in the Slaughterhouse Cases, the Court has been reluctant to interfere in this area of states' rights, although it has upheld the right of an alien to engage in commercial fishing,[9] and has disallowed a presumption of fraud pertaining to a member of a minority group as violative of "equal protection of the laws."[10]

Freedom from Bondage and Arbitrary Punishment

All persons under the control of the United States, however, enjoy the pledge of the Thirteenth Amendment that

> *Neither slavery nor involuntary servitude, except as a punishment for crime whereof the party shall have been duly convicted, shall exist within the United States or any place subject to their jurisdiction.*

No person may hold another in bondage even if he has contracted to be a slave or an indentured servant, since the courts may not enforce such contracts. Suppose that a college student agrees to work for a benefactor for 10 years at $10,000 annually immediately following his graduation, in return for tuition and expense money while at the university. If, upon graduation, he prefers to become a beachcomber on a South Sea island, his

The Thirteenth
Amendment

---

7. When Chinese who were smuggled into the United States were sentenced, by a commissioner of a circuit court, to 60 days at hard labor prior to deportation, the Supreme Court held that although they could be detained, they could not be sentenced to hard labor without a jury trial. Wong Wing v. United States, 133 U.S. 228 (1896).

8. Ludecke v. Watkins, 335 U.S. 160 (1947).

9. Takahashi v. Fish and Game Commission, 334 U.S. 410 (1948).

10. Oyama v. California, 332 U.S. 633 (1948). However, an alien may be presumed to be in the country in violation of the immigration laws if he invokes the Fifth Amendment in lieu of answering questions about his political past. Kimm v. Rosenberg, 363 U.S. 405 (1960).

ex-benefactor might try moral suasion to keep him to his pledge, or, failing, bring a civil action to recover the money paid out and to assuage the broken contract. He cannot make the graduate work for him. Similarly, a sharecropper cannot be kept on the land until his debt to the owner's store has been paid, although he is liable to suit for collection. Since many tenants probably do not understand their rights, obligations, and alternatives, the Department of Justice has devoted a great deal of attention to "peonage cases" to prevent serfdom in this country.

One of the constant threats to freedom that the founders knew first-hand is the punishment of an individual without **Punishment** having afforded him the benefits of trial by the regular courts. **without trial** English (and colonial) legislatures had sometimes used the "bill of attainder" (merely a legislative declaration of guilt) to convict people. By simply announcing a decree or passing a law declaring a person guilty of a crime, a chief of state or an overbearing majority of a legislative body was able to execute or punish an unpopular individual. Article I of the Constitution forbade both Congress and State legislatures from resorting to this convenient method of dealing with enemies by two simple lines, from Sections 9 and 10:

> No bill of attainder . . . shall be passed.
> No State shall . . . pass any bill of attainder. ·

The courts have not been obliged to outlaw any crude attempts of Congress or state legislatures to pass bills of attainder, but they generally have intercepted more sophisticated efforts. They refused to require lawyers practicing before Federal courts to submit to a "test oath" that they had had no complicity in the "rebellion of 1861-65."[11] Again, in 1948, an appropriations act was declared unconstitutional under this clause because it stipulated that none of the money allocated could be used to compensate three government employees whom the House Committee on Un-American Activities had described as "irresponsible, unrepresentative, crackpot, radical bureaucrats."[12]

A traditional technique of tyrants to silence critics has been to declare them guilty of treason. Knowing this, the framers of **Treason** the Constitution built a particularly solid safeguard for their fellow citizens. The requirements to prove treason, found in Article III, Section 3, are:

> Treason against the United States shall consist only in levying war against them, or in adhering to their enemies, giving

11. *Ex Parte* Garland, 4 Wallace 333 (1867).

12. United States v. Lovett, 328 U.S. 303 (1948).

them aid and comfort. No person shall be convicted of trea-
son unless on the testimony of two witnesses to the same
overt act, or on confession in open court.

This careful wording has not only prevented the development
of the "new-fangled and artificial treasons" which Madison
feared, in *Federalist*, Number 43, but has also made it
extremely difficult to convict even those persons whose guilt has
appeared obvious to some.[13] It should be noted that no treason
trials have developed from the opposition to the Vietnam war;
in many other lands, such overt opposition would surely lead
not only to trials but to convictions.[14]

Rights of Those Accused of Crimes

HABEAS CORPUS

It is extremely difficult to convict persons accused of any
crime in American courts. Not only is a person presumed to be
innocent until he has been proved to be guilty, but he is surrounded by important safeguards before, during, and after trial
which increase the obstacles for the government. The escape
hatch of the grand jury in Federal cases has already been mentioned, but there are many more. Consider Article I, Section 9:

> *The privilege of the writ of habeas corpus shall not be sus-*
> *pended, unless when in cases of rebellion or invasion the*
> *public safety may require it.*

Without a doubt, the writ of habeas corpus is one of the most
important guarantees of freedom in the Anglo-American legal
system. The "great writ" is a court order, directed to any person
who has custody of another, stating that the person confined be
brought before a regular judge at a stated time. The judge, after
hearing from both the accuser and the accused, determines
whether or not sufficient legal cause exists to justify holding the
prisoner. The writ may be obtained by anyone who believes
another person has been taken into custody—even a passer-by
may seek the writ, since it is assumed that everybody has an

The "great writ"

13. See, for example, Cramer v. United States, 325 U.S. 1 (1945).

14. Perhaps it is true, as Justice Jackson wrote in the Cramer decision,
that "We have managed to do without treason prosecutions to a degree
that probably would be impossible except while a people was singularly
confident of external security and internal stability." Still, it should be
mentioned, as C. Herman Pritchett does, that prosecutions under the subversive and espionage laws have served as substitutes for treason prosecutions, and that they do not involve the "two witnesses" nor the "overt act"
provisions which make treason convictions difficult to obtain. See Pritchett,
op. cit., pp. 600–601.

331

interest in the freedom of every other person.[15] The judge does not, of course, always free the detained person, but the writ does discourage arrests based upon insufficient grounds. The requirement that the accused be physically present before the judge also diminishes the danger that a prisoner will be tortured or ill-treated following his arrest. The writ may be sought after trial and conviction, if there is cause to believe the trial was improper, and it may thus serve to obtain a new trial. Failure to heed the writ results in a citation of contempt of court against the person to whom it is addressed.

The importance of the writ of habeas corpus in America is underscored by the Court's consistent and unequivocal insist- **Suspending** ence that the danger must be immediate and intense before the **habeas corpus** writ may be suspended, because its suspension signals the close of the civilian courts and the substitution of martial rule. Chief Justice Taney believed that Lincoln had no authority to suspend this guarantee in Baltimore in 1861 even though that city was a strategic railroad center vital to the defense of Washington.[16] A few years later a unanimous Court held that the same President lacked power to suspend the writ in Southern Indiana during the Civil War, in spite of the fact that the area was teeming with secessionists. (A majority of the Court ruled that even Congress might not have constitutionally suspended it at that time and place.)[17] Finally, the Court ruled again, in 1946, that martial rule in Hawaii for the two years following the attack on Pearl Harbor was unjustified.[18]

"UNREASONABLE SEARCHES" AND BAIL

Another preventative against too easy a conviction is found in the Fourth Amendment:

> The right of the people to be secure in their persons, houses, papers, and effects, against unreasonable searches and seizures, shall not be violated, and no warrants shall issue but upon probable cause, supported by oath or affirmation, and

15. Some years ago a movie depicted the peculiar fact that, on petitions for the writ of habeas corpus, an "interest" in the case is not required to give standing in court as in other legal actions. A policeman (the "good guy") arrested an intended, but unsuspecting, victim of some mobsters in order to afford him protection. The lawyer for the "bad guys" sought a writ of habeas corpus, and when it was served, the "prisoner" was immediately released. The mobsters were waiting outside the police station and shot him as he emerged.

16. *Ex parte* Merryman, 17 Fed. Cas. 145.

17. *Ex parte* Milligan, 4 Wallace 2 (1866).

18. Duncan v. Kahanamoku, 327 U.S. 304.

Herblock in *The Herblock Gallery*
(Simon & Schuster, 1968).

particularly describing the place to be searched, and the persons or things to be seized.

The problem is, of course, to determine which searches are "unreasonable." If a person is apprehended in the act of committing a misdemeanor, or is arrested as a probable participant in a felony, he and the premises may be searched immediately. If a person under surveillance is about to remove the suspected evidence by car, airplane, or boat, the officers need not leave the scene in order to procure a warrant—provided there is sufficient cause to detain him on the spot.[19] A man whose reflexes are quick enough to enable him to swallow the evi-

Obtaining evidence

19. Henry v. United States, 361 U.S. 98 (1959). The majority of the judges said that good faith on the part of the officer is not enough.

dence between the time the police burst open his hotel room door and get to his bed, however, may not have his stomach pumped.[20] The guarantee has been important in prevent overzealous officers from searching anybody and everything with the hope that "something will turn up,"[21] but more important is the Court's refusal to permit the fruits of unreasonable searches from being used as evidence in either Federal or state trials.[22]

A difficult aspect of unreasonable search-and-seizure rulings concerns the use of telephone wiretaps, and other electronic **Eavesdropping** devices commonly called "bugs," to record words for use as evidence in a trial—or in an investigation—which an individual thought he was uttering in private. After a considerable review of the subject, which extends as far back as 1928 when the government successfully used wiretap evidence against a gang illegally selling alcoholic beverages, the Supreme Court recently seems to have devised a formula which protects individuals from indiscriminate electronic eavesdropping while providing state and Federal law-enforcement officials the right to use advanced electronic and acoustical technology provided certain procedures are followed. These include the necessity for securing authorization from a court, based upon prior investigation which shows good cause for the "bugging" or wiretapping, before officers may commence the electronic snooping; and the requirement that the eavesdropping must be consistent with a strictly prescribed law-enforcement purpose.[23]

In 1968 Congress acted to make wiretapping and bugging by Federal and state officers a permissible procedure in the investi**Legal eavesdropping** gations of a large number of specific crimes.[24] Congress stipulated such electronic eavesdropping may normally not occur until a warrant authorizing the activity has been obtained from an appropriate court. Exceptions permitted by the law are

20. Rochin v. California, 342 U.S. 165 (1952).

21. In 1968 the Supreme Court ruled that "stop and frisk" action by police was constitutional, but only when there is good cause to believe an individual is up to illegal activity or is illegally armed.

22. The original case excluding illegally obtained evidence from Federal trials is Weeks v. United States, 232 U.S. 383 (1914). In a series of cases the proposition was advanced that the Fourth Amendment's protection against unreasonable searches and seizures should be applied to the states via the due-process clause of the Fourteenth Amendment, and that illegally obtained evidence must not be used in states' trials either. See particularly Mapp v. Ohio, 367 U.S. 643 (1961).

23. Osborn v. United States, 385 U.S. 323 (1966); Katz v. United States, 389 U.S. 347 (1967).

24. See Title III of the Omnibus Crime Control and Safe Streets Act of 1968.

when emergency conditions arise in regard to the operations of organized crime or a threat to national security. Even under these conditions a warrant must be obtained within 48 hours after the electronic listening has begun.[25] In signing the Omnibus Crime Control and Safe Streets Act, President Johnson strongly criticized portions of the wiretap and bugging provisions. He stated, in his message delivered upon the signing of the Act:

> . . . the Congress, in my judgment, has taken an unwise and potentially dangerous step by sanctioning eavesdropping and wiretapping by Federal, state, and local law officials in an almost unlimited variety of situations.
>
> If we are not very careful and cautious in our planning, these legislative provisions could result in producing a nation of snoopers bending through the keyholes of the homes and offices in America, spying on our neighbors. No conversation in the sanctity of the bedroom or relayed over a copper telephone wire would be free of eavesdropping by those who say they want to ferret out crime.
>
> Thus, I believe this action goes far beyond the effective and legitimate needs of law enforcement. The right of privacy is a valued right. But in a technologically advanced society, it is a vulnerable right. That is why we must strive to protect it all the more against erosion.[26]

Most people who are arrested appreciate the assurance in the Constitution that "excessive bail shall not be required." The invention of "bail" (in Old French the word *bailler* meant "to take charge of") was an important milestone in individual liberty, since it permits an accused to leave security as a guarantee of his return to face trial; he becomes free to go about his business instead of being confined in jail to await his turn on the docket. As mentioned in the preceding chapter, not all crimes (or persons) are bailable, but a judge's decision in setting or denying bail may be challenged in the regular courts.

Bail

RIGHTS BEFORE, DURING, AND AFTER TRIAL

If a person faces trial, he is accorded the great advantage of having the prosecution bear the burden of proof. Whether or not this proof is sufficient "beyond reasonable doubt" is deter-

25. Additional provisions of the Omnibus Crime and Safe Streets Act made it a serious crime for unauthorized persons to engage in wiretapping and bugging, or to transport in interstate commerce wiretapping and bugging equipment for use in surreptitious listening activity.

26. The text of the President's message appears in the *Congressional Quarterly Weekly Report*, XXVI (June 28, 1968), pp. 1632–1633.

mined by an impartial jury of 12 which must be in unanimous agreement. Although one has no right to have friends on the jury, an accused who belongs to a minority racial group, and who can show that qualified members of his group have been deliberately excluded from jury service, is considered to have had his right to "equal protection of the laws" denied.[27]

As noted in the previous chapter, the Congress moved in 1968 to alter the jury selection in Federal courts so that larger numbers of black persons will serve in the future. Also in 1968 the Supreme Court handed down an important ruling regarding the composition of juries sitting in cases where the penalty is death.[28] The Court struck down as unconstitutional the common practice in most state and Federal courts of automatically excluding from jury duty in capital-offense cases persons who express opposition to the death penalty. Many believed the practical effect of the Court's ruling would be the further elimination of capital punishment in the United States.[29]

Fair treatment

The Sixth Amendment guarantees a trial by jury in Federal courts unless the defendant wishes to waive the right.[30] The Supreme Court recently stated that states must provide jury trials if the offense charged is "serious."[31] Whatever form of trials the states do provide, however, must be conducted in an atmosphere of calm deliberation.[32] Fairness demands that the judge have no "direct, personal, substantial or pecuniary" interest in

27. Strauder v. West Virginia, 100 U.S. 303 (1880); Hernandez v. Texas, 347 U.S. 475 (1954); Whitus v. Georgia, 385 U.S. 545 (1967). In 1947 the Court came within one vote of disallowing New York's "Blue Ribbon Jury" plan, which provided for the selection of jurors with better-than-average education and hence meant juries so selected would not reflect a cross section of the community. Fay v. New York 332 U.S. 261 (1947). New York abolished the Blue Ribbon Jury in 1965.

28. Witherspoon v. Illinois, 389 U.S. 1035 (1968).

29. The Court has agreed to consider the question whether the death penalty violates the constitutional prohibition against "cruel and unusual punishment." In 1968 Attorney General Ramsey Clark, speaking for the Johnson Administration, recommended that the death penalty be abolished in all Federal crimes including the assassination of a President. Among the states the use of the death penalty has declined in recent years, and 13 states have abolished capital punishment.

30. The Federal kidnapping law stated that only a jury could impose the death penalty in kidnap cases. The Supreme Court recently held this provision unconstitutional because it would impair a defendant's right to jury trial if he sought a trial by judge to escape the possibility of receiving the death penalty. United States v. Jackson, 387 U.S. 929 (1967).

31. Duncan v. Louisiana 391 U.S. 145 (1968).

32. Trials held in surroundings of intense hostility to the accused deny due process. More v. Dempsey, 261 U.S. 86 (1923). In this case the trial lasted only forty-five minutes, and the jury returned a verdict of guilty within five minutes.

the case.[33] In every instance, "fundamental principles of liberty and justice" must be ensured: physical torture, fraud, collusion, and trickery on the part of the Federal or the state government are not permitted.[34] Police have learned that protracted questioning in privacy is dangerous, for if a confession results the Supreme Court may hold it to be involuntary regardless of the decision of the jury at the trial that the confession was voluntarily made. In the case of *Ashcraft* v. *Tennessee*, Mr. Justice Black declared that long questioning creates a situation "so inherently coercive that its very existence is irreconcilable with the possession of mental freedom." How long is too long depends upon the circumstances. Relay questioning of an apparently normal, adult male, with no claim to a minority status, from 7:00 p.m. on Saturday to 9:30 a.m. on Monday was held to be excessive; interrogation for five hours was enough to deny due process of law to a 15-year-old Negro boy who had been arrested at midnight on a murder charge; eight or nine hours was too long for an adult who had a history of mental illness.[35] If a suspect is taken into custody for questioning at length without arraignment, the courts are especially doubtful about the voluntary nature of any confession which may be obtained, even though they recognize that the police often have sufficient evidence to suspect a person although not enough to charge him with a crime.[36]

During the 1960's the Supreme Court handed down a number of "landmark" decisions which further extended the cloak of protection afforded those accused of crimes, and incorporated most of the protections found in the Bill of Rights into the Fourteenth Amendment—making them applicable to the states as well as to the Federal Government. Because of the far-reaching nature of the Court's rulings, students of constitutional law refer to the period as one of "constitutional revolution."[37] In *Malloy* v. *Hogan* the Court extended the Fifth Amendment guarantee against self-incrimination to accused persons in the custody of state officials. The Sixth Amendment guarantee of right of counsel was also extended to

Protecting the accused

33. Tumey v. Ohio, 273 U.S. 510 (1927).

34. Brown v. Mississippi, 297 U.S. 278 (1936); Lisenba v. California, 312 U.S. 219 (1941).

35. Ashcraft v. Tennessee, 332 U.S. 143 (1943); Haley v. Ohio, 322 U.S. 596 (1948); Blackburn v. Alabama, 361 U.S. 199 (1960).

36. Watts v. Indiana, 338 U.S. 49 (1949).

37. Pritchett, *op. cit.*, p. 621. This 840-page book is an excellent source of information regarding constitutional law, as well as other aspects of the Constitution.

persons accused of violating state criminal laws.[38] A difficult question arising from the Gideon decision concerned when in the process of arrest, interrogation, indictment, and trial does the right to counsel begin. In *Escobedo* v. *Illinois* the Court stated that the right to counsel must begin "when the process shifts from investigatory to accusatory—when its focus is on the accused and its purpose is to elicit a confession."[39] Then in 1966 the Supreme Court handed down four decisions collectively called the Miranda decisions which involved confessions being obtained by police questioning of suspects without the latter having been warned of their constitutional rights.[40] The Court stated that in the future, police must carefully conduct their questioning of suspects so that the latter's constitutional safeguards are not violated. Specifically the police must inform suspects that: (a) they may remain silent during questioning, (b) any statement they make may be used against them, (c) they have the right to have counsel with them during questioning, and (d) if they cannot afford counsel an attorney will be appointed for them.

The decisions by the Warren Court regarding the rights of those accused of crimes were greeted with mixed responses.[41] **"Coddling criminals"?** The complaint was heard that the Court's decisions would seriously hamper law-enforcement officials in the performance of their duty. On the other hand it was argued .that some police departments and the FBI already followed the standards set by the Court, that therefore other law-enforcement officials could initiate better investigative work and so rely less upon the questioning of accused persons and the obtaining of confessions. Debate arose as to whether the Court, by its rulings, was "coddling criminals" and contributing to the "breakdown of law

38. Gideon v. Wainwright, 372 U.S. 335 (1963). Gideon was convicted in a Florida court of breaking into a pool hall and stealing goods therefrom. At his trial Gideon requested a court-appointed counsel because he was too poor to hire a defense attorney. His request was refused according to state law which provided for court-appointed counsel only in capital cases. Gideon then defended himself, lost his case, and was sentenced to a prison term. He petitioned the Supreme Court to review his case, which it did. The story of Gideon's successful efforts to change American judicial practice is found in the fascinating book by Anthony Lewis, *Gideon's Trumpet* (New York: Vintage, 1964).

39. Escobedo v. Illinois, 378 U.S. 478 (1964). In United States v. Wade 388 U.S. 218 (1967) the Court ruled that an accused person has the right to have counsel present when he is placed in a "police lineup" for identification before trial.

40. Miranda v. Arizona, 384 U.S. 436 (1966).

41. For an examination of the complaints made about the Warren court to 1968 see Clifford M. Lytle, *The Warren Court & Its Critics* (Tucson: University of Arizona Press, 1968).

and order." Congress reacted to the Court's decisions by over-ruling parts of them in regard to persons accused of Federal crimes. In Title II of the Omnibus Crime Control and Safe Street act of 1968 Congress stipulated that confessions need not be rejected because an accused had not been warned of his constitutional rights; that officers could hold a suspect in custody up to six hours before arraignment and still obtain a confession during that time which could be admitted into evidence; and that an accused need not have an attorney present when he was identified in a police lineup. Less controversial have been the High Court's opinions that a speedy and public trial, right to confront accusers, and right to have witnesses in one's own favor brought into the court by subpoena if necessary, apply to state trials as well as ones in Federal courts.

If a defendant is found guilty, he may receive some comfort from knowing that the Eighth Amendment prohibits the national government from imposing "excessive" fines and both the national and state governments from inflicting "cruel and unusual punishments" on him. This amendment was adopted to prevent the filling of the national treasury by threats and torture—techniques used for two centuries in the infamous "Star Chamber" of medieval England—and to prevent the barbaric and bloody practices, in America, of our ancestors. The courts decide, on appeal, whether or not a fine is excessive or a punishment is cruel or unusual. Certainly, burning, quartering, disemboweling, or starving convicted persons are not permissible, although hanging, shooting, electrocuting, or subjecting prisoners to lethal gas are considered suitable ways of dispatching them.[42]

After conviction

DOUBLE JEOPARDY AND EX POST FACTO

If the court finds the defendant not guilty, he need never fear a retrial in a Federal court because of the clause in the Fifth Amendment that states, "nor shall any person be subject for the same offense to be twice put in jeopardy of life or limb." Federal prosecutors must build the best possible case before the trial since, once an accused has been released, the discovery of new evidence (which could irrefutably convict him) may not be used against him on the same charge. The principle of federalism has had two interesting effects on the question of "double jeopardy." In the first place, one action

42. As noted earlier, the Supreme Court agreed to examine the question of whether capital punishment is "cruel and unusual punishment" in its 1968–1969 term, and former Attorney General Ramsey Clark recommended in 1968 that the death penalty be abolished for Federal offenses.

Federal vs. state laws

may breach the laws of both the national and a state government and so lead to trial in two different courts and harvest two distinct sentences. When this happens, the national government usually defers to the state. If a person brought intoxicants into a "dry" state in violation of its laws, he has offended the Twenty-first Amendment of the Constitution as well as the state law and, if convicted, may serve time in a state penitentiary and then be transferred to a Federal prison to begin a sentence there. Secondly, the prohibition of double jeopardy does not bind the states.[43] One convicted murderer learned this to his sorrow when the Supreme Court refused to have its "principles of liberty and justice" shocked upon learning that a state had appealed his sentence of life imprisonment and, on retrial, obtained the death sentence for him.[44]

Ex post facto laws

Neither the national nor state governments, however, may pass ex post facto laws. Because of an early interpretation, laws passed "after the fact" mean only that retroactive criminal laws which operate to the disadvantage of the accused are without force. For example, there was no penalty for burning leaves within the city limits when Professor Caldwell burned his the day his next-door neighbor's house was being painted. It just happened that the neighbor was the mayor and, in a special session hurriedly convened, the city council adopted an ordinance that subjected leaf-burners to a fine of $500. The ordinance was applicable immediately, of course, but Professor Caldwell didn't have to answer for the leaves he had burned the afternoon before. If his addiction to burning things had eventually brought him to trial for arson and he had received the full sentence in his state of ten years' imprisonment, the prison term would not have been affected if the legislature had increased the maximum to fifteen years the day after he was sentenced. (It could have been decreased, of course, since a new law reducing the maximum imprisonment would have operated to his advantage.) The obvious importance of this guarantee lies in the protection that if behavior which is permitted one day is changed later, a person has an opportunity to change with the law and need not live in fear of being punished for past acts. Recall, however, that ex post

43. It should be noted Pritchett states the prohibition against double jeopardy will likely be added to the list of protections applied to both the state governments and the national one. Pritchett, op. cit., p. 651.

44. Palko v. Connecticut, 302 U.S. 319 (1937). When a robber forced a driver to help him get away and later killed the unfortunate man, he was tried in one county for murder and, because he pleaded guilty, received life imprisonment. A month later another county (where the murder took place) charged him with kidnapping and secured the death penalty. Williams v. Oklahoma, 358 U.S. 576 (1959).

facto laws are limited to *criminal* statutes. If the government should decide to make a tax increase retroactive, we would be obliged to pay any deficiency—it is no crime to pay taxes.

SEDITION AND SLANDER

If we don't approve of the tax policy of the government, we are free to try to do something about it. The First Amendment establishes this right to criticize in these words:

> *Congress shall make no law . . . abridging the freedom of speech or of the press; or the right of the people peaceably to assemble, and to petition the government for a redress of grievances.*

This is really a remarkable concession, for nobody likes to be criticized, and when he has the power to prevent it, he usually does. Governments have been especially notorious for their willingness to silence critics. The common law never has recognized the right of a subject to criticize the government or its officials, and it was not until Fox's Libel Act (1792) that Parliament formally recognized that Englishmen were free to point out the faults of the government provided the purpose was not to incite violence or cause a breach of the law. Americans wrote free speech and press into their Constitution the year before the British equivalent,[45] although in 1798 Congress enacted the Sedition Law which made it a crime to write, print, or speak words "with the intent to defame the said government, **Defamation** or either House of the said Congress, or the same President, or to bring them or either of them, into contempt or disrepute." Since it was the goal of the Jeffersonians to bring the Adams Administration into disrepute, there were convictions under the hated law (the fines levied were later repaid). In times of peace the courts have been inclined to consider that it is a more serious evil to prevent publication of defamatory words about the government than to risk public scandal by their publication.[46] In times of national emergency, however, the courts have exhibited less interest in preserving the right to criticize the government and its policies.[47]

45. Leonard W. Levy, in *Legacy of Suppression* (Cambridge: Harvard University Press, 1960), presents a revisionist interpretation of the origins of the first amendments, stressing that the Bill of Rights was more a product of political expediency than of commitment to personal liberties.

46. Near v. Minnesota, 283 U.S. 697 (1931).

47. Schenk v. United States, 249 U.S. 47 (1919); Abrams v. United States, 250 U.S. 616 (1919). In the Abrams case, Justice Holmes (together with Justice Brandeis) dissented, offering the classic argument:

(Continued on next page)

Problems of "free speech," "free press"

Private citizens are protected from abuse by "free speech" and "free press" by laws which make slander and libel crimes as well as causes for civil actions. Under the common law the truth of the words spoken or written was not considered to be a defense in criminal trials, although it was accepted in civil cases. In America today, although state laws differ, the truth of a statement is always admitted as a defense. The courts have been especially loath to punish calumny against politicians (except false charges of crime)—on the probable ground that those who enter the rough-and-tumble of politics soon develop thick skins! The more serious "free speech and press" problems have come from attempts of cities and states, under their police power, to censor books and movies; forbid the amplification of human speech by mechanical contrivances; or from permitting "captive audiences" to be bombarded by advertisers.[48]

"CLEAR AND PRESENT DANGER"

Determining the boundaries of free speech, free press, free assembly, peaceful picketing, and such related activities is an extremely difficult task. There are those who believe that freedom is more essential than order, and others who consider that the maintenance of order is the primary concern of government. Drawing the line between the permissible and unpermissible is faced every day by those who want to preserve both freedom and an orderly society. In 1950, a New York policeman patrolling in a predominately Negro district of the city, observed that a political orator had attracted a crowd of approximately

48. Burstyn v. Wilson, 343 U.S. 495 (1952); for an excellent study of this case, see Alan F. Westin, *The Miracle Case: The Supreme Court and the Movies*, Inter-University Case Program #64 (University, Ala.: University of Alabama Press, 1961). Saia v. New York, 334 U.S. 558 (1948); Kovacs v. Cooper, 336 U.S. 77 (1949). Public Utilities Commission v. Pollak, 343 U.S. 451 (1952). See in Pritchett, *op. cit.*, Chapter 25, "Obscenity," for a discussion of the effect upon obscenity laws of the revolutions in sexual and moral standards which have taken place in the past two decades.

"But when men have realized that time has upset many fighting faiths, they may come to believe even more than they believe the very foundations of their own conduct that the ultimate good desired is better reached by free trade in ideas—that the best test of truth is the power of the thought to get itself accepted in the competition of the market, and that truth is the only ground upon which their wishes safely can be carried out. That, at any rate, is the theory of our Constitution. It is an experiment, as all life is an experiment. Every year, if not every day, we have to wager our salvation upon some prophecy based upon imperfect knowledge. While that experiment is part of our system I think that we should be eternally vigilant against attempts to check the expression of opinions that we loathe and believe to be fraught with death, unless they so imminently threaten immediate interference with the lawful and pressing purposes of the law that an immediate check is required to save the country."

80 people which filled the sidewalk and spread into the street. The man talked approximately a half hour over a loudspeaker attached to his automobile and attacked the President, the mayor, and certain patriotic organizations. He told the Negroes to rise up in arms against the whites in order to assume their equal rights. The harangue was apparently fairly good-humored and, except for a few who muttered (one of whom told the policeman to "get that man down or I will"), the crowd seemed more amused than angry. What did the policeman do? Three times he told the speaker to get off his soapbox and finally placed him under arrest; his action was approved by the majority of the Supreme Court.[49] If, on the other hand, the policeman had made the decision to protect his right to speak, he would have received the blessing of the minority. The standard Justices Holmes and Brandeis recommended is known as the "clear and present danger" test;[50] are the words delivered in such a way, at such a place, and at such a time as to bring about "substantive evils"? (The courts have, of course, reserved the right to accept or reject an individual's decision.)

The "clear and present danger" test seemed well on its way to judicial acceptance, when the threat of internal Communist conspiracy after World War II brought a change in the situation. In 1940, the Congress had enacted the Alien Registration (Smith) Act, the first peacetime sedition law since 1798. In 1948, the 11 top leaders of the Communist Party of the United States were indicted under the Act, charged with conspiring to teach and advocate the overthrow of the government by force. With public opinion aroused by the dangers of Communist aggression, particularly in light of the Korean conflict, the Supreme Court in 1951 upheld the district court's conviction of the Communist leaders. In doing so, four justices of the Court reformulated and broadened the "clear and present danger" test.[51] Chief Justice Vinson, in revising the formula, said:

> The "clear and present danger" test

49. Feiner v. New York, 340 U.S. 315 (1950).

50. This test was first stated by Justice Holmes, speaking for a unanimous Court in the Schenk case: "The question in every case is whether the words used are used in such circumstances and are of such a nature as to create a clear and present danger that they will bring about the substantive evils that Congress has a right to prevent. It is a question of proximity and degree."

51. Dennis v. United States, 341 U.S. 494 (1951). Justices Frankfurter and Jackson believed that the test should not have been applied at all, but for different reasons. Frankfurter deferred to congressional power to determine whether advocacy or overthrow creates a danger which justifies a restriction of freedom of speech. Jackson believed that the test, if applied, would protect Communist plotting during its period of preliminary preparation. Both Justices Black and Douglas dissented from the Court's ruling, the former saying, "Public opinion being what it now is, few will protest

343

(Continued on next page)

"Chief Judge Learned Hand [Court of Appeals], writing for the majority below, interpreted the phrase as follows: 'In each case [courts] must ask whether the gravity of the "evil," discounted by its improbability, justifies such invasion of free speech as is necessary to avoid the danger.' ... We adopt this statement of the rule." The new test, one of "grave and probable danger," thus held only that the danger to be guarded against need be probable, not that it be "present."

Several years later the Court revised its attitude: international tensions were somewhat abated as a result of Stalin's death and the Korean armistice; the Communist scare at home diminished after the demise of virulent McCarthyism; and a change took place in the membership of the Court. A judicial attitude more protective of civil liberties developed. Although the Supreme Court in 1957 did not rule on the constitutionality of the Smith Act, in *Yates* v. *United States*,[52] it effectively restricted possible prosecutions under that law. In reversing the district court decision convicting second-string Communist Party leaders, Justice Harlan in the majority opinion wrote: "In failing to distinguish between advocacy of forcible overthrow as an abstract doctrine and advocacy of action to that end, the District Court appears to have been led astray by the holding in Dennis that advocacy of violent action to be taken at some future time was enough. ... In other words, the District Court apparently thought that Dennis obliterated the traditional dividing line between advocacy of abstract doctrine and advocacy of action." Such switches in the interpretation of language as well as the line dividing "fundamental" rights from societal security emphasize the power of the Court and also underscore the relative and mutable nature of all individual liberties.[53]

52. 354 U.S. 298 (1957).

53. In 1961 the Court used the strict criteria enunciated in the Yates case to uphold the constitutionality of the section of the Smith Act which makes membership in an organization advocating the forcible overthrow of the United States government unlawful. Scales v. United States, 367 U.S. 203 (1961). For a time attempts were made to force Communists to register themselves with the Federal Government and thereby incur sanctions set forth in the Internal Security (McCarran) Act of 1950; and both state and Federal governments have required public employees to sign so-called "loyalty" oaths. The first practice has been emasculated by Court decisions such as Aptheker v. Secretary of State, 378 U.S. 500 (1964) and United States v. Robel, 389 U.S. 258 (1967). In a series of decisions the Court has indicated that to be considered valid, loyalty oaths must be carefully drawn to avoid vague and uncertain language. Baggett v. Bullitt, 377 U.S. 360 (1964); Knight v. Board of Regents, 390 U.S. 36 (1968).

the conviction of these Communist petitioners. There is hope, however, that in calmer times, when present pressures, passions, and fears subside, this or some later Court will restore the First Amendment liberties to the high preferred place where they belong in a free society."

The "Free Exercise" of Religion

If one reads the First Amendment literally—that Congress may not legislate at all regarding the "fundamental" rights—all sorts of interesting problems arise. Ponder the literal meaning of this simple phrase:

Separation of church and state?

> Congress shall make no law respecting the establishment of religion, or prohibiting the free exercise thereof;

There is no doubt that it means, at least, that no single religion may be declared as official in the United States and be supported out of tax funds; that police may not enforce church attendance nor keep people from attending religious services. On the other hand, if that statement built a wall of separation between church and state, as some experts insist, tax immunity for churches would have to be discontinued, and there would be a constitutional question as to whether or not the military forces could provide chapels and chaplains at public expense. Perhaps prayers would have to cease in Congress and at government schools. Rather than completely separating church and state, it is more accurate to describe the practice in America as allowing governmental encouragement of *religion* but maintaining a position of aloofness from *denominationalism*.

Actually, agencies of both Federal and state governments have frequently interfered in what churches might logically assume to be their own proper "exercises." The courts often have been obliged to decide whether or not such interferences were justified. Legislators, administrators, and courts have wrestled with such decisions as whether or not the free exercise of religion includes the practice of polygamy; supports communicants in their refusal to salute the flag; removes one from the necessity of obtaining a canvasser's license in order to sell and distribute religious literature; excuses a worker from being obliged to join a labor union (it doesn't); or permits a youngster to violate child-labor laws in order to engage in vending church pamphlets which preach the gospel.[54] Courts ponder whether or not citizenship may be granted to a pacifist who, because of religious conviction, is unable to pledge that he will "take up arms in defense of this country'; or if religiously motivated zeal excuses an activist for publicly insulting the doc-

Specific questions

54. Reynolds v. United States, 98 U.S. 145 (1878); a useful collection of the leading cases in the area of freedom of religion is Joseph Tussman, *The Supreme Court on Church and State* (New York: Oxford University Press, 1962). Minersville School District v. Gobitis, 310 U.S. 586 (1940); West Virginia State Board of Education v. Barnette, 319 U.S. 624 (1943). Murdock v. Pennsylvania, 319 U.S. 105 (1943). Wicks v. Southern Pacific Co., 231 Fed. 130 (C.A. 9, 1956), cert. denied, 351 U.S. 946 (1956). Prince v. Massachusetts, 321 U.S. 158 (1943).

trines and beliefs of other people.[55] The Court decided in 1947 that parochial school students could ride to school on buses supported by the public school system, and the following year ruled that religious education could not be given in public school buildings during school hours by volunteer teachers when other children were obliged to wait out the time in the library or gymnasium.[56] But by 1952, the Court reached a compromise solution which allowed state legislatures to permit students to attend religion classes during school hours (on "released time") provided the instruction was given off school grounds.[57] A decade later the justices followed their logic a step further and held that prayers could not be offered in school classrooms.[58] Of course, parents have the liberty of sending their children to church schools, rather than to public schools, provided the standards are comparable.[59] On the other hand, religious objections to compulsory vaccination laws have been waived, and police powers of the state may require blood transfusions for residents even though their religion forbids this form of medical treatment.[60] Although state statutes providing for sexual sterilization of mental incompetents undeniably breach the biblical command to "multiply and replenish the earth," the decision of Mr. Justice Holmes that "three generations of imbeciles are enough" has stood since 1927 and undoubtedly would control challenges on religious grounds.[61]

The state-aid question

The increasing costs of education have caused another church/state question to reach substantial proportions. This is whether the "state," either in the form of the Federal or state governments, may properly use tax funds to assist church-operated schools and colleges. In 1966 the Maryland Supreme Court invalidated the use of state tax funds to assist in the construction of buildings at three church-operated colleges, while

---

55. United States v. Schwimmer, 279 U.S. 644 (1929); United States v. Macintosh, 283 U.S. 605 (1930); reversed by Girouard v. United States, 328 U.S. 61 (1946); the McCarran-Walter Act, passed six years later, excuses conscientious objectors only if they declare their belief in a supreme being and agree to do civilian work if required. Cantwell v. Connecticut, 310 U.S. 296 (1940).

56. Everson v. Board of Education, 330 U.S. 1. McCullum v. Board of Education, 333 U.S. 203 (1948).

57. Zorach v. Clauson, 343 U.S. 306.

58. Engle v. Vitale, 370 U.S. 421 (1962).

59. Pierce v. Society of Sisters, 268 U.S. 510 (1925).

60. Jacobson v. Massachusetts, 197 U.S. 11 (1905), and Wallace v. Labrenz, 411 Ill. 618, cert. denied, 344 U.S. 824 (1952).

61. Buck v. Bell, 274 U.S. 200.

Fitzpatrick in The St. Louis Post Dispatch
"You may come back now."

the use of tax funds was ruled permissible at another college.[62]
The distinction made by the Maryland court was that in the
former instances the colleges had a religious image which was
found lacking in the latter case. It seems unlikely that the Maryland decisions will end all questions regarding government aid
to church-run educational institutions.

"Equal Protection of the Laws"

The leading case of sexual sterilization of inmates in mental
institutions (*Buck* v. *Bell*) was sustained by eight justices because the statute was carefully drawn and due process of law
was guaranteed both in procedure and substance. However,
when a different state decided to apply the same operation to
"habitual criminals," the Supreme Court invalidated that law.
The judges refused to be persuaded that a man who had been
convicted once for stealing chickens and twice for robbery with
firearms was more likely to transmit biologically inheritable
traits than, for example, a man who had been guilty of repeated

62. Board of Public Works of Maryland v. Horace Mann League, 385
U.S. 97 (1966). The United States Supreme Court refused to review the
Maryland case.

Police protection

Classification
necessary

embezzlement—a crime not included under the sterilization law.[63] Because of the faulty classification in this case, the chicken thief who had graduated to more dangerous crimes was protected in his bodily integrity. The principle involved is fundamental: the Fourteenth Amendment prohibits states from denying "equal protection of the laws" to any person within their jurisdictions.

Every resident is entitled to police protection in a community where a police force exists, but reasonable classifications may be made. A decision that the police patrol only the wealthy part of a town could be successfully challenged by residents of less-favored sections, whereas the assignment of a greater number of police to guard the business district than that assigned a residential section would be proper. If the chief of police decided to furnish a bodyguard to a person who had received threats, "equal protection" would not oblige him to do the same for every citizen who merely would appreciate the company or the protection of a policeman. "Equal protection" applied to police protection prevents the hideous spectacle of police standing idly by while members of minority groups and their property are attacked by mobs—a scene which has been and is too familiar in some parts of the world.

Classifications need constantly to be made in order to allow general legislation to be effective. Legislatures frequently divide cities into classes, depending upon population, for a variety of purposes (allowing different degrees of local authority, regulation of school systems, and taxing privileges), but problems arise when they pass laws such as the one which prohibited women in cities of the first and second class from being employed in restaurants between the hours of 10 P.M. and 6 A.M. The question was whether or not such provisions denied equal protection to women who were similarly employed during the wee hours in smaller towns.[64] If a statute brands price-fixing of other than agricultural and livestock products a crime, is the classification reasonable? The Court decided it was, and that equal protection was not denied in a criminal action against a conspirator who sought to fix the price of beer.[65] On the other hand, the Court struck down a state measure which forbade employers of five or more persons from employing fewer than 80 per cent who were electors of the state, as deny-

63. Skinner v. Oklahoma, 316 U.S. 535 (1942).
64. Radice v. New York, 264 U.S. 292 (1924).
65. Tigner v. Texas, 310 U.S. 141 (1940).

ing equal protection to resident aliens.[66] Certainly a city as large and congested as San Francisco was before the earthquake and fire should, by ordinance, prohibit the use of wooden buildings for laundries unless certified for safety, but when the Court learned that 80 non-Chinese proprieters were permitted to operate while 200 alien Chinese were denied permission, it decided that a law fair on its face and impartial in appearance might be applied and administered by public authorities "with an evil eye and an unjust hand" and therefore be incompatible with equal protection of the laws.[67]

The Problems of Discrimination

In America today the mention of "discrimination" is almost certain to bring the words "Negro" or "black" to mind. Waitresses, beer, resident aliens, and Chinese laundries still exist and have their problems, but the attack by the national government on barriers which have kept the nation's largest racial minority from unrestricted participation in the life of the community has accelerated so rapidly in the past two decades that most of the public has forgotten that any other categories have been, or might be, denied equal protection of the laws.

The Civil Rights Acts of 1957, 1960, and 1964, the Voting Rights Act of 1965, and the Civil Rights Act of 1968, together with a number of Court decisions, contain an immense amount of legislation and judicial rulings designed to enable black citizens to participate in American life on a nonsegregated basis. Nevertheless, segregation remains a prominent feature of American society, as the basic conclusion of the President's Advisory Commission on Civil Disorders stated: "Our Nation is moving toward two societies, one black, one white—separate and unequal."[68] The problem of segregation may be examined by dividing the subject into the major areas in which it is practiced—i.e., travel; education; employment; eating, entertainment, and accommodations in public places; housing; and voting.

Civil rights acts and segregation

INTERSTATE AND INTRASTATE TRAVEL

Except for a flurry of interest in ex-slaves after the Civil War, separation by race was accepted as permissible (if not normal)

66. Truax v. Raich, 239 U.S. 33 (1915).

67. Yick Wo v. Hopkins, 118 U.S. 356 (1885).

68. *Report of the National Advisory Commission on Civil Disorders* (Washington: United States Government Printing Office, 1968), p. 1.

by the national and some state governments from the founding of Jamestown in 1607 until the formation of the "Roosevelt court" in 1938. Consider the way the following specific words of the Interstate Commerce Act (passed in 1887) were interpreted: "It shall be unlawful for any common carrier ... to make, give, or cause any undue or unreasonable preference or advantage to any particular person ... in any respect whatsoever; or to subject any particular person ... to any undue or unreasonable prejudice or disadvantage in any respect whatsoever . . ."[69] It apparently never occurred to the Commission that segregation by race on the public carriers under its jurisdiction was an "unreasonable prejudice or disadvantage," even though that body tried to ensure equality of accommodations.[70] In the epoch-making decision of *Plessy* v. *Ferguson* in 1896, the Supreme Court adhered to the view of the Commission that segregation, per se, was not a violation of the Fourteenth Amendment.[71]

Plessy v. Ferguson

For six decades the courts managed to live with a worsening situation by handing down a series of decisions unusual for their logic. A Louisiana statute *forbidding* segregation in intrastate travel had been struck down in 1877 on the ground that it caused an undue burden on interstate commerce; but a Kentucky law *requiring* segregation was upheld as affecting interstate commerce only "incidentally" (over the protests of the streetcar company that 80 percent of its passengers crossed into an unsegregated state).[72] The Court explained that a first-class passenger from Washington, D.C., to Lexington, Kentucky, had been obliged to move into a Negro section of the train at the Kentucky border because of "the act of a private person, to wit, the railroad company."[73] Railroads complained when they were told that they must furnish equal but separate Pullman and dining cars even for a single Negro passenger, but the Court refused to find state segregation laws as burdening interstate commerce.[74] Finally, in 1948, a state law forbidding persons of the two races from occupying contiguous seats on inter-

69. 24 Stat. 380, 49 U.S.C. 3 (1940).

70. See, for example, Councill v. Western & Atlantic R.R. Co., 1 I.C.C. 339 (1887); Heard v. Georgia R.R. Co., 1 I.C.C. 428 (1888); Edwards v. Nashville, C. & S.L. Ry. Co., 12 I.C.C. 247 (1907); Stamps v. Chicago, R.I. & P. Ry. Co., 253 I.C.C. 557 (1942); Henderson v. Southern Ry. Co., 269 I.C.C. 73 (1947).

71. 163 U.S. 537 (1896).

72. Hall v. De Cuir, 95 U.S. 485 (1877). South Covington Ry. Co. v. Kentucky, 252 U.S. 399 (1919).

73. Chiles v. Chesapeake & O. Ry. Co., 218 U.S. 71 (1910).

74. Mitchell v. United States, 313 U.S. 80 (1941).

state buses while within its territory was invalidated.[75] Two years later the Supreme Court reread the Interstate Commerce Act and ruled that racial segregation in dining cars of interstate trains was not permissible.[76]

In 1956 the Court ruled on the matter of segregation in *intra*state transportation. The question arose from the famous bus boycott in Montgomery, Alabama (1955-1956) in which blacks refused to ride buses which were segregated in accordance with Alabama and Montgomery law. The Court stated, in affirming a lower court's ruling, that segregation in intrastate transportation violated the equal protection and due process provisions of the Fourteenth Amendment.[77] In 1960 the Court held that Congress had forbidden racial segregation for interstate travelers even if the services, like depot lunchrooms, were leased by the carriers to private concerns.[78] Two years later the Court set aside the convictions of six Freedom Riders who had tried to enter a "white" bus terminal in Louisiana and were charged with breach of the peace.

The bus-boycott case

EDUCATION AND "SEPARATE BUT EQUAL"

The field of education has long been a bitter and sometimes hysterical battleground between the advocates of integration and segregation. The champions of "separate but equal" schools are armed with the power of tradition reinforced by the principle of federalism; their opponents are equipped with statistics demonstrating the prohibitive expense involved in attempting to support two complete school systems and with the slogan "all men are created equal." Unlike interstate commerce, local education was never conceived to be within the control of Congress, and the Courts had almost automatically accepted segregation laws applying to schools and individuals until 1938.[79] In that year a prospective law student successfully attacked a state statute which provided funds for his education in a neighboring state university since Missouri did not maintain a law school for Negroes. The Court, through Mr. Chief Justice Hughes, ruled that equal protection of the laws required that a qualified student be admitted to a law school in his own state, since one existed.[80] A feverish attempt to establish "sep-

75. Morgan v. Virginia, 328 U.S. 373 (1948).

76. Henderson v. United States, 339 U.S. 816 (1950).

77. Gayle v. Browder, 352 U.S. 903 (1956).

78. Boynton v. Virginia, 364 U.S. 454.

79. Berea College v. Kentucky, 211 U.S. 45 (1904). Gong Lum v. Rice, 275 U.S. 78 (1927).

80. Missouri *ex rel* Gaines v. Canada, 305 U.S. 337.

351

arate but equal" professional schools in Negro colleges was undertaken by other states—only to founder on the hard fact that such facilities are not established overnight. Racial desegregation was then introduced to the universities.[81]

The vindicated foes of segregation, sensing victory through the courts, began a concentrated drive at the primary and secondary **Brown v. Board** school levels and, in 1954, heard a unanimous Court conclude **of Education** that "in the field of public education the doctrine of 'separate but equal' has no place."[82] In the years since the *Brown* v. *Board of Education* decision the high court has on numerous occasions acted, generally by either sustaining or overturning a lower court's decision, to secure implementation of its desegregation ruling.[83] Several times within recent years the Court has indicated its dissatisfaction over the slowness with which desegregation in public education has progressed.[84]

In passing the 1964 Civil Rights Act the other two branches of the national government took forceful steps to "encourage" **The 1964** or "coerce," depending upon one's point of view, desegregation **Civil Rights Act** in public education.[85] Title IV of the act authorized the

81. Sipuel v. Board of Regents, 332 U.S. 631 (1949); McLaurin v. Oklahoma State Regents, 337 U.S. 637 (1950); Sweatt v. Painter, 339 U.S. 629 (1950). However, it was not until the autumn of 1962 that integration came to the University of Mississippi. Newspaper headlines around the world told of the days of uncertainty and the nights of violence before James H. Meredith was enrolled.

82. Brown v. Board of Education, 347 U.S. 483. The Court reasoned that segregation based upon state law was in violation of the equal protection of the laws provision of the Fourteenth Amendment. After the Brown decision lower courts used the logic of that case to desegregate public parks, golf courses, swimming pools, beaches, athletic contests, and auditoriums. For an informative account of the legal stratagems and lower court tests that brought the school segregation cases before the Supreme Court in 1954, see Daniel M. Berman, *It Is So Ordered* (New York: Norton, 1965).

83. Aaron v. Cooper, 357 U.S. 566 (1958); Louisiana Financial Assistance Committee v. Poindexter, 389 U.S. 571 (1968).
The court did not attempt to achieve immediate desegregation of public schools. In apparent recognition of the immense problems associated with reversing a historical pattern of activity deeply ingrained in much of America, the Court stated in 1955 that desegregation would need be made "with all deliberate speed," but it permitted lower courts to grant time to local school authorities to work out the transformation.

84. In declaring unconstitutional the closing of all public schools in Prince Edward County, Virginia, to avoid desegregation, the Court stated there had been "too much deliberation and not enough speed." Griffin v. County School Board of Prince Edward County, 337 U.S. 218 (1964).

85. Federal troops had been employed by President Eisenhower in 1957 to support a court order desegregating Central High School in Little Rock, Arkansas, and by President Kennedy in 1962 to support a court order admitting James Meredith to the University of Mississippi. In 1963 Governor George Wallace of Alabama took his "stand in the schoolhouse door" to dramatize opposition to the entry of two black students to the Univer-

(Continued on next page)

United States Office of Education (located within the Department of Health, Education and Welfare) to assist schools in planning for and making the transition from segregated to integrated operation, and empowered the Attorney General to file suit in behalf of desegregation actions regarding public schools when certain conditions exist.[86] Title VI of the Act authorized the United States Office of Education, as well as all other Federal agencies and departments, to withhold funds from programs (in this case, schools) which are found to be carrying out segregated activities.

Fifteen years after the fateful Brown decision many of the nation's public educational facilities remain segregated. The degree to which the "law of the land" has not been implemented was suggested recently by the retiring United States Commissioner of Education, who said:

Slow pace of school integration

> Some 85 percent of Negro youngsters in the South still go to almost fully segregated schools. In the North, the picture's very much the same.
>
> We still are confronted with a school system in the United States which is divided up on a racial basis.[87]

One may well wonder how such sustained thwarting of clear Federal intent on segregation can be so successful and so pervasive. Several reasons seem to account for it. As mentioned previously, the federal system of government affords local and state interests opposed to integration many opportunities either to circumvent or dilute the policies emanating from Washington. This is of course most true in areas where opposition to integration is both popular and backed by economic wealth. Another reason for the slow pace of school integration is that many black families live in black neighborhoods, a reflection of other forms of discrimination, and consequently schools nearby

86. The conditions include a signed complaint charging segregation which the Attorney General believes is meritorious, the inability of the wronged persons to sustain their own suit, certification the suit would advance the orderly desegregation of schools, provided the subject school authorities fail to correct the condition complained about after notice of a complaint has been made.

87. "Integration Bid Called Frustrating," *Tucson Daily Citizen*, November 14, 1968.

---

sity of Alabama. The governor permitted the students to enter when it appeared President Kennedy was ready to use federalized National Guard troops to support the desegregation move. Such action disturbed many at home while it delighted America's enemies abroad.

The 1964 act also extended the life of the Civil Rights Commission, a body charged with investigating activities such as denials of the right to vote and with the duty to serve as a clearing house for civil-rights information; and created a Community Relation Service. The latter agency was given the responsibility of assisting communities to resolve their racial problems connected with discriminatory practices.

353

are black in composition also.[88] Finally there is the problem of rapidly changing a society which until rather recently accorded legal status to the notion of segregated school facilities.

VOTING: LEGACIES OF THE RECONSTRUCTION

The roots of the problem of restricted black political participation run deep into the unpleasant aspects of human psychology and American history which gave rise to other forms of discrimination. Although it is not surprising that white Southerners were reluctant to accept their ex-slaves as political equals, particularly since their right to vote was secured by Northern bayonets, it is astonishing that a concerted plan for disfranchising Negroes was so late in coming. The useful study of C. Vann Woodward discloses that the great reduction in Negro voting took place 30 years after the Civil War.[89] Strange as it seems now, in 1896 Negroes made up a majority of registrants in 26 parishes in the deep-South state of Louisiana. Six years later they did not comprise a majority in any. Stated numerically, Negro registration plummeted from 130,334 to 1,342 during this brief period.[90]

Disfranchisement of Negroes

Woodward explains that the systematic disfranchisement of Southern Negroes was the by-product of the struggle waged by white Southern conservatives to keep the section solid and secure from the rising tide of white agrarian radicals. Before the Populist movement, conservatives had generally protected Negroes from the wrath of the racists and had encouraged their political integration into the Democratic Party. However, the Populist leader in the South, Tom Watson, had declared that the Negro "is a citizen just as much as we are, and the party that acts on that fact will gain the colored vote of the south."[91] When his party acted on that logic and made a concerted drive for Negro political support, the prospect of Negroes comprising a balance of power between two warring white factions reinforced old fears. When the conservatives decided to abandon the Negro and raise the cry of "white supremacy," the Populists fell into the trap: their rank-and-file was made up of

88. One effort to achieve integrated schools, in spite of the presence of nearly solid black and white neighborhoods, has been the controversial system of "busing,"—i.e., transporting black and white children out of their respective neighborhoods in order to provide a greater racial balance in the schools.

89. *The Strange Career of Jim Crow* (New York: Oxford University Press, 1957).

90. *Ibid.*, p. 68.

91. *Ibid.*, p. 45.

the lower economic class—precisely the type which feared Negro competition most and succumbed most easily to the siren song of racial superiority. The implicit bargain struck was that neither side would muster Negro political support against the other.

A concerted plan of disfranchisement began. A long residence requirement, particularly in the county, effectively curbed the vote of those whose work followed the crops. Opportunities were provided in the administration of literacy tests to discriminate against Negroes who were eligible to register. When the poll tax was harnessed to the task of reducing the Negro vote, the victim was given his receipt without a word while the receipt of the white registrant was filed in the courthouse until election day. The discriminatory suffrage laws appeared almost foolproof.

The manipulation of qualifications had not solved all the problems, however. The poll tax applied equally to the whites; so did the long residence requirements and the literacy and property tests. A plan was needed to permit whites to vote while keeping Negroes away, and a satisfactory solution precluded the use of terror. An answer emerged by 1895: a law provided that if an individual could trace his lineal descent to a person qualified to vote in 1867, the property ownership and literacy tests could be waived. This "grandfather clause" enabled otherwise unqualified whites to be enrolled on the permanent registration lists, while it did nothing to help the Negro. In the next twenty years variations of the "grandfather clause" appeared on the statute books of seven Southern states, and one was elevated to the dignity of a constitutional provision by Oklahoma. Although the various versions of the "grandfather clause" were flagrantly unconstitutional, the Supreme Court did not overrule one until 1915.[92] Even as late as 1961, legislation proposed by the Kennedy administration to make a sixth-grade education sufficient proof of literacy was buried by a Southern filibuster in the Senate. However, the 1964 Civil Rights Act contained the provision making a sixth-grade education (if it were in English) a rebuttable presumption of literacy. In the same year the Twenty-fourth Amendment was added to the Constitution. It provided that the right to vote in primary or general elections for national officials,

> . . . shall not be denied or abridged by the United States or any State by reason of failure to pay any poll tax or other tax.

In 1966 the Supreme Court struck down poll taxes required for

The "grandfather clause"

92. Guinn v. United States, 238 U.S. 347 (1915).

state elections.[93] The justices stated that a Virginia poll tax on voters wishing to participate in state elections violated the equal "protection of the laws" section of the Fourteenth Amendment.

State poll taxes nullified

Another legacy of the Reconstruction period in the South until very recently was the one-party system.[94] The Southern conservatives first used the excesses of the radical Republicans in the post-Civil War era to solidify the "white folks" of Dixie into the Democratic Party and then raised the white-supremacy standard to keep them there. The result has been until 1964, that although an occasional Republican presidential nominee has been able to split the "solid South" and pick up a few electoral votes, generally a Republican candidate for a local, state, or congressional post could employ his time and money profitably in almost any other sort of enterprise.[95] All of this meant that if Southern voters were to have a real political alternative, it had for many years to be among Democratic candidates who sought the nomination of their party. Since the nominee was chosen at a party primary, and because the Democratic nominee was almost certain to win the election, the only voters who had to be wooed and won were those who voted in the primary. This is why Negroes wanted to participate in the Democratic Party primaries in the South and why many whites wanted to keep them from participation.

The one-party system

VOTING RIGHTS

A made-to-order technique for reducing Negro political influence was the "white primary," the blueprint for which was

93. Virginia attempted to dodge the Amendment's provisions by passing a law to give voters a choice of paying a poll tax or filing residence certificates before general elections. The Court invalidated the law. Harman v. Forssenius, 380 U.S. 528 (1965). The state poll-tax case was Harper v. Virginia State Board of Elections, 383 U.S. 663 (1966). Three-judge Federal courts in Alabama and Texas ruled on complaints initiated by the Attorney General, in accord with his responsibilities outlined in the 1965 Voting Rights Act, and found poll taxes for state elections in those states invalid.

94. In 1964 Goldwater carried Louisiana, Mississippi, Alabama, Georgia, and South Carolina. In 1968 President Nixon carried South Carolina and Florida, while American Independent Party candidate George Wallace won the electoral votes of Arkansas, Louisiana, Mississippi, Alabama, and Georgia. Undoubtedly the best analysis of the classic one-party system as it operated in the South is V. O. Key, Jr., *Southern Politics in State and Nation* (New York: Knopf, 1949). See also Alexander Heard, *A Two-Party South?* (Chapel Hill: University of North Carolina Press, 1952).

95. *The Journal of Politics* in its February, 1964, issue (vol. 26) contained a number of articles on politics in the South. See particularly in regard to party development, Donald R. Matthews and James W. Prothro, "Southern Images of Political Parties: An Analysis of White and Negro Attitudes," pp. 82–111; and Samuel Dubois Cook, "Political Movements and Organizations," pp. 130–153.

inspired by the Court's decision in a case which had nothing to do with Negroes. In 1918 two Michigan Republicans, Henry Ford and Truman Newberry, competed for the senatorial nomination. Newberry won and was indicted for spending too much money (900 percent too much!) in violation of a Federal law applicable to candidates for Congress. The Supreme Court split four ways but concluded that Congress could not make such legislation applicable to primaries, since the primary election was only a method by which private organizations called "political parties" made nominations. In brief: the Newberry decision held that primaries were not elections.[96]

The Newberry decision

It was not long until the Texas legislature had enacted a statute which made Negroes ineligible to vote in a Democratic Party primary. In the case fought by a Negro dentist, Dr. Nixon, the law was struck down in short order as a rather crude violation of the "equal protection" clause of the Fourteenth Amendment.[97]

The Texas cases

Texas tried again. This time the legislature invested the executive committee of a political party with authority to prescribe who might vote in its primaries. Under this statute the Democratic executive committee adopted a resolution limiting participation in the Democratic primary to white persons. Dr. Nixon again complained when denied an opportunity to vote in the Democratic primary, and again the Supreme Court vindicated his claim. The Court found that the law had made Texas a party to the discrimination by making the members of the executive committee agents of the state, thus violating the "equal protection" clause of the Fourteenth Amendment.[98]

The Texas law was amended once more. This time the delegation of authority to the executive committee was eliminated, and in the silence of the law the Democratic state convention limited the right to participate in the Democratic primary to white persons. When a Negro who was refused an absentee ballot solely on the ground of color complained, the Court upheld the exclusion as perfectly constitutional on the fiction that the Democratic Party in Texas was like a private club and its refusal of membership to any person was not an act of the state. The Court had fallen into the Newberry trap.[99]

The "white primary"

Just as the "white primary" was given birth by a case having nothing to do with Negroes, so it received its death sentence from the same kind of situation. When election commissioners

96. Newberry v. United States, 256 U.S. 232 (1920).
97. Nixon v. Herndon, 273 U.S. 536 (1927).
98. Nixon v. Condon, 286 U.S. 73 (1932).
99. Grovey v. Townsend, 295 U.S. 45 (1935).

357

in Louisiana were charged with having "willfully altered and falsely counted and certified the ballots of voters cast in a primary election in which nominees for Congress were being determined," the Court had to decide, in *United States* v. *Classic*, whether or not the right of a Louisiana voter to have his ballot counted was "secured by the Constitution." The Supreme Court, now refusing to be governed by the ghost of the Newberry case, said: "We think that the authority of Congress . . . includes the authority to regulate primary elections, when, as in this case, they are a step in the exercise by the people of their choice of representatives in Congress."[100]

If the integrity of *ballots* in a primary election could be protected, could constitutional protection of *voters* be denied? The

The Allwright decision   time seemed ripe for a reconsideration of the premises and conclusions that had legitimized the "white primary." An opportunity came when a Texas Negro was refused a Democratic ballot in the primary election of 1940, and his plea finally reached the Supreme Court. This time the judges had little difficulty linking state action to the denial of the ballot. They held, in *Smith* v. *Allwright*:

> The privilege of membership in a party may be . . . no concern of a state. But when, as here, that privilege is also the essential qualification for voting in a primary to select nominees for a general election, the state makes the action of the party the action of the state. . . . Here we are applying . . . the well-established principle of the Fifteenth Amendment, forbidding the abridgement by a state of a citizen's right to vote. *Grovey v. Townsend* is overruled.[101]

But the "white primary" refused to die with *Grovey* v. *Townsend*. When challenged in South Carolina, Democrats pointed out that the Allwright decision did not apply to them. They argued that the Texas primaries had been conducted under the provisions of the state law, whereas in South Carolina the primaries were entirely managed by party rules. (The Democratic Party had even allowed 18-year-olds to participate in the primary—if they were white.) Spokesmen for the dominant party stated flatly: "Plaintiff has no more right to vote in the Democratic primary in the State of South Carolina than to vote in the election of officers in the Forest Lake Country Club or for the officers of the Colonial Dames of America, which principle is precisely the same."[102]

100. 313 U.S. 299, 317 (1941).
101. Smith v. Allwright, 321 U.S. 649, 666 (1944).
102. Rice v. Elmore, 165 F. 2d 387, 389 (4th Cir. 1947), cert. denied, 333 U.S. 875 (1948).

TABLE 8.1   Voter Registration in the Southern States
Spring-Summer, 1968

State	White Voting Age Population	Negro Voting Age Population	White Registered	Percent White VAP* Registered	Negro Registered (1964 figure in parentheses)		Percent Negro VAP* Registered	Percent Negro
Ala.	1,353,058	481,320	1,117,000	82.5	273,000 (	111,000)	56.7	19.6
Ark.	850,643	192,626	640,000	75.2	130,000 (	105,000)	67.5	16.9
Fla.	2,617,438	470,261	2,195,000	83.8	292,000 (	300,000)	62.1	11.7
Ga.	1,797,062	612,910	1,524,000	84.7	344,000 (	270,000)	56.1	18.4
La.	1,289,216	514,589	1,133,000	87.9	305,000 (	164,700)	59.3	21.2
Miss.	748,266	422,256	691,000	92.4	251,000 (	28,500)	59.4	26.6
N.C.	2,005,955	550,929	1,579,000	78.7	305,000 (	258,000)	55.3	16.2
S.C.	895,147	371,104	587,000	65.6	189,000 (	144,000)	50.8	24.5
Tenn.	1,779,018	313,873	1,448,000	81.3	228,000 (	218,000)	72.6	13.6
Texas	4,884,765	649,512	3,532,000	72.3	540,000 (	375,000)	83.1	13.2
Va.	1,876,167	436,720	1,256,000	67.0	255,000 (	200,000)	58.4	16.9
Totals	20,096,735	5,016,100	15,702,000	78.1	3,112,000 (2,174,200)		62.0	16.5

* *Voting Age Population*
Source: Voter Education Project of the Southern Regional Council

The Court of Appeals, however, saw a distinction between a political party and a country club and ruled for the right of the Negro to vote in the primary. In his opinion for the court, Judge Parker emphasized the statement from *United States* v. *Classic* that "the choice of candidates at the Democratic primary determines the choice of the elected representative," and then added an observation of his own: "The disfranchised can never speak with the same force as those who are able to vote."[103]

Judge Parker's observation takes on greater force if one conceives of politics as involving exchange—a *quid pro quo* (something for something). The voter has something to offer the candidate: electoral support. The candidate has something to give his supporter: a variety of political favors. But the disfranchised has nothing to trade, and so may expect to gain very little.

In 1965 the Congress and President Johnson cooperated to secure passage of the most potent voting-rights legislation in the twentieth century.[104] In contrast to previous laws which relied extensively upon individual suits brought to secure compliance with the law, the 1965 act authorized direct Federal intervention in behalf of those kept from voting for illegal rea-

Voting-rights act of 1965

103. *Id.* at 392. The Court of Appeals for the Fifth Circuit had reached the same conclusion in a similar case from the State of Georgia two years earlier. Chapman v. King, 154 F. 2d 460 (5th Cir. 1945), cert. denied, 327 U.S. 800 (1946).

104. The Civil Rights Acts of 1957, 1960, and 1964 had progressively involved the Justice Department in the investigation of efforts to prevent black citizens from registering and voting, and the bringing of suits intended to correct the "pattern or practice" of depriving blacks of their right to vote.

359

sons. When certain criteria were determined to exist by a Federal court or the Attorney General, Federal officials were empowered to move into a voting district to determine if individuals were qualified to vote, and when they were, to require their enrollment for voting in Federal, state, and local elections, and in elections to select delegates to state party conventions.[105] The 1965 act also authorized Federal courts to suspend literacy and similar tests when a determination was made that such means had been used for or with discriminatory effects. Furthermore, the act directed the Attorney General to commence suits against poll taxes used in state elections.[106]

EMPLOYMENT

In 1948 President Harry Truman requested that Congress create a permanent Fair Employment Practices Commission to guard against discrimination in public and private employment, by labor unions and trade and professional groups.[107] No such organization was created until 1964 when Congress passed the Civil Rights Act of that year, and provision was made therein for an Equal Employment Opportunity Commission. Between 1948 and 1963 Presidents Truman, Eisenhower, and Kennedy issued executive orders to maintain nonpermanent committees charged with preventing discrimination regarding Federal employees and enforcing the antidiscriminatory provisions of government contracts. The 1964 Civil Rights Act contained an Equal Employment Opportunity section (Title VII) which outlawed discrimination in much of the nation's employment based upon race, color, religion, sex, or national origin. The bars against such discrimination included labor unions and employment agencies. The law permitted the hiring or classification upon grounds of religion, sex, or national origin when these constitute legitimate occupational qualifications. The law did not prohibit different amounts of remuneration for persons so long as the aforementioned characteristics were not the basis for the distinctions. Contrary to what some thought, the law

Fair employment practices

105. The conditions needed to actuate the appointment of Federal voting examiners were determination by the Attorney General that a literacy or similar test had been used as a qualification for voting in 1964 and the determination that less than 50 percent of the persons in the district of voting age were registered to vote in 1964, or did vote in the presidential election of that year.

106. The 1968 Civil Rights Act made it a crime to harm, intimidate, or interfere with any person exercising his right to vote for any candidate in a public election.

107. A review of civil rights activity by the Federal Government is "Open-Housing Law Highlights 20-Year Civil Rights Effort," *Congressional Quarterly Weekly Report* (April 19, 1968), pp. 898–901.

did not require a specific percentage of some race to be hired by private concerns. The Equal Employment Opportunity Commission was charged with the responsibility for securing compliance to the employment provisions of the 1964 act, preferably by seeking the cooperation of affected parties, but authorizing the initiation of legal action if necessary. As noted in Chapter 9, both the Johnson and Nixon Administrations favored the encouragement of private business entering the ghetto areas to establish operations providing jobs to the unemployed and underemployed, many of whom were nonwhite.

PUBLIC ACCOMMODATIONS

The 1964 Civil Rights Act represented a major effort by the Federal Government to secure equal access to public accommodations and facilities for black persons as well as other non- **Equal access** white minorities. Title II of the Act prohibited the denial of access of any person to a wide range of facilities because of race, color, religion, or national origin when enumerated condi-

Herblock in *The Herblock Gallery*
(Simon & Schuster, 1968).

The light at the top of the stairs.

tions exist.[108] Facilities covered include lunchrooms and counters; soda counters; restaurants and cafeterias; theaters and motion-picture houses; concert halls and sports stadiums; hotels, motels, and rooming houses (except for owner-occupied dwellings with five or fewer rooms for rent); and public facilities within or containing any of the above. Private clubs were exempted from the provisions of the law. The law authorized the Attorney General to bring suit for relief in behalf of persons seeking their right of access to public accommodations and facilities.

HOUSING

Renting and selling

After several unsuccessful attempts President Johnson succeeded in persuading Congress to pass open-housing legislation.[109] Embodied as the most important feature of the Civil Rights Act of 1968 was a three-stage ban upon discrimination in the selling or renting of housing on the basis of race, religion, or national origin.[110] The first stage, effective in 1968, prohibited discrimination in housing built with Federal loans or grants or with Federally insured or guaranteed loans. The second stage, which went into effect on January 1, 1969, added the prohibition against discrimination in renting and selling regarding single-family dwellings not owned by private individu-

108. The conditions are (1) when discrimination is supported by state laws or official action, (2) when a significant amount of the goods or entertainment sold moves in interstate commerce, and (3) when interstate or transient travelers are lodged.

109. In 1962 President Kennedy issued an executive order prohibiting discrimination in housing which had received Federal assistance or was Federally owned or operated.

110. In 1968 the Supreme Court issued a ruling, Jones v. Alfred H. Mayer Co., 392 U.S. 409 (1968), which went beyond the open-housing provisions of the 1968 statute. The Court stated: "All citizens of the United States shall have the same right, in every state and territory, as is enjoyed by white citizens thereof to inherit, purchase, lease, sell, hold, and convey real and personal property." The Court's ruling was immediately effective, whereas the 1968 Act's provisions do not fully apply until 1970. Furthermore, the Court's ruling applies to dwellings with less than five units, whereas the 1968 law did not. The 1968 Act included other provisions. Among these were the authorization of criminal penalties for harming or intimidating civil-rights workers engaged in assisting persons to use their rights, or persons exercising their civil rights; provision of criminal penalties for those using interstate commerce to facilitate a riot, and persons manufacturing firearms and explosives or giving instruction in their use relative to riots; the prohibition of Indian tribal governments violating constitutional rights of tribal members and of states exercising jurisdiction over Indian tribes without securing the consent of the subject tribes.

als, nonowner-occupied dwellings up to four units and all larger ones. Effective January 1, 1970, the third stage of the discriminatory ban includes all privately owned single-family housing whose occupancy is arranged by a real-estate agent. It is estimated that after 1969 the open-housing provisions will cover 80 percent of American housing which is sold or rented.[111]

OTHER DISCRIMINATORY ACTS

It was President Truman who decided the time had come to end segregation in the military forces, and he proceeded to do so in 1948 in his role as Commander-in-Chief. Up until that same year the courts, which had always understood individual discriminatory acts to be beyond the subject matter of the Fourteenth Amendment,[112] discovered that when state courts enforced restrictive covenants (long used to prevent nonwhite or non-Christian people from buying property in certain neighborhoods), the exercise of the judicial power was a form of state action which violated equal protection of the laws.[113] The courts had never been sympathetic to city zoning ordinances aimed at keeping the races segregated, on the ground that they violated the right of an owner to dispose of his real estate as he chose and thus denied him his property without due process of law.[114]

Restrictive zoning ordinances

For years states had miscegenation laws on their books. In 1964 the Supreme Court declared unconstitutional a Florida law outlawing a white and a black person not married to each other from continuously living in the same room at night.[115] Three years later the Court struck down a Virginia anti-miscegenation law because it was held to violate the due process provisions of the Fourteenth Amendment.[116]

Miscegenation laws

111. See "Open Housing Law to Cover 80% of Dwellings By 1970," *Congressional Quarterly Weekly Report*, XXVI (April 12, 1968), pp. 791–795, 838, for a discussion of the 1968 Civil Rights Act.

112. Civil Rights Cases, 109 U.S. 3 (1883).

113. Shelley v. Kraemer, 334 U.S. 1 (1948). Hurd v. Hodge, 334 U.S. 24, reported the same day, held that since state courts could not enforce restrictive covenants, courts in the District of Columbia were also forbidden to give them effect.

114. Buchanan v. Warley, 245 U.S. 60 (1917); Harmon v. Tyler, 273 U.S. 668 (1927); City of Richmond v. Deans, 281 U.S. 704 (1930).

115. McLaughlin v. Florida, 379 U.S. 184 (1964).

116. Loving v. Virginia, 388 U.S. 1 (1967).

The American Dilemma[117]

Although the recent deluge of legislation and court decisions helped some black Americans to exercise the full spectrum of their civil rights, and to live in a condition akin to that of first-class citizenship, millions have not been so fortunate. After the "long, hot summers" of the 1960's it became obvious to almost everyone that the laws and court decisions by themselves were not solving the racial tensions that beset the nation. A number of studies have appeared which claim to discuss the factors beneath the racial problems and to make recommendations suitable for their solution. Perhaps the most impressive of the studies which call for broad political action is the *Report of the National Advisory Commission on Civil Disorders*.[118] A brief examination of this study will impress the reader with the magnitude of the racial problems still awaiting resolution by the American people.

THE REPORT OF THE NATIONAL ADVISORY COMMISSION ON CIVIL DISORDERS

Many white Americans were shocked in 1968 when the President's National Advisory Commission on Civil Disorders stated that among the complex factors responsible for the nation's racial troubles the most fundamental one was:

Racial tensions: the major causes

. . . the racial attitude and behavior of white Americans toward black Americans.

Race prejudice has shaped our history decisively; it now threatens to affect our future.

White racism is essentially responsible for the explosive mixture which has been accumulating in our cities since the end of World War II.[119]

117. In the early 1940's the Swedish scholar Gunnar Myrdal directed a study of American racial problems entitled *An American Dilemma* (New York: Harper and Brothers, 1944). It has since become a classic.

118. The range of studies available to those interested in theories about and solutions for racial problems are suggested by the following citations which approach the matter in different ways: Harry A. Bailey, Jr., *Negro Politics in America* (Columbus: Merrill Books, 1967); Claude Brown, *Manchild in the Promised Land* (New York: New American Library, 1965); Office of Policy Planning and Research, United States Department of Labor, *The Negro Family: The Case for National Action* (Washington: United States Government Printing Office, 1965). This report was prepared by Daniel P. Moynihan and became known as "The Moynihan Report."

119. *Report of the National Advisory Commission on Civil Disorders*, p. 5.

Other factors were:

> *Pervasive discrimination and segregation* in employment, education, and housing, which have resulted in the continuing exclusion of great numbers of Negroes from the benefits of economic progress.
>
> *Black in-migration and white exodus,* which have produced the massive and growing concentrations of impoverished Negroes in our major cities, creating a growing crisis of deteriorating facilities and services and unmet human needs.
>
> *The black ghettos,* where segregation and poverty converge on the young to destroy opportunity and enforce failure. Crime, drug addiction, dependency on welfare, and bitterness and resentment against society in general and white society in particular are the result.[120]

The ghettos

The commission noted that recently other ingredients have begun to "catalyze" the above mixture:

> *Frustrated hopes* are the residue of the unfulfilled expectations aroused by the great judicial and legislative victories of the civil-rights movement and the dramatic struggle for equal rights in the South.
>
> *A climate that tends toward approval and encouragement of violence* as a form of protest has been created by white terrorism directed against nonviolent protest; by the open defiance of law and Federal authority by state and local officials resisting desegregation; and by some protest groups engaging in civil disobedience who turn their backs on nonviolence, go beyond the constitutionally protected rights of petition and free assembly, and resort to violence to attempt to compel alteration of laws and policies with which they disagree.
>
> *The frustrations of powerlessness* have led some Negroes to the conviction that there is no effective alternative to violence as a means of achieving redress of grievances, and of "moving the system." These frustrations are reflected in alienation and hostility toward the institutions of law and government and the white society which controls them, and in the reach toward racial consciousness and solidarity reflected in the slogan "Black Power."
>
> *A new mood* has sprung up among Negroes, particularly among the young, in which self-esteem and enhanced racial pride are replacing apathy and submission to "the system."
>
> *The police are not merely a "spark" factor.* To some Negroes police have come to symbolize white power, white racism, and white repression. And the fact is that many police do reflect and express these white attitudes. The atmosphere of hostility and cynicism is reinforced by a widespread

Frustrations and violence

The police symbol

120. *Loc. cit.*

belief among Negroes in the existence of police brutality and in a "double standard" of justice and protection—one for Negroes and one for whites.[121]

Looking to the future, the commission noted that by 1985 the black population of the "central cities" will probably increase 68 percent to nearly 20.3 million. This growth, together with the continued exodus of white families to the suburbs, will likely produce black majorities in many of the nation's largest cities, according to the commission. The outlook for such cities and their black millions was held to be "grim":

> Most new employment opportunities are being created in suburbs and outlying areas. This trend will continue unless important changes in public policy are made.
> In prospect, therefore, is further deterioration of already inadequate municipal tax bases in the face of increasing demands for public services, and continuing unemployment and poverty among the urban Negro population.[122]

Unemployment and poverty

The commission held out three choices from which the nation could select regarding its future development:

Three choices

> We can maintain present policies, continuing both the proportion of the nation's resources now allocated to programs for the unemployed and the disadvantaged, and the inadequate and failing effort to achieve an integrated society.
> We can adopt a policy of "enrichment" aimed at improving dramatically the quality of ghetto life while abandoning integration as a goal.
> We can pursue integration by combining ghetto "enrichment" with policies which will encourage Negro movement out of central city areas.[123]

The commission felt that the third alternative ought to be the one chosen for implementation. However it warned that:

> Only a commitment to national action on an unprecedented scale can shape a future compatible with the historic ideals of American society.[124]

121. *Loc. cit.*

122. *Ibid.*, p. 10.

123. *Loc. cit.*

124. *Ibid.*, p. 11. The roster of distinguished Americans on the commission which made this recommendation included Otto Kerner (chairman), former Democratic governor of Illinois; John Lindsay (vice chairman), Republican mayor of New York; I. W. Able, president, United Steelworkers of America; Senator Edward Brooke (R., Mass.); Congressman James C. Corman (D., Cal.); Senator Fred Harris (D., Okla.); Herbert Jenkins,

(Continued on next page)

The commission singled out four areas in which it called for massive efforts. *Employment* was considered important because:

> Pervasive unemployment and underemployment are the persistent and serious grievances in minority areas. They are inextricably linked to the problem of civil disorder.[125]

The commission recommended (1) consolidation of manpower programs operated by the Federal Government and state and local governments; (2) the creation of one million new jobs in the public sector and a similar number in the private sector of the economy within the next three years; (3) provision of more on-the-job training with a reimbursement arrangement for private employers who participate; (4) authorization of tax and other incentives to investment in rural areas to offer life there as an alternative to migration to the cities; and (5) removal of artificial barriers to employment such as lack of a high-school diploma coupled with more active enforcement of Title VI of the 1964 Civil Rights Act (which provides for withholding of Federal funds from activities which discriminate on the basis of color or race).

About *education* the commission stated:

> Education in a democratic society must equip children to develop their potential and to participate fully in American life. For the community at large, the schools have discharged this responsibility well. But for many minorities, and particularly for the children of the ghetto, the schools have failed to provide the educational experience which could overcome the effects of discrimination and deprivation.[126]

The remedial action suggested took two broad forms. One involved the extension and broadening of educational opportunities to disadvantaged children, often with Federal assistance. The other was the elimination of racial discrimination in Northern and Southern schools by more vigorous application of Title VI of the Civil Rights Act of 1964.

The commission criticized the nation's *public-welfare programs* in this fashion:

---

125. *Loc. cit.*
126. *Loc. cit.*

---

chief of police, Atlanta, Georgia; Congressman William M. McCulloch (R., Ohio); Katherine Graham Peden, formerly commissioner of commerce, State of Kentucky; Charles B. Thornton, chairman of the board and chief executive officer, Litton Industries, Inc.; and Roy Wilkins, executive director of the National Association for the Advancement of Colored People.

Our present system of public welfare is designed to save money instead of people, and tragically ends up doing neither. This system has two critical deficiencies.[127]

Public-welfare programs

The first defect was described as the exclusion of millions who require assistance. The second major fault was held to be assistance well below what is needed for those included in welfare programs. Suggestions were made regarding reform of Federal, state, and local welfare programs. As a long-term goal the commission recommended the adoption of a national system of "income supplementation based strictly on need," which "would involve substantially greater Federal expenditures than anything now contemplated."

The commission lodged two complaints against the national housing program. First, it was contended that many ghetto dwellers cannot pay the rent necessary to secure "decent housing." Second, the charge was made that discrimination prevents access to non-slum areas, particularly in the suburbs. Two fundamental points for corrective action were stated: that the prevailing patterns of segregated housing must be broken down by Federal action, and that private industry need be attracted to the production of low and moderate cost housing.[128]

National housing program

THE NEW BLACK LEADERSHIP

As the white community confronted the question of what more, if anything, should be done regarding the black community (and other racial minorities), signs of new political consciousness were appearing among black citizens. Youths particularly tended to gravitate toward militant-to-violent leaders such as Stokely Carmichael, who first attracted attention as the chairman of the Student Non-Violent Coordinating Committee,[129] and Eldridge Cleaver, the Oakland, California, Black Panther activist.[130] Others read the stirring words of slain Malcolm X.[131] The slogan, "Black is beautiful," and the sign of the clenched black fist symbolized pride in race and the unity

Militancy and nonviolence

127. *Ibid.*, p. 12.

128. The open-housing provisions of the 1968 Civil Rights Act and the 1968 Housing Act substantially reflected the commission's recommendations.

129. A *Congressional Quarterly* report credits Carmichael with being one of the first to employ the concept of Black Power. " 'Black Power' Enters Civil Rights Movement," *Revolution in Civil Rights, Congressional Quarterly Service*, 1967, p. 14.

130. See his book *Soul on Ice* (New York: McGraw-Hill, 1967).

131. George Breitman, ed., *Malcolm X Speaks* (New York: Grove Press, 1966).

and power concepts which were being accepted as the necessary basis for the drive to equal rights.[132] The assassinated Rev. Martin Luther King and his nonviolent protests of black injustice were not forgotten, but many believed his teaching and methods were less applicable to the 1970's than to the middle 1960's. Julian Bond, the articulate young member of the Georgia legislature, seemed to represent the young black element still willing to eschew violence as it concentrated upon political and economic means to win actual, as compared with theoretical, rights from the white community. Much older leaders such as Roy Wilkins of the National Association for the Advancement of Colored People were striving to retain their positions of moderate leadership among young people suspicious of moderation.

As black Americans struggled to improve their lot, other racial minorities began to organize for their drives to first-class citizenship. Persons with Spanish surnames, particularly in the Southwest, began to apply pressure to reverse old social relationships, and on the Indian reservations talk was heard of "Red Power."

Protection of Property

Government officials have always been sensitive to the liberty of the people to own, control, and alienate property. This attitude has its roots in the fact that private ownership of property was one of the trinity of fundamental rights enunciated by John Locke—a right accepted by the American Colonials before their independence and guaranteed against abuse by their new national government through the adoption of the Fifth Amendment to the Constitution. With few exceptions,[133] property, which is wealth protected by law, has been defined by the states. For example, New York passed a fish conservation law and declared that nets would be treated as a public nuisance (i.e., not as property). When state officers found nets drying out on a beach, they were summarily

Property rights

132. Some suggested the way to equality lay through the establishment of black communities wherein political and economic power could be amassed, for it was often contended the white community responded only to power.

133. Amendment XIII destroyed slavery and Amendment XIV forbade claims to compensate their loss. Amendment XVIII ended property in intoxicating liquor and equipment for its manufacture a year after its adoption.

destroyed. The fishermen could not recover damages.[134] A slot machine may be classified as "property" in one state and be protected, whereas it may not have the same status in a bordering state and is liable to be confiscated or smashed.

The Constitution now forbids either the national or state governments from depriving any person of property without due

Right of eminent domain

process of law (Amendments V and XIV), and the national government may not take private property for public use without just compensation (Amendment V). These guarantees protect property from discriminatory practices. An owner may not prevent military aircraft from flying over his property at low altitudes, but "just compensation" may be claimed if the flights impair his property.[135] Governments may take private property through purchase, taxation, and a process known as *eminent domain*. For purposes of taxing, reasonable classifications may be made (e.g., amount of income and number of dependents for determining income tax), but blacks, Rotarians, or people with red hair may not be taxed at a rate different from that of other persons. Eminent domain is the power of a government to take private property for public purposes. Usually the amount of reimbursement is fixed in advance by agreement, but if this is impossible, the courts may set a price which both parties must accept. States may destroy one class of property, if necessary, in order to save another.[136]

Fishing nets, slot machines, land, red cedar trees, and apple orchards are all *corporeal* property, but the Constitution also

Property and contracts

protects commitments which are a form of *incorporeal* property. States are forbidden to impair "the obligation of contracts" (Article I, Section 10);[137] Article VI, Section 1 secured "all debts contracted and engagements entered into, before the

134. Lawton v. Steele, 152 U.S. 133 (1894). The Court said that the power of a state legislature to declare what things are innocent in themselves, and still unlawful, "cannot be questioned."

135. United States v. Causby, 328 U.S. 256 (1946).

136. Miller v. Schoene, 276 U.S. 272 (1928). Here an owner was directed to destroy his red cedar trees which were dangerous to the existence of nearby apple orchards. He was allowed $100 to cover the expense of removal and was given the use of the trees felled.

137. See Chap. Two for a brief discussion of the leading cases of Dartmouth College v. Woodward, 4 Wheaton 518 (1819), and Charles River Bridge Co. v. Warren Bridge Co., 11 Peters 420 (1827). A reading of the precedent-shattering decision in Home Building & Loan Association v. Blaisdell, 290 U.S. 398 (1934), is warranted. Here the Court split 5-4 in upholding a state moratorium on the foreclosure of mortgages. This distinct departure from tradition alarmed many people but was accepted as necessary in view of the then critical economic situation. The case does not appear radical today.

adoption of this Constitution." Conversely, the Fourteenth Amendment made illegal and void "any debt or obligation incurred in aid of insurrection or rebellion against the United States"—*i.e.*, by the Confederates in the Civil War. This provision highlights the principle that all kinds of property owe their existence to law. Since laws can be changed from time to time, new kinds of property may be created or old forms nullified. In view of this basic fact, the degree to which individuals are protected in private ownership by the Constitution was well stated in a decision upholding the power of a state to establish price controls for milk. In his opinion for the Court Justice Roberts observed that the use of property and the making of contracts are normally matters of private, rather than public, concern and that the general rule is that both should be free from government interference. He found, however, that neither the Fifth nor the Fourteenth Amendment prohibited governmental regulation for the public welfare if due process were provided. "And," the Justice said, "the guaranty of due process, as has often been held, demands only that the law should not be unreasonable, arbitrary or capricious, and that the means selected shall have a real and substantial relation to the object sought to be attained."[138] The Supreme Court will, of course, continue to determine what is "unreasonable, arbitrary or capricious" and whether or not the "public welfare" requires government interference in private concerns.

The Fourteenth Amendment

SUMMARY

• Traditionally, the Supreme Court has been the defender of the rights set forth in the Bill of Rights. However, in the 1960's both Congress and the executive were unusually active in securing the rights of minority groups.

• The original prohibitions against government action contained in the Bill of Rights pertained only to the Federal Government. The addition of the Fourteenth Amendment containing its guarantee of "due process" and "equal protection of the laws" regarding state activity did not immediately result in the application of the Bill of Rights to the states. However, the Supreme Court has incorporated the guarantees of the Bill of Rights into the Fourteenth Amendment to the point where most of them apply to the states as well as the Federal Government.

138. Nebbia v. New York, 291 U.S. 502 (1934). The Court divided 5-4 on this decision, the dissenters predicting "the end of liberty under the Constitution."

• The Thirteenth Amendment prohibits slavery, and involuntary servitude except that resulting from conviction of a crime. Bills of attainder are also prohibited.

• The rights of persons accused of crimes which were extensive initially have been substantially broadened in recent years. An original protection was the writ of habeas corpus. The Fourth Amendment, now applicable to both state and Federal governments, prohibits "unreasonable searches and seizures." Recent technical developments have created difficult problems as to the degree government may use telephone wiretap and electronic bugging to apprehend criminals. The right of trial by jury has been enhanced recently by provisions to ensure that greater numbers of minority group members will sit on Federal juries. The Supreme Court has also ruled that neither state nor Federal courts may exclude from juries those who are opposed to imposition of the death penalty, and that in state trials the accused must be afforded a jury trial when the charge is "serious."

• In a series of controversial decisions in the 1960's the Supreme Court extended the Fifth Amendment's protection against self-incrimination; the Sixth Amendment's guarantee of counsel, speedy and public trial, confrontation of witnesses, and compulsory process; and the Eighth Amendment's prohibitions regarding "cruel and unusual punishments" to include state governments. Neither the national government or those of the states may pass ex post facto laws; however, the protection against double jeopardy does not yet pertain to state governments.

• Neither freedom of speech nor of the press, two bulwarks of democratic society, are absolute. Private citizens are protected from abuse of free speech by slander laws; libel laws serve the same purpose in regard to written materials. A continuing problem is the determination of boundaries of freedom of expression.

• Freedom of religion, like that of press and speech, is not absolute. Courts and legislatures frequently struggle with the determination of where the line may be properly drawn between the state's authority and the person's exercise of religion. The most pressing problem now concerns the use of tax funds by church schools.

• The idea that all Americans must receive "equal protection of the laws" applies to everyone; however, in recent times the concept has most often been invoked by Federal courts protecting the rights of black Americans. In a series of high-court decisions, executive orders, and Civil Rights Acts, the three branches of the Federal Government have used the legal machinery at their command to attack racial discrimination in public transportation, education, voting, employment, public accommodations and facilities, and housing. Other types of discrimination—for example, in the Armed Forces and in regard to anti-miscegenation laws—have gradually been eliminated, at least in theory, by government action.

• Despite extensive governmental activity at the national level to provide black citizens with the full spectrum of civil rights, millions in effect remain second-class citizens. The racial disorders of the mid- and later 1960's reflect this situation. In 1968 President Johnson's National Advisory Commission on Civil Disorders advised the nation was "moving toward two societies, one black, one white—separate and unequal." The commission recommended massive Federal action in the fields of employment, education, welfare, and housing if the nation were to avoid wrenching racial tensions in the future.

• Property rights are also guaranteed in the Constitution. Persons may not be deprived of their property by either the Federal or state governments without due process of law.

SUGGESTED READING

* *(Books so designated are available in paperbound editions.)*

* Abraham, Henry J., *Freedom and the Court: Civil Rights and Liberties in the U.S.* (New York: Oxford University Press, 1967).

* Bailey, Harry A., Jr., ed., *Negro Politics in America* (Columbus: Merrill Books, 1967).

* Berman, Daniel M., *It Is So Ordered: The Supreme Court Rules on School Segregation* (New York: Norton, 1965).

* Breitman, George, ed., *Malcolm X Speaks* (New York: Grove Press, 1965).

* Carmichael, Stokely and Charles V. Hamilton, *Black Power: The Politics of Liberation in America* (New York: Vintage, 1967).

Carr, Robert K., *Federal Protection of Civil Rights: Quest for a Sword* (Ithaca: Cornell University Press, 1947).

Cleaver, Eldridge, *Soul on Ice* (New York: McGraw-Hill, 1967).

* Hook, Sidney, *Political Power and Personal Freedom: Critical Studies in Democracy, Communism, and Civil Rights* (New York: Collier Books, 1962).

* Konvitz, Milton R. and Theodore Leskes, *A Century of Civil Rights* (New York: Columbia University Press, 1961).

Levy, Leonard W., *Legacy of Suppression* (Cambridge: Harvard University Press, 1960).

* Lewis, Anthony, *Gideon's Trumpet* (New York: Vintage, 1964).

Myrdal, Gunnar, *An American Dilemma: The Negro Problem and Modern Democracy* (New York: Harper and Brothers, 1944).

Lytle, Clifford M., *The Warren Court & Its Critics* (Tucson: University of Arizona Press, 1968).

* Mill, John S., *On Liberty* (New York: Crofts Classics, 1947).

Pritchett, C. Herman, *The American Constitution*, 2nd ed. (New York: McGraw-Hill, 1968).

* *Report of the National Advisory Commission on Civil Disorders* (Washington: United States Government Printing Office, 1968).

* Roche, John P., *Courts and Rights* (New York: Random House, 1961).

* *The Negro Family: The Case For National Action* (Washington: United States Government Printing Office, 1965).

9

The
Business
of
Government

"What is government itself, but the greatest of all reflections on human nature? If men were angels, no government would be necessary." This was the position of James Madison in *The Federalist*, Number 51; were he to hold to the same contention today, he would be forced to conclude that the American people have been growing less angelic and more devilish every decade. Although the original nation, consisting of 13 states along the Atlantic seaboard, has expanded into 50 states stretching far out in the Pacific Ocean, the administrative growth of the national government has managed to outstrip the increase in its physical size. It has been argued that the spectacular increase in government is due to the sinful predispositions of destruction and greed in men which, by paving the way for economic dislocations and threatening global wars, have created situations so formidable that only a rich central government can attempt to meet their challenges with any hope of success. But other thinkers, in the tradition of Plato and Aristotle, believe that government has roles other than to referee the game of life while making sure that the playing field is not invaded. These students of politics suggest that there is more government today because of the increasing awareness that men seek the "good life" and, in a democratic country, can use the political process to obtain it. From this point of view, contemporary Americans can be regarded as a moral cut above their predecessors because they have developed stronger social consciences.

The Size of the National Government

Some Americans contend the growth of government, particularly the central one, can be explained by the insidious efforts

Growth of the welfare state

of proponents of the welfare state to control the nation. Still others credit a weakening of moral fiber and dilution of individual initiative as leading to a desire for "cradle to the grave" security. But it is perhaps best argued that the expansion in population, science, and industry require, and made possible, governmental activity neither necessary nor available in 1789.[1] No matter what the analysis of causes, it is obvious that the central government has become more active and powerful with every passing year. Because this has happened in all countries, talk about any modern government "withering away" (a thought associated with Marxist theory) sounds hopelessly naïve.

Discounting the ethical arguments, one stubborn fact stands out clearly: state legislatures simply could not grapple with

Problems national in scope

problems which had become national in scope. When railroads spanned the continent and their discriminatory practices could not be curbed by local efforts, the national government was obliged to step in with regulatory laws; the same pattern has been repeated with the growth of big business and big labor. When the Great Depression caused a collapse in agriculture, Federal assistance was demanded in the name of the "general welfare"; the same cry was heard from individuals who depended on other types of industries for their livelihood. Uniform national laws to deal with such needs had become generally acceptable by 1950; they would not have been tolerated a century and a half earlier. More recently the deterioration of ghettos in most metropolitan centers, plus the necessity that those same cities face up to problems concerning the quality of life for minority groups, transportation, environmental pollution, crime and justice, have prompted national efforts at solution. The change in attitude was made possible by the modern transportation and communication which has tied the 205,000,000 Americans of today more securely together than the 3,000,000 had been linked in 1789; by the interlocking of modern industrial activity and an interdependent economic system; and by a growing awareness that all Americans need concern themselves with the welfare of their fellow citizens—

1. For an essay on the opportunities and dangers of the "technetronic society" see Zbigniew Brzezinski, "The American Transition," *The New Republic*, 157 (December 23, 1967), pp. 18–21. A provocative article which asks whether the Constitution is adequate for the modern scientific age is Wilbur H. Ferry, "Must We Rewrite the Constitution to Control Technology?" *Saturday Review*, LI (March 2, 1968), pp. 50–54.

either for reasons of self-interest or because of humanitarian concerns, or both.[2]

An alphabetical list of subjects dealt with by the national government today begins before "atomic energy" and continues after "urban renewal." While citizens complain about the Brobdingnagian growth of their government, they petition for more services. Each new addition to the list requires a larger national budget and more Federal employees.

Government and Business

From the beginning, the relationship between government and private business has been intimate. Business interests had a powerful champion in the brilliant Alexander Hamilton, and the managers of the national government early indicated their ability to help friends by providing favorable legislation, which included tariffs, subsidies, bounties, a guaranteed bank, and other boons.[3] Today there is even more aid to business. Private companies reap enormous benefits from the services of the Department of Commerce, which engages in an astonishing number of research projects and makes available the results of its testing data, statistics, and analyses. Loans and tax advantages are common. Domestic firms are given preference in government purchases, and the United States consular offices promote and defend the interests of American industries throughout the world. During much of America's history the government protected "infant" industries (and, some have charged, mature industries as well) from foreign competition by erecting high tariff walls. Since 1934 the official policy changed to the view that more businesses could be assisted by reciprocally lowering tariffs on imported goods in return for the lowering of foreign tariffs upon American-made products. This theory has not been uniformly accepted. Some business and labor groups con-

Government and private enterprise

2. A pithy and succinct statement of this point of view is one credited to President Lyndon B. Johnson, who admonished, "Don't spit in the soup. We've all got to eat." Jack Shepherd and Christopher S. Wren, eds., *Quotations From Chairman LBJ* (New York: Simon and Schuster, 1968), frontpiece.

3. Even more interesting than the national role were the relationships of the states to business. The cases of Massachusetts, Pennsylvania, and New York are explored in the following: Oscar and Mary Handlin, *Commonwealth* (New York: New York University Press, 1947); Louis Hartz, *Economic Policy and Democratic Thought* (Cambridge: Harvard University Press, 1948); and Harry H. Pierce, *Railroads of New York* (Cambridge: Harvard University Press, 1953); Thurman Arnold, *The Folklore of Capitalism* (New Haven: Yale University Press, 1937).

tend that the influx of cheaper foreign products does them a disservice. Business also receives various subsidies, from the Federal Government in the form of franchises, amortization, and lucrative contracts, particularly for materials related to national defense. In times of economic stress public works are inaugurated which support business activity. During long periods of history businessmen frequently dominated not only the political process but American ideas and ideals as well.[4] At one such time it seemed perfectly natural for President Coolidge to say: "The business of the United States is business."

While the national government has been able to make life easier and increasingly prosperous for private enterprisers, it can also hamper their activities. The Founding Fathers wrote clauses into the Constitution which provided three important keys by which Federal regulators and inspectors could enter the domains of entrepreneurs: the power to regulate commerce, the power to tax, and the power to prescribe restrictive measures on business activity during wartime. The commerce power, declared by Chief Justice Marshall in *Gibbons* v. *Ogden* as admitting of no limitations and giving Congress the right to prescribe the rules by which commerce is to be governed, has allowed the national government to control, to prohibit, to promote, and to limit. The clause underlies most of the national regulation of private enterprise—to determine, for example, rates charged, the quality of services rendered, the wages and hours of workers engaged in production, and rules for mergers of companies. The tax power has been used to encourage plant expansion and to discourage production of items as dissimilar as state bank notes and poisonous matches; it has made the government a party to the financial affairs of private concerns. Finally, wartime power gives government almost life-and-death control over business in times of national emergency. During World War II, for example, the central government fixed prices and wages, rationed food and fuel, commandeered factories, and dictated production, distribution, and consumption. This potent key also locked workers to their jobs and confined their rent payments.

There is, then, ample legal power in the Constitution to allow the central government vast control over private enterprise. The only problems which remain are political: to determine what the policy of government toward business will be, and to transform that policy into administration. Both problems need brief consideration.

The commerce, tax, and wartime powers

4. *Cf.* Thomas C. Cochran, *The American Business System* (Cambridge: Harvard University Press, 1957).

GOVERNMENT POLICY TOWARD BUSINESS

Early in our history it was established that private proprietor-
ship and management of the means of production are the rule,
and that public regulation or ownership is the exception. This
concept has, of course, been repeatedly challenged. The champions of change are always at a disadvantage, however, since the
principle of separation of powers requires the conversion of
three branches of government to the same point of view before
changes can be made; because of the principle of checks and
balances, the opposition can usually prevent change merely by
controlling one branch. In addition to these historical and
political factors which discourage government regulation of
(and competition with) business, the American people are by
no means agreed on the basic issue of effective monopolies vs.
vigorous competition. Some forms of business are "naturally"
monopolistic—few telephone subscribers would appreciate competing lines. Without competition to safeguard the interests of
the consumers, the alternatives to allowing natural monopolies
to charge what the traffic will bear seem to be either government ownership and operation or governmental regulation of
private management's rates and services. Other industries, such
as automobile and steel manufacturing, require such an enormous capital outlay that potential competitors dare not enter
the field. If more competition is considered desirable, government must either enter the field itself or use its power to cut
the giants down to a size where they can be challenged successfully by other private companies. Citizens have not been persuaded that increased competition in such areas is worth the
adoption of either of these alternatives. The entry of government into a field which is not essentially of public concern is
foreign to tradition; few consumers are prepared to sacrifice the
dependable and lower-priced products which frequently are the
by-products of bigness to the ideal of a truly competitive
market.[5] Besides, it should not be overlooked that government
has actually contributed to monopolies by its patent and copyright laws which, although designed to reward inventiveness,
actually prevent the widespread adoption of useful devices. The
pendulum of public policy has swung, during the last century,
from tacit approval of the growth of monopolies to a vigorous
effort to "bust the trusts." At the present time the national gov-

Monopolies

5. David E. Lilienthal, former chairman of the Tennessee Valley
Authority (TVA) and the Atomic Energy Commission, writes eloquently
of the contributions of big business to American prosperity and democracy
in *Big Business: A New Era* (New York: Pocket Books, 1956).

ernment is apparently trying to distinguish between "good" and "bad" combinations and to confine its attacks to the latter.

Certain types of scientific and industrial endeavors are so expensive that private companies, even of the size found in the United States, cannot undertake their development. Frequently these gigantic ventures are thought to be so dangerous or so potentially powerful as to offer sound arguments against their control and use by private firms. The development and production of nuclear weapons is a multibillion-dollar enterprise which is an absolute monopoly of the Federal Government. The development of the SST (supersonic transport) to compete with similar jet aircraft being built in Europe and the Soviet Union receives Federal financial support. The program to place a man on the moon, rather like the plan of Columbus to sail west from Spain, can only be financed by central governments, in this case those of the United States and the Soviet Union. The huge linear accelerator at Stanford University was built with government money. And so it goes.

Major government enterprises

There are other types of business activity which the government stimulates and encourages but does not directly undertake itself. For example, in the late 1960's the government was active in urging private business to enter the ghetto areas of the large cities to spark housing construction, create new jobs, and to underwrite the creation of "black business."[6] Hope has been expressed that the latter, operated by black entrepreneurs, will constitute a new means of creating the economic base many feel is necessary to support the full participation of black citizens in the give-and-take of American life. Increasingly Federal money is being made available, and tax incentives are being offered, to attract business to the urgent problem of urban redevelopment.

"Human investment" approach

As one would expect, Republicans tend to look to business as a logical ally in the battle to cope with urban problems. An example of the views many Republican members of Congress hold regarding the role business should have in tackling urban difficulties is found in what has been termed the "human investment" approach.[7] As explained by former Representative

6. The interest of the business community in helping solve the problems found in the cities is suggested by a special report produced by McGraw-Hill in 1968 entitled, *Business and the Urban Crisis*.

7. Representative Thomas B. Curtis, "The Case for the Republican Human Investment Act," in Representative Melvin R. Laird, ed., *Republican Papers* (New York: Anchor Books, 1968), pp. 191–201. This book, which contains a number of chapters devoted to domestic problems, suggests the kinds of proposed solutions some Republicans are discussing for America's internal difficulties.

Thomas Curtis (R., Missouri), "human investment" is a way of attacking the problems of unemployment, poverty, and related matters through government encouragement of business's participation in training individuals to obtain and hold jobs. According to Representative Curtis, the various components of the business community know better than government agencies what kinds of skills are needed for future business expansion, and they are better qualified to conduct the training necessary to upgrade an individual's abilities to the point required for steady employment. Curtis argues that it is more efficient for government to encourage such training programs, by offering tax credits to business, than for the government to do the training directly.

It is difficult to predict exactly what proportion of effort will be carried by government, particularly the Federal Government, and the business community in future attempts to solve the domestic problems facing the nation. The records of the Kennedy and Johnson Administrations in this decade, which include Republican contributions to legislation, suggest the presence of strong forces in both major parties which could agree on large-scale cooperative efforts involving government and business. Should this be the case in the 1970's, few would mourn another step away from the days when government and business often viewed each other as enemies—provided of course that the public interest, involving many more interests than those of business, is well served.

Government and business cooperation

LAWS AND REGULATORY COMMISSIONS

Laws regarding business are, of course, considerably softened by the political compromises required by the American system of government. In the past, the temperate legislation which emerged from the two political branches was frequently further weakened, if not killed outright, by the judicial branch. The Interstate Commerce Act (1887) established a Commission and empowered it to ensure that "reasonable and just" rates were charged by the railroads, but the courts disallowed 90 percent of the commission's determinations during the first decade of its existence. Similarly, the Sherman Antitrust Act (1890) was put on ice for years by a tortured judicial interpretation that the law did not apply to combinations created to monopolize *manufacturing* but only to those attempting to control *commerce*.[8]

Like most pioneering efforts, the interstate commerce and antitrust laws had serious defects, but they were correctible.

8. United States v. E. C. Knight, 156 U.S. 1 (1895).

Interstate commerce and antitrust laws

Strengthened by a series of laws,[9] the Interstate Commerce Commission now has both jurisdiction and effective power over the entire transportation network in the United States, excluding airlines but including pipelines. Returning to the spirit of *Gibbons v. Ogden* after a change of membership,[10] the Court decided that "commerce" included manufacturing. In 1914, the Wilson Administration passed two laws which helped patch the statutory inadequacies of the Sherman Act. The first, the Clayton Act, was intended to list the monopolistic practices which were to be outlawed. Although Congress had to abandon the project as too difficult, the Clayton Act did prohibit price discrimination, exclusive agreements, interlocking directorates, and the purchase of stock in competing companies. It also specifically excluded labor unions from the operation of the antitrust laws. The second, the Federal Trade Commission Act, created a new independent regulatory commission to investigate corporations engaged in interstate commerce, to examine alleged violations of the laws, and to issue "cease and desist" orders to stop unfair competitive methods.

The regulatory commissions

Over the years, as Congress established more and more independent regulatory commissions, most of the American people came to accept them as the normal and most efficient way of implementing the public policy of regulating private business.[11] This conclusion is not, perhaps, entirely justified. Several experts in public administration have objected to the plethora of agencies with overlapping jurisdictions and have urged the creation of a single regulatory body; some have favored a single administrator over a board; still others protest that independence of the President effectively removed commissioners from public control while making them more susceptible to pressure groups.[12] Many citizens mistake the labels of "independent" and "bipartisan" to mean that the commission-

9. Notably the Hepburn Act (1906), the Mann-Elkins Act (1910), the Transportation Act (1920), and the Transportation Act of 1940.

10. Addyston Pipe & Steel Co. v. United States, 175 U.S. 211 (1899). Half a century later the Supreme Court had reached the point where any "substantial" effect, either actual or threatened, on interstate commerce, was under congressional control. Mandevelle Island Farms v. American Crystal Sugar Co., 334 U.S. 219 (1948).

11. Varying views of the regulatory process are set forth in Samuel Krislov and Lloyd D. Musolf, eds., *The Politics of Regulation* (Boston: Houghton Mifflin, 1964).

12. See, for example, Marver Bernstein, *Regulating Business by Independent Commission* (Princeton: Princeton University Press, 1955), and Emmette Redford, *Administration of National Economic Control* (New York: Macmillan, 1952).

ers serve only an administrative purpose while the political struggles rage elsewhere. But as commissions became firmly established, interest groups learned to shift their battle fronts as strategy suggested to the halls of Congress, to the courts of law, or to the offices of the commissioners. Politics flourishes wherever decisions are being made. When an agency such as the Interstate Commerce Commission obtains comprehensive power to approve, disapprove, suspend, or set rates, to control services, to prescribe safety equipment, to control stock issues, to supervise accounting methods, to investigate accidents, and to authorize discontinuance of service, the carriers can be expected to try to influence both the selection of their regulators and the decisions they make. Against such pressure the ICC and other regulatory bodies are expected to maintain the public interest, but at times charges to the contrary are heard.[13] For example, it is national policy to preserve the inherent advantages of each form of transportation, but the Interstate Commerce Commission must decide what they are—and so the ICC has become an arena where truckers, water carriers, and pipelines compete for favorable decisions with the railroads. The commission must also provide different regions of the country with "adequate" services without "discriminatory" rates, which means that delegates of the business interests in the rapidly industrializing area of "prices slightly higher West of the Rockies" come to Twelfth Street and Constitution Avenue for bitter and repeated clashes with their counterparts from the rate-advantaged East. The requirement that transportation companies procure a "certificate of convenience and necessity" before beginning operations or extending services brings floods of conflicting claims to the ICC from common, contract, and private carriers.

The same kinds of struggles are constantly enacted within all of the regulatory agencies because the stakes are high and someone stands to win. The Civil Aeronautics Board is under diverse pressures from established airlines companies and from feeder and nonscheduled lines, because it alone can approve the addition of new routes and the abandonment of old ones, and it has power to assign entry rights into cities. Representatives from towns which want air service and residents living next to airports considering expansion are frequently in conflict. The arguments revolve about the relative merits of expanded jet service

Pressures on the agencies

13. For a scathing editorial attack upon the ICC, which states, "The I.C.C.'s duty is to stop pampering the railroads it is supposed to regulate and to begin protecting the defenseless traveling public," see "Hotfoot for the I.C.C.," *New York Times*, May 13, 1968.

to the community versus the noise problem jet traffic creates for those living near the terminals. The Federal Communications Commission must decide on licensing or refusing to license radio and television stations—and a license is a very valuable form of property. The natural gas interests have fought both the regulatory authority and the individual members of the Federal Power Commission with determination and skill for the past two decades, while private and public power lobbies have made decisions hard and compromises necessary for the Atomic Energy Commission. Individual members of the Board of Governors of the Federal Reserve System frequently find themselves in the center of momentous struggles which involve not only other Governors, but the President, the Secretary of the Treasury, the Congress, and lenders and borrowers, concerning policy on such questions as "tight money" or the most desirable political and economic means of combatting inflation or recession. Reading newspapers and magazines—even advertisements—with political sophistication reveals the nature and scope of the conflicts that constantly swirl around the agencies which are charged by law to control, to prohibit, to promote, and to limit private enterprise in the United States.

Most business transactions ultimately involve two parties, those doing the selling and those doing the buying, *i.e.*, the **Protecting the** consumers. Because the latter are not organized, considerable **consumer** governmental supervision and regulation is conducted on behalf of the consuming public. Many students will remember reading of the "Muckraking" era in the early years of this century. That was a time when crusading journalists exposed various ways in which the public was being victimized by unscrupulous producers, and corrective legislation often followed. A number of books have been published recently which contend that more needs to be done to protect the consumer, and to inform him of the nature of the goods and services now on the market.[14] Congress has been very much interested in these charges and has legislated to protect the consumer in a number of areas. Automobiles, beginning with the 1968 models, carry additional safety equipment which is required by Federal regulations. The Truth-in-Packaging law requires producers to present more complete details on labels and packages so that the buyer can better evaluate what is in the container he contemplates purchasing. Investigations of meat-packing plants which did not ship their products across state lines, and hence escaped Federal

14. Some examples are Rachel Carson, *Silent Spring* (Boston: Houghton Mifflin, 1962), and Ralph Nader, *Unsafe at Any Speed* (New York: Grossman, 1965).

inspection, resulted in legislation requiring states to bring up their inspection standards to those of the Federal Government or have Federal inspectors do the inspecting. A Truth-in-Lending Act, which took effect in July, 1969, is designed to assist consumers who "buy on time" to gain fuller knowledge of the financial agreements into which they enter by requiring sellers to make available the complete details of the proposed transaction. A glance at a cigarette package will indicate another aspect of consumer protection—the warning now required by law that cigarette smoking may be dangerous to health. With the ever-increasing diversity and complexity of goods and services now on the market, many of which are too esoteric for the average purchaser to evaluate fully, one may expect continued controversy as to how far the government should go in pulling the teeth of the old proverb, "Let the buyer beware."

THE GOVERNMENT IN BUSINESS

On the other hand, there are many businessmen who pressure their elected officials for prohibitions and limitations on the business enterprises in which the national government is engaged. It is doubtful if private operators are seriously concerned over government ownership and management of its canal in Panama or of its railroad in Alaska, but one suspects that some manufacturers object to the government production of munitions and ordnance, and that contractors frown on highway and dam construction performed by government.[15] Grazing interests, lumbermen, and miners have long sought to have the national government liquidate its vast amounts of real estate—or, at least, to "return" the public domain to the states (where their influence is greater than in Washington). The Department of the Interior, and the United States Forest Service within the Department of Agriculture, together the supervisors of vast areas of Federally owned land, are scenes of constant battles between conservation groups wanting the land used, or not used in some instances, in particular ways, and various business and agricultural interests wishing to utilize the land, timber, and water upon it—or minerals beneath it—for their purposes. Such controversies often involve the Congress and sometimes the governments of the states in which the Federally owned land is found. A recent argument of major proportions involved the use which would be made of giant redwood

Controversy: business vs. government

15. The classic study of the government and private industry in dam construction is Arthur A. Maass, *Muddy Waters* (Cambridge: Harvard University Press, 1951).

385

forests in Northern California. Lumbering interests were pitted against the Sierra Club and other conservation groups wanting an extensive Redwoods National Park. The result was something of a compromise; a Redwoods National Park was created, but it was not as large as some had hoped.

Oil-shale lands

In recent years a potential controversy has been building up which concerns government in business, or perhaps out of it, in regard to the oil-shale lands of several western states. The problem is roughly this: While oil pumped in the United States is sufficient for the present demand, this happy condition will not continue indefinitely. However, in areas of Colorado, Wyoming, and Utah an oil-bearing shale has been discovered. The oil cannot be exploited by conventional drilling but it may be possible to release it from the rock strata by new technology. Much of the oil shale lies beneath land owned by the Federal Government, and this accounts for the dispute which may occur between conservation groups and the private oil interests. On the one hand an argument can be advanced that the oil-shale deposits should be developed in the traditional fashion. That is, the oil companies would lease or buy the land, extract the mineral wealth, and sell it for a profit in the traditional free-enterprise manner. Running counter to this is the suggestion that the oil shale under Federally owned land belongs to the citizens of the United States, and that the government should exploit the oil, or realize as much of the profit from its exploitation as possible, with the funds thus acquired being used for purposes benefiting the people of the United States. The oil companies and others meet this argument by pointing to the alleged inefficiencies of government-owned companies and the undesirable precedent which might be set if the government entered the oil business on a large scale. Further, if private oil companies developed the reserves there would be a considerable payoff through taxes to various levels of government.[16]

16. Political battles over oil are not a new development. A particularly hard-fought dispute concerned whether the Federal Government or the state governments would control the drilling of oil from beneath the salt-water along America's shallow coasts, in such places as the Gulf of Mexico off Texas and Louisiana, and in the Pacific off Southern California. After World War II President Truman claimed the oil under saltwater (the "tidelands oil" as it is called) for the United States. Counter claims were made by the states which wanted to be able to charge royalties upon the oil taken from beneath the water. President Truman opposed attempts by Congress to pass legislation settling the matter in favor of the states, and also in favor of oil companies which would probably face less restrictive regulation by the states than by the Federal Government. His veto action was effective in preventing the legislation from being passed. However, President Eisenhower signed into law a measure which provided the states would assume control of oil production in the tidelands.

For a study of the oil shale development matter see "The Prospects for Oil Shale Development," published by the Department of Interior in May, 1968.

There is one set of initials which causes the blood pressure of many devotees of private enterprise to rise: TVA.[17] The Tennessee Valley Authority is an autonomous agency which is governed by a board appointed by the President with Senate confirmation.[18] It differs from other governmental agencies in that it has complete administrative authority over the diversified projects under its jurisdiction (rather than sharing them with other bureaus) and because its administration comes from the region (instead of from the national capital). The Authority, a pet project of the early New Deal, was given the comprehensive development of an entire river valley which includes parts of seven southeastern states. After three decades of existence, the general consensus is that TVA has succeded magnificently in most of its accomplishments: the income level of the valley residents climbed from below to well above the national average; the life of the region took on a new tempo; both farming and industry have improved; and the series of multi-purpose dams constructed on the Tennessee and its tributaries have prevented floods, ensured year-round navigation, provided areas for recreation, and produced power.[19] It is the production of power which most disturbs the critics of TVA. They have always objected to the theory of the Authority as a symbol of government ownership in contradiction to the American tradition, but they complain especially about the low cost of its electric power. The private power producers are affronted by the invidious comparisons with their own rates (which are higher, they insist, because they must pay national, state, and local taxes, whereas the TVA, a government corporation, gives smaller payments in lieu of taxes only to state and local governments) and the gigantic extension the Tennessee Valley Authority has given to public power.

Public power is both familiar and widespread in the United States, since many communities have long owned their own plants, but the large-scale entry of the central government into

Achievements of TVA

Objections to TVA

17. In the 1964 Presidential campaign Barry Goldwater caused a considerable stir when he suggested the government could sell the Tennessee Valley Authority. *The Making of the President: 1964*, op. cit., p. 360.

18. If the proposals made by a special presidential Commission are adopted, there will be a new government corporation created to handle the nation's postal service. Should such a move be made it would be to correct the chronic monetary deficit which plagues the Post Office Department, and to improve upon postal service. As recommended to President Johnson in mid-1968, the Postal Corporation would be authorized to set postal rates subject only to the veto of Congress.

19. See Roscoe Martin, ed., *TVA: The First Twenty Years* (University, Ala.: University of Alabama Press, 1956). Also Aaron Wildavsky on efforts by the Eisenhower Administration to stem the expansion of TVA, *Dixon-Yates: A Study in Power Politics* (New Haven: Yale University Press, 1962).

the power business is fairly recent, and it traces to the fact that dams built for irrigation, navigation, and/or flood control impound water which will also produce hydroelectric power. The New Deal idea, under which many multiple-purpose dams were begun, was that electricity should be furnished as cheaply and used as widely as possible in implementation of "the good life." To realize this policy, government dams produced power, and the Rural Electrification Administration was established to aid and encourage the construction of generating plants and transmission systems in areas which private power had avoided as economically unprofitable. When hydroelectric power was made available from the rash of new dams, purchasing preference was given to rural cooperatives and community-owned distribution systems which cooperated under the aims of the REA, while private utilities companies were only permitted to buy whatever electricity was left over. Naturally, electric power could be sold more cheaply at distribution points if it had been transmitted over lines built or aided financially by government rather than over lines constructed by utilities companies. The private power interests, therefore, have long campaigned for the exclusive right to build distribution lines from the sites. They frankly admit that the electricity sold through their companies costs the consumers more, but they argue that the public power is cheaper only because it is subsidized by the taxpayers. Advertisements in national magazines incessantly proclaim that this form of subsidization is inconsistent with the American way of life.[20]

The Farm Problem

Agriculture, which enjoys both the aura of the American tradition and the benefits of subsidies, is another one of the primary concerns of the national government. Surprisingly enough, both of these apparent advantages have contributed to the seriousness of the "farm problem" and have interfered with the attempts of the national policy-makers to solve it.

FARMERS IN TRUTH AND FICTION

At one time the United States was a nation of autonomous farmers—many of them so fiercely independent that they moved on to newer frontiers every time the rapidly increasing westward migration caught up to them. As long as the frontier

20. See David B. Truman, *The Governmental Process* (New York: Knopf, 1958) p. 232.

existed and subsistence agriculture was the rule, farmers
undoubtedly were the most secure and independent element in
the society. Thomas Jefferson believed them to be the best
guarantors of the republican system—an idea which continues
to cast its spell over voters, politicians, and the farmers themselves. The myth accounts for the sentimental determination to
preserve the family farm and explains the failure of many
people to recognize that farming today has become more of a
business than a "way of life."

Public power

The revolution which followed the introduction of mechanization to the farms completely changed the agricultural situation in fact, although fancy continued to endow the farmers
with the attributes, desires, and needs which had characterized
the subsistence farmer of history. Mechanization led to cash
farming, which, to be successful, required expansion and specialization. It also made farmers dependent upon markets to an
extent they had never known before. In short, farming became
a big business, requiring sizable outlays of capital and the adoption of new methods. The farmers who adapted most promptly
and completely were the ones who began incorporating neighboring family farms into their expanding acreage. Subsistence
farmers increasingly found that the only alternatives were to
stay on the land as tenants or to move to the remaining frontier
of industry. They have been reluctant to face the choices, either
because farming *is* a way of life for them or because they are
unfamiliar with city living and are unskilled for industrial jobs:
consequently they are often disinclined to be transplanted. The
old slogan, "the farmer always has something to eat," would be
true today only if the commercial farmer were willing to restrict
his diet to wheat, cotton, corn, artichokes, or whatever specialized crop he grows. Instead of having farms which meet the
family needs for food, modern farmers buy their eggs, milk, and
bread at a supermarket in town.

Mechanization

The handwriting was on the wall shortly after the Civil War,
and, except for times of war; the farming industry has been
depressed for a century. At best, farming has always been risky:
a year of labor can be lost in an hour. But the modern causes of
agricultural troubles add to the ancient foes the farmers have
always faced—flood, drought, hail, and untimely rains. Until
they were organized by government, the farmers, unlike their
business counterparts who combined in ingenious ways to limit
production and force prices up, tried to increase their income
by producing more—and prices fell. This flouting of one of the
primary axioms of the free market became especially serious as
the new science of agriculture increased farm productivity far

Uncertainties

389

more rapidly than the population expanded. Then, just when the American farmer came to depend on the export trade for his survival, foreign competition and retaliatory tariffs played havoc with his overseas markets. The steady rise in per capita income in the United States permitted its urban residents to satisfy their need for food and still have increasing amounts of money remaining to spend for other things, whereas the farm families actually received a diminishing proportion of the national income.

EARLY SOLUTIONS

Evidences of agrarian discontent flared intermittently, but bitterly, from the 1870's until the early 1930's, when they reached revolutionary proportions. To voice their protests, the farmers converted the Grange Movement (organized to provide social and educational opportunities to scattered farm families) into a political nucleus for the inflationary Greenback Party. Then the Farmers' Alliances amassed a formidable (if disunited) strength which prepared the way for the formation of the Populist Party of the 1890's.[21] After the unprecedented prosperity which accompanied the feeding of the nation and its allies during World War I, farm prices began a steady course downward, with the net income shrinking 400 percent in the 12 years between 1920 and 1932. Congress twice passed bills which would have had the national government buy agricultural products in order to force prices up, but both were vetoed by President Coolidge (who privately opined that farmers had never made money and he didn't think much could be done about the situation). President Hoover was persuaded to sign a similar measure (the Agricultural Marketing Act of 1929) which created a Federal Farm Board to encourage farmer-cooperatives and armed it with a half-billion dollars with which to buy up surpluses. The board ran out of money after two years of operation, since the farmers continued their immemorial practice of increasing production in the face of declining farm income.

Declining prices and income

FARM POLICIES FROM THE NEW DEAL TO THE PRESENT

The New Deal of President Franklin D. Roosevelt attempted to meet the farm crisis by curtailing production.[22] The pream-

21. For a brilliant analysis of the farmers' "revolt" of the late nineteenth and early twentieth centuries, see Richard Hofstadter, *The Age of Reform* (New York: Vintage Books, 1960), Chaps. I-III. Also John D. Hicks, *The Populist Revolt* (Lincoln, Nebraska: Bison Books, 1961).

22. See the first chapter, "The Fight for Agricultural Balance," in Arthur M. Schlesinger, Jr., *The Coming of the New Deal* (Boston: Houghton Mifflin, 1959).

ble of the Agricultural Adjustment Act of 1933 cited a breakdown of orderly exchange brought about by the destruction of the farmer's purchasing power, which, in turn, was due to the disparity between prices of agricultural and other commodities. On the theory that this breakdown "burdened and obstructed normal currents of commerce," the Secretary of Agriculture was authorized to contract to pay farmers for reducing their acreage and raising less livestock. The money to finance the program was to come from a tax levied on the processors of basic farm products, such as meat packers, millers, and cotton ginners. The Supreme Court indignantly struck down the first AAA because it discovered that the tax was to benefit only a segment of society rather than the "general welfare." "At best, it is a scheme for purchasing with federal funds submission to federal regulation of a subject reserved to the states." Justice Roberts thundered, "the Congress cannot invade state jurisdiction to compel individual action; no more can it purchase such action."[23] Congress reacted quickly with a "soil conservation" act which paid farmers for taking "soil depleting" crops out of production. Oddly enough, the soil-depleting varieties seemed to be those crops in excess supply. Subsidies were introduced into American agriculture on a vast scale.

New Deal subsidies

The present national policy is to attempt to arrange for the prices a farmer receives for his products to keep pace with the prices he pays for the things he buys. This is accomplished by determining prices for agricultural products which will be in "parity" with prices charged for selected nonfarm products.[24] Parity prices might be set at 100 percent of the base period or at lower percentages. They might be "fixed" (*i.e.*, by law) or "flexible" (*i.e.*, left to the determination of the Secretary of Agriculture). Once prices are set, the Commodity Credit Corporation (a government agency) is instructed to grant loans to farmers at the parity specified and to accept their crops as security. If the prices during the next year exceed the loan figure, the farmer may redeem his crop and sell it on the market at the higher price. If the price falls below the determined support price, the farmer simply fails to redeem his crop, and the CCC takes possession. In this way the farmer receives at least a minimum price for his supported commodities, and surpluses are acquired by the national government.

Parity

Price supports

The lesson learned by the failure of the Federal Farm Board

23. United States v. Butler, 297 U.S. 1 (1936).

24. Parity is determined by computing the ratio of the cost of agricultural products to the cost of products from other industries over a given period of time, the so-called base period.

Controlling production

was that prices cannot be supported if production is not controlled. At first, Congress tried to reduce production by allotting acres to be planted in certain crops, the total number to be divided among the states and then subdivided among counties and individual farms. If a farmer planted more than his allotted share, he was ineligible for full price supports. Since, by more intensive farming, the American farmer demonstrated his ability to cut acreage while increasing production, it was sometimes necessary to impose "marketing quotas." The system compels a farmer to live within his acreage allotment by requiring him to have a marketing card which he must show when he sells his crop. He is not entitled to a card unless he agrees to the limitations, and he may not sell without one. Limitations are imposed after a referendum which ascertains whether or not growers wish to accept the quotas.[25] If the proposal passes by the required two-thirds majority, farmers who exceed their quotas are subjected to severe fines. If growers fail to vote approval for the quotas, the percentage of price support is drastically reduced. Farmers ordinarily vote for the controls.

The constitutionality of farm legislation has not been in doubt since the Supreme Court had a change of membership in 1937. In the leading case on the revised "triple-A," Justice Roberts found that the statute did not purport to control production but merely to regulate interstate commerce. "Any rule," he said for the Court, "which is intended to foster, protect and conserve that commerce or to prevent the flow of commerce from working harm to the people of the nation, is within the competence of Congress."[26] A few years later the Court informed a farmer that the practice of feeding excess wheat to household chickens had a direct effect on interstate commerce and that "Congress has the power to regulate the prices of commodities and the practices affecting such prices."[27]

FARMERS IN THE DEMOCRATIC SYSTEM: RIVALRIES AND PRESSURE GROUPS

When the Court removed itself from active participation in farm politics, political pressures on the members of the legislative and administrative branches of the national government

25. Only farmers are permitted to vote. Some labor leaders complain that this is an undue preference, since voting on "right to work" laws is not limited to workers.

26. Mulford v. Smith, 307 U.S. 38 (1939).

27. Wickard v. Filburn, 317 U.S. 111 (1942).

increased.[28] Congress may decide whether some or all commodities should be supported, or it may leave this determination to the Secretary of Agriculture. It may set the parity standards itself or permit the Secretary of Agriculture to do so. The political struggle, therefore, involves not only classification and amounts, but the question of delegation of power, and interest groups change their positions on the virtues of "fixed" or "flexible" price supports depending on the personality and views of the Secretary of Agriculture. There was a time when a politically overrepresented[29] and united "farm bloc" in Congress was primarily concerned with championing the interests of its constituents against colleagues who represented industrial states, but today, as never before, the representatives of the "farmers" are divided by the types of farms in their constituencies and by the rival farm organizations which are in serious competition.

For example, wheat farmers ordinarily want the firmest protection the central government can make available, because the demand for bread and cereals falls off during times of economic growth. Corn farmers have less interest in protection because their situation is nearly the reverse: they profit from the increased demand for meat in times of economic prosperity since they feed most of their crop to hogs and livestock. Cotton farmers face different threats; synthetic fabrics and foreign producers. Some areas have their own special commodities, such as tobacco, rice, sorghums, peanuts, and range cattle, which take on political importance because their spokesmen in Washington are adept at logrolling.[30] Small-scale farmers need government help if they are to remain on their farms; large-scale farmers would like to see them leave.

Farm products and prosperity

Like political parties, which have many supporters merely because of tradition and geography, the membership of both of the huge farm organizations includes growers of different kinds of crops and in all parts of the country. In the last 15 years,

Farm organizations

28. See, for example, Charles M. Hardin, *The Politics of Agriculture: Soil Conservation and the Struggle for Power in Rural America* (Glencoe, Ill.: The Free Press, 1952), Reo M. Christenson, *The Brannan Plan: Farm Politics and Policy* (Ann Arbor: University of Michigan Press, 1959), and Don Paarlberg, *American Farm Policy* (New York: Wiley, 1964).

29. As noted in earlier chapters, the movement of rural population to urban centers and the reapportionment of congressional districts are reducing the influence of rural inhabitants in Congress.

30. The importance of crop "representation" on the House Agriculture Committee is considered by Charles O. Jones, "Representation in Congress: The Case of the House Agriculture Committee," *American Political Science Review*, LV (June, 1961), 358–67.

however, the National Farmers' Union has shown remarkable growth as it tended to become 'the spokesman for the small wheat farmers, the less prosperous cotton and corn-hog producers, and the "family farmers." Reflecting the desires of this element, the N.F.U. works for maximum government protection, a policy which keeps the small-scale farmers operational. It stresses the theme of farming as a way of life and opposes the designs of the large farming corporations to squeeze the family farmers off the land. The Farmer's Union has demonstrated an ability to work with organized labor groups and has its greatest influence when Democrats are in office. In reaction to the aggressive challenge of the N.F.U., the American Farm Bureau Federation has tended to reflect more strongly than before the interests of the corn-hog producers and those of the prosperous large-scale farmers in other sections. The A.F.B.F. has a strong organizational base in farm counties, since it has traditionally worked closely with the county agents (at one time it helped pay their salaries) and with local businessmen. It is influential on the state government level—particularly the land-grant colleges, where it has been active in extension work. Although the Farm Bureau was instrumental in influencing the direction of New Deal farm legislation, the leadership recently has advocated diminishing national control of, and aid to, agriculture, and it has favored a decentralized program to be administered by the states. The American Farm Bureau Federation has retained the traditional farmer's distrust of organized labor and has edged closer to alliance with the Republican Party.

GOVERNMENT FOOD PROGRAMS

Food for the needy

During the 1960's the Kennedy and Johnson Administrations followed a policy of high price supports coupled with efforts to control production. The government also administered several food programs to assist the needy in the United States, and participated in efforts to help certain food-deficient areas overseas. The domestic food programs included the direct distribution of surplus commodities to individuals qualified to receive them, a Food Stamp program designed to increase the food-buying power of poor people, a School Lunch and Breakfast program, and a School Milk program. The government distributed food abroad under the provisions of the Food for Peace program.[31]

31. The legislative basis for the Food for Peace program is PL 480. See Peter Toma, *The Politics of Food for Peace* (Tucson: University of Arizona Press, 1967), for a discussion of American policy regarding distribution of food abroad looking toward the future.

Criticism has been voiced regarding the government's handling of price and supply matters, and of the food programs for the poor. Complaints against price supports and marketing controls center on the assertion that big landowners receive large agricultural payments which should be granted instead to the small "family" farmer. On the other hand it is charged that artificial efforts to keep people on small farms run counter to the times and will never solve the problems associated with small-scale farming operations in periods of increasing costs and operating complexity. While theorists continue to argue the merits of government-supported prices and marketing controls versus the return to a "free market," the migration of farmers to metropolitan areas continues. Although this movement reduces one kind of problem, it contributes to the difficulties experienced by the urban areas. Arguments over the value and efficiency of food-distribution programs to the poor in America have recently come to the fore and are represented by contradictory reports on the subject. A report issued by a private group charged that the government's agriculture policy is not compatible with the needs of the poor and that it is "dominated by a concern for maximizing agricultural income, especially within the big production categories."[32] The report declared that hunger is a problem facing millions in America and that the matter is becoming more serious.[33] Recommendations made are for extensive modifications in the Food Stamp program so as to provide free food to those who need it, and for food-distribution programs for the poor to be removed from the administration and responsibility of the Department of Agriculture and the Agriculture Committees of Congress.[34]

Criticism

Stung by criticism such as is contained in *Hunger, U.S.A.* and by several programs on the subject of hunger which appeared on television in 1968, the Department of Agriculture and the Agriculture Committee of the House of Representatives entered their side of the story in the public record. The latter made a survey of health officials in the counties where the greatest amount of hunger was said to be found and then issued this statement: "There is much malnutrition but no known current instances of starvation or serious hunger caused either by inability of the individual to buy food or receive

Malnutrition

32. *Hunger, U.S.A.*, prepared by the Citizens' Board of Inquiry into Hunger and Malnutrition in the United States (Washington: New Community Press, 1968), p. 5.

33. *Ibid.*, p. 16.

34. *Ibid.*, p. 5.

public assistance."[35] The Secretary of Agriculture defended his department's handling of the food programs for the needy, and noted the difficulties imposed upon food distribution by fiscal restraints and the necessity for the central government to work through the sometimes frustrating intricacies which result from the Federal system of overlapping governments.[36]

The inability of farm families to break out of the cycle of poverty found in many rural areas of the nation constitutes another type of farm problem. Particularly serious is the plight of whites in portions of Appalachia, of blacks in parts of the South, and of Spanish-Americans and Indians in areas of the Southwest.

Distributing food abroad While Americans may in theory support giving food to those desperately in need of it abroad, and some citizens feel America has not done enough in this area, there remain practical problems to be faced. A very major one is the common belief that the distribution of food without accompanying birth-control measures aggravates the situation. It has been noted that the United States must be careful not to damage the agricultural economies of other nations by acts which have the effect of "dumping" food on the world market and thus depressing prices. Shipping food from the United States to where it is needed costs money, and sometimes the intended recipients cannot easily be reached because of geography and politics. The problem of feeding the world's expanding population may be a matter more suitable for the affluent nations to tackle together than for some of them to attempt to solve alone.

Government and Organized Labor

Although American farmers have banded together in cooperatives to produce, store, or distribute their harvests, most are opposed to efforts at unionization by organized labor. The suspicion farmers have for organized labor is not an occupational disease—it may be found in depth on every stratum of American society, and it traces its roots back to the England of the Common Law. Unlike business and agriculture, which had

35. Press Release, Committee on Agriculture, United States House of Representatives, June 28, 1968.

36. See the Appendix in *Hunger Study*, Committee on Agriculture, House of Representatives, 90th Cong., 2nd Sess. (Washington: United States Government Printing Office, June 11, 1968). This study also contains the survey of county health officials made by the House Agriculture Committee. In 1968 the Congress agreed to provide nearly one billion dollars to feed the poor, partially as a result of pressure toward that end.

such distinguished patriots as Alexander Hamilton and Thomas Jefferson to plead their causes, and whose combinations have been generally accepted as natural and desirable, workingmen's associations have been obliged to fight every inch of the way for acceptance by the bulk of the American people. Some aspects of their fight only made the chasm of distrust wider—but the climb from the status of being a "conspiracy in restraint of trade" (against which the public had to be protected), under an ancient common law doctrine, to the position of power and influence labor unions hold today attests to the dedication of labor leaders and to the adaptability of democratic processes.[37]

LABOR'S STRUGGLES FOR RECOGNITION

One of the main contributing causes of the apprehension over organized labor is the power of labor's traditional weapon—the strike (when workers quit their employment as a group in order to secure their demands). Strikes at best paralyze production and at worst are accompanied by violence and, in the past, even bloodshed. Strikes are not a recent phenomenon. It is said that the bakers of New York were on strike as early as 1741 and that the first "sympathy" strike (by workers not directly involved in a dispute) occurred in Philadelphia 10 years after the adoption of the Constitution. As the nineteenth century wore on, unions gained recognition as legal entities, although attempts to gain their objectives by strikes and boycotts (refusals to trade with an establishment) were considered to be illegal until fairly recent times. The unions had to contend not only with distrustful fellow citizens, but with unsympathetic courts and with the economic power of their employers. The frequent use of court injunctions to forbid strikes was not curbed until 1914, when the Clayton Antitrust Act limited their use and provided jury trial in contempt cases. The power of employers to oblige workers to sign "yellow-dog contracts" (wherein workers promised that they would not join a union) was not outlawed on a national scale until the Norris-LaGuardia Act of 1932. By that year half of the states had prohibited the practice of "blacklisting" workers who were agitators for labor organizations (thus making them unemployable by other companies), but the National Labor Relations Act

Strikes and strikebreaking

37. In some areas the struggle to organize workers into union movements continues, and the current stage of development is somewhat similar to that through which the big national unions passed years ago. An example of a new and struggling labor organization is the National Farm Workers Association, which is particularly active in California among Spanish-American farm laborers.

(1935) effectively blunted that retaliatory weapon of employers.

For approximately the first century under the Constitution, labor disputes were assumed to be local concerns in which the national government did not interfere.[38] It was the common law of the states with which union organizers had to contend and the state militias which striking workers had to face. By 1877 serious labor disputes had become matters for national concern, although the implications of this fact were not completely recognized for an additional 60 years. In that year Federal troops were used when workers struck eastern railroads in protest against a 10 percent pay cut. Before order was restored over 100 people had been killed and twice that number had been wounded. Then followed a series of labor conflicts punctuated by the bloody Haymarket riot in Chicago (1886) and the Homestead strike in Pennsylvania (1892). The devastating Pullman strike of 1894 was triggered by the dismissal of a third of the employees, while the remaining workers suffered wage cuts of 30 to 40 percent with no corresponding reductions in rent at company houses or items at the company store. The strike paralyzed rail shipping between Cincinnati and San Francisco and was accompanied by much violence. President Cleveland sent in Federal troops to protect the United States mails over the vehement protests of the local governor, but the troops actually served as strikebreakers. Four years later Congress passed the Erdman Act, which made it a criminal offense for railroads to dismiss or discriminate against employees because of union activity, but the Supreme Court declared that portion of the law to be unconstitutional.

The Clayton Act, passed during Wilson's first term, was widely hailed as the "Magna Carta of Labor," and the heartened liberals also attempted to end child labor by taxing its products out of existence. But both of these laws, along with attempts by state legislatures and Congress to establish minimum wages for women and children, fared badly in the courts during the "Golden Twenties."[39]

The Clayton Act

38. Perhaps the best study of the development of the American labor movement is Harry A. Millis and Royal E. Montgomery, *Organized Labor* (New York: McGraw-Hill, 1945).

39. Duplex Printing Press v. Deering, 254 U.S. 443 (1921); Bailey v. Drexel Furniture Company, 259 U.S. 20 (1923); and Adkins v. Children's Hospital, 261 U.S. 525 (1923). An earlier Court was more liberal, voting to sustain a state law limiting women to a 10-hour working day, Muller v. Oregon, 208 U.S. 412 (1908).

"FREEDOM OF CONTRACT"

Before child labor could be abolished and the principle of minimum wages and maximum hours solidly established, "freedom of contract," the myth most affectionately cherished by economic conservatives, had to be abolished. The theory of this liberty seemed sound and simple: a prospective worker bargained directly with his employer concerning wages, hours, and conditions of work. If agreement were reached, both parties were presumably satisfied; if agreement failed, the job-seeker would look for a more congenial place to work, and the employer would find some other worker. The theory failed in practice. In the first place, as industries enlarged, the personal contact between employer and employee disappeared. In the second place, the two contracting parties did not meet on the basis of equality because of the chronic oversupply of employables and the undersupply of potential employers. Justice Harlan Fiske Stone probably stated the failure of the theory as accurately and temperately as anyone in a classic dissent: "We have had opportunity to learn that a wage is not always the resultant of free bargaining between employers and employees; that it may be forced upon employees by their economic necessities and upon employers by the most ruthless of their competitors."[40] Although many employers recognized that freedom of contract was largely responsible for the sweatshop conditions they deplored, most of them still championed the "right" as one of the bulwarks of "the American way of life"; others piously invoked it for less defensible reasons. Labor leaders argued that since management spoke with one voice, the give-and-take of genuine bargaining could be guaranteed only if the workers could also speak, collectively, with one voice. Since, except for a few isolated trades, neither side could convince the other, the principle of the freedom of contract poisoned labor relations for a century before the aftermath of the Great Depression swept it away.

Sweatshops

LABOR LEGISLATION UNDER THE NEW DEAL

The Roosevelt administration which came into power in 1933 was friendly to labor, and union leaders were welcomed into the highest councils of the nation. One of the earliest and most influential pieces of legislation passed by the New Deal was the National Industrial Recovery Act (1933). Its famous Section 7a guaranteed the right of collective bargaining. When

40. Morehead v. New York *ex rel* Tipaldo, 298 U.S. 587 (1936).

The Wagner Act

the NIRA was declared unconstitutional two years later by a unanimous Court, Section 7a, with its victory for organized labor, died with it. Within two months, however, Congress had passed the comprehensive National Labor Relations (Wagner) Act. The new law again replaced "freedom of contract" with the "right of collective bargaining" for all workers engaged in interstate commerce. It also specifically forbade employers to engage in certain "unfair labor practices," such as dominating or in any way influencing labor unions, discriminating against union members in either hiring or firing, and refusing to bargain collectively with the properly designated representatives of the employees. A National Labor Relations Board was created to prevent and remedy "unfair labor practices" on the part of employers, and the act forbade retaliation against employees who took advantage of their new rights under the law. The NLRB was also authorized to investigate and certify which union was to represent employees as their bargaining agent—a task which took on new meaning after the American Federation of Labor expelled the gigantic Committee for Industrial Organization in 1938 and set the stage for competition for membership and position between the two huge confederations.[41] In the case testing the constitutionality of the Wagner Act, the Supreme Court distinguished, but did not overrule, the case which had destroyed the National Industrial Recovery Act. By a slender 5-4 decision, the judges found that the power of Congress over interstate commerce reached into labor relations, and declared that industrial strife was harmful to the economy of the nation. The recognition of the "fundamental right" of collective bargaining, Chief Justice Hughes observed, leads to industrial peace.[42]

The Wagner Act proved to be an enormous stimulus to labor organization; its provisions (and especially the spirit in which they were administered) greatly aided organized labor in its drive for higher wages and more advantageous working conditions. Unorganized labor, however, required outside help to better its condition, and President Roosevelt vigorously set out to provide this help, over strong objections from powerful segments in the Southern wing of his party. The Fair Labor Standards Act, passed in 1938 after extended debate, refused to permit products to cross state lines if they had been manufactured under "unfair" conditions. The Act set up a minimum wage (then, 25¢ an hour) and maximum hours of work (then,

The Fair Labor Standards Act

41. The two rival labor groups merged in 1955 to form the AFL-CIO.

42. National Labor Relations Board v. Jones & Laughlin Steel Corp., 301 U.S. 1 (1937).

44 hours per week) and barred the use of oppressive child labor (defined as any person under 16 or, in unhealthful or dangerous occupations, one under 18 years of age).[43] As originally signed, the law reflected the compromises necessary to secure its passage, but it established a firm base for increasingly liberalized provisions. The case testing the constitutionality of the Fair Labor Standards Act was easily won. Justice Stone pointed out that Congress had power over all manufactured products when any part of them were intended or expected to enter interstate commerce.[44]

To reach employees whose work was entirely intrastate, Congress had passed the Public Contracts (Walsh-Healey) Act in 1936. This law required contractors for the national government to meet most requirements for interstate firms, including the minimum wage, the eight-hour day, and the forty-hour week. Because they received grants-in-aid, many state agencies were also included under the operation of the act. The various aspects of labor legislation were enforced by the Department of Labor.

LABOR AFTER WORLD WAR II

After World War II, the tide of public opinion turned against the supposed "excesses" of organized labor. With the war won, the union pledges of "no-strike" no longer held, and in 1946 strike idleness reached the highest percentage of total working time in the history of the United States. The causes for labor discontent were many, but they included such factors as layoffs and cutbacks which resulted from the conversion to peacetime production, when many plants slowed down or closed temporarily. The virtual end of "time-and-a-half" for overtime work, which had greatly increased take-home pay, led to demands for wage increases—particularly in view of the relaxation of rent and price controls, followed by a rise in the

Labor discontent

43. The Fair Labor Standards Act has been amended from time to time in efforts to benefit working people, and controversy still swirls about the effectiveness of such legislation. For example, a 1966 amendment provided for the minimum hourly wage to be increased from $1.40 in 1967 to $1.60 in 1968. This effort to raise wages by law was criticized by an economist on the grounds that employers would be likely to stop employing substandard labor not worth the $1.60 an hour and turn instead to machinery, or more highly skilled labor, or in some instances discontinue the process requiring less productive individuals. Thus his argument is that artificial efforts to improve the conditions of working people by increasing wages by law may actually work to the disadvantage of many for whom the legislation was passed. See Yale Brozen, "The Untruth of the Obvious," in Melvin Laird, *op. cit.*, pp. 143–159.

44. United States v. Darby Lumber Company, 312 U.S. 100 (1941).

The Taft-Hartley Act

cost of living. Groups which had consistently opposed the Wagner Act mobilized enough support to secure Congressional passage of the Labor Management (Taft-Hartley) Act over the President's veto in 1947. The concept of the new law was to reach a "balance" between organized labor and employers. In order to achieve this, a new list of "unfair labor practices"—this time directed against unions—was enacted. The enormous list cited the refusals of unions to bargain in good faith, to engage in secondary boycotts, to attempt to cause an employer to pay for services not performed ("featherbedding"), to restrain or coerce employees in their right not to join a union, to charge excessive initiation fees, and the like. Management was entitled to bring its grievances before an enlarged National Labor Relations Board, and states were specifically permitted to adopt labor legislation more restrictive than the national law.

Shops: "closed," "open," "union"

One of the most controversial aspects of the Taft-Hartley Law was the reversal of the former position on "closed," "open," and "union" shops contained in Section 14(b). The Wagner Act had permitted management and union bargainers to agree upon a "closed shop" (requiring employees to be members of the union before being hired). The new labor law branded bargaining on this arrangement to be an "unfair labor practice." "Union shops" (where an employee must join the union within a given time after beginning work) were permitted if state laws did not prohibit them. Some state legislators read this part of the Taft-Hartley Act as an invitation to outlaw "union shops," and outlaw they did. Well-financed and carefully organized campaigns calling for the "right to work" were undertaken to require an "open shop" (where a worker may join or not join a union, as he sees fit). Dedicated union members saw the "open shop" as a direct assault on their unions: the least damage it could do, they insisted, was to encourage "free-loading"—since a nonmember would enjoy the benefits the organization could provide without paying his share; at the worst, it was condemned as a "union-wrecking" scheme. In a test case, unions attacked several state right-to-work laws as denials of free speech, assembly, and petition, as well as of equal protection of the laws and due process of law. The Supreme Court, after noting that the unions were asking it to return to the old philosophy of judicial interference which had been deliberately discarded in sustaining the New Deal legislation, said, through Mr. Justice Black, that just as the due process clause could not be used to block congressional protection of union members, so it could not be used now to block legislative protection of nonunion members.[45] It was then apparent that organized labor, too, must have recourse to state legislatures and the Congress. Piecemeal changes have been made on the national level from time to time—for instance, ending the requirement for a special election of the membership to validate a "union shop" agreement (members almost always voted overwhelmingly for it)—but there are enormous political difficulties in changing a law as complex and passion-ridden as the Labor Management Relations Act of 1947. Actually, however, the gloomy predictions of those who branded the Taft-Hartley Act as a "slave-labor law" did not come to pass because most employers (especially in big business) had come to recognize the advantages of dealing with strong, disciplined unions. Closed shops exist without complaint from the management, and many employers prefer union shops to open shops as insurance against "wildcat strikes." In right-to-work states management and unions frequently agree to utilize a Canadian invention, the agency shop, which requires nonunion members to contribute money in order to support the recognized union as their "agent" for purposes of collective bargaining, although they need not formally join. Since bargaining between management and unions is accomplished by attorneys for each side (not by the face-to-face confrontation of the owners and the union chiefs which is frequently imagined), considerable expense is involved.

In the late 1950's the union movement received considerable adverse publicity because of the corrupt practices and racketeering in some unions.[46] These activities were brought to the public's attention by the investigation of a Senate Committee headed by Senator John McClellan (D., Arkansas). The Labor-Management Reporting and Disclosure Act (Landrum-

The Landrum-Griffin Act

45. Lincoln Federal Labor Union v. Northwestern Iron & Metal, 335 U.S. 525 (1949).

46. The increasing confidence many employers have indicated in organized labor is not shared by all businessmen or citizens—or even by some union members. In a real sense most of the publicity given the labor movement is bad publicity. Charges and disclosures of corruption (including mismanagement of union funds by officers, "racketeering," the acceptance of "kickbacks" by union bosses, and the lack of democratic participation within some unions) have been front-page news, while the fact that the great majority of organizations are free from such malpractices and present scenes of vigorous democratic participation is even less newsworthy than men bitten by dogs. For a discussion of the operation of democracy in the union movement see Seymour Martin Lipset, Martin Trow, and James S. Coleman, *Union Democracy* (Garden City: Anchor Books, 1962); and Lipset, "The Politics of Private Government: A Case Study" in his *Political Man* (Garden City: Anchor Books, 1963).

Griffin Act) of 1959 followed the investigation. Major provisions of the act include the requirement for unions periodically to file detailed reports regarding financial matters and the operation of union constitutions and bylaws. The right of union members to secret balloting in union elections was established in law. Certain persons such as Communists and those with criminal records were barred from holding union offices. In addition, unions were forbidden to use the "hot cargo" sanction—refusal to transport products consigned to or shipped from firms engaged in a labor dispute—as a means of applying pressure under management. Also prohibited was picketing for organizational purposes if the subject firm legally recognized another union, or if there had been an NLRB supervised election within the preceding year.

Organized labor was not happy with either the Taft-Hartley Act or the Landrum-Griffin Act. However, most efforts at repeal since passage of the acts have been directed at Section 14(b) of the former.[47] This is the section which permits states to pass "right to work" laws. Even though there were large Democratic majorities in both Houses of Congress during President Johnson's occupancy of the White House, and the President announced his support of repeal, Section 14(b) remains "on the books."

UNIONS IN THE DEMOCRATIC SYSTEM

The national interest

At one time in American history industrial strikes did considerable economic harm, although the public was often only mildly inconvenienced by the temporary paralysis of a single industry. In more recent years, as new groups organized and struck—schoolteachers, for example—and as the economy became increasingly tightly woven in a way which meant strikes could more easily disrupt people's lives—by airline strikes for instance—greater concern began to be shown about strikes that involved the "national interest." Cognizance of the problem was taken when the Taft-Hartley Act was passed. That legislation empowered the President, when he judges that a labor stoppage endangers the national interest, to initiate a number of actions designed to protect the public while the dispute is being resolved. The powers include the appointment of a special investigating group to determine the facts in the dispute, and the authority to seek an 80-day "cooling off" injunction which, if granted by a Federal court, prohibits the strike while

47. A campaign to urge union families to write their congressmen in behalf of repeal of Section 14(b) featured this slogan, "A Letter a Day Will Put 14(b) Away."

negotiations proceed. The latter are often participated in by representatives of the government. The President may ask Congress for legislation he feels is required if after secret balloting the striking workers refuse to accept the last offer made by management during the period of injunction. The Taft-Hartley Act also created the Federal Mediation and Conciliation Service, which offers its assistance to labor and management in disputes affecting interstate commerce.[48] Since it possesses no law-enforcement authority, the Federal Mediation and Conciliation Service mediators assist in resolving disputes by relying "wholly on persuasive techniques of mediation and conciliation to perform their duties."[49] The director of the Federal Mediation and Conciliation Service is assisted by the National Labor-Management Panel in his efforts to avoid industrial controversies that would affect the national welfare. The panel's composition of 12 members appointed by the President, 6 representing management and 6 representing labor, is indicative of the theory that management and labor are equal protagonists who must take into consideration the interest of the nation as they seek to advance their own goals.

Mediation

The national unions still have serious disagreements with employers over wages, fringe benefits, and working conditions. Strikes still occur. However the union movement is increasingly turning its attention—research, publication, money, lobbying, and political activity—to broader vistas of social action.[50] Those critical of unions tend to characterize all such functions as being propagandistic in nature. But this interest in matters which transcend wages and working conditions may be observed in the 1968 legislative program supported by the AFL-CIO. The nation's largest union organization endorsed a wide range of health, education, housing, transportation, welfare, antipoverty, and civil rights measures, in addition to specific legislative proposals designed to assist its own members.[51]

AFL-CIO social action

The average nonunion citizen hears a great deal about bargaining demands and organizing drives, but he knows little about such collateral activities as the educational institutes

48. The National Mediation Board, created earlier, acts in a similar fashion in regard to the railroads, express and Pullman companies, and airlines.

49. *United States Government Organization Manual*, p. 449.

50. Unions are barred by law from contributing their funds to political campaigns. However, union members may contribute to whomever they wish and the unions maintain politically oriented research and information staffs. For example, the AFL-CIO has its Committee on Political Education and Department of Legislation.

51. *Labor Looks At Congress 1967*, prepared by the AFL-CIO Department of Legislation, January, 1968, pp. 80–83.

which many unions provide for the improvement of work skills or for the study of subjects like accounting methods or American government, nor is he aware of the social activities available in the union hall. The many factual and analytical research projects undertaken in the last two decades by the large unions are also not generally publicized, nor are the efforts of American unionists to encourage their foreign counterparts to recognize that the existence and effectiveness of the free trade union movement depend on democratic organization within a capitalistic framework. The public is aware of repeated attempts by subversive elements to infiltrate unions, but often forgets that probably no group in American life is more conscious of the threat Communism has to its existence than is organized labor: when Communist-dominated or corrupt unions are expelled from membership, the AFL-CIO organizes rival unions and vigorously proselytes members away from the outcasts.

Labor and lobbying

Samuel Gompers, the first president of the American Federation of Labor, insisted that the primary goals of organized labor were "improved wages, hours, and working conditions," and that these were to be sought through nonrevolutionary means. Subsequent leaders have adhered to this view. This "bread and butter unionism" accepted capitalism and rejected the siren-song of a separate labor party. American organized labor would "help our friends and defeat our enemies" within the two-party system, swinging support to whichever candidate appeared to be the better friend. Although friends differ from district to district, labor leaders obviously have more influence when Democrats control Washington. Labor does not, however, speak with one voice. Surveys demonstrate that although its influence can be determinative in isolated areas, the idea of a "labor vote" on the national level is a stereotype.[52] Labor's ability to influence congressional seats has been particularly unconvincing in off-year elections. In lobbying, too, labor does not always present a united front. The practical autonomy of constituent unions in the giant AFL-CIO accounts for the existence of separate headquarters buildings in the national capital; the varied interests of the individual unions explains the many uncoordinated labor groups at work influencing legislation on Capitol Hill. The labor lobbies do coalesce, however, when broad public policy is before the lawmakers. The different labor pressure groups can usually be enlisted to support Federal aid to

52. An intensive analysis of the voting behavior of American workers is Arthur W. Kornhauser, A. L. Sheppard, and A. J. Mayer, *When Labor Votes* (New York: University Books, 1956).

education, integration of the races, foreign aid, and the broadening of social security programs. This was not always the case: in their earlier history the unions showed no eagerness to enroll non-Caucasians and saw the beginning of government social security legislation as a threat to their own welfare plains.

Public Welfare and Social Security

During the election campaign of 1932, Franklin D. Roosevelt made repeated references to the "forgotten man." In the campaigner's mind, this hypothetical person was the symbol of millions of humble citizens who lived with fear and insecurity in an economy turned topsy-turvy which they did not completely understand and were powerless to control. Actually, the private sector of the American free-enterprise economy had failed to meet the needs of the vast and growing "working" population. Most older workers had probably always looked with dread toward the day of retirement because the termination of their jobs meant the end of their incomes. As the nation became more industrialized and urbanized their numbers grew and their problems intensified. Few average workers in industry were ever prepared to tide themselves over the periods of temporary unemployment which come to most men, but as technology advanced its ceaseless changes enormously increased the rapidity of job dislocations. Long before 1932 many people had come to the conclusion that, somehow, the public sector had to step in to correct the social imbalances which had become chronic in the twentieth century and critical during the Great Depression. It was precisely the "forgotten men" of Germany who were flocking to the Nazi standards of Adolf Hitler in 1932. In America, they turned to Franklin D. Roosevelt because of his implied promises to do something for them. Millions of "forgotten men" voted the Democrats into the White House, sent them to Capitol Hill—and accomplished a revolution in American life.

The Social Security Act, certainly one of the most important and far-reaching pieces of legislation in American history, made public welfare the business of the national government over the objections of a variety of dissimilar groups which have since come to support it. When the law was passed in 1935, it was designed not only to implement the New Deal idea of reform but also, one may suspect, to out-maneuver Roosevelt's political enemies of the left—the extremists who advocated enticing, if

The Social Security Act (1935)

407

fantastic, schemes for "sharing the wealth" or "ending poverty" and who were attracting millions of followers.[53] Like other pilot efforts, the act was more important for accomplishing a constitutional change of direction than for the breadth or liberality of its coverage. Since the specifics of the program have been and are liable to be changed from one session of Congress to another, only the theory and techniques of the program are considered here.[54]

Before 1935, charity was extensive but uncoordinated; there were three primary sources—private, local government, and

Pre-1935 welfare political machines. The recipients of welfare were primarily the insane, the deaf, the blind, mothers with dependent children, orphans, and the very poor. Local government welfare was frankly considered to be charity and was ordinarily administered with the intention of making it difficult to receive and embarrassing to accept, while the national government confined itself to aiding impoverished "VIMS"—veterans, Indians, and merchant seamen. The bright spots on the social welfare horizon were the Workmen's Compensation laws enacted by many states which required employers to be insured for injuries which occurred to their employees on the job. The victims then were reimbursed at a scheduled rate which depended on the seriousness of the injury and their pay status. Without the laws, injured workers were obliged to sue the company and prove it to be liable for damages before claims would be paid.

The aims of the national social security program were to extend protection to unemployed and retired persons; to contribute aid to needy old people; to make all benefits as uniform as the principle of federalism would permit; and to make the program as self-supporting as possible. Backing away from the term "assistance," the lawmakers preferred to use the word "insurance," although unlike traditional insurance plans, the

53. Chief among these were Senator Huey Long, who was estimated to command 3 to 4 million votes on a "third party" ticket; Dr. Francis E. Townsend, with 3 million organized supporters and probably 7 million more friendly voters; Father Charles E. Coughlin, a "radio priest" who crusaded against the "international bankers"; and Gerald L. K. Smith, who mixed racial hatred with his economic radicalism. The most fascinating account of this remarkable era is in Arthur M. Schlesinger, Jr., *The Politics of Upheaval* (Boston: Houghton Mifflin, 1960), pp. 15–207.

54. The general pattern of Social Security legislation has been the gradual increase of the dollar amount of benefits and the extension of the coverage to include more types of persons. The Social Security Act of 1967 increased benefits for most recipients by 13 percent. The minimum monthly benefit for a single person became $55, and for a couple $82.50. Despite the increases some argued that Social Security benefits had failed to keep pace with inflation which reduced the value of the Social Security checks.

Social Security Act does not take into account the factor of risk, is not contractual, and is compulsory. The change from "assistance" to "insurance" was not, however, simply a substitution of words. People covered by social security do contribute to the benefits they now have a right to receive, and, therefore, the stigma of accepting charity has disappeared. The concept of the law has proved to be an inestimable stimulus to the professionalization of the administration of the program. Today, trained persons superintend public welfare and engage in research and follow-up studies of the cases to which they are assigned; the emphasis is on preventing poverty, not merely keeping the poor alive. In spite of professional improvements many Americans believe welfare programs still need much attention.

UNEMPLOYMENT AND OLD AGE INSURANCE

The Social Security Act of 1935 trained its big guns on the twin threats to earning power: unemployment and advancing age. Each of these deserves a brief discussion.

The range of programs

Unemployment. There are many causes for unemployment, ranging from temporary layoffs to the fact that some people are simply unemployable. "Insurance" will tide the former over a limited period, but only direct assistance will solve the problem for the latter. Before the government entered this area, a few states had attempted to provide a form of unemployment compensation supported by taxes, but threats of local industries to leave such states indicated that a national policy was mandatory to prevent all states from sinking to the lowest common denominator. The national law leaves unemployment policy to the states, but it imposes a tax on payrolls and allows a credit of 90 percent of the amount collected to states meeting Federal specifications, thereby enticing all states into providing an unemployment compensation program. The money collected is kept in separate accounts for each state in the United States Treasury. The benefits and coverage vary widely because of the local administration, but this is one of the prices of federalism. In order to help the unemployed find work the government established public employment offices to serve as clearing houses with no cost to employers and potential employees. The function of the United States Employment Service is to assist state employment agencies. It is generally acknowledged that the present system of employment compensation could not continue to operate without huge outlays of national money if there were to be periods of prolonged economic depression, but

Unemployment compensation

in ordinary times unemployment insurance has proved to be feasible and popular.

Old Age. One of the enduring national fictions has been that people prepared for their own retirement (in the "good old days") by thrift. The fact was that most of them have relied upon their children for help when advanced age forced them to cease working. Although family help and private pensions are still important, it is the Old Age and Survivor's Insurance that today gives America's senior citizens the foundation upon which they can build their economic independence. This aspect of the Social Security Law is government-operated and is financed by compulsory payroll deductions from employees and matching contributions by their employers. It reaches all except a few occupational groups. Self-employed persons maintain coverage by paying a percentage higher than one who receives a contribution from his employer. The money collected is invested in government bonds (in order to earn interest), and the payments which are made to a retired worker bear a relation to his family obligations and former earning power. If a worker covered by the law dies before retirement, his family receives a lump sum as a death benefit and regular monthly payments which vary in size depending upon the number of dependents to be supported and the amount of past contributions. Because the benefits are not princely, additional help is often necessary in order to supplement them. Gifts from families, private investments, and pension plans are encouraged by the law, since income from such sources does not decrease the benefit rates. If one who is "retired" accepts other employment, his benefits are reduced if he is within the age bracket of 65-72 and earns more than $1,680 a year.

ASSISTANCE

Despite the general affluence in America and the large Federal programs previously mentioned, there remain individuals who require help of various kinds. These include the aged who for some reason do not receive sufficient benefits from other programs, the blind, individuals with various handicaps, and families with dependent children.[55] The Federal Government

The insurance program

55. The Social Security Act of 1967 extended coverage to certain individuals who become disabled and therefore cannot work. Veterans receive various forms of assistance which range from educational benefits to medical care and are administered by the Veterans Administration. The Railroad Retirement Act of 1937 created a special program of retirement, disability, and survivors' benefits for railroad employees.

extends *assistance* to such groups by providing grants to the states for use in their public assistance program. The Federal funds are extended only when minimum standards are met by the states. Because the programs are administered by the states, the benefits and terms under which they are made available vary widely, reflecting the unequal wealth of the states and differing views of public assistance found among them.

Today the various assistance programs financed by the Federal Government are more sophisticated than the "soup kitchens" or the "dole" of other times. The Department of Health, Education, and Welfare philosophy is that, "Public assistance includes financial aid, medical care, and other social services to help recipients achieve their potentialities for self-care, self-support, and strong family life."[56] However, despite enlightened efforts to assist individuals become self-supporting, considerable criticism has been leveled at the assistance programs in the late 1960's by both Republicans and Democrats. The charges most frequently heard are that the programs are wasteful, hard to administer, demeaning to recipients, and not always helpful in accomplishing their purpose. There is also the possibility that a certain percentage of individuals cannot really be assisted in becoming self-supporting members of society until much greater understanding is gained regarding the nature and causes of poverty.[57]

Areas of public assistance

The problem of the indigent, as well as related problems, continue to generate debate as to the proper course of future government activity. One matter of a highly controversial nature is aid given to dependent children. It can be argued, on the one hand, that such children could be cared for more economically by placing them in public institutions; on the other hand, that the costs of keeping children in private homes is justified because they may live more satisfying and normal lives there than would be the case in state-run institutions. Further complicating the care-for-dependent-children theories is the feeling by some that mothers of such children should not receive public assistance if their children are illegitimate, or if the mother lives with a man out of wedlock. Some critics insist that women continue to bear children in order to increase the welfare payments they receive. Efforts to curb illegitimacy have

Dependent children

56. *United States Government Organization Manual*, p. 371.

57. The economist John Kenneth Galbraith identified two kinds of poverty which need study. "Case" poverty involving particular individuals who cannot effectively compete in modern society, and "insular" poverty involving areas of poverty-stricken individuals. See "The New Position of Poverty," in *The Affluent Society* (Boston: Houghton Mifflin, 1958).

resulted in some states' passing laws which prevent assistance funds being extended to mothers with dependent children if they live with a man to whom they are not married.

In 1968 the Supreme Court ruled that an Alabama law which excluded children from receiving assistance when their mother "cohabited" with a man to whom she was not married was invalid. It was the Court's view (9-0) that Alabama was free to discourage illegitimacy and immorality by other means, but not by the disqualification of needy children from receipt of assistance.[58]

The controversial matter of birth control, and the extent to which government should participate in it, continues to loom behind discussions of alternate means of dealing with low-income families who have dependent children, and other poor parents who require public help to support their offspring.

HEALTH CARE FOR "SENIOR CITIZENS"

In 1965 an energetic President, a receptive Congress, and strong public support combined to add another major landmark to the Social Security program of the United States. The enactment of Medicare, the health-insurance program for the elderly, ended a long-standing dispute among Americans regarding health care. The basic question at issue was whether the Federal Government should commence an activity which could lead in time to the assumption of the responsibility for the health care of all Americans, or whether the government should limit its assistance to certain categories of poor while the bulk of the population continued to prepare for meeting its health needs by accumulating savings and through participation in private health-insurance programs. The latter position was rejected by President Johnson, the majority of Congress, and, it would seem, by the American people, who appear after the implementation of Medicare to approve of its philosophy and practice.

The basic features of Medicare consist of two types of health insurance provided by the Federal Government for those who **Medicare provisions** are 65 years of age or over. Hospital and nursing home care, including outpatient and home health services, are provided to practically all Americans 65 or over whether or not they participate in the Social Security or Railroad Retirement benefit programs. The Federal Government pays most of the bills incurred by such services. The funding for this part of Medicare is provided by increases in the Social Security payroll tax and by drawing upon general revenue funds to cover those not enrolled

58. King v. Smith 392 U.S. 309 (1968).

in the former. Participation in this portion of the Medicare program, at least in terms of paying the Social Security tax, is compulsory. The second kind of Medicare is voluntary and initially cost three dollars a month for those who are 65 and over and who wish to participate. This contribution is matched by an equal contribution by the government. This supplementary program helps to pay doctors' bills and other costs not included in the hospital and nursing home provisions.

If current trends continue, the chances are good that the initial Medicare provisions will be expanded both in terms of benefits to those 65 and over and in terms of persons under 65 who will be made eligible for health insurance. The dire predictions about the bureaucratic malfunctions with which Medicare would infect the medical profession and the dangers of socialism for the entire nation should Medicare become a reality, made by opponents of the 1965 legislation, have not come to pass. Whether or not they will in the future, it is certain the arguments will remain for a while as part of the nation's political dialogue.

A NEW PROPOSAL TO OVERCOME POVERTY: A GUARANTEED INCOME

As previously discussed, a number of Federal programs exist which are administered with a view of extending some kind of assistance to certain categories of people. In practice these programs offer a kind of guarantee that individuals and families will not sink below some level of living standard. Although not reflected in current Federal law, there is a serious search for an alternative means of assisting the poor which in time may replace many of the currently operating welfare programs.[59] During recent years a body of literature has been building which is critical of current welfare programs and which suggests an improvement in welfare activity can be achieved by adoption of some form of income supplements to individuals and families in low or no-income categories.

One plan which has received considerable attention is the "negative income tax" proposal.[60] Under this plan an individual (or family) would receive money from the government to

"Negative income tax"

59. In 1968 President Johnson appointed a Commission on Income Maintenance Programs to study various proposals which have been made regarding income security. A subcommittee of the Joint Economic Committee of Congress has been studying ways of improving upon the maze of Federal welfare programs, and the first bill has been introduced into Congress which would authorize a Federal guaranteed income program.

60. See Milton Friedman, "The Case for the Negative Income Tax," in Laird, op. cit., pp. 202–220.

the extent that his total income fell below an established minimum figure. Presumably such payments would be kept high enough to provide a standard of living considered acceptable by society, but not so high as to encourage persons to eschew employment and other efforts to better their financial condition. It is claimed that the "negative income tax" would be more effective in getting money into the hands of the poor than some current welfare programs which involve various "middlemen" in the administrative process. Another advantage claimed for the proposal is that recipients would be less enveloped by government inspections and "red tape" regarding how they conduct their affairs than is now the case with those applying for and receiving various welfare provisions. The most obvious argument against a "negative income tax" idea which would place money directly in the possession of the needy, is that individual initiative could be substantially dulled if not destroyed. Sharp legislative battles can be expected if and when the Federal Government moves toward some form of annual income provision for the poor.

WELFARE AND POLITICS: THE "NEW FRONTIER" AND THE "GREAT SOCIETY"

"New Frontier" programs

Theodore Sorensen, friend, adviser, and biographer of President Kennedy, wrote of the 1960 presidential primary in West Virginia:

> . . . West Virginia was making a deep and lasting impression on Jack Kennedy. He was appalled by the pitiful conditions he saw, by the children of poverty, by the families living on surplus lard and corn meal, by the waste of human resources.[61]

After he had won the White House the new President set about to redeem his campaign promises to attack the poverty areas such as he had seen in West Virginia. The Area Redevelopment Act provided funds for certain areas to assist in developing industries and tourism and to provide employment to local people, and to improve public facilities. The Manpower Development and Retraining Act was aimed at training the "hard core" poor so that they could become gainfully employed.[62] President Kennedy received the approval of Congress to update and expand New Deal programs such as

---

61. Sorensen, *op. cit.*, p. 140.

62. For a discussion of contributions to this law and others relating to jobs and poverty, written by Republicans, see Charles E. Goodell and Albert H. Quie, "The Republican Opportunity Crusade As An Alternative To The Anti-Poverty Program," Laird, *op. cit.*, pp. 171–190.

expanded coverage of the Social Security program and higher minimum wages for more persons. He revived the Food Stamp program designed to increase food purchasing power by the poor, and expanded the services offered by the United States Employment Office.[63]

Thirty-one years after Franklin Roosevelt inaugurated the New Deal another President, one who had long admired F.D.R., substantially enlarged the principle that the purpose of government is to assist those who need help. Declaring a "War on Poverty" as part of the "Great Society," President Johnson set out to, "eliminate the paradox of poverty in the midst of plenty in this nation by opening to everyone the opportunity for education and training, the opportunity to work, and the opportunity to live in decency and dignity." The coalition of Midwest Republicans and Southern Democrats which often opposes costly and extensive welfare programs was temporarily put to rout by the twin blows of Johnsonian "politicking" and the massive election victory of the President and his political sympathizers in 1964. Johnson saw his opportunity, and the legislative sessions of 1964, 1965, and 1966 were saturated with proposals from the White House to commence or expand this or that activity to assist one group here and another there.

War on poverty

In a burst of Presidential leadership Lyndon B. Johnson secured the passage of much legislation he wanted during his first years as Chief Executive. In 1964 the Office of Economic Opportunity was added to the Executive Office of the President as a kind of command post for the assault upon poverty and associated ills. In 1965 the Department of Housing and Urban Development (HUD) was created by legislation to consolidate various agencies particularly concerned with the development and improvement of the metropolitan areas in which most of the nation's inhabitants live, and where many of the country's domestic problems are found.[64] In 1967 the Department of Transportation (DOT) was created to bring together the Federal Government's agencies working upon the problems of mass

New departments and agencies

63. It is difficult to determine precisely where the "New Frontier" programs merge into the "Great Society" ones. Some of the legislation passed during the Johnson Administration began its life during the Kennedy period. Other laws proposed by Johnson were related to unfulfilled Kennedy plans. Sorensen offers a list of legislation which Kennedy did not live to sign, but which Sorensen states ought to be included in his legislative achievements because of prior association with it. Sorensen, *op. cit.*, pp. 759–760.

64. The first Secretary of HUD was also the first black cabinet officer, Robert C. Weaver. For a sample of his views on urban problems see his *The Urban Complex* (Garden City: Anchor Books, 1966).

transportation in an increasingly complex and mobile society which insists upon getting there and back in the least possible time. Previously established government agencies were energized by the President's interest in a wide spectrum of social problems. Most notable among these was the Department of Health, Education, and Welfare, which dates back to the Eisenhower Administration. Six months before his voluntary retirement from the White House, when some were referring to Johnson as a "lame duck" President, he received congressional approval for the most comprehensive housing bill in American history. The measure is designed to result in the construction or rehabilitation of approximately 1.7 million housing units at a cost slightly exceeding $5 billion. A key feature of the law provides for government subsidies which are designed to permit low-to-moderate income families to obtain mortgage money for purchasing their own homes, or in the case of renters the subsidies would be used to assist builders of rental units to borrow money and then pass on their savings to tenants in the form of lower rents.

The breadth of Federal Government activity regarding social legislation during the Johnson period precludes detailed examination. However, a number of major programs, not previously **Head Start,** discussed, deserve brief mention. The Head Start project was **Teacher Corps,** an effort to assist preschool children from "culturally deprived" **Job Corps** homes make up deficiencies before entering scholastic competition in regular school enrollments. The Teacher Corps was designed to provide specially trained instructors for children in poverty areas. The Job Corps assisted high school "dropouts," young persons who have difficulty in qualifying for gainful employment, or those who have underdeveloped reading and arithmetic skills, to develop skills needed to acquire a job. Education bills to provide Federal funds for construction of academic buildings for colleges and universities were passed,[65] as were measures to provide financial, counseling, and tutorial assistance to college students, often with an emphasis upon "disadvantaged students." As the Federal Government moved steadily into education the problem of whether, and to what extent, funds collected as taxes from all the people could be provided to church schools, most notably the many operated by the Roman Catholic Church, became increasingly ticklish. In

65. The Federal Government has long assisted higher education. More than a century ago, in 1862, the Morrill Act was passed which provided grants of public land for the endowment of colleges to be organized for the instruction of agricultural and mechanical skills.

commenting upon the doctrine of separation of church and state the Supreme Court recently left the door open for considerable argument, which will likely take place over the years as the matter of church-state relationships in education is thrashed out.[66]

Urban and rural community action programs were designed to assist blighted areas in cities and country, including Indian reservations and migrant-worker communities, to develop anti-poverty programs. Employment and investment incentives were offered to encourage the establishing and strengthening of small business operations which hopefully will increase employment opportunities. Some money was made available as loans to low-income farm families and to groups of such families to establish cooperatives or strengthen those in operation. VISTA (Volunteers In Service To America), often called the "domestic Peace Corps," sent its volunteers to live in American poverty areas where their skills contribute to the recipients' attempts to improve their lot. Appalachia, one region of the nation where poverty is particularly widespread, was the subject of the Appalachian Regional Development Act.

Aid to blighted areas

President Johnson's program to meet the problems of the cities was multifaceted. The "Demonstration Cities" program contained funds to assist cities in planning and implementing their transition from less-desirable to more-desirable places to work and live. Slum clearance and urban renewal were continued and expanded. The Rent Supplement program was intended to allow poor families to meet the rent costs of better housing. The Rat Control Bill furnished funds to help control the rodents which infest some areas of the nation.[67] Government funds have been made available to cities to assist in the modernization of mass transit systems, and the government

Urban programs

66. In 1968 the Supreme Court ruled that persons may challenge Federal school aid to parochial schools, and several such cases are on their way to the high bench. The matter of church-state relationships in education is not new. In Cochran v. Louisiana State Board of Education, 281 U.S. 370 (1930), the Supreme Court enunciated the "child benefit" theory which holds that aid to parochial schools is permissible when such aid is given the receiving child, not the church school he attends. This reasoning was used in Everson v. Board of Education, 330 U.S. 1 (1947), to uphold expenditures of county funds to pay for the transportation of school children to a Catholic school.

67. When President Johnson first asked Congress, in 1967, to pass the Rat Control Bill his request was treated by some as a joke. Subsequently, when he took his case "to the people" via the news media, they did not find the matter to be funny, and pressure mounted and Congress passed the measure.

417

Bruce Shanks in The Buffalo Evening News

Siege

continued to supply massive funding for the construction of the nation's highways, with the states contributing much smaller amounts.[68]

THE "GREAT SOCIETY" IN RETROSPECT

As President Johnson left office in January, 1969, his "Great Society" was not a reality for all. Some of the problems he and his immediate predecessor had identified remained unsolved. Many of the Johnson programs continued to be controversial and some did not "amount to a hill of beans," to use the Texas

68. Funds for highway beautification, screening of junkyards, and billboard removal, strongly backed by Mrs. Lyndon Johnson, often received rough handling by the Congress but were passed on several occasions.

idiom to describe the feelings of some Americans. Still, the belief of the New Dealers, that government is meant to serve the people, had been given dramatic new scope and purpose. Specific legislation, such as Medicare, will probably remain as a permanent feature of the American political landscape. Defenders of the retiring President pointed out that the soaring costs of the Vietnamese war, plus the reluctance by many Republicans and some Democrats during the last years of the Johnson Administration, had kept the Johnson programs from receiving the funding necessary for full implementation. Also mentioned was the fact that in some situations—*e.g.*, finding jobs for minority groups—government can only do so much. Beyond certain limits the final act whereby society is changed must be the culmination of millions of individual acts.

Those dissatisfied with the Johnson Administration's health, employment, education, and welfare programs roughly divided into two groups in 1969. There are those, such as the persons **Dissidents** who participated in the Poor People's March on Washington, joined by dissident Democrats and liberal Republicans, who argue that the President became sidetracked by the war in Vietnam. The result, they claim, was a warping of American political perspective and the draining of money and vitality from needed domestic programs. Another group, composed largely of Southern democrats and conservative Republicans, charged that the War on Poverty and allied programs were little·more than political boondoggles designed to win votes from minorities at the expense of hardworking tax-paying citizens. Individuals holding these views suggest that, nearly 40 years after the New Deal began, entire generations of Americans have become accustomed to government "giveaway" programs. Such critics are deeply suspicious of the growing size and expense of the Federal Government which leads, they contend, to increased bureaucratic inefficiency and the danger of totalitarianism. Their citation of big-city riots, soaring crime statistics, inflation, and examples of mismanagement in government activities provides a serious and sobering aspect to their views.[69]

The entry of the national government into active participation in health, employment, education, and welfare programs has had interesting effects upon American politics. On the credit side, even critics admit that one of the primary apologies

69. See the suggestions contained in James M. Gavin (with the collaboration of Arthur Hadley), *Crisis Now* (New York: Random House, 1968); and those by a member of the Kennedy and Johnson Administrations and urban affairs advisor to President Nixon, Daniel P. Moynihan, "Where the Liberals Went Wrong," Laird, *op. cit.*, pp. 129–142.

for the existence of political machines has been destroyed, and that the professionalization of welfare administration has practically ended the use of political appointees in such positions. On the debit side, even the most ardent admirers have indicated concern about the inroads "welfare chiselers" have made in cheating on government programs. Although proponents of Social Security insist that the abandonment of unemployment compensation, Old Age and Survivors' Insurance, Medicare, and other assistance programs would not save money but merely result in the transfer of the burden to others (private charity, family members, or local governments), there are those who believe that if a "means test" (i.e., proof of poverty) were vigorously administered, substantial savings could be made. On the theoretical level, the argument is between those who see the ideals of thrift and personal responsibility disappearing as compulsory insurance plans are coupled with government assistance programs; and those who assert that Federal activities are more realistic, efficient, and humane than any other alternatives. On the practical level, national lawmakers are under constant pressure to keep taxes low and to increase the benefits afforded by government programs. Promises by campaigning politicians to do more for this or that group are of course popular, but the voters often forget that increased costs must be paid for by higher taxes. In either event the benefits acquired may be purchased at the risk of endangering the value of the dollar.

Taxation and Tax Policy

Whenever the national government spends money, of course, it spends money taken from the people. Arranging for such spending money is another of the concerns of governnment.[70] Determining tax policy is difficult in any country since an unwise one could ruin the national economy, but levying taxes is especially delicate in a democratic country where the political futures of the elected representatives of the

70. For extensive discussion of the subject of government financing see Harold M. Groves, *Financing Government*, 6th ed. (New York: Holt, Rinehart and Winston, 1964); *The Price Of the United States Government 1948–1967*, prepared by the American Enterprise Institute for Public Policy Research, September, 1967; Murray L. Weidenbaum, "The Need for Budgetary Reform," and Frank T. Bow, "The Federal Budget," in Laird, *op. cit.*; and Walter W. Heller, *New Dimensions of Political Economy* (New York: Norton, 1967). Professor Heller, a former chairman of the President's Council of Economic Advisers under Kennedy and Johnson, discusses the ideas of the "new economics" and how they relate in his view to the political management of the nation's economy.

people are at stake. Understandably but unfortunately, everyone likes the benefits which government spending brings, but there are few citizens like the late Justice Holmes who pay taxes willingly in order to "buy civilization."

Because of the difficulties and embarrassments encountered by the inability of the government under the Confederation to levy its own taxes, the framers of the Constitution put few restrictions on the taxing power of Congress. The national government is not authorized to levy direct taxes (e.g., on property) or capitation ("head") taxes (e.g., poll taxes), and it must be sure that duties and imposts are uniform. Article I arranged for all bills raising revenue to originate in the House of Representatives, but this exclusive right was compromised once the Senate learned it could strike out every word except the enacting clause of a tax bill and rewrite the measure to suit its fancy. On a few occasions, however, the House has shown its power by promptly adjourning after sending a tax bill to the Senate. When this happens, it means that the upper chamber can "take it or leave it." (The Senate has to take it.) More frequently, the tax-conscious House of Representatives has demonstrated its power in conference committees, since tax bills always go to conference. Tax bills are not considered especially suitable for vehicles in prestige battles, because members of Congress realize that national finance is fraught with danger these days. Not only does more than half of the tax money go for national security, but the national government spends approximately one fifth of all the money spent in the United States; any serious reduction in government spending would decrease the national income.

Forty-three percent of every tax dollar collected by the Treasury Department's Internal Revenue Service comes from individual income taxes and another 18 percent from corporation taxes. Thus slightly over three fifths of the money in the United States Treasury got there because of the Sixteenth Amendment. Moneys collected for social insurance and retirement, the so-called trust funds, represent 22 percent of the funds collected by the government. Excise taxes (i.e., on gasoline, liquor, etc.) add another 9 percent. The balance is divided between what is borrowed (4 percent) and that generated by other taxes (i.e., franchises, etc.). Among these other sources, the graduated inheritance taxes make a substantial contribution in money but not in percentages. The once-controversial and still debated tariff brings in less than one per cent. Naturally, Congress is under enormous pressure from all sides to shift the tax burden to the other fellow, and the resulting compromises

Congress and taxation

Tax sources

421

account for the incredible complexity of the Internal Revenue Code. Repeated efforts have been made to persuade Congress to revise and systematize the tax laws, closing loopholes and exposing hidden subsidies, but the immensity of the project is

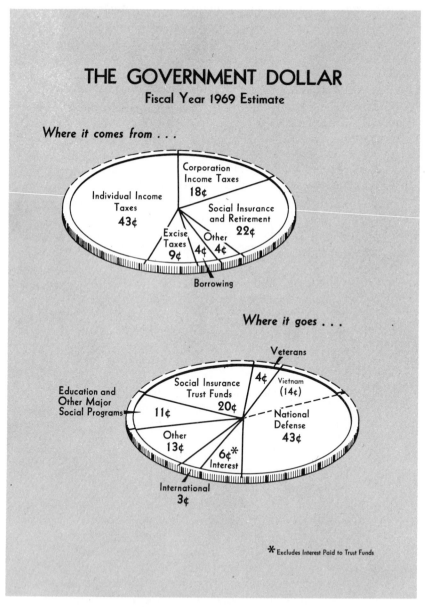

THE GOVERNMENT DOLLAR
Fiscal Year 1969 Estimate

Where it comes from . . .

Corporation Income Taxes
18¢

Individual Income Taxes
43¢

Social Insurance and Retirement
22¢

Excise Taxes
9¢

Other 4¢ 4¢

Borrowing

Where it goes . . .

Veterans
4¢

Vietnam (14¢)

Social Insurance Trust Funds
20¢

Education and Other Major Social Programs
11¢

National Defense
43¢

Other
13¢

6¢*
Interest

International
3¢

*Excludes Interest Paid to Trust Funds

Source: *The Budget in Brief* (Executive Office of the President, Bureau of the Budget, 1968).

disheartening. In 1967 President Johnson called for tax reform which would correct the "undue burdens" placed upon some taxpayers and the "unfair benefits" received by others. His call went unanswered by Congress.

Taxation has uses other than the raising of money. By utilizing the device of tax incentives business activity can be assisted in strengthening itself, or be enticed into activities deemed **Tax incentives** desirable for private enterprise to undertake. Tax reductions can be used to stimulate the entire economy by encouraging business to modernize and expand, and by increasing the spending power of the consuming public.[71] Conversely, increased taxes can be employed to slow economic growth when it is thought by government that inflationary pressures of "boom" times may lead to a "bust" and so bring on depression.[72]

The Budget and Its Preparation

The amount of money raised and spent by the government has not always had such a direct relation to the national economic picture as it does today. In fact, the government managed for nearly a century and a half without a budget at all. Before 1921, when the Budget and Accounting Act was passed, the tax-writing committees and revenue-spending committees in the Congress were not even coordinated. The normal fiscal situation bordered on administrative chaos, but the government managed to limp along—even during World War I when the slipshod arrangement almost broke down completely. National fiscal administration rapidly improved under the constant scrutiny of the Bureau of the Budget, which was created by the act.

The Bureau of the Budget thinks ahead, beginning work on next year's budget on the first day of the current fiscal year (July 1). The director, who has been in close contact with the **Bureau of the Budget** Chief Executive, begins the process by sending letters to all departments and agencies to advise them of the President's budget policy and to request estimates of the amount of money

71. The tax-reduction measure initiated by President Kennedy and passed during the Johnson Administration (1964) was designed to encourage economic expansion.

72. The first general increase in Federal income taxes since the Korean conflict was passed in 1968 when Congress approved a 10 percent "surcharge" on the existing taxation rates. The measure was an attempt to control inflation and stabilize the value of the dollar, as well as to help pay for the Vietnamese war. To obtain passage of the tax increase the President was obliged to accept cuts in his budget and reductions in the number of persons employed by the government.

423

needed for the fiscal year ahead. The executive departments contact their subdivisions, down the chain of command, and these furnish details which creep up the chain to the Washington headquarters. The departmental lists are submitted, usually in September, to the Bureau of the Budget, where expert examiners comb them carefully. The Bureau then arranges for department and agency chiefs to justify their requests during a series of hearings. The examiners make their final recommendations to the director, who makes whatever changes he thinks the chief will want, and forwards the bulky book to the President. Early in January the President delivers a simplified Budget Message to Congress and presents the legislators with the detailed book.[73] Thus ends the first of four steps in the budgetary process.

The budgetary process

On Capitol Hill reviewing the budget and making recommendations to the Congress as to its funding is the primary job of the Appropriations Committees of the House and Senate.[74] Although the budget is presented by the executive branch as a coherent plan, it is considered in fragments by the two Appropriations Committees. Each department or agency estimate of needed funds is first handled separately by one of the several subcommittees of the House Committee on Appropriations, usually after requested items have been previously authorized by one of the legislative committees.[75] The subcommittees— Department of Defense, Public Works, Foreign Operations, Independent Offices, etc.—hold closed hearings to which they summon personnel from both the Bureau of the Budget and the departments or agencies requesting funds. These hearings usually find subcommittee members trying to match expertise

73. In his budget message on the fiscal 1969 budget, President Johnson adopted a new budget accounting system which had been recommended to him by a Commission on Budget Concepts. In place of the old "administrative budget" most familiar to the public, the President discussed the proposed government income and expenditures in terms of the new "unified budget concept." This method of presenting the budgetary information, unlike the "administrative budget," includes the transactions of government-administered trust funds such as that for Social Security. The inclusion of trust fund figures helps explain the $186.1 billion figure which shocked some citizens when they first read the fiscal year 1969 budget request made by President Johnson.

74. Aaron Wildavsky examines fiscal politics in *The Politics of the Budgetary Process* (Boston: Little, Brown, 1964).

75. According to House Rule XXI, Section 2, appropriations must previously have been authorized by law, except in a few instances. In other words, one statute must authorize a governmental activity, while another must provide for its financing. See George B. Galloway, *The Legislative Process in Congress* (New York: Crowell, 1953), p. 124.

with officials of the Executive Branch and occasionally are marked by dramatic testimony, where officials disagree with their chiefs, the Bureau of the Budget, and the President on the amount of money necessary for their agency's program.[76] The subcommittees then make their own uncoordinated recommendations and reports to the full committee, which invariably adopts them. The subsequent appropriation bills are reported to the House, placed on the Union Calendar, and are then voted on by the House of Representatives. After each bill has passed, it is sent to the Senate where it is referred to the Senate Appropriations Committee and then to one of the subcommittees for additional hearings and consideration. Usually cuts made by the House are restored in the Senate and the disagreements are worked out by compromises in a conference committee.

After confirmatory votes in the House and Senate, the conference committee bills are enrolled and sent to the President for signature. Since funds for governmental programs are vital and since the President has no power to veto individual items in a bill, even if he disagrees with certain provisions he inevitably signs the measures as passed by Congress. Many students of American government have argued for the item veto—an arrangement by which the Chief Executive could pick and choose among the provisions offered as many of the state governors do. But other observers fear that to grant this power would be to decrease the already diminished responsibility of Congress vis-à-vis the executive branch.[77] Perhaps the best argument against the item veto is that the President already has the power to curtail expenditures. In 1949 President Truman restricted the Air Force from spending $615 million which Congress over his objections had appropriated for the purchase of airplanes. Since that time there have been several instances where later Presidents refused to spend some specific appropriation made by Congress, and Congress could do little to force compliance with its wishes.

During any congressional session anywhere from 15 to 20 sep-

Appropriations: Congress and the President

76. During the "McNamara years," 1961–1968, budgetary disputes between the Secretary of Defense and the Service Chiefs were not unusual. One of the most controversial of these was in regard to construction of the TFX (now designated the F-111) fighter-bomber. A study of the controversy surrounding this aircraft is Robert J. Art, *The TFX Decision* (Boston: Little, Brown, 1968).

77. This argument is advanced by Pendleton Herring, *Presidential Leadership* (New York: Rinehart, 1940), pp. 76–77. For the pros and cons of the item veto proposal see Bertram M. Gross, *The Legislative Struggle* (New York: McGraw-Hill, 1953), pp. 430–31.

425

arate appropriation bills go through the legislative mill. Taken together, which they never are by either the House or Senate, they bear some resemblance to the budget as formulated by the departments and agencies, Budget Bureau, and President. But the congressional process for budgetary review and appropriation is piecemeal, fragmented, and uncoordinated. Consequently, as one political scientist noted: "Congress does not view the budget as a means of effecting a rational distribution of limited funds among alternatives."[78]

Administration and audit

Once funds have been appropriated, the next stages of the budgetary process are primarily administrative. The Bureau of the Budget apportions money on a quarterly basis to the departments and agencies of the executive branch, and may require periodic reports from them and order them to keep within their allotments. The Treasury, after funds are apportioned, then transfers money from the general fund to the credit of the departments and agencies. Finally, a post-audit is given expended funds by the General Accounting Office, which also may disallow expenditures if they are not proper. The GAO, responsible to Congress, in addition endeavors to facilitate legislative control of expenditures by submitting reports to the Appropriations Committees and the House and Senate Committees on Government Operations.

Government Spending

The Constitution restricts the spending power of Congress by four provisions: (1) *"The Congress shall have power ... to pay the debts and provide for the common defense and general welfare of the United States."* This is to say that spending must be for purposes specified in the Constitution. The clause brings the principle of judicial review into government finance and offers the courts the opportunity to play an important role. (2) *"The Congress shall have power ... to raise and support armies, but no appropriation of money to that use shall be for a longer term than two years."* This clause was drafted with the obvious intent of preventing the military forces from becoming independent of the people's elected representatives. It is not particularly meaningful today because of the annual budget system.

78. Edward C. Banfield, "Congress and the Budget: A Planner's Criticism," *American Political Science Review*, XLIII (December, 1949), p. 1217. See also the suggestions for a "radical incremental approach designed to improve the calculating capability of all government participants in the budgetary process," in Aaron Wildavsky, "Toward A Radical Incrementalism," Alfred de Grazia, *op. cit.*, p. 111.

EXPANSION OF FEDERAL NONMILITARY PROGRAMS 1948-1967

Source: *The Price of the United States Government, 1948–1967* (The American Enterprise Institute, September 1967).

(3) "*No money shall be drawn from the Treasury but in consequence of appropriations made by law.*" This requirement is extremely important since it enables Congress to keep control over the purse. (4) "*. . . a regular statement and account of the receipts and expenditures of all public money shall be published from time to time.*" Although this provision might appear to be similar to locking the proverbial barn after the horse has been stolen, it does attest to the conviction of the founders that the citizens have a right to know how their money is spent.

The citizens also have a responsibility to know where their tax dollars go because it is their money and particularly since so many of them talk about the high cost of big government.[79] In President Johnson's proposed budget for fiscal year 1969, as might have been expected, expenditures for past and present wars, and preparations for future wars should they come, took the largest bite—$86.9 billion, or nearly 50 percent. The next

Where the money goes

79. John Kenneth Galbraith is one of a number of American economists who maintain that spending and production for public services—schools, libraries, hospitals, roads, etc.—is less than it should be in comparison with spending and production for private luxuries. The resulting "social imbalance," Galbraith argues, can be redressed by spending our resources for more and improved governmental services. See *The Affluent Society* (Boston: Houghton Mifflin, 1968).

427

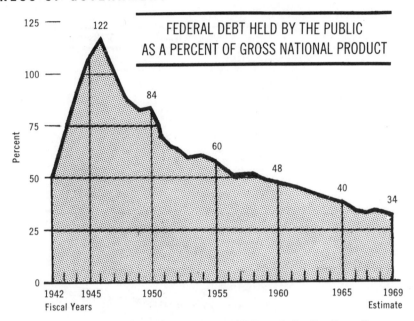

Source: *The Budget in Brief* (Executive Office of the President, Bureau of the Budget, 1968).

largest amount, $56.3 billion, was budgeted for health, education, welfare, and labor. Nearly 75 percent of this sum was to be derived from largely self-financing trust funds such as Social Security. The third largest amount, $14.1 billion, was for the interest on the national debt.[80] Lesser amounts, such as $8 billion for commerce and transportation, $4.6 billion for space research and technology, $4.5 billion for agriculture, $4.5 billion for international affairs and finance, and $2.5 billion for natural resources were included in the President's budget.

Cost of national security

The most staggering aspect about the astronomical figures associated with any discussion of the Federal budget is that since the beginning of the Cold War the United States has spent more than $1,000 billion paying for national security, and there is seemingly no end in sight for such expenditures unless the Cold War can be phased out. Even with the end of the Vietnamese war or its significant reduction in scope, the missile competition with the Soviets and Chinese could cost the United States between $40 billion and $50 billion for just a single new weapons system by 1975. That system is the antimissile defense program barely commenced in 1968. The costs of

80. In his first 1969 budget message President Johnson estimated the Federal debt—held by the public—would be $298 billion as of June 30, 1969. This figure appears less alarming when compared with the estimated Gross National Product—the value of all goods and services produced in the United States for a year. The latter will probably surpass $900 billion in 1969.

other weapons systems run into the billions, as does the maintenance of large military forces to avert or "win" brush-fire wars and major conflagrations.

Some groups may talk of significantly reducing expenditures for health, education, welfare, and the like. However, it is doubtful if such measures would be popular with the bulk of the voters. Therefore it appears evident that if any real reductions in the nation's budget are to be made in the next decade they must accompany an easing of international tension. Otherwise the government must learn to handle increasingly large "guns" and "butter" budgets successfully, with the ever-present danger that the value of the dollar will be decreased further with unhappy results for many citizens. The international situation which received little attention in *The Federalist Papers*, but which is crucial to America's security as well as to the effort to put the American budget in order, is the subject of the next chapter.

Prospects for the nation's budget

SUMMARY

• A highly visible, and to some an objectionable, facet of the Federal Government is its size. Demographic, social, and technological changes since 1789 have been accompanied by increases in the scope and degree of government activity.

• From the beginnings of the republic the Federal Government has substantially assisted business. However, the Constitution contains key clauses which have been interpreted to permit the government to regulate extensively and at times enter into business activity. Through the years Congress has established a number of independent regulatory commissions and empowered them with authority to see that business operated "in the public interest." Specific laws add to the regulation of business activity. The Tennessee Valley Authority is an example of the government operating a business—in this case the development of a river valley system based upon production of electric power and flood control.

• As with business, the government's relationship to agricultural enterprise is a dual one—assistance and regulation. The dimensions of the current "farm problem" have been developing for decades. Increased farm production, resulting from scientific farming, has created farm surpluses and consequent low prices on agricultural products. Much Federal activity since the Franklin Roosevelt Administration has been concerned with regulating farm production to increase prices. Such activ-

429

ity often includes payment of subsidies to farmers. The question has long been debated whether the various programs designed to assist the farmer are worthwhile. Recently the matter of how food is dispensed to needy Americans has become a controversial subject.

- American labor, too, is deeply affected by government actions. During the New Deal era Administration labor legislation such as the Wagner Act enlisted the Federal Government's power to assist the labor movement further organize and collectively bargain with management over better working conditions and higher pay. After World War II a political reaction to big labor's successes and what some described as "excesses" took the form of increased government regulation of the unions. The Taft-Hartley Act and Landrum-Griffin Act were the major pieces of regulatory legislation.

- The most extensive changes in the Federal Government's domestic operations in this century have concerned the nation's health, education, and welfare. The Social Security Act passed during the New Deal firmly embedded into law the belief that the government has wide-ranging responsibilities to care for its citizens when they are unable to do it for themselves. While the Social Security program has been largely accepted, as has the recently added Medicare program, theoretical and practical problems remain. Foremost among these are aid to dependent children who are illegitimate and/or those abandoned by one of their parents, and persons who remain in a condition of deep poverty. A new proposal regarding poverty is for a Federally supported guaranteed annual income which would establish a level of income below which no person or family would be allowed to sink.

- A major responsibility of the Federal Government is formulating tax policy. Taxes, primarily from those upon individual and corporate income, support the nearly $180 billion cost of operating the government. Tax policy may also be used to control the nation's economy. Tax reductions, properly timed, are thought to stimulate a lagging economy. A carefully implemented tax increase is believed to be useful in slowing inflation and lending stability to an economy which is expanding too rapidly. Tax incentives may be used to strengthen business and to attract business to such endeavors as solving the problems of the urban areas.

- A once rather haphazard Federal budgetary process has developed into a highly specialized procedure involving the Bureau of the Budget, the agencies of the executive branch, the President, and Congress. The national security program continues to take the largest slice of the Federal budget, with expenditures for health, education, and welfare requiring the second largest amount.

SUGGESTED READING

* *(Books so designated are available in paperbound editions.)*

* Dahl, Robert and Charles E. Lindblom, *Politics, Economics, and Welfare* (New York: Harper Torchbooks, 1963).

Fainsod, Merle, Lincoln Gordon, and Joseph C. Palamountain, *Government and the American Economy* (New York: Norton, 1959).

Friedrich, Carl J., ed., *The Public Interest* (New York: Atherton Press, 1960).

Gordon, Kermit, ed., *Agenda For The Nation* (Washington: The Brookings Institution, 1968).

* Galbraith, John Kenneth, *The Affluent Society* (Boston: Houghton Mifflin, 1968).

———, *The New Industrial State* (Boston: Houghton Mifflin, 1967).

* Gavin, James M., with the collaboration of Arthur Hadley, *Crisis Now* (New York: Random House, 1968).
Basic Books, 1966).

Haber, William, ed., *Labor in a Changing America* (New York:

* Heller, Walter W., *New Dimensions of Political Economy* (New York: Norton, 1967).

* Hofstadter, Richard, *The Age of Reform: From Bryan to F.D.R.* (New York: Vintage Books, 1960).

* Kaplan, Abraham, *American Ethics and Public Policy* (New York: Oxford University Press, 1963).

* Krislov, Samuel and Lloyd D. Musolf, eds., *The Politics of Regulation* (Boston: Houghton Mifflin, 1964).

* Laird, Melvin R., ed., *Republican Papers* (New York: Anchor Books, 1968).

* Lilienthal, David E., *Big Business: A New Era* (New York: Pocket Books, 1956).

* Lipset, Seymour Martin, Martin Trow, and James S. Coleman, *Union Democracy* (Garden City: Anchor Books, 1962).

Mason, Edward S., ed., *The Corporation in Modern Society* (Cambridge: Harvard University Press, 1959).

Moynihan, Daniel P., *Maximum Feasible Misunderstanding* (New York: Free Press, 1969).

Paarlberg, Don, *American Farm Policy* (New York: Wiley, 1964).

431

Truman, David B., *The Governmental Process* (New York: Knopf, 1958).

Udall, Stewart, *Agenda for Tomorrow* (New York: Harcourt, Brace & World, 1968).

* Weaver, Robert C., *The Urban Complex* (Garden City: Anchor Books, 1966).

* Wildavsky, Aaron, *The Politics of the Budgetary Process* (Boston: Little, Brown, 1964).

10

Foreign
Policy

It is not surprising that Americans, faced with ominous and frustrating situations abroad, and vexing problems at home, may occasionally exhibit a nostalgia for the "good old days"—the halcyon century between 1812 and 1912 when private citizens never, and public servants rarely, occupied themselves with the threat of involvement in war with a first-class adversary. After the War of 1812 the new nation turned its back on the Atlantic and yielded to the attraction of developing the enormous uninhabited continent to the West, which drew like a magnet. Europe seemed farther away than ever, and any other part of the world was so remote as hardly to merit consideration. The Americans engaged in a mild skirmish with Mexico (1846) while rounding out their country's borders and fought a brief war with Spain in Cuba (1898) from the sentimental desire to help the island become politically independent, but neither was a national effort. The symbolic Uncle Sam took on the characteristics of the cowboy type: always attacked when off guard, invariably victorious regardless of odds, and forever riding off alone into the sunset without having been enticed into an "entangling alliance."

The United States in a Changing World

The "Lone Ranger" role adopted by the United States was the result of a combination of strong forces. The policy of isolationism grew from the geographical fact that two broad oceans and the frozen arctic wastes separated America from the danger of a successful attack by great powers. The contiguous nations were sparsely settled and militarily weak. There was no need, therefore, to become concerned about building and maintaining costly fortifications, engaging in military conscription, or

Isolationism

433

building far-flung military alliances. The average American regarded World War I as another "Uncle Sam to the Rescue," although by 1914 some of them recognized the intrinsic involvement of their country in world affairs. In the flush of victory when the war was over, President Wilson's idea of a League of Nations seemed acceptable to many citizens, although few of them were particularly vocal about making the United States part of the League. The idealism which had swept them into war was not sufficient after the end of hostilities to cause the American people to break with tradition and join the European powers in forming the new international organization. Neutrality seemed a better guarantee against any future involvement than did an active policy of seeking peace through international organization, and Wilson's dream was put into storage by the Senate as that body exercised its constitutional obligation to approve or disapprove treaties. The sequel, World War II, ostensibly began with Uncle Sam being ambushed at Pearl Harbor, but it had actually begun with the nation's decision to aid friends on the sides of both oceans.[1] Although doubts still lingered, public opinion strongly favored American involvement in international affairs after 1945 when the war was over. The willingness of the public to accept a change of roles in the international drama was particularly opportune since, unlike World War I, the bloodletting of the great nations involved in World War II had practically obliged the United States to accept the mantle of world leadership.

The change from Lone Ranger to something more akin to the World's Policeman has been difficult for both the American people and their policy-makers. Many citizens yearn for the comparatively "carefree" time when their country assumed only perfunctory responsibilities on the international scene and they had lower taxes, no peacetime military service, and fewer frustrations,[2] and policy-makers need not fight political battles

World's Policeman

1. A study prepared by the Council on Foreign Relations, at the request of the Senate Foreign Relations Committee, put it like this: "The prospect of a German victory had threatened to demolish the protective hedge behind which we had been able to concentrate on cultivating our own garden." Committee Print, 86th Congress, 1st Session, *Committee Print No. 7* (Nov. 25, 1959), p. 20.

2. An excellent study of American attitudes, including those of the mass public, attentive publics, and foreign-policy elites, is Gabriel A. Almond, *The American People and Foreign Policy* (New York: Praeger, 1960). For a study of public opinion during the Vietnamese war see Sidney Verba, Richard A. Brody, Edwin B. Parker, Norman H. Nie, Nelson W. Polsby, Paul Ekman, and Gordon S. Black, "Public Opinion and the War in Vietnam," *The American Political Science Review*, LXI (June, 1967), pp. 317–333.

on both the domestic and international fronts. The democratic framework in which the national leaders work at home requires that they win the support of the electorate for what they think the national strategy demands. The American conception of international order prefers that cooperation of foreign peoples also be based upon persuasion and consent. The political divisions at home, encouraged and nurtured by the opposing views and interests of an open society, pale into insignificance when compared to the divisive forces abroad, which are fanned by the exaggerated pride of established nations, the rampant nationalism of new nations, and the ancient animosities among many countries of the world. These factors which contribute to a lack of harmony in international relations are exacerbated by the economic, social, and political desires of the "poor nations";[3] the widespread acceptance of violent political ideologies as blueprints for bringing about overdue social change; and the political "fallout" from the confrontation between the Soviet Union and the United States.

The nation with the greatest power in the seething maelstrom of international affairs is the United States, and the man

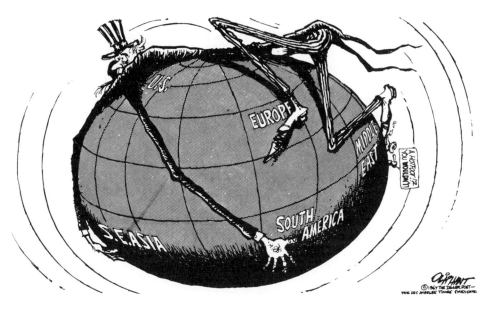

Oliphant in The Denver Post. Copyright, The Denver Post. Reprinted with permission of Los Angeles Times Syndicate.

3. The English economist Barbara Ward has described the antagonisms which divide the wealthy countries from the poor ones in *The Rich Nations and the Poor Nations* (New York: Norton, 1962).

Power of the President

primarily responsible for wielding the power of that nation is the President. The Founding Fathers, who obviously never expected their creation to be a world leader, did little to prepare the President for his vast responsibilities in guiding the conduct of foreign affairs. The Constitution merely made him Commander-in-Chief, provided that he might receive and (with two thirds of the Senate concurring) appoint ambassadors, and arranged for him to make treaties with the advice and consent of two thirds of the Senate. Fortunately, the historical precedents set by Lincoln, Wilson, and Roosevelt during the country's grave hours and the consistent willingness of the Supreme Court to stamp as valid practically everything the executive does as Chief of Foreign Policy have prepared the President of today with all the legal powers he needs to accomplish his work. In fact, as was noted in Chapter 5, the Congress is concerned that the President has acquired too much power, particularly as regards war-making. Unfortunately, neither legal nor historical precedents can provide the necessary personality and skill which the President needs if he is to surmount the political hurdles of American government which were designed precisely to check his power. The President's problem, on the domestic side of international relations, is to keep Congress and the people securely with him, which requires time. As Chief of Foreign Policy, however, he must react swiftly to sudden and sometimes unpredictable developments abroad. Congress has a slower reflex than the President, and the people are slowest to respond of all.[4] The observation of Socrates to the Athenians of the fourth century B.C.—that the state "is a great and noble steed who is tardy in his motions owing to his very size, and requires to be stirred into life"—is still valid in the United States of the twentieth century A.D. The President, as driver, must arouse the "great steed" to the extent that it will meet the threat (*e.g.*, become the "arsenal of democracy," as in 1941) without exciting it to the point of causing a runaway (*e.g.*,

4. Walter Lippmann argues that in matters of foreign policy, the movement of mass opinion is much slower than the movement of events. Public opinion, he writes, has been wrong at critical times: "The people have imposed a veto upon the judgments of informed and responsible officials. They have compelled the governments, which usually knew what would have been wiser, or was necessary, or was more expedient, to be too late with too little, or too long with too much, too pacifist in peace and too bellicose in war, too neutralist or appeasing in negotiation or too intransigent." *The Public Philosophy* (New York: Mentor Books, 1956), p. 24. For a contrasting view see Dexter Perkins, "Public Opinion and Foreign Affairs: A More Optimistic Appraisal," in Reo M. Christenson and Robert O. McWilliams (eds.), *Voice of the People* (New York: McGraw-Hill, 1962) and Almond, *op. cit.*, pp. xx–xxx.

engaging in needlessly belligerent behavior toward Cold War rivals). The relative ease with which substantial changes were made, and are being made, in American foreign policy, seems to attest both to the skill of the drivers and to the temper of the steed. Final judgment as to whether or not the changes were wise can only be made after the passage of considerable time.

Traditional Foreign Policies

In the decade which followed 1935, the United States either abandoned or drastically altered each of three cardinal principles of foreign policy which had been born during the early years of the republic and had flourished for more than a century. Briefly, those policies were as follows:

Isolationism. The keystone of traditional American foreign policy was to keep aloof from European quarrels. The warning against "permanent alliances" was enunciated by Washington in his Farewell Address, restated by Jefferson as "entangling alliances," and pledged anew by every President down to and including Franklin D. Roosevelt. The principle of nonintervention in European affairs was set aside in 1917: at the close of the war Wilson actively championed membership in the League of Nations; but in the election of 1920 the voters chose to return to "normalcy"—which meant, in this case, no alliances. For two decades more the American people kept repeating to themselves that what had happened beyond the Western Hemisphere was of no concern to them, as they watched with increasing apprehensions the powerful nations preying upon weak neighbors in Europe, Asia, and Africa. Then, in the autumn of 1940, while England was bravely withstanding the fury of Hitler's blitzkrieg, a public opinion poll disclosed that over half the American people had concluded that aiding Britain was more important than staying out of the war. The poll was symptomatic of the waning of noninterventionist sentiment; once the United States had entered World War II, a series of conferences among the allied powers brought the United States into international commitments that left the policy of isolationism hopelessly outmoded.

Changing attitudes

Freedom of the Seas. As a commercial nation set apart from its markets by oceans, the United States had always insisted on the right to unmolested use of the high seas; indeed, the War of 1812 had been fought against England to vindicate this claim,

437

as well as others. A century later, the unrestricted submarine warfare of the Germans finally led the United States into the **An obsolete** conflict. It is significant that the second of the famous Four-**principle** teen Points (which Wilson had listed as bases for a peace settlement) provided for "absolute freedom of navigation upon the seas in peace and in war." But the principle had been made archaic by the introduction of submarines and aircraft as war weapons, and it became preposterous to attempt to define any article of commerce as "non-contraband" once great nations had begun the life-and-death struggles which distinguish "total wars" from their less dangerous precursors. The Neutrality Act of 1937 recognized the inapplicability of ancient concepts in modern warfare when it required belligerent nations which bought nonmilitary goods in the United States to carry them in their own ships. Two years later, when Congress forbade American ships from sailing into danger zones, the principle of freedom of the seas was effectively abandoned.

The Monroe Doctrine. In rather ambiguous sentences scattered in an annual message to Congress in 1823, President Monroe **Evolution of** warned European powers not to attempt to extend their **the Doctrine** "system" to the Western Hemisphere. Originally, Great Britain had proposed a joint statement to warn the autocratic rulers of Europe who had banded together as the Holy Alliance against forcing the newly independent Latin American republics back under the Spanish crown, but John Quincy Adams, then Secretary of State, successfully urged the President to make a unilateral declaration. Americans came to regard the Monroe Doctrine with genuine affection as a guarantee of the independence of their southern neighbors. Latin Americans were less enthusiastic—particularly as the "Roosevelt Corollary" was applied. This interpretation of the Monroe Doctrine was given by Theodore Roosevelt in a message to Congress in 1904 when he opined that under the Monroe Doctrine the United States, acting as an "international police force," might be obliged to intervene in the affairs of Latin American republics in order to rectify "chronic wrong-doing." The intent, of course, was to forestall intervention by European powers in countries which threatened foreign investments by failure to pay debts or protect property. Within a year his words were followed by deeds. Armed intervention by North Americans brought social and financial stability to several Caribbean and Central American countries, but it also fostered a tradition of fear and distrust, by Latin Americans, of "Yanqui imperialistas." Then, in 1930, the

State Department published the Clark Memorandum on the

"Hands Off!": Theodore Roosevelt
and the Monroe Doctrine, 1905.

Monroe Doctrine, which repudiated the Roosevelt Corollary and signaled the beginning of honest efforts by the North Americans to become "Good Neighbors" to their sister republics south of the Rio Grande. As confidence was established, the commitment to keep foreign intervention out of the hemisphere became the joint project of the Organization of American States. The Monroe Doctrine had become internationalized.[5]

The Good Neighbor Policy

The President and the Department of State

There is no doubt of the primacy of the President in formulating foreign policy. Like domestic policy, what finally endures has run the hurdles of the principles of separation of powers and checks and balances, even though the hurdles are lower and fewer. By tradition and logic, the President is by far more

5. There is little doubt that the United States would not stand idly by for long, however, if the New World were threatened by an old-world power and the Organization of American States were unable or unwilling to take action. President Kennedy expressed this sentiment forcefully in 1961, although he significantly increased efforts for closer collaboration with the other American republics.

powerful in foreign policy than is the Congress, while the courts have virtually removed themselves from this area of public concern. The President's position as Chief of State gives him an unrivaled platform for explaining his interpretations to the people; his constitutional role as Commander-in-Chief permits him to deploy existing military strength; his power as Chief Executive allows him to manage the agencies concerned with foreign affairs; and his informational sources from diplomatic, military, and intelligence channels provide him a gigantic advantage as Chief of Foreign Policy, although whenever his policies require money, treaties, and/or legislation, the Constitution directs him to Capitol Hill.

CHECKS AND BALANCES

Political checks on the President

The checks and balances which operate in foreign affairs are both political and institutional. The primary political forces consist of pressure groups (spanning from organized economic interests to patriotic societies), opinion makers (politicians, educators, commentators), and government personnel. All of these compete with the President for the creation of a public opinion favorable to their views and, when successful, can modify or change his position. In 1956 opposition by Southern cotton interests probaby influenced Secretary of State John Foster Dulles to reverse his position on the building of a high dam at Aswan on the Egyptian Nile. There is little doubt that a generation of educators, sympathetic to the ideals of Wilson, prepared their students for American membership in the United Nations. And farm-state senators led the fight in Congress which restored the authority of the President to make surplus grains available to Yugoslavia and Poland. It will be interesting, when all the facts are available for examination, to ascertain to what extent the groups opposing the Vietnamese War affected President Johnson's conduct of the struggle, his decision to retire from the Presidency, and the subsequent initiation of the Paris peace talks with the North Vietnamese.[6] But it goes without question that the political checks on foreign policy have genuine potency.

Many of the institutional checks on the President are more

6. In addition to the many demonstrations, speeches, editorials, and articles and books voicing opposition to the war the spring of 1968 was a time when three prominent candidates for the Presidency expressed "dovish" sentiments about the war. These were Senator Eugene McCarthy (D., Minnesota), Governor Nelson Rockefeller (R., New York), and, until his assassination Senator Robert Kennedy (D., New York). In the later stages of the Presidential campaign Vice President Hubert Humphrey moved away somewhat from the war policy of President Johnson.

apparent than real, despite the increased need for treaties and legislation in implementing foreign policy today.[7] Since the United States has become the leader of the free world, Congress has been less willing to refuse to cooperate with the President for fear of weakening the position of the country abroad. However, within recent years the development, particularly within the Senate, of the belief that the United States has overextended itself in foreign affairs has presented the White House with formidable opposition. The budgetary pinch created by the Vietnamese war, inflation, and the need for funding domestic programs as well as diminishing sympathy for providing assistance to foreign nations resulted in Congress' consistently refusing to appropriate the funds requested by the President for foreign-aid programs. In 1968 the Congress slashed such funds to a new low in the 21-year history of the program—$1.75 billion. It should be recognized that Congress has been increasingly disposed to authorize the Chief of Foreign Policy, by law, to handle a growing number of subjects through the swift procedure of the Executive Agreement without debating each situation in its own halls. An idea of the scope and convenience of this method is furnished by an example which is not unusual: within the space of two days the United States loaned additional naval vessels to Brazil and furnished a six-million dollar assistance grant to Iceland.[8] Executive Agreements cover even such important subjects as providing atomic energy materials to other nations, agreements which may be amended merely by an exchange of notes between the diplomatic representatives of the governments concerned. The two great congressional checks which do remain, however, are the power of the purse and the right of the lawmakers to probe the agencies which make and administer foreign policy.[9]

Institutional checks on the President

A kind of intellectual check and balance not mentioned by the authors of *The Federalist Papers* is now found in the ideas and analyses injected into the Federal Government by the so-called "think tanks" which appeared on the scene after

"Think tanks"

7. The role of Congress in foreign policy making is examined in James A. Robinson, *Congress and Foreign Policy Making*, rev. ed., (Homewood, Ill.: Dorsey Press, 1967).

8. *Treaties and Other International Acts of the United States Series* (Dec. 29–30, 1960), 4462, 4467.

9. Particularly prominent among the committees which investigated and criticized the Johnson Administration has been the Senate Foreign Relations Committee chaired by J. William Fulbright (D., Arkansas). The recent hearings of this committee contain many of the arguments in opposition to the Vietnamese war and for selective retrenchment in American overseas commitments.

World War II. The first such collection of mathematicians, engineers, and social and physical scientists was established in Santa Monica, California, where it continues to operate. The organization is the RAND Corporation, the acronym RAND standing for Research and Development. Much credit for the RAND concept of providing government with analyses arrived at by individuals somewhat removed from the normal bureaucratic structures must go to General H. H. Arnold, commander of the Army Air Corps in World War II. Arnold noted that America's success in the war effort could be largely attributed to the government's mobilization of highly educated talent, the most notable of which was the group of scientists, engineers, and military men who produced the atomic bomb. Arnold suggested that an effort should be made in the postwar period to retain a cadre of scientists and scholars as full-time analysts for the government on matters relating to the use of force in support of American foreign policy. Initially RAND, and some of the subsequently formed similar organizations, were almost exclusively devoted to the systematic study of problems relating to national security.[10] Today many of the think tanks scattered about the nation invest considerable time and effort in studying the domestic problems besetting the country. Whether these groups are as useful to the government as their advocates suggest is a matter of controversy. On the one hand, it appears a good idea in theory to confront government planners with a cold analysis of their actions or proposed actions by individuals working in an independent situation. Of course in practice the analysis may on occasions be neither good nor independent. Some have questioned the influence think tanks exercise in Washington and are disturbed by the fact that they are not responsible to the electorate as are Congress and the executive branch. Like other concepts spawned in the Cold War period the think tanks are being re-examined with the view of how best to fit them into the democratic American society.[11]

Programs and influence

10. In the colorful words of a former RAND member, who later founded the Hudson Institute, the "think tanks" have spent considerable time "thinking about the unthinkable," which often meant they have been particularly concerned with the various dimensions of nuclear war. Herman Kahn, *Thinking About the Unthinkable* (New York: Horizon Press, 1961).

11. For a lengthy study of RAND see Bruce L. R. Smith, *The RAND Corporation: Case Study of a Nonprofit Advisory Corporation* (Cambridge: Harvard University Press, 1966). A much shorter piece is William Leavitt, "RAND: The Air Force's Original 'Think-Tank,'" *Air Force & Space Digest*, 50 (May 1967), pp. 100–109.

FOREIGN RELATIONS: THE DEPARTMENT OF STATE

In the beginning of our national history, the Department of State was entrusted with the formulation and administration of foreign affairs. The President *is* constitutionally responsible for both, but except for unusual instances when a Chief Executive decides to be his own Secretary of State, the man who heads the complex hierarchy of "State" undoubtedly has more unfettered opportunity to shape policy than anyone else in the executive branch.[12] He supplies the President with information on foreign affairs which he has gleaned partly from his own personal contacts but especially from his corps of special assistants, undersecretaries, deputy undersecretaries, and assistant secretaries, who advise him on a variety of topics: the state of public opinion, the attitude of Congress, the day-to-day administration of the great department; they report on geographical areas of the world, international organizations, and functions (*e.g.*, economic affairs). In Washington headquarters there is a country "desk" (*e.g.*, the Guatemala Desk), whose occupant reports to a Country Director, Central America who, in turn, consults with the Assistant Secretary of State (for Inter-American Affairs) and U.S. Coordinator, Alliance for Progress, who briefs the Secretary. The desk officer receives reports from the "field."

The Secretary of State

The "field" in 1968 stretched alphabetically from Afghanistan to Zambia and included such unfamiliar countries as Tanzania, Rwanda, and Kuwait—any one of which could create a problem for the United States in the complex and shifting international arena. The United States maintains 112 embassies headed by ambassadors who, as representatives of the President, have the right of audience with the rulers of the countries to which they are appointed. Two legations, in Hungary and Bulgaria, are each staffed by a minister who, although chief of mission, is obliged by his lower rank to deal with the head of the foreign ministry in the country to which he is assigned.

Ambassadors

12. See Don K. Price, ed., *The Secretary of State* (Englewood Cliffs, N.J.: Prentice-Hall, 1960). However, because of the unusual role which military power played in American foreign policy during the 1960's, and the unusual abilities of Robert S. McNamara, who was Secretary of Defense for much of that decade, the State Department shared considerable policy-making responsibility with the Pentagon in that period. A further reduction in State Department influence resulted from the presence of such forceful men as McGeorge Bundy and W. W. Rostow as national security assistants to Presidents Kennedy and Johnson. President Nixon noted, when he announced the appointment of Henry Kissinger as his assistant for national security affairs, that the previous occupant of that office had interfered with State Department operations, and that this would not be the case in his administration for he wanted a "very strong Secretary of State."

Naturally, both ambassadors and ministers are approved by the host government in advance of assignment, since it would be insulting to send an official representative who was "persona non grata" (*i.e.*, unwelcome) to the receiving nation. In the absence of an ambassador or minister, a Chargé d'Affaires serves temporarily as the head of the U.S. delegation. Approximately 170 consulates-general, consulates, and special offices are maintained by the United States in major cities about the world to assist Americans doing business or traveling in foreign lands. In addition the United States operates a number of Special Missions which represent America in such international organizations as the United Nations, the Organization of American States, North Atlantic Treaty Organization, International Atomic Energy Agency, and others.

Traditionally, the posts of ambassador and minister were spoils distributed by Presidents to deserving political friends; although this practice still exists, an increasing number of career diplomats are selected for the top positions. Since ambassadors are personal representatives of the President, they are expected to submit their resignations with each change of administration. Such resignations may or may not be accepted. Ambassadors are, of course, liable to be recalled from their posts and reassigned to other positions at the discretion of the President.

Embassies Embassies are organized into traditional sections (Administration, Consular, Economic, Political) and staffed by Foreign Service Officers. These persons must have passed a series of written examinations on subjects from algebra to world history and survived the close scrutiny of an oral examination. Once in the field, their tasks are to provide information for the use of the Department in formulating foreign policy, to establish friendly relations with the host country, to encourage travel and trade with the United States, and, in general, to represent American interests abroad. The United States Information Agency furnishes the embassies with public affairs officers, cultural attachés, and information officers who explain American goals and ideas to local people. The Agency for International Development sends expert technicians abroad to implement foreign aid. On occasion, the Department of Defense assigns military cadres to train national troops, but in any event the armed forces have attachés at each mission.[13] The Marine Corps

13. Representatives of other Federal agencies are often present in a country. With many Americans pursuing different tasks supported by somewhat different philosophies, the work required to coordinate and implement all American activities into a coherent program takes on the aspect of a major problem at times.

provides a small guard for the Embassy. All of these personnel, whether Foreign Service Officers, military, or contract employees, are expected to cultivate extensive contacts with the local people. This activity not only has personal advantages but may put them in touch with the "next government." Their primary task remains to gain support with the present government for the foreign policies of the United States.

Although the Peace Corps is housed as an agency within the Department of State, its purposes as set forth in the Peace Corps Act are designed to be less "political" than other activities of the government overseas. Of course the United States may gain politically to the extent that volunteers are successful in aiding foreign peoples to meet "their needs for trained manpower, and to help promote a better understanding of the American people on the part of the peoples served and a better understanding of other peoples on the part of the American people."[14]

Peace Corps

World Politics After World War II

Before World War II, it appeared that the foreign policy of the United States was dedicated to preserve her predominance in the Caribbean; to retain her freedom from European entanglements; and, after the acquisition of the Philippines, to rely on cooperation in the Far East.[15] She recognized "spheres of influence" in Africa and the Middle East by European states and thought little more about these areas. During the war, U.S. efforts were directed toward the formation of an international organization which would replace the old "balance of power" strategy of rival alliances. The hope was to begin a concert of action based upon cooperation and agreement. It was believed that such an international organization would provide agencies to promote cooperation among the members; would establish an international police force which would force recalcitrant states to abide by decisions; and would arrange a forum where differences among nations could be discussed and solved. But after World War II, the ideal met reality. Two super-states, America and the Soviet Union, faced each other over the pros-

14. *United States Government Organization Manual*, p. 94.

15. The "Open Door" policy was urged by the United States and was more or less accepted by other powers interested in the Far East. The aim was to prevent the partition of China into European spheres of influence so that all trading nations had equal opportunity in this potential market. The American people were never prepared to go to war in order to preserve this policy.

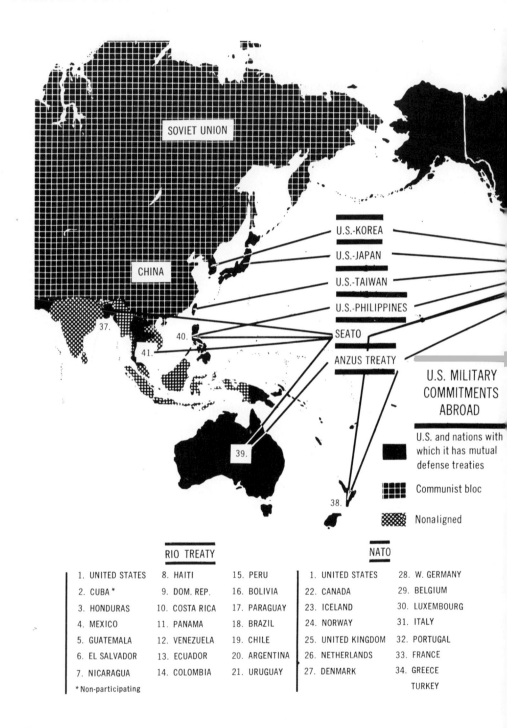

SOVIET UNION

CHINA

U.S.-KOREA

U.S.-JAPAN

U.S.-TAIWAN

U.S.-PHILIPPINES

SEATO

ANZUS TREATY

37.

40.

41.

39.

38.

U.S. MILITARY COMMITMENTS ABROAD

U.S. and nations with which it has mutual defense treaties

Communist bloc

Nonaligned

RIO TREATY

1. UNITED STATES	8. HAITI	15. PERU
2. CUBA *	9. DOM. REP.	16. BOLIVIA
3. HONDURAS	10. COSTA RICA	17. PARAGUAY
4. MEXICO	11. PANAMA	18. BRAZIL
5. GUATEMALA	12. VENEZUELA	19. CHILE
6. EL SALVADOR	13. ECUADOR	20. ARGENTINA
7. NICARAGUA	14. COLOMBIA	21. URUGUAY

* Non-participating

NATO

1. UNITED STATES	28. W. GERMANY
22. CANADA	29. BELGIUM
23. ICELAND	30. LUXEMBOURG
24. NORWAY	31. ITALY
25. UNITED KINGDOM	32. PORTUGAL
26. NETHERLANDS	33. FRANCE
27. DENMARK	34. GREECE
	TURKEY

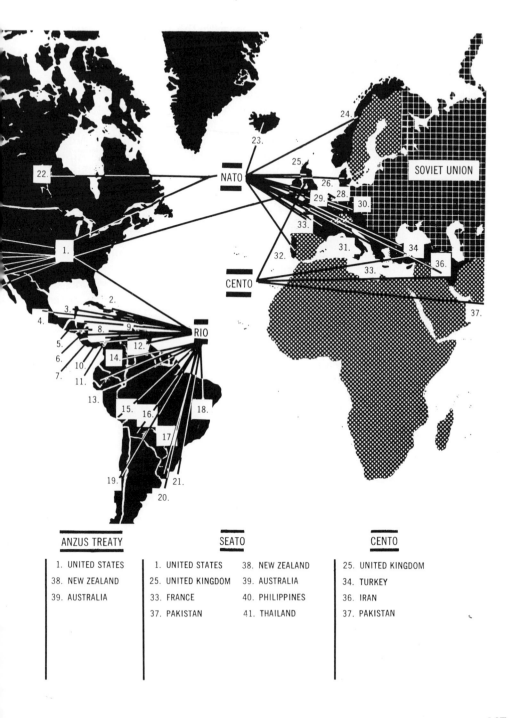

trated old nations of Europe, with the rising new nations of Africa and Asia eagerly accepting their proffers of economic and technical assistance. Each desired to construct a new system of world order to replace the one destroyed by two savage wars.

A polarized situation A polarized international situation was not what the United States had expected; a relapse to the power struggle with herself as a chief antagonist was not what she had intended. She was therefore obliged to rebuild a foreign policy hastily, from the ground up and under the most trying conditions. The American people were caught off-balance by the sudden enmity of their late ally and were psychologically unprepared for the savage give-and-take of *Weltpolitik*. The construction of a new policy was further complicated by the conflict between the idealism in American thinking and the realism of the threat to the security of the United States. The pendulum swung violently from attempted collaboration to "getting tough."[16] Each reaction was criticized on every side. Large segments of the American public were mortified by the defensive character of the new policies; many foreigners were suspicious of the idealistic features; and the policy-makers themselves were embarrassed by the opportunistic appearance of their creations. It was difficult for Americans to accept the fact that their nation could not react consistently and unequivocally to every new world development, and many were angry when introduced to the concept that they must fight wars for "limited objectives"—*i.e.*, not to crush the enemy. Although it became popular to insist that the United States "has no foreign policy," the pattern, which assumed form under the direction of both political parties, is easily discernible.

THE CONTAINMENT OF COMMUNISM

Beginning almost immediately with the end of World War II Communism became the predominant factor with which the foreign policy of the United States has to contend. At times the United States has considered adopting the tactic of "roll back," liberating areas under Communist control and so destroying that force many Americans consider their primary foreign threat; at other times the United States has attempted to "lean over backward" or "walk another mile" in efforts to reach accommodations with the Communists. However, for more than two decades under five Presidents, and with the support of both major parties, the basic foreign policy of the United States has been the containment of Communism.

16. In the study of international politics this "political realism" approach is best illustrated by Hans J. Morgenthau, *Politics Among Nations*, 4th ed., (New York: Knopf, 1966).

Whether or not the Communists actually meant, or mean, to "take over the world" continues to be debated. Because it has lacked sure knowledge of Communist intentions, the American government has been obliged since 1946 to plot its foreign policy course on the basis of perceived Communist acts, Communist statements, and judgments made of Communist political, economic, and military capabilities. These factors have appeared sufficiently ominous to demand the expenditure of nearly incomprehensible sums and the investment of vast human resources to construct an economic, political, and military "shield" against the Communist world in an attempt to prevent its expansion.[17]

U.S. policy: the cost

Although Prime Minister Churchill's warnings of what he held to be Soviet duplicity fell on deaf ears during World War II,[18] cognizance of particular Soviet actions near the end of the war led some Americans to question the postwar intentions of their wartime ally. Several of these events deserve brief mention. The discovery in 1943 of mass graves containing the bodies of thousands of murdered Polish Army officers in the Katyn forest near Smolensk, U.S.S.R., suggested to some that the Soviets had systematically destroyed the men who would have opposed the imposition of Soviet will upon postwar Poland.[19] The stopping of the Red Army before Warsaw, until the Polish underground fighters (who had come out of hiding

Signs of duplicity

17. A few individuals have advanced a revisionist thesis concerning American foreign policy since World War II. It is their contention that the United States is to a large extent responsible for the Cold War because of its hostile attitude toward the Soviet Union, rather than the other way around. See particularly for this point of view D. F. Fleming, *The Cold War And Its Origins*, 2 vols. (Garden City: Doubleday, 1961). Arthur Schlesinger, Jr., examines the revisionist view and the more common explanations concerning the Cold War beginnings in "Origins of the Cold War," *Foreign Affairs*, 46, (October, 1967), pp. 22–52.

18. Churchill sought to have Western armies invade the Balkans and so prevent that area from falling into Soviet hands. Failing in this, Churchill tried to convince the Americans, after the invasion of France, that allied troops should make a drive as far into Eastern Europe as possible. Again his idea was to prevent territory from being occupied by the Red Army, and again his plan failed to persuade American leaders. Finally, at the war's end, with some American forces in areas to be administered by the Soviets, Churchill urged that U.S. forces not be withdrawn until Stalin had offered proof he would truly establish democratic governments in the Eastern European nations as pledged by the Yalta Agreements. For a third time the British leader failed to persuade the Americans to follow his suggestions. Churchill's fears of Soviet postwar designs may be read in his *The Second World War*, particularly Vol. VI, *Triumph and Tragedy* (Cambridge: Houghton Mifflin, 1953).

19. An account of the matter is given in Churchill, Vol IV, *The Hinge of Fate* (Cambridge: Houghton Mifflin, 1950), pp. 757–760. Churchill notes that to believe the Soviet version, which attributed the mass murder to the Germans, "seems an act of faith," p. 760.

449

to attack the occupying German forces) had been destroyed by the Germans, created further doubts as to Soviet plans for an independent Poland.[20] Additional suspicions were aroused by the way the Soviets handled the Polish governments-in-exile. There were two such "governments" during the war composed of Poles who had escaped the Nazi occupation of their homeland. One group was in England and the other in the Soviet Union. Toward the end of the war it became apparent that through Soviet machinations the latter group would be established in Warsaw as the primary force in designing the destiny of postwar Poland, to the general exclusion of the non-Communist group.[21]

Iran

To these and other suspicions generated between the Western Allies and the Soviet Union another problem was added in 1946. Its resolution, in a fashion favorable to the United States, was suggestive of the relationship which soon would obtain between the world's most powerful, and second most powerful, nations. The difficulty arose when Soviet troops were not withdrawn from Northern Iran after the war in accordance with the prior agreements among the British, Americans, and Soviets. The international forces had been placed in Iran during the war to guarantee the operation of a railroad over which supplies were shipped to the Soviet Union by England and the United States. Working with the British through the United Nations, and finally resorting to a "blunt message" sent to Stalin, President Truman pressured the Soviet Union into withdrawing its troops back to its national boundaries.[22]

The Truman Doctrine

Almost exactly one year following his success in blocking Soviet expansion in Iran President Truman faced a similar but more important problem. The British, bled white by World War II, announced they were obliged to abandon their traditional balance-of-power position in the Eastern Mediterranean. The British withdrawal coincided with the Greek government's heavy involvement in guerrilla war against Communists and Turkish efforts to bolster their defenses in the face of the steadily increasing power of the Soviet Union. The President's response, embodied in a request to Congress on March 12, 1947, has come to be known as the Truman Doctrine. This landmark departure from the traditional American foreign policy involved the appropriation of $400 million for assistance

20. *Triumph and Tragedy*, pp. 128–145.

21. *Ibid.*, pp. 418–439.

22. Harry S. Truman, *Memoirs*, Vol. II, *Years of Trial and Hope* (New York: Doubleday, 1956), pp. 93–96.

to Greece and Turkey, and the dispatch of American personnel to both nations to help erect a bulwark against Communism. This segment of the containment shield is still being maintained more than two decades later. The American presence in the Mediterranean is most clearly evident in the form of the 6th Fleet which today confronts an expanding Soviet Navy in the waters off Greece and Turkey.

Speaking at the Harvard commencement exercises on June 5, 1947, Secretary of State George Marshall broached a plan which would be incorporated in the containment policy. His astonishing proposal that one nation finance the economic rehabilitation of others was made after Marshall had surveyed the wreckage of European economies caused by the war and concluded that industrial chaos was an invitation for the rise of extremist, antidemocratic regimes.[23] American idealism and harsh reality merged neatly in support of the Marshall Plan.[24]

The Marshall Plan

The novel idea was violently opposed by isolationists and also by those who objected to the offer's extending to Russia and Eastern European states controlled by the Red Army. Actually, the Soviet Union had no intention of taking part in the program and refused to permit her satellites to do so, but most of the other European governments worked out a comprehensive recovery plan and waited for action by the Congress. The Economic Cooperation Bill was debated for months until the destruction of democratic government in Czechoslovakia by Communists took the fight out of the bill's opponents. Today, when Western Europeans attribute the birth of their Common Market and the upswing of their economies to the Marshall Plan, there are few who regret the $12 billion transfusion which revived the economic life of Western Europe.[25]

In his inaugural address, January 20, 1949, President Truman turned his attention to the Communist threat in areas that were not reached by Marshall Plan aid. On the assumption that the glib promises of Communist agitators would be irresistible to the poor, undeveloped nations, President Truman proposed,

Truman's Point Four

23. A detailed account of the evolution of the Marshall Plan and the Truman Doctrine is Joseph M. Jones, *The Fifteen Weeks* (New York: Viking, 1955).

24. For a penetrating analysis of the uses to which foreign aid can be put see Hans J. Morgenthau, "Preface to a Political Theory of Foreign Aid," in Robert A. Goldwin, ed., *Why Foreign Aid?* (Chicago: Rand McNally, 1963), pp. 70–89.

25. A qualification would be in regard to those Americans who feel the French have shown an improper sense of gratitude as evidenced in the strained relations between the two nations which developed during the 1960's.

451

as "Point Four" in his blueprint for fighting Communism, that the United States export her technical knowhow as a form of foreign aid. Since the program began in 1949, thousands of experts have been sent to many parts of the world where they have engaged in projects as diversified as civil service reform, chicken raising, and community development.

COMMUNIST AGGRESSIONS DURING THE TRUMAN ERA

Response to Soviet expansion

In 1947 an article appeared in the influential journal *Foreign Affairs* which analyzed Soviet behavior and suggested that if Soviet expansion were blocked by

> . . . firm containment, designed to confront the Russians with unalterable counter-force at every point where they show signs of encroaching upon the interests of a peaceful and stable world,

the totalitarian society of the Soviet Union would be weakened and that nation's expansionist policies altered.[26] The Soviets initiated two major acts which convinced additional Americans in 1948 that Josef Stalin indeed was prepared to use brute power in order to Communize the world. In February, Czechoslovakia, remembered as the little nation sacrificed by the infamous Munich Agreement 10 years before, underwent a Communist coup and re-emerged as a Soviet satellite. Late in the spring the Soviets, contrary to understandings the Americans thought they had made with them, blockaded road, rail, and water access routes to the Western sectors in the city of Berlin which lay deep within the Soviet-occupied zone of Germany. Regardless of what the Soviets hoped to gain by the action, the reaction must have been surprising. President Truman refused to accept the Soviet move; he declined to use ground forces to "open up" the access routes to the former German capital. Instead he ordered an airlift which carried supplies to the hard-pressed West Berliners during the severe winter of 1948-49. The Berlin airlift was terminated when the Soviets suddenly opened the access routes in May of 1949.

26. Everyone interested in America's current foreign policy, whether or not he agrees with it, should read the germinal article, "The Sources of Soviet Conduct," *Foreign Affairs*, 25 (July, 1947), pp. 566-582. Because the author of the article, George F. Kennan, was at the time holding a high position within the Department of State, the author was listed simply as "X." Since his famous article Mr. Kennan has written and lectured extensively upon the relationship between the United States and the Soviet Union. Those who argue that containment should be applied to Communism today as it was 22 years ago should read some of Mr. Kennan's later works.

In the United States Senate the Soviet actions in Czechoslovakia and Eastern Germany helped build support for a measure known as the Vandenberg Resolution. This document, prepared by Senator Arthur Vandenberg (R., Michigan) with the cooperation of the Department of State laid the foundation for bipartisan support of the historic military alliance between America and Western Europe—the North Atlantic Treaty Organization, which was formed in 1949 to present a military front against the possibility of Soviet aggression in Europe.[27] In joining NATO the United States agreed that an armed attack upon any one of the signatories would be considered an attack upon them all. To bolster its commitment to NATO the United States assigned military forces to the NATO military command. Navy, Air Force, and Army units (7th Army in West Germany) remain in Western Europe today.[28]

NATO

Communism scored its most impressive victory since the Russian Revolution of 1917 when Mao Tse-tung became master of China in 1949 after a struggle of two decades against General Chiang Kai-shek and his Nationalist Chinese followers, who fled to the island of Taiwan.[29] Although the United States' attitude was favorable toward Chiang during his last years on the mainland, American troops were not committed to the struggle against Mao's Communist armies. In the aftermath of the Communist takeover of China some Americans searched for Washington scapegoats. Secretary of State Dean Acheson was a favorite target but he was stoutly defended by President Truman.[30] Some observers insist that had the containment doctrine been inaugurated in China in 1945, instead of in Greece in 1947, the Republic of China would never have fallen

China: Mao vs. Chiang

27. The initial members were Canada, Great Britain, France, Italy, Belgium, the Netherlands, Luxembourg, Denmark, Norway, Portugal, and Iceland. Greece and Turkey were invited to join in 1952, and the Federal Republic of Germany was granted admission three years later. The 20-year-old pact is being reconsidered for renewal.

28. The reassertion of raw Soviet power to dampen the liberalization of the Czechoslovakian government in 1968 cast serious doubts upon talk that the United States might be able to substantially reduce its military forces in Europe.

29. The political and economic philosophies devised by Mao, plus his military strategy for advancing Communism, are set forth in the four volumes of the English translations of *Selected Works of Mao Tse-tung* (Peking: Foreign Languages Press, 1961–1965).

30. Harry S. Truman, *Memoirs*, Vol. II, *Years of Trial and Hope*, pp. 428–430.

453

to Communism.[31] But in view of the difficulty the United States has encountered in the small nation of South Vietnam, one wonders what success could have been expected had American soldiers been sent to fight in the Chinese Civil War.

War in Korea

To many Americans what seemed the final piece of evidence needed to confirm the worst fears regarding Communist aggression occurred in June of 1950. On the 25th of that month North Korean troops invaded South Korea. That country had been divided at the 38th parallel during the Cairo Conference (1943) for occupation by Russian and American forces until the Japanese had surrendered and Korea could be re-established as an independent country. The Soviets, however, quickly demonstrated their intention to remain until their occupation zone was completely Communized: when they withdrew in 1948, a large and well-equipped army faced the South Koreans—who had been prepared by the United States for self-government, not war. At the time of the invasion, since the Russian representative on the Security Council was absent, the United Nations was able to vote aid for the invaded South Koreans without a veto. The same day, President Truman ordered American military forces into the action. It was never entirely clear whether the goal of this "police action" was to drive the invaders back across the 38th parallel or to unite the divided country. When the U.N. forces, led by General MacArthur, turned the tide and drove toward the northern border of Korea at the Yalu River, Communist Chinese "volunteers" crossed the frontier in numbers sufficient to force the U.N. troops back across the 38th parallel. General MacArthur, wishing to clean out Communism in North Korea, recommended bombing the Chinese bases in Manchuria. The administration, however, pursued a policy of containment and was satisfied to accept an armistice line at approximately the 38th parallel.[32]

The impact of the Korean war upon spending for military purposes can be graphically perceived by observing the dramatic rise of the defense budget from $12½ billion in 1950, to $20.6 billion in 1951, to double that the following year. By 1953,

31. This debate is still not resolved. Defenders of the Administration's policy cite reports of corruption and antidemocratic practices in the Chiang regime which, they insist, prevented saving the Nationalist Chinese government. Opponents of Truman's policy argue that more aid would have turned back the Communist advance. Most students of the Far East believe that only military intervention by the United States could have prevented the Communists from coming to power in 1950 since they were receiving aid from the Soviet Union.

32. See Walter Millis *et al.*, *Arms and the State* (New York: Twentieth Century Fund, 1958), Chapter 7.

defense spending had reached $45.4 billion. Since the Korean conflict the defense budget has never fallen below $37 billion, or three times the pre-Korean budget, and most of the time it has been considerably higher.[33]

FOREIGN POLICY IN THE EISENHOWER ADMINISTRATION

The Truman Administration which had firmly established the containment policy was replaced in 1953 by the Republicans led by Dwight D. Eisenhower. The former five-star general brought new faces to Washington, most notably his Secretary of State, John Foster Dulles, who had some ideas of his own regarding containment. Dulles suggested that America might block Communism without such heavy drains on the budget by relying more upon the threat to destroy the homelands of Communist nations than upon Truman's policy of opposing Communism at whatever point it sought to burst through into the non-Communist world. This proposal, known as Massive Retaliation, seemed a logical way for the world's most technically advanced nation to defend the very long border of the non-Communist world against the vast manpower resources of the Soviet Union and China.[34] As time passed the policy fell partial victim to the progress in nuclear weapons development made by the Communist scientists and the political and military tactics derived from Mao Tse-tung's guerrilla-war experiences. The United States did not resort to Massive Retaliation against China or the Soviet Union to save the French anti-Communist war in Indochina in 1954, and Ho Chi Minh successfully established a Communist regime in North Vietnam. In 1955, when Chinese Communist pressure was mounting against the Nationalist Chinese on Taiwan and the offshore islands of Quemoy and Matsu, the American response was to supply conventional armaments to the Nationalists and for the Congress to pass the Formosa Resolution, which authorized the President to use force to protect Taiwan, the Pescadores, and related islands.[35]

In 1958 President Eisenhower, reacting to the threat of a Communist coup in Lebanon, dispatched several Marine and

"Massive Retaliation"

33. The figures are from *The Price of the United States Government 1948–1967* (Washington: The American Enterprise Institute, 1967), p. 110.

34. See John Foster Dulles, "A Policy of Boldness," *Life*, 32 (May 19, 1952), pp. 148–150.

35. Whether the United States would have used nuclear weapons against the Chinese mainland had an attack been launched across the Taiwan Strait remains a debatable question.

Army battalions to the troubled little country in the Middle East. After stability was restored, the American forces were withdrawn.[36] The political and technical difficulties associated with the policy of Massive Retaliation were recognized by Secretary Dulles before he died. Referring to the continued danger of repeated Communist assaults into the non-Communist world, Dulles suggested that in time small nuclear weapons suitable for use on the battlefield could replace the reliance put upon the threat of attacking Communist homelands with nuclear weapons.[37] Further evidence that the United States was prepared to fight "brush-fire" wars on the spot with American troops, rather than resort to Massive Retaliation, was the development of the Strategic Army Command. This force composed of Army and Marine divisions was kept in reserve in the United States for deployment to trouble spots about the world.[38]

While the Eisenhower Administration was resolute in its opposition to Communist expansion,[39] several attempts were made to reduce Cold War tensions and reach an understanding with the Soviets. One such attempt was the President's Atoms for Peace proposal made before the United Nations during his first year in office. Eisenhower suggested that the United States and the Soviet Union reduce the size of their nuclear weapons stockpiles by making fissionable material available for peaceful purposes to the nations of the world. Cooperation of the two super-powers could not be obtained in the venture, so the

36. The President's actions were in accord with the Middle East Resolution which Congress had passed the previous year.

37. John Foster Dulles, "Challenge and Response in U.S. Policy," *Foreign Affairs*, 36 (October 1957), pp. 25–43.

38. It should be noted, however, that President Eisenhower, writing of the Lebanon intervention and the Strategic Air Command, stated, "that if 'small wars' were to break out in several places in the world simultaneously, then we would not fight on the enemy's terms and be limited to his choice of weapons. We would hold the Kremlin—or Peking—responsible for their actions and would act accordingly." *The White House Years*, Vol. II, *Waging Peace, 1956–1961* (Garden City: Doubleday, 1965), p. 291.

39. Secretary Dulles followed the tradition-shattering NATO alliance by arranging for other military alliances in peacetime. Most notable was the pact signed in Manila in 1954 which established what became known as the Southeast Asia Treaty Organization, or SEATO. The commitment assumed by the nations adhering to the Manila agreement is less than that prescribed in the NATO treaty. Nevertheless, the United States for this and other reasons felt itself obligated to defend Southeast Asia against Communism. Unfortunately in Southeast Asia there were no sturdy building blocks for constructing a containment wall such as were found in the nations of Western Europe. The eight members of SEATO are the United States, Great Britain, France, Australia, New Zealand, the Philippines, Thailand, and Pakistan.

United States unilaterally developed a program for assisting nations to develop the peaceful uses of nuclear energy. The Soviets then offered some assistance to other Communist nations developing nuclear energy programs for peaceful purposes and probably devoutly wish now that the program to assist China had never been started, or had been more tightly controlled. President Eisenhower's Open Skies proposal was another effort to make the Cold War less dangerous. This suggestion was that the Soviet Union and the United States reciprocally permit aerial photography of each other's territory to provide insurance against surprise attack. The Soviets refused to accept the plan, claiming, among other things, that it was a trick to gain espionage access to the Soviet Union. Of course, the United States stood to benefit more from an open-skies inspection since Soviet agents have much more accessibility to American military activity because of the "open society" of the United States than vice versa. Following the Soviet rejection of the American proposition the United States sought to obtain information by sending its high-altitude reconnaissance plane, the U-2, into Russian airspace. The discovery and capture by the Soviets of one of these aircraft scuttled a summit conference between the heads of the two super-states which had been expected to result in a step forward for disarmament. The increased sophistication in building and launching space satellites, however, may have made explicit agreement for aerial inspection unnecessary. Espionage from outer space is less desirable than free inspection teams on the ground, but it could probably provide the verification the United States insists upon before engaging in disarmament, and it may make the Russians less adamant about allowing inspections within their borders.[40]

"Open Skies" plan

FOREIGN POLICY IN THE KENNEDY ADMINISTRATION

Less than three months after assuming office President Kennedy temporarily departed—to his deep regret—from the general containment theme in foreign policy. The result was the fiasco at the Bay of Pigs in Cuba. There, in April, 1961, nearly 1500 Cuban exiles who had been trained, armed, and transported by the United States were killed or captured after landing on the island in an effort to overthrow the Communist regime of Fidel Castro. The plan for the Cuban invasion was begun in 1960 during the Eisenhower Administration. It was accepted by the Kennedy Administration with the new Presi-

40. For a series of studies on opportunities and problems associated with aerial inspection see Frederick J. Ossenbeck and Patricia C. Kroeck, eds., *Open Space and Peace* (Stanford: The Hoover Institution, 1964).

457

dent's proviso that no American forces were to be directly involved in the fighting. The plan as presented to the President was based upon the assumption that the landing force would in time trigger a general uprising against the Castro regime, thus making the use of American military forces unnecessary. But the invaders were overwhelmed scant hours after they landed.

Quickly recovering from the disaster at the Bay of Pigs, an event for which he took full public responsibility, President Kennedy devoted his energies in international affairs to the further development of the general concepts of his predecessors. He relied heavily on arguments advanced by General Maxwell Taylor, chairman of the Joint Chiefs of Staff, to adopt a policy of "flexible response" to Communist expansion.[41] Taylor had criticized the Eisenhower Administration for being too rigid and for placing too much reliance upon nuclear weapons which he contended would neither be used by the United States nor would constitute a credible threat in Communist eyes. He suggested increasing America's nonnuclear forces and strengthening its air- and sea-lift capability to ensure that forces could be moved rapidly to danger spots. He believed that American security could best be safeguarded by possessing the capability to oppose Communist moves, from small guerrilla activity on up to all-out thermonuclear war, by responses which would be generally reciprocal and therefore appropriate to the provocation. President Kennedy agreed.[42]

In Southeast Asia the President was faced with the kind of Communist guerrilla war he feared would become the standard technique for Communist expansion. The danger loomed in Laos and more importantly in South Vietnam. The sending of American troops to Thailand in 1962 apparently convinced the Communists in neighboring Laos to accept a "neutral" regime. In Vietnam Kennedy sought to oppose Communist economic and political appeals, and the threat of guerrilla terror, by joint efforts with the South Vietnamese government to enhance the living conditions of the peasants and by sending American mili-

"Flexible response" policy

"Advisers" to Vietnam

41. Maxwell Taylor, *The Uncertain Trumpet* (New York: Harper, 1959).

42. Kennedy was particularly interested in beefing up American capabilities to respond to the type of political-economic-military threat posed in the guerrilla warfare philosophies of Mao and the late Cuban strategist Che Guevara. Of singular concern to the President was the fact that Premier Khrushchev had delivered a speech on January 6, 1961, in which the Soviet leader pledged support for "wars of national liberation," the Communist term for guerrilla war. Hilsman, *op. cit.*, Chap. 23, "Subterranean War," pp. 413–439.

tary "advisers" to help the South Vietnamese Army destroy the Communist guerrilla forces.[43]

In more successful containment efforts President Kennedy resisted new Soviet pressure upon Berlin. The Berlin crisis of 1961 begain in June at a meeting in Vienna between the President and Premier Khrushchev. The latter informed the United States that the Soviet Union intended to sign a peace treaty with East Germany within six months, thus formally ending World War II in Europe. The danger in such a move was the Soviet contention that a peace treaty would end all commitments based upon the German surrender, among which the most important to the United States were (a) the presence of American and allied troops in West Berlin, and (b) access rights to cross East German territory to reach the Western sections of the former German capital. Kennedy's response to the Soviet threat was to order a substantial increase in conventional armed forces and equipment. In the middle of August the Communists put up the infamous Berlin Wall to prevent East Germans from escaping to the West. Although the United States criticized the wall the government did not consider its construction an act requiring the risk of war to tear it down. Ultimately, Khrushchev decided not to sign a peace treaty with East Germany and many in the United States believed the reversal in Soviet policy resulted from the firm American stance based upon military strength.

The Kennedy Administration's highwater mark in implementing the containment policy was reached during the Cuban missile crisis, discussed in detail in Chapter 6. A Communist intrusion was turned back by a prompt and unequivocal American response based solidly upon possession of superior military force.

While continuing various foreign aid programs, most of which were related to preventing the spread of Communism, the Kennedy Administration inaugurated a kind of Marshall Plan for Latin America which he called the "Alliance for Progress." In some respects more ambitious than the Marshall Plan, which had been designed as temporary aid to re-build shattered economies, the Alliance for Progress was intended to build an industrial base in an area beset with chronic and widespread

The Berlin crisis of 1961

Alliance for Progress

---

43. An extensive literature exists on guerrilla warfare. Any reading should begin with Mao Tse-tung, *On the Protracted War* (Peking: Foreign Languages Press, 1960). The book is composed of lectures delivered by Mao in 1938. After reading this successful practitioner one can better appreciate the problems faced by officials who must devise a way of defeating guerrilla operations.

illiteracy, expanding population, and low per capita income. Both successes and failures can be marked up to the Alliance for Progress. In 1971, when the Alliances' 10-year initial life will terminate, a decision will need to be made by the United States and the Latin-American governments whether to continue their joint attack on problems of housing, tax reform, agriculture, land tenure, and economic development.

President Kennedy's efforts to extend the Truman and Eisenhower attempts to reduce the tensions and dangers of the Cold War were both varied and controversial. They included the installation of a "hot line" Teletype link between Washington and Moscow,[44] the exchange of weather information and other scientific data collected by American and Soviet space satellites, the sale of American wheat to the Soviet Union, and the signing of the Partial Nuclear Test Ban Treaty.[45]

FOREIGN POLICY IN THE JOHNSON ADMINISTRATION

Vietnam

President Johnson continued to work simultaneously upon the twin pillars of United States foreign policy inherited from the previous Cold War Presidents—containment of Communism and easement of the confrontation between the United States and the Communist world. His most persistent problem was the Vietnam war, where he quickly found himself "damned if he did" and "damned if he didn't." On the one hand, "hawk" critics urged a more vigorously prosecuted campaign, for they argued that a stalemate or defeat would open the rest of Asia, possibly Africa and Latin America as well, to Communist guerrilla warfare. On the other hand, "dove" critics accused the President of seeking to crush a small nation fighting for independence from foreign domination. Some suggested that had the United States not intervened in the Vietnamese war the Communist leader Ho Chi Minh would have consolidated both Vietnams into one country which would have sought to maintain its independence of Communist China.[46] Still others voiced concern about the wisdom of involving American fighting forces in a land war in Asia, about the dangers of war escalating up to the thermonuclear level, and about the moneys going to war when they were needed for urgent domestic problems. The Johnsonian mixture of sword and olive

44. The complexities of the nuclear age are suggested by the fact that the "hot line" enables the President to communicate directly with the most powerful of America's possible enemies, but without branch lines to America's allies. The stark truth is that it may be more important to talk with the Soviets who can "blow up the world" than with the British, French, and West Germans, who cannot.

45. The particulars of the treaty are examined in the next chapter.

46. The hoped-for analogy would be one with the independence displayed by the Communist government of Yugoslavia toward Moscow.

"This job is just one dang containment policy after another."

branch employed in Vietnam may be seen in the words of an address he gave in April, 1965. Of Communist expansion the President said:

> The central lesson of our times is that the appetite of aggression is never satisfied. To withdraw from one battlefield means only to prepare for the next. We must say in Southeast Asia—as we did in Europe—in the words of the Bible: "Hitherto shalt thou come, but no further."[47]

47. " 'Pattern for Peace in Southeast Asia': Address by the President at Johns Hopkins University, Baltimore, April 7, 1965," in Richard P. Stebbins, ed., *Documents on American Foreign Relations 1965* (New York: Harper and Row, 1966), p. 142.

The President also noted the harsh life for the peoples of Southeast Asia, and he recalled that Americans had before been generous in assisting the impoverished. Johnson suggested therefore:

> The first step is for the countries of Southeast Asia to associate themselves in a greatly expanded cooperative effort for development. We would hope that North Vietnam would take its place in the common effort just as soon as peaceful cooperation is possible.[48]

Longest U.S. war

By 1969 America's venture in containing Communism in Southeast Asia had stretched into the longest war in American history, and many were questioning the wisdom of this particular effort[49] as well as the general policy. The war, along with domestic problems attributed in part to the war, joined with "law and order" to become central issues in the presidential campaign. President Johnson's Democratic Party became divided over the struggle. After noting the "divisiveness among us all tonight," the President startled the entire world on March 31, 1968, when he said in a televised speech:

> . . . I have concluded that I should not permit the Presidency to become involved in the partisan divisions that are developing in this political year.
>
> With America's sons in the fields far away, with America's future under challenge right here at home, with our hopes and the world's hopes for peace in the balance every day, I do not believe that I should devote an hour or a day of my time to any personal partisan causes or to any duties other than the awesome duties of this office—the Presidency of your country.
>
> Accordingly, I shall not seek, and I will not accept, the nomination of my party for another term as your President.[50]

Cessation of bombing

Earlier in the speech the President had announced the unilateral reduction of the aerial bombardment of North Vietnam as a step made with the hope of bringing the North Vietnamese

48. *Ibid.*, p. 144.

49. A number of books have appeared which examine the Vietnam war from various points of view. See for example: Marvin E. Gettleman, ed., *Viet Nam* (New York: Fawcett, 1965); Richard N. Goodwin, *Triumph or Tragedy* (New York: Vintage, 1966); Marcus G. Raskin and Bernard B. Fall, eds., *The Viet-Nam Reader* (New York: Vintage, 1965); Frank M. Robinson and Earl Kemp, eds., *The Truth About Vietnam* (San Diego: Greenleaf Classics, 1966).

50. "A New Step Toward Peace" (Washington: Government Printing Office, 1968).

to the conference table. After some weeks of negotiation on a site, the United States and North Vietnam began conferences in Paris to discuss peace. On October 31, 1968, as the presidential campaign was drawing to a close, Mr. Johnson announced the cessation of all bombing of North Vietnam as a further effort toward a peace settlement.

President Johnson vigorously contained the threat of Communism, or at least claimed to have done so against some criticism, in another part of the world. The place was the Domini-can Republic and the time was 1965. As with the Vietnamese war the precise facts are controversial and they vary according to the particular account one is reading. But it is generally agreed that there was a revolution in the nation that might have ended in the establishment of a Communist state similar to Castro's Cuba. To counter this threat President Johnson dispatched troops to the Dominican Republic. Later the American troops served as a nucleus of an Organization of American States force which had as its mission the restoration of order and the prevention of a Communist takeover. Whether or not there actually existed the danger of a Communist coup, and how damaging this might have been to the United States had it occurred, remain matters of considerable debate. For his part the President stated in an address:

Dominican Republic affair

> The American nations cannot, must not, and will not permit the establishment of another Communist government in the Western Hemisphere.[51]

Further in his speech the President sought to make a distinction between official American sanction for political change (after all, the United States was born in one of the world's great revolutions), and American opposition to a change brought about by Communist machinations.

> We believe that change comes and we are glad it does, and it should come through peaceful process. But revolution in any country is a matter for that country to deal with. It becomes a matter calling for hemispheric action only—repeat—only when the object is the establishment of a Communist dictatorship.[52]

Actively pursuing what might be called the "guard is up, but the hand is out" philosophy (some would prefer to describe it as the carrot-and-stick approach), President Johnson sought

51. Stebbins, *op. cit.*, "Purposes of the United States Intervention: Broadcast Statement by the President, May 2, 1965," p. 245.

52. *Ibid.*, p. 246.

463

Toward a lessening of the Cold War

means to reduce Cold War tensions and dangers. Among his activities were efforts to increase trade in peaceful goods with the Soviet Union and the Communist nations of Eastern Europe; the establishment of consulate offices between the Soviet Union and the United States; agreement with the Soviet Union to leave outer space free from claims of national sovereignty, and to refrain from orbiting weapons of mass destruction in space; initiation of commercial airline service between the Soviet Union and the United States; the cosponsoring of a treaty by the United States, the Soviet Union, and Great Britain to prohibit the further proliferation of nuclear weapons; and an agreement with the Soviets to commence discussions on ways to reduce the further development of long-range nuclear missiles and anti-missile missiles by both super-powers. Such relationships with the Soviet Union, at a time when Soviet military equipment was being used by the North Vietnamese against American soldiers and airmen, serve to emphasize the complexities of American foreign policy in today's world.

Red China

In regard to the second major Communist power, China, the Johnson Administration refused to extend diplomatic recognition according to the pattern which dates back to the Truman years. President Johnson's diplomats did carry on discussions with the Communist Chinese at the ambassadorial level in Warsaw, a practice begun in 1955. Secretary of State Dean Rusk summed up the official policy of the government toward China in these words, "We do not seek the overthrow by force of the Peiping regime; we do object to its attempt to overthrow other regimes by force."[53]

ASSESSMENT OF CONTAINMENT

Future policies?

As America prepares to enter the 1970's under the leadership of the Nixon Administration, several basic questions regarding foreign policy have emerged for debate.[54] One is whether the threat from the Soviet Union has waned, or whether the Soviet Union is patiently waiting for internal problems and frustrations to take their toll of American power and resolve prior to

53. *United States Policy Toward Communist China*, Department of State Publication, 8078 (Washington: Government Printing Office, May, 1966).

54. At one point in the presidential campaign of 1968 then-Vice President Hubert Humphrey went so far as to advocate a shift in foreign policy from containment of Communism to a policy of "reconciliation and peaceful engagement." Roy Reed, "Humphrey Urges U.S. Stop Trying to Contain Reds," *New York Times*, July 13, 1968.

launching anew an effort to Communize the world.[55] Another question involves the danger from China. If in fact the Soviet Union has "mellowed" and become fully conscious of the constraints imposed by life in the nuclear age, will the same process result in limits being set upon the external policies of China? There also are questions about the trends toward nationalism in lesser Communist states such as Romania, Yugoslavia, and most recently Czechoslovakia, which developed their own brands of "nationalist Communism" apart from the path followed by China and the Soviet Union. Lastly, Americans must confront the tough question of whether their nation need intervene to prevent all Communist movements which may result in Communist governments, or whether the United States can afford to be more selective in employing its power for containment purposes.[56]

The national debate on these matters began several years ago. A prominent critic of the Vietnamese war, the intervention in the Dominican Republic, and one who argues the United States should modify its foreign policy is the chairman of the Senate Foreign Relations Committee, J. William Fulbright (D., Arkansas).[57] One of Senator Fulbright's chief concerns is that Americans have become so engrossed in anti-Communism that they have been transformed into agents of reaction and suppression. An example of his point of view is this statement regarding American policy toward Latin America: **Critique of U.S. policy**

Guided by a reflex bred into them by Fidel Castro, Ameri-

55. One who suggests that the latter view is the correct one is Colonel William Kintner, deputy director of the Foreign Policy Research Institute, University of Pennsylvania. See *Peace and the Strategy Conflict* (New York: Praeger, 1967).

56. It is possible that in the 1970's America will move toward a policy of "eclectic containment." Such a policy would normally require the military confrontation of Soviet and Chinese armies should they move across national boundaries into non-Communist nations, but would not necessarily mean American involvement in all revolutionary situations where status quo governments would be under attack by indigenous Communist movements, even some receiving aid from Moscow and Peiping. The rationale for adopting such a policy would be that in time Communist governments, as they developed their own national interests independent of the Soviet Union and China, would serve more as a brake to Chinese and Soviet imperialism, rather than assisting it. Of course the United States probably would not want to make this kind of policy change unless it did so from a position of impressive strategic nuclear capacity.

57. In addition to many statements uttered in the course of his committee's activities, Senator Fulbright has authored two books on foreign policy. *Old Myths and New Realities* (New York: Random House, 1964); and *The Arrogance of Power,* (New York: Random House, 1966). Senator Fulbright was reelected to the Senate in 1968.

can policy-makers have developed a tendency to identify revolution with communism, assuming, because they have something to do with each other, as indeed they do, that they are one and the same thing, as indeed they are not. The pervading suspicion of social revolutionary movements on the part of the United States policy-makers is unfortunate indeed because there is the strong possibility of more explosions in Latin America and, insofar as the United States makes itself the enemy of revolutionary movements, communism is enabled to make itself their friend. The anti-revolutionary bias in United States policy, which is rooted in the fear of communism on the Cuban model, can only have the effect of strengthening communism.[58]

Another concern expressed by Senator Fulbright and others is that America has embarked upon a "mission" to save and police the world. To attempt the shouldering of such responsibilities is part of what Fulbright calls "the arrogance of power." He warns repeatedly of attempting to assume greater responsibilities than the United States can handle, and he notes that great nations which have over long periods of time invested too much in foreign affairs have neglected their domestic sources of power to their sorrow.[59]

Two options A strong defense of what America has attempted to achieve by containing Communism is found in the writings of Professor W. W. Rostow, who served as a primary foreign policy adviser to President Johnson.[60] Rostow notes that characteristically nations move up a scale of economic and industrial development from "traditional societies" (based upon pre-Newtonian science and technology) to the "high mass-consumption" level, and possibly to an even more advanced state he terms "beyond consumption," as in the case of the United States.[61] Rostow observes that as nations industrialize in their drive toward the high consuming level two options are opened to them: (1) they may use their industrial and scientific muscle to provide for the welfare of their citizens, or (2) they may build the machines of war. In this century the Soviet Union, Germany, and Japan, writes Rostow, were all tempted to use their new-

58. *The Arrogance of Power*, p. 83.

59. *Ibid.*, "Introduction," pp. 3–22.

60. W. W. Rostow, *The Stages of Economic Growth* (London: Cambridge University Press, 1965).

61. The intervening levels in Rostow's description of national growth are "preconditions for take-off," "take-off," and "drive to maturity." *Ibid.*, Chapter 2, "The Five Stages-of-Growth—A Summary," pp. 4–16.

found industrial power to impose their will upon areas of less industrial growth in Eurasia.[62]

> Each effort failed because a fourth power had simultaneously come to maturity—the United States—which shared with Western Europe an interest in frustrating such a unilateral dominance of Eurasia, and which in the end successfully made common cause with the older mature powers, most notably with Great Britain.[63]

Looking to the future, Rostow sees a world in which more nations will harness the secrets of modern science and technology. This means, among other things, that more nations can acquire the weapons of the nuclear age. This somber projection leads Rostow to suggest that American foreign policy must persuade the Soviet Union to accept the diffusion of power on the world scene as setting real limits upon any nation's expansionist tendencies. Rostow suggests three things must be demonstrated to the Soviets in order for them to accept a pluralistic and peaceful world:

Diffusion of power

> We must demonstrate that we shall not permit them to get far enough ahead to make a temporary military resolution rational.
> We must demonstrate that the underdeveloped nations —now the main focus of Communist hopes—can move successfully through the preconditions into a well-established take-off within the orbit of the democratic world, resisting the blandishments and temptations of Communism. This is, I believe, the most important single item on the Western agenda.
> And we must demonstrate to the Russians that there is an interesting and lively alternative for Russia on the world scene to either an arms race or unconditional surrender.[64]

To Rostow the "lively alternative" is for the Soviet Union to join

> . . . the great mature powers of the north in a common effort to ensure that the arrival at maturity of the south and

62. The casual reader of Rostow must beware lest he assume Rostow is spinning out an all-inclusive theory in which the stages-of-growth are the single causes for international action. Rostow clearly states that is not his intention; for example, "The stages-of-growth do, then, throw some light on—but they do not pretend to explain fully—the great power struggles of the twentieth century. But that, after all, is one of the major conclusions of this book—that economic forces and motives are not a unique and overriding determinant of the course of history." *Ibid.*, p. 121.

63. *Ibid.*, p. 118.

64. *Ibid.*, p. 134.

of China will not wrack the world as the arrival at maturity of Japan, Germany, and Russia itself did at an earlier time; for with nuclear weapons, that old self-indulgence—seeing how far you can go towards world power when you reach maturity—this sport of the Kaiser and Hitler and the Japanese militarists and Stalin—can no longer be safely afforded.[65]

Selective intervention

Those concerned about the evolution of the containment policy should consider the views of another prominent participant in the implementation of that policy during the 1960's. Reviewing the American involvement in Vietnam, General Maxwell Taylor concluded that while the defense of South Vietnam was "the right thing," the United States should in the future be careful and selective in its interventions on the behalf of a particular group or government. General Taylor draws a precise lesson from the Vietnam experience: "We must be sure that there are reasonably able leaders with whom we can work, who are cooperative, and who have an attitude like our own toward the problems which we are to resolve in common."[66] Contemplating the future, General Taylor suggests:

> We must be philosophical and recognize that turbulence will be the rule for a long time in a large number of these new countries and be slow to back individuals and parties which, at best, are poor bets in the short term.[67]

The United States and the International Community

While containment of Communism has been the core of American foreign policy since 1947, other activities have been undertaken in the international arena by the United States. Efforts to establish links among the nations of the world often center on the United Nations and its related international organizations.

THE UNITED NATIONS

The radical shift from isolationism to participation in collective action by an international body was symbolized when the Senate, after only six days of debate, voted 89-2 to make the United States a charter member of the United Nations—even after the serious rifts between the Soviet Union and the West-

---

65. *Loc. cit.*

66. Maxwell Taylor, *Responsibility and Response* (New York: Harper and Row, 1967), p. 53.

67. *Loc. cit.*

ern powers had been adequately exposed at the San Francisco conference of 1945. Since each of the five permanent members of the Security Council (the United States, the Soviet Union, the United Kingdom, France, and the Republic of China) was given the veto power, the organizational squabbles were an indication of things to come. Although the preamble of the United Nations Charter begins with the statement of the members' determination "to save succeeding generations from the scourge of war," the veto underscored the fact that world peace would be preserved only if the great powers wished to preserve it. Most of the people of the United States have supported the United Nations steadily because they approve its principles, admire the work of its agencies, and hope to strengthen its machinery, but their policy-makers have not made the organization the cornerstone of American foreign policy.[68]

Entering its third decade of existence the United Nations has both successes and failures behind it.[69] In terms of successes a number of specialized international agencies working in association with the United Nations must be ranked high as worthwhile activities benefiting numbers of the world's population. Examples of such agencies are the Food and Agriculture Organization; the International Atomic Energy Agency; the United Nations Educational, Scientific, and Cultural Organization (UNESCO); the World Health Organization; the International Labor Organization; and the United Nations Children's Fund (UNICEF). While these agencies, along with others, do not solve immediate international difficulties, their proponents point with pride to their beneficial work which depends upon international cooperation for accomplishment. On a number of occasions the injection of United Nations peace-keeping forces has brought relative stability to politically volatile areas. Such

U.N. agencies

68. Stronger commitments to collective security have been made by the United States in terms of various military agreements. A few months before the San Francisco conference convened, the United States joined the Latin-American republics in the Act of Chapultepec. This pact pledged its signatories to "assist in meeting" an armed attack should any of the other members be attacked by an American or non-American state. The Rio Pact (Treaty of Reciprocal Assistance) of 1947 further defined this obligation of member states. Already mentioned have been the NATO and SEATO alliances. In addition the United States has acceded to many mutual defense treaties, some multiple-party (e.g., ANZUS: Australia, New Zealand, and the United States), and several bilateral (e.g., Japan). Some were designed to afford bases for American military forces.

69. For an examination of the relationships of American foreign policy to the United Nations see Lincoln P. Bloomfield, *The United Nations and U.S. Foreign Policy*, rev. ed. (Boston: Little, Brown, 1967). The organization and administration of the United Nations is the subject of Maurice Waters, *The United Nations* (New York: Macmillan, 1967).

has been the case in regard to U.N. military missions sent to Cyprus, the Congo, and the Gaza Strip, which once separated Israel and Egypt before the withdrawal of U.N. forces and the June, 1967 war between the two Middle East countries. The use of a United Nations army, composed predominantly of American forces, stymied North Korean aggression against South Korea. Failures to resolve international disputes also dot the history of the United Nations. The animosity between Jews and Arabs in the Middle East continues to flare intermittently into violence which endangers world peace. Kashmir is still argued over by India and Pakistan. The United Nations has not been successful in halting the Vietnamese war. Perhaps the greatest utility of the United Nations is serving as a world forum before which powerful and weak nations alike can air their views, and in which international discussion can lead to important agreements among nations. Recent examples of such agreements are the banning of weapons of mass destruction from space and the treaty prohibiting nuclear-weapons proliferation which a number of nations signed.

Unless the unlikely happens, and international frictions dissolve, the United Nations may look forward to a rich variety of problems which will require attention in the years ahead. The outlines of several such problems are clearly visible now. For example, there is the controversial exclusion of Communist China from the United Nations in general and from the Security Council in particular. This exclusion does not reflect the change in power status between the weakened government of the Republic of China, which is in the United Nations and occupies a Security Council seat, and the growing power of the Communist government of mainland China, which is equipped with nuclear weapons and controls some 700 million citizens. The exclusion of the Communist government does reflect the desire of the United States and other nations to prevent the Communists from being seated at all until such time as evidence is given of willingness to abide by the peaceful outlines of the U.N. Charter. Large expenditures upon peace-keeping forces, plus a reluctance by some United Nations members to meet their fiscal responsibilities for such activities, has been a recurrent cause of concern for the United Nations. Part of the difficulty is that certain nations, for example the Soviet Union, may not want to support various peace-keeping activities because their particular brand of foreign policy flourishes best in conditions featuring political and economic chaos. For some, another problem has arisen from the seating of new nations in the General Assembly (where each nation has one vote regard-

Successes and failures

Continuing problems

less of size or power) from nonwhite areas of the globe. The expressed fear is that the United Nations will increasingly become the tool of the poor, dark-skinned, and less-industrialized peoples to be used against the more affluent, highly industrialized white societies. And of course the cross-purposes at which the Soviet Union and the United States often find themselves will, to the extent that they continue, hamper a number of United Nations activities.[70]

The United Nations continues to evolve in practice in ways its founders and backers did not plan for initially. First of all, the United Nations has not become an organization wherein the few very powerful nations sitting on the Security Council (the big five policemen theory) would work in concert to bring peace and stability to the world. Because Soviet-United States disagreement, and the veto of the Security Council members, often combined to block Security Council action to maintain peace, the scene of much such activity has shifted to the General Assembly.[71] Since there are Cold War and other divisions in the General Assembly, it is frequently difficult to achieve a working majority of votes in that arena. Those who were looking for the United Nations International Court of Justice to serve the purposes of international law more fully than its predecessor (the Permanent Court of International Justice) have been disappointed. To date the present court has had little business; for nations, unlike individuals living within a state, need not appear before the bar of justice unless they wish to do so. Therefore nations generally continue to settle most of their disputes, and all really major ones, by means other than court decisions. The final arbiter, of course, is war. Those who saw in the creation of the United Nations the beginnings of a world government have also been disappointed, or perhaps they have learned to be very patient. The United Nations in time could prove to be the precursor of a true world govern-

The U.N. record

70. Some Americans contend that the United Nations has been used by the Soviet Union for advancing its national interests to the detriment of American purposes. This view is often disputed by scholars. See for example John C. Stoessinger, *The United Nations and the Super-powers* (New York: Random House, 1965). The major reason why the United Nations is more useful to the United States than to the Soviet Union is that the U.N.'s goals as stated in the charter are much more compatible to the goals of the United States than to those of the Soviet Union.

71. On November 2, 1950 the General Assembly passed the Uniting for Peace resolution proposed by the United States to help solve the impasse created in the Security Council when the Soviet Union sought to veto prosecution of the Korean conflict. The resolution holds that when the Security Council is unable, because of a lack of unanimity, to exercise its responsibility to maintain international peace the General Assembly shall consider making appropriate recommendations to member states for action.

ment—one with a monopoly of force with which to coerce obedience to its laws like any other true government, but that day seems far off down either an evolutionary or revolutionary road. An exception might be a nuclear encounter so frightening as to convince the world's nations to yield enough of their national sovereignty necessary for the building and operation of a world government.[72]

AID AND TRADE

Already mentioned have been the assistance to other nations the United States has provided through specific programs such **AID** as the Marshall Plan, the Point Four Program, and the Alliance for Progress. Except for the last-named program, which is still in effect, American nonmilitary assistance is extended in accord with the Foreign Assistance Act of 1961. Nonmilitary assistance is normally handled through the Agency for International Development (AID), housed within the Department of State. Military assistance to foreign nations, both in terms of weapons and supplies, and training are the responsibility of the Department of Defense. Military Assistance and Advisory Groups operate in various nations whose security against Communism is considered necessary by the government as a part of the security program of the United States. The granting or selling of armaments to foreign governments, and the training of foreign nationals to use such equipment, has become one of the facets of the containment policy severely criticized by those suggesting that extensive modifications be made in American foreign policy.[73] American assistance to less developed nations is also made through established international organizations **World Bank** such as the International Bank for Reconstruction and Development (World Bank), the Inter-American Development Bank, and more recently created international credit institutions such as the Asian Development Bank. While the problems attacked by American aid in the non-Western world are more difficult than those for which American aid was spent in Western Europe two decades ago, some progress is claimed by

72. Perhaps the most detailed study suggesting ways in which the current United Nations could be transformed into a world government with "teeth" may be found in Grenville Clark and Louis B. Sohn, *World Peace Through World Law*, rev. ed. (Cambridge: Harvard University Press, 1962).

73. An explanation and justification of the military assistance programs is contained in *Statement by Secretary of Defense Robert S. McNamara on the Fiscal Year 1969–73 Defense Program and the 1969 Defense Budget* (Washington: U.S. Government Printing Office, January, 1968), pp. 32–36.

Mauldin in The St. Louis Post-Dispatch

"It's beautiful, but we were sort of hoping for a plow."

the government. For example, AID assistance to the Republic of China has been terminated because it is no longer required. Still, the Malthusian nightmare of population growth surpassing food production continues to hover over many areas of the globe.

Within recent years the annual contributions of the United States to military and nonmilitary assistance programs has fallen to hover near the two-billion-dollar mark. There they are likely to remain unless new programs or emergencies develop. Foreign aid has a difficult time when Congress is in a budget-cutting mood, and particularly when segments of the American population are cited as needing massive economic help.

The matter of foreign trade continues to be a problem area for the United States. Chief difficulties are the balance of payments situation and the related matter of gold outflow. Over the years Americans have spent, loaned, or given away more money than they have earned in foreign trade or through the visits of foreign tourists. Since dollars in overseas markets can be redeemed in gold, which shrinks the supply of that metal possessed by the United States, America has had to face the recurrent problem of "raids" on its gold supply. The matter of gold outflow became particularly critical in the "gold crises" of

Balance of payments and gold crises

473

1968, when speculation pushed up the price of gold, dollars were redeemed in gold, American stocks of gold fell, and the value of the dollar became less certain. To meet the crisis, most major Western nations decided to move toward a "paper gold" system. This involves the creation of fiscal units which are substituted for gold, dollars, or pounds sterling in the international money markets.[74] Whether or not the modification in the non-Communist world's international monetary system will require still further moves to establish a more stable and permanent fiscal situation remains to be seen.[75] As the gold problem furrows brows in Washington, the balance of payments difficulty causes anxiety also. Alternative solutions proposed include: limiting American dollars which flow overseas in a number of ways, reducing inflationary pressures which force up the price of American goods in foreign markets, thus causing them to be undersold by foreign products, and increasing American productivity while keeping costs down so as to provide cheaper American goods.

Tariff problems Another aspect of the overall trade problem is the argument about tariffs. As described in Chapter 9, the United States sharply reversed its high-tariff policies in the 1930's. Since World War II the United States has continued its tariff reduction policies by becoming a member of the General Agreement on Tariffs and Trade. This international organization is dedicated to the proposition that international trade can be stimulated by easing trade restrictions. Over the years the United States has participated in extensive reciprocal lowering of tariffs. The most impressive of recent tariff negotiations was the "Kennedy Round" of agreements reached by 53 nations accounting for 80 percent of the world's trade.[76] American participation in these negotiations, finally agreed to in Geneva in 1967, resulted from congressional authorization to the late President (hence the name) to commence wide-ranging negotiations contained in the Trade Expansion Act of 1962. Although the Act provides for Federal assistance to industries hurt by lowered tariffs, some opposition developed against the Kennedy Round agreements. In the last year of his Administration President Johnson issued warnings against the temptation

74. John M. Lee, "9 Nations Vote to Adopt 'Paper Gold' Money Plan: France Refuses to Join," *New York Times*, March 21, 1968.

75. For suggestions regarding international fiscal policy see, C. Fred Bergsten, "Taking the Monetary Initiative," *Foreign Affairs*, 46 (July, 1968), pp. 713–732.

76. "International Trade," *Department of State Foreign Policy Briefs*, XVI (June 2, 1967), pp. 1–2.

to resurrect trade barriers after more than 30 years of American efforts to increase trade by tariff reduction.

Regional Internationalism

Although the world has known eras when people were not banded together in nation-states and when international frontiers had practically no meaning, the idea is difficult for the twentieth-century American to grasp. One of the distinctive characteristics of modern times is "nationalism"—the consciousness that one is closely identified with the people who live on one side of an arbitrary boundary and that one is different from, and therefore probably opposed to, those who live on the other side of it. Acceptance of this idea transformed the world into a system of nation-states whose borders have since been lined with customs officers and soldiers.

The polarization of the world's power since the end of World War II led both super-states to discourage nationalism in other countries. The original Marxist theory insisted that "the working man has no country," and although contemporary Russian nationalism is notorious, the hierarchic control of international Communism has enabled the Soviets to make some headway, at least initially, in reducing the manifestations of nationalism in Eastern Europe. This has been demonstrated vividly when the Soviet Union felt free to use force in crushing nationalist movements in East Germany, Poland, and Hungary in the 1950's, and in Czechoslovakia in 1968. However, the gradual political and economic changes that are taking place in Eastern European countries suggest that basically the Soviet Union has not been able to quench the fires of nationalism within its own bloc.[77]

Eastern Europe

The United States has recognized nationalism as a legitimate expression of emerging countries and has even encouraged the spirit of particularism in some of them.[78] Although doing this is tantamount to using a dangerous drug for the treatment of political immaturity, the assumption apparently is that the

U.S. and nationalism

77. The Russians have tried vainly for years to crush Tito and lead Yugoslavia back into a normal satellite relationship, but they have found nationalism to be stronger than Communism in that country. The United States has attempted to exploit this rift through special aid programs to Yugoslavia.

78. The United States has also reacted in a similar fashion to certain of the Communist states. For example, by using trade policy to help wean away Eastern European states from Soviet domination the United States has hoped to help reestablish greater independence among the satellite states together with an increased sense of nationalism.

heady potion immunizes against Communism in general, and Soviet and Chinese imperialism in particular, while it stimulates and improves the co-ordination of young nations. There is no sure antidote for the side-effects, however, and the people of the United States have often been dismayed when their patient promptly adopted parochial attitudes and practices which are detrimental to other countries and impede international cooperation.

In established nations the United States actively combats nationalism and fosters internationalism. American leaders are **U.S. and** not prepared to begin a crusade for world union, but they do **European Union** pursue a vigorous policy of encouraging regional internationalism. The United States has long favored closer economic and political ties among the countries of Europe with the hope of the establishment of a "European Union." The Marshall Plan encouraged such a partnership by requiring unified planning. The success of such cooperative ventures as the European Common Market, the Iron and Coal Community, and Euratom, which involved West Germany, France, Italy, the Netherlands, Belgium, and Luxembourg, constitutes a fitting tribute to the American encouragement of economic integration. The Alliance for Progress was designed to have a similar effect in Latin America, for the creation of tariff-free common markets is basic to the success of the program. American Presidents have consistently held up the fledgling Central-American Common Market as an example all other Latin-American states should emulate. Then, in April, 1967, President Johnson made a dramatic flight to Uruguay to meet with other hemispheric chiefs of state at Punta del Este, where the necessity for the prompt and positive creation of a truly effective Latin-American Common Market was laid squarely on table—and accepted by most of those present. Such steps have been taken with the recognition that there are potential dangers in the formation of large industrial complexes unrestricted by national boundaries. There is no ironclad guarantee that a United Europe or a Latin American Common Market would not pose economic and/or military threats to the United States in the future. Evidently the policy-makers assume that the cultural and historical bonds which bind the Western nations together will more likely bring about an eventual gigantic community of them all rather than that economic regionalism will set one group against the other. In fact, when Great Britain indicated her interest in joining the European Common Market in 1961, several highly placed Americans suggested that the United

States also begin thinking about membership, and the President proposed legislation to Congress which would enable this country to compete favorably with Common Market members, and President Kennedy also talked of a "declaration of interdependence" which he suggested be discussed between a "United Europe" and the United States.[79] A Frenchman has recently identified a phenomenon which may operate to disrupt the harmony which characterized so much of the relationship between Western Europe and the United States during the first decades following World War II. The problem as discussed by J. J. Servan-Schreiber is that American economic, industrial, scientific, and business progress is overwhelming Western Europe so that in 10 to 15 years the third largest industrial power in the world, behind the United States and the Soviet Union, may be American-owned industry in Europe. This circumstance, according to Servan-Schreiber, helps to explain European distrust of the United States and some of the strained relations between the United States and the Continent.[80]

Europe vis-à-vis U.S. strength

While many Americans favor internationalism for other countries, well-organized and highly vocal groups are steadfastly opposed to further surrender of the sovereignty of their own nation. The same forces reluctantly accepted membership in the United Nations because the project was energetically pushed by internationally oriented Presidents before World War II had ended and because the war was still attributed in some quarters to the refusal of the United States to join the League of Nations in 1920. They agreed to collective security treaties because of the apparent threat of Communist imperialism. They were forced to assent to the principle of foreign aid in peacetime because of the impact of the fall of Czechoslovakia, and they grudgingly adopted the "Truman Doctrine" of containment because a tenacious President insisted that the alternative was the disappearance of the Middle East behind the Iron Curtain. The extent to which the American public will further commit their own country, even to regional internationalism, will depend upon how seriously they view external threats, how much they value the benefits of economic cooperation, and the vigor with which their leaders champion the policy.

Isolationism again

79. The reference to interdependence was made in a speech delivered on the Fourth of July, 1962, in Independence Square, Philadelphia.

80. This thesis is set forth in *The American Challenge* (New York: Atheneum, 1968).

477

Military Strength and Foreign Policy

No matter how angrily Americans may debate the strategy fashioned by their policy-makers at home for their diplomats to pursue abroad, most agree that under present world conditions foreign policy must be backstopped by military force. A few may sincerely believe in the efficacy of moral power without force, but citizens of the United States, now as in 1788, find the realistic words Madison wrote in Number 41 of *The Federalist* more persuasive: "If one nation maintains constantly a disciplined army, ready for service of ambition or revenge, it obliges the most pacific nations who may be within the reach of its enterprises to take corresponding precautions." The development of intercontinental ballistic missiles by two nations which also have thermonuclear capabilities is a sufficient cause of anxiety anywhere in the world. But when those powers have repeatedly insisted that their systems would engulf the globe and "bury" rivals, the need for taking precautions by the leader of those scheduled for subjugation is beyond argument for most Americans.[81]

Negotiating from strength   If military strength were to lend credibility to the new American foreign policy, it would require an abrupt change of direction. When collective security agreements were undertaken and the doctrine of containment was accepted, it became obvious that the traditional attitude of maintaining only token military forces had to be changed. The fantastic gains of military technology had forever nullified the margin of time America had been able to rely upon in order to tool up for war production. During World War II it was patent that the military forces would have been more effective had they been better co-ordinated, while before the end of the war the interaction of foreign and military policies was plainly evident. Still, the pulling and hauling which accompany a democratic system of government, the conviction of elected representatives that the people were basically opposed to compulsory military service and to the diversion of manpower and money to military preparedness, and rivalry among the armed forces, all resulted in greater hesitation and uncertainty over changing military policy than had been exhibited in foreign policy. However, the

81. Some years ago several prominent individuals expressed doubt that the United States would find as much security in armaments as the government contended would be the case. See Albert Einstein and Bertrand Russell, "Scientists Appeal for the Abolition of War," *Bulletin of the Atomic Scientists*, XI (September, 1955), pp. 236–237; and Albert Schweitzer, "An Obligation to Tomorrow," *Saturday Review*, XLI (May, 1958), pp. 21–28.

nation did develop an impressive military capability. The national security strategies which annually take the largest portion of the Federal budget, and which if poorly conceived or badly practiced could cost the nation its existence, are the subject of the next chapter.

SUMMARY

- Little in America's history prepared the nation for the dramatic role it would play in international affairs in the twentieth century. The office charged by the Constitution with the responsibility for foreign affairs, the Presidency, has been enlarged by its occupants to the point where the Commander-in-Chief has full legal powers to devise and implement foreign policy. This development has been supported by the rulings of the Supreme Court.

- America has progressed far from the age when it had only three basic guiding principles in foreign policy: *Isolationism*, which meant keeping aloof from Europe's quarrels; *Freedom of the Seas*, which supported a commercial nation's right to sail its ships unmolested on the oceans in pursuit of trade; and the *Monroe Doctrine*, which was directed at preventing European powers from reestablishing their power in the Western Hemisphere.

- Originally the President, as Chief of Foreign Policy, had to operate under a number of checks and balances. Today many institutional checks and balances have been eroded by strong Presidents operating in grave times. Recently, however, the Senate has begun to reassert itself regarding powers to involve the nation in war.

- In the late stages of World War II, and thereafter, America's wartime ally, the Soviet Union, engaged in a number of acts perceived by the United States as potentially dangerous to it and to the peace of the world. In response America shouldered the responsibility for defending much of the world against Communist aggression. The Truman Doctrine, the Marshall Plan, the Berlin Blockade, NATO the Point Four Program, and the Korean conflict became landmarks in President Truman's new policy of containment.

- President Eisenhower and his Secretary of State, John Foster Dulles, sought to contain Communism by reliance upon strategic nuclear weapons and the policy of Massive Retaliation. The American threat to retaliate upon the homelands of the Soviet Union and China should Communist aggression occur in Asia, Africa, or Latin America was short-lived, mainly because the Soviets developed their own awesome nuclear weapons. Eisenhower then, like Truman before him, resorted to containing Communism by placing American troops in the path of possible Communist expansion.

• President Kennedy, finding the United States unprepared to counter small-scale Communist aggression, built up anti-guerrilla and conventional forces, along with strategic nuclear units, to be used if necessary in a "flexible response." He began using the former to oppose Communism in South Vietnam. Kennedy also blocked a new Soviet threat to Berlin, and in the high point of his foreign policy confrontations with the Soviets he forced the withdrawal of Soviet missiles from Cuba. Kennedy initiated the Alliance for Progress, a foreign aid plan for Latin America based upon humanitarian concerns and the hopes of preventing the spread of Communism by increasing the living standards of millions. Kennedy's efforts to reduce international tensions included the hot-line link with Moscow, the wheat sale to Russia, the exchange of weather information gathered by satellite, and the signing of the partial nuclear test ban treaty with the Soviets.

• President Johnson vigorously prosecuted the growing war in Vietnam. He sent U.S. troops in a controversial move to the Dominican Republic to forestall a feared Communist revolution. He also sought to reduce tension in the Cold War by initiation of joint consulate service with the Soviets and commercial airline flights between the two super-powers. His Administration agreed with the Soviets to refrain from putting weapons of mass destruction into orbit and from making territorial claims upon outer space. Johnson supported a treaty proposed jointly by the Soviet Union and Great Britain to prohibit the further proliferation of nuclear weapons, and he reached agreement upon the necessity for the Soviet Union and the United States to begin talks aimed at curtailing the missile race. Near the end of his Presidency, and under heavy public pressure, Johnson entered into peace talks with the North Vietnamese.

• As the Nixon Administration entered its first year in office serious questions were being asked concerning the containment policy. These involved the nature of the Communist threat, the utility of containing all Communist movements, how to avoid another "Vietnam," and the danger of the arms race.

• The United States has supported and participated in the efforts of international organizations to reduce global tensions. The main forum for international cooperation is the United

Nations and its associated specialized agencies. It is generally felt in the United States that to the extent the United Nations is successful, chaotic conditions in which Communism breeds best will be lessened. However, because of weaknesses in the organization, and the problems facing the United Nations, the United States does not rely heavily upon it for its own security.

• The United States has underwritten foreign aid both to make Communism less appealing and to spur efforts at modernization programs in less-developed nations. A particular aspect of foreign aid is military assistance to nations willing to oppose Communism. Within the last few years the size of American foreign aid has fallen dramatically.

• The United States has encountered difficulties regarding foreign trade because of an adverse balance-of-payments situation and the outflow of gold. The policy of gradually reducing tariffs in a move to stimulate foreign trade has not been popular with all Americans.

• The United States has generally supported plans for regional internationalism. High on the list of such arrangements it favors are the European Common Market and recent ventures in cooperation by the Latin-American states.

• Regardless of which turn its foreign policy takes the United States supports its participation in international politics with an impressive array of military strength. Madison's admonition that the presence of potentially dangerous armed might in the world obliges peaceful nations to arm themselves as a precaution is still heeded.

SUGGESTED READING

*(Books so designated are available in paperbound editions.)

* Almond, Gabriel A., The American People and Foreign Policy (New York: Praeger, 1960).

* Bloomfield, Lincoln P., The United Nations and U.S. Foreign Policy, rev. ed. (Boston: Little, Brown, 1967).

* Churchill, Winston S., The Second World War, 6 vols. (Boston: Houghton Mifflin, 1948).

* Clark, Grenville and Louis B. Sohn, World Peace Through World Law, rev. ed. (Cambridge: Harvard University Press, 1962).

Eisenhower, Dwight D., Waging Peace, 1956–1961, Vol. 2 of The White House Years (Garden City: Doubleday, 1965).

Fleming, D. F., The Cold War and Its Origins, 2 vols. (Garden City: Doubleday, 1961).

481

* Fulbright, J. William, *The Arrogance of Power* (New York: Random House, 1966).

* Goldwin, Robert A., ed., *Why Foreign Aid?* (New York: Rand McNally, 1963).

Halle, Louis J., *The Cold War as History* (New York: Harper & Row, 1967).

* Houghton, Neal, ed., *Struggle Against History* (New York: Simon and Schuster, 1968).

* Kissinger, Henry A., *American Foreign Policy: Three Essays* (New York: Norton, 1969).

* Lippmann, Walter, *The Public Philosophy* (New York: Mentor Books, 1956).

* Mao Tse-tung, *On the Protracted War* (Peiping: Foreign Language Press, 1960).

Morgenthau, Hans J., *Politics Among Nations*, 4th ed. (New York: Knopf, 1966).

* Price, Don K., ed., *The Secretary of State* (Englewood Cliffs: Prentice-Hall, 1960).

* Raskin, Marcus G. and Bernard B. Fall, eds., *Viet-Nam Reader* (New York: Vintage, 1965).

* Rosenau, James N., *Public Opinion and Foreign Policy* (New York: Random House, 1961).

* Rostow, W. W., *The Stages of Economic Growth* (London: Cambridge University Press, 1965).

Strausz-Hupé, Robert, William R. Kintner, Stefan T. Possony, *et al.*, *A Forward Strategy for America* (New York: Harper & Brothers, 1961).

Taylor, Maxwell, *The Uncertain Trumpet* (New York: Harper and Brothers, 1959).

* Truman, Harry S., *Memoirs by Harry S. Truman*, 2 vols. (Garden City: Doubleday, 1955).

11

National
Security

The old adage "war is too important to leave to the generals" came of age for Americans in the past two decades as their nation searched for security in the nuclear era. Perhaps no single development in American history is so foreign to *The Federalist Papers*, the Constitution, and indeed much of the American tradition as the continued maintenance of the most powerful military force in the world's history. But it is essential to study the defense establishment responsible for military strategy and associated technology in order to understand American government today.

Organizing for Defense

The principal achievement in military legislation since World War II was the passage of the National Security Act of 1947. In this law Congress created a new Department of the Air Force and then combined it with the existing Departments of Army and Navy under the control of a civilian Secretary of Defense. At the same time, the Secretaries of Defense and State were linked with the Director of the Office of Civil and Defense Mobilization (since changed to the Office of Emergency Planning), the Vice President, and the President into a National Security Council.[1] This executive-branch committee was then charged with planning responses to immediate threats to security and working out long-range policies for the nation to follow. Finally, the act subordinated several intelligence bodies to one Central Intelligence Agency.

The National
Security Act of 1947

1. The President may include other persons as he wishes. The Secretary of the Treasury, director of the Bureau of the Budget, director of the Central Intelligence Agency, and the chairman of the Joint Chiefs of Staff frequently attend.

Although most observers consider the National Security Act a great stride forward in the management of the defense **Defense: strategic** establishment, some think the stride was not great enough. It **and tactical** has been pointed out that instead of two rival services in competition for funds and prestige there now are three. Some students of military policy continue to urge the creation of a single, completely integrated service; others favor a functional division of the existing Army, Navy, and Air Force between a strategic force (which would be prepared to fight an all-out war) and a tactical force (which would be trained for localized conflicts).

THE DEPARTMENT OF DEFENSE, THE NSC, AND THE CIA

At the present time, the gigantic Department of Defense is headed by a civilian Secretary of Defense and, subordinate to **The Joint** him, the Secretaries of the Departments of Army, Navy and Air **Chiefs of Staff** Force. These civilians meet with senior military men to formulate in the Armed Forces Policy Council.[2] The Secretary of Defense receives advice on military strategy from the Joint Chiefs of Staff (JCS).[3] His top-level administrative staff is currently comprised of a Deputy Secretary of Defense, the director of Defense Research and Engineering and seven Assistant Secretaries (Administration, Comptroller, Installations and Logistics, International Security Affairs, Manpower, Public Affairs, and Systems Analysis). The control of the Secretary of Defense over his military subordinates is partially reduced by the arrangement that any member of the Joint Chiefs may make recommendations directly to Congress, provided that he first notifies the Secretary of his intention. The fact that the Chairman of the Joint Chiefs often represents his colleagues at the meetings of the National Security Council also lessens the Secretary's influence to some extent.

An independent study made for the Senate Foreign Relations Committee in 1959 found the National Security Council "greatly overrated as an instrument of strategic decision-making

2. This 10-member council consists of the Deputy Secretary of Defense, the Secretaries of the Army, Navy, and Air Force, the director of Defense Research and Engineering, and the Joint Chiefs. The Secretary of Defense is chairman. The Commandant of the Marine Corps regularly attends the meetings.

3. The chairman of the JCS is selected by the President from the active list, and the nominee must receive Senate confirmation. The Chiefs of Staff of the Army and Air Force and the Chief of Naval Operations constitute the group. When Marine Corps matters are discussed, the Commandant of the Marine Corps joins the JCS.

but [it] constitutes a useful forum for frequent high-level discussion of foreign policy issues."[4] Constitutional and political factors appear designed to keep it that way.[5] Under the Constitution, the President must make the final decisions, and no committee can aspire to any position other than advisory. Amendment XXII limits any Administration to ten years—hardly time for long-range planning—and the vagaries of politics can reduce even this brief tenure. All the members of the NSC are there because of their appointment to key positions in the executive branch. But administrative and policy-making chores in their own departments leave these officers very little time to devote to the determination of strategic goals. The addition of several full-time civilians to the National Security Council has been suggested, with the hope that they could provide continuity to policy and aid the development of long-range strategy.

National Security Council

The third creation of the National Defense Act, the Central Intelligence Agency, has been a special target for criticism, to some extent because Americans have had a traditional aversion of espionage. Some of the critics are more inclined to trust information gathered by military attachés in American embassies than the intelligence data uncovered by CIA agents. Others fret over the potential threat of a powerful organization which is not directly answerable to the American people. Even watchdog committees established by Presidents Kennedy and Johnson to maintain a check on CIA activities have not stilled all the criticism of the agency. The CIA has been ridiculed for its reputed failures, most notably in the Bay of Pigs invasion; its successes, for the most part, must remain secret.[6]

The CIA

4. Maxwell Graduate School of Citizenship and Public Affairs of Syracuse University, *The Operational Aspects of the United States Foreign Policy*, 86th Congress, 1st Session, Committee Print No. 6 (Nov. 11, 1959), p. 63.

5. A former Chairman of the Joint Chiefs of Staff, General Maxwell Taylor, has written of the National Security Council that by the end of the Eisenhower Administration it "had developed a reputation for being nothing more than an overgrown committee, long on paperwork but short on decisive action." *Responsibility and Response*, p. 62. Taylor further noted that more recently the NSC has tended to be replaced by *ad hoc* task forces, such as the one which served President Kennedy in the Cuban missile crisis, or by informal staffs assembled by presidential assistants. See for a detailed examination of the NSC by a number of experts, Senator Henry M. Jackson, ed., *The National Security Council* (New York: Praeger, 1965).

6. The late Allen W. Dulles, a former CIA director, described the work of the intelligence community in *The Craft of Intelligence* (New York: Harper and Row, 1963).

485

Nuclear Weapons

Although intelligence gathering and evaluation is a necessary part of the nation's defense activity, American national security rests primarily on an immense stockpile of nuclear weapons. The development of these awesome weapons began during World War II with the Manhattan Project, a program of the utmost secrecy in which prominent scientists joined with military men in creating and testing a bomb with destructive effects many times greater than any weapon known before.[7]

Atomic bombs The "primitive" nuclear weapons which ended World War II when used by the United States against two Japanese cities were called "atomic bombs."[8] Their explosive power, equal to 20,000 tons of TNT, was produced by the fission (breaking apart) of certain isotopes of uranium or plutonium. Only one atomic bomb was dropped on Hiroshima and Nagasaki, but they left an estimated 110,000 people dead amid awesome destruction due primarily to blast and heat.[9] Within recent years rather small atomic bombs or shells for artillery pieces have been perfected, as have nuclear charges for mines. Because of their reduced size and minimized radioactivity these *tactical nuclear weapons* can be used in relatively close proximity to one's troops without harm to them.[10]

The H-bomb A second type of nuclear weapon is the "hydrogen" or "thermonuclear" bomb. Its explosive force is produced by the fusion (coming together) of the nuclei of hydrogen isotopes

---

7. A considerable amount of material regarding nuclear weapons is available in nonclassified literature. For example, see Samuel Glasstone, ed., *The Effects of Nuclear Weapons* (Washington: Atomic Energy Commission, 1957); Ralph Lapp, *Kill and Overkill* (New York: Basic Books, 1962) and *The Weapons Culture* (New York: Norton, 1968); and Arnold Kramish, "The Great Chinese Bomb Puzzle and a Solution," *Fortune* LXXIII (June 1966), pp. 157–158ff.

8. An account of the decision to use the atomic bombs against Japan is Herbert Feis, *The Atomic Bomb and the End of World War II*, rev. ed. (Princeton: Princeton University Press, 1966).

9. *The Effects of Atomic Bombs on Hiroshima and Nagasaki* (Washington: The United States Strategic Bombing Survey, 1946), p. 15. The "dirtiness," or degree of radioactivity of atomic bombs, can be increased by exploding the weapons so that the maximum amount of earth, water, or debris are made radioactive.

10. In 1957 Henry Kissinger argued that the use of tactical nuclear weapons could give to the United States a more flexible means of containing Communism than reliance upon the larger nuclear weapons designed for "city-busting." He noted that the tactical nuclear weapons would assist in battlefield situations to redress the unfavorable manpower balance attributed to Communist China and the Soviet Union vis-à-vis the United States. For an elaboration of such views see *Nuclear Weapons and Foreign Policy* (New York: Harper, 1957).

known as deuterium and tritium. The next development was to fabricate devices which employ both the fission and fusion processes, thus increasing the explosive yield dramatically.[11] Apart from the immense increase in blast and heat released by such weapons, thermonuclear bombs differ from the smaller atomic bombs in terms of the radioactivity they produce. The enormous destructive capacity of hydrogen weapons is suggested by the following quotation from a government publication,

> . . . a nuclear explosion occurring at or near the earth's surface can result in severe contamination by the radioactive fallout. In the case of the powerful thermonuclear device tested at Bikini Atoll on March 1, 1954, which was detonated close to the surface of a coral island, the ensuing fallout caused substantial contamination over an area of over 7,000 square miles.[12]

A particular type of thermonuclear weapon is the so-called "clean H-bomb." These are special weapons in which care has been taken to reduce the amount of radioactivity released by the explosion.[13]

The number of nuclear weapons possessed by the United States is a well guarded secret. Nevertheless it is known that the size of the nuclear stockpile is such that should it be used great areas of the globe would be laid waste, and some sections would remain uninhabitable for substantial periods of time. The destruction of civilization would virtually be certain if the two great superpowers—the U.S.A. and the U.S.S.R.—were to engage in a duel with nuclear weapons. It is therefore the policy of the government to prevent any international crisis developing to the point where the stockpiles would actually be used.

The nuclear stockpile

The Evolution of Military Doctrine and Weapons Systems

The major weapons systems deployed by the United States, and the theories for their use—both of which have supported

11. Ralph Lapp, a nuclear physicist, has written that an early American hydrogen weapon test was rated between 15 and 16 megatons. See *Atoms and People* (New York: Harper & Brothers, 1956), p. 122. The Soviets have claimed to have tested weapons exceeding 50 megatons. Instead of developing such large weapons, the United States has elected to destroy enemy nations, if that becomes necessary, with a greater number of "smaller" hydrogen weapons.

12. Glasstone, *op. cit.*, p. 27.

13. For a discussion of such weapons see Eugene Rabinowitch, "H-Bombs Without Fallout," *Bulletin of the Atomic Scientists*, XII (September 1956), pp. 234, 264.

American foreign policy objectives—have frequently been the subject of clashes and changes since the onset of the Cold War period.

During the Truman Administration the United States undertook a military buildup to support its new international responsibilities as the confrontation with the Communist nations became the focus of foreign policy. Truman ordered increased activity in the nuclear weapons program after the Soviets detonated their first atomic bomb in August, 1949, and the program led to the world's first hydrogen explosion in 1952. In order to make possible the delivery of atomic and hydrogen bombs upon a potential enemy, the Truman Administration ordered a postwar bomber, the intercontinental range B-36, to be produced, and work began on the first pure jet medium-range bomber, the B-47. Both conventional and nuclear armament took a sharp turn upward when South Korea was invaded by North Korea in June, 1950.

In support of policy

The Eisenhower Administration, reflecting the Republican desire for balanced budgets, took a "new look" at military policy and defense expenditures. It decided that the twin goals of containing Communism and achieving budget economies could be achieved by threatening Massive Retaliation directly upon Communist homelands, instead of continuing the more expensive tactic of stationing large numbers of troops prepared to fight at points where Communist thrusts might occur. The rapid development of Soviet nuclear power (the first Soviet hydrogen bomb was detonated in 1953, a year after the initial American thermonuclear success) forced a "second look" at the policy which anticipated bombing the Soviet Union in response to Communist aggression not directly involving the United States.[14] The harsh facts of *Realpolitik* in the nuclear age cautioned against attacking a nation which could counterattack with thermonuclear weapons. Thus there was born a mutual deterrent relationship between the United States and the Soviet Union which permits a considerable amount of localized violence to occur without great risk of thermonuclear war. With

Eisenhower policy

14. In 1959 General Maxwell Taylor wrote in *The Uncertain Trumpet* that the threat of a nuclear strike upon the Soviet homeland in retaliation for many kinds of Communist aggression was not credible, and hence such a threat would not deter such aggression. It was his view, soon to be shared by the new Kennedy Administration, that an American nuclear attack upon the Soviet Union was much more credible only in the event of a Soviet attack on the United States, or of indisputable evidence that such an attack was about to occur. Taylor noted what many Europeans would come to believe later: that the United States threat to attack the Soviet Union in response to a Soviet strike on Western Europe was not entirely credible.

the two super-powers unwilling to bring their immense destructive potential into use out of mutual fear of national disaster, guerrilla wars can and do flourish.

Toward the end of President Eisenhower's second term American non-nuclear forces were increased. The initial efforts were considered insufficient by President Kennedy who ordered a much larger increase in non-nuclear forces, particularly those designed to combat Communist insurgency. President Johnson further enlarged non-nuclear strength as the Vietnam war widened in scope. The result, particularly during the 1960's, has been intensive efforts to react to the guerrilla war fighter—that hardy individual who appears as a ragged peasant in the daytime, but who becomes a proficient soldier at night. The countermeasures include the training of Green Beret units, formation of "air-mobile" Army divisions, development of "vertical envelopment" tactics by helicopter-borne forces, and a host of other military techniques. Along with the purely military response to Communist guerrilla activity the United States has invested in political counterinsurgency measures. These techniques, designed to "win the hearts and minds" of the peasants, are attributable to the acceptance of the Mao Tse-tung dictum that guerrilla fighters have the same relationship to the peasant population in the non-Western world as fish have to water. That is, the guerrilla must receive from the peasants nourishment, intelligence information, recruits, first aid, and assistance in hiding if he is to operate effectively against an opposing army. American efforts to turn peasants against Communist guerrillas in their midst revolve about various assistance programs and attempts to assure that local government is responsive to the grievances of the peasants. These efforts have been sorely tested in South Vietnam, where many observers maintain that the United States has failed to wage effectively the "other war" of pacification.

THE BOMBER VS. MISSILE ARGUMENT

In the fall of 1957 the Soviet Union fired a missile which lifted the world's first earth satellite into orbit. Among other things the launching of Sputnik I meant that the Soviets were technically capable of firing a nuclear bomb, in the form of a missile warhead, at the United States. Such a quantum jump in military power, which could be used to support an aggressive foreign policy, caused reverberations which continue to perplex Americans. The American response to the Soviet feat, first by the Eisenhower Administration and then by following

489

Administrations, was to step up the effort to develop intercontinental ballistic missiles (ICBM's) tipped with nuclear warheads.[15]

Emphasis on missiles

The advent of ICBM's, however, caused a lively debate between advocates of the new weapons system and those who defended the utility of the jet bomber fleets then comprised of B-47's, B-58's, and particularly the B-52's. For seven years the debate was largely dominated by Robert McNamara, the strong-willed Secretary of Defense for Kennedy and Johnson. Over the determined objections of many in the Air Force, and others, McNamara began to emphasize missiles (ICBM's located in the United States and Intermediate Range Ballistic Missiles, IRBM's, carried aboard nuclear-powered submarines) rather than bombers as America's major nuclear retaliatory force. McNamara was willing to sacrifice the greater bomb-carrying capacity of the bombers for the smaller warhead capacity of the missiles in order to obtain the increased certainty he believed the latter offered of reaching their targets. In addition McNamara contended that missiles, unlike bombers stationed on runways, could be made relatively invulnerable to surprise attack by placing them deep into concrete silos about the United States, or aboard submarines hidden in the ocean depths. Such dispersal brought two additional peace factors according to McNamara's logic: First, an enemy would be less tempted to make a sneak attack designed to destroy America's retaliatory power; second, with its nuclear strike-back power safe from a Pearl Harbor type of attack, the United States could afford to be less hasty in responding to deteriorating political situations, false alarms, and accidents than if its nuclear forces were vulnerable to sudden attack.[16]

15. During the Kennedy-Nixon campaign of 1960 the Democrats spoke of a "missile gap" which was unfavorable to the United States and laid the blame on the Republicans. The Republicans denied the charges. As it turned out, the United States was not behind the Soviets in ICBM deployment. The matter probably arose from various and differing intelligence sources, changes in Soviet missile programs, and partisan politics in an election year. In the 1968 campaign Nixon charged that the Democrats had failed to maintain strategic superiority vis-à-vis the Soviet Union.

16. An important study of major weapons systems and the subject of vulnerability to surprise attack is Albert Wohlstetter, "The Delicate Balance of Terror," *Foreign Affairs*, 37 (January, 1959), pp. 211–234. Anticipating the future, a Princeton economist wrote in 1959 that it would be well for both the Soviets and the Americans to develop mutually invulnerable strategic nuclear forces which would have the effect of stabilizing the relationship between the two super-powers. He noted that if the Soviet Union and the United States were mutually deterred from using their strategic forces against each other they might nevertheless clash in less violent form. Oskar Morgenstern, *The Question of National Defense* (New York: Random House, 1959).

The "bomber Generals" and their supporters in Congress responded to the McNamara argument by stressing that aircraft could be modified or developed which could penetrate the air defenses of an enemy state; that bombers can carry more "mega-tonnage" than missiles; and that bombers can be kept on constant "air-borne alert." McNamara's critics made their strongest appeal for a "mix" of bombers and missiles in its strategic nuclear arsenal, maintaining that if the United States relied upon only one long-range nuclear delivery system an enemy would concentrate his defensive abilities upon that one system and thus enhance his chances of successfully defending against it. Conversely, a mixture of bombers and various-type missiles would oblige an enemy to spread his resources among several types of defense systems, thus increasing his costs and difficulties.[17]

A "mix" of missiles and bombers

Because of the long lead times involved in developing, testing, and deploying major strategic nuclear weapons systems, America's strategic arsenal will bear the stamp of the McNamara philosophy into the early 1970's, despite the fact he departed from the Pentagon in 1968. This means that missiles will increase in importance as the big bombers, emphasized in the 1950's and early 1960's, gradually continue to be phased out of inventory.

THE MISSILE VS. MISSILE ARGUMENT

Initially, the prospect of an ICBM warhead hurtling through space at many times the speed of sound appeared to be the proverbial absolute weapon that might result in a kind of power balance among the world's most powerful nations and end the strategic arms race. However, once the ICBM appeared, American and Soviet scientists and defense planners began looking for a countermeasure that would stop or at least blunt ICBM attacks. What they claim to have developed is the much discussed and highly controversial Anti-Ballistic Missile (ABM). The anti-missile concept assumes that ICBM warheads may be intercepted somewhere in their trajectory and either significantly damaged or destroyed by other missiles. The destruction technique generally relied upon in ABM systems is a nuclear explosion.[18] Proponents of ABM point to the advances

17. For contrasting views on the missile vs. bomber argument see Robert S. McNamara, *The Essence of Security* (New York: Harper and Row, 1968) and Curtis E. LeMay, *America Is In Danger* (New York: Funk and Wagnalls, 1968).

18. The case for ABM by two prominent backers may be read in Richard C. Foster, "The Impact of Ballistic Missile Defense on Arms Control

(Continued on next page)

in radar technology which, they claim, make possible the detection and tracking of incoming warheads. They hold that defensive missiles with a very high acceleration rate can be produced which can intercept incoming warheads. To others, most notably the former Secretary of Defense and those who share his views in Washington and among the universities, the task of defending against ICBM's appears extremely difficult in a technical sense, prohibitively costly in an economic sense, and unde-

Le Pelley in The Christian Science Monitor © TCSPS

"Okay, where do you want it?"

Prospects," and Edward Teller, "BMD [Ballistic Missile Defense] in a Strategy for Peace," in James E. Dougherty and J. F. Lehman, Jr., *Arms Control for the Late Sixties* (New York: Van Nostrand, 1967). Critical views of ABM are found in the same volume, Jeremy Stone, "Risks, Costs, and Alternatives," and Joseph I. Coffey, "BMD Options: A Critical Appraisal—Arms Control and Ballistic Missile Defenses."

sirable in a political sense.[19] As regards technology, it is contended that any ABM defense can be overwhelmed, or saturated, by sending many more dummy warheads and decoy devices against the defending system than that system can accommodate. Since dummy warheads and decoys are cheaper to build than real anti-missile missiles, the argument against ABM holds that defense against a serious large-scale ICBM attack would entail enormous financial strain. The political danger suggested as being associated with ABM is that its deployment could provide a basis for both the Soviet Union and the United States to enter into a new arms race, thus increasing distrust and tension between the two giants.

Mr. McNamara's logic largely prevailed in 1967 and 1968 and the United States decided to refrain, at least for a time, from deploying a "thick" ABM defense. Instead a "thin," *i.e.*, light, ABM system will be constructed which can be expanded into a much larger operation if the decision is later made to do so. The ABM system approved was described officially as being "Chinese-oriented," *i.e.*, expected to be able to cope only with the unsophisticated and small missile capability that the Chinese are expected to achieve by the early 1970's.[20]

Although published reports differed somewhat, it appeared that the Soviets in the late 1960's were also experimenting with an ABM system, and had in fact installed portions of such a system. The major American response was to provide its offensive missiles with new devices for penetrating the Soviet defenses. The 1968 Soviet response to America's standing offer

Missile systems in U.S.S.R.

19. The complexities of whether or not to deploy a significant ABM system is an excellent illustration of the interface which now exists between science and technology on the one hand, and politics and fiscal policy on the other, in a number of situations affecting national security and the nation's foreign policy. The Chief Scientific Adviser to the British Government, Sir Solly Zuckerman, has addressed the subject in *Scientists and War* (New York: Harper and Row, 1966).

20. In announcing the decision to build the "light" ABM system, Secretary McNamara clearly stated his reservations about the ABM. "Were we to deploy a heavy ABM system throughout the United States, the Soviets would clearly be strongly motivated to so increase their offensive capability as to cancel out our defensive advantage. It is futile for each of us to spend $4 billion, $40 billion, or $400 billion—and at the end of all the spending, and at the end of all the development, and at the end of all the effort, to be relatively at the same point of balance on the security scale that we are now." Address by Honorable Robert S. McNamara, Secretary of Defense, before United Press International Editors and Publishers, San Francisco, California, September 18, 1967, pp. 16–17. Some wondered if the "Chinese-oriented" ABM wasn't more of a "Republican-oriented" ABM, to protect the Democrats from charges of an ABM gap in the 1968 Presidential election.

to talk about reducing the numbers of ICBM's and ABM's each superpower has may indicate that Soviet thinking is moving along the line of McNamara's regarding the foolishness of continued arms competition. It is to be hoped that in time the Soviets will agree with the closing remarks made by McNamara in announcing the decision to build an ABM system:

> In the end, the root of man's security does not lie in his weaponry.
> In the end, the root of man's security lies in his mind.
> What the world requires in its 22nd Year of the Atomic Age is not a new race towards armament.
> What the world requires in its 22nd Year of the Atomic Age is a new race towards reasonableness.
> We had better all run that race.

The Action-Reaction Syndrome

The arms competition between the United States and the Soviet Union has often been described as consisting of an action-reaction relationship imposed on top of the basic distrust and antagonism existing between the two super-powers. Thus as one side undertakes a new weapons acquisition action the other is likely to respond by taking a countering action, and additional impetus is given the arms race. Perhaps the best example of the action-reaction phenomenon is found in the response to the ABM deployment by both the United States and the Soviet Union. As Secretary McNamara predicted, both nations appear to be responding to the other's ABM deployment by developing greater offensive capabilities to offset the ABM defenses. In his last budget message before Congress, McNamara stated, in regard to the Soviet potential for nuclear attack upon the United States,

Impetus to the arms race

> . . . an attempt on our part to reduce their "Assured Destruction" capability below what they might consider necessary to deter us would simply cause them to respond with an offsetting increase in their offensive forces. It is precisely this process of action and reaction upon which the arms race feeds, at great cost to both sides and benefit to neither.[21]

It is difficult to disagree with the former Defense Secretary that successive rounds of action and reaction in the arms competi-

21. *The Fiscal Year 1969–73 Defense Program and the 1969 Defense Budget*, p. 63.

tion for strategic nuclear weapons represent a waste of money, and that neither nation can achieve a position which would enable it to destroy its opponent without suffering a mortal counterattack. However, although the Soviet Union and the United States may come to accept this view, the Chinese, with an extremely large population and possibly a different concept of nuclear war, may not. Until the Chinese do agree to the mutual cessation of strategic nuclear weapons acquisitions, the Soviet Union and the United States may be expected to continue the development and deployment of new systems.[22]

Chinese and Russian views

Strategic Weapons Parity: Opportunity or Threat?

During most of the Cold War period the United States has possessed a clear preponderance in terms of strategic nuclear weapons *vis-à-vis* the Soviet Union. This is often cited as a significant reason why American leaders stood their ground in various confrontations with the Soviets, and why the latter always backed away from a collision course which could have led to a nuclear exchange. If current trends continue, however, this advantage may not extend into the 1970's since, by that time, the Soviet Union will likely match, or even surpass in some categories, the strategic forces of the United States. There are two reasons for this situation: First, regardless of what one may think of the merits of Communism, it must be recognized that the Soviet society (and in time, one must assume, the Chinese society) is fully competent to produce the most advanced strategic nuclear weapons systems. Second, the United States has chosen to place limits upon its acquisition of strategic weapons systems. In part the limits result from fiscal decisions regarding the allocation of funds between defense and nondefense expenditures. Limits upon the acquisition of strategic weapons systems have also resulted from decisions to take unilateral steps to slow the action-reaction spiral. In other instances the government refused to procure certain weapons systems (for example, long-range bombers) or the quantity of weapons the military requested, because high civilian officials

Soviet capability

U.S. weapons procurement

22. For a discussion of the possibility that another kind of action-reaction relationship could be established which would lead to the lessening of tension and reduction of the arms competition between the Soviet Union and the United States, see Charles E. Osgood, *Graduated Reciprocation in Tension-Reduction* (Urbana: University of Illinois Institute of Communications Research, 1960). Osgood, who does not overly trust the Soviets, would have the United States take small unilateral disarming or tension-reducing steps which would not endanger the nation even should the Soviets take advantage of the situation.

believed alternative weapons systems possessed better cost-effectiveness characteristics.[23] The result of Soviet efforts and American restraint, for whatever reason, will likely be a matching of American land-based ICBM's by the Soviets, and significant increases in other forms of Soviet armament in comparison to American forces.[24]

Is parity enough? If one believes the Soviets have largely given up their notions of Communizing the world, or that they never had such ideas in the first place; or that the Soviets will be deterred from attacking the United States even though they still harbor dreams of world domination; and that the Soviets will not seek to push beyond strategic weapons parity to superiority—then a condition of parity is not particularly frightening. In fact, some argue that achievement of parity regarding strategic weapons systems could set the stage for genuine arms-control-and-reduction talks between two equals. Other Americans contend the United States has seriously erred in not attempting to maintain a substantial lead over the Soviet Union in the area of strategic nuclear weapons systems. The underlying fears of those expressing this view are captured in the following remarks:

> For a half-century, Soviet leaders have time and again repeated that Communism's ultimate objective is world domination. But many in the Free World simply refuse to believe that the Soviet leaders mean what they say.
>
> In the realm of strategic military weapons, the United States has, in recent years, demonstrated much the same inclination to disbelieve or to discount Soviet achievements and advances. This is particularly so with respect to the new ballistic missile defenses of the Soviet Union and to Soviet boasts of an orbital bomb capability.
>
> Yet the available evidence indicates that the Soviet Union has a goal of strategic superiority designed to *win* a nuclear war rather than merely *deter* one. Once in a war-winning posture, the U.S.S.R. would be ideally situated to practice nuclear blackmail and would not even have to fight a nuclear

23. The cost-effectiveness criterion is discussed below.

24. George W. Ashworth, "Matching Missiles: U.S. Wary of Soviet Gains," *Christian Science Monitor*, June 19, 1968. In addition to increases in strategic missile forces the Soviets have made impressive gains in the size and quality of their navy and their air force. Submarines have been emphasized, and helicopter carriers have been added for the first time. The air force is equipped with various fighter-bombers, helicopters, and transports which could be utilized in a number of situations below the thermonuclear war level. William R. Kintner and Harriet Fast Scott, eds., *The Nuclear Revolution in Soviet Military Affairs* (Norman: University of Oklahoma Press, 1968), is a collection of translated Soviet military writings which suggest the Soviets are attempting to achieve strategic military superiority over the United States.

war. Some strategic analysts assert that this is the ultimate goal of the Soviet Union, and that it depends upon a defense against nuclear retaliation.[25]

Unless the Soviets were to make their plans known, it would be difficult to determine whether a condition of strategic parity would endanger the United States, or lead to the possibility of better relations between the Soviet Union and America.

COST EFFECTIVENESS

Another controversial aspect of American defense policy is the conceptual means often employed to assist decision-makers answer the vital question concerning military appropriations for weapons systems—"How much is enough?" Strong differences of opinion exist on the subject. There are those who believe that each prospective weapons system should be evaluated by the cost-effectiveness method. This process involves computing the probable costs of a given system and calculating its expected effectiveness in various circumstances, in comparison with alternative systems. Supposedly, the weapons system which promises the greatest effectiveness with the least cost is selected. This particular method of evaluating weapons systems was developed by the civilian planners initially brought to the Pentagon in 1961 by Secretary McNamara. It has been charged, most often by military men whose requests for weapons have been turned down after a cost-effectiveness evaluation, that such civilians place too much reliance upon cost-effectiveness as a criterion, and that such procedures place an undesirable premium upon price instead of emphasizing security.[26] Those who argue against cost-effectiveness in military spending insist that whatever expense is required for the security of the nation can be afforded.

Projected Military Forces and Doctrines

For a number of years the United States has relied upon a policy of nuclear retaliation to deter a nuclear attack upon its homeland, and, to a lesser extent, upon Western Europe. This basic policy is supplemented by plans to reduce damage and

Strategic offense

25. *The Changing Strategic Military Balance, U.S.A. vs. U.S.S.R.*, prepared at the request of the Committee on Armed Services, House of Representatives, 90th Congress, First Session (Washington: U.S. Government Printing Office, July, 1967). This document is signed by retired military men, scientists, and professors such as General Bernard A. Schriever, USAF (Ret.), General Paul D. Adams, USA (Ret.), General Curtis E. LeMay, USAF (Ret.), Admiral Felix B. Stump, USN (Ret.), Professor Stefan T. Possony, and the nuclear scientist, Dr. Edward Teller.

26. Benjamin Welles, "Rickover Charges Lag in Submarines," *New York Times*, July 5, 1968.

retaliate abroad should an attack come.[27] The *Strategic Offensive Force* (SOF) is entrusted with the awesome mission of destroying with nuclear weapons the military units and civilian society of any nation attacking the United States. Each missile and bomber in the SOF is capable of inflicting more devastation than that caused by the atomic bombs which were used against Japan. From time to time the missiles are replaced by later models. Both missiles and aircraft are constantly undergoing refinements designed to assist them in penetrating enemy defenses. The assumed ability of the SOF to destroy an enemy even should the United States be hit first is called the "assured destruction" capability in a "second strike" attack.[28] The

Strategic defense *Strategic Defensive Force* (SDF), which has a "damage limitation" assignment should an enemy attack against the United States come, is comprised of aircraft and missiles entrusted with an anti-bomber role and the new ABM. Both types of defensive weapons rely heavily upon various radars to detect and subsequently track incoming enemy bombers and missile warheads. Apart from the defenses against bombers and missiles, the United States is capable of destroying enemy satellites.

Augmenting the "damage limiting" capacities of the SDF is the Civil Defense program. The major effort of CD activity is

Civil Defense to find, mark, and stock with supplies buildings suitable for providing shelter from radioactive fallout which would result from nuclear attacks. Because of the difficulties and costs, little has been done to protect the population from blast, heat, or immediate radiation produced by nuclear weapons. During all of the Cold War period it has been government policy to emphasize the Strategic Offensive Force and assign a much less important role to the Strategic Defensive Force. The reason, which some debate, is that offensive forces appear to be in the ascendancy relative to forces designed to stop or blunt them.

The *General Purpose Forces* are comprised of the Marines,

General Purpose Forces most Army combat units, from special counterguerrilla groups to regular divisions, Navy units exclusive of the missile-

27. In recent years the public has been able to read detailed descriptions of the nation's military policies and the forces created to implement them in the annual appearances of the Defense Secretary before budget hearings of the Congress. Mr. McNamara's "valedictory" statement of 1968 is a particularly useful source of information regarding the philosophy of the man who has served longest as the architect of defense policy.

28. From time to time suggestions have been made that the United States adopt a "first strike" philosophy, *i.e.*, that the United States launch its retaliatory forces against the enemy before an attack is mounted against America. Although few will have the endurance to read it entirely, an excellent discussion of the many aspects of nuclear war is Herman Kahn *On Thermonuclear War* (Princeton: Princeton University Press, 1960).

launching submarines, and Air Force contingents. These forces stand ready to implement the containment policy, from small antiguerrilla operations up through large-scale conventional war to tactical nuclear war.[29] Such forces were heavily involved in the Korean conflict and in the Vietnamese war.

The relationship between having a nuclear weapon and having the capability of delivering it on target has its counterpart in maintaining a first-class fighting force and deploying it rapidly. Thus, logistical capability has become a prime factor in foreign policy decision making. The real and immediate connection between military "hardware" and national action is well illustrated by the old frontier maxim for guaranteeing success: "Git there fustest with the mostest." General Purpose Forces are taken to the scene, and are supplied after arrival, by the *Airlift and Sealift Forces*. The transportation of men and matériel from the United States overseas is called "strategic air-sea-lift," while the movement of troops and supplies about the battle zone is termed "intra-theater" or "assault transportation." Various aircraft of the Air Force and vessels of the Navy and Marine Corps perform the transportation function.[30]

Airlift and Sealift Forces

Various human and mechanical activities are conducted by different organizations to obtain intelligence data. The information they obtain is used to formulate target lists for the Strategic Offensive Force, to assist in the making of contingency plans for the General Purpose Forces, and to provide insights into the capabilities of possible enemy nations. Little can be said of such activities, for they are kept out of unclassified discussion except when an unplanned event occurs, such as the downing of an American photo-reconnaissance plane over the Soviet Union in 1960 and over Cuba in 1962.

Intelligence

The *National Military Command System* and various

29. A number of books have been published which examine the subject of limited war in general and the particular kind of limited war known as tactical nuclear war. See Klaus Knorr, *On the Uses of Military Power in the Nuclear Age* (Princeton: Princeton University Press, 1966); Robert McClintock, *The Meaning of Limited War* (Boston: Houghton Mifflin, 1967); and Bernard Brodie, *Escalation and the Nuclear Option* (Princeton: Princeton University Press, 1966).

30. For example, the C-5A, largest jet transport in the world, can carry 750 troops or the largest Army equipment, such as the 50-ton main battle tank. These giant planes, supported by the fast Navy supply vessels, greatly increase American ability to crush guerrilla insurgencies with overwhelming firepower. On the other hand, some senators suggest the giant planes could be useful in decreasing American forces in Europe because the troops could be flown back in case of deteriorating situations. For a study of the relationship between war logistics and national security see Frederick C. Thayer, Jr., *Air Transport Policy and National Security* (Chapel Hill: The University of North Carolina Press, 1965).

communication networks are designed to provide continuous command and control of America's far-flung military forces in all circumstances, including thermonuclear war. Many support, training, and research and development activities function to facilitate the operation of the forces more directly involved with combat responsibilities.[31] All the military services maintain reserve components which are kept in varying states of readiness against the possibility of their use on active duty during a national emergency.

The National Military Command System

The Use of American Military Power

Whenever the United States has employed, or threatened, military force in its foreign dealings, considerable effort has been made to assure that the use of force be appropriate to the provocation—at least as far as those officials ordering the use of force viewed the matter. That is, the American response has been tailored to meet the specific threats which have been faced, and no more. Such an operational philosophy seems appropriate to a society which traditionally places a high regard upon human life and property. So it was that President Truman rejected the suggestion to send an armed convoy down the *autobahn* to West Berlin during the Berlin Blockade; instead he ordered the less provocative but fully effective airlift. President Eisenhower refused to order the use of nuclear weapons to assist what apparently was a doomed French effort to resist the Communists in French Indochina. President Kennedy brushed aside suggestions to bomb the Soviet missiles in Cuba in favor of a "quarantine" about the island. President Johnson eschewed the option of employing tactical nuclear weapons in the Vietnamese war. Of course, in each of the cited instances, and in others, some Americans have contended that the government employed too much force, while others have insisted that too little was used. This has particularly been true regarding the debate over the degree of force used in the Vietnam war.

Examples of restraint

One may visualize the graduated response possibilities open to the United States and its enemies by considering a conceptual tool called an "escalation ladder" which is frequently

Escalation of force

31. The importance of "RDT&E" (research, development, test, and evaluation) in today's complex and ever-changing military environment is indicated by the office of Director of Defense Research and Engineering, which is directly under the Secretary of Defense, and the two prominent groups reporting to the director: Advanced Research Projects Agency and the Weapons Systems Evaluation Group.

TABLE 11.1   An Escalation Ladder

AFTERMATHS

CIVILIAN
CENTRAL
WARS
{
44. Spasm or Insensate War
43. Some Other Kinds of Controlled General War
42. Civilian Devastation Attack
41. Augmented Disarming Attack
40. Countervalue Salvo
39. Slow-Motion Countercity War

(CITY TARGETING THRESHOLD)

MILITARY
CENTRAL
WARS
{
38. Unmodified Counterforce Attack
37. Counterforce-with-Avoidance Attack
36. Constrained Disarming Attack
35. Constrained Force-Reduction Salvo
34. Slow-Motion Counterforce War
33. Slow-Motion Counter-"Property" War
32. Formal Declaration of "General" War

(CENTRAL WAR THRESHOLD)

EXEMPLARY
CENTRAL
ATTACKS
{
31. Reciprocal Reprisals
30. Complete Evacuation (Approximately 95 per cent)
29. Exemplary Attacks on Population
28. Exemplary Attacks Against Property
27. Exemplary Attack on Military
26. Demonstration Attack on Zone of Interior

(CENTRAL SANCTUARY THRESHOLD)

BIZARRE
CRISES
{
25. Evacuation (Approximately 70 per cent)
24. Unusual, Provocative, and Significant Countermeasures
23. Local Nuclear War—Military
22. Declaration of Limited Nuclear War
21. Local Nuclear War—Exemplary

(NO NUCLEAR USE THRESHOLD)

INTENSE
CRISES
{
20. "Peaceful" World-Wide Embargo or Blockade
19. "Justifiable" Counterforce Attack
18. Spectacular Show or Demonstration of Force
17. Limited Evacuation (Approximately 20 per cent)
16. Nuclear "Ultimatums"
15. Barely Nuclear War
14. Declaration of Limited Conventional War
13. Large Compound Escalation
12. Large Conventional War (or Actions)
11. Super-Ready Status
10. Provocative Breaking Off of Diplomatic Relations

(NUCLEAR WAR IS UNTHINKABLE THRESHOLD)

TRADITIONAL
CRISES
{
9. Dramatic Military Confrontations
8. Harassing Acts of Violence
7. "Legal" Harassment—Retortions
6. Significant Mobilization
5. Show of Force
4. Hardening of Positions—Confrontation of Wills

(DON'T ROCK THE BOAT THRESHOLD)

SUBCRISIS
MANEUVER-
ING
{
3. Solemn and Formal Declarations
2. Political, Economic, and Diplomatic Gestures
1. Ostensible Crisis

DISAGREEMENT—COLD WAR

Source: Herman Kahn, On Escalation: Metaphors and Scenarios (New
   York: Praeger, 1965), p. 39.

501

employed by the strategist Herman Kahn.[32] The "escalation ladder" contains a number of "rungs" or options for force utilization—or threats of it—which antagonistic nations may employ as they maneuver in a confrontation.[33] As each party to a potential or actual conflict moves up the range of options, the risks and costs to it and the opponent increase, and presumably so do the pressures to resolve the conflict by peaceful means. Actually, the practice of escalating costs and risks to an opponent is not new in international affairs—diplomacy has dealt in threats made, risks taken, and costs paid to achieve some foreign policy goal for centuries. Kahn's particular contribution to the subject lies in relating the potentialities for destruction found in modern weapons to the ancient art of diplomatic maneuver. His purpose is to assist nations rationally to calculate their participation in international conflict in an age when miscalculation could be tragic for many more than just those citizens of the nation making the error.

The Military-Industrial Complex

By 1968 the Vietnamese war had become the longest war in American history, and in that year Congress voted to commence

Threat to democratic values

what may well become the most costly single weapons systems in the saga of arms building.[34] These facts are only two among many others which, when added together, have profoundly disturbed prominent Americans within the last decade. The concern is whether or not the United States can continue to maintain, and at times use, its large and expensive military establishment without sacrificing democratic values to totalitarian ones normally associated with military discipline and the prosecution of war.[35]

Much in the tradition of President George Wash-

32. Kahn has written an entire book regarding the policy of escalation in international relations, *On Escalation, Metaphors, and Scenarios* (New York: Praeger, 1965).

33. The "ladder" certainly does not exhaust the range of options from which nations may select as they bargain, threaten, and fight. Remembrance of history and use of one's imagination will produce many more "rungs." It should also be pointed out that nations need not go "up" the "ladder" in sequence; they may skip options or whole sets of them if desired.

34. The Sentinel ABM system could cost more than $50 billion if it were to be deployed in the "thick," or heavy, configuration.

35. As the Vietnamese war spending increased, coincident with cries for government attention to social problems of a domestic nature, some wondered whether the United States could support both efforts adequately and maintain the value of the dollar.

ington—who warned his countrymen of dangers to be avoided when he left office—President Eisenhower warned of the dangers associated with the "military-industrial complex" when he moved from the White House to a private Gettysburg farm.[36] Seven years later an influential Democratic senator discussed the evolution of the "military-industrial complex" in these terms:

"A major political force"

> Unplanned though it was, this complex has become a major political force. It is the result rather than the cause of American military involvements around the world; but, composed as it is of a vast number of citizens—not tycoons or "merchants of death" but ordinary, good American citizens—whose livelihood depends on defense production, the military industrial complex has become an indirect force for the perpetuation of our global military commitments. This is not—and I emphasize "not"—because anyone favors war but because every one of us has a natural and proper desire to preserve the sources of his livelihood.[37]

Senator Fulbright pointed out that in 1968 the complex would pour $45 billion into 5,000 cities, providing a living for eight million Americans—or 10 percent of our total labor force. He found this a "giant concentration of socialism in our otherwise free enterprise economy." One can hardly deny that a military-industrial complex exists in the sense that many politicians, businessmen, labor groups, university faculty, and military officers cooperate in and profit from preparations for war. However, because the phenomenon is so new in American experience, precise statements cannot yet be made about the effects of military activity on democracy and the economy.[38] Put another way, it is difficult to determine "where 'the national interest' begins and self-interest leaves off."[39]

36. *Cf.* Chapter 1, p. 34.

37. Senator J. William Fulbright, "The War and Its Effects—II," *Congressional Record*, 113 (December 13, 1967), p. 1.

38. A recent book on the subject is Ralph Lapp, *The Weapons Culture* (New York: Norton, 1968). In addition to discussing the military-industrial complex, Dr. Lapp provides considerable information regarding various major weapons systems. See also Jacob K. Javits, Charles J. Hitch, and Arthur F. Burns, *The Defense Sector and the American Economy: The Moskowitz Lectures* (New York: New York University, 1968).

39. "The 'Military Lobby'—Impact on Congress, Nation," in *Legislators and the Lobbyists* (Washington: Congressional Quarterly Service, 1965), p. 29. A good example of the interface between national interest and self-interest is the February, 1961, issue of *Army*, the publication of the Association of the United States Army. This particular issue was devoted to making the case for American deployment of an early ABM system, the Nike-Zeus. The magazine combined articles by active-duty Army officers praising the weapons system together with advertisements by industrial concerns which would have built the system. The magazine contained a map of the United States showing where money would be spent if the Nike-Zeus were constructed.

TABLE 11.2   Prime Defense Contract Awards by State
Fiscal Years 1967 and 1968

	Fiscal Year			
	July 1966-June 1967		July 1967-June 1968	
State	Amount	Percent	Amount	Percent
TOTAL, U.S.	$41,817,093		$41,241,125	
NOT DISTRIBUTED				
BY STATE	4,435,384		3,994,362	
STATE TOTALS	37,381,709	100.0%	37,246,763	100.0%
Alabama	297,065	0.8	409,189	1.1
Alaska	85,648	0.2	106,602	0.3
Arizona	249,559	0.7	287,045	0.8
Arkansas	127,180	0.3	121,272	0.3
California	6,688,812	17.9	6,470,306	17.4
Colorado	210,409	0.6	262,664	0.7
Connecticut	1,935,895	5.2	2,355,135	6.3
Delaware	51,672	0.1	42,614	0.1
District of Columbia	357,666	1.0	349,743	0.9
Florida	799,005	2.1	975,812	2.6
Georgia	1,148,355	3.1	964,223	2.6
Hawaii	65,445	0.2	95,623	0.3
Idaho	14,772	*	17,051	*
Illinois	1,063,776	2.8	932,115	2.5
Indiana	898,247	2.4	1,107,508	3.0
Iowa	279,328	0.8	260,980	0.7
Kansas	398,918	1.1	292,293	0.8
Kentucky	124,294	0.3	60,366	0.2
Louisiana	656,031	1.8	460,659	1.2
Maine	56,558	0.2	75,383	0.2
Maryland	867,990	2.3	703,857	1.9
Massachusetts	1,422,272	3.8	1,618,960	4.3
Michigan	1,033,706	2.8	796,211	2.1
Minnesota	650,584	1.7	620,123	1.7
Mississippi	114,800	0.3	369,261	1.0
Missouri	2,277,597	6.1	1,356,838	3.6
Montana	78,452	0.2	20,467	0.1
Nebraska	103,522	0.3	120,452	0.3
Nevada	29,315	0.1	17,897	*
New Hampshire	162,551	0.4	155,995	0.4
New Jersey	1,234,768	3.3	1,108,458	3.0
New Mexico	80,472	0.2	87,163	0.2
New York	3,261,750	8.7	3,483,885	9.4
North Carolina	447,608	1.2	487,259	1.3
North Dakota	16,729	*	68,072	0.2
Ohio	1,602,593	4.3	1,640,506	4.4
Oklahoma	157,350	0.4	164,806	0.4
Oregon	99,319	0.3	119,749	0.3
Pennsylvania	1,649,091	4.4	1,727,333	4.6
Rhode Island	198,030	0.5	126,362	0.3
South Carolina	180,777	0.5	133,041	0.4
South Dakota	9,486	*	33,585	0.1
Tennessee	538,225	1.4	541,631	1.5
Texas	3,546,978	9.5	4,087,132	11.0
Utah	178,850	0.5	131,195	0.4
Vermont	100,157	0.3	104,957	0.3
Virginia	665,376	1.8	692,671	1.9
Washington	606,114	1.6	529,532	1.4
West Virginia	142,142	0.4	131,522	0.4
Wisconsin	383,602	1.0	406,409	1.1
Wyoming	32,868	0.1	14,851	*

*Less than 0.05 percent.
Source: Department of Defense.

With hope expressed in most quarters that the Cold War may not congeal into a permanent condition of American life, an important question arises: can the United States economy afford peace? The United States Arms Control and Disarmament Agency has been particularly active in making studies of ways in which industry, labor, and communities which lose financial inputs due to reductions in defense spending respond to the new situation.[40] Further official cognizance of the potential problem was taken in 1965 when the Johnson Administration created a Committee on the Economic Impact of Defense and Disarmament. In establishing the committee the President stated:

Adjusting to a peacetime economy

> Federal outlays for defense are of such magnitude that they inevitably have major economic significance. In certain regions of the Nation and in certain communities they provide a significant share of total employment and income. It is therefore important that we improve our knowledge of the economic impacts of such spending, so that appropriate actions can be taken—in cooperation with State and local governments, private industry, and labor—to minimize potential disturbances which may arise from changes in the level and pattern of defense outlays.[41]

Much of the literature on defense spending suggests that while individuals and particular communities may suffer hardship should substantial decreases in defense spending occur, the general economy need not be seriously damaged so long as resources released from defense spending are reinjected into the economy and the aggregate demand for goods and services continues high. Precisely how the resources released from defense purposes will be used and the roles which will be played in their utilization by government and private enterprise are not now clear. However, many would agree with an early government report on the problem that, "Achievement of major national goals will be greatly facilitated by the use of the human and physical resources released from the defense program."[42]

40. A considerable library of studies has been assembled by ACDA, of which the following is an example: United States Arms Control and Disarmament Agency, *Defense Industry Diversification*, a report prepared by John S. Gilmore and Dean C. Coddington, University of Denver Research Institute (Washington: United States Government Printing Office, 1966).

41. *Report of the Committee on the Economic Impact of Defense and Disarmament* (Washington: United States Government Printing Office, July, 1965), p. iv.

42. United States Arms Control and Disarmament Agency, *Economic Impacts of Disarmament* (Washington: United States Government Printing Office, January, 1962), p. iii.

505

The Proliferation of Nuclear Weapons

A major problem in today's world, to which those responsible for American national security must be responsive, is the proliferation of nuclear weapons.[43] The specter of more nations acquiring nuclear weapons cannot be easily dismissed, for there are at least four reasons why the number of nations possessing nuclear capabilities is likely to increase in the next decade.

First, the secrets of nuclear-weapons fabrication, once the monopoly of the United States and Britain, are no longer

Technical capability secret. The Soviets, French, and Chinese have tested nuclear weapons, and there are no technical reasons why scientists in a number of nations cannot duplicate at least the first generation of nuclear weapons.[44] A nation with a less advanced technical and scientific base than the super-powers could cause considerable disturbance; for example, an "old-fashioned" atomic bomb stowed beneath the decks of a freighter could shatter sizable portions of New York or San Francisco.[45]

Second, materials necessary for the fabrication of nuclear weapons are becoming less expensive and easier to obtain. This

Materials is particularly true of plutonium which is produced during the operation of nuclear power plants generating electricity or desalting water. Such plants, in which uranium fuel elements are partially converted into plutonium, are being rapidly constructed about the world as demand for power and water soars. Devising means to prevent modern man from misusing the fruits of nuclear power reactors is a primary concern for many of the world's statesmen.[46]

43. Different views on the subject are set forth in Alastair Buchan, ed., *A World of Nuclear Powers?* (Englewood Cliffs: Prentice-Hall, 1966). See also Richard N. Rosecrance, ed., *The Dispersion of Nuclear Weapons: Strategy and Politics* (New York: Columbia University Press, 1964).

44. For a discussion of the development program leading to the first American nuclear weapons see Lansing Lamont, *Day of Trinity* (New York: Atheneum, 1965).

45. Accounts of the growing danger that small nations, even criminal groups such as the Mafia, could manufacture nuclear weapons are becoming more common. See for example the editorial in the *Christian Science Monitor* which stated only 13 pounds of plutonium are needed to make a nuclear weapon. "The Mafia and the Atom," June 15, 1968.

46. Science has provided still other methods for man to acquire materials for nuclear weapons. The breeder reactor, under development in a number of nations, is capable of producing more nuclear material than the amount with which it is originally fueled. Perfection of the gas centrifuge (a device somewhat resembling a cream separator) may provide a relatively cheap method of separating weapons-grade uranium from ordinary uranium.

Third, the apparent success the military nuclear powers have attained in deterring attack upon their homelands, plus the political prestige associated with nuclear weapons acquisition, serves as an attraction for other nations to develop their own nuclear forces.[47] To some nations the "bomb" is viewed as a symbol of national power. Others understandably consider nuclear weapons as their best guarantee of continued survival in a hostile world. Israel is a good example. It is a tiny land, hemmed in by avowed enemies which are well supplied with Soviet weapons systems. Since the Israelis may not always be able to depend upon the United States or England for protection, they may turn to nuclear weapons which they seem capable of producing.

National prestige

Fourth, it may be argued that the technical work which leads to nuclear weapons development also produces valuable scientific spin-offs which are commercially valuable. This reason for developing a nuclear weapons program, however, is probably the weakest of the various incentives.

Scientific by-products

Since the matter of becoming a military nuclear power is now technically and economically[48] within the grasp of numerous nations, the decision to "go nuclear" will become more and more a political affair. It is to lessen the political pressures to develop nuclear forces that the Nuclear Non-Proliferation Treaty, supported by Britain, the Soviet Union, and the Johnson and Nixon Administrations in the United States, is directed.[49] The treaty requires the signatories which possess nuclear weapons to agree to refrain from transferring nuclear weapons to other states, or assisting them in any way to obtain such weapons. The treaty requires signatory states not possessing nuclear weapons to agree to refrain from acquiring them. A somewhat ambiguous statement accompanying the treaty was issued by the United Nations Security Council, to the effect that the

Non-proliferation treaty

47. The French rationale for acquiring nuclear weapons to deter attack upon France from any quarter was set forth by General D'Armee Ailleret in "Directed Defense," *Survival*, X (February, 1968), pp. 38–43. Another French strategist, Pierre Gallois, has suggested that the proliferation of nuclear weapons about the world could contribute to peace because the deterrence of attacks upon nations possessing such weapons would be strengthened. See his *The Balance of Terror: Strategy for the Nuclear Age* (Boston: Houghton Mifflin, 1961).

48. An Indian strategist has suggested that India could certainly afford a 10-to-15-billion-dollar investment in a nuclear weapons program spread over 10 years if circumstances require it. K. Subrahmanyam, *A Strategy for India for a Credible Posture Against a Nuclear Adversary*, pp. 6–7.

49. In the fall of 1968 ratification of the Nuclear Non-Proliferation Treaty was stalled temporarily because of adverse reaction to the Soviet invasion of Czechoslovakia.

nuclear-weapons states signing the treaty will afford security to those states which agree not to obtain them.[50] The Nuclear Non-Proliferation Treaty serves well to suggest the divergence between idealism and practice in the harsh world of international politics in which nations fight for survival. France and Communist China, two states possessing nuclear weapons, did not sign the treaty, and presumably regard themselves free to participate in nuclear development in an effort to catch up with the leaders. Even more important, perhaps, was the refusal to sign by some of the nations most able to develop nuclear weapons from a technical and economic standpoint, and with the greatest political incentives to do so. Among these are India, Israel, West Germany, and Japan.[51]

Arms Control and Disarmament

Nuclear vs. conventional weaponry

The cataclysmic possibilities which are always present when human beings possess the kinds of weapons systems previously discussed have generated considerable effort on the part of the United States Government to work for disarmament and arms control among the nations of the world.[52] Attempts to disarm or control nonnuclear weapons are not at all new, and their failures liberally dot the pages of history. The problems which have proved generally insoluble stem from mutual suspicion and the lack of real incentives. They are marked by disagreements regarding inspection and verification and by an inability to decide which arms ought to be limited or con-

50. President Johnson discussed this matter in the following fashion: "If a state which has accepted this treaty does not have nuclear weapons and is a victim of aggression or is subject to a threat of aggression involving nuclear weapons, the United States shall be prepared to ask immediate Security Council action to provide assistance in accordance with the charter." "Statement by the President on Missile Talks With Moscow," *New York Times*, July 2, 1968. Under certain conditions implementation of the President's statement could involve the United States in foreign entanglements far more complex and dangerous than anything dreamed of by President Washington.

51. For questions raised about the treaty see George H. Quester, "Is the Treaty Enough?" *Bulletin of the Atomic Scientists*, XXIII (November, 1967), pp. 35–37.

52. Disarmament refers to a reduction of armaments possessed by nations. Arms control can include disarmament, but may also mean making existing, or even increased armaments more stable, less likely to be used, or if used more likely to be employed in a fashion designed to minimize destruction and maximize political settlement of disputes. A useful reader on the subjects of arms control and disarmament is Donald G. Brennan, ed., *Arms Control, Disarmament, and National Security* (New York: Braziller, 1961).

trolled. Since the nuclear age made the once-feared havoc of conventional weapons relatively insignificant compared to the destruction that would result from a 30-minute missile exchange, the emphasis upon arms control and disarmament since 1945 has focused upon nuclear weapons. Furthermore, the characteristics of nuclear weapons, generally detectable tests and large weapons delivery vehicles, make inspection and verification somewhat easier than was the case with Army reserves, or machine guns and other conventional weapons.

The first attempt to control the destructive potential of the atom occurred when Bernard Baruch, speaking for the United States before the United Nations, told those assembled that if **Attempts at control** they failed to find a way to control nuclear weapons "we have damned every man to be the slave of fear."[53] The United States offered to reduce its nuclear weapons stockpile gradually as the United Nations Atomic Energy Authority instigated inspection and control measures to insure that no nations would develop nuclear weapons in secret. At the same time, the United States offered to assist other nations with the development of nuclear energy for peaceful uses. The Soviet Union rejected the Baruch plan. Possibly the Russian dictator, Josef Stalin, did not trust the United States, and presumably he wanted his own nation to obtain nuclear weapons—an event which occurred in 1949. The lines of argument which were developed by the two super-powers in this first discussion of nuclear weapons regulation remain prominent in current discussions: the Soviets want nations to agree on various arms-limitation measures first, with inspection and verification to follow. The United States reverses the priorities, emphasizing implementation of inspection procedures before it is willing to enter into arms limitations or controls.

THE PARTIAL NUCLEAR TEST BAN TREATY

The kinds of difficulties and potential risks inherent in attempts to limit or control nuclear armaments are suggested by the provisions of the Partial Nuclear Test Ban Treaty that was approved by the Senate in 1963 and subsequently signed by President Kennedy.

The use of nuclear weapons is not proscribed. The treaty does prohibit nuclear testing in space, the earth's atmosphere, and underwater. Nuclear explosions may be held underground, **Provisions** as they frequently are by the Soviet Union and the United

53. Bernard M. Baruch, "Proposals for an International Atomic Development Authority," *The Department of State Bulletin*, XIV (June 23, 1946), p. 1057.

States, provided the radioactive debris which sometimes seeps up from such detonations does not spread into the atmosphere beyond the testing nation's borders.[54] A provision for "on-site" inspection of the treaty signatories, to determine whether they are abiding by the treaty restrictions, was not made. The United States accepted this departure from its usual insistence upon inspection because its scientific advisers believed that advances in detection equipment had progressed to the point that above-ground cheating could be detected, even without inspectors physically present in a particular nation. This view was not unanimously held by all American scientists, and the possibilities of Soviet cheating constituted a major fear by those opposing the treaty. Although underground tests are much more difficult to detect by remote sensing devices, the Soviets would not agree to inspection within their country.[55]

The problem inherent in mistrusting a fellow signatory produced two other major arguments against the treaty. First, it **Risks inherent** was contended that the Soviets wanted the treaty so as to pre- **in the treaty** vent American atmospheric tests of an ABM system featuring nuclear weapons. According to this argument the final series of atmospheric tests conducted by the Soviets before they signed the treaty had advanced Soviet ABM technology substantially beyond that achieved by American developments. Second, the argument was made that the Soviet Union would prepare in secret and then suddenly break the test ban. This would provide them with a scientific advantage over the United States which would have adverse military ramifications. President Kennedy frankly acknowledged the presence of the risks involved in signing the treaty, but he argued that unrestricted nuclear testing and an uncontrolled arms race posed greater risks for the nation.[56] To guard against the possibility of Soviet duplicity, the President ordered that facilities be kept ready for the resumption of nuclear testing in the atmosphere should that become necessary, for the deployment of a satellite-borne nuclear explosion detection system, and for continued underground testing. Since no powerful nation will sign an arms control agreement unless means are provided for abrogation in the event of unforeseen circumstances, the treaty permits signator-

54. Neither France nor China signed the treaty, and both continue to conduct nuclear weapons tests in the atmosphere.

55. The matter of banning underground nuclear tests remains a point of discussion between the Soviet Union and the United States. Fear of nuclear proliferation and the development of better detection equipment may in time lead to agreements banning underground tests also.

56. Sorensen, *op. cit.*, p. 738.

ies to resume above-ground nuclear testing should they deem that their national existence requires it because of the actions of the others.

THE UNITED STATES ARMS CONTROL AND DISARMAMENT AGENCY

In 1961 President Kennedy requested Congress to create the United States Arms Control and Disarmament Agency (ACDA). Since then it has coordinated American efforts at limiting the arms race and making the competition for weapons systems less dangerous. Contrary to what some may think, arms control and disarmament is a highly complex business, much more complicated than simply setting aside some particular weapons system, or doing away with all weapons as the Soviets have suggested in their "General and Complete Disarmament" proposal. Some of the diverse elements of arms control and disarmament are suggested in the responsibilities assigned to ACDA by Congress:

> This organization must have the capacity to provide the essential scientific, economic, political, military, psychological, and technological information upon which realistic arms control and disarmament policy must be based.

Legal basis

The concern of Congress that ACDA might endanger national security in its quest for arms control and disarmament led to this provision in the enabling statute:

> That no action shall be taken under this or any other law that will obligate the United States to disarm or to reduce or limit the Armed Forces or armament of the United States, except pursuant to the treaty-making power of the President under the Constitution or unless authorized by further affirmative legislation by the Congress of the United States.

Despite the Congressional control thus exercised, some Congressmen have feared that ACDA would attempt to disarm unwisely in the face of the threat posed by Communism. These worries account in large part for the annual budget fights over ACDA's appropriations, slashes in its budget requests, and occasional suggestions the agency be abolished.

The Outlook

In the third decade of the nuclear age it is still too early to determine whether those, in and out of government, who search for workable arms control and disarmament measures will succeed in some degree or fail as miserably as their pred-

Optimism

ecessors. There are two new and optimistic features of today's quest for the control and reduction of national armaments that ought to be noted. First, it may be true, as Sir Winston Churchill suggested, that badly matched and run arms races, in which one contestant falls so far behind that the other contender is tempted to attack in the expectation of cheap victory, do lead to war.[57] Since the two super-powers, unlike the Allied and Axis powers prior to World War II, have shown little evidence to date they will permit the other to gain a substantial military margin, temptations of easy military conquests involving nuclear war may be far fewer now than formerly.[58] If it should appear to both nuclear giants that, because the other side will simply counter any nuclear increase, their interests cannot be materially advanced by further acquisitions of major strategic systems or the use of such weapons, pressure will perhaps build until the two nations at least reduce, and possibly call off entirely, the arms competition. Any agreements of this type between the Soviet Union and the United States would have to take into consideration the behavior of less-advanced states which seek to increase their military potential. Soviet-United States agreements would not necessarily prevent arms races or even armament programs in the smaller states. However, they could assist the two nuclear heavyweights from being sucked into war because of international disputes tangential to their basic interests.[59]

The other optimistic note, assuming man's rationality, may be found in the awesome characteristics of nuclear weapons whose presence may force nations to forgo international ven-

57. Churchill described the arms race which culminated in World War II in *The Gathering Storm* (Boston: Houghton Mifflin, 1948). According to Churchill the Axis powers were encouraged in their aggressive activities by the failure of England and France, and to a lesser extent the United States, to maintain their armaments when Germany, Japan, and Italy were rapidly arming. For a voluminous prenuclear inquiry into arms races and other aspects of war see Quincy Wright, *A Study of War* (Chicago: Chicago University Press, 1942). Wright's characterization of arms races lasting three or four decades, punctuated by the increasing frequency of small wars, and ending in a major struggle, must appear to some as descriptive of the situation since 1946. See p. 690 of Volume II.

58. For an example of the kind of international stability which appears to be enhanced by the nuclear stalemate existing between the Soviet Union and the United States see Harlan Cleveland. "Pax Ballistica, the Uncertain Peace," *Saturday Review*, LI (June 29, 1968), pp. 11–13.

59. A nuclear-armed China looms as a substantial threat to American-Soviet arms agreements for the next few years. For a report on the status of Chinese nuclear weapons technology see *Impact of Chinese Communist Nuclear Weapons Progress on United States National Security*, Report of the Joint Committee on Atomic Energy, 90th Congress, 1st Session (Washington: United States Government Printing Office, July, 1967).

tures which, in previous times, might have proved to be irresistibly attractive. It is of course a regrettable commentary upon the nature of man to suggest that only the creation of weapons which can erase a metropolis and seed a continent with radioactivity will force him to control his aggressive tendencies and regulate his acquisition of weapons.[60] Nevertheless, it would seem preferable to use constructively that which man has wrought than simply to deplore the results of the weapons laboratories operated by the world's great powers. To suggest that nuclear weapons may yet induce reason and restraint, if not wisdom, among the nations of the world is less of a pious hope than an expression of the pragmatic philosophy which has guided the United States thus far.

SUMMARY

• The National Security Act of 1947 established the framework for the defense establishment which operates today. The act created a Department of the Air Force and placed it, together with the Departments of the Army and Navy, under a Secretary of Defense within the new Department of Defense. The men bearing the greatest official responsibility for the nation's defense, the President, Vice President, Secretaries of Defense and of State, and the director of Emergency Planning (formerly the director of the Office of Civil and Defense Mobilization) were linked together in a group known as the National Security Council. The 1947 act also brought together several intelligence-gathering organizations into one, the Central Intelligence Agency.

• At the time of the defense reorganization the United States possessed few nuclear weapons, little in the way of conventional forces, and no counterguerrilla capability. Since that time the Department of Defense has grown in response to the perceived threat from Communist nations to include: a vast array of nuclear weapons and their delivery systems, modern conventional forces, and specially trained units to combat guerrilla warfare, plus support forces of various types.

• During the last decade, and particularly during the term of Robert S. McNamara as Secretary of Defense (1961-1968) serious policy differences have marked America's search for security. The *Bomber v. Missile* debate concerns the relative

60. The modern combination of man's primitive aggressive instincts and advanced weapons is discussed brilliantly in Konrad Lorenz, *On Aggression* (New York: Harcourt, Brace & World, 1966).

merits of long-range bombers and missiles as the most effective delivery vehicles for nuclear weapons. The *Missile v. Missile* argument revolves about the question of whether an anti-missile missile can be built to counter long-range offensive missiles, and the political questions as to whether such systems ought to be constructed.

• The current defense posture of the United States includes the *Strategic Offensive Forces*, designed to carry nuclear destruction to any nation which attacks the United States. The *Strategic Defensive Forces* are designed to minimize the effect of an enemy attack upon the United States. *General Purpose Forces* are maintained to fight various types of wars, normally those below the level of thermonuclear war. They are transported to battle and supplied by the *Airlift and Sealift Forces*. The *National Military Command System* links political decision-makers with the military forces. *Intelligence Gathering* activities keep the defense community supplied with information regarding possible enemy nations, and other nations. *Research and Development* and *Reserve* forces support the other types of units. Both nuclear and conventional forces are employed according to the philosophy of the graduated response, *i.e.*, that American responses to provocation are to be carefully tailored to the kind and amount of force employed by an enemy.

• As America enters the third decade of the Cold War increased concern has been voiced whether the United States can continue to procure and at times use its military forces without harming its democratic traditions. A particularly thorny problem for defense planners is nuclear-weapon proliferation. The matter is made unusually difficult because the techniques for manufacturing nuclear weapons are now widely known, and the costs can be borne by a number of nations. Despite American efforts to prevent further proliferation, there remain heavy pressures upon several nations to acquire their own nuclear forces.

• The stark aspects of thermonuclear war have led to various plans to control arms or reduce armaments. To date the most significant measure along these lines has been the Partial Nuclear Test Ban Treaty. In the early 1960's the United States created the Arms Control and Disarmament Agency to seek means of safely curtailing the arms competition.

SUGGESTED READING

* (*Books so designated are available in paperbound editions.*)

* Buchan, Alastair, ed., *A World of Nuclear Powers?* (Englewood Cliffs: Prentice-Hall, 1966).

* Department of Defense, *Statement by Secretary of Defense Robert S. McNamara on The Fiscal Year 1969–73 Defense Program and the Defense Budget* (Washington: Government Printing Office, January 22, 1968).

Dougherty, James E., and J. F. Lehman, Jr., eds., *Arms Control for the Late Sixties* (New York: Van Nostrand, 1967).

* Falk, Richard A., and Saul H. Mendlovitz, eds., *Toward a Theory of War Prevention*, Vol. I of *The Strategy of World Order* (New York: World Law Fund, 1966).

Gallois, Pierre, *The Balance of Terror: Strategy for the Nuclear Age* (Boston: Houghton Mifflin, 1961).

Huntington, Samuel P., *The Common Defense: Strategic Programs in National Politics* (Cambridge: Harvard University Press, 1961).

* Kahn, Herman, *On Escalation: Metaphors and Scenarios* (New York: Praeger, 1965).

Kintner, William R. and Harriet Fast Scott, eds., *The Nuclear Revolution in Soviet Military Affairs* (Norman: University of Oklahoma Press, 1968).

* Kissinger, Henry A., *Nuclear Weapons and Foreign Policy*, Reissued (New York: Norton, 1969).

Knorr, Klaus, *On the Uses of Military Power in the Nuclear Age* (Princeton: Princeton University Press, 1966).

Lapp, Ralph, *The Weapons Culture* (New York: Norton, 1968).

LeMay, Curtis E., *America Is in Danger* (New York: Funk and Wagnalls, 1968).

McClintock, Robert, *The Meaning of Limited War* (Boston: Houghton Mifflin, 1967).

McNamara, Robert S., *The Essence of Security* (New York: Harper and Row, 1968).

* Morgenstern, Oskar, *The Question of National Defense* (New York: Random House, 1959).

Taylor, Maxwell, *The Uncertain Trumpet* (New York: Harper and Row, 1959).

* Waltz, Kenneth, *Man, the State, and War* (New York: Columbia University Press, 1965).

Interstate Rendition

Introduction - Preamble

I.   Article I   Legislative ~~Dept~~. Branch

II.   Article II - Executive Branch

III.   Article III   JUDICIAL BRANCH

IV.   Article IV   Relations of States One to Another

V   Article ~~V~~   Amendments - (6 procedures for Amendments)

VI   ~~DEBTS~~ SUPREME LAW

VII   Ratification of Constitution

The Constitution
of the United States

We the People of the United States, in Order to form a more perfect
1. Union,²establish Justice,³insure domestic Tranquillity,⁴provide for the
common defence, promote the general Welfare, and secure the Blessings
of Liberty to ourselves and our Posterity, do ordain and establish this
Constitution for the United States of America.

Article I

Section 1. All legislative Powers herein granted shall be vested in a
Congress of the United States, which shall consist of a Senate and House
of Representatives.

Section 2. The House of Representatives shall be composed of
Members chosen every second Year by the People of the several States,
and the Electors in each State shall have the Qualifications requisite for
Electors of the most numerous Branch of the State Legislature.

No person shall be a Representative who shall not have attained to the
Age of twenty five Years, and been seven Years a Citizen of the United
States, and who shall not, when elected, be an Inhabitant of that State
in which he shall be chosen.

Representatives and direct Taxes shall be apportioned among the
several States which may be included within this Union, according to
their respective Numbers, which shall be determined by adding to the
whole Number of free Persons, including those bound to Service for a
Term of Years, and excluding Indians not taxed, three fifths of all other
Persons. The actual Enumeration shall be made within three Years after
the first Meeting of the Congress of the United States, and within every
subsequent Term of ten Years, in such Manner as they shall by Law
direct. The Number of Representatives shall not exceed one for every
thirty Thousand, but each State shall have at Least one Representative;
and until such enumeration shall be made, the State of New Hampshire
shall be entitled to chuse three, Massachusetts eight, Rhode-Island and
Providence Plantations one, Connecticut five, New-York six, New Jersey
four, Pennsylvania eight, Delaware one, Maryland six, Virginia ten, North
Carolina five, South Carolina five, and Georgia three.

When vacancies happen in the Representation from any State, the
Executive Authority thereof shall issue Writs of Election to fill such
Vacancies.

The House of Representatives shall chuse their speaker and other officers; and shall have the sole power of Impeachment.

Section 3. The Senate of the United States shall be composed of two Senators from each State, chosen by the Legislature thereof, for six Years; and each Senator shall have one Vote.

Immediately after they shall be assembled in Consequence of the first Election, they shall be divided as equally as may be into three Classes. The Seats of the Senators of the first Class shall be vacated at the Expiration of the second Year, of the second Class at the Expiration of the fourth Year, and of the third Class at the Expiration of the sixth Year, so that one third may be chosen every second Year; and if Vacancies happen by Resignation, or otherwise, during the Recess of the Legislature of any State, the Executive thereof may make temporary Appointments until the next meeting of the Legislature, which shall then fill such Vacancies.

No Person shall be a Senator who shall not have attained to the Age of thirty years, and been nine Years a Citizen of the United States, and who shall not, when elected, be an Inhabitant of that State for which he shall be chosen.

The Vice President of the United States shall be President of the Senate, but shall have no Vote, unless they be equally divided.

The Senate shall chuse their other Officers, and also a President pro tempore, in the Absence of the Vice President, or when he shall exercise the Office of President of the United States.

The Senate shall have the sole power to try all Impeachments. When sitting for that Purpose, they shall be on Oath or Affirmation. When the President of the United States is tried, the Chief Justice shall preside: And no Person shall be convicted without the Concurrence of two thirds of the Members present.

Judgment in Cases of Impeachment shall not extend further than to removal from Office, and disqualification to hold and enjoy any Office of honor, Trust or Profit under the United States: but the Party convicted shall nevertheless be liable and subject to Indictment, Trial, Judgment and Punishment, according to law.

Section 4. The Times, Places and Manner of holding Elections for Senators and Representatives, shall be prescribed in each State by the Legislature thereof; but the Congress may at any time by Law make or alter such Regulations, except as to the Places of chusing Senators.

The Congress shall assemble at least once in every Year, and such Meeting shall be on the first Monday in December, unless they shall by Law appoint a different day.

Section 5. Each House shall be the Judge of the Elections, Returns and Qualifications of its own Members, and a Majority of each shall constitute a Quorum to do Business; but a smaller Number may adjourn from day to day, and may be authorized to compel the Attendance of absent Members, in such Manner, and under such Penalties as each House may provide.

Each House may determine the Rules of its Proceedings, punish its Members for disorderly Behaviour, and, with the Concurrence of two thirds, expel a Member.

Each House shall keep a Journal of its Proceedings, and from time to time publish the same, excepting such Parts as may in their Judgment require Secrecy; and the Yeas and Nays of the Members of either House on any question shall, at the Desire of one fifth of those Present, be entered on the Journal.

Neither House, during the Session of Congress, shall, without the Consent of the other, adjourn for more than three days, nor to any other Place than that in which the two Houses shall be sitting.

Section 6. The Senators and Representatives shall receive a Compensation for their Services, to be ascertained by Law, and paid out of the Treasury of the United States. They shall in all Cases, except Treason, Felony and Breach of the Peace, be privileged from Arrest during their attendance at the Session of their respective Houses, and in going to and returning from the same; and for any Speech or Debate in either House, they shall not be questioned in any other Place.

No Senator or Representative shall, during the Time for which he was elected, be appointed to any civil Office under the Authority of the United States, which shall have been created, or the Emoluments whereof shall have been encreased during such time; and no Person holding any Office under the United States, shall be a Member of either House during his Continuance in Office.

Section 7. All Bills for raising Revenue shall originate in the House of Representatives; but the Senate may propose or concur with Amendments as on other Bills.

Every Bill which shall have passed the House of Representatives and the Senate, shall, before it become a Law, be presented to the President of the United States; If he approve he shall sign it, but if not he shall return it, with his Objections to that House in which it shall have originated, who shall enter the Objections at large on their Journal, and proceed to reconsider it. If after such Reconsideration two thirds of that House shall agree to pass the Bill, it shall be sent, together with the Objections, to the other House, by which it shall likewise be reconsidered, and if approved by two thirds of that House, it shall become a Law. But in all such Cases the Votes of both Houses shall be determined by Yeas and Nays, and the Names of the Persons voting for and against the Bill shall be entered on the Journal of each House respectively. If any Bill shall not be returned by the President within ten Days (Sundays excepted) after it shall have been presented to him, the Same shall be a Law, in like Manner as if he had signed it, unless the Congress by their Adjournment prevent its Return, in which Case it shall not be a Law.

Every Order, Resolution, or Vote to which the Concurrence of the Senate and House of Representatives may be necessary (except on a question of Adjournment) shall be presented to the President of the United States; and before the Same shall take Effect, shall be approved by him, or being disapproved by him, shall be repassed by two thirds of the Senate and House of Representatives, according to the Rules and Limitation prescribed in the Case of a Bill.

Section 8. The Congress shall have Power To lay and collect Taxes, Duties, Imposts and Excises, to pay the Debts and provide for the common Defense and general Welfare of the United States; but all

519

Duties, Imposts and Excises shall be uniform throughout the United States;

To Borrow Money on the Credit of the United States;

To regulate Commerce with foreign Nations, and among the several States, and with the Indian Tribes;

To establish an uniform Rule of Naturalization, and uniform Laws on the subject of Bankruptcies throughout the United States;

To coin Money, regulate the Value thereof, and of foreign Coin, and fix the Standard of Weights and Measures;

To provide for the Punishment of counterfeiting the Securities and current Coin of the United States;

To establish Post Offices and post Roads;

To promote the Progress of Science and useful Arts, by securing for limited Times to Authors and Inventors the exclusive Right to their respective Writings and Discoveries;

To constitute Tribunals inferior to the supreme Court;

To define and punish Piracies and Felonies committed on the high Seas, and Offences against the Law of Nations;

To declare War, grant Letters of Marque and Reprisal, and make Rules concerning Captures on Land and Water;

To raise and support Armies, but no Appropriation of Money to that Use shall be for a longer Term than two Years;

To provide and maintain a Navy;

To make Rules for the Government and Regulation of the land and naval Forces;

To provide for calling forth the Militia to execute the Laws of the Union, suppress Insurrections and repel Invasions;

To provide for organizing, arming, and disciplining, the Militia, and for governing such Part of them as may be employed in the Service of the United States, reserving to the States respectively, the Appointment of the Officers, and the Authority of training the Militia according to the discipline prescribed by Congress;

To exercise exclusive Legislation in all Cases whatsoever, over such District (not exceeding ten Miles square) as may, by Cession of particular States, and the Acceptance of Congress, become the Seat of the Government of the United States, and to exercise like Authority over all Places purchased by the Consent of the Legislature of the State in which the Same shall be for the Erection of Forts, Magazines, Arsenals, dock-Yards, and other needful Buildings;—And

To make all Laws which shall be necessary and proper for carrying into Execution the foregoing Powers, and all other Powers vested by this Constitution in the Government of the United States, or in any Department or Officer thereof.

Section 9.   The Migration or Importation of such Persons as any of the States now existing shall think proper to admit, shall not be prohibited by the Congress prior to the Year one thousand eight hundred and eight, but a Tax or duty may be imposed on such Importation, not exceeding ten dollars for each Person.

The Privilege of the Writ of Habeas Corpus shall not be suspended, unless when in Cases of Rebellion or Invasion the public Safety may require it.

No Bill of Attainder or ex post facto Law shall be passed.

No Capitation, or other direct, Tax shall be laid, unless in Proportion to the Census or Enumeration herein before directed to be taken.

No Tax or Duty shall be laid on Articles exported from any State.

No Preference shall be given by any Regulation of Commerce or Revenue to the Ports of one State over those of another: nor shall Vessels bound to, or from, one State, be obliged to enter, clear, or pay Duties in another.

No Money shall be drawn from the Treasury, but in Consequence of Appropriations made by Law; and a regular Statement and Account of the Receipts and Expenditures of all public Money shall be published from time to time.

No Title of Nobility shall be granted by the United States: And no Person holding any Office of Profit or Trust under them, shall, without the Consent of the Congress, accept of any present, Emolument, Office, or Title, of any kind whatever, from any King, Prince, or foreign State.

Section 10. No State shall enter into any Treaty, Alliance, or Confederation; grant Letters of Marque and Reprisal; coin Money; emit Bills of Credit; make any Thing but gold and silver Coin a Tender in Payment of Debts; pass any Bill of Attainder, ex post facto Law, or Law impairing the Obligation of Contracts. or grant any Title of Nobility.

No State shall, without the Consent of the Congress, lay any Imposts or Duties on Imports or Exports, except what may be absolutely necessary for executing its inspection Laws: and the net Produce of all Duties and Imposts, laid by any State on Imports or Exports, shall be for the Use of the Treasury of the United States; and all such Laws shall be subject to the Revision and Controul of the Congress.

No State shall, without the Consent of Congress, lay any Duty of Tonnage, keep Troops, or Ships of War in time of Peace, enter into any Agreement or Compact with another State, or with a foreign Power, or engage in War, unless actually invaded, or in such imminent Danger as will not admit of delay.

Article II

Section 1. The executive Power shall be vested in a President of the United States of America. He shall hold his Office during the Term of four Years, and, together with the Vice President, chosen for the same term, be elected, as follows

Each State shall appoint, in such Manner as the Legislature thereof may direct, a Number of Electors, equal to the whole Number of Senators and Representatives to which the State may be entitled in the Congress: but no Senator or Representative, or Person holding an Office of Trust or Profit under the United States, shall be appointed an Elector.

Amend. 12

The Electors shall meet in their respective States, and vote by Ballot for two Persons, of whom one at least shall not be an Inhabitant of the same State with themselves. And they shall make a List of all the Persons voted for, and of the Number of Votes for each; which List they shall sign and certify, and transmit sealed to the Seat of the Government of the United States, directed to the President of the Senate. The President of the Senate shall, in the Presence of the Senate and House of Representatives, open all the Certificates, and the Votes shall then be counted. The Person having the greatest Number of Votes shall be the President, if such Number be a Majority of the whole Number of Electors appointed; and if there be more than one who have such Majority, and have an equal Number of Votes, then the House of Representatives shall immediately chuse by Ballot one of them for President: and if no Person have a Majority, then from the five highest on the List the said House shall in like Manner chuse the President. But in chusing the President, the Votes shall be taken by States, the Representation from each State having one Vote; A quorum for this purpose shall consist of a Member or Members from two thirds of the States, and a Majority of all the States shall be necessary to a Choice. In every Case, after the Choice of the President, the Person having the greatest Number of Votes of the Electors shall be the Vice President. But if there should remain two or more who have equal Votes, the Senate shall chuse from them by Ballot the Vice President.

The Congress may determine the Time of chusing the Electors, and the Day on which they shall give their Votes; which Day shall be the same throughout the United States.

No Person except a natural born Citizen, or a Citizen of the United States, at the time of the Adoption of this Constitution, shall be elegible to the Office of President; neither shall any Person be eligible to that Office who shall not have attained to the Age of thirty five Years, and been fourteen Years a Resident within the United States.

Amendment 25

In Case of the Removal of the President from Office, or of his Death, Resignation, or Inability to discharge the Powers and Duties of the said Office, the Same shall devolve on the Vice President, and the Congress may by Law provide for the Case of Removal, Death, Resignation or Inability, both of the President and Vice President, declaring what Officer shall then act as President, and such Officer shall act accordingly, until the Disability be removed, or a President shall be elected.

Spkr. of House

The President shall, at stated Times, receive for his Services, a Compensation, which shall neither be encreased nor diminished during the Period for which he shall have been elected, and he shall not receive within that Period any other Emolument from the United States, or any of them.

$200,000

Before he enter on the Execution of his Office, he shall take the following Oath or Affirmation:—"I do solemnly swear (or affirm) that I will faithfully execute the Office of President of the United States, and will to the best of my Ability, preserve, protect and defend the Constitution of the United States."

Section 2. The President shall be Commander in Chief of the Army and Navy of the United States, and of the Militia of the several States, when called into the actual Service of the United States; he may

Armed Forces

522 *(1947)*

Natl. Guard.

require the Opinion, in writing, of the principal Officer in each of the *—Cabinet* executive Departments, upon any Subject relating to the Duties of their respective Offices, and he shall have Power to grant Reprieves and Pardons for Offences against the United States, except in Cases of Impeachment.

He shall have Power, by and with the Advice and Consent of the Senate, to make Treaties, provided two thirds of the Senators present concur; and he shall nominate, and by and with the Advice and Consent of the Senate, shall appoint Ambassadors, other public Ministers and *all officers* Consuls, Judges of the supreme Court, and all other Officers of the *of Armed Forces* United States, whose Appointments are not herein otherwise provided for, and which shall be established by Law: but the Congress may by Law vest the Appointment of such inferior Officers, as they think proper, in the President alone, in the Courts of Law, or in the Heads of Departments.

The President shall have Power to fill up all Vacancies that may happen during the Recess of the Senate, by granting Commissions which shall expire at the End of their next Session.

Section 3. He shall from time to time give to the Congress Information of the State of the Union, and recommend to their Consideration such Measures as he shall judge necessary and expedient; he may, on extraordinary Occasions, convene both Houses, or either of them, and in Case of Disagreement between them, with Respect to the Time of Adjournment, he may adjourn them to such Time as he shall think proper; he shall receive Ambassadors and other public Ministers; he shall take Care that the Laws be faithfully executed, and shall Commission all the Officers of the United States.

Section 4. The President, Vice President and all civil Officers of the United States, shall be removed from Office on Impeachment for, and Conviction of, Treason, Bribery, or other High Crimes and Misdemeanors.

Article III

Section 1. The judicial Power of the United States, shall be vested in one supreme Court, and in such inferior Courts as the Congress may from time to time ordain and establish. The Judges, both of the supreme and inferior Courts, shall hold their Offices during good Behaviour, and shall, at stated Times, receive for their Services, a Compensation, which shall not be diminished during their Continuance in Office.

Section 2. The judicial Power shall extend to all Cases, in Law and Equity, arising under this Constitution, the Laws of the United States, and Treaties made, or which shall be made, under their Authority;—to all Cases affecting Ambassadors, other public Ministers and Consuls;—to all Cases of admiralty and maritime Jurisdiction;—to Controversies to which the United States shall be a Party;—to Controversies between two or more States; between a State and Citizens of another State;—between Citizens of different States;—between Citizens of the same State claiming Lands under Grants of different States, and between a State, or the Citizens thereof, and foreign States, Citizens or Subjects.

In all Cases affecting Ambassadors, or other public Ministers and Consuls, and those in which a State shall be Party, the supreme Court shall have original Jurisdiction. In all the other Cases before mentioned, the supreme Court shall have appellate Jurisdiction, both as to Law and Fact, with such Exceptions, and under such Regulations as the Congress shall make.

The Trial of all Crimes, except in Cases of Impeachment, shall be by Jury; and such Trial shall be held in the State where the said Crimes shall have been committed; but when not committed within any State, the Trial shall be at such Place or Places as the Congress may by Law have directed.

Section 3. Treason against the United States, shall consist only in levying War against them, or in adhering to their Enemies, giving them Aid and Comfort. No person shall be convicted of Treason unless on the Testimony of two Witnesses to the same overt Act, or on Confession in open Court.

The Congress shall have Power to declare the Punishment of Treason, but no Attainder of Treason shall work Corruption of Blood, or Forfeiture except during the Life of the Person attained.

Article IV

Section 1. Full Faith and Credit shall be given in each State to the public Acts, Records, and judicial Proceedings of every other State. And the Congress may by general Laws prescribe the Manner in which such Acts, Records and Proceedings shall be proved, and the Effect thereof.

Section 2. The Citizens of each State shall be entitled to all Privileges and Immunities of Citizens in the several States.

A Person charged in any State with Treason, Felony, or other Crime, who shall flee from Justice, and be found in another State, shall on Demand of the executive Authority of the State from which he fled, be delivered up, to be removed to the State having Jurisdiction of the Crime.

No Person held to Service or Labour in one State, under the Laws thereof, escaping into another, shall, in Consequence of any Law or Regulation therein, be discharged from such Service or Labour, but shall be delivered up on Claim of the Party to whom such Service or Labour may be due.

Section 3. New States may be admitted by the Congress into this Union; but no new State shall be formed or erected within the Jurisdiction of any other State; nor any State be formed by the Junction of two or more States, or Parts of States, without the Consent of the Legislatures of the States concerned as well as of the Congress.

The Congress shall have Power to dispose of and make all needful Rules and Regulations respecting the Territory or other Property belonging to the United States; and nothing in this Constitution shall be so construed as to Prejudice any Claims of the United States, or of any particular State.

Section 4. The United States shall guarantee to every State in this

Union a Republican Form of Government, and shall protect each of them against Invasion; and on Application of the Legislature, or of the Executive (when the Legislature cannot be convened) against domestic Violence.

Article V

The Congress, whenever two thirds of both Houses shall deem it necessary, shall propose Amendments to this Constitution, or on the Application of the Legislatures of two thirds of the several States, shall call a Convention for proposing Amendments, which, in either Case, shall be valid to all Intents and Purposes, as Part of this Constitution, when ratified by the Legislatures of three fourths of the several States, or by Conventions in three fourths thereof, as the one or the other Mode of Ratification may be proposed by the Congress; Provided that no Amendment which may be made prior to the Year One thousand eight hundred and eight shall in any Manner affect the first and fourth Clauses in the Ninth Section of the first Article; and that no State, without its Consent, shall be deprived of its equal Suffrage in the Senate.

al st had to be ratified

Article VI

All Debts contracted and Engagements entered into, before the Adoption of this Constitution, shall be as valid against the United States under this Constitution, as under the Confederation.

This Constitution, and the Laws of the United States which shall be made in Pursuance thereof; and all Treaties made, or which shall be made, under the Authority of the United States, shall be the supreme Law of the Land; and the Judges in every State shall be bound thereby, any Thing in the Constitution or Laws of any State to the Contrary notwithstanding.

The Senators and Representatives before mentioned, and the Members of the several State Legislatures, and all executive and judicial Officers, both of the United States and the several States, shall be bound by Oath or Affirmation, to support this Constitution; but no religious Test shall ever be required as a Qualification to any Office or public Trust under the United States.

Article VII

The Ratification of the Conventions of nine States, shall be sufficient for the Establishment of this Constitution between the States so ratifying the Same.

DONE in Convention by the Unanimous Consent of the States present the Seventeenth Day of September in the Year of our Lord one thousand seven hundred and Eighty seven and of the Independence of the United States of America the Twelfth IN WITNESS whereof We have hereunto subscribed our Names,

G̣o WASHINGTON—Presidt
and deputy from Virginia

New Hampshire
{ JOHN LANGDON
NICHOLAS GILMAN

Massachusetts
{ NATHANIEL GORHAM
RUFUS KING

Connecticut
{ WM SAMḶ JOHNSON
ROGER SHERMAN

New York
ALEXANDER HAMILTON

New Jersey
{ WIL: LIVINGSTON
DAVID BREARLEY.
WM PATERSON.
JONA: DAYTON

Pennsylvania
{ B FRANKLIN
THOMAS MIFFLIN
ROBT MORRIS
GEO. CLYMER
THOS FITZSIMONS
JARED INGERSOLL
JAMES WILSON
GOUV MORRIS

Delaware
{ GEO: READ
GUNNING BEDFORD jun
JOHN DICKINSON
RICHARD BASSETT
JACO: BROOM

Maryland
{ JAMES MCHENRY
DAN OF ST THOS JENIFER
DANL CARROLL

Virginia
{ JOHN BLAIR—
JAMES MADISON JR.

North Carolina
{ WM BLOUNT
RICHD DOBBS SPAIGHT.
HU WILLIAMSON

South Carolina
{ J. RUTLEDGE
CHARLES COTESWORTH
PINCKNEY
CHARLES PICKNEY
PIERCE BUTLER.

Georgia
{ WILLIAM FEW
ABR BALDWIN

AMENDMENTS

[The first 10 Amendments were adopted December 15, 1791, and form
what is known as the "Bill of Rights"]

Amendment 1

Congress shall make no law respecting an establishment of religion, or
prohibiting the free exercise thereof; or abridging the freedom of speech,
or of the press; or the right of the people peaceably to assemble, and to
petition the Government for a redress of grievances.

Amendment 2

A well regulated Militia, being necessary to the security of a free State,
the right of the people to keep and bear Arms, shall not be infringed.

Amendment 3

No Soldier shall, in time of peace be quartered in any house, without
the consent of the Owner, nor in time of war, but in a manner to be
prescribed by law.

Amendment 4

The right of the people to be secure in their persons, houses, papers,
and effects, against unreasonable searches and seizures, shall not be violated, and no Warrants shall issue, but upon probable cause, supported by
Oath or affirmation, and particularly describing the place to be searched,
and the persons or things to be seized.

Amendment 5

No person shall be held to answer for a capital, or otherwise infamous
crime, unless on a presentment or indictment of a Grand Jury, except in
cases arising in the land or naval forces, or in the Militia, when in actual
service in time of War or public danger; nor shall any person be subject
for the same offence to be twice put in jeopardy of life or limb; nor shall
be compelled in any criminal case to be a witness against himself, nor be
deprived of life, liberty, or property, without due process of law; nor shall
private property be taken for public use, without just compensation.

Amendment 6

In all criminal prosecutions, the accused shall enjoy the right to a
speedy and public trial, by an impartial jury of the State and district
wherein the crime shall have been committed, which district shall have
been previously ascertained by law, and to be informed of the nature and
cause of the accusation; to be confronted with the witnesses against him;
to have compulsory process for obtaining witnesses in his favor, and to
have the Assistance of Counsel for his defence.

Amendment 7

In Suits at common law, where the value in controversy shall exceed twenty dollars, the right of trial by jury shall be preserved, and no fact tried by a jury, shall be otherwise re-examined in any Court of the United States, than according to the rules of the common law.

Amendment 8

Excessive bail shall not be required, nor excessive fines imposed, nor cruel and unusual punishments inflicted.

Amendment 9

The enumeration in the Constitution, of certain rights, shall not be construed to deny or disparage others retained by the people.

Amendment 10

The powers not delegated to the United States by the Constitution, nor prohibited by it to the States, are reserved to the States respectively, or to the people.

Amendment 11
[Adopted January 8, 1798]

The Judicial power of the United States shall not be construed to extend to any suit in law or equity, commenced or prosecuted against one of the United States by Citizens of another State, or by Citizens or Subjects of any Foreign State.

Amendment 12
[Adopted September 25, 1804]

The Electors shall meet in their respective states and vote by ballot for President and Vice President, one of whom, at least, shall not be an inhabitant of the same state with themselves; they shall name in their ballots the person voted for as President, and in distinct ballots the person voted for as Vice President, and they shall make distinct lists of all persons voted for as President, and of all persons voted for as Vice President, and of the number of votes for each, which lists they shall sign and certify, and transmit sealed to the seat of the government of the United States, directed to the President of the Senate;—The President of the Senate shall, in the presence of the Senate and House of Representatives, open all the certificates and the votes shall then be counted;—The person having the greatest number of votes for President, shall be the President, if such number be a majority of the whole number of Electors appointed; and if no person have such majority, then from the persons

528

(not 5)

having the highest numbers not exceeding three on the list of those voted for as President, the House of Representatives shall choose immediately, by ballot, the President. But in choosing the President, the votes shall be taken by states, the representation from each state having one vote; a quorum for this purpose shall consist of a member or members from two-thirds of the states, and a majority of all the states shall be necessary to a choice. And if the House of Representatives shall not choose a President whenever the right of choice shall devolve upon them, before the fourth day of March next following, then the Vice President shall act as President, as in the case of death or other constitutional disability of the President.—The person having the greatest number of votes as Vice President, shall be the Vice President, if such number be a majority of the whole number of Electors appointed, and if no person have a majority, then from the two highest numbers on the list, the Senate shall choose the Vice President; a quorum for the purpose shall consist of two-thirds of the whole number of Senators, and a majority of the whole number shall be necessary to a choice. But no person constitutionally ineligible to the office of President shall be eligible to that of Vice President of the United States.

34 states, pres't 26 must vote for a certain candidate

2 not 3

now Jan 20 — 22nd Amend.

Amendment 13
[Adopted December 18, 1865]

Section 1. Neither slavery nor involuntary servitude, except as a punishment for crime whereof the party shall have been duly convicted, shall exist within the United States, or any place subject to their jurisdiction.

Section 2. Congress shall have power to enforce this article by appropriate legislation.

Amendment 14
[Adopted July 28, 1868]

Section 1. All persons born or naturalized in the United States, and subject to the jurisdiction thereof, are citizens of the United States and of the State wherein they reside. No State shall make or enforce any law which shall abridge the privileges or immunities of citizens of the United States; nor shall any State deprive any person of life, liberty, or property, without due process of law; nor deny to any person within its jurisdiction the equal protection of the laws.

Section 2. Representatives shall be apportioned among the several States according to their respective numbers, counting the whole number of persons in each State, excluding Indians not taxed. But when the right to vote at any election for the choice of electors for President and Vice President of the United States, Representatives in Congress, the Executive and Judicial officers of a State, or the members of the Legislature thereof, is denied to any of the male inhabitants of such State, being twenty-one years of age, and citizens of the United States, or in any way abridged, except for participation in rebellion, or other crime, the basis of representation therein shall be reduced in the proportion which the number of such male citizens shall bear to the whole number of male citizens twenty-one years of age in such State.

Section 3. No person shall be a Senator or Representative in Congress, or elector of President and Vice President, or hold any office, civil or military, under the United States, or under any State, who, having previously taken an oath, as a member of Congress, or as an officer of the United States, or as a member of any State legislature, or as an executive or judicial officer of any State, to support the Constitution of the United States, shall have engaged in insurrection or rebellion against the same, or given aid or comfort to the enemies thereof. But Congress may by a vote of two-thirds of each House, remove such disability.

Section 4. The validity of the public debt of the United States, authorized by law, including debts incurred for payment of pensions and bounties for services in suppressing insurrection or rebellion, shall not be questioned. But neither the United States nor any State shall assume or pay any debt or obligation incurred in aid of insurrection or rebellion against the United States, or any claim for the loss or emancipation of any slave; but all such debts, obligations and claims shall be held illegal and void.

Section 5. The Congress shall have power to enforce, by appropriate legislation, the provisions of this article.

Amendment 15
[*Adopted March 30, 1870*]

Section 1. The right of citizens of the United States to vote shall not be denied or abridged by the United States or by any State on account of race, color, or previous condition of servitude.

Section 2. The Congress shall have power to enforce this article by appropriate legislation.

Amendment 16
[*Adopted February 25, 1913*]

The Congress shall have power to lay and collect taxes on incomes, from whatever source derived, without apportionment among the several States, and without regard to any census or enumeration.

Amendment 17
[*Adopted May 31, 1913*]

The Senate of the United States shall be composed of two Senators from each State, elected by the people thereof for six years; and each Senator shall have one vote. The electors in each State shall have the qualifications requisite for electors of the most numerous branch of the State legislatures.

When vacancies happen in the representation of any State in the Senate, the executive authority of such State shall issue writs of election to fill such vacancies: *Provided,* That the legislature of any State may empower the executive thereof to make temporary appointments until the people fill the vacancies by election as the legislature may direct.

This amendment shall not be so construed as to affect the election or term of any Senator chosen before it becomes valid as part of the Constitution.

Amendment 18
[Adopted January 29, 1919]

Section 1. After one year from the ratification of this article the manufacture, sale, or transportation of intoxicating liquors within, the importation thereof into, or the exportation thereof from the United States and all territory subject to the jurisdiction thereof for beverage purposes is hereby prohibited.

Section 2. The Congress and the several States shall have concurrent power to enforce this article by appropriate legislation.

Section 3. This article shall be inoperative unless it shall have been ratified as an amendment to the Constitution by the legislatures of the several States, as provided in the Constitution, within seven years from the date of the submission hereof to the States by the Congress.

Amendment 19
[Adopted August 26, 1920]

The right of citizens of the United States to vote shall not be denied or abridged by the United States or by any State on account of sex.

Congress shall have power to enforce this article by appropriate legislation.

Amendment 20
[Adopted February 6, 1933]

Section 1. The terms of the President and Vice President shall end at noon on the 20th day of January, and the terms of Senators and Representatives at noon on the 3d day of January, of the years in which such terms would have ended if this article had not been ratified; and the terms of their successors shall then begin.

Section 2. The Congress shall assemble at least once in every year, and such meeting shall begin at noon on the 3d day of January, unless they shall by law appoint a different day.

Section 3. If, at the time fixed for the beginning of the term of the President, the President elect shall have died, the Vice President elect shall become President. If a President shall not have been chosen before the time fixed for the beginning of his term, or if the President elect shall have failed to qualify, then the Vice President elect shall act as President

531

until a President shall have qualified; and the Congress may by law provide for the case wherein neither a President elect nor a Vice President elect shall have qualified, declaring who shall then act as President, or the manner in which one who is to act shall be selected, and such person shall act accordingly until a President or Vice President shall have qualified.

Section 4. The Congress may by law provide for the case of the death of any of the persons from whom the House of Representatives may choose a President whenever the right of choice shall have devolved upon them, and for the case of the death of any of the persons from whom the Senate may choose a Vice President whenever the right of choice shall have devolved upon them.

Section 5. Sections 1 and 2 shall take effect on the 15th day of October following the ratification of this article.

Section 6. This article shall be inoperative unless it shall have been ratified as an amendment to the Constitution by the legislatures of three-fourths of the several States within seven years from the date of its submission.

Amendment 21
[Adopted December 5, 1933]

Section 1. The eighteenth article of amendment to the Constitution of the United States is hereby repealed.

Section 2. The transportation or importation into any State, Territory, or possession of the United States for delivery or use therein of intoxicating liquors, in violation of the laws thereof, is hereby prohibited.

Section 3. This article shall be inoperative unless it shall have been ratified as an amendment to the Constitution by conventions in the several States, as provided in the Constitution, within seven years from the date of the submission hereof to the States by the Congress.

Amendment 22   *Revising Terms of office*
[Adopted March 1, 1951]

Section 1. No person shall be elected to the office of the President more than twice, and no person who has held the office of President, or acted as President, for more than two years of a term to which some other person was elected President shall be elected to the office of the President more than once. But this Article shall not apply to any person holding the office of President when this Article was proposed by the Congress, and shall not prevent any persons who may be holding the office of President, or acting as President, during the term within which this Article becomes operative from holding the office of President or acting as President during the remainder of such term.

Sction 2. This article shall be inoperative unless it shall have been ratified as an amendment of the Constitution by the legislatures of three-fourths of the several States within seven years from the date of its submission to the States by the Congress.

Amendment 23
[Adopted March 29, 1961]

Section 1. The District constituting the seat of Government of the United States shall appoint in such manner as the Congress may direct:

A number of electors of President and Vice President equal to the whole number of Senators and Representatives in Congress to which the District would be entitled if it were a State, but in no event more than the least populous State; they shall be in addition to those appointed by the States, but they shall be considered, for the purposes of the election of President and Vice President, to be electors appointed by a State; and they shall meet in the District and perform such duties as provided by the twelfth article of amendment.

Section 2. The Congress shall have power to enforce this article by appropriate legislation.

Amendment 24
[Adopted January 23, 1964]

Section 1. The right of citizens of the United States to vote in any primary or other election for President or Vice President, for electors for President or Vice President, or for Senator or Representative in Congress, shall not be denied or abridged by the United States or any State by reason of failure to pay any poll tax or other tax.

Section 2. The Congress shall have power to enforce this article by appropriate legislation.

Amendment 25
[Adopted February 10, 1967]   *Order of Succession*

Section 1. In case of the removal of the President from office or of his death or resignation, the Vice President shall become President.

Section 2. Whenever there is a vacancy in the office of Vice President, the President shall nominate a Vice President who shall take office upon confirmation by a majority vote of both Houses of Congress.

Section 3. Whenever the President transmits to the President pro tempore of the Senate and the Speaker of the House of Representatives his written declaration that he is unable to discharge the powers and duties of his office, and until he transmits to them a written declaration to the contrary, such powers and duties shall be discharged by the Vice President as Acting President.

Section 4. Whenever the Vice President and a majority of either the principal officers of the executive departments or of such other body as Congress may by law provide, transmit to the President pro tempore of the Senate and the Speaker of the House of Representatives their written declaration that the President is unable to discharge the powers and duties of his office, the Vice President shall immediately assume the powers and duties of the office as Acting President.

533

Thereafter, when the President transmits to the President pro tempore of the Senate and the Speaker of the House of Representatives his written declaration that no inability exists, he shall resume the powers and duties of his office unless the Vice President and a majority of either the principal officers of the executive departments or of such other body as Congress may by law provide, transmit within four days to the President pro tempore of the Senate and the Speaker of the House of Representatives their written declaration that the President is unable to discharge the powers and duties of his office. Thereupon Congress shall decide the issue, assembling within forty-eight hours for that purpose if not in session. If the Congress, within twenty-one days after receipt of the latter written declaration, or, if Congress is not in session, within twenty-one days after Congress is required to assemble, determines by two-thirds vote of both Houses that the President is unable to discharge the powers and duties of his office, the Vice President shall continue to discharge the same as Acting President; otherwise, the President shall resume the powers and duties of his office.

only time Congress can meet without President beckoning

26th — 18 yr. old vote

Index

535

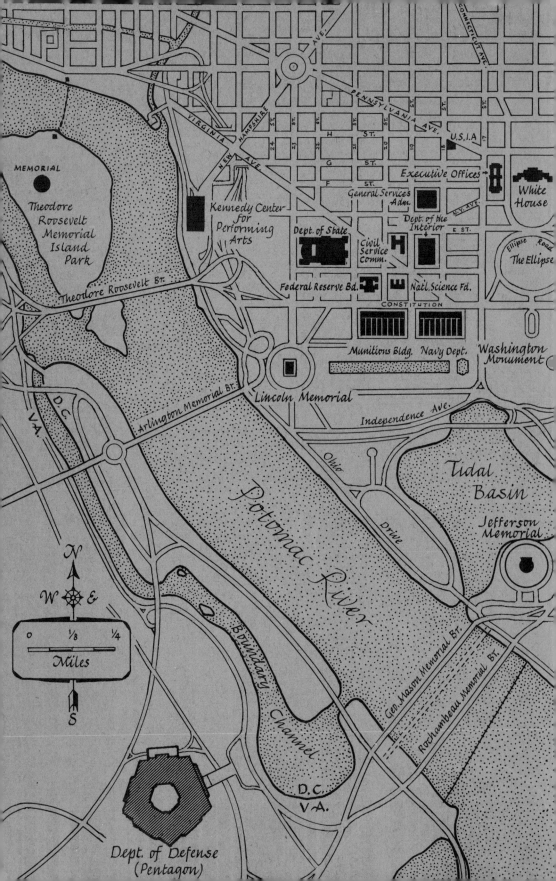

MEMORIAL

Theodore
Roosevelt
Memorial Island
Park

Theodore Roosevelt Br.

D.C.
VA.

Kennedy Center
for
Performing
Arts

Dept. of State

Federal Reserve Bd.

Arlington Memorial Br.

Lincoln Memorial

Potomac River

Boundary

Channel

N
W E
S

0   1/8   1/4
Miles

Dept. of Defense
(Pentagon)

VIRGINIA AVE.
NEW HAMPSHIRE AVE.

24
ST.
23
ST.
22
ST.
21
ST.
20
ST.
19
ST.
18
ST.

PENNSYLVANIA AVE.

H
ST.

G
ST.

F
ST.

General Services
Adm.

Civil
Service
Comm.

Natl. Science Fd.

CONSTITUTION

Munitions Bldg.   Navy Dept.

Independence Ave.

Ohio   Drive

Tidal
Basin

Jefferson
Memorial

Geo. Mason Memorial Br.

Rochambeau Memorial Br.

D.C.
V.A.

U.S.I.A.

Executive Offices →

Dept. of the
Interior

N.Y. AVE.

E ST.

White
House

Ellipse   Road

The Ellipse

Washington
Monument